The History of Protestantism
by
James A. Wylie

Volume III

Hartland Publications
Box 1
Rapidan, VA 22733, U.S.A.

© Copyright 2002
by Hartland Publications, Rapidan, Virginia.
All rights reserved.
Printed in U.S.A.

Published by
Hartland Publications
P.O. Box 1
Rapidan, Virginia, 22733 USA
www.hartlandpublications.com

ISBN 0-923309-80-2

Contents of Volume III

Book Fifteenth
THE JESUITS

1	IGNATIUS LOYOLA	1095
2	LOYOLA'S FIRST DISCIPLES	1100
3	ORGANISATION AND TRAINING OF THE JESUITS	1106
4	MORAL CODE OF THE JESUITS—PROBABILISM, ETC.	1114
5	THE JESUIT TEACHING ON REGICIDE, MURDER, LYING, THEFT, ETC.	1119
6	THE "SECRET INSTRUCTIONS" OF THE JESUITS	1125
7	JESUIT MANAGEMENT OF RICH WIDOWS AND THE HEIRS OF GREAT FAMILIES	1129
8	DIFFUSION OF THE JESUITS THROUGHOUT CHRISTENDOM	1134
9	COMMERCIAL ENTERPRISES AND BANISHMENTS	1139
10	RESTORATION OF THE INQUISITION	1144
11	THE TORTURES OF THE INQUISITION	1148

Book Sixteenth
PROTESTANTISM IN THE WALDENSIAN VALLEYS

1	ANTIQUITY AND FIRST PERSECUTIONS OF THE WALDENSES	1155
2	CATANEO'S EXPEDITION (1488) AGAINST THE DAUPHINESE AND PIEDMONTESE CONFESSORS	1161
3	FAILURE OF CATANEO'S EXPEDITION	1167
4	SYNOD IN THE WALDENSIAN VALLEYS	1172
5	PERSECUTIONS AND MARTYRDOMS	1178
6	PREPARATIONS FOR A WAR OF EXTERMINATION	1186
7	THE GREAT CAMPAIGN OF 1561	1192
8	WALDENSIAN COLONIES IN CALABRIA AND APULIA	1200
9	EXTINCTION OF WALDENSES IN CALABRIA	1205
10	THE YEAR OF THE PLAGUE	1210
11	THE GREAT MASSACRE	1214
12	EXPLOITS OF GIANAVELLO—MASSACRE AND PILLAGE OF RORA	1224
13	THE EXILE	1231
14	RETURN TO THE VALLEYS	1237
15	FINAL RE-ESTABLISHMENT IN THEIR VALLEYS	1242
16	CONDITION OF THE WALDENSES FROM 1690	1248

Book Seventeenth
PROTESTANTISM IN FRANCE FROM DEATH OF FRANCIS I. (1547) TO EDICT OF NANTES (1598)

1	HENRY II. AND PARTIES IN FRANCE	1253
2	HENRY II. AND HIS PERSECUTIONS	1259
3	FIRST NATIONAL SYNOD OF THE FRENCH PROTESTANT CHURCH	1267
4	A GALLERY OF PORTRAITS	1275
5	THE GUISES, AND THE INSURRECTION OF AMBOISE	1282
6	CHARLES IX.—THE TRIUMVIRATE—COLLOQUY AT POISSY	1291
7	MASSACRE AT VASSY AND COMMENCEMENT OF THE CIVIL WARS	1301
8	COMMENCEMENT OF THE HUGUENOT WARS	1309
9	THE FIRST HUGUENOT WAR, AND DEATH OF THE DUKE OF GUISE	1316
10	CATHERINE DE MEDICI AND HER SON, CHARLES IX.—CONFERENCE AT BAYONNE—THE ST. BARTHOLOMEW MASSACRE PLOTTED	1324
11	SECOND AND THIRD HUGUENOT WARS	1331
12	SYNOD OF LA ROCHELLE	1336
13	THE PROMOTERS OF THE ST. BARTHOLOMEW MASSACRE	1341
14	NEGOTIATIONS OF THE COURT WITH THE HUGUENOTS	1346
15	THE MARRIAGE, AND PREPARATIONS FOR THE MASSACRE	1351
16	THE MASSACRE OF ST. BARTHOLOMEW	1355
17	RESURRECTION OF HUGUENOTISM—DEATH OF CHARLES IX	1362
18	NEW PERSECUTIONS—REIGN AND DEATH OF HENRY III	1369
19	HENRY IV. AND THE EDICT OF NANTES	1374

Book Eighteenth
HISTORY OF PROTESTANTISM IN THE NETHERLANDS

1	THE NETHERLANDS AND THEIR INHABITANTS	1384
2	INTRODUCTION OF PROTESTANTISM INTO THE NETHERLANDS	1388
3	ANTWERP: ITS CONFESSORS AND MARTYRS	1393
4	ABDICATION OF CHARLES V. AND ACCESSION OF PHILIP II	1399
5	PHILIP ARRANGES THE GOVERNMENT OF THE NETHERLANDS, AND DEPARTS FOR SPAIN	1403
6	STORMS IN THE COUNCIL, AND MARTYRS AT THE STAKE	1410
7	RETIREMENT OF GRANVELLE—BELGIC CONFESSION OF FAITH	1417
8	THE RISING STORM	1424
9	THE CONFEDERATES OR "BEGGARS"	1431
10	THE FIELD-PREACHINGS	1435
11	THE IMAGE-BREAKINGS	1442
12	REACTION—SUBMISSION OF THE SOUTHERN NETHERLANDS	1450
13	THE COUNCIL OF BLOOD	1457
14	WILLIAM UNFURLS HIS STANDARD—EXECUTION OF EGMONT AND HORN	1465
15	FAILURE OF WILLIAM'S FIRST CAMPAIGN	1470
16	THE "BEGGARS OF THE SEA," AND SECOND CAMPAIGN OF ORANGE	1475
17	WILLIAM'S SECOND CAMPAIGN, AND SUBMISSION OF BRABANT AND FLANDERS	1484

18	THE SIEGE OF HAARLEM	1490
19	SIEGE OF ALKMAAR, AND RECALL OF ALVA	1498
20	THIRD CAMPAIGN OF WILLIAM, AND DEATH OF COUNT LOUIS OF NASSAU	1504
21	THE SIEGE OF LEYDEN	1510
22	MARCH OF THE SPANISH ARMY THROUGH THE SEA—SACK OF ANTWERP	1514
23	THE "PACIFICATION OF GHENT," AND TOLERATION	1521
24	ADMINISTRATION OF DON JOHN, AND FIRST SYNOD OF DORT	1526
25	ABJURATION OF PHILIP, AND RISE OF THE SEVEN UNITED PROVINCES	1535
26	ASSASSINATION OF WILLIAM THE SILENT	1542
27	ORDER AND GOVERNMENT OF THE NETHERLAND CHURCH	1547
28	DISORGANISATION OF THE PROVINCES	1554
29	THE SYNOD OF DORT	1558
30	GRANDEUR OF THE UNITED PROVINCES	1567

Book Nineteenth
PROTESTANTISM IN POLAND AND BOHEMIA

1	RISE AND SPREAD OF PROTESTANTISM IN POLAND	1571
2	JOHN ALASCO, AND REFORMATION OF EAST FRIESLAND	1579
3	ACME OF PROTESTANTISM IN POLAND	1588
4	ORGANISATION OF THE PROTESTANT CHURCH OF POLAND	1594
5	TURNING OF THE TIDE OF PROTESTANTISM IN POLAND	1599
6	THE JESUITS ENTER POLAND—DESTRUCTION OF ITS PROTESTANTISM	1602
7	BOHEMIA — ENTRANCE OF REFORMATION	1611
8	OVERTHROW OF PROTESTANTISM IN BOHEMIA	1619
9	AN ARMY OF MARTYRS	1627
10	SUPPRESSION OF PROTESTANTISM IN BOHEMIA	1634

Syllabus for Volume III

Book Fifteenth
Chapter 1 - page 1095
Rome's New Army—Ignatius Loyola—His Birth—His Wars—He is Wounded—Betakes him to the Legends of the Saints—His Fanaticism Kindled—The Knight-Errant of Mary—The Cave at Manressa—His Mortifications—Comparison between Luther and Ignatius Loyola—An Awakening of the Conscience in both—Luther turns to the Bible, Loyola to Visions—His Revelations.

Chapter 2 - page 1100
Vision of Two Camps—Ignatius Visits Jerusalem—Forbidden to Proselytise—Returns to Spain—Resolves to make Christendom his Field—Puts himself to School—Repairs to Paris—His Two Companions—Peter Fabre—Francis Xavier—Loyola subjects them to a Severe Regimen—They become his Disciples—Loyola's First Nine Followers—Their Vow in the Church of Montmartre—The Book of *Spiritual Exercises*—Its Course of Discipline—Four Weeks of Meditation—Topic of each Week—The *Spiritual Exercises* and the Holy Spirit—Visits Venice—Repairs to Rome—Draft of Rules—Bull Constituting the Society.

Chapter 3 - page 1106
Loyola's Vast Scheme—A General for the Army—Loyola Elected—"Constitutions"—Made Known to only a Select Few—Powers of the General—An Autocrat—He only can make Laws—Appoints all Officers, &c.—Organisation—Six Grand Divisions—Thirty-seven Provinces—Houses, Colleges, Missions, &c.—Reports to the General—His Eye Surveys the World—Organisation—Preparatory Ordeal—Four Classes—Novitiates—Second Novitiate—Its Rigorous Training—The Indifferents—The Scholars—The Coadjutors—The Professed—Their Oath—Their Obedience.

Chapter 4 - page 1114
The Jesuit cut off from Country—from Family—from Property—from the Pope even—The End Sanctifies the Means—The First Great Commandment and Jesuit Morality—When may a Man Love God?—Second Great Commandment—Doctrine of Probabilism—The Jesuit Casuists—Pascal—The Direction of the Intention—Illustrative Cases furnished by Jesuit Doctors—Marvellous Virtues of the Doctrine—A Pious Assassination!

Chapter 5 - page 1119
The Maxims of the Jesuits on Regicide—M. de la Chalotais' Report to the Parliament of Bretagne—Effects of Jesuit Doctrine as shown in History—Doctrine of Mental Equivocation—The Art of Swearing Falsely without Sin—The Seventh Commandment—Jesuit Doctrine on Blasphemy—Murder—Lying—Theft—An Illustrative Case from Pascal—Every Precept of the Decalogue made Void—Jesuit Morality the Consummation of the Wickedness of the Fall.

Chapter 6 - page 1125
The Jesuit Soldier in Armour complete—*Secret Instructions*—How to Plant their First Establishment—Taught to Court the Parochial Clergy—to Visit the Hospitals—to Find out the Wealth of their several Districts—to make Purchases in another Name—to Draw the Youth round them—to Supplant the Older Orders—How to get the Friendship of Great Men—How to Manage Princes—

How to Direct their Policy—Conduct their Embassies—Appoint their Servants, &c.—Taught to Affect a great Show of Lowliness.

Chapter 7 - page 1129

How Rich Widows are to be Drawn to the Chapels and Confessionals of the Jesuits—Kept from Thoughts of a Second Marriage—Induced to Enter an Order, and Bequeath their Estates to the Society—Sons and Daughters of Widows—How to Discover the Revenues and Heirs of Noble Houses—Illustration from Spain—Borrowing on Bond—The *Instructions* to be kept Secret—If Discovered, to be Denied—How the *Instructions* came to Light.

Chapter 8 - page 1134

The Conflict Great—the Arms Sufficient—The Victory Sure—Set Free from Episcopal Jurisdiction—Acceptance in Italy—Venice—Spain—Portugal—Francis Xavier—France—Germany—Their First Planting in Austria—In Cologne and Ingolstadt—Thence Spread over all Germany—their Schools—Wearing of Crosses—Revival of the Popish Faith.

Chapter 9 - page 1139

England—Poland—Cardinal Hosius—Sigismund III.—Ruin of Poland—Jesuit Missions in the East Indies—Numbers of their Converts—Their Missions in Abyssinia—Their Kingdom of Paraguay—Their Trading Establishments in the West Indies—Episode of Father la Valette—Bankruptcy—Trial—Their Constitutions brought to Light—Banished from all Popish Kingdoms—Suppressed by Clement XIV.—The Pope Dies Suddenly—The Order Restored by Pius VII.—The Jesuits the Masters of the Pope.

Chapter 10 - page 1144

Failure of the Ratisbon Conference—What Next to be Done?—Restore the Inquisition—Paul III.—Caraffa—His History—Spread of Protestantism in Italy—Juan di Valdez—His Re-unions at Chiaja—Peter Martyr Vermigli—Bernardino Ochino—Galeazzo Caraccioli—Vittoria Colonna, &c.—Pietro Carnesecchi, &c.—Shall Naples or Geneva Lead in the Reform Movement?

Chapter 11 - page 1148

A Stunning Blow—Three Classes in Italy—Flight of Peter Martyr Vermigli—of Ochino—Caraffa made Pope—The Martyrs, Mollio and Tisserano—Italian Protestantism Crushed—A Notable Epoch—Three Movements—The Inquisition at Nuremberg—The Torture-Chamber—Its Furnishings—Max Tower—The Chamber of Question—The various Instruments of Torture—The Subterranean Dungeons—The Iron Virgin—Her Office—The Burial of the Dead.

Book Sixteenth

Chapter 1 - page 1155

Their Unique Position in Christendom—Their Twofold Testimony—They Witness against Rome and for Protestantism—Hated by Rome—The Cottian Alps—Albigenses and Waldenses—The Waldensian Territory Proper—Papal Testimony to the Flourishing State of their Church in the Fourteenth Century—Early Bulls against them—Tragedy of Christmas, 1400—Constancy of the Waldenses—Crusade of Pope Innocent VIII.—His Bull of 1487—The Army Assembles—Two Frightful Tempests approach the Valleys.

Chapter 2 - page 1161

The Confessors of the Dauphinese Alps—Attacked—Flee to Mont Pelvoux—Retreat into a Cave—Are Suffocated—French Crusaders Cross the Alps—

Enter the Valley of Pragelas—Piedmontese Army Advance against La Torre—
Deputation of Waldensian Patriarchs—The Valley of Lucerne—Villaro—
Bobbio—Cataneo's Plan of Campaign—His Soldiers Cross the Col Julien—
Grandeurs of the Pass—Valley of Prali—Defeat of Cataneo's Expedition.

Chapter 3 - page 1167

The Valley of Angrogna—An Alternative—The Waldenses Prepare for Battle—
Cataneo's Repulse—His Rage—He Renews the Attempt—Enters Angrogna
with his Army—Advances to the Barrier—Enters the Chasm—The Waldenses
on the point of being Cut to Pieces—The Mountain Mist—Deliverance—Utter
Rout of the Papal Army—Pool of Saquet—Sufferings of the Waldenses—
Extinction of the Invading Host—Deputation to their Prince—Vaudois Children—Peace.

Chapter 4 - page 1172

The Old Vine seems Dying—New Life—The Reformation—Tidings Reach the
Waldenses—They Send Deputies into Germany and Switzerland to Inquire—
Joy of Œcolampadius—His Admonitory Letter—Waldensian Deputies at
Strasburg—The Two Churches a Wonder to each other—Martyrdom of One
of the Deputies—Resolution to Call a Synod in the Valleys—Its Catholic
Character—Spot where it Met—Confession of Faith framed—The Spirit of
the Vaudois Revives—They Rebuild their Churches, &c.—Journey of Farel
and Saunier to the Synod.

Chapter 5 - page 1178

A Peace of Twenty-eight Years—Flourishing State—Bersour—A Martyr—Martyrdom of Pastor Gonin—Martyrdoms of a Student and a Monk—Trial and
Burning of a Colporteur—A List of Horrible Deaths—The Valleys under the
Sway of France—Restored to Savoy—Emmanuel Philibert—Persecution
Renewed—Carignano—Persecution Approaches the Mountains—Deputation
to the Duke—The Old Paths—Remonstrance to the Duke—to the Duchess—
to the Council.

Chapter 6 - page 1186

Pastor Gilles Carries the Remonstrance to the Duke—No Tidings for Three
Months—The Monks of Pinerolo begin the Persecution—Raid in San
Martino—Philip of Savoy's Attempt at Conciliation—A Monk's Sermon—
The Duke Declares War against the Vaudois—Dreadful Character of his
Army—The Waldenses hold a Fast, &c.—Skirmishing in Angrogna—Night
Panic—La Trinita Occupies the Val di Lucerna—An Intrigue—Fruitless Concessions—Affecting Incidents—La Trinita Demands 20,000 Crowns from the
Men of the Valleys—He Retires into Winter Quarters—Outrages of his Soldiers.

Chapter 7 - page 1192

Mass or Extermination—Covenant in the Valleys—Their Solemn Oath—How the
Waldenses Recant—Their Energetic Preparations—La Trinita Advances his
Army—Twice attempts to Enter Angrogna, and is Repulsed—A Third attempt—Attacks on Three Points—Repulsed on all Three—Ravages the Valley of Rora—Receives Reinforcements from France and Spain—Commences
a Third Campaign—Six Men against an Army—Utter Discomfiture—Extinction of La Trinita's Host—Peace.

Chapter 8- page 1200

An Inn at Turin—Two Waldensian Youths—A Stranger—Invitation to Calabria—
The Waldenses Search the Land—They Settle there—Their Colony Flourishes—Build Towns—Cultivate Science—They Hear of the Reformation—

Petition for a Fixed Pastor—Jean Louis Paschale sent to them—Apprehended—Brought in Chains to Naples—Conducted to Rome.

Chapter 9 - page 1205
Arrival of Inquisitors in Calabria—Flight of the Inhabitants of San Sexto—Pursued and Destroyed—La Guardia—Its Citizens Seized—Their Tortures—Horrible Butchery—The Calabrian Colony Exterminated—Louis Paschale—His Condemnation—The Castle of St. Angelo—The Pope, Cardinals, and Citizens—The Martyr—His Last Words—His Execution—His Tomb.

Chapter 10 - page 1210
Peace—Reoccupation of their Homes—Partial Famine—Contributions of Foreign Churches—Castrocaro, Governor of the Valleys—His Treacheries and Oppressions—Letter of Elector Palatine to the Duke—A Voice raised for Toleration—Fate of Castrocaro—The Plague—Awful Ravages—10,000 Deaths—Only Two Pastors Survive—Ministers come from Switzerland, &c.—Worship conducted henceforward in French.

Chapter 11 - page 1214
Preliminary Attacks—The Propaganda de Fide—Marchioness de Pianeza—Gastaldo's Order—Its Barbarous Execution—Greater Sorrows—Perfidy of Pianeza—The Massacring Army—Its Attack and Repulse—Treachery—The Massacre Begins—Its Horrors—Modes of Torture—Individual Martyrs—Leger Collects Evidence on the Spot—He Appeals to the Protestant States—Interposition of Cromwell—Mission of Sir Samuel Morland—A Martyr's Monument.

Chapter 12 - page 1224
Ascent of La Combe—Beauty and Grandeur of Valley of Rora—Gianavello—His Character—Marqis di Pianeza—His First Assault—Brave Repulse—Treachery of the Marquis—No Faith with Heretics—Gianavello's Band—Repulse of Second and Third Attacks—Death of a Persecutor—An Army Raised to Invade Rora—Massacre and Pillage—Letter of Pianeza—Gianavello's Heroic Reply—Gianavello Renews the War—500 against 15,000—Success of the Waldenses—Horror at the Massacre—Interposition of England—Letter of Cromwell—Treaty of Peace.

Chapter 13 - page 1231
New Troubles—Louis XIV. and his Confessor—Edict against the Vaudois—Their Defenceless Condition—Their Fight and Victory—They Surrender—The Whole Nation Thrown into Prison—Utter Desolation of the Land—Horrors of the Imprisonment—Their Release—Journey across the Alps—Its Hardships—Arrival of the Exiles at Geneva—Their Hospitable Reception.

Chapter 14 - page 1237
Longings after their Valleys—Thoughts of Returning—Their Reassembling—Cross the Leman—Begin their March—The "Eight Hundred"—Cross Mont Cenis—Great Victory in the Valley of the Dora—First View of their Mountains—Worship on the Mountain-top—Enter their Valleys—Pass their First Sunday at Prali—Worship.

Chapter 15 - page 1242
Cross the Col Julien—Seize Bobbio—Oath of Sibaud—March to Villaro—Guerilla War—Retreat to La Balsiglia—Its Strength—Beauty and Grandeur of San Martino—Encampment on the Balsiglia—Surrounded—Repulse of the Enemy—Depart for the Winter—Return of French and Piedmontese Army in Spring—The Balsiglia Stormed—Enemy Driven Back—Final Assault with Cannon—Wonderful Deliverance of the Vaudois—Overtures of Peace.

Chapter 16 - page 1248

Annoyances—Burdens—Foreign Contributions—French Revolution—Spiritual Revivals—Felix Neff—Dr. Gilly—General Beckwith—Oppressed Condition previous to 1840—Edict of Carlo Alberto—Freedom of Conscience—The Vaudois Church, the Door by which Religious Liberty Entered Italy—Their Lamp Kindled at Rome.

Book Seventeenth

Chapter 1 - page 1253

Francis I.—His Last Illness—Waldensian Settlement in Provence—Fertility and Beauty—Massacre—Remorse of the King—His Death—Lying in State—Henry II.—Parties at Court—The Constable de Montmorency—The Guises—Diana of Poictiers—Marshal de St. André—Catherine de Medici.

Chapter 2 - page 1259

Bigotry of Henry II.—Persecution—The Tailor and Diana of Poictiers—The Tailor Burned—The King Witnesses his Execution—Horror of the King—Martyrdoms—Progress of the Truth—Bishop of Maçon—The Gag—First Protestant Congregation—Attempt to Introduce the Inquisition—National Disasters—Princes and Nobles become Protestants—A Mercuriale—Arrest of Du Bourg—A Tournament—The King Killed—Strange Rumours.

Chapter 3 - page 1267

Early Assemblies of French Protestants—Colportage—Holy Lives—The Planting of Churches throughout France—Play at La Rochelle—First National Synod—Confession of Faith of the French Church—Constitution and Government—Gradation of Courts—Order and Liberty—Piety Flourishes.

Chapter 4 - page 1275

National Decadence—Francis II.—Scenes Shift at Court—The Guises and the Queen-mother—Anthony de Bourbon—His Paltry Character—Prince of Condé—His Accomplishments—Admiral Coligny—His Conversion—Embraces the Reformed Faith—His Daily Life—Great Services—Jeanne d'Albret, Queen of Navarre—Greatness of her Character—Services to French Protestantism—Her Kingdom of Navarre—Edict Establishing the Reformed Worship in it—Her Code—Her Fame.

Chapter 5 - page 1282

Francis II.—Pupilage of the King—The Guises Masters of France—Their Tool, the Mob—*Chambres Ardentes*—Wreckings—Odious Slanders—Confiscation of Huguenot Estates—Retribution—Conspiracy of Amboise—Its Failure—Executions—Tragedies on the Loire—Carrier of Nantes Renews these Tragedies in 1790—Progress of Protestantism—Condemnation of Condé—Preparations for his Execution—Abjuration Test—Death of Francis II.—His Funeral.

Chapter 6 - page 1291

Mary Stuart—Charles IX.—Catherine de Medici Regent—Meeting of States-General—Chancellor de l'Hôpital on Toleration—Speeches of the Deputies—The Church's Advocate calls for the Sword—Sermons at Fontainebleau—The Triumvirate—Debt of France—Colloquy at Poissy—Roman Members—Protestant Deputies—Beza—His Appearance—Points of Difference—Commotion in the Conference—Cardinal of Lorraine's Oration—End of Colloquy—Lesson—Impulse to Protestantism—Preaching of Pierre Viret—Dogmas and their Symbols—Huguenot Iconoclasts.

Chapter 7 - page 1301
Spring-time of French Protestantism—Edict of January—Toleration of Public Worship—Displeasure of the Romanists—Extermination—The Duke of Guise—Collects an Army—Massacres the Protestants of Vassy—The Duke and the Bible—He Enters Paris in Triumph—His Sword Supreme—Shall the Protestants take up Arms?—Their Justification—Massacres—Frightful State of France—More Persecuting Edicts—Charlotte Laval—Coligny sets out for the Wars.

Chapter 8 - page 1309
Condé Seizes Orleans—His Compatriot Chiefs—Prince of Porcian—Rochefoucault—Rohan-Grammont—Montgomery—Soubise—St. Phale—La Mothe—Genlis—Marvellous Spread of the Reformed Faith—The Popish Party—Strength of Protestantism in France—Question of the Civil Wars—Justification of the Huguenots—Finance—Foreign Allies.

Chapter 9 - page 1316
Final Overtures—Rejection—The Two Standards—Division of France—Orleans the Huguenot Headquarters—Condé the Leader—Coligny—The Two Armies Meet—Catherine's Policy—No Battle—Rouen Besieged—Picture of the Two Camps—Fall of Rouen—Miseries—Death of the King of Navarre—Battle of Dreux—Duke of Guise sole Dictator—Condé a Prisoner—Orleans Besieged—The Inhabitants to be put to the Sword—The Duke of Guise Assassinated—Catherine de Medici Supreme—Pacification of Amboise.

Chapter 10 - page 1324
The Peace Satisfactory to Neither Party—Catherine de Medici comes to the Front—The Dance of Death at the Louvre—What will Catherine's Policy be—the Sword or the Olive Branch?—Charles IX.—His Training—A Royal Progress—Iconoclast Outrages—Indignation of Charles IX.—The Envoys of the Duke of Savoy and the Pope—Bayonne—Its Château—Nocturnal Interviews between Catherine de Medici and the Duke of Alva—Agreed to Exterminate the Protestants of France and England—Testimony of Davila—of Tavannes—of Maimbourg—Plot to be Executed at Moulins, 1566—Postponed.

Chapter 11 - page 1331
Peace of Longjumeau—Second Huguenot War—Its One Battle—A Peace which is not Peace—Third Huguenot War—Conspiracy—An Incident—Protestant Chiefs at La Rochelle—Joined by the Queen of Navarre and the Prince of Bearn—Battle of Jarnac—Death of the Prince of Condé—Heroism of Jeanne d'Albret—Disaster at Montcontour—A Dark Night—Misfortunes of Coligny—His Sublimity of Soul.

Chapter 12 - page 1336
Success as Judged by Man and by God—Coligny's Magnanimous Counsels—A New Huguenot Army—Dismay of the Court—Peace of St. Germain-en-Laye—Terms of Treaty—Perfidiousness—Religion on the Battlefield—Synod of La Rochelle—Numbers and Rank of its Members—It Ratifies the Doctrine and Constitution of the French Church as Settled at its First Synod.

Chapter 13 - page 1341
Theocracy and the Punishment of Heresy—The League—Philip II.—Urges Massacre—Position of Catherine de Medici—Hopelessness of Subduing the Huguenots on the Battlefield—Pius V.—His Austerities—Fanaticism—Becomes Chief Inquisitor—His Habits as Pope—His Death—Correspondence of Pius V. with Charles IX. and Catherine de Medici—Massacre distinctly Outlined by the Pope.

Chapter 14 - page 1346

Dissimulation on a Grand Scale—Proposed Expedition to Flanders—The Prince of Orange to be Assisted—The Proposal brings Coligny to Court—The King's Reception of him—Proposed Marriage of the King's Sister with the King of Navarre—Jeanne d'Albret comes to Court—Her Sudden Death—Picture of the French Court—Interview between Charles IX. and the Papal Legate—The King's Pledge—His Doublings.

Chapter 15 - page 1351

Auguries—The King of Navarre and his Companions arrive in Paris—The Marriage—The Rejoicings—Character of Pius V.—The Admiral Shot—The King and Court Visit him—Behaviour of the King—Davila on the Plot—The City-gates Closed—Troops introduced into Paris—The Huguenot Quarter Surrounded—Charles IX. Hesitates—Interview between him and his Mother—Shall Navarre and Condé be Massacred?

Chapter 16 - page 1355

Final Arrangements—The Tocsin—The First Pistol-shot—Murder of Coligny—His Last Moments—Massacre throughout Paris—Butchery at the Louvre—Sunrise, and what it Revealed—Charles IX. Fires on his Subjects—An Arquebus—The Massacres Extend throughout France—Numbers of the Slain—Variously Computed—Charles IX. Excusing Accuses himself—Reception of the News in Flanders—in England—in Scotland—Arrival of the Escaped at Geneva—Rejoicings at Rome—The Three Frescoes—The St. Bartholomew Medal.

Chapter 17 - page 1362

After the Storm—Revival—Siege of Sancerre—Horrors—Bravery of the Citizens—The Siege Raised—La Rochelle—The Capital of French Protestantism—Its Prosperous Condition—Its Siege—Brave Defence—The Besiegers Compelled to Retire—A Year after St. Bartholomew—Has Coligny Risen from the Dead?—First Anniversary of the St. Bartholomew—The Huguenots Reappear at Court—New Demands—Mortification of the Court—A Politico-Ecclesiastical Confederation formed by the Huguenots—The Tiers Parti—Illness of Charles IX.—His Sweat of Blood—Remorse—His Huguenot Nurse—His Death.

Chapter 18 - page 1369

Henry III.—A Sensualist and Tyrant—Persecuting Edict—Henry of Navarre—His Character—The Protestants Recover their Rights—The League—War—Henry III. Joins the League—Gallantry of "Henry of the White Plume"—Dissension between Henry III. and the Duke of Guise—Murder of Guise—Murder of the Cardinal of Lorraine—Henry III. and Henry of Navarre Unite their Arms—March on Paris—Henry III. Assassinated—Death of Catherine de Medici.

Chapter 19 - page 1374

Henry IV.—Birth and Rearing—Assumes the Crown—Has to Fight for the Kingdom—Victory at Dieppe—Victory at Ivry—Henry's Vacillation—His Double Policy—Wrongs of the Huguenots—Henry turns towards Rome—Sully and Duplessis—Their Different Counsel—Henry's Abjuration—Protestant Organisation—The Edict of Nantes—Peace—Henry as a Statesman—His Foreign Policy—Proposed Campaign against Austria—His Forebodings—His Assassination—His Character.

Book Eighteenth
Chapter 1 - page 1384
Batavia—Formed by Joint Action of the Rhine and the Sea—Dismal Territory—The First Inhabitants—Belgium—Holland—Their First Struggles with the Ocean—Their Second with the Roman Power—They Pass under Charlemagne—Rise and Greatness of their Commerce—Civic Rights and Liberties—These Threatened by the Austro-burgundian Emperors—A Divine Principle comes to their Aid.

Chapter 2 - page 1388
Power of the Church of Rome in the Low Countries in the Thirteenth and Fourteenth Centuries—Causes, Forerunners—Waldenses and Albigenses—Romaunt Version of the Scriptures—Influence of Wicliffe's Writings and Huss's Martyrdom—Influence of Commerce, &c—Charles V. and the Netherlands—Persecuting Edicts—Great Number of Martyrs.

Chapter 3 - page 1393
Antwerp—The Convent of Augustines—Jacob Spreng—Henry of Zutphen—Convent Razed—A Preacher Drowned—Placards of the Emperor Charles V.—Well of Life—Long and Dreadful Series of Edicts—Edicts of 1540—The Inquisition—Spread of Lutheranism—Confessors—Martyrdom of John de Bakker.

Chapter 4 - page 1399
Decrepitude of the Emperor—Hall of Brabant Palace—Speech of the Emperor—Failure of his Hopes and Labours—Philip II.—His Portrait—Slender Endowments—Portrait of William of Orange—Other Netherland Nobles—Close of Pageant.

Chapter 5 - page 1403
Philip II. Renews the Edict of 1535 of his Father—Other Atrocious Edicts—Further Martyrdoms—Inquisition introduced into the Low Countries—Indignation and Alarm of the Netherlanders—Thirteen New Bishops—The Spanish Troops to be left in the Country—Violations of the Netherland Charters—Bishop of Arras—His Craft and Ambition—Popular Discontent—Margaret, Duchess of Parma, appointed Regent—Three Councils—Assembly of the States at Ghent—The States request the Suppression of the Edicts—Anger of Philip—He sets Sail from Flushing—Storm—Arrival in Spain.

Chapter 6 - page 1410
Three Councils—These Three but One—Margaret, Duchess of Parma—Cardinal Granvelle—Opposition to the New Bishops—Storms at the Council-board—Position of Prince of Orange, and Counts Egmont and Horn—Their joint Letter to the King—Smouldering Discontent—Persecution—Peter Titlemann—Severity of the Edicts—Father and Son at the Stake—Heroism of the Flemish Martyrs—Execution of a Schoolmaster—A Skeleton at a Feast—Burning of Three Refugees—Great Numbers of Flemish Martyrs—What their Country Owed them.

Chapter 7 - page 1417
Tumults at Valenciennes—Rescue of Two Martyrs—Terrible Revenge—Rhetoric Clubs—The Cardinal Attacked in Plays, Farces, and Lampoons—A Caricature—A Meeting of the States Demanded and Refused—Orders from Spain for the more Vigorous Prosecution of the Edicts—Orange, Egmont, and Horn Retire from the Council—They Demand the Recall of Granvelle—Doublings of Philip II.—Granvelle under pretence of Visiting his Mother Leaves the Netherlands—First Belgic Confession of Faith—Letter of Flemish Protestants to Philip II.—Toleration.

Chapter 8 - page 1424
Speech of Prince of Orange at the Council-table—Egmont sent to Spain—Demand for the States-General, and the Abolition of the Edicts—Philip's Reply—More Martyrs—New and More Rigorous Instructions from Philip—The Nobles and Cities Remonstrate—Arrogance of the Inquisitors—New Mode of putting Protestants to Death—Rising Indignation in the Low Countries—Rumours of General Massacre—Dreadful Secret Imparted to Prince of Orange—Council of Trent—Programme of Massacre.

Chapter 9 - page 1431
League of the Flemish Nobles—Franciscus Junius—The "Confederacy"—Its Object—Number of Signatories—Meeting of the Golden Fleece and States-General—How shall Margaret Steer?—Procession of the Confederates—Their Petition—Perplexity of the Duchess—Stormy Debate in the Council—The Confederates first styled "Beggars"—Medals Struck in Commemoration of the Name—Livery of the Beggars—Answer of the Duchess—Promised Moderation of the Edicts—Martyrdoms Continued—Four Martyrs at Lille—John Cornelius Beheaded.

Chapter 10 - page 1435
The Protestants Resolve to Worship in Public—First Field-Preaching near Ghent—Herman Modet—Seven Thousand Hearers—The Assembly Attacked, but Stands its Ground—Second Field-Preaching—Arrangements at the Field-Preaching—Wall of Waggons—Sentinels, &c.—Numbers of the Worshippers—Singing of the Psalms—Field-Preaching near Antwerp—The Governor Forbids them—The Magistrates unable to put them down—Field-Preaching at Tournay—Immense Congregations—Peregrine de la Grange—Ambrose Wille—Field-Preaching in Holland—Peter Gabriel and John Arentson—Secret Consultations—First Sermon near Horn—Enormous Conventicle near Haarlem—The Town Gates Locked—The Imprisoned Multitude Compel their Opening—Grandeur of the Conventicle—Difference between the Field-Preachers and the Confederates—Preaching at Delft—Utrecht—The Hague—Arrival of more Preachers.

Chapter 11 - page 1442
The Confederate Envoys—Philip's Cruel Purpose—The Image-Breakers—Their Character—Their Devastations—Overspread the Low Countries in a Week—Pillage of 400 Churches—Antwerp Cathedral—Its Magnificence—Its Pillage—Pillage of the Rest of the Churches—The True Iconoclast Hammer—The Preachers and their People take no part in the Image-Breaking—Image-Breaking in Holland—Amsterdam and other Towns—What Protestantism Teaches concerning Image-Breaking—The Popular Outbreaks at the Reformation and at the French Revolution Compared.

Chapter 12 - page 1450
Treaty between the Governor and Nobles—Liberty given the Reformed to Build Churches—Remonstrances of Margaret—Reply of Orange—Anger of Philip—His Cruel Resolve—Philip's Treachery—Letters that Read Two Ways—the Governor raises Soldiers—A Great Treachery Meditated—Egmont's and Horn's Compliance with the Court, and Severities against the Reformed—Horn at Tournay—Forbids the Reformed to Worship inside the Walls—Permitted to erect Churches outside—Money and Materials—the Governor Violates the Accord—Reformed Religion Forbidden in Tournay and Valenciennes—Siege of Valenciennes by Noircarmes—Sufferings of the Besieged—They Surrender—Treachery of Noircarmes—Execution of the Two

Protestant Ministers—Terror inspired by the Fall of Valenciennes—Abject Submission of the Southern Netherlands.

Chapter 13 - page 1457

Orange's Penetration of Philip's Mind—Conference at Dendermonde—Resolution of Egmont—William Retires to Nassau in Germany—Persecution Increased—The Gallows Full—Two Sisters—Philip resolves to send an Army to the Netherlands—Its Command given to the Duke of Alva—His Character—His Person—His Fanaticism and Bloodthirstiness—Character of the Soldiers—An Army of Alvas—Its March—Its *Morale*—Its Entrance Unopposed—Margaret Retires from the Netherlands—Alva Arrests Egmont and Horn—Refugees—Death of Berghen and Montigny—The Council of Blood—Sentence of Death upon all the Inhabitants of the Netherlands—Constitution of the Blood Council—Its Terrible Work—Shrove-tide—A proposed Holocaust—Sentence of Spanish Inquisition upon the Netherlands.

Chapter 14 - page 1465

William cited by the Blood Council—His Estates Confiscated—Solicited to Unfurl the Standard against Spain—Funds raised—Soldiers Enlisted—The War waged in the King's Name—Louis of Nassau—The Invading Host Marches—Battle at Dam—Victory of Count Louis—Rage of Alva—Executions—Condemnation of Counts Egmont and Horn—Sentence intimated to them—Egmont's Conduct on the Scaffold—Executed—Death of Count Horn—Battle of Gemmingen—Defeat of Count Louis.

Chapter 15 - page 1470

Execution of Widow van Dieman—Herman Schinkel—Martyrdoms at Ghent—at Bois-le-Duc—Peter van Kulen and his Maid-servant—A New Gag Invented—William Approaches with his Army—His Manifesto—His Avowal of his Faith—William Crosses the Rhine—Alva Declines Battle—William's Supplies Fail—Flanders Refuses to Rise—William Retires—Alva's Elation—Erects a Statue to himself—Its Inscription—The Pope sends him Congratulations, &c.—Synod of the Church of the Netherlands—Presbyterian Church Government Established.

Chapter 16 - page 1475

Brabant Inactive—Trials of the Blood Council—John Hassels—Executions at Valenciennes—The Year 1568—More Edicts—Individual Martyrdoms—A Martyr Saving the Life of his Persecutor—Burning of Four Converted Priests at the Hague—William enters on his Second Campaign—His Appeal for Funds—The Refugees—The "Beggars of the Sea"—Discipline of the Privateer Fleet—Plan for Collecting Funds—Elizabeth—De la Marck—Capture of Brill by the Sea Beggars—Foundations laid of the Dutch Republic—Alva's Fury—Bossu Fails to Retake Brill—Mons—Alva Besieges it—The Tenth Penny—Meeting of the States of Holland—Speech of St. Aldegonde—Toleration—William of Orange declared Stadtholder of Holland.

Chapter 17 - page 1484

William's New Levies—He crosses the Rhine—Welcome from Flemish Cities—Sinews of War—Hopes in France—Disappointed by the St. Bartholomew Massacre—Reverses—Mutiny—William Disbands his Army—Alva takes Revenge on the Cities of Brabant—Cruelties in Mons—Mechlin Pillaged—Terrible Fate of Zutphen and Naarden—Submission of the Cities of Brabant—Holland Prepares for Defence—Meeting of Estates at Haarlem—Heroic Resolution—Civil and Ecclesiastical Reorganisation of Holland—Novel Battle on the Ice—Preparations for the Siege of Haarlem.

Chapter 18 - page 1490

Haarlem—Its Situation—Its Defences—Army of Amazons—Haze on the Lake—Defeat of a Provisioning Party—Commencement of the Cannonade—A Breach—Assault—Repulse of the Foe—Haarlem Reinforced by William—Reciprocal Barbarities—The Siege Renewed—Mining and Countermining—Battles below the Earth—New Breach—Second Repulse of the Besiegers—Toledo contemplates Raising the Siege—Alva Forbids him to do so—The City Fails—Citizens offer to Capitulate—Toledo's Terms of Surrender—Accepted—The Surrender—Dismal Appearance of the City—Toledo's Treachery—Executions and Massacres—Moral Victory to the Protestant Cause—William's Inspiriting Address to the States.

Chapter 19 - page 1498

Alkmaar—Its Situation—Its Siege—Sonoy's Dismay—Courageous Letter of the Prince—Savage Threats of Alva—Alkmaar Cannonaded—Breach—Stormed—Fury of the Attack—Heroism of the Repulse—What Ensign Solis saw within the Walls—The Spaniards Refuse to Storm the Town a Second Time—The Dutch Threaten to Cut the Dykes, and Drown the Spanish Camp—The Siege Raised—Amsterdam—Battle of the Dutch and Spanish Fleets before it—Defeat of the Spaniards—Admiral Bossu taken Prisoner—Alva Recalled—His Manner of Leaving—Number Executed during his Government—Medina Cœli appointed Governor—He Resigns—Requesens appointed—Assumes the Guise of Moderation—Plain Warning of William—Question of Toleration of Roman Worship—Reasonings—The States at Leyden Forbid its Public Celebration—Opinions of William of Orange.

Chapter 20 - page 1504

Middelburg—Its Siege—Capture by the Sea Beggars—Destruction of One-half of the Spanish Fleet—Sea-board of Zealand and Holland in the hands of the Dutch—William's Preparations for a Third Campaign—Funds—France gives Promises, but no Money—Louis's Army—Battle of Mook—Defeat and Death of Louis—William's Misfortunes—His Magnanimity and Devotion—His Greatness of the First Rank—He Retires into Holland—Mutiny in Avila's Army—The Mutineers Spoil Antwerp—Final Destruction of Spanish Fleet—Opening of the Siege of Leyden—Situation of that Town—Importance of the Siege—Stratagem of Philip—Spirit of its Citizens.

Chapter 21 - page 1510

Leyden—Provisions Fail—William's Sickness—His Plan of Letting in the Sea—The Dykes Cut—The Waters do not Rise—The Flotilla cannot be Floated—Dismay in Leyden—Terrors of the Famine—Pestilence—Deaths—Unabated Resolution of the Citizens—A Mighty Fiat goes forth—The Wind Shifts—The Ocean Overflows the Dykes—The Flotilla Approaches—Fights on the Dykes—The Fort Lammen—Stops the Flotilla—Midnight Noise—Fort Lammen Abandoned—Leyden Relieved—Public Solemn Thanksgiving—Another Prodigy—The Sea Rolls Back.

Chapter 22 - page 1514

The Darkest Hour Passed—A University Founded in Leyden—Its Subsequent Eminence—Mediation—Philip Demands the Absolute Dominancy of the Popish Worship—The Peace Negotiations Broken off—The Islands of Zealand—The Spaniards March through the Sea—The Islands Occupied—The Hopes that Philip builds on this—These Hopes Dashed—Death of Governor Requesens—Mutiny of Spanish Troops—They Seize on Alost—Pillage the Country around—The Spanish Army Join the Mutiny—Antwerp Sacked—

Terrors of the Sack—Massacre, Rape, Burning—The "Antwerp Fury"—Retribution.

Chapter 23 - page 1521

William of Orange more than King of Holland—The "Father of the Country"—Policy of the European Powers—Elizabeth—France—Germany—Coldness of Lutheranism—Causes—Hatred of German Lutherans to Dutch Calvinists—Instances —William's New Project—His Appeal to all the Provinces to Unite against the Spaniards—The "Pacification of Ghent"—Its Articles—Toleration—Services to Toleration of John Calvin and William the Silent.

Chapter 24 - page 1526

Little and Great Countries—Their respective Services to Religion and Liberty—The Pacification of Ghent brings with it an Element of Weakness—Divided Counsels and Aims—Union of Utrecht—The new Governor Don John of Austria—Asked to Ratify the Pacification of Ghent—Refuses—At last Consents—"The Perpetual Edict"—Perfidy meditated—A Martyr—Don John Seizes the Castle of Namur—Intercepted Letters—William made Governor of Brabant—His Triumphal Progress to Brussels—Splendid Opportunity of achieving Independence—Roman Catholicism a Dissolvent—Prince Matthias—His Character—Defeat of the Army of the Netherlands—Bull of the Pope—Amsterdam—Joins the Protestant Side—Civic Revolution—Progress of Protestantism in Antwerp, Ghent, &c.—First National Synod—Their Sentiments on Toleration—"Peace of Religion"—The Provinces Disunite—A Great Opportunity Lost—Death of Don John.

Chapter 25 - page 1535

Alexander, Duke of Parma—His Character—Divisions in the Provinces—Siege of Maestricht—Defection of the Walloons—Union of Utrecht—Bases of Union—Germ of the United Provinces—Their Motto—Peace Congress at Cologne—Its Grandeur—Philip makes Impossible Demands—Failure of Congress—Attempts to Bribe William—His Incorruptibility—Ban Fulminated against him—His "Apology"—Arraignment of Philip—The Netherlands Abjure Philip II. as King—Holland and Zealand confer their Sovereignty on William—Greatness of the Revolution—Its Place in the History of Protestantism.

Chapter 26 - page 1542

What the United Provinces are to become—The Walloons Return to Philip—William's Sovereignty—Brabant and the Duke of Anjou—His Entry into the Netherlands—His Administration a Failure—Matthias Departs—The Netherlands offer their Sovereignty to William—He Declines—Defection of Flanders—Attempt on William's Life—Anastro, the Spanish Banker—The Assassin—He Wounds the Prince—Alarm of the Provinces—Recovery of William—Death of his Wife—Another Attempt on William's Life—Balthasar Gérard—His Project of Assassinating the Prince—Encouraged by the Spanish Authorities—William's Murder—His Character.

Chapter 27 - page 1547

The Spiritual Movement beneath the Armed Struggle — The Infant Springs — Gradual Development of the Church of the Netherlands — The "Forty Ecclesiastical Laws" — Their Enactments respecting the Election of Ministers — Examination and Admission of Pastors — Care for the Purity of the Pulpit — The "Fortnightly Exercise" — Yearly Visitation — Worship and Schools — Elders and Deacons — Power of the Magistrate in the Church — Controversy respecting it — Efforts of the States to Compose these Quarrels —

Synod at Middelburg — It Completes the Constitution of the Dutch Church.
Chapter 28 - page 1554
Vessels of Honour and of Dishonour — Memorial of the Magistrates of Leyden — They demand an Undivided Civil Authority — The Pastors demand an Undivided Spiritual Authority — The Popish and Protestant Jurisdictions — Oaths to Observe the Pacification of Ghent Refused by many of the Priests — The Pacification Violated — Disorders — Tumults in Ghent, &c. — Dilemma of the Romanists — Their Loyalty — Miracles — The Prince obliged to Withdraw the Toleration of the Roman Worship — Priestly Charlatanries in Brussels — William and Toleration.
Chapter 29 - page 1558
First Moments after William's Death — Defection of the Southern Provinces — Courage of Holland — Prince Maurice — States offer their Sovereignty to Henry III. of France — Treaty with Queen Elizabeth — Earl of Leicester — Retires from the Government of the Netherlands — Growth of the Provinces — Dutch Reformed Church — Calvinism the Common Theology of the Reformation — Arminius — His Teaching — His Party — Renewal of the Controversy touching Grace and Free-will — The Five Points — The Remonstrants — The Synod of Dort — Members and Delegates — Remonstrants Summoned before it — Their Opinions Condemned by it — Remonstrants Deposed and Banished — The Reformation Theology of the Second Age as compared with that of the First.
Chapter 30 - page 1567
The One Source of Holland's Strength — Prince Maurice made Governor — His Character — Dutch Statesmen — Spanish Power Sinking — Philip's Many Projects — His Wars in France — Successes of Maurice — Death of the Duke of Parma — Mighty Growth of Holland — Its Vast Commerce — Its Learning — Desolation of Brabant and Flanders — Cause of the Decline of Holland — The Stadtholder of Holland becomes King of England.

Book Nineteenth
Chapter 1 - page 1571
The "Catholic Restoration" — First Introduction of Christianity into Poland — Influence of Wicliffe and Huss — Luther — The Light Shines on Dantzic — The Ex-Monk Knade — Rashness of the Dantzic Reformers — The Movement thrown back — Entrance of Protestantism into Thorn and other Towns — Cracow — Secret Society, and Queen Bona Sforza — Efforts of Romish Synods to Arrest the Truth — Entrance of Bohemian Protestants into Poland — Their great Missionary Success — Students leave Cracow: go to Protestant Universities — Attempt at Coercive Measures — They Fail — Cardinal Hosius — A Martyr — The Priests in Conflict with the Nobles — National Diet of 1552 — Auguries — Abolition of the Temporal Jurisdiction of the Bishops.
Chapter 2 - page 1579
No One Leader — Many Secondary Ones — King Sigismund Augustus — His Character — Favourably Disposed to Protestantism — His Vacillations — Project of National Reforming Synod — Opposed by the Roman Clergy — John Alasco — Education — Goes to Louvain — Visits Zwingle — His Stay with Erasmus — Recalled to Poland — Purges himself from Suspicion of

Heresy — Proffered Dignities — He Severs himself from the Roman Church — Leaves Poland — Goes to East Friesland — Begins its Reformation — Difficulties — Triumph of Alasco — Goes to England — Friendship with Cranmer — Becomes Superintendent of the Foreign Church in London — Retires to Denmark on Death of Edward VI. — Persecutions and Wanderings — Returns to Poland — His Work there — Prince Radziwill — His Attempts to Reform Poland — His Dying Charge to his Son — His Prophetic Words to Sigismund Augustus.

Chapter 3 - page 1588

Arts of the Pope's Legate — Popish Synod — Judicial Murder — A Miracle — The King asks the Pope to Reform the Church — Diet of 1563 — National Synod craved — Defeated by the Papal Legate — His Representations to the King — The King Gained over — Project of a Religious Union — Conference of the Protestants — Union of Sandomir — Its Basis — The Eucharistic Doctrine of the Polish Protestant Church — Acme of Protestantism in Poland.

Chapter 4 - page 1594

Several Church Organisations in Poland — Causes — Church Government in Poland a Modified Episcopacy — The Superintendent — His Powers — The Senior &c. — The Civil Senior — The Synod the Supreme Authority — Local and Provincial Synods — General Convocation — Two Defects in this Organisation — Death of Sigismund Augustus — Who shall Succeed him? — Coligny proposes the Election of a French Prince — Montluc sent as Ambassador to Poland — Duke of Anjou Elected — Pledges — Attempted Treacheries — Coronation — Henry Attempts to Evade the Oath — Firmness of the Polish Protestants — The King's Unpopularity and Flight.

Chapter 5 - page 1599

Stephen Bathory Elected to the Throne — His Midnight Interview — Abandons Protestantism, and becomes a Romanist — Takes the Jesuits under his Patronage — Builds and Endows Colleges for them — Roman Synod of Piotrkow — Subtle Policy of the Bishops for Recovering their Temporal Jurisdiction — Temporal Ends gained by Spiritual Sanctions — Spiritual Terrors *versus* Temporal Punishments — Begun Decadence of Poland — Last Successes of its Arms — Death of King Stephen — Sigismund III. Succeeds — "The King of the Jesuits."

Chapter 6 - page 1602

Cardinal Hosius — His Acquirements — Prodigious Activity — Brings the Jesuits into Poland — They rise to vast Influence — Their Tactics — Mingle in all Circles — Labour to Undermine the Influence of Protestant Ministers — Extraordinary Methods of doing this — Mob Violence — Churches, &c., Burned — Graveyards Violated — The Jesuits in the Saloons of the Great — Their Schools and Method of Teaching — They Dwarf the National Mind — They Extinguish Literature — Testimony of a Popish Writer — Reign of Vladislav — John Casimir, a Jesuit, ascends the Throne — Political Calamities — Revolt of the Cossacks — Invasion of the Russians and Swedes — Continued Decline of Protestantism and Oppression of Protestants — Exhaustion and Ruin of Poland — Causes which contributed along with the Jesuits to the Overthrow of Protestantism in Poland.

Chapter 7 - page 1611

Darkness Concealing Bohemian Martyrs — John Huss — First Preachers of the

Reformed Doctrine in Bohemia — False Brethren — Zahera — Passek — They Excite to Persecutions — Martyrs — Nicolas Wrzetenarz — The Hostess Clara — Martha von Porzicz — The Potter and Girdler — Fate of the Persecutors — Ferdinand I. Invades Bohemia — Persecutions and Emigrations — Flight of the Pastors — John Augusta &c. — A Heroic Sufferer — The Jesuits brought into Bohemia — Maximilian II. — Persecution Stopped — Bohemian Confession — Rudolph — The Majestäts-Brief — Full Liberty given to the Protestants.

Chapter 8 - page 1619

Protestantism Flourishes — Constitution of Bohemian Church — Its Government — Concord between Romanists and Protestants — Temple of Janus Shut — Joy of Bohemia — Matthias Emperor — Election of Ferdinand II. as King of Bohemia — Reaction — Intrigues and Insults — Council-chamber — Three Councillors Thrown out at the Window — Ferdinand II. elected Emperor — War — Battle of the White Hill — Defeat of the Protestants — Atrocities — Amnesty — Apprehension of Nobles and Senators — Their Frightful Sentences — Their Behaviour on the Scaffold — Their Deaths.

Chapter 9 - page 1627

Count Schlik — His Cruel Sentence — The Baron of Budowa — His Last Hours — Argues with the Jesuits — His Execution — Chrostopher Harant — His Travels — His Death — Baron Kaplirz — His Dream — Attires himself for the Scaffold — Procopius Dworschezky — His Martyrdom — Otto Losz — His Learning — His Interview with the Jesuits — Cruel Death — Khobr — Schulz — Kutnauer — His great Courage — His Death — Talents and Rank of these Martyrs — Their Execution the Obsequies of their Country.

Chapter 10 - page 1634

Policy of Ferdinand II. — Murder of Ministers by the Troops — New Plan of Persecution — Kindness and its Effects — Expulsion of Anabaptists from Moravia — The Pastors Banished — Sorrowful Partings — Exile of Pastors of Kuttenberg — The Lutherans "Graciously Dismissed" — The Churches Razed — The New Clergy — Purification of the Churches — The Schoolmasters Banished — Bibles and Religious Books Burned — Spanish Jesuits and Lichtenstein's Dragoons — Emigration of the Nobles — Reign of Terror in the Towns — Oppressive Edicts — Ransom-Money — Unprotestantising of Villages and Rural Parts — Protestantism Trampled out — Bohemia a Desert — Testimony of a Popish Writer.

The History of Protestantism

Book Fifteenth
THE JESUITS

CHAPTER I
IGNATIUS LOYOLA

PROTESTANTISM had marshalled its spiritual forces a second time, and placing itself at the heart of Christendom—at a point where three great empires met—it was labouring with redoubled vigour to propagate itself on all sides. It was expelling from the air of the world that ancient superstition, born of Paganism and Judaism, which, like an opaque veil, had darkened the human mind: a new light was breaking on the eyes and a new life stirring in the souls of men: schools of learning, pure Churches, and free nations were springing up in different parts of Europe; while hundreds of thousands of disciples were ready, by their holy lives or heroic deaths, to serve that great cause which, having broken their ancient fetters, had made them the heirs of a new liberty and the citizens of a new world. It was clear that if let alone, for only a few years, Protestantism would achieve a victory so complete that it would be vain for any opposing power to think of renewing the contest. If that power which was seated in Geneva was to be withstood, and the tide of victory which was bearing it to dominion rolled back, there must be no longer delay in the measures necessary for achieving such a result.

It was further clear that armies would never effect the overthrow of Protestantism. The serried strength of Popish Europe had been put forth to crush it, but all in vain: Protestantism had risen only the stronger from the blows which, it was hoped, would overwhelm it. It was plain that other weapons must be forged, and other armies mustered, than those which Charles and Francis had been accustomed to lead into the field. It was now that the Jesuit corps was embodied. And it must be confessed that these new soldiers did more than all the armies of France and Spain to stem the tide of Protestant success, and bind victory once more to the banners of Rome.

We have seen Protestantism renew its energies: Rome, too, will show what she is capable of doing. As the tribes of Israel were approaching the frontier of the Promised Land, a Wizard-prophet was summoned from the East to bar their entrance by his divinations and enchantments. As the armies of Protestantism neared their final victory, there started up the Jesuit host, with a subtler casuistry and a darker divination than Balaam's, to dispute with the Reformed the possession of Christendom. We shall consider that host in its rise, its equipments, its discipline, its diffusion, and its successes.

Don Inigo Lopez de Recalde, the Ignatius Loyola of history, was the founder of the Order of Jesus, or the Jesuits. His birth was nearly contemporaneous with that of Luther. He was the youngest son of one of the highest Spanish grandees, and was born in his father's Castle of Loyola, in the province of Guipuzcoa, in 1491. His youth was passed at the splendid and luxurious court of Ferdinand the Catholic. Spain at that time was fighting to expel the Moors, whose presence on her soil she accounted at once an insult to her independence and an affront to her faith. She was ending the conflict in Spain, but continuing it in Africa. The naturally ardent soul of Ignatius was set on fire by the religious fervour around him. He grew weary of the gaieties and frivolities of the court; nor could even the dalliances and adventures of knight-errantry satisfy him. He thirsted to earn renown on the field of arms. Embarking in the war which at that time engaged the religious enthusiasm and military chivalry of his countrymen, he soon distinguished himself by his feats of daring. Ignatius was bidding fair to take a high place among warriors, and transmit to posterity a name encompassed with the halo of military glory—but with that halo only. At this stage of his career an incident befell him which cut short his exploits on the battlefield, and transferred his enthusiasm and chivalry to another sphere.

It was the year 1521. Luther was uttering his famous "No!" before the emperor and his princes, and summoning, as with trumpet-peal, Christendom to arms. It is at this moment the young Ignatius, the intrepid soldier of Spain, and about to become the yet more intrepid soldier of Rome, appears before us. He is shut up in the town of Pampeluna, which the French are besieging. The garrison are hard pressed: and after some whispered consultations they openly propose to surrender. Ignatius deems the very thought of such a thing dishonour; he denounces the proposed act of his comrades as cowardice, and re-entering the citadel with a few companions as courageous as himself, swears to defend it to the last drop of his blood. By-and-by famine leaves him no alternative save to die within the walls, or cut his way sword in hand through the host of the besiegers. He goes forth and joins battle with the French. As he is fighting desperately he is struck by a musket-ball, wounded dangerously in both legs, and laid senseless on the field. Ignatius had ended the last campaign he was ever to fight with the sword: his valour he was yet to display on other fields, but he would mingle no more on those which resound with the clash of arms and the roar of artillery.

The bravery of the fallen warrior had won the respect of the foe. Raising him from the ground, where he was fast bleeding to death, they carried him to the hospital of Pampeluna, and tended him with care, till he was able to be conveyed in a litter to his father's castle. Thrice had he to undergo the agony of having his wounds opened. Clenching his teeth and closing his fists he bade defiance to pain. Not a groan escaped him while under the torture of the surgeon's knife. But the tardy passage of the weeks and months during which he waited the slow healing of his wounds, inflicted on his ardent spirit a keener pain than had the probing-knife on his quivering limbs. Fettered to his couch he chafed at the inactivity to which he was doomed. Romances of chivalry and tales of war were brought him to beguile the hours. These exhausted, other books were produced, but of a somewhat different character. This time it was the legends of the saints that were brought to the bed-rid knight. The tragedy of the early Christian martyrs passed before him as he read. Next came the monks and hermits of the Thebaic deserts and the Sinaitic mountains. With an imagination on fire he perused the story of the hunger and cold they had braved; of the self-conquests they had achieved; of the battles they had waged with evil spirits; of the glorious visions that had been vouchsafed them; and the brilliant rewards they had gained in the lasting reverence of earth and the felicities and dignities of heaven. He panted to rival these heroes, whose glory was of a kind so bright and pure, that compared with it the renown of the battlefield was dim and sordid. His enthusiasm and ambition were as boundless as ever, but now they were directed into a new channel. Henceforward the current of his life was changed. He had lain down "a knight of the burning sword"—to use the words of his biographer, Vieyra—he rose up from it "a saint of the burning torch."

The change was a sudden and violent one, and drew after it vast consequences not to Ignatius only, and the men of his own age, but to millions of the human race in all countries of the world, and in all the ages that have elapsed since. He who lay down on his bed the fiery soldier of the emperor, rose from it the yet more fiery soldier of the Pope. The weakness occasioned by loss of blood, the morbidity produced by long seclusion, the irritation of acute and protracted suffering, joined to a temperament highly excitable, and a mind that had fed on miracles and visions till its enthusiasm had grown into fanaticism, accounts in part for the transformation which Ignatius had undergone. Though the balance of his intellect was now sadly disturbed, his shrewdness, his tenacity, and his daring remained. Set free from the fetters of calm reason, these qualities had freer scope than ever. The wing of his earthly ambition was broken, but he could take his flight heavenward. If earth was forbidden him, the celestial domains stood open, and there worthier exploits and more brilliant rewards awaited his prowess.

The heart of a soldier plucked out, and that of a monk given him, Ignatius vowed, before leaving his sick-chamber, to be the slave, the champion, the knight-errant of Mary. She was the lady of his soul, and after the manner of dutiful knights he immediately repaired to her shrine at Montserrat, hung up his arms before her image, and spent the night in watching them. But reflecting that he was a soldier of Christ, that great Monarch who had gone forth to subjugate all the earth, he resolved to eat no other food, wear no other raiment than his King had done, and endure the same hardships and vigils. Laying aside his plume, his coat of mail, his shield and sword, he donned the cloak of the mendicant. "Wrapped in sordid rags," says Duller, "an iron chain and prickly girdle pressing on his naked body, covered with filth, with uncombed hair and untrimmed nails," he retired to a dark mountain in the vicinity of Manressa, where was a gloomy cave, in which he made his abode for some time. There he subjected himself to all the penances and mortifications of the early anchorites whose holiness he emulated. He wrestled with the evil spirit, talked to voices audible to no ear but his own, fasted for days on end, till his weakness was such that he fell into a swoon, and one day was found at the entrance of his cave, lying on the ground, half dead.

The cave at Manressa recalls vividly to our memory the cell at Erfurt. The same austerities, vigils, mortifications, and mental efforts and agonies which were undergone by Ignatius Loyola, had but a very few years before this been passed through by Martin Luther. So far the career of the founder of the Jesuits and that of the champion of Protestantism were the same. Both had set before them a high standard of holiness, and both had all but sacrificed life to reach it. But at the point to which we have come the courses of the two men widely diverge. Both hitherto in their pursuit of truth and holiness had travelled by the same road; but now we see Luther turning to the Bible, "the light that shineth in a dark place," "the sure Word of Prophecy." Ignatius Loyola, on the other hand, surrenders himself to visions and revelations. As Luther went onward the light grew only the brighter around him. He had turned his face to the sun. Ignatius had turned his gaze inward upon his own beclouded mind, and verified the saying of the wise man, "He who wandereth out of the way of understanding shall remain in the congregation of the dead."

Finding him half exanimate at the mouth of his cave, sympathising friends carried Ignatius to the town of Manressa. Continuing there the same course of penances and self-mortifications which he had pursued in solitude, his bodily weakness greatly increased, but he was more than recompensed by the greater frequency of those heavenly visions with which he had now begun to be favoured. In Manressa he occupied a cell in the Dominican convent, and as he was then projecting a pilgrimage to Jerusalem, he began to qualify himself for this holy journey by a course of the severest penances. "He scourged himself thrice a day," says Ranke, "he rose up to prayer at midnight, and passed seven hours of each day on his knees."[2237]

It will hardly do to say that this marvellous case is merely an instance of an unstrung bodily condition, and of vicious mental stimulants abundantly supplied, where the thirst for adventure and distinction was still unquenched. A closer study of the case will show that there was in it an awakening of the conscience. There was a sense of sin—its awful demerit, and its fearful award. Loyola, too, would seem to have felt the "terrors of death, and the pains of hell." He had spent three days in Montserrat in confessing the sins of all his past life.[2236] But on a more searching review of his life, finding that he had omitted many sins, he renewed and amplified his confession at Manressa. If he found peace it was only for a short while; again his sense of sin would return, and to such a pitch did this anguish rise, that thoughts of self-destruction came into his mind. Approaching the window of his cell, he was about to throw himself from it, when it suddenly flashed upon him that the act was abhorrent to the Almighty, and he withdrew, crying out, "Lord, I will not do aught that may offend thee."[2237]

One day he awakened as if from a dream. Now I know, he said to himself, that all these torments are from the assaults of Satan. I am tossed between the promptings of the good spirit, who would have me be at peace, and the dark suggestions of the evil one, who seeks continually to terrify me. I will have done with this warfare. I will forget my past life; I will open these wounds not again. Luther in the midst of tempests as terrible had come to a similar resolution. Awaking as from a frightful dream, he lifted up his eyes and saw One who had borne his sins upon His cross: and like the mariner who clings amid the surging billows to the rock, Luther was at peace because he had anchored his soul on an Almighty foundation. But says Ranke, speaking of Loyola and the course he had now resolved to pursue, "this was not so much the restoration of his peace as a resolution, it was an engagement entered into by the will rather than a conviction to which the submission of the will is inevitable. It required no aid from Scripture, it was based on the belief he entertained of an immediate connection between himself and the world of spirits. This would never have satisfied Luther. No inspirations—no visions would Luther admit; all were in his opinion alike injurious. He would have the simple, written, indubitable Word of God alone."[2238]

From the hour that Ignatius resolved to think no more of his sins his spiritual horizon began, as he believed, to clear up. All his gloomy terrors receded with the past which he had consigned to oblivion. His bitter tears were dried up, and his heavy sighs no longer resounded through the convent halls. He was taken, he felt, into more intimate communion with God. The heavens were opened that he might have a clearer insight into Divine mysteries. True, the Spirit had revealed these things in the morning of the world, through chosen and accredited channels, and inscribed them on the page of inspiration that all might learn from that infallible source. But Ignatius did not search for these mysteries in the Bible; favoured above the sons of men, he received them, as he thought, in revelations made specially to himself. Alas! his hour had come and passed, and the gate that would have ushered him in amid celestial realities and joys was shut, and henceforward he must dwell amid phantasies and dreams.

It was intimated to him one day that he should yet see the Saviour in person. He had not long to wait for the promised revelation. At mass his eyes were opened, and he saw the incarnate God in the Host. What farther proof did he need of transubstantiation, seeing the whole process had been shown to him? A short while thereafter the Virgin revealed herself with equal plainness to his bodily eyes. Not fewer than thirty such visits did Loyola receive. One day as he sat on the steps of the Church of St. Dominic at Manressa, singing a hymn to Mary, he suddenly fell into a reverie, and had the symbol of the ineffable mystery of the Trinity shown to him, under the figure of "three keys of a musical instrument." He sobbed for very joy, and entering the church, began publishing the miracle. On another occasion, as he walked along the banks of the Llobregat, that waters Manressa, he sat down, and fixing his eyes intently on the stream, many Divine mysteries became apparent to him, such "as other men," says his biographer Maffei, "can with great difficulty understand, after much reading, long vigils, and study."

This narration places us beside the respective springs of Protestantism and Ultramontanism. The source from which the one is seen to issue is the Word of God. To it Luther swore fealty, and before it he hung up his sword, like a true knight, when he received ordination. The other is seen to be the product of a clouded yet proud and ambitious imagination, and a wayward will. And therewith have corresponded the fruits, as the past three centuries bear witness. The one principle has gathered round it a noble host clad in the panoply of purity and truth. In the wake of the other has come the dark army of the Jesuits.

CHAPTER II
LOYOLA'S FIRST DISCIPLES

AMONG the wonderful things shown to Ignatius Loyola by special revelation was a vision of two great camps. The centre of the one was placed at Babylon; and over it there floated the gloomy ensign of the prince of darkness. The Heavenly King had erected his standard on Mount Zion, and made Jerusalem his headquarters. In the war of which these two camps were the symbols, and the issues of which were to be grand beyond all former precedent, Loyola was chosen, he believed, to be one of the chief captains. He longed to place himself at the centre of action. The way thither was long. Wide oceans and gloomy deserts had to be traversed, and hostile tribes passed through. But he had an iron will, a boundless enthusiasm, and what was more, a Divine call—for such it seemed to him in his delusion. He set out penniless (1523), and begging his bread by the way, he arrived at Barcelona. There he embarked in a ship which landed him on the shore of Italy. Thence, travelling on foot, he entered in safety the gates of Jerusalem. But the reception that awaited him in the "Holy City" was not such as he had fondly anticipated. His rags, his uncombed locks, which almost hid his emaciated features, but ill accorded with the magnificence of the errand which had brought him to that shore. Loyola thought of doing in his single person what the armies of the Crusaders had failed to do by their combined strength. The head of the Romanists in Jerusalem saw in him rather the mendicant than the warrior, and fearing doubtless that should he offer battle to the Crescent, he was more likely to provoke a tempest of Turkish fanaticism than drive back the hordes of the infidel, he commanded him to desist under the threat of excommunication. Thus withstood Loyola returned to Barcelona, which he reached in 1524.

Derision and insults awaited his arrival in his native Spain. His countrymen failed to see the grand aims he cherished beneath his rags; nor could they divine the splendid career, and the immortality of fame, which were to emerge from this present squalor and debasement. But not for one moment did Loyola's own faith falter in his great destiny. He had the art, known only to those fated to act a great part, of converting impediments into helps, and extracting new experience and fresh courage from disappointment. His repulsion from the "holy fields" had taught him that Christendom, and not Asia, was the predestined scene of his warfare, and that he was to do battle, not with the infidels of the East, but with the ever-growing hosts of heretics in Europe. But to meet the Protestant on his own ground, and to fight him with his own weapons, was a still more difficult task than to convert the Saracen. He felt that meanwhile he was destitute of the necessary qualifications, but it was not too late to acquire them.

Though a man of thirty-five, he put himself to school at Barcelona, and there, seated amid the youth of the city, he prosecuted the study of Latin. Having acquired some mastery of this tongue, he removed (1526) to the University of Alcala to commence theology. In a little space he began to preach. Discovering a vast zeal in the propagation of his tenets, and no little success in making disciples, male and female, the Inquisition, deeming both the man and his aims somewhat mysterious, arrested him. The order of the Jesuits was on the point of being nipped in the bud. But finding in Loyola no heretical bias, the Fathers dismissed him on his promise of holding his peace. He repaired to Salamanca, but there too he encountered similar obstacles. It was not agreeable thus to champ the curb of privilege and canonical authority; but it ministered to him a wholesome discipline. It sharpened his circumspection and shrewdness, without in the least abating his ardour. Holding fast by his grand purpose, he quitted his native land, and repairing in 1528 to Paris, entered himself as a student in the College of St. Barbara.

In the world of Paris he became more practical; but the flame of his enthusiasm still burned on. Through penance, through study, through ecstatic visions, and occasional checks, he pursued with unshaken faith and unquenched resolution his celestial calling as the leader of a mighty spiritual army, of which he was to be the creator, and which was to wage victorious battle with the hosts of Protestantism. Loyola's residence in Paris, which was from 1528 to 1535,[2239] coincides with the period of greatest religious excitement in the French capital. Discussions were at that time of hourly occurrence in the streets, in the halls of the Sorbonne, and at the royal table. Loyola must have witnessed all the stirring and tragic scenes we have already described; he may have stood by the stake of Berquin; he had seen with indignation, doubtless, the saloons of the Louvre opened for the Protestant sermon; he had felt the great shock which France received from the Placards, and taken part, it may be, in the bloody rites of her great day of expiation. It is easy to see how, amid excitements like these, Loyola's zeal would burn stronger every hour; but his ardour did not hurry him into action till all was ready. The blow he meditated was great, and time, patience, and skill were necessary to prepare the instruments by whom he was to inflict it.

It chanced that two young students shared with Loyola his rooms, in the College of St. Barbara. The one was Peter Fabre, from Savoy. His youth had been passed amid his father's flocks; the majesty of the silent mountains had sublimed his natural piety into enthusiasm; and one night, on bended knee, under the star-studded vault, he devoted himself to God in a life of study. The other companion of Loyola was Francis Xavier, of Pampeluna, in Navarre. For 500 years his ancestors had been renowned as warriors, and his ambition was, by becoming a scholar, to enhance the fame of his house by adding to its glory in arms the yet purer glory of learning. These two, the humble Savoyard and the high-born Navarrese, Loyola had resolved should be his first disciples.

As the artist selects his block, and with skilful eye and plastic hand bestows touch after touch of the chisel, till at last the superfluous parts are cleared away, and the statue stands forth so complete and perfect in its symmetry that the dead stone seems to breathe, so did the future general of the Jesuit army proceed to mould and fashion his two companions, Fabre and Xavier. The former was soft and pliable, and easily took the shape which the master-hand sought to communicate. The other was obdurate, like the rocks of his native mountains, but the patience and genius of Loyola finally triumphed over his pride of family and haughtiness of spirit. He first of all won their affection by certain disinterested services; he next excited their admiration by the loftiness of his own asceticism;

he then imparted to them his grand project, and fired them with the ambition of sharing with him in the accomplishment of it. Having brought them thus far he entered them on a course of discipline, the design of which was to give them those hardy qualities of body and soul, which would enable them to fulfil their lofty vocation as leaders in an army, every soldier in which was to be tried and hardened in the fire as he himself had been. He exacted of them frequent confession; he was equally rigid as regarded their participation in the Eucharist; the one exercise trained them in submission, the other fed the flame of their zeal, and thus the two cardinal qualities which Loyola demanded in all his followers were developed side by side. Severe bodily mortifications were also enjoined upon them. "Three days and three nights did he compel them to fast. During the severest winters, when carriages might be seen to traverse the frozen Seine, he would not permit Fabre the slightest relaxation of discipline." Thus it was that he mortified their pride, taught them to despise wealth, schooled them to brave danger and contemn luxury, and inured them to cold, hunger, and toil; in short, he made them dead to every passion save that of the "Holy War," in which they were to bear arms.

A beginning had been made. The first recruits had been enrolled in that army which was speedily to swell into a mighty host, and unfurl its gloomy ensigns and win its dismal triumphs in every land. We can imagine Loyola's joy as he contemplated these two men, fashioned so perfectly in his own likeness. The same master-artificer who had moulded these two could form others—in short, any number. The list was soon enlarged by the addition of four other disciples. Their names—obscure then, but in after years to shine with a fiery splendour—were Jacob Lainez, Alfonso Salmeron, Nicholas Bobadilla, and Simon Rodriguez. The first three were Spaniards, the fourth was a Portuguese. They were seven in all; but the accession of two others increased them to nine: and now they resolved on taking their first step.

On the 15th of August, 1534, Loyola, followed by his nine companions, entered the subterranean chapel of the Church of Montmartre, at Paris, and mass being said by Fabre, who had received the priest's orders, the company, after the usual vow of chastity and poverty, took a solemn oath to dedicate their lives to the conversion of the Saracens, or, should circumstances make that attempt impossible, to lay themselves and their services unreservedly at the feet of the Pope. They sealed their oath by now receiving the Host. The day was chosen because it was the anniversary of the Assumption of the Virgin, and the place because it was consecrated to Mary, the queen of saints and angels, from whom, as Loyola firmly believed, he had received his mission. The army thus enrolled was little, and it was great. It was little when counted, it was great when weighed. In sublimity of aim, and strength of faith—using the term in its mundane sense—it wielded a power before which nothing on earth—one principle excepted—should be able to stand.[2240]

To foster the growth of this infant Hercules, Loyola had prepared beforehand his book entitled *Spiritual Exercises*. This is a body of rules for teaching men how to conduct the work of their "conversion." It consists of four grand meditations, and the penitent, retiring into solitude, is to occupy absorbingly his mind on each in succession, during the space of the rising and setting of seven suns.

It may be fitly styled a journey from the gates of destruction to the gates of Paradise, mapped out in stages so that it might be gone in the short period of four weeks. There are few more remarkable books in the world. It combines the self-denial and mortification of the Brahmin with the asceticism of the anchorite, and the ecstasies of the school men. It professes, like the Koran, to be a revelation. "The Book of Exercises," says a Jesuit, "was truly written by the finger of God, and delivered to Ignatius by the Holy Mother of God."[2241]

The *Spiritual Exercises*, we have said, was a body of rules by following which one could effect upon himself that great change which in Biblical and theological language is termed "conversion." The book displayed on the part of its author great knowledge of the human heart. The method prescribed was an adroit imitation of that process of conviction, of alarm, of enlightenment, and of peace, through which the Holy Spirit leads the soul that undergoes that change in very deed. This Divine transformation was at that hour taking place in thousands of instances in the Protestant world. Loyola, like the magicians of old who strove to rival Moses, wrought with his enchantments to produce the same miracle. Let us observe how he proceeded.

The person was, first of all, to go aside from the world, by entirely isolating himself from all the affairs of life. In the solemn stillness of his chamber he was to engage in four meditations each day, the first at daybreak, the last at midnight. To assist the action of the imagination on the soul, the room was to be artificially darkened, and on its walls were to be suspended pictures of hell and other horrors. Sin, death, and judgment were exclusively to occupy the thoughts of the penitent during the first week of his seclusion. He was to ponder upon them till in a sense "he beheld the vast conflagration of hell; its wailings, shrieks, and blasphemies; felt the worm of conscience; in fine, touched those fires by whose contact the souls of the reprobate are scorched."

The second week he was to withdraw his eye from these dreadful spectacles and fix it upon the Incarnation. It is no longer the wailings of the lost that fill the ear as he sits in his darkened chamber, it is the song of the angel announcing the birth of Christ, and "Mary acquiescing in the work of redemption." At the feet of the Trinity he is directed to pour out the expression of the gratitude and praise with which continued meditation on these themes causes his soul to overflow.

The third week is to witness the solemn act of the soul's enrolment in the army of that Great Captain, who "bowed the heavens and came down" in his Incarnation. Two cities are before the devotee—Jerusalem and Babylon—in which will he choose to dwell? Two standards are displayed in his sight—under which will he fight? Here a broad and brave pennon floats freely on the wind. Its golden folds bear the motto, "Pride, Honour, Riches." Here is another, but how unlike the motto inscribed upon it, "Poverty, Shame, Humility." On all sides resounds the cry "To arms!" He must make his choice, and he must make it now, for the seventh sun of his third week is hastening to the setting. It is under the banner of Poverty that he elects to win the incorruptible crown.

Now comes his fourth and last week, and with it there comes a great change in the subjects of his meditation. He is to dismiss all gloomy ideas, all images of terror; the gates of Hades are to be closed, and those of a new life opened. It is morning with him, it is a spring-time that has come to him, and he is to surround himself with light, and flowers, and odours. It is the Sabbath of a spiritual creation; he is to rest, and to taste in that rest the prelude of the everlasting joys. This mood of mind he is to cultivate while seven suns rise and set upon him. He is now perfected and fit to fight in the army of the Great Captain.

A not unsimilar course of mental discipline, as our history has already shown, did Wicliffe, Luther, and Calvin pass through before they became captains in the army of Christ. They began in a horror of great darkness; through that cloud there broke upon them the revelation of the "Crucified;" throwing the arms of their faith around the Tree of Expiation, and clinging to it, they entered into peace, and tasted the joys to come. How like, yet how unlike, are these two courses! In the one the penitent finds a Saviour on whom he leans; in the other he lays hold on a rule by which he works, and works as methodically and regularly as a piece of machinery. Beginning on a certain day, he finishes, like stroke of clock, duly as the seventh sun of the fourth week is sinking below the horizon. We trace in the one the action of the imagination, fostering one over-mastering passion into strength, till the person becomes capable of attempting the most daring enterprises, and enduring the most dreadful sufferings. In the other we behold the intervention of a Divine Agent, who plants in the soul a new principle, and thence educes a new life.

The war in which Loyola and his nine companions enrolled themselves when on the 15th of August, 1534, they made their vow in the Church of Montmartre, was to be waged against the Saracens of the East. They acted so far on their original design as to proceed to Venice, where they learned that their project was meanwhile impracticable. The war which had just broken out between the Republic and the Porte had closed the gates of Asia. They took this as an intimation that the field of their operations was to be in the Western world. Returning on their path they now directed their steps towards Rome. In every town through which they passed on their way to the Eternal City, they left behind them an immense reputation for sanctity by their labours in the hospitals, and their earnest addresses to the populace on the streets. As they drew nigh to Rome, and the hearts of some of his companions were beginning to despond, Loyola was cheered by a vision, in which Christ appeared and said to him, "In Rome will I be gracious unto thee."[2242] The hopes this vision inspired were not to be disappointed. Entering the gates of the capital of Christendom, and throwing themselves at the feet of Paul III., they met a most gracious reception. The Pope hailed their offer of assistance as most opportune. Mighty dangers at that hour threatened the Papacy, and with the half of Europe in revolt, and the old monkish orders become incapable, this new and unexpected aid seemed sent by Heaven. The rules and constitution of the new order were drafted, and ultimately approved, by the Pope. Two peculiarities in the constitution of the proposed order specially recommended it in the eyes of Paul III. The first was its vow of unconditional obedience. The society swore to obey the Pope as an army obeys its general. It was not *canonical* but *military* obedience which its members offered him. They would go to whatsoever errand he should be pleased to order them. They were, in short, to be not so much monks as soldiers. The second peculiarity was that their services were to be wholly gratuitous; never would they ask so much as a penny from the Papal See.

It was resolved that the new order should bear the name of *The Company of Jesus*. Loyola modestly declined the honour of being accounted its founder. Christ himself, he affirmed, had dictated to him its constitution in his cave at Manressa. He was its real Founder: whose name then could it so appropriately bear as His? The bull constituting it was issued on the 27th of September, 1540, and was entitled *Regimini Militantis Ecclesiæ*,[2243] and bore that the persons it enrolled into an army were to bear "the standard of the Cross, to wield the arms of God, to serve the only Lord and the Roman Pontiff, His Vicar on earth."

CHAPTER III
ORGANISATION AND TRAINING OF THE JESUITS

THE long-delayed wishes of Loyola had been realised, and his efforts, abortive in the past, had now at length been crowned with success. The Papal bull had given formal existence to the order, what Christ had done in heaven his Vicar had ratified on the earth. But Loyola was too wise to think that all had been accomplished; he knew that he was only at the beginning of his labours. In the little band around him he saw but the nucleus of an army that would multiply and expand till one day it should be as the stars in multitude, and bear the standard of victory to every land on earth. The gates of the East were meanwhile closed against him; but the Western world would not always set limits to the triumphs of his spiritual arms. He would yet subjugate both hemispheres, and extend the dominion of Rome from the rising to the setting sun. Such were the schemes that Loyola, who hid under his mendicant's cloak an ambition vast as Alexander's, was at that moment revolving. Assembling his comrades one day about this time, he addressed them, his biographer Bouhours tells us, in a long speech, saying, "Ought we not to conclude that we are called to win to God, not only a single nation, a single country, *but all nations, all the kingdoms of the world?*"

An army to conquer the world, Loyola was forming. But he knew that nothing is stronger than its weakest part, and therefore the soundness of every link, the thorough discipline and tried fidelity of every soldier in this mighty host was with him an essential point. That could be secured only by making each individual, before enrolling himself, pass through an ordeal that should sift, and try, and harden him to the utmost.

But first the Company of Jesus had to elect a head. The dignity was offered to Loyola. He modestly declined the post, as Julius Cæsar did the diadem. After four days spent in prayer and penance, his disciples returned and humbly supplicated him to be their chief. Ignatius, viewing this as an intimation of the will of God, consented. He was the first General of the order. Few royal sceptres bring with them such an amount of real power as this election bestowed on Loyola. The day would come when the tiara itself would bow before that yet mightier authority which was represented by the cap of the General of the Jesuits.

The second step was to frame the "Constitutions" of the society. In this labour Loyola accepted the aid of Lainez, the ablest of his converts. Seeing it was at God's command that Ignatius had planted the tree of Jesuitism in the spiritual vineyard, it was to be expected that the Constitutions of the Company would proceed from the same high source. The Constitutions were declared to be a revelation from God, the inspiration of the Holy Spirit.[2245] This gave them absolute authority over the members, and paved the way for the substitution of the Constitution and canons of the Society of Jesus in the room of Christianity itself. These canons and Instructions were not published: they were not communicated to all the members of the society even; they were made known to a few only—in all their extent to a very few. They took care to print them in their own college at Prague; and if it happened that they were printed elsewhere, they secured and destroyed the edition. "I cannot discover," says M. de la Chalotais, "that the Constitutions of the Jesuits have ever been seen or examined by any tribunal whatsoever, secular or ecclesiastic; by any sovereign—not even by the Court of Chancery of Prague, when permission was asked to print them . . . They have taken all sorts of precautions to keep them a secret."[2246] For a century they were concealed from the knowledge of the world; and it was an accident which at last dragged them into the light from the darkness in which they had so long been buried.

It is not easy, perhaps it is not possible, to say what number of volumes of the Constitutions of the Jesuits form. M. Louis René de la Chalotais, Procurator-General of King Louis XV., in his *Report on the Constitutions of the Jesuits*, given in to the Parliament of Bretagne, speaks of fifty volumes folio. That was in the year 1761, or 221 years after the founding of the order. This code, then enormous, must be greatly more so now, seeing every bull and brief of the Pope addressed to the society, every edict of its General, is so much more added to a legislation that is continually augmenting. We doubt whether any member of their order is found bold enough to undertake a complete study of them, or ingenious enough to reconcile all their contradictions and inconsistencies. Prudently abstaining from venturing into a labyrinth from which he may never emerge, he simply asks, not what do the Constitutions say, but what does the General command? Practically the *will* of his chief is the *code* of the Jesuit.

We shall first consider the powers of the General. The original bull of Paul III. constituting the Company gave to "Ignatius de Loyola, with nine priests, his companions," the power to make Constitutions and particular rules, and also to alter them. The legislative power thus rested in the hands of the General and his company—that is, in a "Congregation" representing them. But when Loyola died, and Lainez succeeded him as General, one of his first acts was to assemble a Congregation, and cause it to be decided that the General only had the right to make rules.[2247] This crowned the autocracy of the General, for while he has the power of legislating for all others, no one may legislate for him. He acts without control, without responsibility, without law. It is true that in certain cases the society may depose the General. But it cannot exercise its powers unless it be assembled, and the General alone can assemble the Congregation. The whole order, with all its authority, is, in fact, comprised in him.

In virtue of his prerogative the General can command and regulate everything in the society. He may make special Constitutions for the advantage of the society, and he may alter them, abrogate them, and make new ones, dating them at any time he pleases. These new rules must be regarded as confirmed by apostolic authority, not merely from the time they were made, but the time they are dated.

The General assigns to all provincials, superiors, and members of the society, of whatever grade, the powers they are to exercise, the places where they are to labour, the missions they are to discharge, and he may annul or confirm their acts at his pleasure. He has the right to nominate provincials and rectors, to admit or exclude members, to say what proffered dignity they are or are not to accept, to change the destinations of legacies, and, though to give money to his relatives exposes him to deposition, "he may yet give alms to any amount that he may deem conducive to the glory of God." He is invested moreover with the entire government and regulation of the colleges of the society. He may institute missions in all parts of the world. When commanding in the name of Jesus Christ, and in virtue of obedience, he commands under the penalty of mortal and venial sin. From his orders there is no appeal to the Pope. He can release from vows; he can examine into the consciences of the members; but it is useless to particularise—the General is the society.[2248]

The General alone, we have said, has power to make laws, ordinances, and declarations. This power is *theoretically* bounded, though *practically* absolute. It has been declared that everything *essential* (Substantia Institutionis) to the society is immutable, and therefore removed beyond the power of the General. But it has never yet been determined what things belong to the *essence* of the institute. Many attempts have been made to solve this question, but no solution that is comprehensible has ever been arrived at; and so long as this question remains without an answer, the powers of the General will remain without a limit.

Let us next attend to the organisation of the society. The Jesuit monarchy covers the globe. At its head, as we have said, is a sovereign, who rules over all, but is himself ruled over by no one. First come six grand divisions termed *Assistanzen*, satrapies or princedoms. These comprehend the space stretching from the Indus to the Mediterranean; more particularly India, Spain and Portugal, Germany and France, Italy and Sicily, Poland and Lithuania.[2249] Outside this area the Jesuits have established missions. The heads of these six divisions act as coadjutors to their General; they are his staff or cabinet.

These six great divisions are subdivided into thirty-seven Provinces.[2250] Over each province is placed a chief, termed a Provincial. The provinces are again subdivided into a variety of houses or establishments. First come the houses of the *Professed*, presided over by their Provost. Next come the colleges, or houses of the novices and scholars, presided over by their Rector or Superior. Where these cannot be established, "residences" are erected, for the accommodation of the priests who perambulate the district, preaching and hearing confessions. And lastly may be mentioned "mission-houses," in which Jesuits live unnoticed as secular clergy, but seeking, by all possible means, to promote the interests of the society.[2251]

From his chamber in Rome the eye of the General surveys the world of Jesuitism to its farthest bounds; there is nothing done in it which he does not see; there is nothing spoken in it which he does not hear. It becomes us to note the means by which this almost superhuman intelligence is acquired. Every year a list of the houses and members of the society, with the name, talents, virtues, and failings of each, is laid before the General. In addition to the annual report, every one of the thirty-seven provincials must send him a report monthly of the state of his province. He must inform him minutely of its political and ecclesiastical condition. Every superior of a college must report once every three months. The heads of houses of residence, and houses of novitiates, must do the same. In short, from every quarter of his vast dominions come a monthly and a trimonthly report. If the matter reported on has reference to persons outside the society, the Constitutions direct that the provincials and superiors shall write to the General in cipher. "Such precautions are taken against enemies," says M. de Chalotais. "Is the system of the Jesuits inimical to all governments?"

Thus to the General of the Jesuits the world lies "naked and open." He sees by a thousand eyes, he hears by a thousand ears; and when he has a behest to execute, he can select the fittest agent from an innumerable host, all of whom are ready to do his bidding. The past history, the good and evil qualities of every member of the society, his talents, his dispositions, his inclinations, his tastes, his secret thoughts, have all been strictly examined, minutely chronicled, and laid before the eye of the General. It is the same as if he were present in person, and had seen and conversed with each.

All ranks, from the nobleman to the day-labourer; all trades, from the opulent banker to the shoemaker and porter; all professions, from the stoled dignitary and the learned professor to the cowled mendicant; all grades of literary men, from the philosopher, the mathematician, and the historian, to the schoolmaster and the reporter on the provincial newspaper, are enrolled in the society. Marshalled, and in continual attendance, before their chief, stand this host, so large in numbers, and so various in gifts. At his word they go, and at his word they come, speeding over seas and mountains, across frozen steppes, or burning plains, on his errand. Pestilence, or battle, or death may lie on his path, the Jesuit's obedience is not less prompt. Selecting one, the General sends him to the royal cabinet. Making choice of another, he opens to him the door of Parliament. A third he enrols in a political club; a fourth he places in the pulpit of a church, whose creed he professes that he may betray it; a fifth he commands to mingle in the saloons of the *literati*; a sixth he sends to act his part in the Evangelical Conference; a seventh he seats beside the domestic hearth; and an eighth he sends afar off to barbarous tribes, where, speaking a strange tongue, and wearing a rough garment, he executes, amidst hardships and perils, the will of his superior. There is no disguise which the Jesuit will not wear, no art he will not employ, no motive he will not feign, no creed he will not profess, provided only he can acquit himself as a true soldier in the Jesuit army, and accomplish the work on which he has been sent forth. "We have men," exclaimed a General exultingly, as he glanced over the long roll of philosophers, orators, statesmen, and scholars who stood before him, ready to serve him in the State or in the Church, in the camp or in the school, at home or abroad—"We have men for martyrdom if they be required."

No one can be enrolled in the Society of Jesus till he has undergone a severe and long-continued course of training. Let us glance at the several grades of that great army, and the preparatory discipline in the case of each. There are four classes of Jesuits. We begin with the lowest. The *Novitiates* are the first in order of admission, the last in dignity. When one presents himself for admission into the order, a strict scrutiny takes place into his talents, his disposition, his family, his former life; and if it is seen that he is not likely to be of service to the society, he is at once dismissed. If his fitness appears probable, he is received into the House of Primary Probation.[2252] Here he is forbidden all intercourse with the servants within and his relations outside the house. A *Compend* of the Institutions is submitted for his consideration; the full body of laws and regulations being withheld from him as yet. If he possesses property he is told that he must give it to the poor—that is, to the society. His tact and address, his sound judgment and business talent, his health and bodily vigour, all are closely watched and noted; above all, his *obedience* is subjected to severe experiment. If he acquits himself on the trial to the satisfaction of his examiners, he receives the Sacrament, and is advanced to the House of Second Probation.[2253]

Here the discipline is of a yet severer kind. The novitiate first devotes a certain period to confession of sins and meditation. He next fulfills a course of service in the hospitals, learning humility by helping the poor and ministering at the beds of the sick. To further his advance in this grace, he next spends a certain term in begging his bread from door to door. Thus he learns to live on the coarsest fare and to sleep on the hardest couch. To perfect himself in the virtue of self-abnegation, he next discharges for awhile the most humiliating and repulsive offices in the house in which he lives. And now, this course of service ended, he is invited to show his powers of operating on others, by communicating instruction to boys in Christian doctrine, by hearing confessions, and by preaching in public. This course is to last two years, unless the superior should see fit to shorten it on the ground of greater zeal, or superior talent.

The period of probation at an end, the candidate for admission into the Order of Jesus is to present himself before the superior, furnished with certificates from those under whose eye he has fulfilled his six *experimenta*, or trials, as to the manner in which he has acquitted himself. If the testimonials should prove satisfactory to the superior, the novitiate is enrolled, not as yet in the Company of the Jesuits, but among the *Indifferents*. He is presumed to have no choice as regards the place he is to occupy in the august corps he aspires to enter; he leaves that entirely to the decision of the superior; he is equally ready to stand at the head or at the foot of the body; to discharge the most menial or the most dignified service; to play his part in the saloons of the great, encompassed by luxury and splendour, or to discharge his mission in the hovels of the poor, in the midst of misery and filth; to remain at home, or to go to the ends of the earth. To have a preference, though unexpressed, is to fall into deadly sin. Obedience is not only the letter of the vow, it is the lesson that his training has written in his heart.[2254]

This further trial gone through, the approved novitiate may now take the three simple vows—poverty, chastity, and obedience—which, with certain modifications, he must ever after renew twice every year. The novitiate is now admitted into the class of *Scholars*. The Jesuits have colleges of their own, amply endowed by wealthy devotees, and to one of these the novitiate is sent, to receive instruction in the higher mysteries of the society. His intellectual powers are here more severely tested and trained, and according to the genius and subtlety he may display, and his progress in his studies, so is the post assigned to him in due time in the order. "The qualities to be desired and commended in the scholars," say the Constitutions, "are acuteness of talent, brilliancy of example, and soundness of body."[2255] They are to be chosen men, picked from the flower of the troop, and the General has absolute power in admitting or dismissing them according to his expectations of their utility in promoting the designs of the institute.[2256] Having finished his course, first as a simple scholar, and secondly as an approved scholar, he renews his three vows, and passes into the third class, or *Coadjutors*.

The coadjutors are divided into temporal and spiritual. The temporal coadjutor is never admitted into holy orders.[2257] Such are retained to minister in the lowest offices. They become college cooks, porters, or purveyors. For these and similar purposes it is held expedient that they should be "lovers of virtue and perfection," and "content to serve the society in the careful office of a Martha."[2258] The spiritual coadjutor must be a priest of adequate learning, that he may assist the society in hearing confessions, and giving instructions in Christian doctrine. It is from among the spiritual coadjutors that the rectors of colleges are usually selected by the General. It is a further privilege of theirs that they may be assembled in congregation to deliberate with the *Professed* members in matters of importance,[2259] but no vote is granted them in the election of a General. Having passed with approbation the many stringent tests to which he is here subjected, in order to perfect his humility and obedience, and having duly deposited in the exchequer of the society whatever property he may happen to possess, the spiritual coadjutor, if a candidate for the highest grade, is admitted to the oblation of his vows, which are similar in form and substance to those he has already taken, with this exception, that they assign to the General the place of God. "I promise," so runs the oath, "to the Omnipotent God, in presence of his virgin mother, and of all the heavenly hierarchy, and to thee, Father General of the Society of Jesus, *holding the place of God*," &c.[2260] With this oath sworn on its threshold, he enters the inner circle of the society, and is enrolled among the *Professed*.

The *Professed Members* constitute the society *par excellence*. They alone know its deepest secrets, and they alone wield its highest powers. But perfection in Jesuitism cannot be reached otherwise than by the loss of manhood. Will, judgment, conscience, liberty, all the Jesuit lays down at the feet of his General. It is a tremendous sacrifice, but to him the General is God. He now takes his fourth, or peculiar vow, in which he binds himself to go, without question, delay, or repugnance, to whatever region of the earth, and on whatever errand, the Pope may be pleased to send him. This he promises to the Omnipotent God, and to his General, *holding the place of God*. The wisdom, justice, righteousness of the command he is not to question; he is not even to permit his mind to dwell upon it for a moment; it is the command of his General, and the command of his General is the precept of the Almighty. His superiors are "over him in the place of the Divine Majesty."[2261] "In not fewer than 500 places in the Constitutions," says M. de la Chalotais, "are expressions used similar to the following:—'We must always see Jesus Christ in the General; be obedient to him in all his behests, as if they came directly from God himself.'"[2262] When the command of the superior goes forth, the person to whom it is directed "is not to stay till he has finished the letter his pen is tracing," say the Constitutions; "he must give instant compliance, so that holy obedience may be perfect in us in every point—in execution, in will, in intellect."[2263] Obedience is styled "the tomb of the will," "a blessed blindness, which causes the soul to see the road to salvation," and the members of the society are taught to "immolate their will as a sheep is sacrificed." The Jesuit is to be in the hands of his superior, "as the axe is in the hands of the wood-cutter," or "as a staff is in the hands of an old man, which serves him wherever and in whatever thing he is pleased to use it." In fine, the Constitutions enjoin that "they who live under obedience shall permit themselves to be moved and directed under Divine Providence by their superiors *just as if they were a corpse*, which allows itself to be moved and handled in any way."[2265] The annals of mankind do not furnish another example of a despotism so finished. We know of no other instance in which the members of the body are so numerous, or the ramifications so wide, and yet the centralisation and cohesion is so perfect.

We have traced at some length the long and severe discipline which every member must undergo before being admitted into the select class that by way of eminence constitute the society. Before arriving on the threshold of the inner circle of Jesuitism, three times has the candidate passed through that terrible ordeal—first as a novice, secondly as a scholar, thirdly as a coadjutor. Is his training held to be complete when he is admitted among the Professed? No: a fourth time must he undergo the same dreadful process. He is thrown back again into the crucible, and kept amid its fires, till pride, and obstinacy, and self-will, and love of ease—till judgment, soul, and conscience have all been purged out of him, and then he comes forth, fully refined, completely attempered and hardened, "a vessel fully fitted" for the use of his General; prepared to execute with a conscience that never remonstrates his most terrible command, and to undertake with a will that never rebels the most difficult and dangerous enterprises he may assign him. In the words of an eloquent writer—"Talk of drilling and discipline! why, the drilling and the discipline which gave to Alexander the men that marched in triumph from Macedon to the Indus; to Cæsar, the men that marched in triumph from Rome to the wilds of Caledonia; to Hannibal, the men that marched in triumph from Carthage to Rome; to Napoleon, the men whose achievements surpassed in brilliance the united glories of the soldiers of Macedon, of Carthage, and of Rome; and to Wellington, the men who smote into the dust the very flower of Napoleon's chivalry—why, the drilling and the discipline of all these combined cannot, in point of stern, rigid, and protracted severity, for a moment be compared to the drilling and discipline which fitted and moulded men for becoming full members of the militant institute of the Jesuits."[2265]

Such Loyola saw was the corps that was needed to confront the armies of Protestantism and turn back the advancing tide of light and liberty. Touched with a Divine fire, the disciples of the Gospel attained at once to a complete renunciation of self, and a magnanimity of soul which enabled them to brave all dangers and endure all sufferings, and to bear the standard of a recovered Gospel over deserts and oceans, in the midst of hunger and pestilence, of dungeons and racks and fiery stakes. It was vain to think of overcoming warriors like these unless by combatants of an equal temper and spirit, and Loyola set himself to fashion such. He could not clothe them with the panoply of light, he could not inspire them with that holy and invincible courage which springs from faith, nor could he so enkindle their souls with the love of the Saviour, and the joys of the life eternal, as that they should despise the sufferings of time; but he could give them their counterfeits: he could enkindle them with fanaticism, inspire them with a Luciferian ambition, and so pervert and indurate their souls by evil maxims, and long and rigorous training, that they should be insensible to shame and pain, and would welcome suffering and death. Such were the weapons of the men he sent forth to the battle.

CHAPTER IV

MORAL CODE OF THE JESUITS—PROBABILISM, ETC.

WE have not yet surveyed the full and perfect equipment of those troops which Loyola sent forth to prosecute the war against Protestantism. Nothing was left unthought of and unprovided for which might assist them in covering their opponents with defeat, and crowning themselves with victory. They were set free from every obligation, whether imposed by the natural or the Divine law. Every stratagem, artifice, and disguise were lawful to men in whose favour all distinction between right and wrong had been abolished. They might assume as many shapes as Proteus, and exhibit as many colours as the chameleon. They stood apart and alone among the human race. First of all, they were cut off from country. Their vow bound them to go to whatever land their General might send them, and to remain there as long as he might appoint. Their country was the society. They were cut off from family and friends. Their vow taught them to forget their father's house, and to esteem themselves holy only when every affection and desire which nature had planted in their breasts had been plucked up by the roots. They were cut off from property and wealth. For although the society was immensely rich, its individual members possessed nothing. Nor could they cherish the hope of ever becoming personally wealthy, seeing they had taken a vow of perpetual poverty. If it chanced that a rich relative died, and left them his heirs, the General relieved them of their vow, and sent them back into the world, for so long a time as might enable them to take possession of the wealth of which they had been named the heirs; and, resuming their vow as Jesuits, laid every penny of their newly-acquired riches at the feet of the General.

They were cut off, moreover, from the State. They were discharged from all civil and national relationships and duties. They were under a higher code than the national one—the *Institutions*, namely, which Loyola had edited, and the Spirit of God had inspired; and they were the subjects of a higher monarch than the sovereign of the nation—their own General. Nay, more, the Jesuits were cut off even from the Pope. For if their General "held the place of the Omnipotent God," much more did he hold the place of "his Vicar." And so was it in fact; for soon the members of the Society of Jesus came to recognise no laws but their own, and though at their first formation they professed to have no end but the defence and glory of the Papal See, it came to pass when they grew to be strong that, instead of serving the tiara, they compelled the tiara to serve the society, and made their own wealth, power, and dominion the one grand object of their existence. They were a Papacy within the Papacy—a Papacy whose organisation was more perfect, whose instincts were more cruel, whose workings were more mysterious, and whose dominion was more destructive than that of the old Papacy.

So stood the Society of Jesus. A deep and wide gulf separated it from all other communities and interests. Set free from the love of family, from the ties of kindred, from the claims of country, and from the rule of law, careless of the happiness they might destroy, and the misery and pain and woe they might inflict, the members were at liberty, without control or challenge, to pursue their terrible end, which was the dethronement of every other power, the extinction of every other interest but their own, and the reduction of mankind into abject slavery, that on the ruins of the liberty, the virtue, and the happiness of the world they might raise themselves to supreme, unlimited dominion. But we have not yet detailed all the appliances with which the Jesuits were careful to furnish themselves for the execution of their unspeakably audacious and diabolical design. In the midst of these abysses there opens to our eye a yet profounder abyss. To enjoy exemption from all human authority and from every earthly law was to them a small matter; nothing would satisfy their lust for licence save the entire abrogation of the moral law, and nothing would appease their pride save to trample under foot the majesty of heaven. We now come to speak of the moral code of the Jesuits.

The key-note of their ethical code is the famous maxim that *the end sanctifies the means*. Before that maxim the eternal distinction of right and wrong vanishes. Not only do the stringency and sanctions of human law dissolve and disappear, but the authority and majesty of the Decalogue are overthrown. There are no conceivable crime, villainy, and atrocity which this maxim will not justify. Nay, such become dutiful and holy, provided they be done for "the greater glory of God," by which the Jesuit means the honour, interest, and advancement of his society. In short, the Jesuit may do whatever he has a mind to do, all human and Divine laws notwithstanding. This is a very grave charge, but the evidence of its truth is, unhappily, too abundant, and the difficulty lies in making a selection.

What the Popes have attempted to do by the plenitude of their power, namely, to make sin to be no sin, the Jesuit doctors have done by their casuistry. "The first and great commandment in the law," said the same Divine Person who proclaimed it from Sinai, "is to love the Lord thy God." The Jesuit casuists have set men free from this obligation to love God. Escobar[2266] collects the different sentiments of the famous divines of the Society of Jesus upon the question, *When is a man obliged to have actually an affection for God?* The following are some of these:—Suarez says, "It is sufficient a man love him before he dies, not assigning any particular time. Vasquez, that it is sufficient even at the point of death. Others, when a man receives his baptism: others, when he is obliged to be contrite: others, upon holidays. But our Father Castro-Palao[2267] disputes all these opinions, and that justly. Hurtado de Mendoza pretends that a man is obliged to do it once every year. Our Father Coninck believes a man to be obliged once in three or four years. Henriquez, once in five years. But Filiutius affirms it to be probable that in rigour a man is not obliged every five years. What then? He leaves the point to the wise." "We are not," says Father Sirmond, "so much commanded to love him as not to hate him."[2268] Thus do the Jesuit theologians make void "the first and great commandment of the law."

The second commandment in the law is, "Thou shalt love thy neighbour as thyself." This second great commandment meets with no more respect at the hands of the Jesuits than the first. Their morality dashes both tables of the law in pieces; charity to man it makes void equally with the love of God. The methods by which this may be done are innumerable.[2269]

The first of these is termed *probabilism*. This is a device which enables a man to commit any act, be it ever so manifest a breach of the moral and Divine law, without the least restraint of conscience, remorse of mind, or guilt before God. What is probabilism? By way of answer we shall suppose that a man has a great mind to do a certain act, of the lawfulness of which he is in doubt. He finds that there are two opinions upon the point: the one *probably* true, to the effect that the act is lawful; the other *more probably* true, to the effect that the act is sinful. Under the Jesuit regimen the man is at liberty to act upon the *probable* opinion. The act is probably right, but more probably wrong, nevertheless he is safe in doing it, in virtue of the doctrine of probabilism. It is important to ask, what makes an opinion probable? To make an opinion probable a Jesuit finds easy indeed. If a single doctor has pronounced in its favour, though a score of doctors may have condemned it, or if the man can imagine in his own mind something like a tolerable reason for doing the act, the opinion that it is lawful becomes probable. It will be hard to name an act for which a Jesuit authority may not be produced, and harder still to find a man whose invention is so poor as not to furnish him with what he deems a good reason for doing what he is inclined to, and therefore it may be pronounced impossible to instance a deed, however manifestly opposed to the light of nature and the law of God, which may not be committed under the shield of the monstrous dogma of probabilism.[2270]

We are neither indulging in satire nor incurring the charge of false-witness-bearing in this picture of Jesuit theology. "A person may do what he considers allowable," says Emmanuel Sa, of the Society of Jesus, "according to a probable opinion, although the contrary may be the more probable one. The opinion of a single grave doctor is all that is requisite." A yet greater doctor, Filiutius, of Rome, confirms him in this. "It is allowable," says he, "to follow the less probable opinion, even though it be the less safe one. That is the common judgment of many authors." "Of two contrary opinions," says Paul Laymann, "touching the legality or illegality of any human action, every one may follow in practice or in action that which he should prefer, although it may appear to the agent himself less probable in theory." He adds: "A learned person may give contrary advice to different persons according to contrary probable opinions, whilst he still preserves discretion and prudence." We may say with Pascal, "These Jesuit casuists give us elbow-room at all events.!"[2271]

It is and *it is not* is the motto of this theology. It is the true Lesbian rule which shapes itself according to that which we wish to measure by it. Would we have any action to be sinful, the Jesuit moralist turns this side of the code to us; would we have it to be lawful, he turns the other side. Right and wrong are put thus in our own power; we can make the same action a sin or a duty as we please, or as we deem it expedient. To steal the property, slander the character, violate the chastity, or spill the blood of a fellow-creature, is *most probably* wrong, but let us imagine some good to be got by it, and it is *probably* right. The Jesuit writers, for the sake of those who are dull of understanding and slow to apprehend the freedom they bring them, have gone into particulars and compiled lists of actions, esteemed sinful, unnatural, and abominable by the moral sense of all nations hitherto, but which, in virtue of this new morality, are no longer so, and they have explained how these actions may be safely done, with a minuteness of detail and a luxuriance of illustration, in which it were tedious in some cases, immodest in others, to follow them.

One would think that this was licence enough. What more can the Jesuit need, or what more can he possibly have, seeing by a little effort of invention he can overleap every human and Divine barrier, and commit the most horrible crimes, on the mightiest possible scale, and neither feel remorse of conscience nor fear of punishment? But this unbounded liberty of wickedness did not content the sons of Loyola. They panted for a liberty, if possible, yet more boundless; they wished to be released from the easy condition of imagining some good end for the wickedness they wished to perpetrate, and to be free to sin without the trouble of assigning even to themselves any end at all. This they have accomplished by the method of *directing the intention*.

This is a new ethical science, unknown to those ages which were not privileged to bask in the illuminating rays of the Society of Jesus, and it is as simple as convenient. It is the soul, they argue, that does the act, so far as it is moral or immoral. As regards the body's share in it, neither virtue nor vice can be predicated of it. If, therefore, while the hand is shedding blood, or the tongue is calumniating character, or uttering a falsehood, the soul can so abstract itself from what the body is doing as to occupy itself the while with some holy theme, or fix its meditation upon some benefit or advantage likely to arise from the deed, which it knows, or at least suspects, the body is at that moment engaged in doing, the soul contracts neither guilt nor stain, and the man runs no risk of ever being called to account for the murder, or theft, or calumny, by God, or of incurring his displeasure on that ground. We are not satirising; we are simply stating the morality of the Jesuits. "We never," says the Father Jesuit in Pascal's *Letters*, "suffer such a thing as the formal intention to sin with the sole design of sinning; and if any person whatever should persist in having no other end but evil in the evil that he does, we break with him at once—such conduct is diabolical. This holds true without exception of age, sex, or rank. But when the person is not of such a wretched disposition as this, we try to put in practice our method of *directing the intention*, which simply consists in his proposing to himself, as the end of his actions, some allowable object. Not that we do not endeavour, as far as we can, to dissuade men from doing things forbidden; but when we cannot prevent the action, we at least purify the motive, and thus correct the viciousness of the means by the goodness of the end. Such is the way in which our Fathers [of the society] have contrived to permit those acts of violence to which men usually resort in vindication of their honour. They have no more to do than to turn off the intention from the desire of vengeance, which is criminal, and to direct it to a desire to defend their honour, which, according to us, is quite warrantable. And in this way our doctors discharge all their duty towards God and towards man. By permitting the action they gratify the world; and by purifying the intention they give satisfaction to the Gospel. This is a secret, sir, which was entirely unknown to the ancients; the world is indebted for the discovery entirely to our doctors. You understand it now, I hope."[2272]

Let us take a few illustrative cases, but only such as Jesuit casuists themselves have furnished. "A military man," says Reginald,[2273] "may demand satisfaction on the spot from the person who has injured him, not indeed with the intention of rendering evil for evil, but with that of preserving his honour." Lessius[2274] observes that if a man has received a blow on the face, he must on no account have an intention to avenge himself; but he may lawfully have an intention to avoid infamy, and may, with that view, repel the insult immediately, even at the point of the sword. "If your enemy is disposed to injure you," says Escobar, "you have no right to wish his death by a movement of hatred, though you may to save yourself from harm." And says Hurtado de Mendoza,[2275] "We may pray God to visit with speedy death those who are bent on persecuting us, if there is no other way of escaping from it." "An incumbent," says Gaspar de Hurtado,[2276] "may, without any mortal sin desire the decease of a life-renter on his benefice, and a son that of a father, and rejoice when it happens, provided always it is for the sake of the profit that is to accrue from the event, and not from personal aversion." Sanchez teaches that it is lawful to kill our adversary in a duel, or even privately, when he intends to deprive us of our honour or property unjustly in a law-suit, or by chicanery, and when there is no other way of preserving them.[2277] It is equally right to kill in a private way a false accuser, and his witness, and even the judge who has been bribed to favour them. "A most pious assassination!" exclaims Pascal.

CHAPTER V

THE JESUIT TEACHING ON REGICIDE, MURDER, LYING, THEFT, ETC.

THE three great rules of the code of the Jesuits, which we have stated in the foregoing chapter—namely, (1) that the end justifies the means; (2) that it is safe to do any action if it be probably right, although it may be more probably wrong; and (3) that if one know to direct the intention aright, there is no deed, be its moral character what it may, which one may not do—may seem to give a licence of acting so immense that to add thereto were an altogether superfluous, and indeed an impossible task. But if the liberty with which these three maxims endow the Jesuit cannot be made larger, its particular applications may nevertheless be made more pointed, and the man who holds back from using it in all its extent may be emboldened, despite his remaining scruples, or the dullness of his intellectual perceptions, to avail himself to the utmost of the advantages it offers, "for the greater glory of God." He is to be taught, not merely by general rules, but by specific examples, how he may sin and yet not become sinful; how he may break the law and yet not suffer the penalty. But, further, these sons of Loyola are the kings of the world, and the sole heirs of all its wealth, honours, and pleasures; and whatever law, custom, sacred and venerable office, august and kingly authority, may stand between them and their rightful lordship over mankind, they are at liberty to throw down and tread into the dust as a vile and accursed thing. The moral maxims of the Jesuits are to be put in force against kings as well as against peasants.

The lawfulness of killing excommunicated, that is Protestant, kings, the Jesuit writers have been at great pains to maintain, and by a great variety of arguments to defend and enforce. The proof is abundant as it is painful. M. de la Chalotais reports to the Parliament of Bretagne, as the result of his examination of the laws and doctrines of the Jesuits, that on this point there is complete and startling unanimity in their teaching. By the same logical track do the whole host of Jesuit writers arrive at the same terrible conclusion, the slaughter, namely, of the sovereign on whom the Pope has pronounced sentence of deposition. If he shall take meekly his extrusion from power, and seek neither to resist nor revenge his being hurled from his throne, his life may be spared; but should "he persist in disobedience," says M. de la Chalotais, himself a Papist, and addressing a Popish Parliament, "he may be treated as a tyrant, in which case anybody may kill him."[2278] Such is the course of reasoning established by all authors of the society, who have written *ex professo* on these subjects—Bellarmine, Suarez, Molina, Mariana, Santarel—all the Ultramontanes without exception, since the establishment of the society."[2279]

But have not the writers of this school expressed in no measured terms their abhorrence of murder? Have they not loudly exclaimed against the sacrilege of touching him on whom the Church's anointing oil has been poured as king? In short, do they not forbid and condemn the crime of regicide? Yes: this is true; but they protest with a warmth that is fitted to awaken suspicion. Rome can take back her anointing, and when she has stripped the monarch of his office he becomes the lawful victim of her consecrated dagger. On what grounds, the Jesuits demand, can the killing of one who is no longer a king be called regicide? Suarez tells us that when a king is deposed he is no longer to be regarded as a king, but as a tyrant: "he therefore loses his authority, and from that moment may be lawfully killed." Nor is the opinion of the Jesuit Mariana less decided. Speaking of a prince, he says: "If he should overthrow the religion of the country, and introduce a public enemy within the State, *I shall never consider that man to have done wrong, who, favouring the public wishes, would attempt to kill him.* . . . It is useful that princes should be made to know, that if they oppress the State and become intolerable by their vices and their pollution, they hold their lives upon this tenure, *that to put them to death is not only laudable, but a glorious action.* . . . It is a glorious thing to exterminate this pestilent and mischievous race from the community of men."[2280]

Wherever the Jesuits have planted missions, opened seminaries, and established colleges, they have been careful to inculcate these principles in the minds of the youth; thus sowing the seeds of future tumults, revolutions, regicides, and wars. These evil fruits have appeared sometimes sooner, sometimes later, but they have never failed to show themselves, to the grief of nations and the dismay of kings. John Chatel, who attempted the life of Henry IV., had studied in the College of Clermont, in which the Jesuit Guignard was Professor of Divinity. In the chamber of the would-be regicide, a manuscript of Guignard was found, in which, besides other dangerous articles, that Father approved not only of the assassination of Henry III. by Clement, but also maintained that the same thing ought to be attempted against *le Bearnois*, as he called Henry IV., which occasioned the first banishment of the order out of France, as a society *detestable and diabolical*. The sentence of the Parliament, passed in 1594, ordained "that all the priests and scholars of the College of Clermont, and others calling themselves the Society of Jesus, as being corrupters of youth, disturbers of the public peace, and enemies of the king and State, should depart in three days from their house and college, and in fifteen days out of the whole kingdom."

But why should we dwell on these written proofs of the disloyal and murderous principles of the Jesuits, when their *acted deeds* bear still more emphatic testimony to the true nature and effects of their principles? We have only to look around, and on every hand the melancholy monuments of these doctrines meet our afflicted sight. To what country of Europe shall we turn where we are not able to track the Jesuit by his bloody footprints? What page of modern history shall we open and not read fresh proofs that the Papal doctrine of killing excommunicated kings was not meant to slumber in forgotten tomes, but to be acted out in the living world? We see Henry III. falling by their dagger. Henry IV. perishes by the same consecrated weapon. The King of Portugal dies by their order. The great Prince of Orange is dispatched by their agent, shot down at the door of his own dining-room. How many assassins they sent to England to murder Elizabeth, history attests. That she escaped their machinations is one of the marvels of history. Nor is it only the palaces of monarchs into which they have crept with their doctrines of murder and assassination; the very sanctuary of their own Popes they have defiled with blood. We behold Clement XIV. signing the order for the banishment of the Jesuits, and soon thereafter he is overtaken by their vengeance, and dies by poison. In the Gunpowder Plot we see them deliberately planning to destroy at one blow the nobility and gentry of England. To them we owe those civil wars which for so many years drenched with blood the fair provinces of France. They laid the train of that crowning horror, the St. Bartholomew massacre. Philip II. and the Jesuits share between them the guilt of the "Invincible Armada," which, instead of inflicting the measureless ruin and havoc which its authors intended, by a most merciful Providence became the means of exhausting the treasures and overthrowing the prestige of Spain. What a harvest of plots, tumults, seditions, revolutions, torturings, poisonings, assassinations, regicides, and massacres has Christendom reaped from the seed sown by the Jesuits! Nor can we be sure that we have yet seen the last and greatest of their crimes.

We can bestow only the most cursory glance at the teaching of the Jesuits under the other heads of moral duty. Let us take their doctrine of mental reservation. Nothing can be imagined more heinous and, at the same time, more dangerous. "The doctrine of equivocation," says Blackwell, "is for the consolation of afflicted Roman Catholics and the instruction of all the godly." It has been of special use to them when residing among infidels and heretics. In heathen countries, as China and Malabar, they have professed conformity to the rites and the worship of paganism, while remaining Roman Catholics at heart, and they have taught their converts to venerate their former deities in appearance, on the strength of directing aright the intention, and the pious fraud of concealing a crucifix under their clothes.

Equivocation they have carried into civil life, as well as into religion. "A man may swear," says Sanchez, "that he hath not done a thing though he really have, by understanding within himself that he did it not *on such and such a day, or before he was born*; or by reflecting on some other circumstance of the like nature; and yet the words he shall make use of shall not have a sense employing any such thing; and this is a thing of great convenience on many occasions, and is always justifiable when it is necessary or advantageous in anything that concerns a man's health, honour, or estate."[2281] Filiutius, in his *Moral Questions*, asks, "Is it wrong to use equivocation in swearing? I answer, first, that it is not in itself a sin to use equivocation in swearing . . . This is the common doctrine after Suarez." "Is it perjury or sin to equivocate in a just cause?" he further asks. "It is not perjury, " he answers. "As, for example, in the case of a man who has outwardly made a promise without the intention of promising; if he is asked whether he has promised, he may deny it, *meaning that he has not promised with a binding promise*; and thus he may *swear*.

Filiutius asks yet again, "With what precaution is equivocation to be used? When we begin, for instance, to say, *I swear*, we must insert in a subdued tone the mental restriction, *that today*, and then continue aloud, *I have not eaten such a thing*; or, *I swear*—then insert *I say*—then conclude in the same loud voice, "*that I have not done this or that thing*; for thus the whole speech is most true."[2282] What an admirable lesson in the art of speaking the truth to one's self, and lying and swearing falsely to everybody else![2283]

We shall offer no comment on the teaching of the Jesuits under the head of the seventh commandment. The doctrines of the society which relate to chastity are screened from exposure by the very enormity of their turpitude. We pass them as we would the open grave, whose putrid breath kills all who inhale it. Let all who value the sweetness of a pure imagination, and the joy of a conscience undefiled, shun the confessional as they would the chamber in which the plague is shut up, or the path in which lurks the deadly scorpion. The teaching of the Jesuits—everywhere deadly—is here a poison that consumes flesh, and bones, and soul.

Which precept of the Decalogue is it that the theology of the Jesuits does not set aside? We are commanded "to fear the great and dreadful name of the Lord our God." The Jesuit Bauny teaches us to blaspheme it. "If one has been hurried by passion into *cursing and doing despite to his Maker*, it may be determined that he has only sinned *venially*."[2284] This is much, but Casnedi goes a little farther. "Do what your conscience tells you to be good, and commanded," says this Jesuit; "if through invincible error you believe lying or blasphemy to be commanded by God, *blaspheme*."[2285] The licence given by the Jesuits to regicide we have already seen; not less ample is the provision their theology makes for the perpetration of ordinary homicides and murders. Reginald says it is lawful to kill a false witness, seeing otherwise one should be killed by him.[2286] Parents who seek to turn their children from the faith, says Fagundez, *"may justly be killed by them."*[2287] The Jesuit Amicus teaches that it is lawful for an ecclesiastic, or one in a religious order, *to kill a calumniator* when other means of defence are wanting.[2288] And Airult extends the same privilege to laymen. If one brings an impeachment before a prince or judge against another, and if that other cannot by any means avert the injury to his character, *he may kill him secretly*. He fortifies his opinion by the authority of Bannez, who gives the same latitude to the right of defence, with this slight qualification, that the calumniator should first be warned that he desist from his slander, *and if he will not, he should be killed, not openly, on account of the scandal, but secretly*.[2289]

Of a like ample kind is the liberty which the Jesuits permit to be taken with the property of one's neighbour. Dishonesty in all its forms they sanction. They encourage cheats, frauds, purloinings, robberies, by furnishing men with a ready justification of these misdeeds, and especially by persuading their votaries that if they will only take the trouble of doing them in the way of directing the *intention* according to their instructions, they need not fear being called to a reckoning for them hereafter. The Jesuit Emmanuel Sa teaches "that it is not a mortal sin to *take secretly* from him who would give if he were asked;" that "it is *not theft* to take a *small thing* from a husband or a father;" that if one has taken what he *doubts* to have been his own, that *doubt* makes it *probable* that it is *safe to keep it*; that if one, from an urgent necessity, or without causing much loss, *takes wood* from another man's pile, *he is not obliged to restore it*. One who has stolen small things at different times, is not obliged to make restitution till such time as they amount to a considerable sum. But should the purloiner feel restitution burdensome, it may comfort him to know that some Fathers *deny it with probability*.[2290]

The case of merchants, whose gains may not be increasing so fast as they could wish, has been kindly considered by the Fathers. Francis Tolet says that if a man cannot sell his wine at a fair price—that is, at a fair profit—he may mix a little water with his wine, or diminish his measure, and sell it for pure wine of full measure. Of course, if it be lawful to mix wine, it is lawful to adulterate all other articles of merchandise, or to diminish the weight, and go on vending as if the balance were just and the article genuine. Only the trafficker in spurious goods, with false balances, must be careful not to tell a lie; or if he should be compelled to equivocate, he must do it in accordance with the rules laid down by the Fathers for enabling one to say what is not true without committing falsehood.[2291]

Domestic servants also have been taken by the Fathers under the shield of their casuistry. Should a servant deem his wages not enough, or the food, clothing, and other necessaries provided for him not equal to that which is provided for the servants of similar rank in other houses, he may recompense himself by abstracting from his master's property as much as shall make his wages commensurate with his services. So has Valerius Reginald decided.[2292]

It is fair, however, that the pupil be cautioned that this lesson cannot safely be put in practice against his teacher. The story of John d'Alba, related by Pascal, shows that the Fathers do not relish these doctrines *in praxi* nearly so well as *in thesi*, when they themselves are the sufferers by them. D'Alba was a servant to the Fathers in the College of Clermont, in the Rue St. Jacques, and thinking that his wages were not equal to his merits, he stole somewhat from his masters to make up the discrepancy, never dreaming that they would make a criminal of him for following their approved rules. However, they threw him into prison on a charge of larceny. He was brought to trial on the 16th April, 1647. He confessed before the court to having taken some pewter plates, but maintained that the act was not to be regarded as a theft on the strength of this same doctrine of Father Bauny, which he produced before the judges, with attestation from another of the Fathers under whom he had studied these cases of conscience. Whereupon the judge, M. de Montrouge, gave sentence as follows:— "That the prisoner should not be acquitted upon the writings of these Fathers, containing a doctrine so unlawful, pernicious, and contrary to all laws, natural, Divine, and human, such as might confound all families, and authorise all domestic frauds and infidelities;" but that the over-faithful disciple "should be whipt before the College gate of Clermont by the common executioner, who at the same time should burn all the writings of those Fathers treating of theft; and that they should be prohibited to teach any such doctrine again *under pain of death.*"[2293]

But we should swell beyond all reasonable limit our enumeration, were we to quote even a tithe of the "moral maxims" of the Jesuits. There is not one in the long catalogue of sins and crimes which their casuistry does not sanction. Pride, ambition, avarice, luxury, bribery, and a host of vices which we cannot specify, and some of which are too horrible to be mentioned, find in these Fathers their patrons and defenders. The alchemists of the Middle Ages boasted that their art enabled them to operate on the essence of things, and to change what was vile into what was noble. But the still darker art of the Jesuits acts in the reverse order; it changes all that is noble into all that is vile. Theirs is an accursed alchemy by which they transmute good into evil, and virtue into vice. There is no destructive agency with which the world is liable to be visited, that penetrates so deep, or inflicts so remediless a ruin, as the morality of the Jesuits. The tornado sweeps along over the surface of the globe, leaving the earth naked and bare as before tree or shrub beautified it; but the summers of after years reclothe it with verdure and beautify it with flowers, and make it smile as sweetly as before. The earthquake overturns the dwelling of man, and swallows up the proudest of his cities; but his skill and power survive the shock, and when the destroyer has passed, the architect sets up again the fallen palace, and rebuilds the ruined city, and the catastrophe is effaced and forgotten in the greater splendour and the more solid strength of the restored structures. Revolution may overturn thrones, abolish laws, and break in pieces the framework of society; but when the fury of faction has spent its rage, order emerges from the chaos, law resumes its supremacy, and the institutions which had been destroyed in the hour of madness, are restored in the hour of calm wisdom that succeeds. But the havoc the Jesuit inflicts is irremediable. It has nothing in it counteractive or restorative; it is only evil. It is not upon the works of man or the institutions of man merely that it puts forth its fearfully destructive power; it is upon man himself. It is not the body of man that it strikes, like the pestilence; it is the soul. It is not a part, but the whole of man that it consigns to corruption and ruin. Conscience it destroys, knowledge it extinguishes, the very power of discerning between right and wrong it takes away, and shuts up the man in a prison whence no created agency or influence can set him free. The Fall defaced the image of God in which man was made; we say, defaced; it did not totally obliterate or extinguish it. Jesuitism, more terrible than the Fall, totally effaces from the soul of man the image of God. Of the "knowledge, righteousness, and true holiness" in which man was made it leaves not a trace. It plucks up by its very roots the moral constitution which God gave man. The full triumph of Jesuitism would leave nothing spiritual, nothing moral, nothing intellectual, nothing strictly and properly human existing upon the earth. Man it would change into the animal, impelled by nothing but appetites and passions, and these more fierce and cruel than those of the tiger. Society would become simply a herd of wolves, lawless, ravenous, greedy of each other's blood, and perpetually in quest of prey. Even Jesuitism itself would perish, devoured by its own progeny. Our earth at last would be simply a vast sepulchre, moving round the sun in its annual circuit, its bosom as joyless, dreary, and waste as are those silent spaces through which it rolls.

CHAPTER VI

THE "SECRET INSTRUCTIONS" OF THE JESUITS

So far we have traced the enrolment and training of that mighty army which Loyola had called into existence for the conquest of Protestantism. Their leader, who was quite as much the shrewd calculator as the fiery fanatic, took care before sending his soldiers into the field to provide them with armour, every way fitted for the combatants they were to meet, and the campaign they were to wage. The war in which they were to be occupied was one against right and truth, against knowledge and liberty, and where could weapons be found for the successful prosecution of a conflict like this, save in the old-established arsenal of sophisms?

The schoolmen, those Vulcans of the Middle Ages, had forged these weapons with the hammers of their speculation on the anvil of their subtlety, and having made them sharp of edge, and given them an incomparable flexibility, they stored them up, and kept them in reserve against the great coming day of battle. To this armoury Loyola, and the chiefs that succeeded him in command, had recourse. But not content with these weapons as the schoolmen had left them, the Jesuit doctors put them back again into the fire; they kept them in a furnace heated seven times, till every particle of the dross of right and truth that cleaved to them had been purged out, and they had acquired a flexibility absolutely and altogether perfect, and a keenness of edge unattained before, and were now deemed every way fit for the hands that were to wield them, and every way worthy of the cause in which they were to be drawn. So attempered, they could cut through shield and helmet, through body and soul of the foe.

Let us survey the soldier of Loyola, as he stands in the complete and perfect panoply his General has provided him with. How admirably harnessed for the battle he is to fight! He has his "loins girt about with" mental and verbal equivocation; he has "on the breast-plate of" probabilism; his "feet are shod with the preparation of the" *Secret Instructions*. "Above all, taking the shield of" intention, and rightly handling it, he is "able to quench all the fiery darts of" human remorse and Divine threatenings. He takes "for an helmet the hope of" Paradise, which has been most surely promised him as the reward of his services; and in his hand he grasps the two-edged sword of a fiery fanaticism, wherewith he is able to cut his way, with prodigious bravery, through truth and righteousness.[2294]

Shrewd, practical, and precise are the instructions of the Jesuits. First of all they are told to select the best points in that great field, all of which they are in due time to subjugate and possess. That field is Christendom. They are to begin by establishing convents, or colleges, in the chief cities. The great centres of population and wealth secured, the smaller places will be easily occupied.

Should any one ask on what errand the good Fathers have come, they are instructed to make answer that their "sole object is the salvation of souls." What a pious errand! Who would not strive to be the first to welcome to their houses, and to seat at their tables, men whose aims are so unselfish and heavenly? They are to be careful to maintain a humble and submissive deportment; they are to pay frequent visits to the hospitals, the sick-chamber, and the prisons. They are to make great show of charity, and as they have nothing of their own to give to the poor, they are "to go far and near" to receive even the "smallest atoms." These good deeds will not lose their reward if only they take care not to do them in secret. Men will begin to speak of them and say, What a humble, pious, charitable order of men these Fathers of the Society of Jesus are! How unlike the Franciscans and Dominicans, who were wont to care for the sick and the poor, but have now forgotten the virtues of a former time, and are grown proud, indolent, luxurious, and rich! Thus the "new-comers," the *Instructions* hint, will supplant the other and older orders, and will receive "the respect and reverence of the best and most eminent in the neighbourhood."[2295]

Further, they are enjoined to conduct themselves very deferentially towards the parochial clergy, and not to perform any sacred function till first they have piously and submissively asked the bishop's leave. This will secure their good graces, and dispose the secular clergy to protect them; but by-and-by, when they have ingratiated themselves with the people, they may abate somewhat of this subserviency to the clergy.

The individual Jesuit takes a vow of poverty, but the society takes no such vow, and is qualified to hold property to any amount. Therefore, while seeking the salvation of souls, the members are carefully to note the rich men in the community. They must find out who own the estates in the neighbourhood, and what are their yearly values. They are to secure these estates by gift, if possible; if not, by purchase. When it happens that they get anything that is considerable, let the purchase be made under a strange name, by some of our friends, that our poverty may still seem the greater."[2296] And let our provincial "assign such revenues to some other colleges, more remote, that neither prince nor people may discover anything of our profits"[2297]—a device that combines many advantages. Every day their acres will increase, nevertheless their apparent poverty will be as great as ever, and the flow of benefactions and legacies to supply it will remain undiminished, although the sea into which all these rivers run will never be full.

Among the multifarious duties laid upon the Jesuits, special prominence is given to the *instruction of youth*. It was by this arm that they achieved their most brilliant success. "Whisper it sweetly in their [the people's] ears, that they are come to catechise the children *gratis*."[2298] Wherever the Jesuits came they opened schools, and gathered the youth around them; but despite their zeal in the work of education, knowledge somehow did not increase. The intellect refused to expand and the genius to open under their tutelage. Kingdoms like Poland, where they became the privileged and only instructors of youth, instead of taking a higher place in the commonwealth of letters, fell back into mental decrepitude, and lost their rank in the community of nations. The Jesuits communicated to their pupils little besides a knowledge of Latin. History, philosophy, and science were sealed books. They initiated their disciples into the mysteries of probabilism, and the art of directing their intention, and the youth trained in these paths, when old did not depart from them. They dwarfed the intellect and narrowed the understanding, but they gained their end. They stamped anew the Roman impress upon many of the countries of Europe.

The second chapter of the *Instructions* is entitled, "What must be done to get the ear and intimacy of great men?" To stand well with monarchs and princes is, of course, a matter of such importance that no stone is to be left unturned to attain it. The *Instructions* here, as we should expect them to be, are full and precise. The members of the Society of Jesus are first of all to imbue princes and great men with the belief that they cannot dispense with their aid if they would maintain the pomp of their State, and the government of their realms. Should princes be filled with a conceit of their own wisdom, the Fathers must find some way of dispelling this egregious delusion. They are to surround them with confessors chosen from their society; but by no means are they to bear hard on the consciences of their royal penitents. They must treat them "sweetly and pleasantly," oftener administering opiates than irritants. They are to study their humours, and if, in the matter of marriage, they should be inclined—as often happens with princes—to contract alliance with their own kindred, they are to smooth their way, by hinting at a dispensation from the Pope, or finding some palliative for the sin from the pharmacopœia of their theology. They may tell them that such marriages, though forbidden to the commonalty, are sometimes allowed to princes, "for the greater glory of God."[2299] If a monarch is bent on some enterprise—a war, for example—the issue of which is doubtful, they are to be at pains so to shape their counsel in the matter, that if the affair succeeds they shall have all the praise, and if it fails, the blame shall rest with the king alone. And, lastly, when a vacancy occurs near the throne, they are to take care that the empty post shall be filled by one of the tried friends of the society, of whom they are enjoined to have, at all times, a list in their possession. It may be well, in order still more to advance their interests at courts, to undertake embassies at times. This will enable them to draw the affairs of Europe into their own hands, and to make princes feel that they are indispensable to them, by showing them what influence they wield at the courts of other sovereigns, and especially how great their power is at that of Rome. Small services and trifling presents they are by no means to overlook. Such things go a great way in opening the hearts of princes. Be sure, say the *Instructions*, to paint the men whom the prince dislikes in the same colours in which his jealousy and hatred teach him to view them. Moreover, if the prince is unmarried, it will be a rare stroke of policy to choose a wife for him from among the beautiful and noble ladies known to their society. "This is seen," say the *Instructions*, "by experience in the House of Austria, and in the Kingdoms of Poland and France, and in many other principalities."[2300]

"We must endeavour," say the *Instructions*, with remarkable plainness, but in the belief, doubtless, that the words would meet the faithful eyes of the members of the Society of Jesus only—"We must endeavour to breed dissension among great men, and raise seditions, or anything a prince would have us to do to please him. If one who is chief Minister of State to a monarch who is our friend oppose us, and that prince cast his whole favours upon him, so as to add titles to his honour, we must present ourselves before him, and court him in the highest degree, as well by visits as all humble respect."[2301]

Having specified the arts by which princes may be managed, the *Instructions* next prescribe certain methods for turning to account others "of great authority in the commonwealth, that by their credit we obtain profit and preferment." "If," say the *Instructions*,[2302] "these lords be seculars, we ought to have recourse to their aid and friendship against our adversaries, and to their favour in our own suits, and those of our friends, and to their authority and power in the purchase of houses, manors, and gardens, and of stones to build with, especially in those places that will not endure to hear of our settling in them, because the authority of these lords serveth very much for the appeasing of the populace, and making our ill-willers quiet."

Nor are they less sedulously to make court to the bishops. Their authority—great everywhere—is especially so in some kingdoms, "as in Germany, Poland, and France;" "and, the bishops conciliated, they may expect to obtain a gift of "new-erected churches, altars, monasteries, foundations, and in some cases the benefice of the secular priests and canons, with the preferable right of preaching in all the great towns." And when bishops so befriend them, they are to be taught that there is no less profit than merit in the deed; inasmuch as, done to the Order of Jesus, they are sure to be repaid with most substantial services; whereas, done to the other orders, they will have nothing in return for their pains "but a song."[2303]

To love their neighbour, and speak well of him, while they held themselves in lowly estimation, was not one of the failings of the Jesuits. Their own virtues they were to proclaim as loudly as they did the faults of their brother monks. Their *Instructions* commanded them to "imprint upon the spirits of those princes who love us, that our order is more perfect than all other orders." They are to supplant their rivals, by telling monarchs that no wisdom is competent to counsel in the affairs of State but "ours," and that if they wish to make their realms resplendent with knowledge, they must surrender the schools to Jesuit teachers. They are especially to exhort princes that they owe it as a duty to God to consult them in the distribution of honours and emoluments, and in all appointments to have a list in their possession of the names of all persons in authority and power throughout Christendom, in order that they may change or continue them in their several posts, as may be expedient. But so covertly must this delicate business be gone about, that their hand must not be seen in it, nor must it once be suspected that the change comes from them.[2304]

While slowly and steadily climbing up to the control of kings, and the government of kingdoms, they are to study great modesty of demeanour and simplicity of life. The pride must be worn in the heart, not on the brow; and the foot must be set down softly that is to be planted at last on the neck of monarchs. "Let ours that are in the service of princes," say the *Instructions*, "keep but a very little money, and a few movables, contenting themselves with a little chamber, modestly keeping company with persons in humble station; and so being in good esteem, they ought prudently to persuade princes to do nothing without their counsel, whether it be in spiritual or temporal affairs."[2305]

CHAPTER VII
JESUIT MANAGEMENT OF RICH WIDOWS AND THE HEIRS OF GREAT FAMILIES

THE sixth chapter of the *Instructions* treats "of the Means to acquire the Friendship of Rich Widows." On opening this new chapter, the reflection that forces itself on one is—how wide the range of objects to which the Society of Jesus is able to devote its attention! The greatest matters are not beyond its strength, and the smallest are not beneath its notice! From counselling monarchs, and guiding ministers of State, it turns with equal adaptability and dexterity to caring for widows. The *Instructions* on this head are minute and elaborate to a degree, which shows the importance the society attaches to the due discharge of what it owes to this class of clients.

True, some have professed to doubt whether the action of the society in this matter be wholly and purely disinterested, from the restriction it puts upon the class of persons taken under its protection. The *Instructions* do not say "widows," but "rich widows." But all the more on that account do widows need defence against the arts of chicanery and the wiles of avarice and how can the Fathers better accord them such than by taking measures to convey their bodies and their goods alike within the safe walls of a convent? There the cormorants and vultures of a wicked world cannot make them their prey. But let us mark how they are to proceed. First, a Father of suitable gifts is to be selected to begin operations. He must not, in point of years, exceed middle age; he must have a fresh complexion, and a gracious discourse. He is to visit the widow, to touch feelingly on her position, and the snares and injuries to which it exposes her, and to hint at the fraternal care that the society of which he is a member delights to exercise over all in her condition who choose to place themselves under its guardianship. After a few visits of this sort, the widow will probably appear at one of the chapels of the society. Should it so happen, the next step is to appoint a confessor of their body for the widow. Should these delicate steps be well got over, the matter will begin to be hopeful. It will be the confessor's duty to see that the wicked idea of marrying again does not enter her mind, and for this end he is to picture to her the delightful and fascinating freedom she enjoys in her widowhood, and over against it he is to place the cares, vexations, and tyrannies which a second matrimony would probably draw upon her. To second these representations, the confessor is empowered to promise exemption from purgatory, should the holy estate of widowhood be persevered in. To maintain this pious frame of mind on the part of the object of these solicitudes, the *Instructions* direct that it may be advisable to have an oratory erected in her house, with an altar, and frequent mass and confession celebrated thereat. The adorning of the altar, and the accompanying rites, will occupy the time of the widow, and prevent the thoughts of a husband entering into her mind. The matter having been conducted to this stage, it will be prudent now to change the persons of trust about her, and to replace them with persons devoted to the society. The number of religious services must also be increased, especially confession, "so that," say the *Instructions*, "knowing their former accusations, manners, and inclinations, the whole may serve as a guide to make them obey our wills."[2306]

These steps will have brought the widow very near the door of a convent. A continuance a little longer in the same cautious and skilful tactics is all that will be necessary to land her safely within its walls. The confessor must now enlarge on the quietude and eminent sanctity of the cloister—how surely it conducts to Paradise; but should she be unwilling to assume the veil in regular form, she may be induced to enter some religious order, such as that of Paulina, "so that being caught in the vow of chastity, all danger of her marrying again may be over."[2307] The great duty of Alms, that queen of the graces, "without which, it is to be represented to her, she cannot inherit the kingdom of heaven," is now to be pressed upon her; "which alms, notwithstanding, she ought not to dispose to every one, if it be not by the advice and with the consent of her spiritual father." Under this *Direction* it is easy to see in what exchequer the lands, manors, and revenues of widows will ultimately be garnered.

But the Fathers deemed it inexpedient to leave such an issue to the least uncertain, and accordingly the seventh chapter enters largely into the "Means of keeping in our hands the Disposition of the Estates of Widows." To shut out worldly thoughts, and especially matrimonial ones, the time of such widows must be occupied with their devotions; they are to be exhorted to curtail their expenditure and abound yet more in alms "to the Church of Jesus Christ." A dexterous confessor is to be appointed them. They are to be frequently visited, and entertained with pleasant discourse. They are to be persuaded to select a patron, or tutelary saint, say St. Francis or St. Xavier. Provision is to be made that all they do may be known, by placing about them only persons recommended by the society. We must be excused for not giving in words of the Fathers the fourteenth section of this chapter. That section gives their *protégées* great licence, indeed all licence, "provided they be liberal and well-affected to our society, and that all things be carried cunningly and without scandal." But the one great point to be aimed at is to get them to make an entire surrender of their estates to the society. This is to reach perfection now, and it may be to attain in the future the yet higher reward of canonisation. But should it so happen, from love of kindred, or other motives, that they have not endowed the "poor companions of Jesus" with all their worldly goods, when they come to die, the preferable claims of "the Church of Jesus Christ" to those of kindred are to be urged upon them, and they are to be exhorted "to contribute to the finishing of our colleges, which are yet imperfect, for the greater glory of God, giving us lamps and pixes, and for the building of other foundations and houses, which we, poor servants of the Society of Jesus, do still want, that all things may be perfected."[2309] "Let the same be done with princes," the *Instructions* go on to say, "and our other benefactors, who build us any sumptuous pile, or erect any foundation, representing to them, in the first place, that the benefits they thus do us are consecrated to eternity; that they shall become thereby perfect models of piety; that we will have thereof a very particular memory, and that in the next world they shall have their reward. But if it be objected that Jesus Christ was born in a stable, and had not where to lay his head, and that we, who are his *companions*, ought not to enjoy perishing goods, we ought to imprint strongly on their spirits that in truth, at first, the Church was also in the same state, but now that by the providence of God she is raised to a *monarchy*, and that in those times the Church was nothing but a *broken rock*, which is now become a *great mountain*.[2310]

In the chapter that follows—the eighth, namely—the net is spread still wider. It is around the feet of "the sons and daughters of devout widows" that its meshes are now drawn. The scheme of machination and seduction unfolded in this chapter differs only in its minor points from that which we have already had disclosed to us. We pass it therefore, and go on to the ninth chapter, where we find the scheme still widening, and wholesale rapacity and extortion, sanctified of course by the end in view, still more openly avowed and enjoined. The chapter is entitled, "Of the Means to Augment the Revenues of our Colleges," and these means, in short, are the astute and persistent deception, circumvention, and robbery of every class. The net is thrown, almost without disguise, over the whole community, in order that the goods, heritages, and possessions of all ranks—prince, peasant, widow, and orphan—may be dragged into the convents of the Jesuits. The world is but a large preserve for the mighty hunters of the Society of Jesus. "Above and before all other things," says the Instruction, "we ought to endeavour our own greatness, by the direction of our superiors, who are the only judges in this case, and who should labour that the Church of God may be in the highest degree of splendour, for the greater glory of God."[2311]

In prosecution of this worthy end, the *Secret Instructions* enjoin the Fathers to visit frequently at rich and noble houses, and to "inform themselves, prudently and dexterously, whether they will not leave something to our Churches, in order to the obtaining remission of their sins, and of the sins of their kindred."[2312] Confessors—and only able and eloquent men are to be appointed as confessors to princes and statesmen—are to ascertain the name and surname of their penitents, the names of their kindred and friends, whether they have hopes of succeeding to anything, and how they mean to dispose of what they already have, or may yet have; whether they have brothers, sisters, or heirs, and of what age, inclination, and education they are. And they "should persuade them that all these questions do tend much to the clearing of the state of their conscience."[2313]

There is a refreshing plainness about the following Instructions. They are given with the air of men who had so often repeated their plea "for the greater glory of God," that they themselves had come at last to believe it:—

"Our provincial ought to send expert men into all those places where there is any considerable number of rich and wealthy persons, to the end they may give their superiors a true and faithful account"

"Let the stewards of our college get an exact knowledge of the houses, gardens, quarries of stone, vineyards, manors, and other riches of every one who lives near the place where they reside, and if it be possible, what degree of affection they have for us."

"In the next place we should discover every man's office, and the revenue of it, their possessions, and the articles of their contracts, which they may surely do by confessions, by meetings, and by entertainments, or by our trusty friends. And generally when any confessor lights upon a wealthy person, from whom he hath good hopes of profit, he is obliged forthwith to give notice of it, and discover it at his return."

"They should also inform themselves exactly whether there be any hope of obtaining bargains, goods, possessions,[2314] pious gifts, and the like, in exchange for the admission of their sons into our society."[2315]

"If a wealthy family have daughters only, they are to be drawn by caresses to become nuns, in which case a small portion of their estate may be assigned for their use, and the rest will be ours."

"The last heir of a family is by all means to be induced to enter the society. And the better to relieve his mind from all fear of his parents, he is to be taught that it is more pleasing to God that he take this step without their knowledge or consent.[2316] "Such a one," the *Instructions* add, "ought to be sent to a distance to pass his novitiate."

These directions were but too faithfully carried out in Spain, and to this among other causes is owing the depopulation of that once-powerful country. A writer who resided many years in the Peninsula, and had the best opportunities of observing its condition, says: "If a gentleman has two or three sons and as many daughters, the confessor of the family adviseth the father to keep the eldest son at home, and send the rest, both sons and daughters, into a convent or monastery; praising the monastic life, and saying that to be retired from the world is the safest way to heaven. . . .The fathers of these families, glad of lessening the expenses of the house, and of seeing their children provided for, do send them into the desert place of a convent, which is really the middle of the world. Now observe that it is twenty to one that their heir dieth before he marrieth and have children, so the estate and everything else falls to the second, who is a professed friar, or nun, and as they cannot use the expression of *meum* or *tuum*, all goes that way to the society. And this is the reason why many families are extinguished, and their names quite out of memory, the convent so crowded, the kingdom so thin of people, and the friars, nuns, and monasteries so rich."[2317]

Further, the Fathers are counselled to raise large sums of money on bond. The advantage of this method is, that when the bond-holder comes to die, it will be easy to induce him to part with the bond in exchange for the salvation of his soul. At all events, he is more likely to make a gift of the deed than to bequeath the same amount in gold. Another advantage of borrowing in this fashion, is that their pretence of poverty may still be kept up. Owners of a fourth or of a half of the property of a county, they will still be "the poor companions of Jesus."[2318]

We make but one other quotation from the *Secret Instructions*. It closes this series of pious advices and is, in one respect, the most characteristic of them all. "Let the superior keep these secret advices with great care, and let them not be communicated but to a very few discreet persons, and that only by parts; and let them instruct others with them, when they have profitably served the society. And then let them not communicate them as rules they have received, but as the effects of their own prudence. But if they should happen to fall into the hands of strangers, who should give them an ill sense or construction, let them be assured the society owns them not in that sense, which shall be confirmed by instancing those of our order who assuredly know them not."[2319]

It was some time before the contingency of exposure here provided against actually happened. But in the beginning of the seventeenth century the accidents of war dragged these *Secret Instructions* from the darkness in which their authors had hoped to conceal them from the knowledge of the world. The Duke of Brunswick, having plundered the Jesuits' college at Paderborn in Westphalia, made a present of their library to the Capuchins of the same town. Among the books which had thus come into their possession was found a copy of the *Secret Instructions*. Another copy is said to have been discovered in the Jesuits' college at Prague. Soon thereafter reprints and translations appeared in Germany, Holland, France, and England. The authenticity of the work was denied, as was to be expected; for any society that was astute enough to compile such a book would be astute enough to deny it. To only the fourth or highest order of Jesuits were these *Instructions* to be communicated; the others, who were ignorant of them, in their written form, were brought forward to deny on oath that such a book existed, but their protestations weighed very little against the overwhelming evidence on the other side. The perfect uniformity of the methods followed by the Jesuits in all countries favoured a presumption that they acted upon a prescribed rule; and the exact correspondence between their methods and the *secret advices* showed that *this* was the rule. Gretza, a well-known member of the society, affirmed that the *Secreta Monita* was a forgery by a Jesuit who had been dismissed with ignominy from the society in Poland, and that he published it in 1616. But the falsehood of the story was proved by the discovery in the British Museum of a work printed in 1596, twenty years before the alleged forgery, in which the *Secreta Monita* is copied.[2320]

Since the first discovery in Paderborn, copies of the *Secreta Monita* have been found in other libraries, as in Prague, noted above. Numerous editions have since been published, and in so many languages, that the idea of collusion is out of the question. These editions all agree with the exception of a few unimportant variations in the reading.[2321] "These private directions," says M. l'Estrange, "are quite contrary to the rules, constitutions, and instructions which this society professeth publicly in those books which it hath printed on this subject. So that without difficulty we may believe that the greatest part of their governors (if a very few be excepted especially) have a double rule as well as a double habit—one for their private and particular use, and another to flaunt with before the world.[2322]

CHAPTER VIII
DIFFUSION OF THE JESUITS THROUGHOUT CHRISTENDOM

THE soldiers of Loyola are about to go forth. Before beginning the campaign we see their chief assembling them and pointing out the field on which their prowess is to be displayed. The nations of Christendom are in revolt: it will be theirs to subjugate them, and lay them once more, bound in chains, at the feet of the Papal See. They must not faint; the arms he has provided them with are amply sufficient for the arduous warfare on which he sends them. Clad in that armour, and wielding it in the way he has shown them, they will expel knowledge as night chases away the day. Liberty will die wherever their foot shall tread. And in the ancient darkness they will be able to rear again the fallen throne of the great Hierarch of Rome. But if the service is hard, the wages will be ample. As the saviours of that throne they will be greater than it. And though meanwhile their work is to be done in great show of humility and poverty, the silver and the gold of Christendom will in the end be theirs; they will be the lords of its lands and palaces, the masters of the bodies and souls of its inhabitants, and nothing of all that the heart can desire will be withholden from them if only they will obey him.

The Jesuits rapidly multiplied, and we are now to follow them in their peregrinations over Europe. Going forth in little bands, animated with an entire devotion to their General, schooled in all the arts which could help to further their mission, they planted themselves in a few years in all the countries of Christendom, and made their presence felt in the turning of the tide of Protestantism, which till then had been on the flow.

There was no disguise they could not assume, and therefore there was no place into which they could not penetrate. They could enter unheard the closet of the monarch, or the cabinet of the statesman. They could sit unseen in Convocation or General Assembly, and mingle unsuspected in the deliberations and debates. There was no tongue they could not speak, and no creed they could not profess, and thus there was no people among whom they might not sojourn, and no Church whose membership they might not enter, and whose functions they might not discharge. They could execrate the Pope with the Lutheran, and swear the Solemn League with the Covenanter. They had their men of learning and eloquence for the halls of nobles and the courts of kings; their men of science and letters for the education of youth; their unpolished but ready orators to harangue the crowd; and their plain, unlettered monks, to visit the cottages of the peasantry and the workshops of the artisan. "I know these men," said Joseph II. of Austria, writing to Choiseul, the Prime Minister of Louis XV.—"I know these men as well as any one can do: all the schemes they have carried on, and the pains they have taken to spread darkness over the earth, as well as their efforts to rule and embroil Europe from Cape Finisterre to Spitzbergen! In China they were mandarins; in France, academicians, courtiers, and confessors; in Spain and Portugal, grandees; and in Paraguay, kings. Had not my grand-uncle, Joseph I., become emperor, we had in all probability seen in Germany, too, a Malagrida or an Alvieros."

In order that they might be at liberty to visit what city and diocese they pleased, they were exempted from episcopal jurisdiction. They could come and go at their pleasure, and perform all their functions without having to render account to any one save to their superior. This arrangement was resisted at first by certain prelates; but it was universally conceded at last, and it greatly facilitated the wide and rapid diffusion of the Jesuit corps.

Extraordinary success attended their first efforts throughout all Italy. Designed for the common people, the order found equal acceptance from princes and nobles. In Parma the highest families submitted themselves to the "Spiritual Exercises." In Venice, Lainez expounded the Gospel of St. John to a congregation of nobles; and in 1542 a Jesuits' college was founded in that city. The citizens of Montepulciano accompanied Francisco Strada through the streets begging. Their chief knocked at the doors, and his followers received the alms. In Faenza, they succeeded in arresting the Protestant movement, which had been commenced by the eloquent Bernardino Ochino, and by the machinery of schools and societies for the relief of the poor, they brought back the population to the Papacy. These are but a few instances out of many of their popularity and success.[2323]

In the countries of Spain and Portugal their success was even greater than in Italy. A son of the soil, its founder had breathed a spirit into the order which spread among the Spaniards like an infection. Some of the highest grandees enrolled themselves in its ranks. In the province of Valencia, the multitudes that flocked to hear the Jesuit preacher, Araoz, were such that no cathedral could contain them, and a pulpit was erected for him in the open air. From the city of Salamanca, where in 1548 they had opened their establishment in a small, wretched house, the Jesuits spread themselves over all Spain. Two members of the society were sent to the King of Portugal, at his own request: the one he retained as his confessor, the other he dispatched to the East Indies. This was that Francis Xavier who there gained for himself, says Ranke, "the name of an apostle, and the glory of a saint." At the courts of Madrid and Lisbon they soon acquired immense influence. They were the confessors of the nobles and the counsellors of the monarch.

The Jesuits found it more difficult to force their way into France. Much they wished to found a college in that city where their first vow had been recorded, but every attempt was met by the determined opposition of the Parliament and the clergy, who were jealous of their enormous privileges. The wars between the Guises and the Huguenots at length opened a door for them. Lainez, who by this time had become their General, saw his opportunity, and in 1561 succeeded in effecting his object, although on condition of renouncing the peculiar privileges of the order, and submitting to episcopal jurisdiction. "The promise was made, but with a mental reservation, which removed the necessity of keeping it."[2324] They immediately founded a college in Paris, opened schools—which were taught by clever teachers—and planted Jesuit seminaries at Avignon, Rhodes, Lyons, and other places. Their intrigues kept the nation divided, and much inflamed the fury of the civil wars. Henry III. was massacred by an agent of theirs: they next attempted the life of Henry IV. This crime led to their first banishment from France, in 1594; but soon they crept back into the kingdom in the guise of traders and operatives. They were at last openly admitted by the monarch—a service which they repaid by slaughtering him in the streets of his capital. Under their rule France continued to bleed and agonise, to plunge from woe into crime, and from crime into woe, till the crowning wickedness of the revocation of the Edict of Nantes laid the country prostrate; and it lay quiet for more than half a century, till, recovering somewhat from its exhaustion, it lifted itself up, only to encounter the terrible blow of its great Revolution.

We turn to Germany. Here it was that the Church of Rome had suffered her first great losses, and here, under the arms of the Jesuits, was she destined to make a beginning of those victories which recovered not a little of the ground she had lost. A generation had passed away since the rise of Protestantism. It is the year 1550: the sons of the men who had gathered round Luther occupy the stage when the van of this great invading host makes its appearance. They come in silence; they are plain in their attire, humble and submissive in their deportment; but behind them are the stakes and scaffolds of the persecutor, and the armies of France and Spain. Their quiet words find their terrible reverberations in those awful tempests of war which for thirty years desolated Germany.

Ferdinand I. of Austria, reflecting on the decay into which Roman Catholic feeling had fallen in Germany, sent to Ignatius Loyola for a few zealous teachers to instruct the youth of his dominions. In 1551, thirteen Jesuits, including Le Jay, arrived at Vienna. They were provided with pensions, placed in the university chairs, and crept upwards till they seized the entire direction of that seminary. From that hour date the crimes and misfortunes of the House of Austria.[2325]

A little colony of the disciples of Loyola had, before this, planted itself at Cologne. It was not till some years later that they took root in that city; but the initial difficulties surmounted they began to effect a change in public sentiment, which went on till Cologne became, as it is sometimes called, the "Rome of the North." About the same time, the Jesuits became flourishing in Ingolstadt. They had been driven away on their first entrance into that university seat, the professors dreading them as rivals; but in 1556 they were recalled, and soon rose to influence, as was to be expected in a city where the memory of Dr. Eck was still fresh. Their battles, less noisy than his, were fated to accomplish much more for the Papacy.

From these three centres—Vienna, Cologne, and Ingolstadt—the Jesuits extended themselves over all Germany. They established colleges in the chief cities for the sons of princes and nobles, and they opened schools in town and village for the instruction of the lower classes. From Vienna they distributed their colonies throughout the Austrian dominions. They had schools in the Tyrol and the cities at the foot of its mountains. From Prague they ramified over Bohemia, and penetrated into Hungary. Their colleges at Ingolstadt and Munich gave them the possession of Bavaria, Franconia, and Swabia. From Cologne they extended their convents and schools over Rhenish Prussia, and, planting a college at Spires, they counteracted the influence of Heidelberg University, then the resort of the most learned men of the German nation.

Wherever the Jesuits came, there was quickly seen a manifest revival of the Popish faith. In the short space of ten years, their establishments had become flourishing in all the countries in which they were planted. Their system of education was adapted to all classes. While they studied the exact sciences, and strove to rival the most renowned of the Protestant professors, and so draw the higher youth into their schools, they compiled admirable catechisms for the use of the poor. They especially excelled as teachers of Latin; and so great was their zeal and their success, that "even Protestants removed their children from distant schools, to place them under the care of the Jesuits."[2326]

The teachers seldom failed to inspire the youth in their schools with their own devotion to the Popish faith. The sons of Protestant fathers were drawn to confession, and by-and-by into general conformity to Popish practice. Food which the Church had forbidden they would not touch on the interdicted days, although it was being freely used by the other members of the family. They began, too, to distinguish themselves by the use of Popish symbols. The wearing of crosses and rosaries is recorded by Ranke as one of the first signs of the setting of the tide toward Rome. Forgotten rites began to be revived; relics which had been thrown aside and buried in darkness, were sought out and exhibited to the public gaze. The old virtue returned into rotten bones, and the holiness of faded garments flourished anew. The saints of the Church came out in bold relief, while those of the Bible receded into the distance. The light of candles replaced the Word of Life in the temples; the newest fashions of worship were imported from Italy, and music and architecture in the style of the Restoration were called in to reinforce the movement. Customs which had not been witnessed since the days of their grandfathers, began to receive the reverent observance of the new generation. "In the year 1560, the youth of Ingolstadt belonging to the Jesuit school walked, two and two, on a pilgrimage to Eichstadt, in order to be strengthened for their confirmation by the dew that dropped from the tomb of St. Walpurgis."[2327] The modes of thought and feeling thus implanted in the schools were, by means of preaching and confession, propagated through the whole population.

While the Jesuits were busy in the seminaries, the Pope operated powerfully in the political sphere. He had recourse to various arts to gain over the princes. Duke Albert V. of Bavaria had a grant made him of one-tenth of the property of the clergy. This riveted his decision on the side of Rome, and he now set himself with earnest zeal and marked success to restore, in its ancient purity and vigour, the Popery of his territories. The Jesuits lauded the piety of the duke, who was a second Josias, a new Theodosius.[2328]

The Pope saw clearly that they could never hope to restore the ancient discipline and rules of their Church without the help of the temporal sovereigns. Besides Duke Albert, who so powerfully contributed to re-establish the sway of Rome over all Bavaria, the ecclesiastical princes, who governed so large a part of Germany, threw themselves heartily into the work of restoration. The Jesuit Canisius, a man of blameless life, of consummate address, and whose great zeal was regulated by an equal prudence, was sent to counsel and guide them. Under his management they accepted provisionally the edicts of the Council of Trent. They required of all professors in colleges subscription to a confession of the Popish faith. They exacted the same pledge from ordinary schoolmasters and medical practitioners. In many parts of Germany no one could follow a profession till first he had given public proof of his orthodoxy. Bishops were required to exercise a more vigilant superintendence of their clergy than they had done these twenty years past. The Protestant preachers were banished; and in some parts the entire Protestant population was driven out. The Protestant nobles were forbidden to appear at court. Many withdrew into retirement, but others purchased their way back by a renunciation of their faith. By these and similar arts Protestantism was conquered on what may be regarded as its native soil. If not wholly rooted up it maintained henceforward but a languishing existence; its leaf faded and its fruit died in the mephitic air around it, while Romanism shot up in fresh strength and robustness. A whole century of calamity followed the entrance of the Jesuits into Germany. The troubles they excited culminated at last in the Thirty Years' War. For the space of a generation the thunder of battle continued to roll over the Fatherland. But the God of their fathers had not forsaken the Germans; it pleased him to summon from the distant Sweden, Gustavus Adolphus, and by his arm to save the remnants of Protestant liberty in that country. Thus the Jesuits failed in their design of subjugating the whole of Germany, and had to content themselves with dominating over those portions, unhappily large, of which the ecclesiastical princes had given them possession at the first.

CHAPTER IX
COMMERCIAL ENTERPRISES AND BANISHMENTS

OF the entrance of the Jesuits into England, the arts they employed, the disguises they wore, the seditions they sowed, the snares they laid for the life of the sovereign, and the plots they concocted for the overthrow of the Protestant Church, we shall have an opportunity of speaking when we come to narrate the history of Protestantism in Great Britain. Meanwhile, we consider their career in Poland.

Cardinal Hosius opened the gates of this country to the Jesuits. Till then Poland was a flourishing country, united at home and powerful abroad. Its literature and science during the half-century preceding had risen to an eminence that placed Poland on a par with the most enlightened countries of Christendom. It enjoyed a measure of toleration which was then unknown to most of the nations of Europe. Foreign Protestants fled to it as a refuge from the persecution to which they were exposed in their native land, bringing to their adopted country their skill, their wealth, and their energy. Its trade increased, and its towns grew in population and riches. Italian, German, French, and Scottish Protestant congregations existed at Cracow, Vilna, and Posnania.[2329] Such was Poland before the foot of Jesuit had touched its soil.

But from the hour that the disciples of Loyola entered the country Poland began to decline. The Jesuits became supreme at court; the monarch, Sigismund III., gave himself entirely up to their guidance; no one could hope to rise in the State who did not pay court to them; the education of youth was wholly in their hands, and the effects became speedily visible in the decay of literature,[2330] and the growing decrepitude of the national mind. At home the popular liberties were attacked in the persons of the Protestants, and abroad the nation was humiliated by a foreign policy inspired by the Jesuits, which drew upon the country the contempt and hostility of neighbouring powers. These evil courses of intrigue and faction within the country, and impotent and arrogant policy outside of it, were persisted in till the natural issue was reached in the partition of Poland. It is at the door of the Jesuits that the fall of that once-enlightened, prosperous, and powerful nation is to be laid.

It concerns us less to follow the Jesuits into those countries which lie beyond the boundaries of Christendom, unless in so far as their doings in these regions may help to throw light on their principles and tactics. In following their steps among heathen nations and savage races, it is alike impossible to withhold our admiration of their burning zeal and intrepid courage, or our wonder at their prodigiously rapid success. No sooner had the Jesuit missionary set foot on a new shore, or preached, by an interpreter it might be, his first sermon in a heathen city, than his converts were to be counted in tens of thousands. Speaking of their missions in India, Sacchinus, their historian, says that "ten thousand men were baptised in the space of one year."[2331] When the Jesuit mission to the East Indies was set on foot in 1559, Torrez procured royal letters to the Portuguese viceroys and governors, empowering them to lend their assistance to the missionaries for the conversion of the Indians. This shortened the process wonderfully. All that had to be done was to ascertain the place where the natives were assembled for some religions festival, and surround them with a troop of soldiers, who, with levelled muskets, offered them the alternative of baptism. The rite followed immediately upon the acceptance of the alternative; and next day the baptised were taught the sign of the cross. In this excellent and summary way was the evangelisation of the island of Goa effected![2332]

By similar methods did they attempt to plant the Popish faith and establish their own dominion in Abyssinia, and also at Mozambique (1560) on the opposite coast of Africa. One of the pioneers, Oviedo, who had entered Ethiopia, wrote thus to the Pope:—"He must be permitted to inform his Holiness that, with the assistance of 500 or 600 Portuguese soldiers, he could at any time reduce the Empire of Abyssinia to the obedience of the Pontificate; and when he considered that it was a country surrounded with territories abounding with the finest gold, and promising a rich harvest of souls to the Church, he trusted his Holiness would give the matter further consideration."[2333] The Emperor of Ethiopia was gained by flatteries and miracles; a terrible persecution was raised against the native Christians; thousands were massacred; but at last, the king having detected the authors of these barbarities plotting against his own life and throne, they were ignominiously expelled the country.

Having secured the territory of Paraguay, a Portuguese possession in South America, the Jesuits founded a kingdom there, and became its sovereigns. They treated the natives at first with kindness, and taught them several useful arts, but by-and-by they changed their policy, and, reducing them to slavery, compelled them to labour for their benefit. Dealing out to the Paraguayan peasant from the produce of his own toil as much as would suffice to feed and clothe him, the Fathers laid up the rest in large storehouses, which they had erected for the purpose. They kept carefully concealed from the knowledge of Europe this seemingly exhaustless source of wealth, that no one else might share its sweets. They continued all the while to draw from it those vast sums wherewith they carried on their machinations in the Old World. With the gold wrung from the Paraguayan peasants' toil, they hired spies, bribed courtiers, opened new missions, and maintained that pomp and splendour of their establishments by which the populace were dazzled.[2334]

Their establishments in Brazil formed the basis of a great and enriching trade, of which Santa Fé and Buenos Ayres were the chief depôts. But the most noted episode of this kind in their history is that of Father Lavalette (1756). He was Visitor-General and Apostolic Prefect of their Missions in the West Indies. "He organised offices in St. Domingo, Granada, St. Lucia, St. Vincent, and other islands, and drew bills of exchange on Paris, London, Bordeaux, Nantes, Lyons, Cadiz, Leghorn, and Amsterdam." His vessels, loaded with riches, comprising, besides colonial produce, negro slaves, "crossed the sea continually."[2335] Trading on credit, they professed to give the property of the society as security. Their methods of business were abnormal. Treaties obeyed by other merchants they disregarded. Neutrality laws were nothing to them. They hired ships which were used as traders or privateers, as suited them, and sailed under whatever flag was convenient. At last, however, came trouble to these Fathers, who were making, as the phrase is, "the best of both worlds." The Brothers Lioncy and Gouffre, of

Marseilles, had accepted their bills for a million and a half of livres, to cover which two vessels had been dispatched for Martinique with merchandise to the value of two millions. Unfortunately for the Fathers, the ships were captured at sea by the English.

The house of Lioncy and Gouffre asked the superior of the Jesuits in Marseilles for four thousand livres as part payment of their debt, to save them from bankruptcy. The Father replied that the society was not answerable, but he offered the Brothers Lioncy and Gouffre the aid of their prayers, fortified by the masses which they were about to say for them. The masses would not fill the coffers which the Jesuits had emptied, and accordingly the merchants appealed to Parliament craving a decree for payment of the debt. The appeal was allowed, and the Jesuits were condemned to honour the bills drawn by their agent. At this critical moment the General of the society sent all the funds he could raise; but before these supplies could reach Marseilles, Lioncy and Gouffre had become bankrupt, involving in their misfortune their connections in all parts of France.

Now that the ruin had come and publicity was inevitable, the Jesuits refused to pay the debt, pleading that they were protected from the claims of their creditors by their Constitutions. The cause now came to a public hearing. After several pleas had been advanced and abandoned, the Jesuits took their final stand on the argument which, in an evil hour for themselves, they had put forth at first in their defence. Their rules, they said, forbade them to trade; and the fault of individual members could not be punished upon the Order: they were shielded by their Constitutions. The Parliament ordered these documents to be produced. They had been kept secret till now. They were laid before Parliament on the 16th of April, 1761. The result was disastrous for the Jesuits. They lost their cause, and became much more odious than before. The disclosure revealed Jesuitism to men as an organisation based on the most iniquitous maxims, and armed with the most terrible weapons for the accomplishment of their object, which was to plant their own supremacy on the ruin of society. The Constitutions were one of the principal grounds of the decree for the extinction of the order in France, in 1762.[2336]

That political kingdom and civil communities should feel the Order a burden too heavy to be borne, is not to be wondered at when we reflect that even the Popes, of whose throne it was the pillar, have repeatedly decreed its extinction. Strange as it may seem, the first bolt in later times that fell on the Jesuits was launched by the hand of Rome. Benedict IV., by a bull issued in 1741, prohibited them from engaging in trade and making slaves of the Indians. In 1759, Portugal, finding itself on the brink of ruin by their intrigues, shook them off. This example was soon followed in France, as we have already narrated. Even in Spain, with all its devotion to the Papal See, all the Jesuit establishments were surrounded, one night in 1767, with troops, and the whole fraternity, amounting to 7,000, were caught and shipped off to Italy. Immediately thereafter a similar expulsion befell them in South America. Naples, Malta, and Parma were the next to drive them from their soil. The severest blow was yet to come. Clement XIII., hitherto their firm friend, yielding at last to the unanimous demands of all the Roman Catholic courts, summoned a secret conclave for the suppression of the

Order: "a step necessary," said the brief of his successor, "in order to prevent Christians rising one against another, and massacring one another in the very bosom of our common mother the Holy Church." Clement died suddenly the very evening before the day appointed for the conclave. Lorenzo Ganganelli was elevated to the vacant chair under the title of Clement XIV. Ganganelli was studious, learned, of pure morals, and of genuine piety. From the schoolmen he turned to the Fathers, forsaking the Fathers he gave himself to the study of the Holy Scriptures, where he learned on what Rock to fix the anchor of his faith. Clement XIV. strove for several years, with honest but mistaken zeal, to reform the Order. His efforts were fruitless. On the 21st of July, 1773, he issued the famous bull, "Dominus ac Redemptor noster," by which he "dissolved and for ever annihilated the Order as a corporate body," at a moment when it counted 22,000 members.[2337]

The bull justifies itself by a long and formidable list of charges against the Jesuits. Had this accusation proceeded from a Protestant pen it might have been regarded as not free from exaggeration, but coming from the Papal chair it must be accepted as the sober truth. The bull of Clement charged them with raising various insurrections and rebellions, with plotting against bishops, undermining the regular monastic orders, and invading pious foundations and corporations of every sort, not only in Europe, but in Asia and America, to the danger of souls and the astonishment of all nations. It charged them with engaging in trade, and that, instead of seeking to convert the heathen, they had shown themselves intent only on gathering gold and silver and precious jewels. They had interpolated pagan rites and manners with Christian beliefs and worship: they had set aside the ordinances of the Church, and substituted opinions which the apostolic chair had pronounced *fundamentally erroneous and evidently subversive of good morals*. Tumults, disturbances, violences, had followed them in all countries. In fine, they had broken the peace of the Church, and so incurably that the Pontificates of his predecessors, Urban VIII., Clements IX., X., XI., and XII., Alexanders VII. and VIII., Innocents X., XI., XII., and XIII., and Benedict XIV., had been passed in abortive attempts to re-establish the harmony and concord which they had destroyed. It was now seen that the peace of the Church would never be restored while the Order existed, and hence the necessity of the bull which dispossessed the Jesuits of "every office, service, and administration;" took away from them "their houses, schools, hospitals, estates;" withdrew "all their statutes, usuages, decrees, customs, and ordinances;" and pronounced "all the power of the General, Provincial, Visitors, and every other head of the same Order, whether spiritual or secular, to be for ever annulled and suppressed." The present ordinance," said the bull, in conclusion, "shall remain in full force and operation from henceforth and for ever."

Nothing but the most tremendous necessity could have made Clement XIV. issue this bull. He knew well how unforgiving was the pride and how deadly the vengeance of the Society, and he did not conceal from himself the penalty he should have to pay for decreeing its suppression. On laying down his pen, after having put his name to the bull, he said to those around him that he had subscribed his death-warrant.[2338] The Pope was at that time in robust health, and his vigorous constitution and temperate habits promised a long life. But now dark rumours began to be whispered in Italy that the Pontiff would die soon. In April of the following year he began to decline without any apparent cause: his illness increased: no medicine was of any avail: and after lingering in torture for months, he died, September 22nd, 1774. "Several days before his death," says Caraccioli, "his bones exfoliated and withered like a tree which, attacked at its roots, withers away and throws off its bark. The scientific men who were called in to embalm his body found the features livid, the lips black, the abdomen inflated, the limbs emaciated, and covered with violet spots. The size of the heart was diminished, and all the muscles were shrunk up, and the spine was decomposed. They filled the body with perfumed and aromatic substances, but nothing could dispel the mephitic effluvia."[2339]

The suppression with which Clement XIV. smote the Society of Jesus was eternal; but the "for ever" of the bull lasted only in actual deed during the brief interval that elapsed between 1773 and 1814. That short period was filled up with the awful tempest of the French Revolution—to the fallen thrones and desecrated altars of which the Jesuits pointed as the monuments of the Divine anger at the suppression of their Order. Despite the bull of Clement, the Jesuits had neither ceased to exist nor ceased to act. Amid the storms that shook the world they were energetically active. In revolutionary conventions and clubs, in war-councils and committees, on battle-fields they were present, guiding with unseen but powerful touch the course of affairs. Their maxim is, if despotism will not serve them, to demoralise society and render government impossible, and from chaos to remodel the world anew. Thus the Society of Jesus, which had gone out of existence before the Revolution, as men believed, started up in full force the moment after, prepared to enter on the work of moulding and ruling the nations which had been chastised but not enlightened. Scarcely had Pius V. returned to the Vatican, when, by a bull dated August 7th, 1814, he restored the Order of Jesus. Thaddeus Borzodzowsky was placed at their head. Once more the brotherhood stalked abroad in their black birettas. In no long time their colleges, seminaries, and novitiates began to flourish in all the countries of Europe, Ireland and England not excepted. Their numbers, swelled by the sodalities of "St. Vincent de Paul," "Brothers of the Christian Doctrine," and other societies affiliated with the order, became greater, perhaps, than they ever were at any former period. And their importance was vastly enhanced by the fact that the contest between the "Order " and the "Papal Chair" ended—temporarily, at any rate—in the enslavement of the Popedom, of which they inspired the policy, indited the decrees, and wielded the power.

CHAPTER X
RESTORATION OF THE INQUISITION

*T*HERE is one arm of the Jesuits to which we have not yet adverted. The weapon that we refer to was not indeed unknown to former times, but it had fallen out of order, and had to be refurbished, and made fit for modern exigencies. No small part of the success that attended the operations of the Jesuits was owing to their use of it. That weapon was the Inquisition.

We have narrated in a former chapter the earnest attempt made at the Conference of Ratisbon to find a basis of conciliation between the Protestant and Popish Churches. The way had been paved at Rome for this attempted reconcilement of the two creeds by an infusion of new blood into the College of Cardinals. Gaspar Contarini, a senator of Venice, who was known to hold opinions on the doctrine of justification differing very little, if at all, from those of Luther,[2340] was invested with the purple of the cardinalate. The chair of the Doge almost within his reach, Contarini was induced to come to Rome and devote the influence of his high character and great talents to the doubtful experiment of reforming the Papacy. By his advice, several ecclesiastics whose sentiments approximated to his own were added to the Sacred College, among others Sadoleto, Gioberto Caraffa, and Reginald Pole.

In the end, these new elections but laid a basis for a more determined and bloody resistance to Protestantism. This was in the future as yet; meanwhile the reforming measures, for which this change in the cardinalate was to pave the way, were taken. Deputies were sent to the Ratisbon Conference, with instructions to make such concessions to the Reformers as might not endanger the fundamental principles of the Papacy, or strip the tiara of its supremacy. The issue was what we have announced in a previous part of our history. When the deputies returned from the Diet, and told Paul III. that all their efforts to frame a basis of agreement between the two faiths had proved abortive, and that there was not a country in Christendom where Protestantism was not spreading, the Pope asked in alarm, "What then is to be done?" Cardinal Caraffa, and John Alvarez de Toledo, Bishop of Burgos, to whom the question was addressed, immediately made answer, Re-establish the Inquisition.

The proposal accorded well with the gloomy genius, unbending opinions, and stern bigotry of the men from whom it came. Caraffa and Toledo were old Dominicans, the same order to whom Innocent III. had committed the working of the "Holy Tribunal," when it was first set up. Men of pure but austere life, they were prepared to endure in their own persons, or to inflict on the persons of others, any amount of suffering and pain, rather than permit the Roman Church to be overthrown. Re-establish the Inquisition, said Caraffa; let the supreme tribunal be set up in Rome, with subordinate branches ramifying over all Europe. "Here in Rome must the successors of Peter destroy all the heresies of the world."[2341] The Jesuit historians take care to tell us that Caraffa's proposal was seconded by a special memorial from the founder of their order, Ignatius Loyola. The bull re-establishing the Inquisition was published July 21st, 1542.

The "Holy Office" revived with terrors unknown to it in former ages. It had now a plenitude of power. Its jurisdiction extended over all countries, and not a man in all Christendom, however exalted in rank or dignity, but was liable to be made answerable at its bar. The throne was no protection; the altar was no shield; withered age and blooming youth, matron and maiden, might any hour be seized by its familiars, and undergo the question in the dark underground chamber, where, behind a table, with its crucifix and taper, sat the inquisitor, his stern pitiless features surmounted by his black cowl, and all around the instruments of torture. Till the most secret thought had been wrung out of the breast, no mercy was to be shown. For the inquisitor to feel the least pity for his writhing victim was to debase himself. Such were the instructions drafted by Caraffa.

The history of the man who restored the Inquisition is one of great interest, and more than ordinary instruction, but it is touchingly sad. Caraffa had been a member of the Oratory of *Divine Love*, which was a little circle of moderate Reformers, that held its sittings in the Trastavere at Rome, and occupied, as regarded the Reform of the Roman Church, a position midway between the champions of things as they were, and the company of decided adherents of the Gospel, which held its re-unions at Chiaja, in Naples, and of which we shall speak below. Caraffa had "tasted the good word of God, and the powers of the world to come," but the gracious stirrings of the Spirit, and the struggles of his own conscience, he had quelled, and from the very threshold of Rest which he was seeking in the Gospel, he had cast himself again into the arms of an infallible Church. With such a history it was not possible that Caraffa could act a middle part. He threw himself with sterner zeal into the dreadful work of reviving the Inquisition than did even Paul III., under whom he served, and whom he was destined to succeed. "Caraffa," says the historian Ranke, "lost not a moment in carrying this edict into execution; he would have thought it a waste of time to wait for the usual issue of means from the apostolic treasury, and, though by no means rich, he hired a house for immediate proceedings at his own expense; this he fitted up with rooms for the officers, and prisons for the accused, supplying the latter with strong bolts and locks, with dungeons, chains, blocks, and every other fearful appurtenance of his office. He appointed commissioners-general for the different countries."[2342]

The resolution to restore the Inquisition was taken at a critical moment for Italy, and all the countries south of the Alps. The dawn of the Protestant day was breaking around the very throne of the Pope. From the city of Ferrara in the north, where the daughter of Louis XII., the correspondent of Calvin, sheltered in her palace the disciples of the Gospel, to the ancient Parthenope, which looks down from its fig and aloe covered heights upon the calm waters of its bay, the light was breaking in a clearness and fulness that gave promise that in proportion to the depth of the previous darkness, so would be the splendours of the coming day. Distinguished as the land of the Renaissance, Italy seemed about to become yet more distinguished as the land of Protestantism. At the foot of Fiesole, and in that Florence on which Cosmo and the brilliant group of scholars around him had so often looked down, while they talked of Plato, there were men who had learned a better knowledge than that which the Greek sage had taught. In Padua, in Bologna, in Lucca, in Modena, in Rome,[2343] and in other cities of classic fame, some of the first families had embraced the Gospel. Men of rank in the State, and of eminence in the Church, persons of mark in the republic of letters, orators, poets, and some noble ladies, as eminent for their talents as for their birth, were not ashamed to enrol themselves among the disciples of that faith which the Lutheran princes had confessed at Augsberg, and which Calvin was propagating from the little town on the shores of the Leman, then beginning to attract the notice of the world. But of all the Protestant groups now forming in Italy, none equalled in respect of brilliance of rank, lustre of talent, and devotion of faith, that which had gathered round Juan di Valdez on the lovely shore of Naples.

This distinguished Spaniard had been forced to leave the court of Charles V. and his native land for the sake of the Gospel. On the western arm of the Bay of Naples, hard by the tomb of Virgil, looking forth on the calm sea, and the picturesque island of Capri, with the opposite shore, on which Vesuvius, with its pennon of white vapour atop, kept watch over the cities which 1,400 years before it had wrapped in a winding-sheet of ashes, and enclosed in a tomb of lava, was placed the villa of Valdez. There his friends often assembled to discuss the articles of the Protestant creed, and confirm one another in their adherence to the Gospel. Among these was Peter Martyr Vermigli, Prior of St. Peter's *ad aram*. In the wilderness of Romanism the prior had become parched with thirst, for no water could he find that could refresh his soul. Valdez led him to a fountain, whereat Martyr drank, and thirsted no more. In his turn he zealously led others to the same living stream. Another member of the Protestant band was Caserta, a Neapolitan nobleman. He had a young relative, then wholly absorbed in the gaieties and splendours of Naples; him Caserta introduced to Valdez. This was Galeazzo Caraccioli, only son of the Marquis of Vico, who embraced the Gospel with his whole heart, and when the tempest dispersed the brilliant company to which he had joined himself, leaving his noble palace, his rich patrimony, his virtuous wife, his dear children, and all his flourishing honours, he cleaved to the cross, and repairing to Geneva was there, in the words of Calvin, "content with our littleness, and lives frugally according to the habits of the commonalty—neither more nor less than any one of us."[2344]

In 1536 this select society received another member. Bernardino Ochino, the great orator of Italy, came at that time to Naples to preach the Lent Sermons. A native of Sienna, he assumed the cowl of St. Francis, which he afterwards exchanged for the frock of the more rigid order of the Capuchins. He was so eloquent that Charles V. said of him, "That man is enough to make the stones weep." His discourses were impregnated with the great principles of the Protestant faith, and his eloquence drew overwhelming crowds to the Church of St. Giovanni Maggiore, where he was now preaching. His accession to the society around Valdez gave it great additional strength, for the preacher was daily scattering the seeds of Divine truth among the common people. And not among these only, for persons of all ranks crowded to hear the eloquent Capuchin. Among his audience might be seen Giulia de Gonzaga, widow of the Duke of Trajetto, reputed the most beautiful woman in Italy, and, what was higher praise, one of the most humble and sincere of its Christians. And there was Vittoria Colonna, Marchioness of Pescaro, also renowned for the loveliness of her person, and not less renowned for her talents and virtues. And there was Pietro Carnesechhi, a patrician of Florence, and a former secretary of Clement VII., now a disciple, and afterwards to be a martyr, of the Gospel. Such were the illustrious men and the high-born women that formed this Protestant propaganda in Naples. It comprehended elements of power which promised brilliant results in the future. It formed a galaxy of rank, talent, oratory, genius, and tact, adapted to all classes of the nation, and constituted, one would have thought, such an organisation or "Bureau" as was sure to originate, and in due time accomplish, the Reformation of Italy. The ravages the Gothic nations had inflicted, and the yet greater ravages of the Papacy, were on the point of being repaired, and the physical loveliness which Italy had known in her first days, and a moral beauty greater than she had ever known, were about to be restored to her. It was during those same years that Calvin was beginning his labours at Geneva, and fighting with the Pantheistic Libertines for a secure foothold on which to place his Reformation, that this little phalanx of devoted Protestant champions was formed on the shore of Naples.

Of the two movements, the southern one appeared at that hour by much the more hopeful. Contemplated from a human point of view, it had all the elements of success. Here the flower of an ancient nation was gathering on its own soil to essay the noble task of evoking into a second development those mighty energies which had long slumbered, but were not dead, in the bosom of a race that had given arts and letters and civilisation to the West. Every needful power and gift was present in the little company here confederate for the glorious enterprise. Though small in numbers this little host was great in names, comprehending as it did men of ancient lineage, of noble birth, of great wealth, of accomplished scholarship, of poetical genius, and of popular eloquence. They could appeal, moreover, to a past of renown, the traditions of which had not yet perished, and the memory of which might be helpful in the struggle to shake off the yoke of the present. These were surpassing advantages compared with the conditions of the movement at Geneva—a little town which had borrowed glory from neither letters nor arms; with a population rude, lawless, and insolent; a diminutive territory, overshadowed on all sides by powerful and hostile monarchs, who stood with arm uplifted to strike down Protestantism should it here raise its head; and, most discouraging of all, the movement was guided by but one man of note, and he a stranger, an exile, without the prestige of birth, or rank, or wealth. The movement at Geneva cannot succeed; that at Naples cannot fail: so would we have said. But the battle of Protestantism was not to the strong. The world needs to have the lesson often repeated, that it is the truth of principles and not the grandeur of names that gives assurance of victory. The young vine planted beneath the towers of the ancient Parthenope, and which was shooting forth so hopefully in the golden air of that classic region, was to wither and die, while that which had taken root beneath the shadow of the Alps was to expand amid the rude blasts of the Swiss mountains, and stretch its boughs over Christendom.

CHAPTER XI
THE TORTURES OF THE INQUISITION

THE re-establishment of the Inquisition decided the question of the Reformation of Italy. The country, struck with this blow as it was lifting itself up, instantly fell back into the old gulf. It had become suddenly apparent that religious reform must be won with a great fight of suffering, and Italy had not strength to press on through chains, and dungeons, and scaffolds to the goal she wished to reach. The prize was glorious, she saw, but the price was great. Pallavicino has confessed that it was the Inquisition that saved Italy from lapsing into Protestantism.[2345]

The religious question had divided the Italians of that day into three classes. The bulk of the nation had not thought on the question at all, and harboured no purpose of leaving the Church of Rome. To them the restoration of the Inquisition had no terrors. There was another and large class who had abandoned Rome, but who had not clearness to advance to the open profession of Protestantism. They were most to be pitied of all should they fall into the hands of the inquisitors, seeing they were too undecided either to decline or to face the horrors of the Holy Office. The third class were in no doubt as to the course they must pursue. They could not return to a Church which they held to be superstitious, and they had no alternative before them but provide for their safety by flight, or await death amid the fires of the Inquisition. The consternation was great; for the Protestants had not dreamed of their enemies having recourse to such violent measures. Numbers fled, and these fugitives were to be found in every city of Switzerland and Germany.[2346] Among these was Bernardino Ochino, on whose eloquent orations all ranks of his countrymen had been hanging but a few months before, and in whose audience the emperor himself might be seen when he visited Italy. Not, however, till he had been served with a citation from the Holy Office at Rome did Ochino make his escape. Flight was almost as bitter as death to the orator. He was leaving behind him the scene of those brilliant triumphs which he could not hope to renew on foreign soil. Pausing on the summit of the Great St. Bernard, he devoted a few moments to those feelings of regret which were so natural on abandoning so much that he could not hope ever again to enjoy. He then went forward to Geneva. But, alas! the best days of the eloquent monk were past. At Geneva, Ochino's views became tainted and obscured with the new philosophy, which was beginning to air itself at that young school of pantheism.

Peter Martyr Vermigli soon followed. He was presiding over the convent of his order in Lucca, when the storm came with such sudden violence. He set his house in order and fled; but it was discovered after he was gone that the heresy remained although the heretic had escaped, his opinions having been embraced by many of the Luccese monks. The same was found to be the case with the order to which Ochino belonged, the Capuchins namely, and the Pope at first meditated, as the only cure, the suppression of both orders. Peter Martyr went ultimately to Strasburg, and a place was found for him in its university, where his lamp continued to burn clearly to the close. Juan di Valdez died before the tempest burst, which drove beyond the Alps so many of the distinguished group that had formed around him at Pausilippo, and saw not the evil days which came on his adopted country. But the majority of those who had embraced the Protestant faith were unable to escape. They were immured in the prisons of the various Holy Offices throughout Italy; some were kept in dark cells for years, in the hope that they would recant, others were quickly relieved by martyrdom. The restorer of the Inquisition, the once reforming Caraffa, mounted the Papal chair, under the name of Paul IV. The rigours of the Holy Office were not likely to be relaxed under the new Pope; but twenty years were needed to enable the torture and the stake to annihilate the Protestants of Italy.[2347]

Of those who suffered martyrdom we shall mention only two—Mollio, a Bolognese professor, renowned throughout Italy for his learning and his pure life; and Tisserano, a native of Perugia. On the 15th of September, 1553, an assembly of the Inquisition, consisting of six cardinals with their episcopal assessors, was held with great pomp at Rome. A train of prisoners, with burning tapers in their hands, was led in before the tribunal. All of them recanted save Mollio and Tisserano. On leave being given them to speak, Mollio broke out, says McCrie, "in a strain of bold and fervid invective, which chained them to their seats, at the same time that it cut them to the quick." He rebuked his judges for their lewdness, their avarice, and their blood-thirsty cruelty, and concluded as follows:—"'Wherefore I appeal from your sentence, and summon you, cruel tyrants and murderers, to answer before the judgement-seat of Christ at the last day, where your pompous titles and gorgeous trappings will not dazzle,. nor your guards and torturing apparatus terrify us. And in testimony of this, take back that which you have given me.' In saying this, he threw the flaming torch which he held in his hand on the ground, and extinguished it. Galled, and gnashing upon him with their teeth, like the persecutors of the first Christian martyrs, the cardinals ordered Mollio, together with his companion, who approved of the testimony he had borne, to instant execution. They were conveyed, accordingly, to the Campo del Fior, where they died with the most pious fortitude.[2348]

The eight years that elapsed between 1534 and 1542 are notable ones in the annals of Protestant Christianity. That epoch witnessed the birth of three movements which were destined to stamp a character upon the future of Europe, and powerfully to modify the conflict then in progress in Christendom. In 1534 the Jesuits recorded their first vow in the Church of Montmartre, in Paris. In 1540 their society was regularly launched by the Papal edict. In 1542, Paul III. issued the bull for the re-establishment of the Inquisition; and in 1541, Calvin returned to Geneva, to prepare that spiritual army that was to wage battle with Jesuitism backed by the Inquisition. The meeting of these dates—the contemporaneous rise of these three instrumentalities, is sufficiently striking, and is one of the many proofs which we meet in history that there is an Eye watching all that is done on earth, and that never does an agency start up to destroy the world, but there is set over against it a yet more powerful agency to convert the evil it would inflict into good.

It is one of these great epochs at which we have arrived. Jesuitism, the consummation of error—the Inquisition, the maximum of force, stand up and array themselves against a now fully developed Protestantism. In following the steps of the combatants, we shall be led in succession to the mountains of the Waldenses, to the cities of France, to the swamps of Holland, to the plains of Germany, to Italy, to Spain, to England and Scotland. Round the whole of Christendom will roll the tide of this great battle, casting down one nation into the darkness of slavery, and lifting up another into the glory of freedom, and causing the gigantic crimes of the persecutor and the despot to be forgotten in the excelling splendour of the patriot and the martyr. This is the struggle with the record of which we shall presently be occupied. Meanwhile we proceed to describe one of those few Inquisitions that remain to this day in almost the identical state in which they existed when the Holy Office was being vigorously worked. This will enable us to realise more vividly the terror of that weapon which Paul III. prepared for the hands of the Jesuits, and the Divine power of that faith which enabled the confessors of the Gospel to withstand and triumph over it.

Turn we now to the town of Nuremberg, in Bavaria. The zeal with which Duke Albert, the sovereign of Bavaria, entered into the restoration of Roman Catholicism, we have already narrated. To further the movement, he provided every one of the chief towns of his dominions with a Holy Office, and the Inquisition of Nuremberg still remains—an anomalous and horrible monument in the midst of a city where the memorials of an exquisite art, and the creations of an unrivalled genius, meet one at every step. We shall first describe the *Chamber of Torture*.[2349]

The house so called immediately adjoins the Imperial Castle, which from its lofty side looks down on the city, whose Gothic towers, sculptured fronts, and curiously ornamented gables are seen covering both banks of the Pegnitz, which rolls below. The house may have been the guard-room of the castle. It derives its name, the *Torture-chamber*, not from the fact that the torture was here inflicted, but because into this one chamber has been collected a complete set of the instruments of torture gleaned from the various Inquisitions that formerly existed in Bavaria. A glance suffices to show the whole dreadful apparatus by which the adherents of Rome sought to maintain her dogma. Placed next to the door, and greeting the sight as one enters, is a collection of hideous masks. These represent creatures monstrous of shape, and malignant and fiendish of nature. It is in beholding them that we begin to perceive how subtle was the genius that devised this system of coercion, and that it took the mind as well as the body of the victim into account. In gazing on them, one feels as if he had suddenly come into polluting and debasing society, and had sunk to the same moral level with the creatures here figured before him. He suffers a conscious abatement of dignity and fortitude. The persecutor had calculated, doubtless, that the effect produced upon the mind of his victim by these dreadful apparitions, would be that he would become morally relaxed, and less able to sustain his cause. Unless of strong mind, indeed, the unfortunate prisoner, on entering such a place, and seeing himself encompassed with such unearthly and hideous shapes, must have felt as if he were the vile heretic which the persecutor styled him, and as if already the infernal den had opened its portals, and sent forth its venomous swarms to bid him welcome. Yourself accursed, with accursed beings are you henceforth to dwell—such was the silent language of these abhorred images.

We pass on into the chamber, where more dreadful sights meet our gaze. It is hung round and round with instruments of torture, so numerous that it would take a long while even to name them, and so diverse that it would take a much longer time to describe them. We must take them in groups, for it were hopeless to think of going over them one by one, and particularising the mode in which each operated, and the ingenuity and art with which all of them have been adapted to their horrible end. There were instruments for probing below the finger-nails till an exquisite pain, like a burning fire, would run along the nerves. There were instruments for tearing out the tongue, for scooping out the eyes, for grubbing-up the ears. There were bunches of iron cords, with a spiked circle at the end of every whip, for tearing the flesh from the back till bone and sinew were laid bare. There were iron cases for the legs, which were tightened upon the limb placed in them by means of a screw, till flesh and bone were reduced to a jelly. There were cradles set full of sharp spikes, in which victims were laid and rolled from side to side, the wretched occupant being pierced at each movement of the machine with innumerable sharp points. There were iron ladles with long handles, for holding molten lead or boiling pitch, to be poured down the throat of the victim, and convert his body into a burning cauldron. There were frames with holes to admit the hands and feet, so contrived that the person put into them had his body bent into unnatural and painful positions, and the agony grew greater and greater by moments, and yet the man did not die. There were chestfuls of small but most ingeniously constructed instruments for pinching, probing, or tearing the more sensitive parts of the body, and continuing the pain up to the very verge where reason or life gives way. On the floor and walls of the apartment were other and larger instruments for the same fearful end—lacerating, mangling, and agonising living men; but these we shall meet in other dungeons we are yet to visit.

The first impression on entering the chamber was one of bewildering horror; a confused procession of mangled, mutilated, agonising men, speechless in their great woe, the flesh peeled from off their livid sinews, the sockets where eyes had been, hollow and empty, seemed to pass before one. The most dreadful scenes which the great genius of Dante has imagined, appeared tame in comparison with the spectral groups which this chamber summoned up. The first impulse was to escape, lest images of pain, memories of tormented men, who were made to die a hundred deaths in one, should take hold of one's mind, never again to be effaced from it.

The things we have been surveying are not the mere models of the instruments made use of in the Holy Office; they are the veritable instruments themselves. We see before us the actual implements by which hundreds and thousands of men and women, many of them saints and confessors of the Lord Jesus, were torn, and mangled, and slain. These terrible realities the men of the sixteenth century had to face and endure, or renounce the hope of the life eternal. Painful they were to flesh and blood—nay, not even endurable by flesh and blood unless sustained by the Spirit of the mighty God.

We leave the Torture-chamber to visit the Inquisition proper. We go eastward, about half a mile, keeping close to the northern wall of the city, till we come to an old tower, styled in the common *parlance* of Nuremberg the Max Tower. We pull the bell, the iron handle and chain of which are seen suspended beside the door-post. The cicerone appears, carrying a bunch of keys, a lantern, and some half-dozen candles. The lantern is to show us our way, and the candles are for the purpose of being lighted and stuck up at the turnings in the dark underground passages which we are about to traverse. Should mischance befall our lantern, these tapers, like beacon-lights in a narrow creek, will pilot us safely back into the day. The cicerone, selecting the largest from the bunch of keys, inserts it in the lock of the massy portal before which we stand, bolt after bolt is turned, and the door, with hoarse heavy groan as it turns on its hinge, opens slowly to us. We begin to descend. We go down one flight of steps; we go down a second flight; we descend yet a third. And now we pause for a moment. The darkness is intense, for here never came the faintest glimmer of day; but a gleam thrown forward from the lantern showed us that we were arrived at the entrance of a horizontal, narrow passage. We could see, by the flickering light upon its sides and roof, that the corridor we were traversing was hewn out of the rock. We had gone only a few paces when we were brought up before a massy door. As far as the dim light served us, we could see the door, old, powdery with dust, and partly worm-eaten. Passing in, the corridor continued, and we went forward other three paces or so, when we found ourselves before a second door. We opened and shut it behind us as we did the first. Again we began to thread our way: a third door stopped us. We opened and closed it in like manner. Every step was carrying us deeper into the heart of the rock, and multiplying the barriers between us and the upper world. We were shut in with the thick darkness and the awful silence. We began to realise what must have been the feelings of some unhappy disciple of the Gospel, surprised by the familiars of the Holy Office, led through the midnight streets of Nuremberg, conducted to Max Tower, led down flight after flight of stairs, and along this horizontal shaft in the rock, and at every few paces a massy door, with its locks and bolts, closing behind him! He must have felt how utterly he was beyond the reach of human pity and human aid. No cry, however piercing, could reach the ear of man through those roofs of rock. He was entirely in the power of those who had brought him thither.

At last we came to a side-door in the narrow passage. We halted, applied the key, and the door, with its ancient mould, creaking harshly as if moving on a hinge long disused, opened to let us in. We found ourselves in a rather roomy chamber, it might be about twelve feet square. This was the *Chamber of Question*. Along one side of the apartment ran a low platform. There sat of old the inquisitors, three in number—the first a divine, the second a casuist, and the third a civilian. The only occupant of that platform was the crucifix, or image of the Saviour on the cross, which still remained. The six candles that usually burned before the "holy Fathers" were, of course, extinguished, but our lantern supplied their place, and showed us the grim furnishings of the apartment. In the middle was the horizontal rack or bed of torture, on which the victim was stretched till bone started from bone, and his dislocated frame became the seat of agony, which was suspended only when it had reached a pitch that threatened death.

Leaning against the wall of the chamber was the upright rack, which is simpler, but as an instrument of torture not less effectual, than the horizontal one. There was the iron chain which wound over a pulley, and hauled up the victim to the vaulted roof; and there were the two great stone weights which, tied to his feet, and the iron cord let go, brought him down with a jerk that dislocated his limbs, while the spiky rollers, which he grazed in his descent, cut into and excoriated his back, leaving his body a bloody, dislocated mass.[2350]

Here, too, was the cradle of which we have made mention above, amply garnished within with cruel knobs on which the sufferer, tied hand and foot, was thrown at every movement of the machine, to be bruised all over, and brought forth discoloured, swollen, bleeding, but still living.

All round, ready to hand, were hung the minor instruments of torture. There were screws and thumbkins for the fingers, spiked collars for the neck, iron boots for the legs, gags for the mouth, cloths to cover the face, and permit the slow percolation of water, drop by drop, down the throat of a person undergoing this form of torture. There were rollers set round with spikes, for bruising the arms and back; there were iron scourges, pincers, and tongs for tearing out the tongue, slitting the nose and ears, and otherwise disfiguring and mangling the body till it was horrible and horrifying to look upon it. There were other things of which an expert only could tell the name and the use. Had these instruments a tongue, and could the history of this chamber be written, how awful the tale!

We shall suppose that all this has been gone through; that the confessor has been stretched on the bed of torture; has been gashed, broken, mangled, and yet, by power given him from above, has not denied his Saviour: he has been "tortured not accepting deliverance:" what further punishment has the Holy Office in reserve for those from whom its torments have failed to extort a recantation? These dreadful dungeons furnish us with the means of answering this question.

We return to the narrow passage, and go forward a little way. Every few paces there comes a door, originally strong and massy, and garnished with great iron knobs but now old and mouldy, and creaking when opened with a noise painfully loud in the deep stillness. The windings are numerous, but at every turning of the passage a lighted candle is placed, lest peradventure the way should be missed, and the road back to the living world be lost for ever. A few steps are taken downwards, ever cautiously, for the lantern can barely show the ground. Here there is a vaulted chamber, entirely dug out of the living rock, except the roof, which is formed of hewn stone. It contains an iron image of the Virgin; and on the opposite wall, suspended by an iron hook, is a lamp, which when lighted shows the goodly proportions of "Our Lady." On the instant of touching a spring the image flings open its arms, which resemble the doors of a cupboard, and which are seen to be stuck full on the inside with poignards, each about a foot in length. Some of these knives are so placed as to enter the eyes of those whom the image enfolded in its embrace, others are set so as to penetrate the ears and brain, others to pierce the breast, and others again to gore the abdomen.

The person who had passed through the terrible ordeal of the Question-chamber, but had made no recantation, would be led along the tortuous passage by which we had come, and ushered into this vault, where the first object that would greet his eye, the pale light of the lamp falling on it, would be the iron Virgin. He would be bidden to stand right in front of the image. The spring would be touched by the executioner—the Virgin would fling open her arms, and the wretched victim would straightway be forced within them. Another spring was then touched—the Virgin closed upon her victim; a strong wooden beam, fastened at one end to the wall by a movable joint, the other placed against the doors of the iron image, was worked by a screw, and as the beam was pushed out, the spiky arms of the Virgin slowly but irresistibly closed upon the man, cruelly goring him.

When the dreadful business was ended, it needed not that the executioner should put himself to the trouble of making the Virgin unclasp the mangled carcase of her victim; provision had been made for its quick and secret disposal. At the touching of a third spring, the floor of the image would slide aside, and the body of the victim drop down the mouth of a perpendicular shaft in the rock. We look down this pit, and can see, at a great depth, the shimmer of water. A canal had been made to flow underneath the vault where stood the iron Virgin, and when she had done her work upon those who were delivered over to her tender mercies, she let them fall, with quick descent and sullen plunge, into the canal underneath, where they were floated to the Pegnitz, and from the Pegnitz to the Rhine, and by the Rhine to the ocean, there to sleep beside the dust of Huss and Jerome.

The History of Protestantism

Book Sixteenth
PROTESTANTISM IN THE WALDENSIAN VALLEYS

CHAPTER I
ANTIQUITY AND FIRST PERSECUTIONS OF THE WALDENSES

THE Waldenses stand apart and alone in the Christian world. Their place on the surface of Europe is unique; their position in history is not less unique; and the end appointed them to fulfill is one which has been assigned to them alone, no other people being permitted to share it with them.

The Waldenses bear a twofold testimony. Like the snow-clad peaks amid which their dwelling is placed, which look down upon the plains of Italy on the one side, and the provinces of France on the other, this people stand equally related to primitive ages and modern times, and give by no means equivocal testimony respecting both Rome and the Reformation. If they are old, then Rome is new; if they are pure, then Rome is corrupt; and if they have retained the faith of the apostles, it follows incontestibly that Rome has departed from it. That the Waldensian faith and worship existed many centuries before Protestantism arose is undeniable; the proofs and monuments of this fact lie scattered over all the histories and all the lands of mediæval Europe; but the antiquity of the Waldenses is the antiquity of Protestantism. The Church of the Reformation was in the loins of the Waldensian Church ages before the birth of Luther; her first cradle was placed amid those terrors and sublimities, those ice-clad peaks and great bulwarks of rock. In their dispersions over so many lands—over France, the Low Countries, Germany, Poland, Bohemia, Moravia, England, Calabria, Naples—the Waldenses sowed the seeds of that great spiritual revival which, beginning in the days of Wicliffe, and advancing in the times of Luther and Calvin, awaits its full consummation in the age to come.

In the place which the Church of the Alps has held, and the office she has discharged, we see the reason of that peculiar and bitter hostility which Rome has ever borne this holy and venerable community. It was natural that Rome should wish to efface so conclusive a proof of her apostasy, and silence a witness whose testimony so emphatically corroborates the position of Protestantism. The great bulwark of the Reformed Church is the Word of God; but next to this is the pre-existence of a community spread throughout Western Christendom, with doctrines and worship substantially one with those of the Reformation.

The persecutions of this remarkable people form one of the most heroic pages of the Church's history. These persecutions, protracted through many centuries, were endured with a patience, a constancy, a bravery honourable to the Gospel, as well as to those simple people, whom the Gospel converted into heroes and martyrs. Their resplendent virtues illumined the darkness of their age; and we turn with no little relief from a Christendom sunk in barbarism and superstition to this remnant of an ancient people, who here in their mountain-engirdled territory practised the simplicity, the piety, and the heroism of a better age. It is mainly those persecutions of the Waldenses which connect themselves with the Reformation, and which were, in fact, part of the mighty effort made by Rome to extinguish Protestantism, on which we shall dwell. But we must introduce ourselves to the great tragedy by a brief notice of the attacks which led up to it.

That part of the great Alpine chain that extends between Turin on the east and Grenoble on the west is known as the Cottian Alps. This is the dwelling-place of the Waldenses, the land of ancient Protestantism. On the west the mountains slope towards the plains of France, and on the east they run down to those of Piedmont. That line of glittering summits, conspicuous among which is the lofty snow-clad peak of Monte Viso on the west, and the craggy escarpments of Genèvre on the east, forms the boundary between the Albigenses and the Waldenses, the two bodies of these early witnesses. On the western slope were the dwellings of the former people, and on the eastern those of the latter. Not entirely so, however, for the Waldenses, crossing the summits, had taken possession of the more elevated portion of the western declivities, and scarcely was there a valley in which their villages and sanctuaries were not to be found. But in the lower valleys, and more particularly in the vast and fertile plains of Dauphiné and Provence, spread out at the foot of the Alps, the inhabitants were mainly of the cis-Alpine or Gallic extraction, and are known in history as the Albigenses. How flourishing they were, how numerous and opulent their towns, how rich their corn-fields and vineyards, and how polished the manners and cultured the genius of the people, we have already said. We have also described the terrible expiation Innocent III. exacted of them for their attachment to a purer Christianity than that of Rome. He launched his bull; he sent forth his inquisitors; and soon the fertility and beauty of the region were swept away; city and sanctuary sank in ruins; and the plains so recently covered with smiling fields were converted into a desert. The work of destruction had been done with tolerable completeness on the west of the Alps; and after a short pause it was commenced on the east, it being resolved to pursue these confessors of a pure faith across the mountains, and attack them in those grand valleys which open into Italy, where they lay entrenched, as in a fastness formed of massy chestnut forests and mighty pinnacles of rock.

We place ourselves at the foot of the eastern declivity, about thirty miles to the west of Turin. Behind us is the vast sweep of the plain of Piedmont. Above us in front tower the Alps, here forming a crescent of grand mountains, extending from the escarped summit that leans over Pinerole on the right, the pyramidal peak of Monte Viso, which cleaves the ebon like a horn of silver, and marks the furthest limit of the Waldensian territory on the left. In the bosom of that mountain crescent, shaded by its chestnut forests, and encircled by its glittering peaks, are hung the famous valleys of that people whose martyrdoms we are now to narrate.

In the centre of the picture, right before us, rises the pillar-like Castelluzzo; behind it is the towering mass of the Vandalin; and in front, as if to bar the way against the entrance of any hostile force into this sacred territory, is drawn the long, low hill of Bricherasio, feathery with woods, bristling with great rocks, and leaving open, between its rugged mass and the spurs of Monte Friolante on the west, only a narrow avenue, shaded by walnut and acacia trees, which leads up to the point where the valleys, spreading out fan-like, bury themselves in the mountains that open their stony arms to receive them. Historians have enumerated some thirty persecutions enacted on this little spot.

One of the earliest dates in the martyr-history of this people is 1332, or thereabouts, for the time is not distinctly marked. The reigning Pope was John XXII. Desirous of resuming the work of Innocent III., he ordered the inquisitors to repair to the Valleys of Lucerna and Perosa, and execute the laws of the Vatican against the heretics that peopled them. What success attended the expedition is not known, and we instance it chiefly on this account, that the bull commanding it bears undesigned testimony to the then flourishing condition of the Waldensian Church, inasmuch as it complains that synods, which the Pope calls chapters, were used to assemble in the Valley of Angrogna, attended by 500 delegates.[2351] This was before Wicliffe had begun his career in England.

After this date scarcely was there a Pope who did not bear unintentional testimony to their great numbers and wide diffusion. In 1352 we find Pope Clement VI. charging the Bishop of Embrun, with whom he associates a Franciscan friar and inquisitor, to essay the purification of those parts adjoining his diocese which were known to be infected with heresy. The territorial lords and city syndics were invited to aid him. While providing for the heretics of the Valleys, the Pope did not overlook those farther off. He urged the Dauphin, Charles of France, and Louis, King of Naples, to seek out and punish those of their subjects who had strayed from the faith. Clement referred doubtless to the Vaudois colonies, which are known to have existed in that age at Naples. The fact that the heresy of the Waldensian mountains extended to the plains at their feet, is attested by the letter of the Pope to Joanna, wife of the King of Naples, who owned lands in the Marquisate[2352] of Saluzzo, near the Valleys, urging her to purge her territory of the heretics that lived in it.

The zeal of the Pope, however, was but indifferently seconded by that of the secular lords. The men they were enjoined to exterminate were the most industrious and peaceable of their subjects; and willing as they no doubt were to oblige the Pope, they were naturally averse to incur so great a loss as would be caused by the destruction of the flower of their populations. Besides, the princes of that age were often at war among themselves, and had not much leisure or inclination to make war on the Pope's behalf. Therefore the Papal thunder sometimes rolled harmlessly over the Valleys, and the mountain-home of these confessors was wonderfully shielded till very nearly the era of the Reformation. We find Gregory XI., in 1373, writing to Charles V. of France, to complain that his officers thwarted his inquisitors in Dauphiné; that the Papal judges were not permitted to institute proceedings against the suspected without the consent of the civil judge; and that the disrespect to the spiritual tribunal was sometimes carried so far as to release condemned heretics from prison.[2353] Notwithstanding this leniency—so culpable in the eyes of Rome—on the part of princes and magistrates, the inquisitors were able to make not a few victims. These acts of violence provoked reprisals at times on the part of the Waldenses. On one occasion (1375) the Popish city of Susa was attacked, the Dominican convent forced, and the inquisitor put to death. Other Dominicans were called to expiate their rigour against the Vaudois with the penalty of their lives. An obnoxious inquisitor of Turin is said to have been slain on the highway near Bricherasio.[2354]

There came evil days to the Popes themselves. First, they were chased to Avignon; next, the yet greater calamity of the "schism" befell them; but their own afflictions had not the effect of softening their hearts towards the confessors of the Alps. During the clouded era of their "captivity," and the tempestuous days of the schism, they pursued with the same inflexible rigour their policy of extermination. They were ever and anon fulminating their persecuting edicts, and their inquisitors were scouring the Valleys in pursuit of victims. An inquisitor of the name of Borelli had 150 Vaudois men, besides a great number of women, girls, and even young children, brought to Grenoble and burned alive.[2355]

The closing days of the year 1400 witnessed a terrible tragedy, the memory of which has not been obliterated by the many greater which have followed it. The scene of this catastrophe was the Valley of Pragelas, one of the higher reaches of Perosa, which opens near Pinerolo, and is watered by the Clusone. It was the Christmas of 1400, and the inhabitants dreaded no attack, believing themselves sufficiently protected by the snows which then lay deep on their mountains. They were destined to experience the bitter fact that the rigours of the season had not quenched the fire of their persecutor's malice. The man named above, Borelli, at the head of an armed troop, broke suddenly into Pragelas, meditating the entire extinction of the population. The miserable inhabitants fled in haste to the mountains, carrying on their shoulders their old men, their sick and their infants, knowing what fate awaited them should they leave them behind. In their flight a great many were overtaken and slain. Night-fall brought them deliverance from the pursuit, but no deliverance from horrors not less dreadful. The main body of the fugitives wandered in the direction of Macel, in the storm-swept and now ice-clad valley of San Martino, where they encamped on a summit which has ever since, in memory of the event, borne the name of the Alberge or Refuge. Without shelter, without food, the frozen snow around them, the winter's sky overhead, their sufferings were inexpressibly great. When morning broke what a heart-rending spectacle did day disclose! Of the miserable group the hands and feet of many were frozen; while others were stretched out on the snow, stiffened corpses. Fifty young children, some say eighty, were found dead with cold, some lying on the bare ice, others locked in the frozen arms of their mothers, who had perished on that dreadful night along with their babes.[2356] In the Valley of Pragelas, to this day, sire recites to son the tale of that Christmas tragedy.

The century, the opening of which had been so fearfully marked, passed on amid continuous executions of the Waldenses. In the absence of such catastrophes as that of Christmas, 1400, individual Vaudois were kidnapped by the inquisitors, ever on the track for them, or waylaid, whenever they ventured down into the plain of Piedmont, were carried to Turin and other towns, and burned alive. But Rome saw that she was making no progress in the extermination of a heresy which had found a seat amid these hills, as firm as it was ancient. The numbers of the Waldenses were not thinned; their constancy was not shaken, they still refused to enter the Roman Church, and they met all the edicts and inquisitors, all the torturings and burnings of their great persecutor with a resistance as unyielding as that which their rocks offer to the tempests of hail and snow, which the whirlwinds of winter hurl against them.

It was the year 1487. A great blow was meditated. The process of purging the Valleys languished. Pope Innocent VIII., who then filled the Papal chair, remembered how his renowned namesake, Innocent III., by an act of summary vengeance, had swept the Albigensian heresy from the south of France. Imitating the vigour of his predecessor, he would purge the Valleys as effectually and as speedily as Innocent III. had done the plains of Dauphiné and Provence.

The first step of the Pope was to issue a bull, denouncing as heretical those whom he delivered over to slaughter. This bull, after the manner of all such documents, was expressed in terms as sanctimonious as its spirit was inexorably cruel. It brings no charge against these men, as lawless, idle, dishonest, or disorderly; their fault was that they did not worship as Innocent worshipped, and that they practised a "simulated sanctity," which had the effect of seducing the sheep of the true fold, therefore he orders "that malicious and abominable sect of malignants," if they "refuse to abjure, to be crushed like venomous snakes."[2357]

To carry out his bull, Innocent VIII. appointed Albert Cataneo, Archdeacon of Cremona, his legate, devolving upon him the chief conduct of the enterprise. He fortified him, moreover, with Papal missives to all princes, dukes, and powers within whose dominions any Vaudois were to be found. The Pope especially accredited him to Charles VIII. of France, and Charles II. of Savoy, commanding them to support him with the whole power of their arms. The bull invited all Catholics to take up the cross against the heretics; and to stimulate them in this pious work, it "absolved from all ecclesiastical pains and penalties, general and particular; it released all who joined the crusade from any oaths they might have taken; it legitimatised their title to any property they might have illegally acquired, and promised remission of all their sins to such as should kill any heretic. It annulled all contracts made in favour of Vaudois, ordered their domestics to abandon them, forbade all persons to give them any aid whatever, and empowered all persons to take possession of their property."

These were powerful incentives, plenary pardon and unrestrained licence. They were hardly needed to awaken the zeal of the neighbouring populations, always too ready to show their devotion to Rome by spilling the blood and harrying the lands and goods of the Waldenses. The King of France and the Duke of Savoy lent a willing ear to the summons from the Vatican. They made haste to unfurl their banners, and enlist soldiers in this holy cause, and soon a numerous army was on its march to sweep from the mountains where they had dwelt from immemorial time, these confessors of the Gospel faith pure and undefiled. In the train of this armed host came a motley crowd of volunteers, "vagabond adventurers," says Muston, "ambitious fanatics, reckless pillagers, merciless assassins, assembled from all parts of Italy,"[2358] a horde of brigands in short, the worthy tools of the man whose bloody work they were assembled to do.

Before all these arrangements were finished, it was the June of 1488. The Pope's bull was talked of in all countries; and the din of preparation rung far and near, for it was not only on the Waldensian mountains, but on the Waldensian race, wherever dispersed, in Germany, in Calabria, and in other countries, that this terrible blow was to fall.[2359] All kings were invited to gird on the sword, and come to the help of the Church in the execution of so total and complete an extermination of her enemies as should never need to be repeated. Wherever a Vaudois foot trod, the soil was polluted, and had to be cleansed; wherever a Vaudois breathed, the air was tainted, and must be purified; wherever Vaudois psalm or prayer ascended, there was the infection of heresy; and around the spot a cordon must be drawn to protect the spiritual health of the district. The Pope's bull was thus very universal in its application, and almost the only people left ignorant of the commotion it had excited, and the bustle of preparation it had called forth, were those poor men on whom this terrible tempest was about to burst.

The joint army numbered about 18,000 regular soldiers. This force was swelled by the thousands of ruffians, already mentioned, drawn together by the spiritual and temporal rewards to be earned in this work of combined piety and pillage.[2360] The Piedmontese division of this host directed their course towards the "Valleys" proper, on the Italian side of the Alps. The French division, marching from the north, advanced to attack the inhabitants of the Dauphinese Alps, where the Albigensian heresy, recovering somewhat its terrible excision by Innocent III., had begun again to take root. Two storms, from opposite points, or rather from all points, were approaching those mighty mountains, the sanctuary and citadel of the primitive faith. That lamp is about to be extinguished at last, which has burned here during so many ages, and survived so many tempests. The mailed hand of the Pope is uplifted, and we wait to see the blow fall.

CHAPTER II
CATANEO'S EXPEDITION (1488) AGAINST THE DAUPHINESE AND PIEDMONTESE CONFESSORS

WE see at this moment two armies on the march to attack the Christians inhabiting the Cottian and Dauphinese Alps. The sword now un sheathed is to be returned to its scabbard only when there breathes no longer in these mountains a single confessor of the faith condemned in the bull of Innocent VIII. The plan of the campaign was to attack at the same time on two opposite points of the great mountain-chain; and advancing, the one army from the south-east, and the other from the north-west, to meet in the Valley of Angrogna, the centre of the territory, and there strike the final blow. Let us attend first to the French division of this host, that which is advancing from the south against the Alps of Dauphiné.

This portion of the crusaders was led by a daring and cruel man, skilled in such adventures, the Lord of La Palu. He ascended the mountains with his fanatics, and entered the Vale of Loyse, a deep gorge overhung by towering mountains. The inhabitants, seeing an armed force, twenty times their own number, enter their valley, despaired of being able to resist them, and prepared for flight. They placed their old people and children in rustic carts, together with their domestic utensils, and such store of victuals as the urgency of the occasion permitted them to collect, and driving their herds before them, they began to climb the rugged slopes of Mount Pelvoux, which rises some six thousand feet over the level of the valley. They sang canticles as they climbed the steeps, which served at once to smooth their rugged path, and to dispel their terrors. Not a few were overtaken and slaughtered, and theirs was perhaps the happier lot.

About half-way up there is an immense cavern, called Aigue-Froid, from the cold springs that gush out from its rocky walls. In front of the cavern is a platform of rock, where the spectator sees beneath him only fearful precipices, which must be clambered over before one can reach the entrance of the grotto. The roof of the cave forms a magnificent arch, which gradually subsides and contracts into a narrow passage, or throat, and then widens once more, and forms a roomy hall of irregular form. Into this grotto, as into an impregnable castle, did the Vaudois enter. Their women, infants, and old men they placed in the inner hall; their cattle and sheep they distributed along the lateral cavities of the grotto. The able-bodied men posted themselves at the entrance. Having barricaded with huge stones both the doorway of the cave and the path that led to it, they deemed themselves secure. They had provisions to last, Cataneo says in his *Memoirs*, "two years;" and it would cost them little effort to hurl headlong down the precipices, anyone who should attempt to scale them in order to reach the entrance of the cavern.

But a device of their pursuer rendered all these precautions and defences vain. La Palu ascended the mountain on the other side, and approaching the cave from above, let down his soldiers by ropes from the precipice that overhangs the entrance of the grotto. The platform in front was thus secured by his soldiers. The Vaudois might have cut the ropes, and dispatched their foes as they were being lowered one by one, but the boldness of the manœuvre would seem to have paralysed them. They retreated into the cavern to find in it their grave. La Palu saw the danger of permitting his men to follow them into the depths of their hiding-place. He adopted the easier and safer method of piling up at its entrance all the wood he could collect and setting fire to it. A huge volume of black smoke began to roll into the cave, leaving to the unhappy inmates the miserable alternative of rushing out and falling by the sword that waited for them, or of remaining in the interior to be stifled by the murky vapour.[2361] Some rushed out, and were massacred; but the greater part remained till death slowly approached them by suffocation. "When the cavern was afterwards examined," says Muston, "there were found in it 400 infants, suffocated in their cradles, or in the arms of their dead mothers. Altogether there perished in this cavern more than 3,000 Vaudois, including the entire population of Val Loyse. Cataneo distributed the property of these unfortunates among the vagabonds who accompanied him, and never again did the Vaudois Church raise its head in these blood-stained valleys."[2362]

The terrible stroke that fell on the Vale of Loyse was the shielding of the neighbouring valleys of Argentière and Fraissinière. Their inhabitants had been destined to destruction also, but the fate of their co-religionists taught them that their only chance of safety lay in resistance. Accordingly barricading the passes of their valleys, they showed such a front to the foe when he advanced, that he deemed it prudent to turn away and leave them in peace. This devastating tempest now swept along to discharge its violence on other valleys. "One would have thought," to use the words of Muston, "that the plague had passed along the track over which its march lay: it was only the inquisitors."

A detachment of the French army struck across the Alps in a south-west direction, holding their course toward the Waldensian Valleys, there to unite with the main body of the crusaders under Cataneo. They slaughtered, pillaged, and burned as they went onward, and at last arrived with dripping swords in the Valley of Pragelas.

The Valley of Pragelas, where we now see these assassins, sweeps along, from almost the summit of the Alps, to the south, watered by the rivers Clusone and Dora, and opens on the great plain of Piedmont, having Pinerolo on the one side and Susa on the other. It was then and long after under the dominion of France. "Prior to the revocation of the Edict of Nantes," says Muston, "the Vaudois of these valleys [that is, Pragelas, and the lateral vales branching out from it] possessed eleven parishes, eighteen churches, and sixty-four centres of religious assembling, where worship was celebrated morning and evening, in as many hamlets. It was in Laus, in Pragelas, that was held the famous synod where, 200 years before the Protestant Reformation, 140 Protestant pastors assembled, each accompanied by two or three lay deputies; and it was from the Val di Pragelas that the Gospel of God made its way into France prior to the fifteenth century."[2363]

This was the Valley of Pragelas which had been the scene of the terrible tragedy of Christmas, 1400. Again terror, mourning, and death were carried into it. The peaceful inhabitants, who were expecting no such invasion, were busy reaping their harvests, when this horde of assassins burst upon them. In the first panic they abandoned their dwellings and fled. Many were overtaken and slain; hamlets and whole villages were given to the flames; nor could the caves in which multitudes sought refuge afford any protection. The horrible barbarity of the Val Loyse was repeated in the Valley of Pragelas. Combustible materials were piled up and fires kindled at the mouths of these hiding-places; and when extinguished, all was silent within. Folded together in one motionless heap lay mother and babe, patriarch and stripling; while the fatal smoke, which had cast them into that deep sleep, was eddying along the roof, and slowly making its exit into the clear sunlit summer sky. But the course of this destruction was stayed. After the first surprise the inhabitants took heart, and turning upon their murderers drove them from their valley, exacting a heavy penalty in the pursuit for the ravages they had committed in it.

We now turn to the Piedmontese portion of this army. It was led by the Papal legate, Cataneo, in person. It was destined to operate against those valleys in Piedmont which were the most ancient seat of these religionists, and were deemed the stronghold of the Vaudois heresy. Cataneo repaired to Pinerolo, which adjoins the frontier of the doomed territory. Thence he dispatched a band of preaching monks to convert the men of the Valleys. These missionaries returned without having, so far as appears, made a single convert. The legate now put his soldiers in motion. Traversing the glorious plain, the Clusone gleaming out through rich corn-fields and vineyards on their left, and the mighty rampart of the hills, with their chestnut forests, their pasturages, and snows, rising grandly on their right, and turning round the shoulder of the copse-clad Bricherasio, this army, with another army of pillagers and cut-throats in its rear, advanced up the long avenue that leads to La Torre, the capital of the Valleys, and sat down before it. They had come against a simple, unarmed people, who knew to tend their vines, and lead their herds to pasture, but were ignorant of the art of war. It seemed as if the last hour of the Waldensian race had struck.

Seeing this mighty host before their Valleys, the Waldenses sent two of their patriarchs to request an interview with Cataneo, and turn, if possible, his heart to peace. John Campo and John Desiderio were dispatched on this embassy. "Do not condemn us without hearing us," said they, "for we are Christians and faithful subjects; and our Barbes are prepared to prove, in public or in private, that our doctrines are conformable to the Word of God.... Our hope in God is greater than our desire to please men; beware how you draw down upon yourselves his anger by persecuting us; for remember that, if God so wills it, all the forces you have assembled against us will nothing avail."

These were weighty words, and they were meekly spoken, but as to changing Cataneo's purpose, or softening the hearts of the ruffian-host which he led, they might as well have been addressed to the rocks which rose around the speakers. Nevertheless, they fell not to the ground.

Cataneo, believing that the Vaudois herdsmen would not stand an hour before his men-at-arms, and desirous of striking a finishing blow, divided his army into a number of attacking parties, which were to begin the battle on various points at the same time. The folly of extending his line so as to embrace the whole territory led to Cataneo's destruction; but his strategy was rewarded with a few small successes at first.

One troop was stationed at the entrance of the Val Lucerna; we shall follow its march till it disappears on the mountains it hopes to conquer, and then we shall return and narrate the more decisive operations of the campaign under Cataneo in the Val Angrogna.

The first step of the invaders was to occupy the town of La Torre, situated on the angle formed by the junction of the Val Lucerna and the Val Angrogna, the silver Pelice at its feet and the shadow of the Castelluzzo covering it. The soldiers were probably spared the necessity or denied the pleasure of slaughter, the inhabitants having fled to the mountains. The valley beyond La Torre is too open to admit of being defended, and the troop advanced along it unopposed. Than this theatre of war nothing in ordinary times is more peaceful, nothing more grand. A carpet of rich meadows clothes it from side to side; fruitful trees fleck it with their shadows; the Pelice waters it; and on either hand is a wall of mountains, whose sides display successive zones of festooned vines, golden grain, dark chestnut forests, and rich pasturages. Over these are hung stupendous battlements of rock; and above all, towering high in air, are the everlasting peaks in their robes of ice and snow. But the sublimities of nature were nothing to men whose thoughts were only of blood.

Pursuing their march up the valley, the soldiers next came to Villaro. It is situated about midway between the entrance and head of Lucerna, on a ledge of turf in the side of the great mountains, raised some 200 feet above the Pelice, which flows past at about a quarter-mile's distance. The troop had little difficulty in taking possession. Most of the inhabitants, warned of the approach of danger, had fled to the Alps. What Cataneo's troop inflicted on those who had been unable to make their escape, no history records. The half of Lucerna, with the towns of La Torre and Villaro and their hamlets, was in the occupation of Cataneo's soldiers; their march so far had been a victorious one, though certainly not a glorious one, such victories as they had gained being only over unarmed peasants and bed-rid women.

Resuming their march the troop came next to Bobbio. The name of Bobbio is not unknown in classic story. It nestles at the base of gigantic cliffs, where the lofty summit of the Col la Croix points the way to France, and overhangs a path which apostolic feet may have trodden. The Pelice is seen forcing its way through the dark gorges of the mountains in a thundering torrent, and meandering in a flood of silver along the valley.

At this point the grandeur of the Val Lucerna attains its height. Let us pause to survey the scene that must have met the eyes of Cataneo's soldiers, and which, one would suppose, might have turned them from their cruel purpose. Immediately behind Bobbio shoots up the "Barion," symmetrical as Egyptian obelisk, but far taller and massier. Its summit rises 3,000 feet above the roofs of the little town. Compared with this majestic monolith the proudest monument of Europe's proudest capital is a mere toy. Yet even the Barion is but an item in this assemblage of glories. Overtopping it behind, and sweeping round the extremity of the valley, is a glorious amphitheatre of crags and precipices, enclosed by a background of great mountains, some rounded like domes, others sharp as needles; and rising out of this sea of hills, are the grander and loftier forms of the Alp des Rousses and the Col de Malaure, which guard the gloomy pass that winds its way through splintered rocks and under overhanging precipices, till it opens into the valleys of the French Protestants, and lands the traveller on the plains of Dauphiné. In this unrivalled amphiteatre sits Bobbio, in summer buried in blossoms and fruit, and in winter wrapped in the shadows of its great mountains, and the mists of their tempests. What a contrast between the still repose and grand sublimity of nature and the dreadful errand on which the men now pressing forward to the little town are bent! To them, nature speaks in vain; they are engrossed with but one thought.

The capture of Bobbio—an easy task—put the soldiers in possession of the entire Valley of Lucerna: its inhabitants had been chased to the Alps, or their blood mingled with the waters of their own Pelice. Other and remoter expeditions were now projected. Their plan was to traverse the Col Julien, sweep down on the Valley of Prali, which lies on the north of it, chastise its inhabitants, pass on to the Valleys of San Martino and Perosa, and pursuing the circuit of the Valleys, and clearing the ground as they went onward of its inveterate heresy, at least its heretics, join the main body of crusaders, who, they expected, would by this time have finished their work in the Valley of Angrogna, and unitedly celebrate their victory. They would then be able to say that they had gone the round of the Waldensian territory, and had at last effected the long-meditated work, so often attempted, but hitherto in vain, of the utter extirpation of its heresy. But the war was destined to have a very different termination.

The expedition across the Col Julien was immediately commenced. A corps of 700 men was detached from the army in Lucerna for this service.[2364] The ascent of the mountain opens immediately on the north side of Bobbio. We see the soldiers toiling upwards on the track, which is a mere foot-path formed by the herdsmen. At every short distance they pass the thick-planted châlets and hamlets sweetly embowered amid mantling vines, or the branches of the apple and cherry tree, or the goodlier chestnut, but the inhabitants have fled. They have now reached a great height on the mountain-side. Beneath is Bobbio, a speck of brown. There is the Valley of Lucerna, a ribbon of green, with a thread of silver woven into it, and lying along amid masses of mighty rocks. There, across Lucerna, are the great mountains that enclose the Valley of Rora, standing up in the silent sky; on the right are the spiky crags that bristle along the Pass of Mirabouc, that leads to France, and yonder in the east is a glimpse of the far-extending plains of Piedmont.

But the summit is yet a long way off, and the soldiers of the Papal legate, bearing their weapons, to be employed, not in venturesome battle, but in cowardly massacre, toil up the ascent. As they gain on the mountain, they look down on pinnacles which half an hour before had looked down on them. Other heights, tall as the former, still rise above them; they climb to these airy spires, which in their turn sink beneath their feet. This process they repeat again and again, and at last they come out upon the downs that clothe the shoulders of the mountain. Now it is that the scene around them becomes one of stupendous and inexpressible grandeur. Away to the east, now fully under the eye, is the plain of Piedmont, green as garden, and level as the ocean. At their feet yawn gorges and abysses, while spiky pinnacles peer up from below as if to buttress the mountain. The horizon is filled with Alps, conspicuous among which, on the east, is the Col la Vêchera, whose snow-clad summit draws the eye to the more than classic valley over which it towers, where the Barbes in ancient days were wont to assemble in synod, and whence their missionaries went forth, at the peril of life, to distribute the Scriptures and sow the seed of the Kingdom. It was not unmarked, doubtless, by this corps, forming, as they meant it should do, the terminating point of their expedition in the Val di Angrogna. On the west, the crowning glory of the scene was Monte Viso, standing up in bold relief in the ebon vault, in a robe of silver. But in vain had Nature spread out her magnificence before men who had neither eyes to see nor hearts to feel her glory.

Climbing on their hands and knees the steep grassy slope in which the pass terminates, they looked down from the summit on the Valley of Prali, at that moment a scene of peace. Its great snow-clad hills, conspicuous among which is the Col d'Abries, kept guard around it. Down their sides rolled foaming torrents, which, uniting in the valley, flowed along in a full and rapid river. Over the bosom of the plain were scattered numerous hamlets. The peasants were at work in the meadows and corn-fields; their children were at play; their herds were browsing in their pastures. Suddenly on the mountains above had gathered this flock of vultures that with greedy eyes were looking down upon their prey. A few hours, and these dwellings would be in flames, their inmates slaughtered, and their herds and goods carried off as booty. Impatient to begin their work, these 700 assassins rushed down on the plain.

The troop had reckoned that, no tidings of their approach having reached this secluded valley, they would fall upon its unarmed peasants as falls the avalanche, and crush them. But it was not to be so. Instead of fleeing, panic-struck, as the invaders expected, the men of Prali hastily assembled, and stood to their defence. Battle was joined at the hamlet of Pommiers. The weapons of the Vaudois were rude, but their trust in God, and their indignation at the cowardly and bloody assault, gave them strength and courage. The Piedmontese soldiers, wearied with the rugged, slippery tracks they had traversed, fell beneath the blows of their opponents. Every man of them was cut down with the exception of one ensign.[2365] Of all the 700, he alone survived. During the carnage, he made his escape, and ascending the banks of a mountain torrent, he crept into a cavity which the summer heats had formed in a mass of snow. There he remained hid for some days; at last, cold and hunger drove him forth to cast himself upon the mercy of the men of Prali. They were generous enough to pardon this solitary survivor of the host that had come to massacre them. They sent him back across the Col Julien, to tell those from whom he had come that the Vaudois had courage to fight for their hearths and altars, and that of the army of 700 which they had sent to slay them, he only had escaped to carry tidings of the fate which had befallen his companions.

CHAPTER III
FAILURE OF CATANEO'S EXPEDITION

THE camp of Cataneo was pitched almost at the gates of La Torre, beneath the shadow of the Castelluzzo. The Papal legate is about to try to force his way into the Val di Angrogna. This valley opens hard by the spot where the legate had established his camp, and runs on for a dozen miles into the Alps, a magnificent succession of narrow gorges and open dells, walled throughout by majestic mountains, and terminating in a noble circular basin—the Pra del Tor—which is set round with snowy peaks, and forms the most venerated spot in all the Waldensian territory, inasmuch as it was the seat of their college, and the meeting-place of their Barbes.

In the Pra del Tor, or Meadow of the Tower, Cataneo expected to surprise the mass of the Waldensian people, now gathered into it as being the strongest refuge which their hills afforded. There, too, he expected to be joined by the corps which he had sent round by Lucerna to make the circuit of the Valleys, and after devastating Prali and San Martino, to climb the mountain barrier and join their companions in the "Pra," little imagining that the soldiers he had dispatched on that errand of massacre were now enriching with their corpses the Valleys they had been sent to subdue. In that same spot where the Barbes had so often met in synod, and enacted rules for the government of their Church and the spread of their faith, the Papal legate would reunite his victorious host, and finish the campaign by proclaiming that now the Waldensian heresy, root and branch, was extinct.

The Waldenses—their humble supplication for peace having been contemptuously rejected, as we have already said—had three courses in their choice—to go to mass, to be butchered as sheep, or to fight for their lives. They chose the last, and made ready for battle. But first they must remove to a place of safety all who were unable to bear arms.

Packing up their kneading-troughs, their ovens, and other culinary utensils, laying their aged on their shoulders, and their sick in couches, and leading their children by the hand, they began to climb the hills, in the direction of the Pra del Tor, at the head of the Val di Angrogna. Transporting their household stuff, they could be seen traversing the rugged paths, and making the mountains resound with psalms, which they sweetly sung as they journeyed up the ascent. Those who remained busied themselves in manufacturing pikes and other weapons of defence and attack, in repairing the barricades, in arranging themselves into fighting parties, and assigning to the various corps the posts they were to defend.

Cataneo now put his soldiers in motion. Advancing to near the town of La Torre, they made a sharp turn to the right, and entered the Val di Angrogna. Its opening offers no obstruction, being soft and even as any meadow in all England. By-and-by it begins to swell into the heights of Roccomaneot, where the Vaudois had resolved to make a stand. Their fighting men were posted along its ridge. Their armour was of the simplest. The bow was almost their only weapon of attack. They wore bucklers of skin, covered with the bark of the chestnut-tree, the better to resist thrust of pike or cut of sword. In the hollow behind, protected by the rising ground on which their fathers, husbands, and brothers were posted, were a number of women and children, gathered there for shelter. The Piedmontese host pressed up the acclivity, discharging a shower of arrows as they advanced, and the Waldensian line on which these missiles fell, seemed to waver, and to be on the point of giving way. Those behind, espying the danger, fell on their knees and, extending their hands in supplication to the God of battles, cried aloud, "O God of our fathers, help us! O God, deliver us!" That cry was heard by the attacking host, and especially by one of its captains, Le Noir of Mondovi, or the Black Mondovi, a proud, bigoted, blood-thirsty man. He instantly shouted out that his soldiers would give the answer, accompanying his threat with horrible blasphemies. The Black Mondovi raised his visor as he spoke. At the instant an arrow from the bow of Pierre Revel, of Angrogna, entering between his eyes, transfixed his skull, and he fell on the earth a corpse. The fall of this daring leader disheartened the Papal army. The soldiers began to fall back. They were chased down the slopes by the Vaudois, who now descended upon them like one of their own mountain torrents. Having driven their invaders to the plain, cutting off not a few in their flight, they returned as the evening began to fall, to celebrate with songs, on the heights where they had won it, the victory with which it had pleased the God of their fathers to crown their arms.

Cataneo burned with rage and shame at being defeated by these herdsmen. In a few days, reassembling his host, he made a second attempt to enter the Angrogna. This promised to be successful. He passed the height of Roccomaneot, where he had encountered his first defeat, without meeting any resistance. He led his soldiers into the narrow defiles beyond. Here great rocks overhang the path: mighty chestnut-trees fling their branches across the way, veiling it in gloom, and far down thunders the torrent that waters the valley. Still advancing, he found himself, without fighting, in possession of the ample and fruitful expanse into which, these defiles passed, the valley opens. He was now master so far of the Val di Angrogna, comprehending the numerous hamlets, with their finely cultivated fields and vineyards, on the left of the torrent. But he had seen none of the inhabitants. These, he knew, were with the men of Lucerna in the Pra del Tor. Between him and his prey rose the "Barricade," a steep unscaleable mountain, which runs like a wall across the valley, and forms a rampart to the famous "Meadow," which combines the solemnity of sanctuary with the strength of citadel.

Must the advance of the Papal legate and his army here end? It seemed as if it must. Cataneo was in a vast *cul-de-sac*. He could see the white peaks round the Pra, but between him and the Pra itself rose, in Cyclopean strength and height, the Barricade. He searched and unhappily for himself, found an entrance. Some convulsion of nature has here rent the mountains, and through the long, narrow, and dark chasm thus formed lies the one only path that leads to the head of Angrogna. The leader of the Papal host boldly ordered his men to enter and traverse this frightful gorge, not knowing how few of them he should ever lead back. The only pathway through this chasm is a rocky ledge on the side of the mountain, so narrow that not more than two abreast can advance along it. If assailed either in front, or in rear, or from above, there is absolutely no retreat.

Nor is there room for the party attacked to fight. The pathway is hung midway between the bottom of the gorge, along which rolls the stream, and the summit of the mountain. Here the naked cliff runs sheer up for at least one thousand feet; there it leans over the path in stupendous masses, which look as if about to fall. Here lateral fissures admit the golden beams of the sun, which relieve the darkness of the pass, and make it visible. There a half-acre or so of level space gives standing-room on the mountain's side to a clump of birches, with their tall silvery trunks, or a châlet, with its bit of bright close-shaven meadow. But these only partially relieve the terrors of the chasm, which runs on from one to two miles, when, with a burst of light, and a sudden flashing of white peaks on the eye, it opens into an amphitheatre of meadow of dimensions so goodly, that an entire nation might find room to encamp in it.

It was into this terrible defile that the soldiers of the Papal legate now marched. They kept advancing, as best they could, along the narrow ledge. They were now nearing the Pra. It seemed impossible for their prey to escape them. Assembled on this spot the Waldensian people had but one neck, and the Papal soldiers, so Cataneo believed, were to sever that neck at a blow. But God was watching over the Vaudois. He had said of the Papal legate and his army, as of another tyrant of former days, "I will put my hook in thy nose, and my bridle in thy lips, and I will cause thee to return by the way which thou camest." But by what agency was the advance of that host to be stayed? Will some mighty angel smite Cataneo's army, as he did Sennacherib's? No angel blockaded the pass. Will thunder-bolts and hailstones be rained upon Cataneo's soldiers, as of old on Sisera's? The thunders slept; the hail fell not. Will earthquake and whirlwind discomfit them? No earthquake rocked the ground; no whirlwinds rent the mountains. The instrumentality now put in motion to shield the Vaudois from destruction was one of the lightest and frailest in all nature; yet no bars of adamant could have more effectually shut the pass, and brought the march of the host to an instant halt.

A white cloud, no bigger than a man's hand, unobserved by the Piedmontese, but keenly watched by the Vaudois, was seen to gather on the mountain's summit, about the time the army would be entering the defile. That cloud grew rapidly bigger and blacker. It began to descend. It came rolling down the mountain's side, wave on wave, like an ocean tumbling out of heaven—a sea of murky vapour. It fell right into the chasm in which was the Papal army, sealing it up, and filling it from top to bottom with a thick black fog. In a moment the host were in night; they were bewildered, stupefied, and could see neither before nor behind, could neither advance nor retreat. They halted in a state bordering on terror.[2366]

The Waldenses interpreted this as an interposition of Providence in their behalf. It had given them the power of repelling the invader. Climbing the slopes of the Pra, and issuing from all their hiding-places in its environs, they spread themselves over the mountains, the paths of which were familiar to them, and while the host stood riveted beneath them, caught in the double toils of the defile and the mist, they tore up the great stones and rocks, and sent them thundering down into the ravine. The Papal soldiers were crushed where they stood. Nor was this all. Some of the Waldenses boldly entered the chasm, sword in hand, and attacked them in front. Consternation seized the Piedmontese host. Panic impelled them to flee, but their effort to escape was more fatal than the sword of the Vaudois, or the rocks that, swift as an arrow, came bounding down the mountain. They jostled one another; they threw each other down in the struggle; some were trodden to death; others were rolled over the precipice, and crushed on the rocks below, or drowned in the torrent, and so perished miserably.[2367]

The fate of one of these invaders has been preserved in story. He was a certain Captain Saquet, a man, it is said, of gigantic stature, from Polonghera, in Piedmont. He began, like his Philistine prototype, to vent curses on the Waldensian dogs. The words were yet in his mouth when his foot slipped. Rolling over the precipice, and tumbling into the torrent of the Angrogna, he was carried away by the stream, and his body finally deposited in a deep eddy or whirlpool, called in the *patois* of the country a "tompie," from the noise made by its waters. It bears to this day the name of the Tompie de Saquet, or Gulf of Saquet.[2368]

This war hung above the Valleys, like a cloud of tempest, for a whole year. It inflicted much suffering and loss upon the Waldenses; their homes were burned, their fields devastated, their goods carried off, and their persons slain; but the invaders suffered greatly more than they inflicted. Of the 18,000 regular troops, to which we may add about an equal number of desperadoes, with which the campaign opened, few ever returned to their homes. They left their bones on the mountains they had come to subdue. They were cut off mostly in detail. They were led weary chases from valley to mountain and from mountain to valley. The rocks rolled upon them gave them at once death and burial. They were met in narrow defiles and cut to pieces. Flying parties of Waldenses would suddenly issue from the mist, or from some cave known only to themselves, attack and discomfit the foe, and then as suddenly retreat into the friendly vapour or the sheltering rock. Thus it came to pass that, in the words of Muston, "this army of invaders vanished from the Vaudois mountains as rain in the sands of the desert."[2369]

"God," says Leger, "turned the heart of their prince toward this poor people." He sent a prelate to their Valleys, to assure them of his good-will, and to intimate his wish to receive their deputies. They sent twelve of their more venerable men to Turin, who being admitted into the duke's presence, gave him such an account of their faith, that he candidly confessed that he had been misled in what he had done against them, and would not again suffer such wrongs to be inflicted upon them. He several times said that he "had not so virtuous, so faithful, and so obedient subjects as the Vaudois."[2370]

He caused the deputies a little surprise by expressing a wish to see some of the Vaudois children. Twelve infants, with their mothers, were straightway sent for from the Valley of Angrogna, and presented before the prince. He examined them narrowly. He found them well formed, and testified his admiration of their healthy faces, clear eyes, and lively prattle. He had been told, he said, that "the Vaudois children were monsters, with only one eye placed in the middle of the forehead, four rows of black teeth, and other similar deformities." [2371] He expressed himself as not a little angry at having been made to believe such fables.

The prince, Charles II.,[2372] a youth of only twenty years, but humane and wise, confirmed the privileges and immunities of the Vaudois, and dismissed them with his promise that they should be unmolested in the future. The Churches of the Valleys now enjoyed a short respite from persecution.

CHAPTER IV
SYNOD IN THE WALDENSIAN VALLEYS

THE DUKE OF SAVOY was sincere in his promise that the Vaudois should not be disturbed, but fully to make it good was not altogether in his power. He could take care that such armies of crusaders as that which mustered under the standard of Cataneo should not invade their Valleys, but he could not guard them from the secret machinations of the priesthood. In the absence of the armed crusader, the missionary and the inquisitor assailed them. Some were seduced, others were kidnapped, and carried off to the Holy Office. To these annoyances was added the yet greater evil of a decaying piety. A desire for repose made many conform outwardly to the Romish Church. "In order to be shielded from all interruption in their journeys on business, they obtained from the priests, who were settled in the Valleys, certificates or testimonials of their being Papists." To obtain this credential it was necessary to attend the Romish chapel, to confess, to go to mass, and to have their children baptised by the priests. For this shameful and criminal dissimulation they fancied that they made amends by muttering to themselves when they entered the Romish temples, "Cave of robbers, may God confound thee!"[2374] At the same time they continued to attend the preaching of the Vaudois pastors, and to submit themselves to their censures. But beyond all question the men who practised these deceits, and the Church that tolerated them, had greatly declined. That old vine seemed to be dying. A little while and it would disappear from off those mountains which it had so long covered with the shadow of its boughs.

But He who had planted it "looked down from heaven and visited it." It was now that the Reformation broke out. The river of the Water of Life was opened a second time, and began to flow through Christendom. The old and dying stock in the Alps, drinking of the celestial stream, lived anew; its boughs began to be covered with blossoms and fruit as of old.

The Reformation had begun its career, and had already stirred most of the countries of Europe to their depths before tidings of the mighty change reached these secluded mountains. When at last the great news was announced, the Vaudois "were as men who dreamed." Eager to have them confirmed, and to know to what extent the yoke of Rome had been cast off by the nations of Europe, they sent forth Pastor Martin, of the Valley of Lucerna on a mission of inquiry. In 1526 he returned with the amazing intelligence that the light of the old Evangel had broken on Germany, on Switzerland, on France, and that every day was adding to the number of those who openly professed the same doctrines to which the Vaudois had borne witness from ancient times. To attest what he said, he produced the books he had received in Germany containing the views of the Reformers.[2275]

The remnant of the Vaudois on the north of the Alps also sent out men to collect information respecting that great spiritual revolution which had so surprised and gladdened them. In 1530 the Churches of Provence and Dauphiné commissioned George Morel, of Merindol, and Pierre Masson, of Burgundy, to visit the Reformers of Switzerland and Germany, and bring them word touching their doctrine and manner of life. The deputies met in conference with the members of the Protestant Churches of Neuchâtel, Morat, and Bern. They had also interviews with Berthold Haller and William Farel. Going on to Basle they presented to Œcolampadius, in October, 1530, a document in Latin, containing a complete account of their ecclesiastical discipline, worship, doctrine, and manners. They begged in return that Œcolampadius would say whether he approved of the order and doctrine of their Church, and if he held it to be defective, to specify in what points and to what extent. The elder Church submitted itself to the younger.

The visit of these two pastors of this ancient Church gave unspeakable joy to the Reformer of Basle. He heard in them the voice of the Church primitive and apostolic speaking to the Christians of the sixteenth century, and bidding them welcome within the gates of the City of God. What a miracle was before him! For ages had this Church been in the fires, yet she had not been consumed. Was not this encouragement to those who were just entering into persecutions not less terrific? "We render thanks," said Œcolampadius in his letter, October 13th, 1530, to the Churches of Provence, "to our most gracious Father that he has called you into such marvellous light, during ages in which such thick darkness has covered almost the whole world under the empire of Antichrist. We love you as brethren."

But his affection for them did not blind him to their declensions, nor make him withhold those admonitions which he saw to be needed. "As we approve of many things among you," he wrote, "so there are several which we wish to see amended. We are informed that the fear of persecution has caused you to dissemble and to conceal your faith. . . . There is no concord between Christ and Belial. You commune with unbelievers; you take part in their abominable masses, in which the death and passion of Christ are blasphemed. . . . I know your weakness, but it becomes those who have been redeemed by the blood of Christ to be more courageous. It is better for us to die than to be overcome by temptation." It was thus that Œcolampadius, speaking in the name of the Church of the Reformation, repaid the Church of the Alps for the services she had rendered to the world in former ages. By sharp, faithful, brotherly rebuke, he sought to restore to her the purity and glory which she had lost.

Having finished with Œcolampadius, the deputies went on to Strasburg. There they had interviews with Bucer and Capito. A similar statement of their faith to the Reformers of that city drew forth similar congratulations and counsels. In the clear light of her morning the Reformation Church saw many things which had grown dim in the evening of the Vaudois Church; and the Reformers willingly permitted their elder sister the benefit of their own wider views. If the men of the sixteenth century recognised the voice of primitive Christianity speaking in the Vaudois, the latter heard the voice of the Bible, or rather of God himself, speaking in the Reformers, and submitted themselves with modesty and docility to their reproofs. The last had become first.

A manifold interest belongs to the meeting of these two Churches. Each is a miracle to the other. The preservation of the Vaudois Church for so many ages, amid the fires of persecution, made her a wonder to the Church of the sixteenth century. The bringing up of the latter from the dead made her a yet greater wonder to the Church of the first century. These two Churches compare their respective beliefs: they find that their creeds are not twain, but one. They compare the sources of their knowledge: they find that they have both of them drawn their doctrine from the Word of God; they are not two Churches, they are one. They are the elder and younger members of the same glorious family, the children of the same Father. What a magnificent monument of the true antiquity and genuine catholicity of Protestantism!

Only one of the two Provence deputies returned from their visit to the Reformers of Switzerland. One their way back, at Dijon, suspicion, from some cause or other, fell on Pierre Masson. He was thrown into prison, and ultimately condemned and burned. His fellow-deputy was allowed to go on his way. George Morel, bearing the answers of the Reformers, and especially the letters of Œcolampadius, happily arrived in safety in Provence.

The documents he brought with him were much canvassed. Their contents caused these two ancient Churches mingled joy and sorrow; the former, however, greatly predominating. The news touching the numerous body of Christians, now appearing in many lands, so full of knowledge, and faith, and courage, was literally astounding. The confessors of the Alps thought that they were alone in the world; every successive century saw their numbers thinning, and their spirit growing less resolute; their ancient enemy, on the other hand, was steadfastly widening her dominion and strengthening her sway. A little longer, they imagined, and all public faithful profession of the Gospel would cease. It was at that moment they were told that a new army of champions had arisen to maintain the old battle. This announcement explained and justified the past to them, for now they beheld the fruits of their fathers' blood. They who had fought the battle were not to have the honour of the victory. That was reserved for combatants who had come newly into the field. They had forfeited this reward, they painfully felt, by their defections; hence the regret that mingled with their joy.

They proceeded to discuss the answers that should be made to the Churches of the Protestant faith, considering especially whether they should adopt the reforms urged upon them by the communications which their deputies had brought back from the Swiss and German Reformers. The great majority of the Vaudois barbes were of opinion that they ought. A small minority, however, were opposed to this, because they thought that it did not become the new discipline to dictate to the old, or because they themselves were secretly inclined to the Roman superstitions. They went back again to the Reformers for advice; and, after repeated interchange of views, it was finally resolved to convene a synod in the Valleys, at which all the questions between the two Churches might be debated, and the relations which they were to sustain towards each other in time to come, determined. If the Church of the Alps was to continue apart, as before the Reformation, she felt that she must justify her position by proving the existence of great and substantial differences in doctrine between herself and the newly-arisen Church. But if no such differences existed, she would not, and dared not, remain separate and alone; she must unite with the Church of the Reformation.

It was resolved that the coming synod should be a truly oecumenical one—

a general assembly of all the children of the Protestant faith. A hearty invitation was sent forth, and it was cordially and generally responded to. All the Waldensian Churches in the bosom of the Alps were represented in this synod. The Albigensian communities on the north of the chain, and the Vaudois Churches in Calabria, sent deputies to it. The Churches of French Switzerland chose William Farel and Anthony Saunier to attend it.[2376] From even more distant lands, as Bohemia, came men to deliberate and vote in this famous convention.

The representatives assembled on the 12th of October, 1532. Two years earlier the Augsburg Confession had been given to the world, marking the culmination of the German Reformation. A year before, Zwingle had died on the field of Cappel. In France, the Reformation was beginning to be illustrated by the heroic deaths of its children. Calvin had not taken his prominent place at Geneva, but he was already enrolled under the Protestant banner. The princes of the Schmalkald League were standing at bay in the presence of Charles V. It was a critical yet glorious era in the annals of Protestantism which saw this assembly convened. It met at the town of Chamforans, in the heart of the Valley of Angrogna. There are few grander or stronger positions in all that valley than the site occupied by this little town. The approach to it was defended by the heights of Roccomaneot and La Serre, and by defiles which now contract, now widen, but are everywhere overhung by great rocks and mighty chestnut-trees, behind and above which rise the taller peaks, some of them snow-clad. A little beyond La Serre is the plateau on which the town stood, overlooking the grassy bosom of the valley, which is watered by the crystal torrent, dotted by numerous châlets, and runs on for about two miles, till shut in by the steep, naked precipices of the Barricade, which, stretching from side to side of Angrogna, leaves only the long, dark chasm we have already described, as the pathway to the Pra del Tor, whose majestic mountains here rise on the sight and suggest to the traveller the idea that he is drawing nigh some city of celestial magnificence. The town of Chamforans does not now exist; its only representative at this day is a solitary farmhouse.

The synod sat for six consecutive days. All the points raised in the communications received from the Protestant Churches were freely ventilated by the assembled barbes and elders. Their findings were embodied in a "Short Confession of Faith," which Monastier says "may be considered as a supplement to the ancient Confession of Faith of the year 1120, which it does not contradict in any point."[2377] It consists of seventeen articles,[2378] the chief of which are the *Moral inability of man; election to eternal life; the will of God, as made known in the Bible, the only rule of duty; and the doctrine of two Sacraments only, baptism and the Lord's Supper.*

The lamp which had been on the point of expiring began, after this synod, to burn with its former brightness. The ancient spirit of the Waldenses revived. They no longer practised those dissimulations and cowardly concealments to which they had had recourse to avoid persecution. They no longer feared to confess their faith. Henceforward they were never seen at mass, or in the Popish churches. They refused to recognise the priests of Rome as ministers of Christ, and under no circumstances would they receive any spiritual benefit or service at their hands.

Another sign of the new life that now animated the Vaudois was their setting about the work of rebuilding their churches. For fifty years previous public worship may be said to have ceased in their Valleys. Their churches had been razed by the persecutor, and the Vaudois feared to rebuild them lest they should draw down upon themselves a new storm of violence and blood. A cave would serve at times as a place of meeting. In more peaceful years the house of their barbe, or of some of their chief men, would be converted into a church; and when the weather was fine, they would assemble on the mountain-side, under the great boughs of their ancestral trees. But their old sanctuaries they dared not raise from the ruins into which the persecutor had cast them. They might say with the ancient Jews, "The holy and beautiful house in which our fathers praised thee is burned with fire, and all our pleasant things are laid waste." But now, strengthened by the fellowship and counsels of their Protestant brethren, churches arose, and the worship of God was reinstituted. Hard by the place where the synod met, at Lorenzo namely, was the first of these post-Reformation churches set up; others speedily followed in the other valleys; pastors were multiplied; crowds flocked to their preaching, and not a few came from the plains of Piedmont, and from remote parts of their valleys, to drink of these living waters again flowing in their land.

Yet another token did this old Church give of the vigorous life that was now flowing in her veins. This was a translation of the Scriptures into the French tongue. At the synod, the resolution was taken to translate and print both the Old and New Testaments, and, as this was to be done at the sole charge of the Vaudois, it was considered as their gift to the Churches of the Reformation. A most appropriate and noble gift! That Book which the Waldenses had received from the primitive Church—which their fathers had preserved with their blood—which their barbes had laboriously transcribed and circulated—they now put into the hands of the Reformers, constituting them along with themselves the custodians of this the ark of the world's hopes. Robert Olivetan, a near relative of Calvin, was asked to undertake the translation, and he executed it—with the help of his great kinsman, it is believed. It was printed in folio, in black letter, at Neuchâtel, in the year 1535, by Pierre de Wingle, commonly called Picard. The entire expense was defrayed by the Waldenses, who collected for this object 1,500 crowns of gold, a large sum for so poor a people. Thus did the Waldensian Church emphatically proclaim, at the commencement of this new era in her existence, that the Word of God was her one sole foundation.

As has been already mentioned, a commission to attend the synod had been given by the Churches of French Switzerland to Farel and Saunier. Its fulfilment necessarily involved great toil and peril. One crosses the Alps at this day so easily, that it is difficult to conceive the toil and danger that attended the journey then. The deputies could not take the ordinary tracks across the mountains for fear of pursuit; they were compelled to travel by unfrequented paths. The way often led by the edge of precipices and abysses, up steep and dangerous ascents, and across fields of frozen snow. Nor were their pursuers the only dangers they had to fear; they were exposed to death from the blinding drifts and tempests of the hills. Nevertheless, they arrived in safety in the Valleys, and added by their presence and their counsels to the dignity of this the first great ecclesiastical assembly of modern times. Of this we have a somewhat remarkable proof. Three years thereafter, a Vaudois, Jean Payrel, of Angrogna, being cast into prison, deposed on his trial that "he had kept guard for the ministers who taught the good law, who were assembled in the town of Chamforans, in the centre of Angrogna; and that amongst others present there was one called Farel, who had a read beard, and a beautiful white horse; and two others accompanied him, one of whom had a horse, almost black, and the other was very tall, and rather lame."[2380]

CHAPTER V
PERSECUTIONS AND MARTYRDOMS

THE Church of the Alps had peace for twenty-eight years. This was a time of great spiritual prosperity. Sanctuaries arose in all her Valleys; her pastors and teachers were found too few, and men of learning and zeal, some of them from foreign lands, pressed into her service. Individuals and families in the cities on the plain of Piedmont embraced her faith; and the crowds that attended her worship were continually growing.[2379] In short, this venerable Church had a second youth. Her lamp, re-trimmed, burned with a brightness that justified her time-honoured motto, "A light shining in darkness." The darkness was not now so deep as it had been; the hours of night were drawing to a close. Nor was the Vaudois community the only light that now shone in Christendom. It was one of a constellation of lights, whose brilliance was beginning to irradiate the skies of the Church with an effulgence which no former age had known.

The exemption from persecution, which the Waldenses enjoyed during this period, was not absolute, but comparative. The lukewarm are seldom molested; and the quickened zeal of the Vaudois brought with it a revival of the persecutor's malignity, though it did not find vent in violences so dreadful as the tempests that had lately smitten them. Only two years after the synod—that is, in 1534—wholesale destruction fell upon the Vaudois Churches of Provence; but the sad story of their extinction will more appropriately be told elsewhere. In the valleys of Piedmont events were from time to time occurring that showed that the inquisitor's vengeance had been scotched, not killed. While the Vaudois as a race were prosperous, their churches multiplying, and their faith extending its geographical area from one year to another, individual Vaudois were being at times seized, and put to death, at the stake, on the rack, or by the cord.

Three years after, the persecution broke out anew, and raged for a short time. Charles III. of Savoy, a prince of mild manners, but under the rule of the priests, being solicited by the Archbishop of Turin and the inquisitor of the same city, gave his consent to "hunting down" the heretics of the Valleys. The commission was given to a nobleman of the name of Bersour, whose residence was at Pinerolo, near the entrance of the Valley of Perosa. Bersour, a man of savage disposition, collected a troop of 500 horse and foot, and attacked the Valley of Angrogna. He was repulsed, but the storm which had rolled away from the mountains fell upon the plains. Turning to the Vaudois who resided around his own residence, he seized a great number of persons, whom he threw into the prisons and convents of Pinerolo and the Inquisition of Turin. Many of them suffered in the flames. One of these martyrs, Catalan Girard, quaintly taught the spectators a parabolic lesson, standing at the pile. From amid the flames he asked for two stones, which were instantly brought him. The crowd looked on in silence, curious to know what he meant to do with them. Rubbing them against each other, he said, "You think to extinguish our poor Churches by your persecutions. You can no more do so that I with my feeble hands can crush these stones."

Heavier tempests seemed about to descend, when suddenly the sky cleared above the confessors of the Alps. It was a change in the politics of Europe in this instance, as in many others, that stayed the arm of persecution. Francis I. of France demanded of Charles, Duke of Savoy, permission to march an army through his dominions. The object of the French king was the recovery of the Duchy of Milan, a long-contested prize between himself and Charles V. The Duke of Savoy refused the request of his brother monarch; but reflecting that the passes of the Alps were in the hands of the men whom he was persecuting, and that should he continue his oppressions, the Vaudois might open the gates of his kingdom to the enemy, he sent orders to Bersour to stop the persecution in the Valleys.

In 1536, the Waldensian Church had to mourn the loss of one of the more distinguished of her pastors. Martin Gonin, of Angrogna—a man of public spirit and rare gifts—who had gone to Geneva on ecclesiastical affairs, was returning through Dauphiné, when he was apprehended on suspicion of being a spy. He cleared himself of that charge, but the gaoler searching his person, and discovering certain papers upon him, he was convicted of what the Parliament of Grenoble accounted a much greater crime—heresy. Condemned to die, he was led forth at night, and drowned in the river Isère. He would have suffered at the stake had not his persecutors feared the effects of his dying words upon the spectators.[2382]

There were others, also called to ascend the martyr-pile, whose names we must not pass over in silence. Two pastors returning from Geneva to their flocks in the Valleys, in company of three French Protestants, were seized at the Col de Tamiers, in Savoy, and carried to Chambéry. There all five were tried, condemned, and burned. The fate of Nicholas Sartoire is yet more touching. He was a student of theology at Geneva, and held one of those bursaries which the Lords of Bern had allotted for the training of young men as pastors in the Churches of the Valleys. He set out to spend his holiday with his family in Piedmont. We know how Vaudois heart yearns for its native mountains; nor would the coming of the youth awaken less lively anticipations on the part of his friends. The paternal threshold, alas! he was never to cross; his native Valleys he was to tread no more. Travelling by the pass of St. Bernard, and the grand Valley of Aosta, he had just passed the Italian frontier, when he was apprehended on the suspicion of heresy. It was the month of May, when all was life and beauty in the vales and mountains around him; he himself was in the spring-time of existence; it was hard to lay down life at such a moment; but the great captain from whose feet he had just come, had taught him that the first duty of a soldier of Christ is obedience. He confessed his Lord, nor could promises or threats—and both were tried—make him waver. He continued steadfast unto the end, and on the 4th of May, 1557, he was brought forth from his dungeon at Aosta, and burned alive.[2383]

The martyr who died thus heroically at Aosta was a youth, the one we are now to contemplate was a man of fifty. Geofroi Varaile was a native of the town of Busco, in Piedmont. His father had been a captain in that army of murderers who, in 1488, ravaged the Valleys of Lucerna and Angrogna. The son in 1520 became a monk, and possessing the gift of a rare eloquence, he was sent on a preaching tour, in company with another cowled ecclesiastic, yet more famous,

Bernardo Ochino of Sienna, the founder of the order of the Capuchins. The arguments of the men he was sent to convert staggered Varaile. He fled to Geneva, and in the city of the Reformers he was taught more fully the "way of life." Ordained as a pastor, he returned to the Valleys, where "like another Paul," says Leger, "he preached the faith he once destroyed." After a ministry of some months, he set out to pay a visit of a few days to his native town of Busco. He was apprehended by the monks who were lying in wait for him. He was condemned to death by the Inquisition of Turin. His execution took place in the castle-piazza of the same city, March 29th, 1558. He walked to the place where he was to die with a firm step and a serene countenance; he addressed the vast multitude around his pile in a way that drew tears from many eyes; after this, he began to sing with a loud voice, and so continued till he sank amid the flames.[2384]

Two years before this, the same piazza, the castle-yard at Turin, had witnessed a similar spectacle. Barthelemy Hector was a bookseller in Poictiers. A man of warm but well-tempered zeal, he travelled as far as the valleys, diffusing that knowledge that maketh wise unto salvation. In the assemblage of white peaks that looks down on the Pra del Tor is one named La Vêchera, so called because the cows love the rich grass that clothes its sides in summer-time. Barthelemy Hector would take his seat on the slopes of the mountain, and gathering the herdsmen and agriculturists of the Pra round him, would induce them to buy his books, by reading passages to them. Portions of the Scriptures also would he recite to the grandames and maidens as they watched their goats, or plied the distaff. His steps were tracked by the inquisitor, even amid these wild solitudes. He was dragged to Turin, to answer for the crime of selling Genevese books. His defence before his judges discovered an admirable courage and wisdom.

"You have been caught in the act," said his judge, "of selling books that contain heresy. What say you?"

"If the Bible is heresy to you, it is truth to me," replied the prisoner.

"But you use the Bible to deter men from going to mass," urged the judge.

"If the Bible deters men from going to mass," responded Barthelemy, "it is proof that God disapproves of it, and that the mass is idolatry."

The judge, deeming it expedient to make short shrift with such a heretic, exclaimed, "Retract."

"I have spoken only truth," said the bookseller, "can I change truth as I would a garment?"

His judges kept him some months in prison, in the hope that his recantation would save them the necessity of burning him. This unwillingness to have resort to the last penalty was owing to no feeling of pity for the prisoner, but entirely to the conviction that these repeated executions were endangering the cause of their Church. "The smoke of these martyr-piles," as was said with reference to the death of Patrick Hamilton, "was infecting those on whom it blew." But the constancy of Barthelemy compelled his persecutors to disregard these prudential considerations. At last, despairing of his abjuration, they brought him forth and consigned him to the flames. His behaviour at the stake "drew rivers of tears," says Leger, "from the eyes of many in the Popish crowd around his stake, while others vented reproaches and invectives against the cruelty of the monks and the inquisitors."[2385]

These are only a few of the many martyrs by whom, even during this period of comparative peace and prosperity, the Church of the Valleys was called to testify against Rome. Some of these martyrs perished by cruel, barbarous, and most horrible methods. To recite all these cases would be beyond our purpose, and to depict the revolting and infamous details would be to narrate what no reader could peruse. We shall only quote part of the brief summary of Muston. "There is no town in Piedmont," says he, "under a Vaudois pastor, where some of our brethren have not been put to death . . . Hugo Chiamps of Vinestrelle had his entrails torn from his living body, at Turin. Peter Geymarali of Bobbio, in like manner, had his entrails taken out at Luzerna, and a fierce cat thrust in their place to torture him further; Maria Romano was buried alive at Rocco-patia; Magdalen Foulano underwent the same fate at San Giovanni; Susan Michelini was bound hand and foot, and left to perish of cold and hunger at Saracena. Bartholomew Fache, gashed with sabres, had the wounds filled up with quicklime, and perished thus in agony at Fenile; Daniel Michelini had his tongue torn out at Bobbio for having praised God. James Baridari perished covered with sulphurous matches, which had been forced into his flesh under the nails, between the fingers, in the nostrils, in the lips, and over all his body, and then lighted. Daniel Revelli had his mouth filled with gunpowder, which, being lighted, blew his head to pieces. Maria Monnen, taken at Liousa, had the flesh cut from her cheek and chin bones, so that her jaw was left bare, and she was thus left to perish. Paul Garnier was slowly sliced to pieces at Rora. Thomas Margueti was mutilated in an indescribable manner at Miraboco, and Susan Jaquin cut in bits at La Torre. Sara Rostagnol was slit open from the legs to the bosom, and so left to perish on the road between Eyral and Luzerna. Anne Charbonnier was impaled and carried thus on a pike, as a standard, from San Giovanni to La Torre. Daniel Rambaud, at Paesano, had his nails torn off, then his fingers chopped off, then his feet and his hands, then his arms and his legs, with each successive refusal on his part to abjure the Gospel."[2386] Thus the roll of martyrs runs on, and with each new sufferer comes a new, a more excruciating and more horrible mode of torture and death.

We have already mentioned the demand which the King of France made upon the Duke of Savoy, Charles III., that he would permit him to march an army through his territories. The reply was a refusal; but Francis I. must needs have a road into Italy. Accordingly he seized upon Piedmont, and held possession of it, together with the Waldensian Valleys, for twenty-three years. The Waldenses had found the sway of Francis I. more tolerant than that of their own princes; for though Francis hated Lutheranism, the necessities of his policy often compelled him to court the Lutherans, and so it came to pass that while he was burning heretics at Paris he spared them in the Valleys. But the general peace of Château Cambrésis, April 3rd, 1559, restored Piedmont, with the exception of Turin, to its former rulers of the House of Savoy.[2387] Charles III. had been succeeded in 1553 by Emmanuel Philibert. Philibert was a prince of superior talents and humane disposition, and the Vaudois cherished the hope that under him they would be permitted to live in peace, and to worship as their fathers had done. What strengthened these just expectations was the fact that Philibert had married a sister of the King of France, Henry II., who had been carefully instructed in the Protestant faith by her illustrious relations, Margaret, Queen of Navarre, and Rénée of France, daughter of Louis XII. But, alas! the treaty that restored Emmanuel Philibert to the throne of his ancestors, contained a clause binding the contracting parties to extinguish heresy. This was to send him back to his subjects with a dagger in his hand.

Whatever the king might incline—and we dare say, strengthened by the counsels of his Protestant queen, he intended dealing humanely by his faithful subjects the Vaudois—his intentions were overborne by men of stronger wills and more determined resolves. The inquisitors of his kingdom, the nuncio of the Pope, and the ambassadors of Spain and France, united in urging upon him the purgation of his dominions, in terms of the agreement in the treaty of peace. The unhappy monarch, unable to resist these powerful solicitations, issued on the 15th February, 1560, an edict forbidding his subjects to hear the Protestant preachers in the Valley of Lucerna, or anywhere else, under pain of a fine of 100 dollars of gold for the first offence, and of the galleys for life for the second. This edict had reference mainly to the Protestants on the plain of Piedmont, who resorted in crowds to hear sermon in the Valleys. There followed, however, in a short time a yet severer edict, commanding attendance at mass under pain of death. To carry out this cruel decree a commission was given to a prince of the blood, Philip of Savoy, Count de Raconis, and with him was associated George Costa, Count de la Trinita, and Thomas Jacomel, the Inquisitor-General, a man as cruel in disposition as he was licentious in manners. To these was added a certain Councillor Corbis, but he was not of the stuff which the business required, and so, after witnessing a few initial scenes of barbarity and horror, he resigned his commission.[2388]

The first burst of the tempest fell on Carignano. This town reposes sweetly on one of the spurs of the Apennines, about twenty miles to the south-west of Turin. It contained many Protestants, some of whom were of good position. The wealthiest were selected and dragged to the burning-pile, in order to strike terror into the rest. The blow had not fallen in vain; the professors of the Protestant creed in Carignano were scattered; some fled to Turin, then under the domination of France, some to other places, and some, alas! frightened by the tempest in front, turned back and sought refuge in the darkness behind them. They had desired a "better country," but could not enter in at the cost of exile and death.

Having done its work at Carignano, this desolating tempest held its way across the plain of Piedmont, towards those great mountains which were the ancient fortress of the truth, marking its track through the villages and country communes in terror, in pillage and blood. It moved like one of those thunder-clouds which the traveller on the Alps may often descry beneath him, traversing the same plain, and shooting its lightnings earthwards as it advances. Wherever it was known that there was a Vaudois congregation, thither did the cloud turn. And now we behold it at the foot of the Waldensian Alps—at the entrance of the Valleys, within whose mighty natural bulwarks crowds of fugitives from the towns and villages on the plain have already found asylum.

Rumours of the confiscations, arrests, cruel tortures, and horrible deaths which had befallen the Churches at the foot of their mountains, had preceded the appearance of the crusaders at the entrance of the Valleys. The same devastation which had befallen the flourishing Churches on the plain of Piedmont, seemed to impend over the Churches in the bosom of the Alps. At this juncture the pastors and leading laymen assembled to deliberate on the steps to be taken. Having fasted and humbled themselves before God, they sought by earnest prayer the direction of the Holy Spirit.[2389] They resolved to approach the throne of their prince, and by humble remonstrance and petition, set forth the state of their affairs and the justice of their cause. Their first claim was to be heard before being condemned—a right denied to no one accused, however criminal. They next solemnly disclaimed the main offence laid to their charge, that of departing from the true faith, and of adopting doctrines unknown to the Scriptures, and the early ages of the Church. Their faith was that which Christ himself had taught; which the apostles, following their Great Master, had preached; which the Fathers had vindicated with their pens, and the martyrs with their blood, and which the first four Councils had ratified, and proclaimed to be the faith of the Christian world. From the "old paths," the Bible and all antiquity being witnesses, they had never turned aside; from father to son they had continued these 1,500 years to walk therein. Their mountains shielded no novelties; they had bowed the knee to no strange gods, and, if they were heretics, so too were the first four Councils; and so too were the apostles themselves. If they erred, it was in the company of the confessors and martyrs of the early ages. They were willing any moment to appeal their cause to a General Council, provided that Council were willing to decide the question by the only infallible standard they knew, the Word of God. If on this evidence they should be convicted of even one heresy, most willingly would they surrender it. On this, the main point of their indictment, what more could they promise? Show us, they said, what the errors are which you ask us to renounce under the penalty of death, and you shall not need to ask a second time.[2390]

Their duty to God did not weaken their allegiance to their prince. To piety they added loyalty. The throne before which they now stood had not more faithful and devoted subjects than they. When had they plotted treason, or disputed lawful command of their sovereign? Nay, the more they feared God, the more they honoured the king. Their services, their substance, their life, were all at the disposal of their prince; they were willing to lay them all down in defence of his lawful prerogative; one thing only they could not surrender—their conscience.

As regarded their Romanist fellow-subjects of Piedmont, they had lived in good-neighbourhood with them. Whose person had they injured—whose property had they robbed—whom had they overreached in their bargains? Had they not been kind, courteous, honest? If their hills had vied in fertility with the naturally richer plains at their feet, and if their mountain-homes had been filled with store of corn and oil and wine, not always found in Piedmontese dwellings, to what was this owing, save to their superior industry, frugality, and skill? Never had marauding expedition descended from their hills to carry off the goods of their neighbours, or to inflict retaliation for the many murders and robberies to which they had had to submit. Why, then, should their neighbours rise against them to exterminate them, as if they were a horde of evil-doers, in whose neighbourhood no man could live in peace; and why should their sovereign unsheathe the sword against those who had never been found disturbers of his kingdom, nor plotters against his government, but who, on the contrary, had ever striven to maintain the authority of his law and the honour of his throne? "One thing is certain, most serene prince," say they, in conclusion, "that the Word of God will not perish, but will abide for ever. If, then, our religion is the pure Word of God, as we are persuaded it is, and not a human invention, no human power will be able to abolish it."[2391]

Never was there a more solemn, or a more just, or a more respectful remonstrance presented to any throne. The wrong about to be done them was enormous, yet not an angry word, nor a single accusatory sentence, do the Vaudois permit themselves to utter. But to what avail this solemn protest, this triumphant vindication? The more complete and conclusive it is, the more manifest does it make the immense injustice and the flagrant criminality of the House of Savoy. The more the Vaudois put themselves in the right, the more they put the Church of Rome in the wrong; and they who have already doomed them to perish are but the more resolutely determined to carry out their purpose.

This document was accompanied by two others: one to the queen, and one to the Council. The one to the queen is differently conceived from that to the duke. They offer no apology for their faith: the queen herself was of it. They allude in a few touching terms to the sufferings they had already been subjected to, and to the yet greater that appeared to impend. This was enough, they knew, to awaken all her sympathies, and enlist her as their advocate with the king, after the example of Esther, and other noble women in former times, who valued their lofty station less for its dazzling honours, than for the opportunities it gave them of shielding the persecuted confessors of the truth.[2392]

The remonstrance presented to the Council was couched in terms more plain and direct, yet still respectful. They bade the counsellors of the king beware what they did; they warned them that every drop of innocent blood they should spill they would one day have to account for; that if the blood of Abel, though only that of one man, cried with a voice so loud that God heard it in heaven, and came down to call its shedder to a reckoning, how much mightier the cry that would arise from the blood of a whole nation, and how much more terrible the vengeance with which it would be visited! In fine, they reminded the Council that what they asked was not an unknown privilege in Piedmont, nor would they be the first or the only persons who had enjoyed that indulgence if it should be extended to them. Did not the Jew and the Saracen live unmolested in their cities? Did they not permit the Israelite to build his synagogue, and the Moor to read his Koran, without annoyance or restraint? Was it a great thing that the faith of the Bible should be placed on the same level in this respect with that of the Crescent, and that the descendants of the men who for generations had been the subjects of the House of Savoy, and who had enriched the nations with their virtues, and defended them with their blood, should be treated with the same humanity that was shown to the alien and the unbeliever?

These petitions the confessors of the Alps dispatched to the proper quarter, and having done so, they waited an answer with eyes lifted up to heaven. If that answer should be peace, with what gratitude to God and to their prince would they hail it! should it be otherwise, they were ready to accept that alternative too; they were prepared to die.

CHAPTER VI
PREPARATIONS FOR A WAR OF EXTERMINATION

WHERE was the Vaudois who would put is life in his hand, and carry this remonstrance to the duke? The dangerous service was undertaken by M. Gilles, Pastor of Bricherasio, a devoted and courageous man. A companion was associated with him, but wearied out with the rebuffs and insults he met with, he abandoned the mission, and left its conduct to Gilles alone. The duke then lived at Nice, for Turin, his capital was still in the hands of the French, and the length of the journey very considerably increased its risks. Gilles reached Nice safely, however, and after many difficulties and delays he had an interview with Queen Margaret, who undertook to place the representations of which he was the bearer in the hands of her husband, the duke. The deputy had an interview also with Philip of Savoy, the Duke's brother, and one of the commissioners under the Act for the purgation of the Valleys. The Waldensian pastor was, on the whole well received by him. Unequally yoked with the cruel and bigoted Count La Trinita, Philip of Savoy soon became disgusted, and left the bloody business wholly in the hands of his fellow-commissioner.[2393] As regarded the queen, her heart was in the Valleys; the cause of the poor Vaudois was her cause also. But she stood alone as their intercessor with the duke; her voice was drowned by the solicitations and threats of the prelates, the King of Spain, and the Pope.[2394]

For three months there came neither letter nor edict from the court at Nice. If the men of the Valleys were impatient to know the fate that awaited them, their enemies, athirst for plunder and blood, were still more so. The latter, unable longer to restrain their passions, began the persecution on their own account. They thought they knew the sovereign's intentions, and made bold to anticipate them.

The tocsin was rung out from the Monastery of Pinerolo. Perched on the frontier of the Valleys, the monks of this establishment kept their eyes fixed upon the heretics of the mountains, as vultures watch their prey, ever ready to sweep down upon hamlet or valley when they found it unguarded. They hired a troop of marauders, whom they sent forth to pillage. The band returned, driving before them a wretched company of captives whom they had dragged from their homes and vineyards in the mountains. The poorer sort they burned alive, or sent to the galleys; the rich they imprisoned till they had paid the ransom to which they were held.

The example of the monks was followed by certain Popish landlords in the Valley of San Martino. The two seigneurs of Perrier attacked, before day-break of April 2nd, 1560, the villagers of Rioclareto, with an armed band. Some they slaughtered, the rest they drove out, without clothes or food, to perish on the snow-clad hills. The ruffians who had expelled them, took possession of their dwellings, protesting that no one should enter them unless he were willing to go to mass. They kept possession only three days, for the Protestants of the Valley of Clusone, to the number of 400, hearing of the outrage, crossed the mountains, drove out the invaders, and reinstated their brethren.[2396]

Next appeared in the Valleys, Philip of Savoy, Count de Raconis, and Chief Commissioner. He was an earnest Roman Catholic, but a humane and upright man. He attended sermon one day in the Protestant church of Angrogna, and was so much pleased with what he heard, that he obtained from the pastor an outline of the Vaudois faith, so as to send it to Rome, in the hope that the Pope would cease to persecute a creed that seemed so little heretical. A sanguine hope truly! Where the honest count had seen very little heresy, the Pope, Pius IV., saw a great deal; and would not even permit a disputation with the Waldensian pastors, as the count had proposed. He would stretch his benignity no farther than to absolve "from their past crimes" all who were willing to enter the Church of Rome. This was not very encouraging, still the count did not abandon his idea of conciliation. In June, 1560, he came a second time to the Valley of Lucerna, accompanied by his colleague La Trinita, and assembling the pastors and heads of families, he told them that the persecution would cease immediately, provided they would consent to hear the preachers he had brought with him, *Brothers of the Christian Doctrine*. He further proposed that they should silence their own ministers while they were making trial of his. The Vaudois expressed their willingness to consent, provided the count's ministers preached the pure Gospel; but if they preached human traditions, they (the Vaudois) would be under the necessity of withholding their consent; and, as regarding silencing their own ministers, it was only reasonable that they should be permitted first to make trial of the count's preachers. A few days after, they had a taste of the new expositors. Selecting the ablest among them, they made him ascend the pulpit and hold forth to a Vaudois congregation. He took a very effectual way to make them listen. "I will demonstrate to you," said he, "that the mass is found in Scripture. The word *massah* signifies 'sent,' does it not?" "Not precisely," replied his hearers, who knew more about Hebrew than was convenient for the preacher. "The primitive expression," continued he, "*Ite missa est*, was employed to dismiss the auditory, was it not?" "That is quite true," replied his hearers, without very clearly seeing how it bore on his argument. "Well, then, you see, gentlemen, that the mass is found in Holy Scripture."[2397] The congregation were unable to determine whether the preacher was arguing with them or simply laughing at them.

Finding the Waldenses obdurate, as he deemed them, the Duke of Savoy, in October, 1560, declared war against them. Early in that month a dreadful rumour reached the Valleys, namely, that the duke was levying an army to exterminate them. The news was but too true. The duke offered a free pardon to all "outlaws, convicts, and vagabonds" who would enrol as volunteers to serve against the Vaudois. Soon an army of truly dreadful character was assembled. The Vaudois seemed doomed to total and inevitable destruction. The pastors and chief persons assembled to deliberate on the measures to be taken at this terrible crisis. Feeling that their refuge was in God alone, they resolved that they would take no means for deliverance which might be offensive to him, or dishonourable to themselves. The pastors were to exhort every one to apply to God, with true faith, sincere repentance, and ardent prayer; and as to defensive measures, they recommended that each family should collect their provisions, clothes, utensils, and herds, and be ready at a moment's notice to convey them, together with all infirm persons, to their strongholds in the mountains. Meanwhile, the duke's army—if the collected ruffianism of Piedmont could be so called—came nearer every day.[2398]

On the 31st of October, a proclamation was posted throughout the Valley of Angrogna, calling on the inhabitants to return within the Roman pale, under penalty of extermination by fire and sword. On the day following, the 1st of November, the Papal army appeared at Bubiana, on the right bank of the Pelice, at the entrance to the Waldensian Valleys. The host numbered 4,000 infantry and 200 horse;[2399] comprising, besides the desperadoes that formed its main body, a few veterans, who had seen a great deal of service in the wars with France.

The Vaudois, the enemy being now in sight, humbled themselves, in a public fast, before God. Next, they partook together of the Lord's Supper. Refreshed in soul by these services, they proceeded to put in execution the measures previously resolved on. The old men and the women climbed the mountains, awakening the echoes with the psalms which they sung on their way to the Pra del Tor, within whose natural ramparts of rock and snow-clad peaks they sought asylum. The Vaudois population of the Valleys at that time was not more than 18,000; their armed men did not exceed 1,200;[2400] these were distributed at various passes and barricades to oppose the enemy, who was now near.

On the 2nd of November the Piedmontese army, putting itself in motion, crossed the Pelice, and advanced along the narrow defile that leads up to the Valleys, having the heights of Bricherasio on the right, and the spurs of Monte Friolante on the left, with the towering masses of the Vandalin and Castelluzzo in front. The Piedmontese encamped in the meadows of San Giovanni, within a stone's-throw of the point where the Val di Lucerna and the Val di Angrogna divide, the former to expand into a noble breadth of meadow and vineyard, running on between magnificent mountains, with their rich clothing of pastures, chestnut groves, and châlets, till it ends in the savage Pass of Mirabouc; and the latter, to wind and climb in a grand succession of precipice, and gorge, and grassy dell, till it issues in the funnel-shaped valley around which the ice-crowned mountains stand the everlasting sentinels.

It was the latter of these two valleys (Angrogna) that La Trinita first essayed to enter. He marched 1,200 men into it, the wings of his army deploying over its bordering heights of La Cotière. His soldiers were opposed by only a small body of Vaudois, some of whom were armed solely with the sling and the crossbow. Skirmishing with the foe, the Vaudois retired, fighting, to the higher grounds. When the evening set in, neither side could claim a decided advantage. Wearied with skirmishing, both armies encamped for the night—the Vaudois on the heights of Roccomaneot, and the Piedmontese, their camp-fires lighted, on the lower hills of La Cotière.

Suddenly the silence of the evening was startled by a derisive shout that rose from the Piedmontese host. What had happened to evoke these sounds of contempt? They had descried, between them and the sky, on the heights above them, the bending figures of the Vaudois. On their knees the Waldensian warriors were supplicating the God of battles. Hardly had the scoffs with which the Piedmontese hailed the act died away, when a drum was heard to beat in a side valley. A child had got hold of the instrument, and was amusing itself with it.

The soldiers of La Trinita saw in imagination a fresh body of Waldensians advancing from this lateral defile to rush upon them. They seized their arms in no little disorder. The Vaudois, seeing the movement of the foe, seized theirs also, and rushed down-hill to anticipate the attack. The Piedmontese army threw away their arms and fled, chased by the Waldenses, thus losing in half an hour the ground it had cost them a day's fighting to gain. The weapons abandoned by the fugitives formed a much-needed and most opportune supply to the Vaudois. As the result of the combats of the day, La Trinita had sixty-seven men slain; of the Vaudois only three had fallen.[2401]

Opening on the left of La Trinita were the corn-clad, vine-clad, and mountain-ramparted Valley of Lucerna, with its towns, La Torre, Villaro, Bobbio, and others, forming the noblest of the Waldensian Valleys. La Trinita now occupied this valley with his soldiers. This was comparatively an easy achievement, almost all its inhabitants having fled to the Pra del Tor. Those that remained were mostly Romanists, who were, at that time, mixed with the Waldensian population, and even they, committing their wives and daughters to the keeping of their Vaudois neighbours, had sent them with them to the Pra del Tor, to escape the brutal outrages of the Papal army. On the following days La Trinita fought some small affairs with the Vaudois, in all of which he was repulsed with considerable slaughter. The arduous nature of the task he had in hand now began to dawn upon him.

The mountaineers, he saw, were courageous, and determined to die rather than submit their conscience to the pope, and their families to the passions of his soldiers. He discovered, moreover, that they were a simple and confiding people, utterly unversed in the ways of intrigue. He was delighted to find these qualities in them, because he thought he saw how he could turn them to account. He had tools with him as cunning and vile as himself—Jacomel, the inquisitor; and Gastaud, his secretary; the latter feigned a love for the Gospel. These men he set to work. When they had prepared matters, he assembled the leading men of the Waldenses, and recited to them some flattering words, which he had heard or professed to have heard the duke and duchess make use of towards them; he protested that this was no pleasant business in which he was engaged, and that he would be glad to have it off his hands; peace, he thought, could easily be arranged, if they would only make a few small concessions to show that they were reasonable men; he would propose that they should deposit their arms in the house of one of their syndics, and permit him, for form's sake, to go with a small train, and celebrate mass in the Church of St. Laurenzo, in Angrogna, and afterwards pay a visit to the Pra del Tor. La Trinita's proposal proved the correctness of the estimate he had formed of Vaudois confidingness. The people spent a whole night in deliberation over the count's proposition, and, contrary to the opinion of their pastors and some of their laymen, agreed to accept of it.[2402]

The Papal general said his mass in the Protestant church. After this he traversed the gloomy defiles that lead up to the famous Pra, on whose green slopes, with their snowy battlements, he was so desirous to feast his eyes, though, it is said, he showed evident trepidation when he passed the black pool of Tompie, with its memories of retribution. Having accomplished these feats in safety, he returned to wear the mask a little longer.

He resumed the efforts on which he professed to be so earnestly and laudably bent, of effecting peace. The duke had now come nearer, and was living at Vercelli, on the plains of Piedmont; La Trinita thought that the Vaudois ought by all means to send deputies thither. It would strengthen their supplication—indeed, all but insure its success—if they would raise a sum of 20,000 crowns. On payment of this sum he would withdraw his army, and leave them to practise their religion in peace.[2403] The Vaudois, unable to conceive of dissimulation like La Trinita's, made concession after concession. They had previously laid down their arms; they now sent deputies to the duke; next, they taxed themselves to buy off his soldiers; and last and worst of all, at the demand of La Trinita, they sent away their pastors. It was dreadful to think of a journey across the Col Julien at that season; yet it had to be gone. Over its snowy summits, where the winter drifts were continually obliterating the track, and piling up fresh wreathes; across the Valleys of Prali and San Martino, and over the ice-clad mountains beyond, had this sorrowful band of pastors to pursue their way, to find refuge among the Protestants in the French Valley of Pragelas. This difficult and dangerous route was forced upon them, the more direct road through the Valley of Perosa being closed by the marauders and assassins that infested it, and especially by those in the pay of the monks of Pinerolo.

The count believed that the poor people were now entirely in his power. His soldiers did their pleasure in the Valley of Lucerna. They pillaged the houses abandoned by the Vaudois. The few inhabitants who had remained, as well as those who had returned, thinking that during the negotiations for peace hostilities would be suspended, were fain to make their escape a second time, and to seek refuge in the woods and caves of the higher reaches of the Valleys. The outrages committed by the ruffians to whom the Valley of Lucerna was now given over were of a kind that cannot be told. The historian Gilles has recorded a touching instance. A helpless man, who had lived a hundred and three years, was placed in a cave, and his granddaughter, a girl of seventeen, was left to take care of him. The soldiers found out his hiding-place; the old man was murdered, and outrage was offered to his granddaughter. She fled from the brutal pursuit of the soldiers, leaped over a precipice, and died. In another instance, an old man was pursued to the brink of a precipice by one of La Trinita's soldiers. The Vaudois had no alternative but to throw himself over the brink or die by the sword of his pursuer. He stopped, turned round, and dropped on his knees, as if to supplicate for his life. The trooper was raising his sword to strike him dead, when the Vaudois, clasping him tightly round the legs, and swaying himself backward with all his might, rolled over the precipice, dragging the soldier with him into the abyss.

Part of the sum agreed on between La Trinita and the Waldenses had now been paid to him. To raise this money the poor people were under the necessity of selling their herds. The count now withdrew his army into winter quarters at Cavour, a point so near the Valleys that a few hours' march would enable him to re-enter them at any moment. The corn and oil and wine which he had not been able to carry away he destroyed. Even the mills he broke in pieces. His design appeared to be to leave the Vaudois only the alternative of submission, or of dying of hunger on their mountains. To afflict them yet more he placed garrisons here and there in the Valleys; and, in the very wantonness of tyranny, required those who themselves were without bread to provide food for his soldiers. These soldiers were continually prowling about in search of victims on whom to gratify their cruelty and their lust. Those who had the unspeakable misfortune to be dragged into their den, had to undergo, if men, excruciating torture; if women, revolting outrage.[2404]

CHAPTER VII
THE GREAT CAMPAIGN OF 1561

THESE frightful inflictions the Waldenses had submitted to in the hope that the deputies whom they had sent to the duke would bring back with them an honourable peace. The impatience with which they waited their return may well be conceived. At last, after an absence of six weeks, the commissioners reappeared in the Valleys; but their dejected faces, even before they had uttered a word, told that they had not succeeded. They had been sent back with an order, enjoining on the Vaudois unconditional submission to the Church of Rome on pain of extermination. To enforce that order to the uttermost a more numerous army was at that moment being raised. The mass or universal slaughter—such was the alternative now presented to them.

The spirit of the people woke up. Rather than thus disgrace their ancestors, imperil their own souls, and entail a heritage of slavery on their children, they would die a thousand times. Their depression was gone; they were as men who had awakened from heavy sleep; they had found their arms. Their first care was to recall their pastors, their next to raise up their fallen churches, and their third to resume public service in them. Daily their courage grew, and once more joy lighted up their faces.

There came letters of sympathy and promises of help from their fellow-Protestants of Geneva, Dauphiné, and France. Over the two latter countries persecution at that hour impended, but their own dangers made them all the more ready to succour their brethren of the Valleys. "Thereupon," says an historian, "took place one of those grand and solemn scenes which, at once heroic and religious, seem rather adapted for an epic poem than for grave history."[2405]

The Waldenses of Lucerna sent deputies across the mountains, then covered to a great depth with snow, to propose an alliance with the Protestants of the Valley of Pragelas, who were at that time threatened by their sovereign Francis I. The proposed alliance was joyfully accepted. Assembling on a plateau of snow facing the mountains of Sestrières, and the chain of the Guinevert, the deputies swore to stand by each other and render mutual support in the coming struggle.[2406] It was agreed that this oath of alliance should be sworn with like solemnity in the Waldensian Valleys.

The deputies from Pragelas, crossing the Mount Julien, arrived at Bobbio on the 21st January, 1561. Their coming was singularly opportune. On the evening before a ducal proclamation had been published in the Valleys, commanding the Vaudois, within twenty-four hours, to give attendance at mass, or abide the consequences—"fire, sword, the cord: the three arguments of Romanism," says Muston. This was the first news with which the Pragelese deputies were met on their arrival. With all the more enthusiasm they proceeded to renew their oath. Ascending a low hill behind Bobbio, the deputies from Pragelas, and those from Lucerna, standing erect in the midst of the assembled heads of families, who knelt around, pronounced these words—

"In the name of the Vaudois Churches of the Alps, of Dauphiné and of Piedmont, which have ever been united, and of which we are the representatives, we here promise, our hands on our Bible, and in the presence of God, that all our Valleys shall courageously sustain each other in matters of religion, without prejudice to the obedience due to their legitimate superiors.

"We promise to maintain the Bible, whole and without admixture, according to the usage of the true Apostolic Church, persevering in this holy religion, though it be at the peril of our lives, in order that we may transmit it to our children, intact and pure, as we received it from our fathers.

"We promise aid and succour to our persecuted brothers, not regarding our individual interests, but the common cause; and not relying upon man, but upon God."

The physical grandeurs of the spot were in meet accordance with the moral sublimity of the transaction. Immediately beneath was spread out the green bosom of the valley, with here and there the silver of the Pelice gleaming out amid vineyards and acacia groves. Filling the horizon on all sides save one stood up an array of magnificent mountains, white with the snows of winter. Conspicuous among them were the grand peaks of the Col de Malaure and the Col de la Croix. They looked the silent and majestic witnesses of the oath in which a heroic people bound themselves to die rather than permit the defilement of their hearths, and the profanation of their altars, by the hordes of an idolatrous tyranny. It was in this grand fashion that the Waldenses opened one of the most brilliant campaigns ever waged by their arms.

The next morning, according to the duke's order, they must choose between the mass and the penalty annexed to refusal. A neighbouring church—one of those which had been taken from them—stood ready, with altar decked and tapers lighted, for the Vaudois to hear their first mass. Hardly had the day dawned when the expected penitents were at the church door. They would show the duke in what fashion they meant to read their recantation. They entered the building. A moment they stood surveying the strange transformation their church had undergone, and then they set to work. To extinguish the tapers, pull down the images, and sweep into the street rosary and crucifix and all the other paraphernalia of the Popish worship, was but the work of a few minutes. The minister, Humbert Artus, then ascended the pulpit, and reading out as his text Isaiah xlv. 20—"Assemble yourselves and come; draw near together, ye that are escaped of the nations: they have no knowledge that set up the wood of their graven image, and pray unto a God that cannot save"—preached a sermon which struck the key-note of the campaign then opening.

The inhabitants of the hamlets and châlets in the mountains rushed down like their own winter torrents into Lucerna, and the army of the Vaudois reinforced set out to purge the temple at Villaro. On their way they encountered the Piedmontese garrison. They attacked and drove them back; the monks, seigneurs, and magistrates, who had come to receive the abjuration of the heretics, accompanying the troops in their ignominious flight. The whole band of fugitives—soldiers, priests, and judges—shut themselves up in the town of Villaro, which was now besieged by the Vaudois. Thrice did the garrison from La Torre attempt to raise the siege, and thrice were they repulsed. At last, on the tenth day, the garrison surrendered, and had their lives spared, two Waldensian pastors accompanying them to La Torre, the soldiers expressing greater confidence in them than in any other escort.

The Count La Trinita, seeing his garrison driven out, struck his encampment at Cavour, and moved his army into the Valleys. He again essayed to sow dissension amongst the Vaudois by entangling them in negotiations for peace, but by this time they had learned too well the value of his promises to pay the least attention to them, or to intermit for an hour their preparations for defence. It was now the beginning of February, 1561.

The Vaudois laboured with the zeal of men who feel that their cause is a great and a righteous one. They erected barricades; they planted ambushes; they appointed signals, to telegraph the movements of the enemy from post to post. "Every house," says Muston, "became a manufactory of pikes, bullets, and other weapons." They selected the best marksmen their Valleys could furnish, and formed them into the "Flying Company," whose duty it was to hasten to the point where danger pressed the most. To each body of fighting men they attached two pastors, to maintain the *morale* of their army. The pastors, morning and evening, led the public devotions; they prayed with the soldiers before going into battle; and when the fighting was over, and the Vaudois were chasing the enemy down their great mountains, and through their dark gorges, they exerted themselves to prevent the victory being stained by any unnecessary effusion of blood.

La Trinita knew well that if he would subjugate the Valleys, and bring the campaign to a successful end, he must make himself master of the Pra del Tor. Into that vast natural citadel was now gathered the main body of the Waldensian people. What of their herds and provisions remained to them had been transported thither; there they had constructed mills and baking ovens; there, too, sat their council, and thence directed the whole operations of the defence. A blow struck there would crush the Vaudois' heart, and convert what the Waldenses regarded as their impregnable castle into their tomb.

Deferring the chastisement of the other valleys meanwhile, La Trinita directed all his efforts against Angrogna. His first attempt to enter it with his army was made on the 4th February. The fighting lasted till night, and ended in his repulse. His second attempt, three days after, carried him some considerable way into Angrogna, burning and ravaging, but his partial success cost him dear, and the ground won had ultimately to be abandoned.[2408]

The 14th of February saw the severest struggle. Employing all his strategy to make himself master of the much-coveted Pra, with all in it, he divided his army into three corps, and advanced against it from three points. One body of troops, marching along the gorges of the Angrogna, and traversing the narrow chasm that leads up to the Pra, attacked it on the south. Another body, clinging the heights from Pramol, and crossing the snowy flanks of La Vêchere, tried to force an entrance on the east; while a third, ascending from San Martino, and crossing the lofty summits that wall in the Pra on the north, descended upon it from that quarter. The count's confident expectation was that if his men should be unable to force an entrance at one point they were sure to do so at another.

No scout had given warning of what was approaching. While three armies were marching to attack them, the Waldenses, in their grand valley, with its rampart of ice-crowned peaks, were engaged in their morning devotions. Suddenly the cries of fugitives, and the shouts of assailants, issuing from the narrow chasm on the south, broke upon their ear, together with the smoke of burning hamlets. Of the three points of attack this was the easiest to be defended. Six brave Waldensians youths strode down the valley, to stop the way against La Trinita's soldiers. They were six against an army.

The road by which the soldiers were advancing is long and gloomy, and overhung by great rocks, and so narrow that only two men can march abreast. On this side rises the mountain: on that, far down, thunders the torrent; a ledge in the steep face of the cliff, running here in the darkness, there in the sunshine, serves as a pathway. It leads to what is termed the gate of the Pra. That gateway is formed by an angle of the mountain, which obtrudes upon the narrow ledge on the one side, while a huge rock rises on the other and still further narrows the point of ingress into the Pra del Tor. Access into the famous Pra, of which La Trinita was now striving to make himself master, there is not on this side save through this narrow opening; seeing that on the right rises the mountain; on the left yawns the gulf, into which, if one steps aside but in the least, he tumbles headlong. To friend and foe alike the only entrance into the Pra del Tor on the south is by this gate of Nature's own erecting. It was here that the six Waldensian warriors took their stand.[2409] Immovable as their own Alps, they not only checked the advance of the host, but drove it back in a panic-stricken mass, which made the precipices of the defile doubly fatal.

Others would have hastened to their aid, had not danger suddenly presented itself in another quarter. On the heights of La Vêchera, crossing the snow, was descried an armed troop, making their entrance into the valley on the east. Before they had time to descend they were met by the Waldenses, who dispersed them, and made them flee. Two of the attacking parties of the count have failed: will the third have better success?

As the Waldenses were pursuing the routed enemy on La Vêchera, they saw yet another armed troop, which had crossed the mountains that separate the Val San Martino from the Pra del Tor on the north, descending upon them. Instantly the alarm was raised. A few men only could they dispatch to meet the invaders. These lay in ambush at the mouth of a defile through which the attacking party was making its way down into the Pra. Emerging from the defile, and looking down into the valley beneath them, they exclaimed, "Haste, haste! Angrogna is ours." The Vaudois, starting up, and crying out, "It is you that are ours," rushed upon them sword in hand. Trusting in their superior numbers, the Piedmontese soldiers fought desperately. But a few minutes sufficed for the men of the Valleys to hurry from the points where they were now victorious, to the assistance of their brethren. The invaders, seeing themselves attacked on all sides, turned and fled up the slopes they had just descended. Many were slain, nor would a man of them have recrossed the mountains but for the pastor of the Flying Company, who, raising his voice to the utmost pitch, entreated the pursuers to spare the lives of those who were no longer able to resist. Among the slain was Charles Truchet, who so cruelly ravaged the commune of Rioclaret a few months before. A stone from a sling laid him prostrate on the ground, and his head was cut off with his own sword. Louis de Monteuil, another noted persecutor of the Vaudois, perished in the same action.

Furious at his repulse, the Count La Trinita turned his arms against the almost defenceless Valley of Rora. He ravaged it, burning its little town, and chasing away its population of eighty families, who escaped over the snows of the mountains to Villaro, in the Valley of Lucerna. That valley he next entered with his soldiers, and though it was for the moment almost depopulated, the Popish general received so warm a welcome from those peasants who remained that, after being again and again beaten, he was fain to draw off his men-at-arms, and retreat to his old quarters at Cavour, there to chew the cud over his misfortunes, and hatch new stratagems and plan new attacks, which he fondly hoped would retrieve his disgraces.

La Trinita spent a month in reinforcing his army, greatly weakened by the losses it had sustained. The King of France sent him ten companies of foot, and some other choice soldiers.[2410] There came a regiment from Spain; and numerous volunteers from Piedmont, comprising many of the nobility. From 4,000, the original number of his army, it was now raised to 7,000.[2411] He thought himself strong enough to begin a third campaign. He was confident that this time he would wipe out the disgrace which had befallen his arms, and sweep from the earth once and for ever the great scandal of the Waldenses. He again directed all his efforts against Angrogna, the heart and bulwark of the Valleys.

It was Sunday, the 17th of March, 1561. The whole of the Vaudois assembled in the Pra del Tor had met on the morning of that day, soon after dawn, as was their wont, to unite in public devotion. The first rays of the rising sun were beginning to light up the white hills around them, and the last cadences of their morning psalm were dying away on the grassy slopes of the Pra, when a sudden alarm was raised. The enemy was approaching by three routes. On the ridges of the eastern summits appeared one body of armed men; another was defiling up the chasm, and in a few minutes would pour itself, through the gateway already described, into the Pra; while a third was forcing itself over the rocks by a path intermediate between the two. Instantly the enemy was met on all the points of approach. A handful of Waldensians sufficed to thrust back along the narrow gorge the line of glittering cuirassed men, who were defiling through it. At the other two points, where bastions of rock and earth had been erected, the fighting was severe, and the dead lay thick, but the day at both places went against the invaders. Some of the ablest captains were among the slain. The number of the soldiers killed was so great that Count La Trinita is said to have sat down and wept when he beheld the heaps of the dead.[2412] It was a matter of astonishment at the time that the Waldenses did not pursue the invaders, for had they done so, being so much better acquainted with the mountain-paths, not one of all that host would have been left alive to carry tidings of its dicomfiture to the inhabitants of Piedmont. Their pastors restrained the victorious Vaudois, having laid it down as a maxim at the beginning of the campaign, that they would use with moderation and clemency whatever victories the "God of battles" might be pleased to give them, and that they would spill no blood unless when absolutely necessary to prevent their own being shed. The Piedmontese dead was again out of all proportion to those who had fallen on the other side; so much so, that it was currently said in the cities of Piedmont that "God was fighting for the barbets."[2413]

More deeply humiliated and disgraced than ever, La Trinita led back the remains of his army to its old quarters. Well had it been for him if he had never set foot within the Waldensian territory, and not less so for many of those who followed him, including not a few of the nobles of Piedmont, whose bones were now bleaching on the mountains of the Vaudois. But the Popish general was slow to see the lesson of these events. Even yet he harboured the design of returning to assail that fatal valley where he had lost so many laurels, and buried so many soldiers; but he covered his purpose with craft. Negotiations had been opened between the men of the Valleys and the Duke of Savoy, and as they were proceeding satisfactorily, the Vaudois were without suspicions of evil. This was the moment that La Trinita chose to attack them. He hastily assembled his troops, and on the night of the 16th April he marched them against the Pra del Tor, hoping to enter it unopposed, and give the Vaudois "as sheep to the slaughter."

The snows around the Pra were beginning to burn in the light of morning when the attention of the people, who had just ended their united worship, was attracted by unusual sounds which were heard to issue from the gorge that led into the valley. On the instant six brave mountaineers rushed to the gateway that opens from the gorge. The long file of La Trinita's soldiers was seen advancing two abreast, their helmets and cuirasses glittering in the light. The six Vaudois made their arrangements, and calmly waited till the enemy was near. The first two Vaudois, holding loaded muskets, knelt down. The second two stood erect, ready to fire over the heads of the first two. The third who undertook the loading of the weapons as they were discharged. The invaders came on. As the first two of the enemy turned the rock they were shot down by the two foremost Vaudois. The next two of the attacking force fell in like manner by the shot of the Vaudois in the rear. The third rank of the enemy presented themselves only to be laid by the side of their comrades. In a few minutes a little heap of dead bodies blocked the pass, rendering impossible the advance of the accumulating file of the enemy in the chasm.

Meanwhile, other Vaudois climbed the mountains that overhang the gorge in which the Piedmontese army was imprisoned. Tearing up great stones with which the hill-side was strewn, the Vaudois sent them rolling down upon the host. Unable to advance from the wall of dead in front, and unable to flee from the ever-accumulating masses behind, the soldiers were crushed in dozens by the falling rocks. Panic set in: and panic in such a position how dreadful! Wedged together on the narrow ledge, with a murderous rain of rocks falling on them, their struggle to escape was frightful. They jostled one another, and trod each other under foot, while vast numbers fell over the precipice, and were dashed on the rocks or drowned in the torrent.[2414] When those at the entrance of the valley, who were watching the result, saw the crystal of the Angrogna begin about midday to be changed into blood, "Ah!" said they, "the Pra del Tor has been taken; La Trinita has triumphed; there flows the blood of the Vaudois." And, indeed, the count on beginning his march that morning is said to have boasted that by noon the torrent of the Angrogna would be seen to change colour; and so in truth it did. Instead of a pellucid stream, rolling along on a white gravelly bed, which is its usual appearance at the mouth of the valley, it was now deeply dyed from the recent slaughter. But when the few who had escaped the catastrophe returned to tell what had that day passed within the defiles of the Angrogna, it was seen that it was not the blood of the Vaudois, but the blood of their ruthless invaders, which dyed the waters of the Angrogna. The count withdrew on that same night with his army, to return no more to the Valleys.

Negotiations were again resumed, not this time through the Count La Trinita, but through Philip of Savoy, Count of Raconis, and were speedily brought to a satisfactory issue. The Duke of Savoy had but small merit in making peace with the men whom he found he could not conquer. The capitulation was signed on the 5th of June, 1561, and its first clause granted an indemnity for all offences. It is open to remark that this indemnity was given to those who had suffered, not to those who had committed the offences it condoned. The articles that followed permitted the Vaudois to erect churches in their Valleys, with the exception of two or three of their towns, to hold public worship—in short, to celebrate all the offices of their religion. All the "ancient franchises, immunities, and privileges, whether conceded by his Highness, or by his Highness's predecessors," were renewed, provided they were vouched by public documents.[2415] Such was the arrangement that closed this war of fifteen months. The Vaudois ascribed it in great part to the influence of the good Duchess Margaret. The Pope designated it a "pernicious example," which he feared would not want imitators in those times when the love of many to the Roman See was waxing cold. It stank in the nostrils of the prelates and monks of Piedmont, to whom the heretics had been a free booty. Nevertheless, Duke Emmanuel Philibert faithfully maintained its stipulations, the duchess being by his side to counteract any pressure in the contrary direction. This peace, together with the summer that was now opening, began to slowly efface the deep scars the persecution had left on the Valleys; and what further helped to console and reanimate this brave but afflicted people, was the sympathy and aid universally tendered them by Protestants abroad, in particular by Calvin and the Elector Palatine, the latter addressing a spirited letter to the duke on behalf of his persecuted subjects.[2416]

Nothing was more admirable than the spirit of devotion which the Vaudois exhibited all through these terrible conflicts. Their Valleys resounded not less with the voice of prayer and praise, than with the din of arms. Their opponents came from carousing, from blaspheming, from murdering, to engage in battle; the Waldenses rose from their knees to unsheathe the sword, and wield it in a cause which they firmly believed to be that of Him to whom they had bent in supplication. When their little army went afield their barbes always accompanied it, to inspirit the soldiers by suitable exhortations before joining battle, and to moderate in the hour of victory a vengeance which, however excusable, would yet have lowered the glory of the triumph. When the fighting men hastened to the bastion or to the defile, the pastors betook them to the mountain's slope, or to its summit, and there with uplifted hands supplicated help from the "Lord, strong and mighty, the Lord mighty in battle." When the battle had ceased, and the enemy were in flight, and the victors had returned from chasing their invaders from their Valleys, the grey-haired pastor, the lion-hearted man of battle, the matron, the maiden, the stripling, and the little child, would assemble in the Pra del Tor, and while the setting sun was kindling into glory the mountain-tops of their once more ransomed land, they would raise their voices together, and sing the old war-song of Judah, in strains so heroic that the great rocks around them would send back the thunder of their praise in louder echoes than those of the battle whose triumphant issue they were celebrating.

CHAPTER VIII
WALDENSIAN COLONIES IN CALABRIA AND APULIA

ONE day, about the year 1340, two Waldensian youths were seated in an inn in Turin, engaged in earnest conversation respecting their home prospects. Shut up in their valleys, and cultivating with toil their somewhat sterile mountains, they sighed for wider limits and a more fertile land. "Come with me, and I will give you fertile fields for your barren rocks." The person who now courteously addressed the youths, and whose steps Providence had directed to the same hotel with themselves, was a gentleman from Calabria, at the southern extremity of the Italian Peninsula.

On their return to the Valleys the youths reported the words of the stranger, and the flattering hopes he had held out should they be willing to migrate to this southern land, where skies more genial, and an earth more mollient, would reward their labour with more bounteous harvests. The elders of the Vaudois people listened not without interest. The population of their Valleys had recently received a great accession in the Albigensian refugees, who had escaped from the massacres of Innocent III. in the south of France; and the Waldenses, feeling themselves overcrowded, were prepared to welcome any fair scheme that promised an enlargement of their boundaries. But before acceding to the proposition of the stranger they thought it advisable to send competent persons to examine this new and to them unknown land. The Vaudois explorers returned with a flattering account of the conditions and capabilities of the country they had been invited to occupy. Compared with their own more northern mountains, whose summits Winter covers all the year through with his snows, whose gorges are apt to be swept by furious gusts, and their sides stripped of their corn and vines by devastating torrents, Calabria was a land of promise. "There are beautiful hills," says the historian Gilles, describing this settlement, "clothed with all kinds of fruit-trees spontaneously springing up according to their situation—in the plains, vines and chestnuts; on the rising ground, walnuts and every fruit-tree. Everywhere were seen arable land and few labourers." A considerable body of emigrants set out for this new country. The young men were accompanied to their future homes with partners. They carried with them the Bible in the Romance version, "that holy ark of the New Covenant, and of everlasting peace."

The conditions of their emigration offered a reasonable security for the free and undisturbed exercise of their worship. "By a convention with the local seigneurs, ratified later by the King of Naples, Ferdinand of Arragon, they were permitted to govern their own affairs, civil and spiritual, by their own magistrates, and their own pastors."[2417] Their first settlement was near the town of Montalto. Half a century later rose the city of San Sexto, which afterwards became the capital of the colony. Other towns and villages sprang up, and the region, which before had been thinly inhabited, and but poorly cultivated, was soon transformed into a smiling garden. The swelling hills were clothed with fruit-trees, and the plains waved with luxuriant crops.

So struck was the Marquis of Spinello with the prosperity and wealth of the settlements, that he offered to cede lands on his own vast and fertile estates where these colonists might build cities and plant vineyards. One of their towns he authorised them to surround with a wall; hence its name, La Guardia. This town, situated on a height near the sea, soon became populous and opulent.[2418]

Towards the close of the same century, another body of Vaudois emigrants from Provence arrived in the south of Italy. The new-comers settled in Apulia, not far from their Calabrian brethren, villages and towns arose, and the region speedily put on a new face under the improved arts and husbandry of the colonists. Their smiling homes, which looked forth from amid groves of orange and myrtle, their hills covered with the olive and the vine, their corn-fields and pasture-lands, were the marvel and the envy of their neighbours.

In 1500 there arrived in Calabria yet another emigration from the Valleys of Pragelas and Fraissinières. This third body of colonists established themselves on the Volturata, a river which flows from the Apennines into the Bay of Tarento. With the increase of their numbers came an increase of prosperity to the colonists. Their neighbours, who knew not the secret of this prosperity, were lost in wonder and admiration of it. The physical attributes of the region occupied by the emigrants differed in no respect from those of their own lands, both were placed under the same sky, but how different the aspect of the one from that of the other! The soil, touched by the plough of Vaudois, seemed to feel a charm that made it open its bosom and yield a tenfold increase. The vine tended by Vaudois hands bore richer clusters, and strove in generous rivalry with the fig and the olive to outdo them in enriching with its produce the Vaudois board. And how delightful the quiet and order of their towns; and the air of happiness on the faces of the people! And how sweet to listen to the bleating of the flocks on the hills, the lowing of the herds in the meadows, the song of the reaper and grape-gatherer, and the merry voices of children at play around the hamlets and villages! For about 200 years these colonies continued to flourish.

"It is a curious circumstance," says the historian McCrie, that the first gleam of light, at the revival of letters, shone on that remote spot of Italy where the Vaudois had found an asylum. Petrarch first acquired a knowledge of the Greek tongue from Barlaam, a monk of Calabria; and Boccaccio was taught it from Leontius Pilatus, who was a hearer of Barlaam, if not also of native of the same place."[2419] Muston says that "the sciences flourished among them."[2420] The day of the Renaissance had not yet broken. The flight of scholars, which was to bear with it the seeds of ancient learning to the West, had not yet taken place; but the Vaudois of Calabria would seem to have anticipated the great literary revival. They had brought with them the Scriptures in the Romance version. They possessed doubtless the taste and genius for which the Romance nations were then famous; and, moreover, in their southern settlement they may have had access to some knowledge of those sciences which the Saracens then so assiduously cultivated; and what so likely, with their leisure and wealth, that these Vaudois should turn their attention to letters as well as to husbandry, and make their adopted country vocal with the strains of that minstrelsy with which Provence and Dauphiné had resounded so melodiously, till its music was quenched at once and for ever by the murderous arms of Simon de Montfort? But here we can only doubtfully guess, for the records of this interesting people are scanty and dubious.

These colonists kept up their connection with the mother country of the Valleys, though situated at the opposite extremity of Italy. To keep alive their faith, which was the connecting link, pastors were sent in relays of two to minister in the Churches of Calabria and Apulia; and when they had fulfilled their term of two years they were replaced by other two. The barbes, on their way back to the Valleys, visited their brethren in the Italian towns; for at that time there were few cities in the peninsula in which the Vaudois were not to be found. The grandfather of the Vaudois historian, Gilles, in one of these pastoral visits to Venice, was assured by the Waldenses whom he there conversed with, that there were not fewer than 6,000 of their nation in that city. Fear had not yet awakened the suspicions and kindled the hatred of the Romanists, for the Reformation was not yet come. Nor did the Waldenses care to thrust their opinions upon the notice of their neighbours. Still the priests could not help observing that the manners of these northern settlers were, in many things, peculiar and strange. They eschewed revels and fêtes; they had their children taught by foreign schoolmasters; in their churches was neither image nor lighted taper; they never went on pilgrimage; they buried their dead without the aid of the priests; and never were they known to bring a candle to the Virgin's shrine, or purchase a mass for the help of their dead relatives. These peculiarities were certainly startling, but one thing went far to atone for them—they paid with the utmost punctuality their stipulated tithes; and as the value of their lands was yearly increasing, there was a corresponding yearly increase in both the tithe due to the priest and the rent payable to the landlord, and neither was anxious to disturb a state of things so beneficial to himself, and which was every day becoming more advantageous.[2421]

But in the middle of the sixteenth century the breath of Protestantism from the North began to move over these colonies. The pastors who visited them told them of the synod which had been held in Angrogna in 1532, and which had been as the "beginning of months" to the ancient Church of the Valleys. More glorious tidings still did they communicate to the Christians of Calabria. In Germany, in France, in Switzerland, and in Denmark the old Gospel had blazed forth in a splendour unknown to it for ages. The Lamp of the Alps was no longer the one solitary light in the world: around it was a circle of mighty torches, whose rays, blending with those of the older luminary, were combining to dispel the night from Christendom. At the hearing of these stupendous things their spirit revived: their past conformity appeared to them like cowardice; they, too, would take part in the great work of the emancipation of the nations, by making open confession of the truth; and no longer content with the mere visit of a pastor, they petitioned the mother Church to send them one who might statedly discharge amongst them the office of the holy ministry.[2422]

There was at that time a young minister at Geneva, a native of Italy, and him the Church of the Valleys designated to the perilous but honourable post. His name was John Louis Paschale; he was a native of Coni in the Plain of Piedmont. By birth a Romanist, his first profession was that of arms; but from a knight of the sword he had become, like Loyola, but in a truer sense, a knight of the Cross. He had just completed his theological studies at Lausanne. He was betrothed to a young Piedmontese Protestant, Camilla Guerina.[2423] "Alas!"

she sorrowfully exclaimed, when he intimated to her his departure for Calabria, "so near to Rome and so far from me." They parted, nevermore to meet on earth.

The young minister carried with him to Calabria the energetic spirit of Geneva. His preaching was with power; the zeal and courage of the Calabrian flock revived, and the light formerly hid under a bushel was now openly displayed. Its splendour attracted the ignorance and awoke the fanaticism of the region. The priests, who had tolerated a heresy that had conducted itself so modestly, and paid its dues so punctually, could be blind no longer. The Marquis of Spinello, who had been the protector of these colonists hitherto, finding his kindness more than repaid in the flourishing condition of his states, was compelled to move against them. "That dreadful thing, Lutheranism," he was told, "had broken in, and would soon destroy all things."

The marquis summoned the pastor and his flock before him. After a few moments' address from Paschale, the marquis dismissed the members of the congregation with a sharp reprimand, but the pastor he threw into the dungeons of Foscalda. The bishop of the diocese next took the matter into his own hands, and removed Paschale to the prison of Cosenza, where he remained shut up during eight months.

The Pope heard of the case, and delegated Cardinal Alexandrini, Inquisitor-General, to extinguish the heresy in the Kingdom of Naples.[2424] Alexandrini ordered Paschale to be removed from the Castle of Cosenza, and conducted to Naples. On the journey he was subjected to terrible sufferings. Chained to a gang of prisoners—the handcuffs so tight that they entered the flesh—he spent nine days on the road, sleeping at night on the bare earth, which was exchanged on his arrival at Naples for a deep, damp dungeon,[2425] the stench of which almost suffocated him.

On the 16th of May, 1560, Paschale was taken in chains to Rome, and imprisoned in the Torre di Nona, where he was thrust into a cell not less noisome than that which he had occupied at Naples.

His brother, Bartolomeo, having obtained letters of recommendation, came from Coni to procure, if possible, some mitigation of his fate. The interview between the two brothers, as told by Bartolomeo, was most affecting. "It was quite hideous to see him," says he, "with his bare head, and his hands and arms lacerated by the small cords with which he was bound, like one about to be led to the gibbet. 'My brother,' said he, 'if you are a Christian, why do you distress yourself thus? Do you know that a leaf cannot fall to the ground without the will of God? Comfort yourself in Christ Jesus, for the present troubles are not worthy to be compared with the glory to come.'" His brother, a Romanist, offered him half his fortune if only he would recant, and save his life. Even this token of affection could not move him. "Oh, my brother!" said he, "the danger in which you are involved gives me more distress than all that I suffer."[2426]

He wrote to his affianced bride with a pen which, if it softened the picture of his own great sufferings, freely expressed the affection he bore for her, which "grows," said he, "with that I feel for God." Nor was he unmindful of his flock in Calabria. "My state is this," said he, in a letter which he addressed to them, "I feel my joy increase every day, as I approach nearer the hour in which I shall be offered a sweet-smelling sacrifice to the Lord Jesus Christ, my faithful Saviour; yea, so inexpressible is my joy that I seem to myself to be free from captivity, and am prepared to die for Christ, and not only once, but ten thousand times, if it were possible; nevertheless, I persevere in imploring the Divine assistance by prayer, for I am convinced that man is a miserable creature when left to himself, and not upheld and directed by God."[2327]

CHAPTER IX
EXTINCTION OF WALDENSES IN CALABRIA

LEAVING the martyr for a little while in his dungeon at Rome, we shall return to his flock in Calabria, on whom the storm which we saw gathering had burst in terrific vengeance.

When it was known that Protestant ministers had been sent from Geneva to the Waldensian Churches in Calabria, the Inquisitor-General, as already mentioned, and two Dominican monks, Valerio Malvicino and Alfonso Urbino, were dispatched by the Sacred College to reduce these Churches to the obedience of the Papal See, or trample them out. They arrived at San Sexto, and assembling the inhabitants, they assured them no harm was intended them, would they only dismiss their Lutheran teachers and come to mass. The bell was rung for the celebration of the Sacrament, but the citizens, instead of attending the service, left the town in a body, and retired to a neighbouring wood. Concealing their chagrin, the inquisitors took their departure from San Sexto, and set out for La Guardia, the gates of which they locked behind them when they had entered, to prevent a second flight. Assembling the inhabitants, they told them that their co-religionists of San Sexto had renounced their errors, and dutifully attended mass, and they exhorted them to follow their good example, and return to the fold of the Roman shepherd; warning them, at the same time, that should they refuse they would expose themselves as heretics to the loss of goods and life. The poor people taken unawares, and believing what was told them, consented to hear mass; but no sooner was the ceremony ended, and the gates of the town opened, than they learned the deceit which had been practised upon them. Indignant, and at the same time ashamed of their own weakness, they resolved to leave the place in a body, and join their brethren in the woods, but were withheld from their purpose by the persuasion and promises of their feudal superior, Spinello.

The Inquisitor-General, Alexandrini, now made request for two companies of men-at-arms, to enable him to execute his mission. The aid requested was instantly given, and the soldiers were sent in pursuit of the inhabitants of San Sexto. Tracking them to their hiding-places, in the thickets and the caves of the mountains, they slaughtered many of them; others, who escaped, they pursued with bloodhounds, as if they had been wild beasts. Some of these fugitives scaled the craggy summits of the Apennines, and hurling down the stones on the soldiers who attempted to follow them, compelled them to desist from the pursuit.

Alexandrini dispatched a messenger to Naples for more troops to quell what he called the rebellion of the Vaudois. The viceroy obeyed the summons by coming in person with an army. He attempted to storm the fugitives now strongly entrenched in the great mountains, whose summits of splintered rock, towering high above the pine forests that clothe their sides, presented to the fugitives an almost inaccessible retreat. The Waldenses offered to emigrate; but the viceroy would listen to nothing but their return within the pale of the Church of Rome. They were prepared to yield their lives rather than accept peace on such conditions. The viceroy now ordered his men to advance; but the shower of rocks that met his soldiers in the ascent hurled them to the bottom, a discomfited mass in which the bruised, the maimed, and the dying were confusedly mingled with the corpses of the killed.

The viceroy, seeing the difficulty of the enterprise, issued an edict promising a free pardon to all bandits, outlaws, and other criminals, who might be willing to undertake the task of scaling the mountains and attacking the strongholds of the Waldenses. In obedience to this summons, there assembled a mob of desperadoes, who were but too familiar with the secret paths of the Apennines. Threading their way through the woods, and clambering over the great rocks, these assassins rushed from every side on the barricades on the summit, and butchered the poor Vaudois. Thus were the inhabitants of San Sexto exterminated, some dying by the sword, some by fire, while others were torn by bloodhounds, or perished by famine.[2428]

While the outlaws of the Neapolitan viceroy were busy in the mountains, the Inquisitor-General and his monks were pursuing their work of blood at La Guardia. The military force at their command not enabling them to take summary measures with the inhabitants, they had recourse to a stratagem. Enticing the citizens outside the gates, and placing soldiers in ambush, they succeeded in getting into their power upwards of 1,600 persons.[2429] Of these, seventy were sent in chains to Montalto, and tortured, in the hope of compelling them to accuse themselves of practising shameful crimes in their religious assemblies. No such confession, however, could the most prolonged tortures wring from them. "Stefano Carlino," says McCrie, was tortured till his bowels gushed out;" and another prisoner, named Verminel, "was kept during eight hours on a horrid instrument called the *hell*, but persisted in denying the atrocious calumny."[2430] Some were thrown from the tops of towers, or precipitated over cliffs; others were torn with iron whips, and finally beaten to death with fiery brands; and others, smeared with pitch, were burned alive.

But these horrors pale before the blood tragedy of Montalto, enacted by the Marquis di Buccianici, whose zeal was quickened, it is said, by the promise of a cardinal's hat to his brother, if he would clear Calabria of heresy. One's blood runs cold at the perusal of the deed. It was witnessed by a servant to Ascanio Caraccioli, himself a Roman Catholic, and described by him in a letter, which was published in Italy, along with other accounts of the horrible transaction, and has been quoted by McCrie. "Most illustrious sir, I have now to inform you of the dreadful justice which began to be executed on these Lutherans early this morning, being the 11th of June. And, to tell you the truth, I can compare it to nothing but the slaughter of so many sheep. They were all shut up in one house as in a sheep-fold. The executioner went, and bringing out one of them, covered his face with a napkin, or *benda*, as we call it, led him out to a field near the house, and causing him to kneel down, cut his throat with a knife. Then, taking off the bloody napkin, he went and brought out another, whom he put to death after the same manner. In this way the whole number, amounting to eighty-eight men, were butchered. I leave you to figure to yourself the lamentable spectacle, for I can scarcely refrain from tears while I write; nor was there any person, after witnessing the execution of one, could stand to look on a second. The meekness and patience with which they went to martyrdom and death was incredible. Some of them at their death professed themselves of the same faith with us, but the greater part died in their cursed obstinacy. All the old met their death with cheerfulness, but the young exhibited symptoms of fear. I still shudder when I think of the executioner with the bloody knife in his teeth, the dripping napkin in his hand, and his arms besmeared with gore, going to the house, and taking out one victim after another, just as a butcher does the sheep which he means to kill."[2431] Their bodies were quartered, and stuck up on pikes along the high road leading from Montalto to Château-Vilar, a distance of thirty-six miles.

Numbers of men and women were burned alive, many were drafted off to the Spanish galleys, some made their submission to Rome, and a few, escaping from the scene of these horrors, reached, after infinite toil, their native Valleys, to tell that the once-flourishing Waldensian colony and Church in Calabria no longer existed, and that they only had been left to carry tidings to their brethren of its utter extermination.

Meanwhile, preparations had been made at Rome for the trial of Jean Louis Paschale. On the 8th of September, 1560, he was brought out of his prison, conducted to the Convent della Minerva, and cited before the Papal tribunal. He confessed his Saviour, and, with a serenity to which the countenances of his judges were strangers, he listened to the sentence of death, which was carried into execution on the following day.

Standing upon the summit of the Janiculum Mount, vast crowds could witness the spectacle. In front the Campagna spreads out its once glorious but now desolated bosom; and winding through it like a thread of gold is seen the Tiber, while the Apennines sweeping round it in craggy grandeur enclose it like a vast wall. Immediately beneath, uprearing her domes and monuments and palaces, with an air that seems to say, "I sit a queen," is the city of Rome. Yonder, asserting an easy supremacy amid the other fabrics of the Eternal City, is the scarred and riven yet Titanic form of the Coliseum, with its stains of early Christian blood not yet washed out. By its side, the partner of its guilt and doom, lies the Palatine, once the palace of the world's master, now a low mound of ruins, with its row of melancholy cypresses, the only mourners on that site of vanished glory and fallen empire. Nearer, burning in the midday sun, is the proud cupola of St. Peter's, flanked on the one side by the buildings of the Inquisition, and on the other by the huge Mole of Hadrian, beneath whose gloomy ramparts old Tiber rolls sluggishly and sullenly along. But what shout is this which we hear? Why does Rome keep holiday? Why do all her bells ring? Lo! from every street and piazza eager crowds rush forth, and uniting in one overwhelming and surging stream, they are seen rolling across the Bridge of St. Angelo, and pressing in at the gates of the old fortress, which are thrown open wide to admit this mass of human beings.

Entering the court-yard of the old castle, an imposing sight meets the eye. What a confluence of ranks, dignities, and grandeurs! In the centre is placed a chair, the emblazonry of which tells us that it claims to rise in authority and dignity over the throne of kings. The Pontiff, Pius IV., has already taken his seat upon it, for he has determined to be present at the tragedy of today. Behind his chair, in scarlet robes, are his cardinals and counsellors, with many dignitaries besides in mitres and cowls, ranged in circles, according to their place in the Papal body. Behind the ecclesiastics are seated, row on row, the nobility and beauty of Rome. Plumes wave, stars gleam, and seem to mock the frocks and cowls gathered near them, whose wearers, however, would not exchange these mystic garments for all the bravery that blazes around them. The vast sweep of the Court of St. Angelo is densely occupied. Its ample floor is covered from end to end with a closely-wedged mass of citizens, who have come to see the spectacle. In the centre of the throng, rising a little way over the sea of human heads, is seen a scaffold, with an iron stake, and beside it a bundle of faggots.

A slight movement begins to be perceptible in the crowd beside the gate. Some one is entering. The next moment a storm of hissing and execration salutes the ear. It is plain that the person who has just made his entrance is the object of universal dislike. The clank of irons on the stone floor of the court, as he comes forward, tells how heavily his limbs are loaded with fetters. He is still young; but his face is pale and haggard with suffering. He lifts his eyes, and with countenance undismayed surveys the vast assembly, and the dismal apparatus that stands in the midst of it, waiting its victim. There sits a calm courage on his brow; the serene light of deep, untroubled peace beams in his eye. He mounts the scaffold, and stands beside the stake. Every eye is now turned, not on the wearer of the tiara, but on the man who is clad in the sanbenito. "Good people," says the martyr—and the whole assembly keep silence—"I am come here to die for confessing the doctrine of my Divine Master and Saviour, Jesus Christ." Then turning to Pius IV. he arraigned him as the enemy of Christ, the persecutor of his people, and the Antichrist of Scripture, and concluded by summoning him and all his cardinals to answer for their cruelties and murders before the throne of the Lamb. "At his words," says the historian Crespin, "the people were deeply moved, and the Pope and the cardinals gnashed their teeth."[2432]

The inquisitors hastily gave the signal. The executioners came round him, and having strangled him, they kindled the faggots, and the flames blazing up speedily reduced his body to ashes. For once the Pope had performed his function. With his key of fire, which he may truly claim to carry, he had opened the celestial doors, and had sent his poor prisoner from the dark dungeons of the Inquisition, to dwell in the palace of the sky.

So died, or rather passed into life eternal, Jean Louis Paschale, the Waldensian missionary and pastor of the flock in Calabria. His ashes were collected and thrown into the Tiber, and by the Tiber they were borne to the Mediterranean. And this was the grave of the preacher-martyr, whose noble bearing and undaunted courage before the very Pope himself, gave added value to his splendid testimony for the Protestant cause. Time may consume the marble, violence or war may drag down the monumental pile;

"The pyramids that cleave heaven's jewelled portal;
Eleän Jove's star-spangled dome; the tomb
Where rich Mausolus sleeps—are not immortal."[2433]

But the tomb of the far-sounding sea to which the ashes of Paschale were committed, with a final display of impotent rage, was indeed a nobler mausoleum than ever Rome raised to any of her Pontiffs, and it will remain through all the ages, until time shall be no more.

CHAPTER X
THE YEAR OF THE PLAGUE

A whole century nearly wore away between the trampling out of the Protestant Church in Calabria, and the next great persecution which befell that venerable people whose tragic history we are recording. We can touch on a few only, and those the more prominent, of the events which fill up the interval.

The war that La Trinita, so ingloriously for himself, had waged against the Waldenses, ended, as we have seen, in a treaty of peace, which was signed at Cavour on the 5th of June, 1561, between Philip of Savoy and the deputies of the Valleys. But though the cloud had rolled past, it had left numerous and affecting memorials of the desolation it had inflicted. The inhabitants descended from the mountains to exchange the weapons of war for the spade and the pruning-knife. With steps slow and feeble the aged and the infirm were led down into the vales, to sit once more at noon or at eve beneath the shadow of their vines and ancestral chestnut-trees. But, alas! how often did the tear of sorrow moisten the eye as it marked the desolation and ruin that deformed those scenes lately so fair and smiling! The fruit-bearing trees cut down; vineyard and cornfield marred; hamlets burned; villages, in some cases, a heap of ruins, all testified to the rage of the enemy who had invaded their land. Years must pass before these deep scars could be effaced, and the beauty of their Valleys restored. And there were yet tenderer griefs weighing upon them. How many were there who had lived under the same roof-tree with them, and joined night and morning in the same psalm, who would return no more!

Distress, bordering on famine, began to invade the Valleys. Seven months of incessant fighting had left them no time to cultivate the fields; and now the stock of last year's provisions was exhausted, and starvation stared them in the face. Before the treaty of peace had been signed, the time of sowing was past, and when the autumn came there was scarcely anything to reap. Their destitution was further aggravated by the fugitives from Calabria, who began about this time to arrive in the Valleys. Escaping with nothing but their lives, they presented themselves in hunger and nakedness. Their brethren opened their arms to receive them, and though their own necessities were great, they nevertheless shared with them the little they had.

The tale of the suffering now prevailing in the Valleys was known in other countries, and evoked the sympathy of their Protestant brethren. Calvin, with characteristic promptness and ardour, led in the movement for their relief. By his advice they sent deputies to represent their case to the Churches of Protestantism abroad, and collections were made for them in Geneva, France, Switzerland, and Germany. The subscriptions were headed by the Elector Palatine, after whom came the Duke of Wurtemberg, the Canton of Bern, the Church at Strasburg, and others.

By-and-by, seed-time and harvest were restored in the Valleys; smiling châlets began again to dot the sides of their mountains, and to rise by the banks of their torrents; and the miseries which La Trinita's campaign had entailed upon them were passing into oblivion, when their vexations were renewed by the appointment of a deputy-governor of their Valleys, Castrocaro, a Tuscan by birth.

This man had served against the Vaudois as a colonel of militia under La Trinita; he had been taken prisoner in an encounter with them, but honourably treated, and at length generously released. He returned the Waldenses evil for good. His appointment as governor of the Valleys he owed mainly to his acquaintance with the Duchess Margaret, the protectress of the Vaudois, into whose favour he had ingratiated himself by professing a warm affection for the men of the Valleys; and his friendship with the Archbishop of Turin, to whom he had pledged himself to do his utmost to convert the Vaudois to Romanism. When at length Castrocaro arrived in the Valleys in the character of governor, he forgot his professions to the duchess, but faithfully set about fulfilling the promise he had made to the archbishop.

The new governor began by restricting the liberties guaranteed to their Churches in the treaty of peace; he next ordered the dismissal of certain of the pastors, and when their congregations refused to comply, he began to fine and imprison the recusants. He sent false and calumnious reports to the court of the duke, and introduced a troop of soldiers into the country, on the pretext that the Waldenses were breaking out into rebellion. He built the fortress at Mirabouc, at the foot of the Col de la Croix, in the narrow gorge that leads from Bobbio to France, to close this gate of exit from their territory, and overawe the Valley of Lucerna. At last, he threatened to renew the war unless the Waldenses should comply with his wishes.

What was to be done? They carried their complaints and remonstrances to Turin; but, alas! the ear of the duke and duchess had been poisoned by the malice and craft of the governor. Soon again the old alternative would be presented to them, the mass or death.[2434]

In their extremity they sought the help of the Protestant princes of Germany. The cry from the Alps found a responsive echo from the German plains. The great Protestant chiefs of the Fatherland, especially Frederick, Elector Palatine, saw in these poor oppressed herdsmen and vine-dressers his brethren, and with zeal and warmth espoused their cause. He indited a letter to the duke, distinguished for its elevation of sentiment, as well as the catholicity of its views. It is a noble defence of the rights of conscience, and an eloquent pleading in behalf of toleration. "Let your highness," says the elector, "know that there is a God in heaven, who not only contemplates the actions, but also tries the hearts and reins of men, and from whom nothing is hid. Let your highness take care not voluntarily to make war upon God, and not to persecute Christ in his members. . . . Persecution, moreover, will never advance the cause it pretends to defend. The ashes of the martyrs are the seed of the Christian Church. For the Church resembles the palm-tree, whose stem only shoots up the taller, the greater the weights that are hung upon it. Let your highness consider that the Christian religion was established by persuasion, and not by violence; and as it is certain that religion is nothing else than a firm and enlightened persuasion of God, and of his will, as revealed in his Word, and engraven in the hearts of believers by his Holy Spirit, it cannot, when once rooted, be torn away by tortures."[2435] So did the Elector Palatine warn the duke.

These are remarkable words when we think that they were written in the middle of the sixteenth century. We question whether our own age could express itself more justly on the subject of the rights of conscience, the spirituality of religion, and the impolicy, as well as the criminality, of persecution. We sometimes apologise for the cruel deeds of Spain and France, on the ground of the intolerance and blindness of the age. But six years before the St. Bartholomew Massacre was enacted, this great voice had been raised in Christendom for toleration.

What effect this letter had upon the duke we do not certainly know, but from about this time Castrocaro moderated his violence, though he still continued at intervals to terrify the poor people he so basely oppressed by fulminating against them the most atrocious threats. On the death of Emmanuel Philibert, in 1580, the villany of the governor came to light. The young Duke Charles Emmanuel ordered his arrest; but the execution of it was a matter of difficulty, for Castrocaro had entrenched himself in the Castle of La Torre, and surrounded himself with a band of desperadoes, to which he had added, for his yet greater defence, a pack of ferocious blood-hounds of unusual size and strength.[2436] A captain of his guard betrayed him, and thus as he had maintained himself by treachery, so by treachery did his doom at last overtake him. He was carried to Turin, where he perished in prison.[2437]

Famine, persecution, war—all three, sometimes in succession and sometimes together—had afflicted this much-enduring people, but now they were visited from the hand of God. For some years they had enjoyed an unusual peace; and this quiet was the more remarkable inasmuch as all around their mountains Europe was in combustion. Their brethren of the Reformed Church in France, in Spain, and in Italy, were falling on the field, perishing by massacre, or dying at the stake, while they were guarded from harm. But now a new calamity carried gloom and mourning into their Valleys. On the morning of the 23rd of August, 1629, a cloud of unusual blackness gathered on the summit of the Col Julien. It burst in a water-spout or deluge. The torrents rolled down the mountain on both sides, and the villages of Bobbio and Prali, situated the one in the southern and the other in the northern valley, were overflown by the sudden inundation. Many of the houses were swept away, and the inhabitants had barely time to save their lives by flight. In September of the same year, there came an icy wind, accompanied by a dry cloud, which scathed their Valleys and destroyed the crop of the chestnut-tree. There followed a second deluge of rain, which completely ruined the vintage. These calamities were the more grievous inasmuch as they succeeded a year of partial famine. The Vaudois pastors assembled in solemn synod, to humble themselves and to lift up their voices in prayer to God. Little did they imagine that at that moment a still heavier calamity hung over them, and that this was the last time they were ever to meet one another on earth.

In 1630, a French army, under Marshal Schomberg, suddenly occupied the Valleys. In that army were many volunteers, who had made their escape from a virulent contagious disease then raging in France. The weather was hot, and the seeds of the pestilence which the army had brought with it speedily developed themselves. The plague showed itself in the first week of May in the Valley of Perosa; it next broke out in the more northern Valley of Martino; and soon it spread throughout all the Valleys. The pastors met together to supplicate the Almighty, and to concert practical measures for checking the ravages of this mysterious and terrible scourge. They purchased medicine and collected provisions for the poor.[2439] They visited the sick, consoled the dying, and preached in the open air to crowds, solemnised and eager to listen.

In July and August the heat was excessive, and the malady raged yet more furiously. In the month of July four of the pastors were carried off by the plague; in August seven others died; and in the following month another, the twelfth, was mortally stricken. There remained now only three pastors, and it was remarked that they belonged to three several valleys—Lucerna, Martino, and Perosa. The three survivors met on the heights of Angrogna, to consult with the deputies of the various parishes regarding the means of providing for the celebration of worship. They wrote to Geneva and Dauphiné requesting that pastors might be sent to supply the place of those whom the plague had struck down, that so the venerable Church of the Valleys, which had survived so many calamities, might not become extinct. They recalled Antoine Leger from Constantinople.[2440]

The plague subsided during the winter, but in spring (1631) it rose up again in renewed force. Of the three surviving pastors, one other died; leaving thus only two, Pierre Gilles of Lucerna, and Valerius Gross of Martino. With the heats of the summer the pestilence waxed in strength. Armies, going and coming in the Valleys, suffered equally with the inhabitants. Horsemen would be seen to drop from the saddle on the highway, seized with sudden illness. Soldiers and sutlers, struck in by-paths, lay there infecting the air with their corpses. In La Torre alone fifty families became extinct. The most moderate estimate of the numbers cut off by the plague is 10,000, or from a half to two-thirds of the entire population of the Valleys. The corn in many places remained uncut, the grapes rotted on the bough, and the fruit dropped from the tree. Strangers who had come to find health in the pure mountain air, obtained from the soil nothing but a grave. Towns and villages, which had rung so recently with the sounds of industry, were now silent. Parents were without children, and children were without parents. Patriarchs, who had been wont with pride and joy to gather round them their numerous grandchildren, had seen them sicken and die, and were now alone. The venerable pastor Gilles lost his four elder sons. Though continually present in the homes of the stricken, and at the bed-sides of the dying, he himself was spared to compile the monuments of his ancient Church, and narrate among other woes that which had just passed over his native land, and "part of which he had been."

Of the Vaudois pastors only two now remained; and ministers hastened from Geneva and other places to the Valleys, lest the old lamp should go out. The services of the Waldensian Churches had hitherto been performed in the Italian tongue, but the new pastors could speak only French. Worship was henceforward conducted in that language, but the Vaudois soon came to understand it, their own ancient tongue being a dialect between the French and Italian. Another change introduced at this time was the assimilation of their ritual to that of Geneva. And farther, the primitive and affectionate name of *Barba* was dropped, and the modern title substituted, Monsieur le Ministre.[2441]

CHAPTER XI
THE GREAT MASSACRE

THE first labour of the Waldenses, on the departure of the plague, was the re-organisation of society. There was not a house in all their Valleys where death had not been. All ties rent, the family relationship all but extinct; but the destroyer being gone, the scattered inhabitants began to draw together, and to join hand and heart in restoring the ruined churches, raising up the fallen habitations, and creating anew family and home.

Other events of an auspicious kind, which occurred at this time, contributed to revive the spirits of the Waldenses, and to brighten with a gleam of hope the scene of the recent great catastrophe. The army took its departure, peace having been signed between the French monarch and the duke, and the Valleys returned once more under the dominion of the House of Savoy. A decade and a half of comparative tranquillity allowed the population to root itself anew, and their Valleys and mountain-sides to be brought again under tillage. Fifteen years—how short a breathing-space amid storms so awful!

These fifteen years draw to a close; it is now 1650, and the Vaudois are entering within the shadow of their greatest woe. The throne of Savoy was at this time filled by Charles Emmanuel II., a youth of fifteen. He was a prince of mild and humane disposition; but he was counselled and ruled by his mother, the Duchess Christina, who had been appointed regent of the kingdom during his minority. That mother was sprung of a race which have ever been noted for their dissimulation, their cruelty, and their bigoted devotion to Rome. She was the daughter of Henry IV. of France and his second wife, Mary de Medici, daughter of Francis II., Duke of Tuscany. The ferocious temper and gloomy superstition of her ancestors, the Medici—a name so conspicuously mixed up with the world-execrated massacre of St. Bartholomew—had descended to the Duchess Christina. In no other reign did the tears and blood of the Waldenses flow so profusely, a fact for which we cannot satisfactorily account, unless on the supposition that the sufferings which now overwhelmed them came not from the mild prince who occupied the throne, but from the cold, cruel, and bloodthirsty regent who governed the kingdom. In short, there is reason to believe that it was not the facile spirit of the House of Savoy, but the astute spirit of the Medici, prompted by the Vatican, that enacted those scenes of carnage that we are now to record.

The blow did not descend all at once; a series of lesser attacks heralded the great and consummating stroke. Machinations, chicaneries, and legal robberies paved the way for an extermination that was meant to be complete and final.

First of all came the monks. We have seen the plague with which the Valleys were visited in 1630; there came a second plague—not this time the pestilence, but a swarm of Capuchins. They had been sent to convert the heretics, and they began by eagerly challenging the pastors to a controversy, in which they felt sure of triumphing. A few attempts, however, convinced them that victory was not to be so easily won as they had fondly thought. The heretics made "a Pope of their Bible," they complained, and as this was a book which the Fathers had not studied, they did not know where to find the passages which they felt sure would confute the Vaudois pastors. They could silence them only by banishing them, and among others whom they drove into exile was the accomplished Antoine Leger, the uncle of the historian. Thus were the people deprived of their natural leaders.[2442] The Vaudois were forbidden on pain of confiscation and death to purchase or farm lands outside their own narrow territories. Certain of their churches were closed. Their territory was converted into a prison by an order forbidding them to cross the frontier even for a few hours, unless on fair-days. The wholly Protestant communes of Bobbio, Villaro, Angrogna, and Rora were ordered to maintain each a mission of Capuchins; and foreign Protestants were interdicted from settling in the Valleys under pain of death, and a fine of 1,000 gold crowns upon the communes that should receive them. This law was levelled against their pastors, who, since the plague, were mostly French or Swiss. It was hoped that in a few years the Vaudois would be without ministers. *Monts-de-Piété* were established to induce the Vaudois, whom confiscations, bad harvests, and the billeting of soldiers had reduce to great straits, to pawn their goods, and when all had been put in pledge they were offered restitution in full on condition of renouncing their faith. Dowries were promised to young maidens on the same terms.[2443] These various arts had a success surprisingly small. Some dozen of Waldensian perverts were added to the Roman Church. It was plain that the good work of proselytising was proceeding too slowly. More efficient measures must be had recourse to.

The Society for the "Propagation of the Faith," established by Pope Gregory XV. in 1622, had already been spread over Italy and France. The object of the society was originally set forth in words sufficiently simple and innocent—"De Propagandâ Fidei" (for the Propagation of the Faith). Since the first institution of this society, however, its object had undergone enlargement, or, if not its object, at all events its title. Its first modest designation was supplemented by the emphatic words, "et Extirpandis Hæreticis" (and the Extirpation of Heretics). The membership of the society soon became numerous: it included both laymen and priests; all ranks, from the noble and the prelate to the peasant and the pauper, pressed forward to enrol themselves in it—the inducement being a plenary indulgence to all who should take part in the good work so unmistakably indicated in the one brief and pithy clause, "et Extirpandis Hæreticis." The societies in the smaller towns reported to the metropolitan cities; the metropolitan cities to the capital; and the capitals to Rome, where, in the words of Leger, "sat the great spider that held the threads of this mighty web."

In 1650 the "Council of the Propagation of the Faith" was established at Turin. The chief councillors of state, the great lords of the country, and the dignitaries of the Church enrolled themselves as a presiding board. Societies of women were formed, at the head of which was the Marchioness di Pianeza. She was the first lady at court; and as she had not worn "the white rose of a blameless life," she was all the more zealous in this cause, in the hope of making expiation for the errors of the past. She was at infinite pains to further the object of the society; and her own eager spirit she infused into all under her. "The lady propagandists," says Leger,[2444] "distributed the towns into districts, and each visited the district assigned to her twice a week, suborning simple girls, servant maids, and young children by their flattering allurements and fair promises, and doing evil turns to such as would not listen to them. They had their spies everywhere, who, among other information, ascertained in what Protestant families disagreements existed, and hither would the propagandists repair, stirring up the flame of dissension in order to separate the husband from the wife, the wife from the husband, the children from the parents; promising them, and indeed giving them, great advantages, if they would consent to attend mass. Did they hear of a tradesman whose business was falling off, or of a gentleman who from gambling or otherwise was in want of money, these ladies were at hand with their *Dabo tibi* (I will give thee), on condition of apostacy; and the prisoner was in like manner relieved from his dungeon, who would give himself up to them. To meet the very heavy expenses of this proselytising, to keep the machinery at work, to purchase the souls that sold themselves for bread, regular collections were made in the chapels, and in private families, in the shops, in the inns, in the gambling-houses, in the streets—everywhere was alms-begging in operation. The Marchioness of Pianeza herself, great lady as she was, used every second or third day to make a circuit in search of subscriptions, even going into the taverns for that purpose. . . . If any person of condition, who was believed able to contribute a coin, chanced to arrive at any hotel in town, these ladies did not fail to wait upon him, purse in hand, and solicit a donation. When persons of substance known to belong to the religion [Reformed] arrived in Turin, they did not scruple to ask money of them for the propagation of the faith, and the influence of the marchioness, or fear of losing their errand and ruining their affairs, would often induce such to comply."

While busied in the prosecution of these schemes the Marchioness de Pianeza was stricken with death. Feeling remorse, and wishing to make atonement, she summoned her lord, from whom she had been parted for many years, to her bedside, and charged him, as he valued the repose of her soul and the safety of his own, to continue the good work, on which her heart had been so much set, of converting the Vaudois. To stimulate his zeal, she bequeathed him a sum of money, which, however, he could not touch till he had fulfilled the condition on which it was granted. The marquis undertook the task with the utmost goodwill.[2445] A bigot and a soldier, he could think of only one way of converting the Vaudois. It was now that the storm burst.

On the 25th of January, 1655, came the famous order of Gastaldo. This decree commanded all the Vaudois families domiciled in the communes of Lucerna, Fenile, Bubiana, Bricherasio, San Giovanni, and La Torre—in short, the whole of that rich district that separates their capital from the plain of Piedmont—to quit their dwellings within three days, and retire into the Valleys of Bobbio, Angrogna, and Rora. This they were to do on pain of death. They were farther required to sell their lands to Romanists within twenty days. Those who were willing to abjure the Protestant faith were exempted from the decree.

Anything more inhuman and barbarous in the circumstances than this edict it would not be easy to imagine. It was the depth of winter, and an Alpine winter has terrors unknown to the winters of even more northern regions. However could a population like that on which the decree fell, including young children and old men, the sick and bed-ridden, the blind and the lame, undertake a journey across swollen rivers, through valleys buried in snow, and over mountains covered with ice? They must inevitably perish, and the edict that cast them out was but another form of condemning them to die of cold and hunger. "Pray ye," said Christ, when warning his disciples to flee when they should see the Roman armies gathering round Jerusalem, "Pray ye that your flight be not in the winter." The Romish Propaganda at Turin chose this season for the enforced flight of the Vaudois. Cold were the icy peaks that looked down on this miserable troop, who were now fording the torrents and struggling up the mountain tracks, but the heart of the persecutor was colder still. True, an alternative was offered them: they might go to mass. Did they avail themselves of it? The historian Leger informs us that he had a congregation of well-nigh 2,000 persons, and that not a man of them all accepted the alternative. "I can well bear them this testimony," he observes, "seeing I was their pastor for eleven years, and I knew every one of them by name; judge, reader whether I had not cause to weep for joy, as well as for sorrow, when I saw that all the fury of these wolves was not able to influence one of these lambs, and that no earthly advantage could shake their constancy. And when I marked the traces of their blood on the snow and ice over which they had dragged their lacerated limbs, had I not cause to bless God that I had seen accomplished in their poor bodies what remained of the measure of the sufferings of Christ, and especially when I beheld this heavy cross borne by them with a fortitude so noble?"[2446]

The Vaudois of the other valleys welcomed these poor exiles, and joyfully shared with them their own humble and scanty fare. They spread the table for all, and loaded it with polenta and roasted chestnuts, with the milk and butter of their mountains, to which they did not forget to add a cup of the red wine which their valleys produce.[2447] Their enemies were amazed when they saw the whole community rise up as one man and depart.

Greater woes trod fast upon the heels of this initial calamity. A part only of the Vaudois nation had suffered from the cruel decree of Gastaldo, but the fixed object of the Propaganda was the extirpation of the entire race, and the matter was gone about with consummate perfidy and deliberate cruelty. From the upper valleys, to which they had retired, the Waldenses sent respectful representations to the court of Turin. They described their piteous condition in terms so moving—and it would have been hard to have exaggerated it—and besought the fulfilment of treaties in which the honour and truth of the House of Savoy were pledged, in language so temperate and just, that one would have thought that their supplication must needs prevail. Alas, no! The ear of their prince had been poisoned by falsehood. Even access to him was denied them. As regarded the Propaganda, their remonstrances, though accompanied with tears and groans, were wholly unheeded. The Vaudois were but charming deaf adders. They were put off with equivocal answers and delusive promises till the fatal 17th of April had arrived, when it was no longer necessary to dissemble and equivocate.[2448]

On the day above named, April 17th, 1655, the Marquis di Pianeza departed secretly at midnight from Turin, and appeared before the Valleys at the head of an army of 15,000 men.[2449] The Waldensian deputies were by appointment knocking at the door of the marquis in Turin, while he himself was on the road to La Torre. He appeared under the walls of that town at eight o'clock on Saturday evening, the same 17th of April, attended by about 300 men; the main body of his army he had left encamped on the plain. That army, secretly prepared, was composed of Piedmontese, comprehending a good many banditti, who were promised pardon and plunder should they behave themselves well, some companies of Bavarians, six regiments of French, whose thirst for blood the Huguenot wars had not been able to slake, and several companies of Irish Romanists, who, banished by Cromwell, arrived in Piedmont dripping from the massacre of their Protestant fellow-subjects in their native land.[2450]

The Waldenses had hastily constructed a barricade at the entrance of La Torre. The marquis ordered his soldiers to storm it; but the besieged resisted so stoutly that, after three hours' fighting, the enemy found he had made no advance. At one o'clock on the Sunday morning, Count Amadeus of Lucerna, who knew the locality, made a flank movement along the banks of the Pelice, stole silently through the meadows and orchards, and, advancing from the opposite quarter, attacked the Vaudois in the rear. They faced round, pierced the ranks of their assailants, and made good their retreat to the hills, leaving La Torre in the hands of the enemy. The Vaudois had lost only three men in all that fighting. It was now between two and three o'clock on Sunday morning, and though the hour was early, the Romanists repaired in a body to the church and chanted a *Te Deum*.[2451] The day was Palm-Sunday, and in this fashion did the Roman Church, by her soldiers, celebrate the great festival of love and goodwill in the Waldensian Valleys.

The Vaudois were once more on their mountains. Their families had been previously transported to their natural fastnesses. Their sentinels kept watch night and day along the frontier heights. They could see the movements of Pianeza's army on the plains beneath. They beheld their orchards falling by the axes, and their dwellings being consumed by the torches of the soldiers. On Monday the 19th, and Tuesday the 20th, a series of skirmishes took place along the line of their mountain passes and forts. The Vaudois, though poorly armed and vastly outnumbered—for they were but as one to a hundred—were victorious on all points. The Popish soldiers fell back in ignominious rout, carrying wondrous tales of the Vaudois' valour and heroism to their comrades on the plain, and infusing incipient panic into the camp.[2452]

Guilt is ever cowardly. Pianeza now began to have misgivings touching the issue. The recollection that mighty armies had aforetime perished on these mountains haunted and disquieted him. He betook him to a weapon which the Waldenses have ever been less able to cope with than the sword. On Wednesday, the 21st, before daybreak, he announced, by sound of trumpet at the various Vaudois entrenchments, his willingness to receive their deputies and treat for peace. Delegates set out for his camp, and on their arrival at headquarters were received with the utmost urbanity, and sumptuously entertained. Pianeza expressed the utmost regret for the excesses his soldiers had committed, and which had been done, he said, contrary to orders. He protested that he had come into their valleys only to track a few fugitives who had disobeyed Gastaldo's order, that the higher communes had nothing to fear, and that if they would admit a single regiment each for a few days, in token of their loyalty, all would be amicably ended. The craft of the man conquered the deputies, and despite the warnings of the more sagacious, the pastor Leger in particular, the Waldenses opened the passes of their valleys and the doors of their dwellings to the soldiers of Pianeza.

Alas! alas! these poor people were undone. They had received under their roof the murderers of themselves and their families. The first two days, the 22nd and 23rd of April, were passed in comparative peace, the soldiers eating at the same table, sleeping under the same roof, and conversing freely with their destined victims. This interval was needed to allow every preparation to be made for what was to follow. The enemy now occupied the towns, the villages, the cottages, and the roads throughout the valleys. They hung upon the heights. Two great passes led into France: the one over the snows of the lofty Col Julien, and the other by the Valley of Queyras into Dauphiné. But, alas! escape was not possible by either outlet. No one could traverse the Col Julien at this season and live, and the fortress of Mirabouc, that guarded the narrow gorge which led into the Valley of Queyrás, the enemy had been careful to secure.[2453] The Vaudois were enclosed as in a net—shut in as in a prison.

At last the blow fell with the sudden crash of the thunderbolt. At four o'clock on the morning of Saturday, the 24th of April, 1655, the signal was given from the castle-hill of La Torre.[2454] But who shall rehearse the tragedy that followed? "It is Cain a second time," says Monastier, "shedding the blood of his brother, Abel."[2455] On the instant a thousand assassins began the work of death. Dismay, horror, agony, woe in a moment overspread the Valleys of Lucerna and Angrogna. Though Pandemonium had sent forth its fiends to riot in crime and revel in blood, they could not have outdone the soldiers of the Propaganda. We see the victims climbing the hills with what speed they are able, the murderer on their track. We see the torrents as they roll down from the heights beginning to be tinged with blood. Gleams of lurid light burst out through the dark smoke that is rolling through the vales, for a priest and a monk accompany each party of soldiers, to set fire to the houses as soon as the inmates have been dispatched. Alas! what sounds are these that fall upon our ears? The cries and groans of the dying are echoed and re-echoed from the rocks around, and it seems as if the mountains had taken up a wailing for the slaughter of their children. "Our Valley of Lucerna," exclaims Leger, "which was like a Goshen, was now converted into a Mount Etna, darting forth cinders and fire and flames. The earth resembled a furnace, and the air was filled with a darkness like that of Egypt, which might be felt, from the smoke of towns, villages, temples, mansions, granges, and buildings, all burning in the flames of the Vatican.[2456]

The soldiers were not content with the quick dispatch of the sword, they invented new and hitherto unheard-of modes of torture and death. No man at this day dare write in plain words all the disgusting and horrible deeds of these men; their wickedness can never be all known, because it never can be all told.

From the awful narration of Leger, we select only a few instances; but even these few, however mildly stated, grow, without our intending it, into a group of horrors. Little children were torn from the arms of their mothers, clasped by their tiny feet, and their heads dashed against the rocks; or were held between two soldiers and their quivering limbs torn up by main force. Their mangled bodies were then thrown on the highways or fields, to be devoured by beasts. The sick and the aged were burned alive in their dwellings. Some had their hands and arms and legs lopped off, and fire applied to the severed parts to staunch the bleeding and prolong their suffering. Some were flayed alive, some were roasted alive, some disembowelled; or tied to trees in their own orchards, and their hearts cut out. Some were horribly mutilated, and of others the brains were boiled and eaten by these cannibals. Some were fastened down into the furrows of their own fields, and ploughed into the soil as men plough manure into it. Others were buried alive. Fathers were marched to death with the heads of their sons suspended round their necks. Parents were compelled to look on while their children were first outraged, then massacred, before being themselves permitted to die. But here we must stop. We cannot proceed farther in Leger's awful narration. There come vile, abominable and monstrous deeds, utterly and overwhelmingly disgusting, horrible and fiendish, which we dare not transcribe. The heart sickens, and the brain begins to swim. "My hand trembles," says Leger, "so that I scarce can hold the pen, and my tears mingle in torrents with my ink, while I write the deeds of these children of darkness—blacker even than the Prince of Darkness himself."[2457]

No general account, however awful, can convey so correct an idea of the horrors of this persecution as would the history of individual cases; but this we are precluded from giving. Could we take these martyrs one by one—could we describe the tragical fate of Peter Simeon of Angrogna—the barbarous death of Magdalene, wife of Peter Pilon of Villaro—the sad story—but no, that story could not be told—of Anne, daughter of John Charbonier of La Torre—the cruel martyrdom of Paul Garnier of Rora, whose eyes were first plucked out, who next endured other horrible indignities, and, last of all, was flayed alive, and his skin, divided into four parts, extended on the window gratings of the four principal houses in Lucerna—could we describe these cases, with hundreds of others equally horrible and appalling, our narrative would grow so harrowing that our readers, unable to proceed, would turn from the page. Literally did the Waldenses suffer all the things of which the apostle speaks, as endured by the martyrs of old, with other torments not then invented, or which the rage of even a Nero shrank from inflicting:—"They were stoned, they were sawn asunder, were tempted, were slain with the sword; they wandered about in sheep-skins and goat-skins; being destitute, afflicted, tormented (of whom the world was not worthy); they wandered in deserts, and in mountains, and in dens, and caves of the earth."

These cruelties form a scene that is unparalleled and unique in the history of at least civilised countries. There have been tragedies in which more blood was spilt, and more life sacrificed, but none in which the actors were so completely dehumanised, and the forms of suffering so monstrously disgusting, so unutterably cruel and revolting. The "Piedmontese Massacres" in this respect stand alone. They are more fiendish than all the atrocities and murders before or since, and Leger may still advance his challenge to "all travellers, and all who have studied the history of ancient and modern pagans, whether among the Chinese, Tartars and Turks, they ever witnessed or heard tell of such execrable perfidies and barbarities."

The authors of these deeds, thinking it may be that their very atrocity would make the world slow to believe them, made bold to deny that they had ever been done, even before the blood was well dry in the Valleys. Pastor Leger took instant and effectual means to demonstrate the falsehood of that denial, and to provide that clear, irrefragable, and indubitable proof of these awful crimes should to down to posterity. He travelled from commune to commune, immediately after the massacre, attended by notaries, who took down the depositions and attestations of the survivors and eye-witnesses of these deeds, in presence of the council and consistory of the place.[2458] From the evidence of these witnesses he compiled and gave to the world a book, which Dr. Gilly truly characterised as one of the most "dreadful" in existence.[2459] The originals of these depositions Leger gave to Sir Samuel Morland, who deposited them, together with other valuable documents pertaining to the Waldenses, in the Library of the University of Cambridge.

Uncontrollable grief seized the hearts of the survivors at the sight of their brethren slain, their country devastated, and their Church overthrown. "Oh that my head were waters," exclaims Leger, "and mine eyes a fountain of tears, that I might weep day and night for the slain of the daughter of my people! Behold and see if there be any sorrow like unto my sorrow." "It was then," he adds, "that the fugitives, who had been snatched as brands from the burning, could address God in the words of the 79th Psalm, which literally as emphatically describes their condition:—

"O God, the heathen are come into thine inheritances,
Thy holy temple have they defiled;
They have laid Jerusalem on heaps.
The dead bodies of thy servants have they given
To be meat unto the fowls of heaven,
The flesh of thy saints unto the beasts of the earth,
Their blood have they shed like water; . . .
And there was none to bury them!'"[2460]

When the storm had abated, Leger assembled the scattered survivors, in order to take counsel with them as to the steps to be now taken. It does not surprise us to find that some had begun to entertain the idea of abandoning the Valleys altogether. Leger strongly dissuaded them against the thought of forsaking their ancient inheritance. They must, he said, rebuild their Zion in the faith that the God of their fathers would not permit the Church of the Valleys to be finally overthrown. To encourage them, he undertook to lay a representation of their sufferings and broken condition before their brethren of other countries, who, he was sure, would hasten to their help at this great crisis. These counsels prevailed. "Our tears are no longer of water," so wrote the remnant of the slaughtered Vaudois to the Protestants of Europe, "they are of blood; they do not merely obscure our sight, they choke our very hearts. Our hands tremble and our heads ache by the many blows we have received. We cannot frame an epistle answerable to the intent of our minds, and the strangeness of our desolations. We pray you to excuse us, and to collect amid our groans the meaning of what we fain would utter." After this touching introduction, they proceed with a representation of their state, expressing themselves in terms the moderation of which contrasts strongly with the extent of their wrongs. Protestant Europe was horror-struck when the tale of the massacre was laid before it.

Nowhere did these awful tidings awaken a deeper sympathy or kindle a stronger indignation than in England. Cromwell, who was then at the head of the State, proclaimed a fast, ordered a collection for the sufferers,[2461] and wrote to all the Protestant princes, and to the King of France, with the intent of enlisting their sympathy and aid in behalf of the Vaudois. One of the noblest as well as most sacred of the tasks ever undertaken by the great poet, who then acted as the Protector's Latin secretary, was the writing of these letters. Milton's pen was not less gloriously occupied when writing in behalf of these venerable sufferers for conscience sake, than when writing "Paradise Lost." In token of the deep interest he took in this affair, Cromwell sent Sir Samuel Morland with a letter to the Duke of Savoy, expressive of the astonishment and sorrow he felt at the barbarities which had been committed on those who were his brethren in the faith. Cromwell's ambassador visited the Valleys on his way to Turin, and saw with his own eyes the frightful spectacle which the region still presented. "If," said he, addressing the duke, the horrors he had just seen giving point to his eloquence, and kindling his republican plainness into Puritan fervour, "If the tyrants of all times and ages were alive again, they would doubtless be ashamed to find that nothing barbarous nor inhuman, in comparison of these deeds, had ever been invented by them. In the meantime," he continued, "the angels are stricken with horror; men are dizzy with amazement; heaven itself appears astonished with the cries of the dying, and the very earth to blush with the gore of so many innocent persons. Avenge not thyself, O God, for this mighty wickedness, this parricidal slaughter! Let thy blood, O Christ, wash out this blood!"[2462]

We have repeatedly mentioned the Castelluzzo in our narrative of this people and their many martyrdoms. It is closely connected with the Massacre of 1655, and as such kindled the muse of Milton. It stands at the entrance of the Valleys, its feet swathed in feathery woods; above which is a mass of débris and fallen rocks, which countless tempests have gathered like a girdle round its middle. From amidst these the supreme column shoots up, pillar-like, and touches that white cloud which is floating past in mid-heaven. One can see a dark spot on the face of the cliff just below the crowning rocks of the summit. It would be taken for the shadow of a passing cloud upon the mountain, were it not that it is immovable. That is the mouth of a cave so roomy, it is said, as to be able to contain some hundreds. To this friendly chamber the Waldenses were wont to flee when the valley beneath was a perfect Pandemonium, glittering with steel, red with crime, and ringing with execrations and blasphemies. To this cave many of the Vaudois fled on occasion of the great massacre. But, alas! thither the persecutor tracked them, and dragging them forth rolled them down the awful precipice.

The law that indissolubly links great crimes with the spot where they were perpetrated, has written the Massacre of 1655 on this mountain, and given it in eternal keeping to its rock. There is not another such martyr's monument in the whole world. While the Castelluzzo stands the memory of this great crime cannot die; through all the ages it will continue to cry, and that cry our sublimest poet has interpreted in his sublime sonnet:—

"Avenge, O Lord, thy slaughter'd saints, whose bones
Lie scattered on the Alpine mountains cold;
Even them who kept thy truth so pure of old,
When all our fathers worshipt stocks and stones,
Forget not: in thy book record their groans
Who were thy sheep, and in their ancient fold
Slain by the bloody Piedmontese, that roll'd
Mother with infant down the rocks. Their moans
The vales redoubled to the hills, and they
To heaven. Their martyr'd blood and ashes now
O'er all the Italian fields, where still doth sway
The triple tyrant; that from these may grow
A hundredfold, who, having learned thy way,
Early may fly the Babylonian woe."

———————————————

CHAPTER XII
EXPLOITS OF GIANAVELLO—MASSACRE AND PILLAGE OF RORA

THE next tragic episode in the history of the Waldenses takes us to the Valley of Rora. The invasion and outrages of which this valley became the scene were contemporaneous with the horrors of the Great Massacre. In what we are now to relate, feats of heroism are blended with deeds of suffering, and we are called to admire the valour of the patriot, as well as the patience of the martyr.

The Valley of Rora lies on the left as one enters La Torre; it is separated from Lucerna by a barrier of mountains. Rora has two entrances: one by a side ravine, which branches off about two miles before reaching La Torre, and the other by crossing the Valley of Lucerna and climbing the mountains. This last is worthy of being briefly described. We start, we shall suppose, from the town of La Torre; we skirt the Castelluzzo on the right, which high in air hangs its precipices, with their many tragic memories, above us. From this point we turn to the left, descend into the valley, traverse its bright meadows, here shaded by the vine which stretches its arms in classic freedom from tree to tree. We cross the torrent of the Pelice by a small bridge, and hold on our way till we reach the foot of the mountains of La Combe, that wall in the Valley of Rora. We begin to climb by a winding path. Pasturage and vineyard give place to chestnut forest; the chestnut in its turn yields to the pine; and, as we mount still higher, we find ourselves amid the naked ledges of the mountain, with their gushing rills, margined by moss or other Alpine herbage.

An ascent of two hours brings us to the summit of the pass. We have here a pedestal, some 4,000 feet in height, in the midst of a stupendous amphitheatre of Alps, from which to view their glories. How profoundly deep the valley from which we have just climbed up A thread of silver is now the Pelice; a patch of green a few inches square is now the meadow; the chestnut-tree is a mere dot, hardly visible; and yonder are La Torre and the white Villaro, so tiny that they look as if they could be packed into a child's toy-box.

But while all else has diminished, the mountains seem to have enlarged their bulk and increased their stature. High above us towers the summit of the Castelluzzo; still higher rise the rolling masses of the Vandalin, the lower slopes of which form a vast and magnificent hanging garden, utterly dwarfing those of which we read as one of the wonders of Babylon. And in the far distance the eye rests on a tumultuous sea of mountains, here rising in needles, there running off in long serrated ridges, and there standing up in massy peaks of naked granite, wearing the shining garments which winter weaves for the giants of the Alps.

We now descend into the Valley of Rora. It lies at our feet, a cup of verdure, some sixty miles in circumference, its sides and bottom variously clothed with corn-field and meadow, with vineyard and orchard, with the walnut, the cherry, and all fruit-bearing trees, from amid which numerous brown châlets peep out. The great mountains sweep round the valley like a wall, and among them, pre-eminent in glory as in stature, stands the monarch of the Cottian Alps—Monte Viso.

As among the Jews of old, so among the Waldenses, God raised up, from time to time, mighty men of valour to deliver his people. One of the most remarkable of these men was Gianavello, commonly known as Captain Joshua Gianavello, a native of this same Valley of Rora. He appears, from the accounts that have come down to us, to have possessed all the qualities of a great military leader. He was a man of daring courage, of resolute purpose, and of venturous enterprise. He had the faculty, so essential in a commander, of skilful combination. He was fertile in resource, and self-possessed in emergencies; he was quick to resolve, and prompt to execute. His devotion and energy were the means, under God, of mitigating somewhat the horrors of the Massacre of 1655, and his heroism ultimately rolled back the tide of that great calamity, and made it recoil upon its authors. It was the morning of the 24th of April, 1655, the day which saw the butchery commenced that we have described above. On that same day 500 soldiers were dispatched by the Marquis di Pianeza to the Valley of Rora, to massacre its unoffending and unsuspecting inhabitants. Ascending from the Valley of the Pelice, they had gained the summit of the pass, and were already descending on the town of Rora, stealthily and swiftly, as a herd of wolves might descend upon a sheepfold, or as, says Leger, "a brood of vultures might descend upon a flock of harmless doves." Happily Gianavello, who had known for weeks before that a storm was gathering, though he knew not when or where it would burst, was on the outlook. He saw the troop, and guessed their errand. There was not a moment to be lost; a little longer, and not a man would be left alive in Rora to carry tidings of its fate to the next commune. But was Gianavello single-handed to attack an army of 500 men? He stole up-hill, under cover of the rocks and trees, and on his way he prevailed on six peasants, brave men like himself, to join him in repelling the invaders. The heroic little band marched on till they were near the troop, then hiding in the bushes, they lay in ambush by the side of the path. The soldiers came on, little suspecting the trap into which they were marching. Gianavello and his men fired, and with so unerring an aim that seven of the troop fell dead. Then, reloading their pieces, and dexterously changing their ground, they fired again with a like effect. The attack was unexpected; the foe was invisible; the frightened imaginations of Pianeza's soldiers multiplied tenfold the number of their assailants. They began to retreat. But Gianavello and his men, bounding from cover to cover like so many chamois, hung upon their rear, and did deadly execution with their bullets. The invaders left fifty-four of their number dead behind them; and thus did these seven peasants chase from the Valley of the Rora the 500 assassins who had come to murder its peaceful inhabitants.

That same afternoon the people of Rora, who were ignorant of the fearful murders which were at that very moment proceeding in the valleys of their brethren, repaired to the Marquis de Pianeza to complain of the attack. The marquis affected ignorance of the whole affair. "Those who invaded your valley," said he, "were a set of banditti. You did right to repel them. Go back to your families and fear nothing; I pledge my word and honour that no evil shall happen to you."

These deceitful words did not impose upon Gianavello. He had a wholesome recollection of the maxim enacted by the Council of Constance, and so often put in practice in the Valleys, "No faith is to be kept with heretics." Pianeza, he knew, was the agent of the "Council of Extirpation." Hardly had the next morning broke when the hero-peasant was abroad, scanning with eagle-eye the mountain paths that led into his valley. It was not long till his suspicions were more than justified. Six hundred men-at-arms, chosen with special reference to this difficult enterprise, were seen ascending the mountain Cassuleto, to do what their comrades of the previous day had failed to accomplish. Gianavello had now mustered a little host of eighteen, of whom twelve were armed with muskets and swords, and six with only the sling. These he divided into three parties, each consisting of four musketeers and two slingers, and he posted them in a defile, through which he saw the invaders must pass. No sooner had the van of the enemy entered the gorge than a shower of bullets and stones from invisible hands saluted them. Every bullet and stone did its work. The first discharge brought down an officer and twelve men. That volley was succeeded by others equally fatal. The cry was raised, "All is lost, save yourselves!" The flight was precipitate, for every bush and rock seemed to vomit forth deadly missiles. Thus a second ignominious retreat rid the Valley of Rora of the murderers.

The inhabitants carried their complaints a second time to Pianeza. "Concealing," as Leger says, "the ferocity of the tiger under the skin of the fox," he assured the deputies that the attack had been the result of a misunderstanding; that certain accusations had been lodged against them, the falsity of which had since been discovered, and now they might return to their homes, for they had nothing to fear. No sooner were they gone than Pianeza began vigorously to prepare for a third attack.[2464]

He organised a battalion of from 800 to 900 men. Next morning, this host made a rapid march on Rora, seized all the avenues leading into the valley, and chasing the inhabitants to the caves in Monte Friolante, set fire to their dwellings, having first plundered them. Captain Joshua Gianavello, at the head of his little troop, saw the enemy enter, but their numbers were so overwhelming that he waited a more favourable moment for attacking them. The soldiers were retiring, laden with their booty, and driving before them the cattle of the peasants. Gianavello knelt down before his hero-band, and giving thanks to God, who had twice by his hand saved his people, he prayed that the hearts and arms of his followers might be strengthened, to work yet another deliverance. He then attacked the foe. The spoilers turned and fled up-hill, in the hope of escaping into the Valley of the Pelice, throwing away their booty in their flight. When they had gained the pass, and begun their descent, their flight became yet more disastrous; great stones, torn up and rolled after them, were mingled with the bullets, and did deadly execution upon them, while the precipices over which they fell in their haste consummated their destruction. The few who survived fled to Villaro.[2465]

The Marquis de Pianeza, instead of seeing in these events the finger of God, was only the more inflamed with rage, and the more resolutely bent on the extirpation of every heretic from the Valley of Rora. He assembled all the royal troops then under his command, or which could be spared from the massacre in which they were occupied in the other valleys, in order to surround the little territory. This was now the fourth attack on the commune of Rora, but the invaders were destined once more to recoil before the shock of its heroic defenders. Some 8,000 men had been got under arms, and were ready to march against Rora, but the impatience of a certain Captain Mario, who had signalised himself in the massacre at Bobbio, and wished to appropriate the entire glory of the enterprise, would not permit him to await the movement of the main body. He marched two hours in advance, with three companies of regular troops, few of whom ever returned. Their ferocious leader, borne along by the rush of his panic-stricken soldiers, was precipitated over the edge of the rock into the stream, and badly bruised. He was drawn out and carried to Lucerna, where he died two days afterwards, in great torment of body, and yet greater torment of mind. Of the three companies which he led into this fatal expedition, one was composed of Irish, who had been banished by Cromwell, and who met in this distant land the death they had inflicted on others in their own, leaving their corpses to fatten those valleys which were to have been theirs, had they succeeded in purging them of heresy and heretics.[2466]

This series of strange events was now drawing to an end. The fury of Pianeza knew no bounds. This war of his, though waged only with herdsmen, had brought him nothing but disgrace, and the loss of his bravest soldiers. Victor Amadeus once observed that "the skin of every Vaudois cost him fifteen of his best Piedmontese soldiers." Pianeza had lost some hundreds of his best soldiers, and yet not one of the little troop of Gianavello, dead or alive, had he been able to get into his hands. Nevertheless, he resolved to continue the struggle, but with a much greater army. He assembled 10,000, and attacked Rora on three sides at once. While Gianavello was bravely combating with the first troop of 3,000, on the summit of the pass that gives entrance from the Valley of the Pelice, a second of 6,000 had entered by the ravine at the foot of the valley; and a third of 1,000 had crossed the mountains that divide Bagnolo from Rora. But, alas! who shall describe the horrors that followed the entrance of these assassins? Blood, burning, and rapine in an instant overwhelmed the little community. No distinction was made of age or sex. None had pity for their tender years; none had reverence for their grey hairs. Happy they who were slain at once, and thus escaped horrible indignities and tortures. The few spared from the sword were carried away as captives, and among these were the wife and the three daughters of Gianavello.[2467]

There was now nothing more in the Valley of Rora for which the patriot-hero could do battle. The light of his hearth was quenched, his village was a heap of smoking ruins, his fathers and brethren had fallen by the sword; but rising superior to these accumulated calamities, he marched his little troop over the mountains, to await on the frontier of his country whatever opportunities Providence might yet open to him of wielding his sword in defence of the ancient liberties and the glorious faith of his people.

It was at this time that Pianeza, intending to deal the finishing blow that should crush the hero of Rora, wrote to Gianavello as follows:—"I exhort you for the last time to renounce your heresy. This is the only hope of your obtaining the pardon of your prince, and of saving the life of your wife and daughters, now my prisoners, and whom, if you continue obstinate, I will burn alive. As for yourself, my soldiers shall no longer pursue you, but I will set such a price upon your head, as that were you Beelzebub himself, you shall infallibly be taken; and be assured that, if you fall alive into my hands, there are no torments with which I will not punish your rebellion." To these ferocious threats Gianavello magnanimously and promptly replied: "There are no torments so terrible, no death so barbarous, that I would not choose rather than deny my Saviour. Your threats cannot cause me to renounce my faith; they but fortify me in it. Should the Marquis di Pianeza cause my wife and daughters to pass through the fire, it can but consume their mortal bodies; their souls I commend to God, trusting that he will have mercy on them, and on mine, should it please him that I fall into the marquis's hands."[2468] We do not know whether Pianeza was capable of seeing that this was the most mortifying defeat he had yet sustained at the hands of the peasant-hero of Rora; and that he might as well war against the Alps themselves as against a cause that could infuse a spirit like this into its champions. Gianavello's reply, observes Leger, "certified him as a chosen instrument in the hands of God for the recovery of his country seemingly lost."

Gianavello had saved from the wreck of his family his infant son, and his first care was to seek a place of safety for him. Laying him on his shoulders, he passed the frozen Alps which separate the Valley of Lucerna from France, and entrusted the child to the care of a relative resident at Queyras, in the Valleys of the French Protestants. With the child he carried thither the tidings of the awful massacre of his people. Indignation was roused. Not a few were willing to join his standard, brave spirits like himself; and, with his little band greatly recruited, he repassed the Alps in a few weeks, to begin his second and more successful campaign. On his arrival in the Valleys he was joined by Giaheri, under whom a troop had been assembling to avenge the massacre of their brethren.

In Giaheri, Captain Gianavello had found a companion worthy of himself, and worthy of the cause for which he was now in arms. Of this heroic man Leger has recorded that, "though he possessed the courage of a lion, he was as humble as a lamb, always giving to God the glory of his victories; well versed in Scripture, and understanding controversy, and of great natural talent. The massacre had reduced the Vaudois race to all but utter extermination, and 500 men were all that the two leaders could collect around their standard. The army opposed to them, and at this time in their Valleys, was from 15,000 to 20,000 strong, consisting of trained and picked soldiers. Nothing but an impulse from the God of battles could have moved these two men, with such a handful, to take the field against such odds. To the eye of a common hero all would have seemed lost; but the courage of these two Christian warriors was based on faith. They believed that God would not permit his cause to perish, or the lamp of the Valleys to be extinguished; and, few though they were, they knew that God was able by their humble instrumentality to save their country and Church. In this faith they unsheathed the sword; and so valiantly did they wield it, that soon that sword became the terror of the Piedmontese armies. The ancient promise was fulfilled, "The people that do know their God shall be strong and do exploits."

We cannot go into details. Prodigies of valour were performed by this little host. "I had always considered the Vaudois to be men," said Descombies, who had joined them, "but I found them lions." Nothing could withstand the fury of their attack. Post after post and village after village were wrested from the Piedmontese troops. Soon the enemy was driven from the upper valleys. The war now passed down into the plain of Piedmont, and there it was waged with the same heroism and the same success. They besieged and took several towns, they fought not a few pitched battles; and in nearly all of them they were victorious, though opposed by more than ten times their number. Their success could hardly be credited had it not been recorded by historians whose veracity is above suspicion, and the accuracy of their statements was attested by eye-witnesses. Not unfrequently did it happen at the close of a day's fighting, that 1,400 Piedmontese dead covered the field of battle, while not more than six or seven of the Waldenses had fallen. Such success might well be termed miraculous; and not only did it appear so to the Vaudois themselves, but even to their foes, who could not refrain from expressing their conviction "that surely God was on the side of the Barbets."

While the Vaudois were thus heroically maintaining their cause by arms, and rolling back the chastisement of war on those from whom its miseries had come, tidings of their wrongs were travelling to all the Protestant States of Europe. Wherever these tidings came a feeling of horror was evoked, and the cruelty of the Government of Savoy was universally and loudly execrated. All confessed that such a tale of woe they had never before heard. But the Protestant States did not content themselves with simply condemning these deeds; they judged it to be their clear duty to move in behalf of this poor and greatly oppressed people; and foremost among those who did themselves lasting honour by interposing in behalf of a people "drawn unto death and ready to perish," was, as we have already said, England, then under the Protectorate of Cromwell. We mentioned in the previous chapter the Latin letter, the composition of Milton, which the Protector addressed to the Duke of Savoy. In addition, Cromwell wrote to Louis XIV. of France, soliciting his mediation with the duke in behalf of the Vaudois. The letter is interesting as containing the truly catholic and noble sentiments of England, to which the pen of her great poet gave fitting expression:—

"Most Serene and Potent King,

... "After a most barbarous slaughter of persons of both sexes, and of all ages, a treaty of peace was concluded, or rather secret acts of hostility were committed the more securely under the name of a pacification. The conditions of the treaty were determined in your town of Pinerolo: hard conditions enough, but such as these poor people would gladly have agreed to, after the horrible outrages to which they had been exposed, provided that they had been faithfully observed. But they were not observed; the meaning of the treaty is evaded and violated, by putting a false interpretation upon some of the articles, and by straining others. Many of the complainants have been deprived of their patrimonies, and many have been forbidden the exercise of their religion. New payments have been exacted, and a new fort has been built to keep them in check, from whence a disorderly soldiery make frequent sallies, and plunder or murder all they meet. In addition to these things, fresh levies of troops are clandestinely preparing to march against them; and those among them who profess the Roman Catholic religion have been advised to retire in time; so that everything threatens the speedy destruction of such as escaped the former massacre. I do therefore beseech and conjure your Majesty not to suffer such enormities, and not to permit (I will not say any prince, for surely such barbarity never could enter into the heart of a prince, much less of one of the duke's tender age, or into the mind of his mother) those accursed murderers to indulge in such savage ferocity, who, while they profess to be the servants and followers of Christ, who came into the world to save sinners, do blaspheme his name, and transgress his mild precepts, by the slaughter of innocent men. Oh, that your Majesty, who has the power, and who ought to be inclined to use it, may deliver so many supplicants from the hands of murderers, who are already drunk with blood, and thirst for it again, and who take pleasure in throwing the odium of their cruelty upon princes! I implore your Majesty not to suffer the borders of your kingdom to be polluted by such monstrous wickedness. Remember that this very race of people threw themselves upon the protection of your grandfather, King Henry IV., who was most friendly disposed towards the Protestants, when the Duke of Lesdiguieres passed victoriously through their country, as affording the most commodious passage into Italy at the time he pursued the Duke of Savoy in his retreat across the Alps. The act or instrument of that submission is still extant among the public records of your kingdom, in which it is provided that the Vaudois shall not be transferred to any other government, but upon the same condition that they were received under the protection of your invincible grandfather. As supplicants of his grandson, they now implore the fulfilment of this compact.

* * * * * * * * * * * * * *

"Given at our Court at Westminster, this 26th of May, 1658."

The French King undertook the mediation, as requested by the Protestant princes, but hurried it to a conclusion before the ambassadors from the Protestant States had arrived. The delegates from the Protestant cantons of Switzerland were present, but they were permitted to act the part of onlookers simply. The Grand Monarch took the whole affair upon himself, and on the 18th of August, 1655, a treaty of peace was concluded of a very disadvantageous kind. The Waldenses were stripped of their ancient possessions on the right bank of the Pelice, lying toward the plains of Piedmont. Within the new boundary they were guaranteed liberty of worship; an amnesty was granted for all offences committed during the war; captives were to be restored when claimed; and they were to be exempt from all imposts for five years, on the ground that they were so impoverished as not to be able to pay anything.

When the treaty was published it was found to contain two clauses that astonished the Protestant world. In the preamble the Vaudois were styled rebels, whom it had pleased their prince graciously to receive back into favour; and in the body of the deed was an article, which no one recollected to have heard mentioned during the negotiations, empowering the French to construct a fort above La Torre. This looked like a preparation for renewing the war.

By this treaty the Protestant States were outwitted; their ambassadors were duped; and the poor Vaudois were left as much as ever in the power of the Duke of Savoy and of the Council for the Propagation of the Faith, and the Extirpation of Heretics.

CHAPTER XIII
THE EXILE

AFTER the great Massacre of 1655, the Church of the Valleys had rest from persecution for thirty years. This period, however, can be styled one of rest only when contrasted with the frightful storms which had convulsed the era that immediately preceded it. The enemies of the Vaudois still found innumerable ways in which to annoy and harass them. Ceaseless intrigues were continually breeding new alarms, and the Vaudois had often to till their fields and prune their vines with their musket slung across their shoulders. Many of their chief men were sent into exile. Captain Gianavello and Pastor Leger, whose services to their people were too great ever to be forgiven, had sentence of death passed on them. Leger was "to be strangled; then his body was to be hung by one foot on a gibbet for four-and-twenty hours; and, lastly, his head was to be cut off and publicly exposed at San Giovanni. His name was to be inserted in the list of noted outlaws; his houses were to be burned."[2469] Gianavello retired to Geneva, where he continued to watch with unabated interest the fortunes of his people. Leger became pastor of a congregation at Leyden, where he crowned a life full of labour and suffering for the Gospel, by a work which has laid all Christendom under obligations to him; we refer to his *History of the Churches of the Vaudois*—a noble monument of his Church's martyr-heroism and his own Christian patriotism.

Hardly had Leger unrolled to the world's gaze the record of the last awful tempest which had smitten the Valleys, when the clouds returned, and were seen rolling up in dark, thunderous masses against this devoted land. Former storms had assailed them from the south, having collected in the Vatican; the tempest now approaching had its first rise on the north of the Alps. It was the year 1685; Louis XIV. was nearing the grave, and with the great audit in view he inquired of his confessor by what good deed as a king he might atone for his many sins as a man. The answer was ready. He was told that he must extirpate Protestantism in France.

The Grand Monarch, as the age styled him, bowed obsequiously before the shaven crown of the priest, while Europe was trembling before his armies. Louis XIV. did as he was commanded; he revoked the Edict of Nantes. This gigantic crime, which inflicted so much misery on the Protestants in the first place, and brought so many woes on the throne and nation of France in the second, will be recorded in its place. It is the nation of the Vaudois, and the persecution which the counsel of Father la Chaise brought upon them, with which we have here to do. Wishing for companionship in the sanguinary work of purging France from Protestantism, Louis XIV. sent an ambassador to the Duke of Savoy, with a request that he would deal with the Waldenses as he was now dealing with the Huguenots. The young and naturally humane Victor Amadeus was at the moment on more than usually friendly terms with his subjects of the Valleys. They had served bravely under his standard in his late war with the Genoese, and he had but recently written them a letter of thanks. How could he unsheathe his sword against the men whose devotion and valour had so largely contributed to his victory? Victor Amadeus deigned no reply to the French ambassador. The request was repeated; it received an evasive answer; it was urged a third time, accompanied by a hint from the potent Louis that if it was not convenient for the duke to purge his dominions, the King of France would do it for him with an army of 14,000 men, and would keep the Valleys for his pains. This was enough. A treaty was immediately concluded between the duke and the French King, in which the latter promised an armed force to enable the former to reduce the Vaudois to the Roman obedience, or to exterminate them.[2470] On the 31st of January, 1686, the following edict was promulgated in the Valleys:—

"I. The Vaudois shall henceforth and for ever cease and discontinue all the exercises of their religion.

"II. They are forbidden to have religious meetings, under pain of death, and penalty of confiscation of all their goods.

"III. All their ancient privileges were abolished.

"IV. All the churches, prayer-houses, and other edifices consecrated to their worship shall be razed to the ground.

"V. All the pastors and schoolmasters of the Valleys are required either to embrace Romanism or to quit the country within fifteen days, under pain of death and confiscation of goods.

"VI. All the children born, or to be born, of Protestant parents, shall be compulsorily trained up as Roman Catholics. Every such child yet unborn shall, within a week after its birth, be brought to the curé of its parish, and admitted of the Roman Catholic Church, under pain, on the part of the mother, of being publicly whipped with rods, and on the part of the father of labouring five years in the galleys.

"VII. The Vaudois pastors shall abjure the doctrine they have hitherto publicly preached; shall receive a salary, greater by one-third than that which they previously enjoyed; and one-half thereof shall go in reversion to their widows.

"VIII. All Protestant foreigners settled in Piedmont are ordered either to become Roman Catholics, or to quit the country within fifteen days.

"IX. By a special act of his great and paternal clemency, the sovereign will permit persons to sell, in this interval, the property they may have acquired in Piedmont, provided the sale be made to Roman Catholic purchasers."

This monstrous edict seemed to sound the knell of the Vaudois as a Protestant people. Their oldest traditions did not contain a decree so cruel and unrighteous, nor one that menaced them with so complete and summary a destruction as that which now seemed to impend over them. What was to be done? Their first step was to send delegates to Turin, respectfully to remind the duke that the Vaudois had inhabited the Valleys from the earliest times; that they had led forth their herds upon their mountains before the House of Savoy had ascended the throne of Piedmont; that treaties and oaths, renewed from reign to reign, had solemnly secured them in the freedom of their worship and other liberties; and that the honour of princes and the stability of States lay in the faithful observance of such covenants; and they prayed him to consider what reproach the throne and kingdom of Piedmont would incur if he should become the executioner of those of whom he was the natural protector. The Protestant cantons of Switzerland joined their mediation to the intercessions of the Waldenses. And when the almost incredible edict came to be known in Germany and Holland, these countries threw their shield over the Valleys, by interceding with the duke that he would not inflict so great a wrong as to cast out from a land which was theirs by irrevocable charters, a people whose only crime was that they worshipped as their fathers had worshipped, before they passed under the sceptre of the duke. All these powerful parties pleaded in vain. Ancient charters, solemn treaties, and oaths, made in the face of Europe, the long-tried loyalty and the many services of the Vaudois to the House of Savoy, could not stay the uplifted arm of the duke, or prevent the execution of the monstrously criminal decree. In a little while the armies of France and Savoy arrived before the Valleys.

At no previous period of their history, perhaps, had the Waldenses been so entirely devoid of human aid as now. Gianavello, whose stout heart and brave arm had stood them in such good stead formerly, was in exile. Cromwell, whose potent voice had stayed the fury of the great massacre, was in his grave. An avowed Papist filled the throne of Great Britain. It was going ill at this hour with Protestantism everywhere. The Covenanters of Scotland were hiding on the moors, or dying in the Grass-market of Edinburgh. France, Piedmont, and Italy were closing in around the Valleys; every path guarded, all their succours cut off, an overwhelming force waited the signal to massacre them. So desperate did their situation appear to the Swiss envoys, that they counselled them to "transport elsewhere the torch of the Gospel, and not keep it here to be extinguished in blood."

The proposal to abandon their ancient inheritance, coming from such a quarter, startled the Waldenses. It produced, at first, a division of opinion in the Valleys; but ultimately they united in rejecting it. They remembered the exploits their fathers had done, and the wonders God had wrought in the mountain passes of Rora, in the defiles of Angrogna, and in the field of the Pra del Tor, and their faith reviving, they resolved, in a reliance on the same Almighty Arm which had been stretched out in their behalf in former days, to defend their hearths and altars. They repaired the old defences, and made ready for resistance. On the 17th of April, being Good Friday, they renewed their covenant, and on Easter Sunday their pastors dispensed to them the Communion. This was the last time the sons of the Valleys partook of the Lord's Supper before their great dispersion.

Victor Amadeus II. had pitched his camp on the plain of San Gegonzo before the Vaudois Alps. His army consisted of five regiments of horse and foot. He was here joined by the French auxiliaries who had crossed the Alps, consisting of some dozen battalions, the united force amounting to between 15,000 and 20,000 men. The signal was to be given on Easter Monday, at break of day, by three cannon-shots, fired from the hill of Bricherasio. On the appointed morning, the Valleys of Lucerna and San Martino, forming the two extreme opposite points of the territory, were attacked, the first by the Piedmontese host, and the last by the French under the command of General Catinat, a distinguished soldier. In San Martino the fighting lasted ten hours, and ended in the complete repulse of the French, who retired at night with a loss of more than 500 killed and wounded, while the Vaudois had lost only two.[2471] On the following day the French, burning with rage at their defeat, poured a more numerous army into San Martino, which swept along the valley, burning, plundering, and massacring, and having crossed the mountains descended into Pramol, continuing the same indiscriminate and exterminating vengeance. To the rage of the sword were added other barbarities and outrages too shocking to be narrated.[2472]

The issue by arms being deemed uncertain, despite the vast disparity of strength, treachery, on a great scale, was now had recourse to. Wherever, throughout the Valleys, the Vaudois were found strongly posted, and ready for battle, they were told that their brethren in the neighbouring communes had submitted, and that it was vain for them, isolated and alone as they now were, to continue their resistance. When they sent deputies to headquarters to inquire—and passes were freely supplied for that purpose—they were assured that the submission had been universal, and that none save themselves were now in arms. They were assured, moreover, that should they follow the example of the rest of their nation, all their ancient liberties would be held intact.[2473] This base artifice was successfully practiced at each of the Vaudois posts in succession, till at length the Valleys had all capitulated. We cannot blame the Waldenses, who were the victims of an act so dishonourable and vile as hardly to be credible; but the mistake, alas! was a fatal one, and had to be expiated afterwards by the endurance of woes a hundred times more dreadful than any they would have encountered in the rudest campaign. The instant consequence of the submission was a massacre which extended to all their Valleys, and which was similar in its horrors to the great butchery of 1655. In that massacre upwards of 3,000 perished. The remainder of the nation, amounting, according to Arnaud, to between 12,000 and 15,000 souls, were consigned to the various gaols and fortresses of Piedmont.[2474]

We now behold these famous Valleys, for the first time in history, empty. The ancient lamp burns no longer. The school of the prophets in the Pra del Tor is razed. No smoke is seen rising from cottage, no psalm is heard ascending from dwelling or sanctuary. No herdsman leads forth his kine on the mountains, and no troop of worshippers, obedient to the summons of the Sabbath-bell, climbs the mountain paths. The vine flings wide her arms, but no skilful hand is nigh to train her boughs and prune her luxuriance. The chestnut-tree rains its fruits, but there is no group of merry children to gather them, and they lie rotting on the ground. The terraces of the hills, that were wont to overflow with flowers and fruitage, and which presented to the eye a series of hanging gardens, now torn and breached, shoot in a mass of ruinous rubbish down the slope. Nothing is seen but dismantled forts, and the blackened ruins of churches and hamlets. A dreary silence overspreads the land, and the beasts of the field strangely multiply. A few herdsmen, hidden here and there in forests and holes of the rocks, are now the only inhabitants. Monte Viso, from out the silent vault, looks down with astonishment at the absence of that ancient race over whom, from immemorial time, he had been wont to dart his kindling glories at dawn, and let fall at eve the friendly mantle of his purple shadows.

We know not if ever before an entire nation were in prison at once. Yet now it was so. All of the Waldensian race that remained from the sword of their executioners were immured in the dungeons of Piedmont! The pastor and his flock, the father and his family, the patriarch and the stripling had passed in, in one great procession, and exchanged their grand rock-walled Valleys, their tree-embowered homes, and their sunlit peaks, for the filth, the choking air, and the Tartarean walls of an Italian gaol. And how were they treated in prison? As the African slave was treated on the "middle passage." They had a sufficiency of neither food nor clothing. The bread dealt out to them was fetid. They had putrid water to drink. They were exposed to the sun by day and to the cold by night. They were compelled to sleep on the bare pavement, or on straw so full of vermin that the stone-floor was preferable. Disease broke out in these horrible abodes, and the mortality was fearful. "When they entered these dungeons," says Henri Arnaud, "they counted 14,000 healthy mountaineers, but when, at the intercession of the Swiss deputies, their prisons were opened, 3,000 skeletons only crawled out." These few words portray a tragedy so awful that the imagination recoils from the contemplation of it.

Well, at length the persecutor looses their chains, and opening their prison doors he sends forth these captives—the woe-worn remnant of a gallant people. But to what are they sent forth? To people again their ancient Valleys? To rekindle the fire on their ancestral hearths? To rebuild "the holy and beautiful house" in which their fathers had praised God? Ah, no! They are thrust out of prison only to be sent into exile—to Vaudois a living death.

The barbarity of 1655 was repeated. It was in December (1686) that the decree of liberation was issued in favour of these 3,000 men who had escaped the sword, and now survived the not less deadly epidemic of the prison. At that season, as every one knows, the snow and ice are piled to a fearful depth on the Alps; and daily tempests threaten with death the too adventurous traveller who would cross their summits. It was at this season that these poor captives, emaciated with sickness, weakened by hunger, and shivering from insufficient clothing, were commanded to rise up and cross the snowy hills. They began their journey on the afternoon of that very day on which the order arrived; for their enemies would permit no delay. One hundred and fifty of them died on their first march. At night they halted at the foot of the Mont Cenis. Next morning, when they surveyed the Alps they saw evident signs of a gathering tempest, and they besought the officer in charge to permit them, for the sake of their sick and aged, to remain where they were till the storm had spent its rage. With heart harder than the rocks they were to traverse, the officer ordered them to resume their journey. That troop of emaciated beings began the ascent, and were soon struggling with the blinding drifts and fearful whirlwinds of the mountain. Eighty-six of their number, succumbing to the tempest, dropped by the way. Where they lay down, there they died. No relative or friend was permitted to remain behind to watch their last moments or tender them needed succour. That ever-thinning procession moved on and on over the white hills, leaving it to the falling snow to give burial to their stricken companions. When spring opened the passes of the Alps, alas! what ghastly memorials met the eye of the horror-stricken traveller. Strewed along the track were the now unshrouded corpses of these poor exiles, the dead child lying fast locked in the arms of the dead mother.

But why should we prolong this harrowing tale? The first company of these miserable exiles arrived at Geneva on Christmas Day, 1686, having spent about three weeks on the journey. They were followed by small parties, who crossed the Alps one after the other, being let out of prison at different times. It was not till the end of February, 1687, that the last band of these emigrants reached the hospitable gates of Geneva. But in what a plight! way-worn, sick, emaciated, and faint through hunger. Of some the tongue was swollen in their mouth, and they were unable to speak; of others the arms were bitten with the frost, so that they could not stretch them out to accept the charity offered to them; and some there were who dropped down and expired on the very threshold of the city, "finding," as one has said, "the end of their life at the beginning of their liberty." Most hospitable was the reception given them by the city of Calvin. A deputation of the principal citizens of Geneva, headed by the partriarch, Gianavello, who still lived, went out to meet them on the frontier, and taking them to their homes, they vied with each other which should show them the greatest kindness. Generous city! If he who shall give a cup of cold water to a disciple shall in nowise lose his reward, how much more shalt thou be requited for this thy kindness to the suffering and sorrowing exiles of the Saviour!

CHAPTER XIV
RETURN TO THE VALLEYS

WE now open the bright page of the Vaudois history. We have seen nearly 3,000 Waldensian exiles enter the gates of Geneva, the feeble remnant of a population of from 14,000 to 16,000. One city could not contain them all, and arrangements were made for distributing the expatriated Vaudois among the Reformed cantons. The revocation of the Edict of Nantes had a little before thrown thousands of French Protestants upon the hospitality of the Swiss; and now the arrival of the Waldensian refugees brought with it yet heavier demands on the public and private charity of the cantons; but the response of Protestant Helvetia was equally cordial in the case of the last comers as in that of the first, and perhaps even more so, seeing their destitution was greater. Nor were the Vaudois ungrateful. "Next to God, whose tender mercies have preserved us from being entirely consumed," said they to their kind benefactors, "we are indebted to you alone for life and liberty."

Several of the German princes opened their States to these exiles; but the influence of their great enemy, Louis XIV., was then too powerful in these parts to permit of their residence being altogether an agreeable one. Constantly watched by his emissaries, and their patrons tampered with, they were moved about from place to place. The question of their permanent settlement in the future was beginning to be anxiously discussed. The project of carrying them across the sea in the ships of Holland, and planting them at the Cape, was even talked of. The idea of being separated for ever from their native land, dearer in exile than when they dwelt in it, gave them intolerable anguish. Was it not possible to reassemble their scattered colonies, and marching back to their Valleys, rekindle their ancient lamp in them? This was the question which, after three years of exile, the Vaudois began to put to themselves. As they wandered by the banks of the Rhine, or traversed the German plains, they feasted their imaginations on their far-off homes. The chestnuts shading their former abodes, the vine bending gracefully over their portal, and the meadow in front, which the crystal torrent kept perpetually bright, and whose murmur sweetly blended with the evening psalm, all rose before their eyes. They never knelt to pray but it was with their faces turned toward their grand mountains, where slept their martyred fathers. Attempts had been made by the Duke of Savoy to people their territory by settling in it a mongrel race, partly Irish and partly Piedmontese; but the land knew not the strangers, and refused to yield its strength to them. The Vaudois had sent spies to examine its condition;[2475] its fields lay untilled, its vines unpruned, nor had its ruins been raised up; it was almost as desolate as on the day when its sons had been driven out of it. It seemed to them that the land was waiting their return.

At length the yearning of the heart could no longer be repressed. The march back to their Valleys is one of the most wonderful exploits ever performed by any people. It is famous in history by the name of "La Rentrée Glorieuse." The parallel event which will recur to the mind of the scholar is, of course, the retreat of "the ten thousand Greeks." The patriotism and bravery of both will be admitted, but a candid comparison will, we think, incline one to assign the palm of heroism to the return of "the eight hundred."

The day fixed for beginning their expedition was the 10th of June, 1688. Quitting their various cantonments in Switzerland, and travelling by by-roads, they traversed the country by night, and assembled at Bex, a small town in the southern extremity of the territory of Bern. Their secret march was soon known to the senates of Zurich, Bern, and Genera; and, foreseeing that the departure of the exiles would compromise them with the Popish powers, their Excellencies took measures to prevent it. A bark laden with arms for their use was seized on the Lake of Geneva. The inhabitants of the Vallais, in concert with the Savoyards, at the first alarm seized the Bridge of St. Maurice, the key of the Rhone Valley, and stopped the expedition. Thus were they, for the time, compelled to abandon their project.

To extinguish all hopes of their return to the Valleys, they were anew distributed over Germany. But scarcely had this second dispersion been effected, when war broke out; the French troops overran the Palatinate, and the Vaudois settled there, dreading not without reason, the soldiers of Louis XIV., retired before them, and retook the road to Switzerland. The Protestant cantons, pitying these poor exiles, tossed from country to country by political storms, settled them once more in their former allotments. Meanwhile, the scenes were shifting rapidly around the expatriated Vaudois, and with eyes uplifted they waited the issue. They saw their protector, William of Orange, mount the throne of England. They saw their powerful enemy, Louis XIV., attacked at once by the emperor and humiliated by the Dutch. They saw their own Prince Victor Amadeus withdraw his soldiers from Savoy, seeing that he needed them to defend Piedmont. It seemed to them that an invisible Hand was opening their path back to their own land. Encouraged by these tokens, they began to arrange a second time for their departure.

The place of appointed rendezvous was a wood on the northern shore of the Leman, near the town of Noyon. For days before they continued to converge in scattered bands, and by stealthy marches, on the selected point. On the decisive evening, the 16th of August, 1689, a general muster took place under cover of the friendly wood of Prangins. Having by solemn prayer commended their enterprise to God, they embarked on the lake, and crossed by star-light. Their means of transport would have been deficient but for a circumstance which threatened at first to obstruct their expedition, but which, in the issue, greatly facilitated it. Curiosity had drawn numbers to this part of the lake, and the boats that brought hither the sightseers furnished more amply the means of escape to the Vaudois.

At this crisis, as on so many previous ones, a distinguished man arose to lead them. Henri Arnaud, whom we see at the head of the 800 fighting men who are setting out for their native possessions, had at first discharged the office of pastor, but the troubles of his nation compelling him to leave the Valleys, he had served in the armies of the Prince of Orange. Of decided piety, ardent patriotism, and of great decision and courage, he presented a beautiful instance of the union of the pastoral and the military character. It is hard to say whether his soldiers listened more reverentially to the exhortations he at times delivered to them from the pulpit, or to the orders he gave them on the field of battle.

Arriving on the south shore of the lake, these 800 Vaudois bent their knees in prayer, and then began their march through a country covered with foes. Before them rose the great snow-clad mountains over which they were to fight their way. Arnaud arranged his little host into three companies—an advanced-guard, a centre, and a rear-guard. Seizing some of the chief men as hostages, they traversed the Valley of the Arve to Sallenches, and emerged from its dangerous passes just as the men of the latter place had completed their preparations for resisting them. Occasional skirmishes awaited them, but mostly their march was unopposed, for the terror of God had fallen upon the inhabitants of Savoy. Holding on their way they climbed the Haut Luce Alp,[2476] and next that of Bon Homme, the neighbouring Alp to Mont Blanc; sinking sometimes to their middle in snow. Steep precipices and treacherous glaciers subjected them to both toil and danger. They were wet through with the rain, which at times fell in torrents. Their provisions were growing scanty, but their supply was recruited by the shepherds of the mountains, who brought them bread and cheese, while their huts served them at night. They renewed their hostages at every stage; sometimes they "caged"—to use their own phrase—a Capuchin monk, and at other times an influential landlord, but all were treated with uniform kindness.

Having crossed the Bon Homme, which divides the basin of the Arve from that of the Isère, they descended on Wednesday, the fifth day of their march, into the valley of the latter stream. They had looked forward to this stage of their journey with great misgivings, for the numerous population of the Val Isère was known to be well armed, and decidedly hostile, and might be expected to oppose their march, but the enemy was "still as a stone" till the people had passed over. They next traversed Mount Iseran, and the yet more formidable Mont Cenis, and finally descended into the Valley of the Dora. It was here, on Saturday, the 24th of August, that they encountered for the first time a considerable body of regular troops.

As they traversed the valley they were met by a peasant, of whom they inquired whether they could have provisions by paying for them. "Come on this way," said the man, in a tone that had a slight touch of triumph in it, "you will find all that you want; they are preparing an excellent supper for you."[2477] They were led into the defile of Salabertrand, where the Col d'Albin closes in upon the stream of the Dora, and before they were aware they found themselves in presence of the French army, whose camp-fires—for night had fallen—illumined far and wide the opposite slope. Retreat was impossible. The French were 2,500 strong, flanked by the garrison of Exiles, and supported by a miscellaneous crowd of armed followers.

Under favour of the darkness, they advanced to the bridge which crossed the Dora, on the opposite bank of which the French were encamped. To the challenge, "Who goes there?" the Vaudois answered, "Friends." The instant reply shouted out was "Kill, kill!" followed by a tremendous fire, which was kept up for a quarter of an hour. It did no harm, however, for Arnaud had bidden his soldiers lie flat on their faces, and permit the deadly shower to pass over them. But now a division of the French appeared in their rear, thus placing them between two fires. Someone in the Vaudois army, seeing that all must be risked, shouted out, "Courage! the bridge is won!" At these words the Vaudois started to their feet, rushed across the bridge sword in hand, and clearing it, they threw themselves with the impetuosity of a whirlwind upon the enemy's entrenchments. Confounded by the suddenness of the attack, the French could only use buttends of their muskets to parry the blows. The fighting lasted two hours, and ended in the total rout of the French. Their leader, the Marquis de Larrey, after a fruitless attempt to rally his soldiers, fled wounded to Briançon, exclaiming, "Is it possible that I have lost the battle and my honour?"

Soon thereafter the moon rose and showed the field of battle to the victors. On it, stretched out in death, lay 600 French soldiers, besides officers; and strewn promiscuously with the fallen, all over the field, were arms, military stores, and provisions. Thus had been suddenly opened an armoury and magazines to men who stood much in need both of weapons and of food. Having amply replenished themselves, they collected what they could not carry away into a heap, and set fire to it. The loud and multifarious noises formed by the explosions of the gunpowder, the sounding of the trumpets, and the shouting of the captains, who, throwing their caps in the air, exclaimed, "Thanks be to the Lord of hosts who hath given us the victory," echoed like the thunder of heaven, and reverberating from hill to hill, formed a most extraordinary and exciting scene, and one that is seldom witnessed amid these usually quiet mountains. This great victory cost the Waldenses only fifteen killed and twelve wounded.

Their fatigue was great, but they feared to halt on the battlefield, and so, rousing those who had already sunk into sleep, they commenced climbing the lofty Mount Sci. The day was breaking as they gained the summit. It was Sunday, and Henri Arnaud, halting till all should assemble, pointed out to them, just as they were becoming visible in the morning light, the mountain-tops of their own land. Welcome sight to their longing eyes! Bathed in the radiance of the rising sun, it seemed to them, as one snowy peak began to burn after another, that the mountains were kindling into joy at the return of their long-absent sons. This army of soldiers resolved itself into a congregation of worshippers, and the summit of Mt. Sci became their church. Kneeling on the mountain-top, the battlefield below them, and the solemn and sacred peaks of the Col du Pis, the Col la Vêchera, and the glorious pyramid of Monte Viso looking down upon them in reverent silence, they humbled themselves before the Eternal, confessing their sins, and giving thanks for their many deliverances. Seldom has worship more sincere or more rapt been offered than that which this day ascended from this congregation of warrior-worshippers gathered under the dome-like vault that rose over them.

Refreshed by the devotions of the Sunday, and exhilarated by the victory of the day before, the heroic band now rushed down to take possession of their inheritance, from which the single Valley of Clusone only parted them. It was three years and a half since they had crossed the Alps, a crowd of exiles, worn to skeletons by sickness and confinement, and now they were returning a marshalled host, victorious over the army of France, and ready to encounter that of Piedmont. They traversed the Clusone, a plain of about two miles in width, watered by the broad, clear, blue-tinted Germagnasca, and bounded by hills, which offer to the eye a succession of terraces, clothed with the richest vines, mingled with the chestnut and the apple-tree. They entered the narrow defile of Pis, where a detachment of Piedmontese soldiers had been posted to guard the pass, but who took flight at the approach of the Vaudois, thus opening to them the gate of one of the grandest of their Valleys, San Martino. On the twelfth day after setting out from the shores of the Leman they crossed the frontier, and stood once more within the limits of their inheritance. When they mustered at Balsiglia, the first Vaudois village which they entered, in the western extremity of San Martino, they found that fatigue, desertion, and battle had reduced their numbers from 800 to 700.

Their first Sunday after their return was passed at the village of Prali. Of all their sanctuaries, the church of Prali alone remained standing; of the others only the ruins were to be seen. They resolved to recommence this day their ancient and scriptural worship. Purging the church of its Popish ornaments, one half of the little army, laying down their arms at the door, entered the edifice, while the other half stood without, the church being too small to contain them all. Henri Arnaud, the soldier-pastor, mounting a table which was placed in the porch, preached to them. They began their worship by chanting the 74th Psalm—"O God, why hast thou cast us off for ever? Why doth thine anger smoke against the sheep of thy pasture?" &c. The preacher then took as his text the 129th Psalm—"Many a time have they afflicted me from my youth, may Israel now say." The wonderful history of his people behind him, so to speak, and the re-conquest of their land before him, we can imagine how thrilling every word of his discourse must have been, and how it must have called up the glorious achievements of their fathers, provoking the generous emulation of their sons. The worship was closed by these 700 warriors chanting in magnificent chorus the psalm from which their leader had preached. So passed their first Sunday in their land.

To many it seemed significant that here the returned exiles should spend their first Sunday, and resume their sanctuary services. They remembered how this same village of Prali had been the scene of a horrible outrage at the time of their exodus. The Pastor of Prali, M. Leidet, a singularly pious man, had been discovered by the soldiers as he was praying under a rock, and being dragged forth, he was first tortured and mutilated, and then hanged; his last words being, "Lord Jesus, receive my spirit." It was surely appropriate, after the silence of three years and a half, during which the rage of the persecutor had forbidden the preaching of the glorious Gospel, that its reopening should take place in the pulpit of the martyr Leidet.

CHAPTER XV
FINAL RE-ESTABLISHMENT IN THEIR VALLEYS

THE Vaudois had entered the land, but they had not yet got possession of it. They were a mere handful; they would have to face the large and well-appointed army of Piedmont, aided by the French. But their great leader to his courage added faith. The "cloud" which had guided them over the great mountains, with their snows and abysses, would cover their camp, and lead them forth to battle, and bring them in with victory. It was not surely that they might die in the land, that they had been able to make so marvellous a march back to it. Full of these courageous hopes, the "seven hundred" now addressed themselves to their great task.

They began to climb the Col Julien, which separates Prali from the fertile and central valley of the Waldenses, that of Lucerna. As they toiled up and were now near the summit of the pass, the Piedmontese soldiers, who had been stationed there, shouted out, "Come on, ye Barbets; we guard the pass, and there are 3,000 of us!" They did come on. To force the entrenchments and put to flight the garrison was the work of a moment. In the evacuated camp the Vaudois found a store of ammunition and provisions, which to them was a most seasonable booty. Descending rapidly the slopes and precipices of the great mountain, they surprised and took the town of Bobbio, which nestles at its foot. Driving out the Popish inhabitants to whom it had been made over, they took possession of their ancient dwellings, and paused a little while to rest after the march and conflict of the previous days. Here their second Sunday was passed, and public worship again celebrated, the congregation chanting their psalm to the clash of arms. On the day following, repairing to the "Rock of Sibaud," where their fathers had pledged their faith to God and to one another, they renewed on the same sacred spot their ancient oath, swearing with uplifted hands to abide steadfastly in the profession of the Gospel, to stand by one another, and never to lay down their arms till they had re-established themselves and their brethren in those Valleys, which they believed had as really been given to them by the God of heaven, as Palestine had been to the Jews.

Their next march was to Villaro, which is situated half-way between Bobbio at the head and La Torre at the entrance of the valley. This town they stormed and took, driving away the new inhabitants. But here their career of conquest was suddenly checked. The next day a strong reinforcement of regular troops coming up, the Vaudois were under the necessity of abandoning Villaro, and falling back on Bobbio.[2478] This patriot army now became parted into two bands, and for many weeks had to wage a sort of guerilla war on the mountains. France on the one side, and Piedmont on the other, poured in soldiers, in the hope of exterminating this handful of warriors. The privations and hardships which they endured were as great as the victories which they won in their daily skirmishes were marvellous. But though always conquering, their ranks were rapidly thinning. What though a hundred of the enemy were slain for one Waldensian who fell? The Piedmontese could recruit their numbers, the Vaudois could not add to theirs. They had now neither ammunition nor provisions, save what they took from their enemies; and, to add to their perplexities, winter was near, which would bury their mountains beneath its snows, and leave them without food or shelter. A council of war was held, and it was ultimately resolved to repair to the Valley of San Martino, and entrench themselves on La Balsiglia.

This brings us to the last heroic stand of the returned exiles. But first let us sketch the natural strength and grandeur of the spot on which that stand was made. The Balsiglia is situated at the western extremity of San Martino, which in point of grandeur yields to few things in the Waldensian Alps. It is some five miles long by about two in width, having as its floor the richest meadowland; and for walls, mountains superbly hung with terraces, overflowing with flower and fruitage, and ramparted atop with splintered cliffs and dark peaks. It is closed at the western extremity by the naked face of a perpendicular mountain, down which the Germagnasca is seen to dash in a flood of silver. The meadows and woods that clothe the bosom of the valley are seamed by a broad line of white, formed by the torrent, the bed of which is strewn with so many rocks that it looks like a continuous river of foam.

Than the clothing of the mountains that form the bounding walls of this valley nothing could be finer. On the right, as one advances up it, rises a succession of terraced vineyards, finely diversified with corn-fields and massy knolls of rock, which rise crowned with cottages or hamlets, looking out from amid their rich embowerings of chestnut and apple-tree. Above this fruit-bearing zone are the grassy uplands, the resort of herdsmen, which in their turn give place to the rocky ridges that rise in wavy and serrated lines, and run off to the higher summits, which recede into the clouds.

On the left the mountain-wall is more steep, but equally rich in its clothing. Swathing its foot is a carpeting of delicious sward. Trees, vast of girth, part, with their over-arching branches, the bright sunlight. Higher up are fields of maize and forests of chestnut; and higher still is seen the rock-loving birch, with its silvery stem and graceful tresses. Along the splintered rocks atop runs a bristling line of firs, forming a mighty *chevaux-de-frise*.

Toward the head of the valley, near the vast perpendicular cliff already mentioned, which shuts it in on the west, is seen a glorious assemblage of mountains. One mighty cone uplifts itself above and behind another mighty cone, till the last and highest buries its top in the rolling masses of cloud, which are seen usually hanging like a canopy above this part of the valley. These noble *aiguilles*, four in number, rise feathery with firs, and remind one of the fretted pinnacles of some colossal cathedral. This is La Balsiglia. It was on the terraces of this mountain that Henri Arnaud, with his patriot-warriors, pitched his camp, amid the dark tempests of winter, and the yet darker tempests of a furious and armed bigotry. The Balsiglia shoots its gigantic pyramids heavenward, as if proudly conscious of having once been the resting-place of the Vaudois ark. It is no castle of man's erecting; it had for its builder the Almighty Architect himself.

It only remains, in order to complete this picture of a spot so famous in the wars of conscience and liberty, to say that behind the Balsiglia on the west rises the lofty Col du Pis. It is rare that this mountain permits to the spectator a view of his full stature, for his dark sides run up and bury themselves in the clouds.

Face to face with the Col du Pis, stands on the other side of the valley, the yet loftier Mont Guinevert, with, most commonly, a veil of cloud around him, as if he too were unwilling to permit to the eye of visitor a sight of his stately proportions. Thus do these two Alps, like twin giants, guard this famous valley.

It was on the lower terrace of this pyramidal mountain, the Balsiglia, that Henri Arnaud—his army, now, alas! reduced to 400—sat down. Viewed from the level of the valley, the peak seems to terminate in a point, but on ascending, the top expands into a level grassy plateau. Steep and smooth as escarped fortress, it is unscalable on every side save that on which a stream rushes past from the mountains. The skill of Arnaud enabled him to add to the natural strength of the Vaudois position, the defences of art. They enclosed themselves within earthen walls and ditches; they erected covered ways; they dug out some four-score cellars in the rock, to hold provisions, and they built huts as temporary barracks. Three springs that gushed out of the rock supplied them with water. They constructed similar entrenchments on each of the three peaks that rose above them, so that if the first were taken they could ascend to the second, and so on to the fourth. On the loftiest summit of the Balsiglia, which commanded the entire valley, they placed a sentinel, to watch the movements of the enemy.

Only three days elapsed till four battalions of the French army arrived, and enclosed the Balsiglia on every side. On the 29th of October, an assault was made on the Vaudois position, which was repulsed with great slaughter of the enemy, and the loss of not one man of the defenders. The snows of early winter had begun to fall, and the French general thought it best to postpone the task of capturing the Balsiglia till spring. Destroying all the corn which the Vaudois had collected and stored in the villages, he began his retreat from San Martino, and, taking laconic farewell of the Waldenses, he bade them have patience till Easter, when he would again pay them a visit.[2479]

All through the winter of 1689–90, the Vaudois remained in their mountain fortress, resting after the marches, battles, and sieges of the previous months, and preparing for the promised return of the French. Where Henri Arnaud had pitched his camp, there had he also raised his altar, and if from that mountain-top was pealed forth the shout of battle, from it ascended also, morning and night, the prayer and the psalm. Besides the daily devotions, Henri Arnaud preached two sermons weekly, one on Sunday and another on Thursday. At stated times he administered the Lord's Supper. Nor was the commissariat overlooked. Foraging parties brought in wine, chestnuts, apples, and other fruits, which the autumn, now far advanced, had fully ripened. A strong detachment made an incursion into the French valleys of Pragelas and Queyras, and returned with salt, butter, some hundred head of sheep, and a few oxen. The enemy, before departing, had destroyed their stock of grain, and as the fields were long since reaped, they despaired of being able to repair their loss. And yet bread to last them all the winter through had been provided, in a way so marvellous as to convince them that He who feeds the fowls of the air was caring for them. Ample magazines of grain lay all around their encampment, although unknown as yet to them. The snow that year began to fall earlier than usual, and it covered up the ripened corn, which the Popish inhabitants had not time to cut when the approach of the Vaudois compelled them to flee. From this unexpected storehouse the garrison drew as they had need. Little did the Popish peasantry, when they sowed the seed in spring, dream that Vaudois hands would reap the harvest.

Corn had been provided for them, and, to Vaudois eyes, provided almost as miraculously as was the manna for the Israelites, but where were they to find the means of grinding it into meal? At almost the foot of the Balsiglia, on the stream of the Germagnasca, is a little mill. The owner, M. Tron-Poulat, three years before, when going forth into exile with his brethren, threw the mill-stone into the river; "for," said he, "it may yet be needed." It was needed now, and search being made for it, it was discovered, drawn out of the stream, and the mill set a-working. There was another and more distant mill at the entrance of the valley, to which the garrison had recourse when the immediate precincts of the Balsiglia were occupied by the enemy, and the nearer mill was not available. Both mills exist to this day, their roofs of brown slate may be seen by the visitor, peering up through the luxuriant foliage of the valley, the wheel motionless, it may be, and the torrent which turned it shooting idly past in a volley of spray.

With the return of spring, the army of France and Piedmont reappeared. The Balsiglia was now completely invested, the combined force amounting to 22,000 in all—10,000 French and 12,000 Piedmontese. The troops were commanded by the celebrated De Catinat, lieutenant-general of the armies of France. The "four hundred" Waldenses looked down from their "camp of rock" on the valley beneath them, and saw it glittering with steel by day, and shining with camp-fires by night. Catinat never doubted that a single day's fighting would enable him to capture the place. That the victory, which he looked upon as already won, might be duly celebrated, he ordered four hundred ropes to be sent along with the army, in order to hang at once the four hundred Waldenses; and he had commanded the inhabitants of Pinerolo to prepare *feux-de-joie* to grace his return from the campaign. The headquarters of the French were at Great Passet—so called in contradistinction to Little Passet, situated a mile lower in the valley. Great Passet counts some thirty roofs, and is placed on an immense ledge of rock that juts out from the foot of Mont Guinevert, some 800 feet above the stream, and right opposite the Balsiglia. On the flanks of this rocky ledge are still to be seen the ruts worn by the cannon and baggage-waggons of the French army. There can be no doubt that these marks are the memorials of the siege, for no other wheeled vehicles ever were in these mountains.[2480]

Having reconnoitred, Catinat ordered the assault (1st May, 1690). Only on that side of Balsiglia, where a stream trickles down from the mountains, and which offers a gradual slope, instead of a wall of rock as everywhere else, could the attack be made with any chance of success. But this point Henri Arnaud had taken care to fortify with strong palisades. Five hundred picked men, supported by seven thousand musketeers, advanced to storm the fortress.[2481] They rushed forward with ardour: they threw themselves upon the palisades; but they found it impossible to tear them down, formed as they were of great trunks fastened by mighty boulders. Massed behind the defence were the Vaudois, the younger men loading the muskets, and the veterans taking steady aim, while the besiegers were falling in dozens at every volley. The assailants beginning to waver, the Waldensians made a fierce sally, sword in hand, and cut in pieces those whom the musket had spared. Of the five hundred picked soldiers only some score lived to rejoin the main body, which had been spectators from the valley of their total rout. Incredible as it may appear, we are nevertheless assured of it as a fact, that not a Vaudois was killed or wounded: not a bullet had touched one of them. The fireworks which Catinat had been so provident as to bid the men of Pinerolo get ready to celebrate his victory, were not needed that night.

Despairing of reducing the fortress by other means, the French now brought up cannon, and it was not till the 14th of May that all was ready, and that the last and grand assault was made. Across the ravine in which the conflict we have just described took place, an immense knoll juts out, at an equal level with the lower entrenchments of the Waldenses. To this rock the cannons were hoisted up to play upon the fortress.[2482] Never before had the sound of artillery shaken the rocks of San Martino. It was the morning of Whit-Sunday, and the Waldenses were preparing to celebrate the Lord's Supper, when the first boom from the enemy's battery broke upon their ear.[2483] All day the cannonading continued, and its dreadful noises re-echoed from rock to rock, and rolled upwards to the summits of the Col du Pis and the Mont Guinevert, were still further heightened by the thousands of musketeers who were stationed all round the Balsiglia. When night closed in the ramparts of the Waldenses were in ruins, and it was seen that it would not be possible longer to maintain the defence. What was to be done? The cannonading had ceased for the moment, but assuredly the dawn would see the attack renewed.

Never before had destruction appeared to impend so inevitably over the Vaudois. To remain where they were was certain death, yet whither could they flee? Behind them rose the unscalable precipices of the Col du Pis, and beneath them lay the valley swarming with foes. If they should wait till the morning broke it would be impossible to pass the enemy without being seen; and even now, although it was night, the numerous camp-fires that blazed beneath them made it almost as bright as day. But the hour of their extremity was the time of God's opportunity. Often before it had been seen to be so, but perhaps never so strikingly as now. While they looked this way and that way, but could discover no escape from the net that enclosed them, the mist began to gather on the summits of the mountains around them. They knew the old mantle that was wont to be cast around their fathers in the hour of peril. It crept lower and yet lower on the great mountains. Now it touched the supreme peak of the Balsiglia.

Will it mock their hopes? Will it only touch, but not cover their mountain camp? Again it is in motion; downward roll its white fleecy billows, and now it hangs in sheltering folds around the war-battered fortress and its handful of heroic defenders. They dared not as yet attempt escape, for still the watch-fires burned brightly in the valley. But it was only for a few minutes longer. The mist kept its downward course, and now all was dark. A Tartarean gloom filled the gorge of San Martino.

At this moment, as the garrison stood mute, pondering whereunto these things would grow, Captain Poulat, a native of these parts, broke silence. He bade them be of good courage, for he knew the paths, and would conduct them past the French and Piedmontese lines, by a track known only to himself. Crawling on their hands and knees, and passing close to the French sentinels, yet hidden from them by the mist, they descended frightful precipices, and made their escape. "He who has not seen such paths," says Arnaud in his *Rentrée Glorieuse*, cannot conceive the danger of them, and will be inclined to consider my account of the march a mere fiction. But it is strictly true; and I must add, the place is so frightful that even some of the Vaudois themselves were terror-struck when they saw by daylight the nature of the spot they had passed in the dark." When the day broke, every eye in the plain below was turned to the Balsiglia. That day the four hundred ropes which Catinat had brought with him were to be put in requisition, and the *feux-de-joie* so long prepared were to be lighted at Pinerolo. What was their amazement to find the Balsiglia abandoned! The Vaudois had escaped and were gone, and might be seen upon the distant mountains, climbing the snows, far out of the reach of their would-be captors. Well might they sing—

"Our soul is escaped as a bird out of the snare of the fowlers.
The snare is broken, and we are escaped."

There followed several days, during which they wandered from hill to hill, or lay hid in woods, suffering great privations, and encountering numerous perils. At last they succeeded in reaching the Pra del Tor. To their amazement and joy, on arriving at this celebrated and hallowed spot, they found deputies from the prince, the Duke of Savoy, waiting them with an overture of peace. The Vaudois were as men that dreamed. An overture of peace! How was this? A coalition, including Germany, Great Britain, Holland, and Spain, had been formed to check the ambition of France, and three days had been given Victor Amadeus to say to which side he would join himself—The Leaguers or Louis XIV. He resolved to break with Louis and take part with the coalition. In this case, to whom could he so well commit the keys of the Alps as to his trusty Vaudois? Hence the overture that met them in the Pra del Tor. Ever ready to rally round the throne of their prince the moment the hand of persecution was withdrawn, the Vaudois closed with the peace offered them. Their towns and lands were restored: their churches were reopened for Protestant worship: their brethren still in prison at Turin were liberated, and the colonists of their countrymen in Germany had passports to return to their homes; and thus, after a dreary interval of three and a half years, the Valleys were again peopled with their ancient race, and resounded with their ancient songs. So closed the famous period of their history, which, in respect of the wonders, we might say the miracles that attended it, we can compare only to the march of the chosen people through the wilderness to the Land of Promise.

CHAPTER XVI
CONDITION OF THE WALDENSES FROM 1690

WITH this second planting of the Vaudois in their Valleys, the period of their great persecutions may be said to have come to an end. Their security was not complete, nor their measure of liberty entire. They were still subject to petty oppressions; enemies were never wanting to whisper things to their prejudice; little parties of Jesuits would from time to time appear in their Valleys, the forerunners, as they commonly found them, of some new and hostile edict; they lived in continual apprehension of having the few privileges which had been conceded to them swept away; and on one occasion they were actually threatened with a second expatriation. They knew, moreover, that Rome, the real author of all their calamities and woes, still meditated their extermination, and that she had entered a formal protest against their rehabilitation, and given the duke distinctly to understand that to be the friend of the Vaudois was to be the enemy of the Pope.[2484] Nevertheless, their condition was tolerable compared with the frightful tempests which had darkened their sky in previous eras.

The Waldenses had everything to begin anew. Their numbers were thinned; they were bowed down by poverty; but they had vast recuperative power; and their brethren in England and Germany hastened to aid them in reorganising their Church, and bringing once more into play that whole civil and ecclesiastical economy which the "exile" had so rudely broken in pieces. William III. of England incorporated a Vaudois regiment at his own expense, which he placed at the service of the duke, and to this regiment it was mainly owing that the duke was not utterly overwhelmed in his wars with his former ally, Louis XIV. At one point of the campaign, when hard pressed, Victor Amadeus had to sue for the protection of the Vaudois, on almost the very spot where the deputies of Gianavello had sued him for peace, but had sued in vain.

In 1692 there were twelve churches in the Valleys; but the people were unable to maintain a pastor to each. They were ground down by military imposts. Moreover, a peremptory demand was made upon them for payment of the arrears of taxes which had accrued in respect of their lands during the three years they had been absent, and when to them there was neither seed-time nor harvest. Anything more extortionate could not be imagined. In their extremity, Mary of England, the consort of William III., granted them a "Royal Subsidy," to provide pastors and schoolmaster, and this grant was increased with the increased number of parishes, till it reached the annual sum of £550. A collection which was made in Great Britain at a subsequent period (1770) permitted an augmentation of the salaries of the pastors. This latter fund bore the name of the "National Subsidy," to distinguish it from the former, the "Royal Subsidy." The States-General of Holland followed in the wake of the English sovereign, and made collections for salaries to schoolmasters, gratuities to superannuated pastors, and for the founding of a Latin school. Nor must we omit to state that the Protestant cantons of Switzerland appropriated bursaries to students from the Valleys at their academies—one at Basle, five at Lausanne, and two at Geneva.[2485]

The policy of the Court of Turin towards the Waldenses changed with the shiftings in the great current of European politics. At one unfavourable moment, when the influence of the Vatican was in the ascendant, Henri Arnaud, who had so gloriously led back the Israel of the Alps to their ancient inheritance, was banished from the Valleys, along with others, his companions in patriotism and virtue, as now in exile. England, through William, sought to draw the hero to her own shore, but Arnaud retired to Schoenberg, where he spent his last years in the humble and most affectionate discharge of the duties of a pastor among his expatriated countrymen, whose steps he guided to the heavenly abodes, as he had done those of their brethren to their earthly land. He died in 1721, at the age of four-score years.

The century passed without any very noticeable event. The spiritual condition of the Vaudois languished. The year 1789 brought with it astounding changes. The French Revolution rung out the knell of the old times, and introduced amidst those earthquake-shocks that convulsed nations, and laid thrones and altars prostrate, a new political age. The Vaudois once again passed under the dominion of France. There followed an enlargement of their civil rights, and an amelioration of their social condition; but, unhappily, with the friendship of France came the poison of its literature, and Voltairianism threatened to inflict more deadly injury to the Church of the Alps than all the persecutions of the previous centuries. At the Restoration the Waldenses were given back to their former sovereign, and with their return to the House of Savoy they returned to their ancient restrictions, though the hand of bloody persecution could no more be stretched out.

The time was now drawing near when this venerable people was to obtain a final emancipation. That great deliverance rose on them, as day rises on the earth, by slow stages. The visit paid them by the apostolic Felix Neff, in 1808, was the first dawning of their new day. With him a breath from heaven, it was felt, had passed over the dry bones. The next stage in their resurrection was the visit of Dr. William Stephen Gilly, in 1828. He cherished, he tells us, the conviction that "this is the spot from which it is likely that the great Sower will again cast his seed, when it shall please him to permit the pure Church of Christ to resume her seat in those Italian States from which Pontifical intrigues have dislodged her."[2486] The result of Dr. Gilly's visit was the erection of a college at La Torre, for the instruction of youth and the training of ministers, and an hospital for the sick; besides awakening great interest on their behalf in England.[2487]

After Dr. Gilly there stood up another to befriend the Waldenses, and prepare them for their coming day of deliverance. The career of General Beckwith is invested with a romance not unlike that which belongs to the life of Ignatius Loyola. Beckwith was a young soldier, and as brave, and chivalrous, and ambitious of glory as Loyola. He had passed unhurt through battle and siege. He fought at Waterloo till the enemy was in full retreat, and the sun was going down. But a flying soldier discharged his musket at a venture, and the leg of the young officer was hopelessly shattered by the bullet. Beckwith, like Loyola, passed months upon a bed of pain, during which he drew forth from his portmanteau his neglected Bible, and began to read and study it. He had lain down, like Loyola, a knight of the sword, and like him he rose up a knight of the Cross, but in a truer sense.

One day in 1827 he paid a visit to Apsley House, and while he waited for the duke, he took up a volume which was lying on the table. It was Dr. Gilly's narrative of his visit to the Waldenses. Beckwith found himself drawn irresistibly to a people with whose wonderful history this book made him acquainted for the first time. From that hour his life was consecrated to them. He lived among them as a father—as a king. He devoted his fortune to them. He built schools, and churches, and parsonages. He provided improved school-books, and suggested better modes of teaching. He strove above all things to quicken their spiritual life. He taught them how to respond to the exigencies of modern times. He specially inculcated upon them that the field was wider than their Valleys; and that they would one day be called to arise and to walk through Italy, in the length of it and in the breadth of it. He was their advocate at the Court of Turin; and when he had obtained for them the possession of a burying-ground outside their Valleys, he exclaimed, "Now they have got infeftment of Piedmont, as the patriarchs did of Canaan, and soon all the land will be theirs."[2488]

But despite the efforts of Gilly and Beckwith, and the growing spirit of toleration, the Waldenses continued to groan under a load of political and social disabilities. They were still a proscribed race.

The once goodly limits of their Valleys had, in later times, been greatly contracted, and like the iron cell in the story, their territory was almost yearly tightening its circle round them. They could not own, or even farm, a foot-breadth of land, or practise any industry, beyond their own boundary. They could not bury their dead save in their Valleys; and when it chanced that any of their people died at Turin or elsewhere, their corpses had to be carried all the way to their own graveyards. They were not permitted to erect a tombstone above their dead, or even to enclose their burial-grounds with a wall. They were shut out from all the learned and liberal professions—they could not be bankers, physicians, or lawyers. No avocation was left them but that of tending their herds and pruning their vines. When any of them emigrated to Turin, or other Piedmontese town, they were not permitted to be anything but domestic servants. There was no printing-press in their Valleys—they were forbidden to have one; and the few books they possessed, mostly Bibles, catechisms, and hymn-books, were printed abroad, chiefly in Great Britain; and when they arrived at La Torre, the Moderator had to sign before the Reviser-in-Chief an engagement that not one of these books should be sold, or even lent, to a Roman Catholic.[2489]

They were forbidden to evangelise or make converts. But though fettered on the one side they were not equally protected on the other, for the priests had full liberty to enter their Valleys and proselytise; and if a boy of twelve years or a girl of ten professed their willingness to enter the Roman Church, they were to be taken from their parents, that they might with more freedom carry out their intention. They could not marry save among their own people. They could not erect a sanctuary save on the soil of their own territory. They could take no degree at any of the colleges of Piedmont. In short, the duties, rights, and privileges that constitute *life* they were denied. They were reduced as nearly as was practicable to simple existence, with this one great exception—which was granted them not as a right, but as a favour—namely, the liberty of Protestant worship within their territorial limits.

The Revolution of 1848, with trumpet-peal, sounded the overthrow of all these restrictions. They fell in one day. The final end of Providence in preserving that people during long centuries of fearful persecutions now began to be seen. The Waldensian Church became the door by which freedom of conscience entered Italy. When the hour came for framing a new constitution for Piedmont, it was found desirable to give standing-room in that constitution to the Waldenses, and this necessitated the introduction into the edict of the great principle of freedom of worship as a right. The Waldenses had contended for that principle for ages—they had maintained and vindicated it by their sufferings and martyrdoms; and therefore they were necessitated to demand, and the Piedmontese Government to grant, this great principle. It was the only one of the many new constitutions framed for Italy at that same time in which freedom of conscience was enacted. Nor would it have found a place in the Piedmontese constitution, but for the circumstance that here were the Waldenses, and that their great distinctive principle demanded legal recognition, otherwise they would remain outside the constitution. The Vaudois alone had fought the battle, but all their countrymen shared with them the fruits of the great victory. When the news of the Statuto of Carlo Alberto reached La Torre there were greetings on the streets, psalms in the churches, and blazing bonfires at night on the crest of the snowy Alps.

At the door of her Valleys, with lamp in hand, its oil unspent and its light unextinguished, is seen, at the era of 1848, the Church of the Alps, prepared to obey the summons of her heavenly King, who has passed by in earthquake and whirlwind, casting down the thrones that of old oppressed her, and opening the doors of her ancient prison. She is now to go forth and be "The Light of all Italy,"[2490] as Dr. Gilly, twenty years before, had foretold she would at no distant day become. Happily not all Italy as yet, but only Piedmont, was opened to her. She addressed herself with zeal to the work of erecting churches and forming congregations in Turin and other towns of Piedmont. Long a stranger to evangelistic work, the Vaudois Church had time and opportunity thus given her to acquire the mental courage and practical habits needed in the novel circumstances in which she was now placed. She prepared evangelists, collected funds, organised colleges and congregations, and in various other ways perfected her machinery in anticipation of the wider field that Providence was about to open to her.

It is now the year 1859, and the drama which had stood still since 1849 begins once more to advance. In that year France declared war against the Austrian occupation of the Italian peninsula. The tempest of battle passes from the banks of the Po to those of the Adige, along the plain of Lombardy, rapid, terrible, and decisive as the thunder-cloud of the Alps, and the Tedeschi retreat before the victorious arms of the French. The blood of the three great battles of the campaign was scarcely dry before Austrian Lombardy, Modena, Parma, Tuscany, and part of the Pontifical States had annexed themselves to Piedmont, and their inhabitants had become fellow-citizens of the Waldenses. With scarcely a pause there followed the brilliant campaign of Garibaldi in Sicily and Naples, and these rich and ample territories were also added to the kingdom of the patriotic Victor Emmanuel. We now behold the whole of Italy—one little spot excepted, the greatly diminished "States of the Church"—comprehended in the Kingdom of Piedmont, and brought under the operation of that constitution which contained in its bosom the beneficent principle of freedom of conscience. The whole of Italy, from the Alps to Etna, with the exception already stated, now became the field of the Waldensian Church. Nor was this the end of the drama. Another ten years pass away: France again sends forth her armies to battle, believing that she can command victory as aforetime. The result of the brief but terrible campaign of 1870, in which the French Empire disappeared and the German uprose, was the opening of the gates of Rome. And let us mark—for in the little incident we hear the voice of ten centuries—in the first rank of the soldiers whose cannon had burst open the old gates, there enters a Vaudois colporteur with a bundle of Bibles. The Waldenses now kindle their lamp at Rome, and the purpose of the ages stands revealed!

Who can fail to see in this drama, advancing so regularly and majestically, that it is the Divine Mind that arranges, and the Divine Hand that executes? Before this Power it becomes us to bow down, giving thanks that he does his will, nor once turns aside for the errors of those that would aid or the strivings of those that would oppose his plan; and, by steps unfathomably wise and sublimely grand, carries onward to their full accomplishment his infinitely beneficent purposes.

The History of Protestantism

Book Seventeenth
PROTESTANTISM IN FRANCE FROM DEATH OF FRANCIS I. (1547) TO EDICT OF NANTES (1598)

CHAPTER I
HENRY II. AND PARTIES IN FRANCE

WE have rapidly traced the line of Waldensian story from those early ages when the assembled barbes are seen keeping watch around their lamp in the Pra del Tor, with the silent silvery peaks looking down upon them, to those recent days when the Vaudois carried that lamp to Rome and set it in the city of Pius IX. Our desire to pursue their conflicts and martyrdoms till their grand issues to Italy and the world had been reached has carried us into modern times. We shall return, and place ourselves once more in the age of Francis I.

We resume our history at the death-bed of that monarch. Francis died March 31st, 1547, at the age of fifty-two, "of that shameful distemper," says the Abbé Millot, "which is brought on by debauchery, and which had been imported with the gold of America."[2491] The character of this sovereign was adorned by some fine qualities, but his reign was disgraced by many great errors. It is impossible to withhold from him the praise of a generous disposition, a cultivated taste, and a chivalrous bearing; but it is equally impossible to vindicate him from the charge of rashness in his enterprises, negligence in his affairs, fickleness in his conduct, and excess in his pleasures. He lavished his patronage upon the scholars of the Renaissance, but he had nothing but stakes wherewith to reward the disciples of Protestantism. He built Fontainebleau, and began the Louvre. And now, after all his great projects for adorning his court with learned men, embellishing his capital with gorgeous fabrics, and strengthening his throne by political alliances, there remains to him only "darkness and the worm."

Let us enter the royal closet, and mark the setting of that sun which had shed such a brilliance during his course. Around the bed upon which Francis I. lies dying is gathered a clamorous crowd of priests, courtiers, and courtesans,[2492] who watch his last moments with decent but impatient respect, ready, the instant he has breathed his last, to turn round and bow the knee to the rising sun. Let us press through the throng and observe the monarch. His face is haggard. He groans deeply, as if he were suffering in soul. His starts are sudden and violent. There flits at times across his face a dark shadow, as if some horrible sight, afflicting him with unutterable woe, were disclosed to him; and a quick tremor at these moments runs through all his frame. He calls his attendants about him and, mustering all the strength left him, he protests that it is not he who is to blame, inasmuch as his orders were exceeded. What orders? we ask; and what deed is it the memory of which so burdens and terrifies the dying monarch?

We must leave the couch of Francis while we narrate one of the greatest of the crimes that blackened his reign. The scene of the tragedy which projected such dismal shadows around the death-bed of the king was laid in Provence. In ancient times Provence was comparatively a desert. Its somewhat infertile soil was but thinly peopled, and but indifferently tilled and planted. It lay strewn all over with great boulders, as if here the giants had warred, or some volcanic explosion had rained a shower of stones upon it. The Vaudois who inhabited the high-lying valleys of the Piedmontese Alps, cast their eyes upon this more happily situated region, and began to desire it as a residence. Here, said they, is a fine champaign country, waiting for occupants; let us go over and possess it. They crossed the mountains, they cleared the land of rocks, they sowed it with wheat, they planted it with the vine, and soon there was seen a smiling garden, where before a desert of swamps, and great stones, and wild herbage had spread out its neglected bosom to be baked by the summer's sun, and frozen by the winter's winds. "An estate which before their establishment hardly paid four crowns as rental, now produced from three to four hundred."[2493] The successive generations of these settlers flourished here during a period of three hundred years, protected by their landlords, whose revenues they had prodigiously enriched, loved by their neighbours, and loyal to their king.

When the Reformation arose, this people sent delegates—as we have related in the previous book—to visit the Churches of Switzerland and Germany, and ascertain how far they agreed with, and how far they differed from, themselves. The report brought back by the delegates satisfied them that the Vaudois faith and the Protestant doctrine were the same; that both had been drawn from the one infallible fountain of truth; and that, in short, the Protestants were Vaudois, and the Vaudois were Protestants. This was enough. The priests, who so anxiously guarded their territory against the entrance of Lutheranism, saw with astonishment and indignation a powerful body of Protestants already in possession. They resolved that the heresy should be swept from off the soil of France as speedily as it had arisen. On the 18th of November, 1540, the Parliament of Aix passed an *arrêt* to the following effect:— "Seventeen inhabitants of Mérindol shall be burnt to death" (they were all the heads of families in that place); "their wives, children, relatives, and families shall be brought in trial, and if they cannot be laid hold on, they shall be banished the kingdom for life. The houses in Mérindol shall be burned and razed to the ground, the woods cut down, the fruit-trees torn up, and the place rendered uninhabitable, so that none may be built there."[2494]

The president of the Parliament of Aix, a humane man, had influence with the king to stay the execution of this horrible sentence. But in 1545 he was succeeded by Baron d'Oppède, a cruel, intolerant, bloodthirsty man, and entirely at the devotion of Cardinal Tournon—a man, says Abbé Millot, "of greater zeal than humanity, who principally enforced the execution of this barbarous *arrêt*.[2495] Francis I. offered them pardon if within three months they should enter the pale of the Roman Church. They disdained to buy their lives by apostacy; and now the sword, which had hung for five years above their heads, fell with crushing force. A Romanist pen shall tell the sequel:—

"Twenty-two towns or villages were burned or sacked, with an inhumanity of which the history of the most barbarous people hardly presents examples. The unfortunate inhabitants, surprised during the night, and pursued from rock to rock by the light of the fires which consumed their dwellings, frequently escaped one snare only to fall into another; the pitiful cries of the old men, the women, and the children, far from softening the hearts of the soldiers, mad with rage like their leaders, only set them on following the fugitives, and pointed out the places whither to direct their fury. Voluntary surrender did not exempt the men from execution, nor the women from excesses of brutality which made Nature blush. It was forbidden, under pain of death, to afford them any refuge. At Cabrières, one of the principal towns of that canton, they murdered more than seven hundred men in cold blood; and the women, who had remained in their houses, were shut up in a barn filled with straw, to which they set fire; those who attempted to escape by the window were driven back by swords and pikes. Finally, according to the tenor of the sentence, the houses were razed, the woods cut down, the fruit-trees pulled up, and in a short time this country, so fertile and so populous, became uncultivated and uninhabited."[2496]

Thus did the red sword and the blazing torch purge Provence. We cast our eyes over the purified land, but, alas! we are unable to recognise it. Is this the land which but a few days ago was golden with the yellow grain, and purple with the blushing grape; at whose cottage doors played happy children; and from whose meadows and mountain-sides, borne on the breeze, came the bleating of flocks and herds? Now, alas! its bosom is scarred and blackened by smouldering ruins, its mountain torrents are tinged with blood, and its sky is thick with the black smoke of its burning woods and cities.

We return to the closet of the dying monarch. Francis is still protesting that the deed is not his, and that too zealous execution exceeded his orders. Nevertheless he cannot banish, we say not from his memory, but from his very sight, the awful tragedy enacted on the plains of Provence. Shrieks of horror, wailings of woe, and cries for help seem to resound through his chamber. Have his ministers and courtiers no word of comfort wherewith to assuage his terrors, and fortify him in the prospect of that awful Bar to which he is hastening with the passing hours? They urged him to sanction the crime, but they leave him to bear the burden of it alone. He summons his son, who is so soon to mount his throne, to his bedside, and charges him with his last breath to execute vengeance on those who had shed this blood.[2497] With this slight reparation the unhappy king goes his dark road, the smoking and blood-sprinkled Provence behind him, the great Judgment-seat before him.

Having breathed his last, the king lay in state, preparatory to his being laid in the royal vaults at St. Dénis. Two of his sons who had pre-deceased him—Francis and Charles—were kept unburied till now, and their corpses accompanied that of their father to the grave. Of the king's lying-in-state, the following very curious account is given us by Sleidan:—

"For some days his effigies, in most rich apparel, with his crown, sceptre, and other regal ornaments, lay upon a bed of state, and at certain hours dinner and supper were served up before it, with the very same solemnity as was commonly performed when he was alive. When the regal ornaments were taken off, they clothed the effigies in mourning; and eight-and-forty Mendicant friars were always present, who continually sung masses and dirges for the soul departed. About the corpse were placed fourteen great wax tapers, and over against it two altars, on which from daylight to noon masses were said, besides what were said in an adjoining chapel, also full of tapers and other lights. Four-and-twenty monks, with tapers in their hands, were ranked about the hearse wherein the corpse was carried, and before it marched fifty more men in mourning, every one with a taper in his hand. Amongst other nobles, there were eleven cardinals present."

Henry II. now mounted the throne of France. At the moment of his accession all seemed to promise a continuance of that prosperity and splendour which had signalised the reign of his father. The kingdom enjoyed peace, the finances were flourishing, the army was brave and well-affected to the throne; and all men accepted these as auguries of a prosperous reign. This, however, was but a brief gleam before the black night. France had missed the true path.

Henry had worn the crown for only a short while when the clouds began to gather, and that night to descend which is only now beginning to pass away from France. His father had early initiated him into the secrets of governing, but Henry loved not the business. The young king sighed to get away from the council-chamber to the gay tournament, where mailed and plumed warriors pursued, amid applauding spectators, the mimic game of war. What good would this princedom do him if it brought him not pleasure? At his court there lacked not persons, ambitious and supple, who studied to flatter his vanity and gratify his humours. To lead the king was to govern France, and to govern France was to grasp boundless riches and vast power. It was under this feeble king that those factions arose, whose strivings so powerfully influenced the fate of Protestantism in that great kingdom, and opened the door for so many calamities to the nation. Four parties were now formed at court, and we must pause here to describe them, otherwise much that is to follow would be scarcely intelligible. In the passions and ambitions of these parties, we unveil the springs of those civil wars which for more than a century deluged France with blood.

At the head of the first party was Anne de Montmorency, High Constable of France. Claiming descent from a family which had been one of the first to be baptised into the Christian faith, he assumed the glorious title of *First Christian* and Premier Baron[2498] of France. He possessed great strength of will, and whatever end he proposed to himself he pursued, without much caring whom he trod down in his way to it. He had the misfortune on one occasion to give advice to Francis I. which did not prosper, and this, together with his headstrongness, made that monarch in his latter days banish him from the court. When Francis was dying he summoned his son Henry to his bedside, and earnestly counselled him never to recall Montmorency, fearing that the obstinacy and pride which even he had with difficulty repressed, the weaker hands to which he was now bequeathing his crown[2499] would be unequal to the task of curbing.

No sooner had Henry assumed the reins of government than he recalled the Constable. Montmorency's recall did not help to make him a meeker man. He strode back to court with brow more elate, and an air more befitting one who had come to possess a throne than to serve before it. The Constable was beyond measure devout, as became the *first Christian* in France. Never did he eat flesh on forbidden days; and never did morning dawn or evening fall but his beads were duly told. It is true he sometimes stopped suddenly in the middle of his chaplet to issue orders to his servants to hang up this or the other Huguenot, or to set fire to the corn-field or plantation of some neighbour of his who was his enemy; but that was the work of a minute only, and the Constable was back again with freshened zeal to his Pater-nosters and his Ave-Marias. It became a proverb, says Brantôme, "God keep us from the Constable's beads."[2500] These singularities by no means lessened his reputation for piety, for the age hardly placed acts of religion and acts of mercy in the same category. Austere, sagacious, and resolute, he constrained the awe if not the love of the king, and as a consequence his heavy hand was felt in every part of the kingdom.

The second party was that of the Guises. The dominancy of that family in France marks one of the darkest eras of the nation. The House of Lorraine, from which the Lords of Guise are descended, derived its original from Godfrey Bullen, King of Jerusalem, and on the mother's side from a daughter of Charlemagne. Anthony, flourishing in wealth and powerful in possessions, was Duke of Lorraine; Claude, a younger brother, crossed the frontier in 1513, staff in hand, attended by but one servant, to seek his fortunes in France. He ultimately became Duke of Guise. This man had six sons, to all of whom wealth seemed to come at their wish. Francis I., perceiving the ambition of these men, warned his son to keep them at a distance.[2501] But the young king, despising the warning, recalled Francis de Lorraine as he had done the Constable Montmorency, and the power of the Guises continued to grow, till at last they became the scourge of the country in which they had firmly rooted themselves, and the terror of the throne which they aspired to mount.

The two brothers, Francis and Charles, stood at the head of the family, and figured at the court. Francis, now in the flower of his age, was sprightly and daring; Charles was crafty, but timid; Laval says of him that he was "the cowardliest of all men." The qualities common to both brothers, and possessed by each in inordinate degree, were cruelty and ambition. Rivals they never could become, for though their ambitions were the same, their spheres lay apart, Francis having chosen the profession of arms, and Charles the Church. This division of pursuits doubled their strength, for what the craft of the one plotted, the sword of the other executed. They were the acknowledged heads of the Roman Catholic party. "But for the Guises," says Mezeray, "the new religion would perhaps have become dominant in France."

The third party at the court of France was that of Diana of Poictiers. This woman was the daughter of John of Poictiers, Lord of St. Valier, and had been the wife of the Seneschal of Normandy. She was twenty years older than the king, but this disparity of age did not hinder her from becoming mistress of his heart. The populace could not account for the king's affection for her, save by ascribing it to the philtres which she made him drink. A more likely cause was her brilliant wit and sprightly manners, added to her beauty, once dazzling, and not yet wholly faded. But her greed was enormous. The people cursed her as the cause of the taxes that were grinding them into poverty; the nobility hated her for her insulting airs; but access there was none to the king, save through the good graces of Diana of Poictiers, whom the king created Duchess of Valentinois. The title by embellishing made only the more conspicuous the infamy of her relation to the man who had bestowed it. The Constable on the one side, and the Guises on the other, sought to buttress their own power by paying court to Diana.[2502] To such a woman the holy doctrine of Protestantism could not be other than offensive; in truth, she very thoroughly hated all of the religion, and much of the righteous blood shed in the reign of Henry II. is to be laid at the door of the lewd, greedy, and cruel Diana of Poictiers.

The fourth and least powerful faction was that of the Marshal de St. André. He was as brave and valiant as he was witty and polite; but he was drowned in debt. Though a soldier he raised himself not by his valour, but by court intrigues; "under a specious pretence for the king's service he hid a boundless ambition, and an unruly avarice," said his Romanist friends, "and was more eager after the forfeited estates than after the overthrow of the rebels and Huguenots."[2503] Neither court nor country was likely to be quiet in which such a man figured.

To these four parties we may add a fifth, that of Catherine de Medici, the wife of Henry. Of deeper passions but greater self-control than many of those around her, Catherine meanwhile was "biding her time." There were powers in this woman which had not yet disclosed themselves, perhaps not even to herself; but when her husband died, and the mistress no longer divided with the wife the ascendancy over the royal mind, then the hour of revelation came, and it was seen what consummate guile, what lust of power, what love of blood and revenge had slumbered in her dark Italian soul. As one after another of her imbecile sons—each more imbecile than he who had preceded him—mounted the throne, the mother stood up in a lofty and yet loftier measure of truculence and ambition. As yet, however, her cue was not to form a party of her own, but to maintain the poise among the other factions, that by weakening all of them she might strengthen herself.

Such were the parties that divided the court of Henry II. Thrice miserable monarch! without one man of real honour and sterling patriotism in whom to confide. And not less miserable courtiers! They made a brave show, no doubt, living in gilded saloons, wearing sumptuous raiment, and feasting at luxuriant tables, but their hearts all the while are torn with envy, or tortured with fear, lest this gay life of theirs should come to a sudden end by the stiletto or the poison-cup. "Two great sins," says an old historian, "crept into France under this prince's reign—atheism and magic."

CHAPTER II
HENRY II. AND HIS PERSECUTIONS

HENRY II walked in the ways of his father, Francis, who first made France to sin by beginning a policy of persecution. To the force of paternal example was added, in the case of Henry, the influence of the maxims continually poured into his ear by Montmorency, Guise, and Diana of Poictiers. These councillors inspired him with a terror of Protestantism as pre-eminently the enemy of monarchs and the source of all disorders in States; and they assured him that should the Huguenots prevail they would trample his throne into the dust, and lay France at the feet of atheists and revolutionists. The first and most sacred of duties, they said, was to uphold the old religion. To cut off its enemies was the most acceptable atonement a prince could make to Heaven. With such schooling, is it any wonder that the deplorable work of burning heretics, begun by Francis, went on under Henry; and that the more the king multiplied his profligacies, the greater his zeal in kindling the fires by which he thought he was making atonement for them?[2504]

The historians of the time record a sad story, which unhappily is not a solitary instance of the bigotry of the age, and the vengeance that was beginning to animate France against all who favoured Protestantism. It affectingly displays the heartless frivolity and wanton cruelty—two qualities never far apart—which characterised the French court. The coronation of the queen, Catherine de Medici, was approaching, and Henry, who did his part so ill as a husband in other respects, resolved to acquit himself with credit in this. He wished to make the coronation fêtes of more than ordinary splendour; and in order to this he resolved to introduce what would form a new feature in these rejoicings, and give variety and piquancy to them, namely, the burning piles of four Huguenots. Four victims were selected, and one of these was a poor tailor, who, besides having eaten flesh on a day on which its use was forbidden, had given other proofs of being not strictly orthodox. He was to form, of course, one of the coronation torches; but to burn him was not enough. It occurred to the Cardinal of Lorraine that a little amusement might be extracted from the man. The cardinal pictured to himself the confusion that would overwhelm the poor tailor, were he to be interrogated before the king, and how mightily the court would be diverted by the incoherence of his replies. He was summoned before Henry, but the matter turned out not altogether as the Churchman had reckoned it would. The promise was fulfilled to the confessor, "When ye shall be brought before kings and rulers for my sake and the Gospel's, it shall be given you in that hour what ye shall speak." So far from being abashed, the tailor maintained perfect composure in the royal presence, and replied so pertinently to all interrogatories and objections put by the Bishop of Maçon, that it was the king and the courtiers who were disconcerted. Diana of Poictiers—whose wit was still fresh, if her beauty had faded—stepped boldly forward, in the hope of rescuing the courtiers from their embarrassment; but, as old Crespin says, "the tailor cut her cloth otherwise than she expected; for he, not being able to endure such unmeasured arrogance in her whom he knew to be the cause of these cruel persecutions, said to her, 'Be satisfied, Madam, with having infected France, without mingling your venom and filth in a matter altogether holy and sacred, as is the religion and truth of our Lord Jesus Christ.'"[2505] The king took the words as an affront, and ordered the man to be reserved for the stake. When the day of execution came (14th July, 1549), the king bade a window overlooking the pile be prepared, that thence he might see the man, who had had the audacity to insult his favourite, slowly consuming in the fire. Both parties had now taken their places, the tailor burning at the stake, the king reposing luxuriously at the window, and Diana of Poictiers seated in haughty triumph by his side. The martyr looked up to the window where the king was seated, and fixed his eye on Henry. From the midst of the flames that eye looked forth with calm, steady gaze upon the king. They eye of the monarch quailed before that of the burning man. He turned away to avoid it, but again his glance wandered back to the stake. The flames were still blazing around the martyr; his limbs were dropping off, his face was growing fearfully livid, but his eye, unchanged, was still looking at the king; and the king felt as if, with Medusa-power, it was changing him into stone.

The execution was at an end: not so the terror of the king. The tragedy of the day was reacted in the dreams of the night. The terrible apparition rose before Henry in his sleep. There again was the blazing pile, there was the martyr burning in the fire, and there was the eye looking forth upon him from the midst of the flames. For several successive nights was the king scared by this terrible vision. He resolved, nay, he even took an oath, that never again would he be witness to the burning of a heretic. It had been still better had he given orders that never again should these horrible executions be renewed.

So far, however, was the persecution from being relaxed, that its rigour was greatly increased. Piles were erected at Orleans, at Poictiers, at Bordeaux, at Nantes—in short, in all the chief cities of the kingdom. These cruel proceedings, however, so far from arresting the progress of the Reformed opinions, only served to increase the number of their professors. Men of rank in the State, and of dignity in the Church, now began, despite the disfavour in which all of the "religion" were held at court, to enrol themselves in the Protestant army. But the Gospel in France was destined to owe more to men of humble faith than to the possessors of rank, however lofty. We have mentioned Châtelain, Bishop of Mâçon, who disputed with the poor tailor before Henry II. As Beza remarks, one thing only did he lack, even grace, to make him one of the most brilliant characters and most illustrious professors of the Gospel in France. Lowly born, Châtelain had raised himself by his great talents and beautiful character. He sat daily at the table of Francis I., among the scholars and wise men whom the king loved to hear discourse. To the accomplishments of foreign travel he added the charms of an elegant latinity. He favoured the new opinions, and undertook the defence of Robert Stephens, the king's printer, when the Sorbonne attacked him for his version of the Bible.[2507] These acquirements and gifts procured his being made Bishop of Mâçon. But the mitre would seemed to have cooled his zeal for the Reformation, and in the reign of Henry II. we find him persecuting the faith he had once defended. Soon after his encounter with the tailor he was promoted to the See of Orleans, and he set out to take possession of his new bishopric. Arriving at a monastery in the neighbourhood of Orleans, he halted there, intending to make his entry into the city on the morrow. The Fathers persuaded him to preach; and, as Beza remarks, to see a bishop in a pulpit was so great a wonder in those days, that the sight attracted an immense crowd. As the bishop was thundering against heretics, he was struck with a sudden and violent illness, and had to be carried out of the pulpit. He died the following night.[2508] At the very gates of his episcopal city, on the very steps of his episcopal throne, he encountered sudden arrest, and gave up the ghost.

Five days thereafter (9th July, 1550), Paris was lighted up with numerous piles. Of these martyrs, who laid gloriously with their blood the foundations of the French Protestant Church, we must not omit the names of Leonard Galimar, of Vendôme, and Florent Venot, of Sedan. The latter endured incredible torments, for no less a period than four years, in the successive prisons into which he was thrown. His sufferings culminated when he was brought to Paris. He was there kept for six weeks in a hole where he could neither lie, nor stand upright, nor move about, and the odour of which was beyond measure foul and poisonous, being filled with all manner of abominable filth. His keepers said they had never known any one inhabit that dreadful place for more than fifteen days, without losing either life or reason. But Venot surmounted all these sufferings with a most admirable courage. Being burned alive in the Place Maubert, he ceased not at the stake to sing and magnify the Saviour, till his tongue was cut out, and even then he continued to testify his joy by signs.[2509]

In the following year (1551) a quarrel broke out between Henry and Pope Julius III., the cause being those fruitful sources of strife, the Duchies of Parma and Placentia. The king showed his displeasure by forbidding his subjects to send money to Rome, and by protesting against the Council of Trent, the Fathers having returned for the second time to that town. But this contention between the king and the Pope only tended to quicken the flames of persecution. Henry wished to make it clear to his subjects that it was against the Pope in his temporal and not his spiritual character that he had girded on the sword; that if he was warring against the Prince of the Roman States, his zeal had not cooled for the Holy See; and that if Julius the monarch was wicked, and might be resisted, Julius the Pope was none the less entitled to the obedience of all Christians.[2510]

To teach the Protestants, as Maimbourg observes, that they must not take advantage of these quarrels to vent their heresies, there was published at this time (27th June) the famous Edict of Chateaubriand, so called from the place where it was given. By this law, all former severities were re-enacted; the cognisance of the crime of heresy was given to the secular power; informers were rewarded with the fourth part of the forfeited goods; the possessions and estates of all those who had fled to Geneva were confiscated to the king; and no one was to hold any office under the crown, or teach any science, who could not produce a certificate of being a good Romanist.[2511] This policy has at all times been pursued by the monarchs of France when they quarrelled with the Pope. It behoved them, they felt, all the more that they had incurred suspicion, to vindicate the purity of their orthodoxy, and their claim to the proud title of "the Eldest Son of the Church."

Maurice, Elector of Saxony, was at this time prosecuting his victorious campaign against Charles V. The relations which the King of France had contracted with the Protestant princes, and which enabled him to make an expedition into Lorraine, and to annex Metz and other cities to his crown, moderated for a short while the rigours of persecution. But the Peace of Passau (1552), which ratified the liberties of the Protestants in Germany, rekindled the fires in France. "Henry having no more measures to observe with the Protestant princes," says Laval, "nothing was to be seen in his kingdom but fires kindled throughout all the provinces against the poor Reformed."[2512] Vast numbers were executed in this and the following year. It was now that the gag was brought into use for the first time. It had been invented on purpose to prevent the martyrs addressing the people at the stake, or singing psalms to solace themselves when on their way to the pile. "The first who suffered it," says Laval, "was Nicholas Noil, a book-hawker, who was executed at Paris in the most barbarous manner."[2513]

The scene of martyrdom was in those days at times the scene of conversion. Of this, the following incident is a proof. Simon Laloe, of Soisson, was offering up his life at Dijon. As he stood at the stake, and while the faggots were being kindled, he delivered an earnest prayer for the conversion of his persecutors. The executioner, Jacques Sylvester, was so affected that his tears never ceased to flow all the time he was doing his office. He had heard no one before speak of God, or of the Gospel, but he could not rest till he was instructed in the Scriptures. Having received the truth, he retired to Geneva, where he died a member of the Reformed Church.[2514] The same stake that gave death to the one, gave life to the other.

The insatiable avarice of Diana of Poictiers, to whom the king had gifted the forfeited estates of the Reformed, not less than zeal for Romanism, occasioned every day new executions. The truth continued notwithstanding to spread. "When the plague," says Maimbourg, "attacks a great city, it matters little what effort is made to arrest it. It enters every door; it traverses every street; it invades every quarter, and pursues its course till the whole community have been enveloped in its ravages: so did this dangerous sect spread through France. Every day it made new progress, despite the edicts with which it was assailed, and the dreadful executions to which so many of its members were consigned."[2515] It was in the midst of this persecution that the first congregation of the Reformed Church in France were settled with pastors, and began to be governed by a regular discipline.

The first Church to be thus constituted was in Paris; "where," says Laval, "the fires never went out." At that time the disciples of the Gospel were wont to meet in the house of M. de la Ferrière, a wealthy gentleman of Maine, who had come to reside in the capital. M. de la Ferrière had a child whom he wished to have baptised, and as he could not present him to the priests for that purpose, nor undertake a journey to Geneva, he urged the Christians, who were wont to assemble in his house, to elect one of themselves to the office of pastor, with power to administer the Sacraments. They were at last prevailed upon, and, after prayer and fasting, their choice fell on Jean Maçon de la Rivière. He was the son of the king's attorney at Angers, a rich man, but a bitter enemy of Protestantism. He was so offended at his son for embracing the Reformed faith, that he would have given him up to the judges, had he not fled to Paris. The sacrifice which M. de la Rivière had made to preserve the purity of his conscience, fixed the eyes of the little flock upon him. In him we behold the first pastor of the Reformed Church of France,[2516] elected forty years after Lefevre had first opened the door for the entrance of the Protestant doctrines. "They chose likewise," says Laval, speaking of this little flock, "some amongst them to be elders and deacons, and made such other regulations for the government of their Church as the times would allow. Such were the first beginnings of the Church of Paris in the month of September, 1555, which increased daily during the war of Henry II. with Charles V."[2517]

If France blazed with funeral piles, it was day by day more widely illuminated with the splendour of truth. This gave infinite vexation and torment to the friends of Rome, who wearied themselves to devise new methods for arresting the progress of the Gospel. Loud accusations and reproaches passed between the courts of jurisdiction for not showing greater zeal in executing the edicts against heresy. The cognisance of that crime was committed sometimes to the royal and sometimes to the ecclesiastical judges, and sometimes parted between them. The mutual recriminations still continued. A crime above all crimes, it was said, was leniently treated by those whose duty it was to pursue it without mercy. At last, in the hope of attaining the requisite vigour, the Cardinal of Lorraine stripped the Parliament and the civil judge of the right of hearing such causes, and transferred it to the bishops, leaving nothing to the others but the mere execution of the sentence against the condemned. This arrangement the cardinal thought to perfect by establishing the Inquisition in France on the Spanish model. In this, however, he did not succeed, the Parliament having refused its consent thereto.[2518]

The calamities that befell the kingdom were a cover to the evangelisation. Henry II. had agreed on a truce with the Emperor Charles for five years. It did not, however, suit the Pope that the truce should be kept. Paul IV. sent his legate to France to dispense Henry from his oath, and induce him to violate the peace. The flames of war were rekindled, but the French arms were disgraced. The battle of St. Quentin was a fatal blow to France, and the Duke of Guise was recalled from Italy to retrieve it. He recovered in the Low Countries the reputation which he had lost in Sicily;[2519] but even this tended in the issue to the weakening of France. The duke's influence at court was now predominant, and the intrigues which his great rival, Montmorency, set on foot to supplant him, led to the Treaty of Cateau Cambrésis (1559), by which France lost 198 strongholds,[2520] besides the deepening of the jealousies and rivalships between the House of Lorraine and that of the Constable, which so nearly proved the ruin of France. One main inducement with Henry to conclude this treaty with Philip of Spain, was that it left him free to prosecute the design formed by the Cardinal of Lorraine and the Bishop of Arras for the utter extirpation of the Reformed. In fact, the treaty contained a secret clause binding both monarchs to combine their power for the utter extirpation of heresy in their dominions.

But despite the growing rigour of the persecution, the shameful slanders which were propagated against the Reformed, and the hideous deaths inflicted upon persons of all ages and both sexes, the numbers of the Protestants and their courage daily increased. It was now seen that scarcely was there a class of French society which did not furnish converts to the Gospel. Mezeray says that there was no town, no province, no trade in the kingdom wherein the new opinions had not taken root. The lawyers, the learned, nay, the ecclesiastics, against their own interest, embraced them.[2521] Some of the greatest nobles of France now rallied round the Protestant standard. Among these was Antoine de Bourbon, Duke of Vendôme, and first prince of the blood, and Louis de Bourbon, Prince of Condé, his brother. With these were joined two nephews of the Constable Montmorency, the Admiral Gaspard de Coligny and his brother, François de Chàtillon, better known as the Sire d'Andèlot. A little longer and all France would be Lutheran. The king's alarm was great: the alarm of all about him was not less so, and all united in urging upon him the adoption of yet more summary measures against an execrable belief, which, if not rooted out, would most surely overthrow his throne, root out his house, and bring his kingdom to ruin. Might not the displeasure of Heaven, evoked by that impious sect, be read in the many dark calamities that were gathering round France?

It was resolved that a "Mercuriale," as it is called in France, should be held, and that the king, without giving previous notice of his coming, should present himself in the assembly. He would thus see and hear for himself, and judge if there were not, even among his senators, men who favoured this pestilent heresy. It had been a custom from the times of Charles VIII. (1493), when corruption crept into the administration, that representatives of all the principal courts of the realm should meet, in order to inquire into the evil, and admonish one another to greater vigilance. Francis I. had ordered that these "Censures" should take place once every three months, and from the day on which they were held—namely, Wednesday (*Dies Mercurii*)—they were named "Mercuriales."[2522]

On the 10th of June, 1559, the court met in the house of the Austin Friars, the Parliament Hall not being available, owing to the preparations for the wedding of the king's daughter and sister. The king suddenly appeared in the assembly, attended by the princes of the blood, the Constable, and the Guises. Having taken his seat on the throne, he delivered a discourse on religion; he enlarged on his own labours for the peace of Christendom, which he was about to seal by giving in marriage his daughter Elizabeth to Philip of Spain, and his only sister Margaret to Philibert Emmanuel, Duke of Savoy; and he concluded by announcing his resolution to devote himself henceforward to the healing of the wounds of the Christian world. He then ordered the senators to go on with their votes.

Though all felt that the king was present to overawe them in the expression of their sentiments, many of the senators declared themselves with that ancient liberty which became their rank and office. They pointed to the fact that a Council was at that moment convened at Trent to pronounce on the faith, and that it was unjust to burn men for heresy before the Council had decreed what was heresy. Arnold du Ferrier freely admitted that the troubles of France sprang out of its religious differences, but then they ought to inquire who was the real author of these differences, lest, while pursuing the sectaries, they should expose themselves to the rebuke, "Thou art the man that troubles Israel." Annas du Bourg, who next rose, came yet closer to the point. There were, he said, many great crimes and wicked actions, such as oaths, adulteries, and perjuries, con-

Book Seventeenth

demned by the laws, and deserving of the severest punishment, which went without correction, while new punishments were every day invented for men who as yet had been found guilty of no crime. Should those be held guilty of high treason who mentioned the name of the prince only to pray for him? and should the rack and the stake be reserved, not for those who raised tumults in the cities, and seditions in the provinces, but for those who were the brightest patterns of obedience to the laws, and the firmest defenders of order? It was a very grave matter, he added, to condemn to the flames men who died calling on the name of the Lord Jesus. Other speakers followed in the same strain. Not so the majority, however. They recalled the examples of old days, when the Albigensian heretics had been slaughtered in thousands by Innocent III.; and when the Waldenses, in later times, had been choked with smoke in their own dwellings, and the dens of the mountains; and they urged the instant adoption of these time-honoured usages. When the opinions of the senators had been marked, the king took possession of the register in which the votes were recorded, then rising up, he sharply chid those members who had avowed a preference for a moderate policy; and, to show that under a despot no one could honestly differ from the royal opinion and be held guiltless, he ordered the Constable to arrest Du Bourg. The captain of the king's guard instantly seized the obnoxious senator, and carried him to the Bastile. Other members of Parliament were arrested next day at their own houses.[2523]

The king's resolution was fully taken to execute all the senators who had opposed him, and to exterminate Lutheranism everywhere throughout France. He would begin with Du Bourg, who, shut up in an iron cage in the Bastile, waited his doom. But before the day of Du Bourg's execution arrived, Henry himself had gone to his account. We have already mentioned the delight the king took in jousts and tournaments. He was giving his eldest daughter in marriage to the mightiest prince of his time—Philip II. of Spain—and so great an occasion he must needs celebrate with fêtes of corresponding magnificence. Fourteen days have elapsed since his memorable visit to his Parliament, and now Henry presents himself in a very different assemblage. It is the last day of June, 1559, and the rank and beauty of Paris are gathered in the Faubourg St. Antoine, to see the king tilting with selected champions in the lists. The king bore himself "like a sturdy and skilful cavalier" in the mimic war. The last passage-of-arms was over, the plaudits of the brilliant throng had saluted the royal victor, and every one thought that the spectacle was at an end. But no; it was to close with a catastrophe of which no one present so much as dreamed. A sudden resolve seizing the king yet farther to display his prowess before the adoring multitude, he bade the Count Montgomery, the captain of his guard, make ready and run a tilt with him. Montgomery excused himself, but the king insisted. Mounting his horse and placing his lance in rest, Montgomery stood facing the king. The trumpet sounded. The two warriors, urging their steeds into a gallop, rushed at each other: Montgomery's lance struck the king with such force that the shaft was shivered. The blow made Henry's visor fly open, and a splinter from the broken beam entered his left eye and drove into his brain. The king fell from his horse to the ground. A thrill of horror ran through the spectators. Was the king slain? No; but he was mortally wounded, and the death-blow had been dealt by the same hand—that of the captain of his guard—which he had employed to arrest Du Bourg. He was carried to the Hôtel de Tournelles, where he died on the 10th of July, in the forty-first year of his age.[2524]

Many strange things were talked of at the time, and have been related by contemporary historians, in connection with the death of Henry II. His queen, Catherine de Medici, had a dream the night before, in which she saw him tilting in the tournament, and so hard put to, that in the morning when she awoke she earnestly begged him that day not to stir abroad; but, says Beza, he no more heeded the warning than Julius Cæsar did that of his wife, who implored him on the morning of the day on which he was slain, not to go to the Senate-house. Nor did it escape observation that the same palace which had been decked out with so much magnificence for the two marriages was that in which the king breathed his last, and so "the hall of triumph was changed into the chamber of mourning." And, finally, it was thought not a little remarkable that when the bed was prepared on which Henry was to lie in state, and the royal corpse laid upon it, the attendants, not thinking of the matter at all, covered it with a rich piece of tapestry on which was represented the conversion of St. Paul, with the words in large letters, "Saul, Saul, why persecutest thou me?" This was remarked upon by so many who saw it, that the officer who had charge of the body ordered the coverlet to be taken away, and replaced with another piece.[2525] The incident recalled the last words of Julian, who fell like Henry, warring against Christ: "Thou hast overcome, O Galilean!"

CHAPTER III

FIRST NATIONAL SYNOD OF THE FRENCH PROTESTANT CHURCH

THE young vine which had been planted in France, and which was beginning to cover with its shadow the plains of that fair land, was at this moment sorely shaken by the tempests; but the fiercer the blasts that warred around it, the deeper did it strike its roots in the soil, and the higher did it lift its head into the heavens. There were few districts or cities in France in which there was not to be found a little community of disciples. These flocks had neither shepherd to care for them, nor church in which to celebrate their worship. The violence of the times taught them to shun observation; nevertheless, they neglected no means of keeping alive the Divine life in their souls, and increasing their knowledge of the Word of God. They assembled at stated times, to read together the Scriptures, and to join in prayer, and at these gatherings the more intelligent or the more courageous of their number expounded a passage from the Bible, or delivered a word of exhortation. These teachers, however, confined themselves to doctrine. They did not dispense the Sacraments, for Calvin, who was consulted on the point, gave it as his opinion that, till they had obtained the services of a regularly ordained ministry, they should forgo celebrating the Lord's Supper. They were little careful touching the fashion of the place in which they offered their united prayer and sang their psalm. It might be a garret, or a cellar, or a barn. It might be a cave of the mountains, or a glen in the far wilderness, or some glade shaded by the ancient trees of the forest. Assemble where they might, they knew that there was One ever in the midst of them, and where he was, there was the Church. One of their number gave notice to the rest of the time and place of meeting. If in a city, they took care that the house should have several secret doors, so that, entering by different ways, their assembling might attract no notice. And lest their enemies should break in upon them, they took the precaution of bringing cards and dice with them, to throw upon the table in the room of their Bibles and psalters, as a make-believe that they had been interrupted at play, and were a band of gamblers instead of a congregation of Lutherans.[2526]

In the times we speak of, France was traversed by an army of book-hawkers. The printing-presses of Geneva, Lausanne, and Neuchàtel supplied Bibles and religious books in abundance, and students of theology, and sometimes even ministers, assuming the humble office of colporteurs carried them into France. Staff in hand, and pack slung on their back, they pursued their way, summer and winter, by highways and cross-roads, through forests and over marshes, knocking from door to door, often repulsed, always hazarding their lives, and at times discovered, and dragged to the pile. By their means the Bible gained admission into the mansions of the nobles, and the cottages of the peasantry. They employed the same methods as the ancient Vaudois colporteur to conceal their calling. Their precious wares they deposited at the bottom of their baskets, so that one meeting them in city alley, or country highway, would have taken them for vendors of silks and jewellery—a deception for which Florimond de Ræmond rebukes them, without, however, having a word in condemnation of the violence that rendered the concealment necessary. The success of these humble and devoted evangelists was attested by the numbers whom they prepared for the stake, and who, in their turn, sowed in their blood the seed of new confessors and martyrs.

At times, too, though owing to the fewness of pastors it was only at considerable intervals, these little assemblies of believing men and women had the much-prized pleasure of being visited by a minister of the Gospel. From him they learned how it was going with their brothers in other parts of France. Their hearts swelled and their eyes brightened as he told them that, despite the fires everywhere burning, new converts were daily pressing forward to enrol themselves in the army of Christ, and that the soldiers of the Cross were multiplying faster than the stake was thinning them. Then covering the table, and placing upon it the "bread" and "cup," he would dispense the Lord's Supper, and bind them anew by that holy pledge to the service of their heavenly King, even unto the death. Thus the hours would wear away, till the morning was on the point of breaking, and they would take farewell of each other as men who would meet no more till, by way of the halter or the stake, they should reassemble in heaven.

The singular beauty of the lives of these men attracted the notice, and extorted even the praise, of their bitterest enemies. It was a new thing in France. Florimond de Ræmond, ever on the watch for their halting, could find nothing of which to accuse them save that "instead of dances and Maypoles they set on foot Bible-readings, and the singing of spiritual hymns, especially the psalms after they had been turned into rhyme. The women, by their deportment and modest apparel, appeared in public like sorrowing Eves, or penitent Magdalenes, as Tertullian said of the Christian women of his day. The men too, with their mortified air, seemed to be overpowered by the Holy Ghost."[2527] It does not seem to have occurred to the monkish chronicler to inquire why it was that what he considered an evil tree yielded fruits like these, although a true answer to that question would have saved France from many crimes and woes. If the facts were as Ræmond stated them—if the confessors of an heretical and diabolical creed were men of pre-eminent virtue—the conclusion was inevitable, either that he had entirely misjudged regarding their creed, or that the whole moral order of things had somehow or other come to be reversed. Even Catherine de Medici, in her own way, bore her testimony to the moral character of Protestantism. "I have a mind," observed she one day, "to turn to the new religion, to pass for a prude and a pious woman." The persecutors of that age are condemned out of their own mouths. They confess that they "killed the innocent."

Truly wonderful was the number of Protestant congregations already formed in France at the time of the death of Henry II. "Burning," yet "not consumed," the Reformed Church was even green and flourishing, because refreshed with a secret dew, which was more efficacious to preserve its life than all the fury of the flames to extinguish it. We have already recorded the organisation of the Church in Paris, in 1555. It was followed in that and the five following years by so many others in all parts of France, that we can do little save recite the names of these Churches. The perils and martyrdoms through which each struggled into existence, before taking its place on the soil of France, we cannot recount. The early Church of Meaux, trodden into the dust years before, now rose from its ruins. In 1546 it had seen fourteen of its members burned; in 1555 it obtained a settled pastor.[2528] At Angers (1555) a congregation was formed, and placed under the care of a pastor from Geneva. At Poictiers, to which so great an interest belongs as the flock that Calvin gathered together, and to whom he dispensed, for the first time in France, the Sacrament of the Lord's Supper, a congregation was regularly organised (1555). It happened that the plague came to Poictiers, and drove from the city the bitterest enemies of the Reformation; whereupon its friends, taking heart, formed themselves into a Church, which soon became so flourishing that it supplied pastors to the congregations that by-and-by sprang up in the neighbourhood.[2529] At Alevert, an island lying off the coast of Saintonge, a great number of the inhabitants received the truth, and were formed into a congregation in 1556. At Agen, in Guienne, a congregation was the same year organised, of which Pierre David, a converted monk, became pastor. He was afterwards chaplain to the King of Navarre.

At Bourges, at Aubigny, at Issoudun, at Blois, at Tours, at Montoine, at Pau in Bearn, Churches were organised under regular pastors in the same year, 1556. To these are to be added the Churches of Montauban and Angoulême.[2530]

In the year following (1557), Protestant congregations were formed, and placed under pastors, at Orleans, at Sens, at Rouen in Normandy, and in many of the towns and villages around, including Dieppe on the shores of the English Channel. Protestantism had penetrated the mountainous region of the Cevennes, and left the memorials of its triumphs amid a people proverbially primitive and rude, in organised Churches. In Brittany numerous Churches arose, as also along both banks of the Garonne, in Nerac, in Bordeaux, and other towns too numerous to be mentioned. In Provence, the scene of recent slaughter, there existed no fewer than sixty Churches in the year 1560.[2531]

The beginnings of the "great and glorious" Church of La Rochelle are obscure. So early as 1534 a woman was burned in Poitou, who said she had been instructed in the truth at La Rochelle. From that year we find no trace of Protestantism there till 1552, when its presence there is attested by the barbarous execution of two martyrs, one of whom had his tongue cut out for having acted as the teacher of others; from which we may infer that there was a little company of disciples in that town, though keeping themselves concealed for fear of the persecutor.[2532]

In 1558 the King and Queen of Navarre, on their way to Paris, visited La Rochelle, and were splendidly entertained by its citizens. In their suite was M. David, the ex-monk, and now Protestant preacher, already referred to. He proclaimed openly the pure Word of God in all the places through which the court passed, and so too did he in La Rochelle. One day during their majesties' stay at this city, the town-crier announced that a company of comedians had just arrived, and would act that day a new and wonderful piece. The citizens crowded to the play; the king, the queen, and the court being also present.

When the curtain rose, a sick woman was seen at the point of death, shrieking in pain, and begging to be confessed. The parish priest was sent for. He arrived in breathless haste, decked out in his canonicals. He began to shrive his penitent, but to little purpose. Tossing from side to side, apparently in greater distress than ever, she cried out that she was not well confessed. Soon a crowd of ecclesiastics had assembled around the sick woman, each more anxious than the other to give her relief. One would have thought that in such a multitude of physicians a cure would be found; but no: her case baffled all their skill. The friars next took her in hand. Opening great bags which they had brought with them, they drew forth, with solemn air, beads which they gave her to count, relics which they applied to various parts of her person, and indulgences which they read to her, with a perfect confidence that these would work an infallible cure. It was all in vain. Not one of these renowned specifics gave her the least mitigation of her sufferings. The friars were perfectly non-plussed. At last they bethought them of another expedient. They put the habit of St. Francis upon her. Now, thought they, as sure as St. Francis is a saint, she is cured. But, alas! attired in cowl and frock, the poor sick woman sat rocking from side to side amid the friars, still grievously tormented by the pain in her conscience, and bemoaning her sad condition, that those people understood not how to confess her. At that point, when priest and friar had exhausted their skill, and neither rosary nor holy habit could work a cure, one stepped upon the stage, and going up to the woman, whispered into her ear that he knew a man who would confess her right, and give her ease in her conscience; but, added he, he goes abroad only in the night-time, for the day-light is hurtful to him. The sick person earnestly begged that that man might be called to her. He was straightway sent for: he came in a lay-dress, and drawing near the bolster, he whispered something in the woman's ear which the spectators did not hear. They saw, however, by her instant change of expression, that she was well pleased with what had been told her. The mysterious man next drew out of his pocket a small book, which he put into her hand, saying aloud, "This book contains the most infallible recipes for the curing of your disease; if you will make use of them, you will recover your health perfectly in a few days." Hereupon he left the stage, and the sick woman, getting out of bed with cheerful air, as one perfectly cured, walked three times round the stage, and then turning to the audience, told them that that unknown man had succeeded where friar and priest had failed, and that she must confess that the book he had given her was full of most excellent recipes, as they themselves might see from the happy change it had wrought in her; and if any of them was afflicted with the same disease, she would advise them to consult that book, which she would readily lend them; and if they did not mind its being somewhat hot in the handling, and having about it a noisome smell like that of a fagot, they might rest assured it would certainly cure them. If the audience desired to know her name, and the book's name, she said, they were two riddles which they might guess at.[2533]

The citizens of La Rochelle had no great difficulty in reading the riddle. Many of them made trial of the book, despite its associations with the stake and the fagot, and they found that its efficacy was sufficiently sovereign to cure them. They obtained deliverance from that burden on the conscience which had weighed them down in fear and anguish, despite all that friar or penance could do to give them ease. From that time Protestantism flourished in La Rochelle; a Church was formed, its members not daring as yet, however, to meet for worship in open day, but assembling under cloud of night, as was still the practice in almost all places in France.

We are now arrived at a new and most important development of Protestantism in France. As has been already maintained, the crowns of France and Spain made peace between themselves, that they might be at liberty to turn their arms against Protestantism, and effect its extermination. Both monarchs were preparing to inflict a great blow. It was at that hour the scattered sections of the French Protestant Church drew together, and, rallying around a common standard, presented a united front to their enemies.

It was forty years since Lefevre had opened the door of France to the Gospel. All these years there had been disciples, confessors, martyrs, but no congregations in our sense of the term. The little companies of believing men and women, scattered over the country, were cared for and fed only by the Great Shepherd, who made them lie down in the green pastures of the Word, and by the still waters of the Spirit. But this was an incomplete and defective condition. Christ's people are not only a "flock" but a "kingdom," and it is the peculiarity of a kingdom that it possesses "order and government" as well as subjects. The former exists for the edification and defence of the latter. In 1555 congregations began to be formed on the Genevan model. A pastor was appointed to teach, and with him was associated a small body of laymen to watch over the morals of the flock. The work of organising went on vigorously, and in 1560 from one to two thousand Protestant congregations existed in France. Thus did the individual congregations come into existence. But the Church of God needs a wider union, and a more centralised authority.

Scattered over the wide space that separates the Seine from the Rhone and the Garonne, the Protestant Churches of France were isolated and apart. In the fact that they had common interests and common dangers, a basis was laid, they felt, for confederation. In this way would the wisdom of all be available for the guidance of each, and the strength of each be combined for the defence of all.

As the symbol of such a confederation it was requisite that a creed should be drafted which all might confess, and a code of discipline compiled to which all would submit. Not to fetter the private judgment of individual Christians, nor to restrict the rights of individual congregations, was this creed framed; on the contrary, it was intended as a shield of both liberty of opinion and liberty of Christian action. But in order to effect this, it was essential that it should be drawn from the doctrines of the Bible and the models of apostolic times, with the same patient investigation, and the same accurate deduction, with which men construct a science from the facts which they observe in nature, but with greater submission of mind, inasmuch as the facts observed for the framing of a creed are of supernatural revelation, and with a more anxious vigilance to avoid error where error would be so immensely more pernicious and destructive, and above all, with a dependence on that Spirit who inspired the Word, and who has been promised to enlighten men in the true sense of it. As God has revealed himself in his Word, so the Church is bound to reveal the Word to the world. The French Protestant Church now discharged that duty to its nation.

It was agreed between the Churches of Paris and Poictiers, in 1558, that a National Synod should be held for the purpose of framing a common confession and a code of discipline. In the following spring, circular letters were addressed to all the Churches of the kingdom, and they, perceiving the benefit to the common cause likely to accrue from the step, readily gave their consent. It was unanimously agreed that the Synod should be held in Paris. The capital was selected, says Beza, not because any pre-eminence or dignity was supposed to belong to the Church there, but simply because the confluence of so many ministers and elders was less likely to attract notice in Paris than in a provincial town.[2534] As regards rank, the representative of the smallest congregation stood on a perfect equality with the deputy of the metropolitan Church.

The Synod met on the 25th of May, 1559. At that moment the Parliament was assembling for the Mercuriale, at which the king avowed his purpose of pursuing the Reformed with fire and sword till he had exterminated them. From eleven Churches only came deputies to this Synod: Paris, St. Lô, Dieppe, Angers, Orleans, Tours, Poictiers, Saintes, Marennes, Châtellerault, and St. Jean d'Angely.[2535] Pastor François Morel, Sieur of Collonges, was chosen to preside. Infinite difficulties had to be overcome, says Beza, before the Churches could be advertised of the meeting, but greater risks had to be run before the deputies could assemble: hence the fewness of their number. The gibbet was then standing in all the public places of the kingdom, and had their place of meeting been discovered, without doubt, the deputies would have been led in a body to the scaffold.

There is a simplicity and a moral grandeur appertaining to this assembly that compels our homage. No guard stands sentinel at the door. No mace or symbol of authority graces the table round which the deputies of the Churches are gathered; no robes of office dignify their persons; on the contrary, royal edicts have proclaimed them outlaws, and the persecutor is on their track. Nevertheless, as if they were assembled in peaceful times, and under the shadow of law, they go on day by day, with calm dignity and serene power, planting the foundations of the House of God in their native land. They will do their work, although the first stones should be cemented with their blood.

We can present only an outline of their great work. Their Confession of Faith was comprehended in forty articles, and agrees in all essential points with the Creed of the Church of England. They received the Bible as the sole infallible rule of faith and manners. They confessed the doctrine of the Trinity; of the Fall; of the entire corruption of man's nature, and his condemnation; of the election of some to everlasting life; of the call of sovereign and omnipotent grace; of a free redemption by Christ, who is our righteousness; of that righteousness as the ground of our justification; of faith, which is the gift of God, as the instrument by which we obtain an interest in that righteousness; of regeneration by the Spirit to a new life, and to good works; of the Divine institution of the ministry; of the equality of all pastors under one chief Pastor and Universal Bishop, Jesus Christ; of the true Church, as composed of the assembly of believers, who agree to follow the rule of the Word; of the two Sacraments, baptism and the Lord's Supper; of the policy which Christ has established for the government of his Church; and of the obedience and homage due to rulers in monarchies and commonwealths, as God's lieutenants whom he has set to exercise a lawful and holy office.[2536]

Their code of discipline was arranged also in forty articles. Dismissing details, let us state in outline the constitution of the Reformed Church of France, as settled at its first National Synod. Its fundamental idea was that which had been taught both at Wittemberg and Geneva, namely, that the government of the Church is diffused throughout the whole body of the faithful, but that the exercise of it is to be restricted to those to whom Christ, the fountain of that government, has given the suitable gifts, and whom their fellow Church members have called to its discharge. On this democratic basis there rose four grades of power:— 1. The Consistory. 2. The Colloquy. 3. The Provincial Synod. 4. The National Synod. Corresponding with these four grades of power there were four circles or areas—the Parish, the District, the Province, and the Kingdom. Each grade of authority narrowed as it ascended, while the circle within which it was exercised widened. What had its beginning in a democracy, ended in a constitutional monarchy, and the interests of each congregation and each member of the Church were, in the last resort, adjudicated upon by the wisdom and authority of all. There was perfect liberty, combined with perfect order.

Let us sketch briefly the constitution of each separate court, with the sphere within which, and the responsibilities under which, it exercised its powers. First came the Consistory. It bore rule over the congregation, and was composed of the minister, elders, and deacons. The minister might be nominated by the Consistory, or by the Colloquy, or by the Provincial Synod, but he could not be ordained till he had preached three several Sundays to the congregation, and the people thus had had an opportunity of testing his gifts, and his special fitness to be their pastor. The elders and deacons were elected by the congregation.

The Colloquy came next, and was composed of all the congregations of the district. Each congregation was represented in it by one pastor and one elder or deacon. The Colloquy met twice every year, and settled all questions referred to it from the congregations within its limits.

Next came the Provincial Synod. It comprehended all the Colloquies of the Province, every congregation sending a pastor and an elder to it. The Provincial Synod met once a year, and gave judgment in all cases of appeal from the court below, and generally in all matters deemed of too great weight to be determined in the Colloquy.

At the head of this graduation of ecclesiastical authority came the National Synod. It was composed of two pastors and two elders from each of the Provincial Synods, and had the whole kingdom for its domain or circle. It was the court of highest judicature; it determined all great causes, and heard all appeals, and to its authority, in the last resort, all were subject. It was presided over by a pastor chosen by the members. His pre-eminence was entirely official, and ended at the moment the Synod had closed its sittings.

In the execution of this great task, these first builders of the Protestant Church in France availed themselves of the counsel of Calvin. Nevertheless, their eyes were all the while directed to a higher model than Geneva, and they took their instructions from a higher authority than Calvin. They studied the New Testament, and what they aimed at following was the pattern which they thought stood revealed to them there, and the use they made of Calvin's advice was simply to be able to see that plan more clearly, and to follow it more closely. Adopting as their motto the words of the apostle—"One is your Master, even Christ, and all ye are brethren"—they inferred that there must be government in the Church—

"One is your Master"—that the source of that government is in heaven, namely, Christ; that the revelation of it is in the Bible, and that the depository of it is in the Church—"All ye are brethren." Moving between the two great necessities which their motto indicated, authority, and liberty, they strove to adjust and reconcile these two different but not antagonistic forces—Christ's royalty and his people's brotherhood. Without the first there could not be order, without the second there could not be freedom. Their scheme of doctrine preceded their code of discipline; the first had been accepted before the second was submitted to; thus all the bonds that held that spiritual society together, and all the influences that ruled it, proceeded out of the throne in the midst of the Church. If they, as constituted officers, stood between the Monarch and the subjects of this spiritual empire, it was neither as legislators nor as rulers, strictly so called. "One" only was Master, whether as regarded law or government. Their power was not legislative but administrative, and their rule was not lordly but ministerial; they were the fellow-servants of those among whom, and for whom, their functions were discharged.

The Synod sat four days; its place of meeting was never discovered, and its business finished, its members departed for their homes, which they reached in safety. Future councils have added nothing of moment to the constitution of the French Protestant Church, as framed by this first National Synod.[2537]

The times subsequent to the holding of this assembly were times of great prosperity to the Protestants of France. The Spirit of God was largely given them; and though the fires of persecution continued to burn, the pastors were multiplied, congregations waxed numerous, and the knowledge and purity of their members kept pace with their increase. The following picture of the French Church at this era has been drawn by Quick:—"The holy Word of God is duly, truly, and powerfully preached in churches and fields, in ships and houses, in vaults and cellars, in all places where the Gospel ministers can have admission and conveniency, and with singular success. Multitudes are convinced and converted, established and edified. Christ rideth out upon the white horse of the ministry, with the sword and bow of the Gospel preached, conquering and to conquer. His enemies fall under him, and submit themselves unto him.

"Oh! the unparalleled success of the plain and earnest sermons of the first Reformers! Multitudes flock in like doves into the windows of God's ark. As innumerable drops of dew fall from the womb of the morning, so hath the Lord Christ the dew of his youth. The Popish churches are drained, the Protestant churches are filled. The priests complain that their altars are neglected; their masses are now indeed solitary. Dagon cannot stand before God's ark. Children and persons of riper years are catechised in the rudiments and principles of the Christian religion, and can give a satisfactory account of their faith, a reason of the hope that is in them. By this ordinance do their pious pastors prepare them for communion with the Lord at his holy table."[2538]

CHAPTER IV
A GALLERY OF PORTRAITS

HENRY II went to his grave amid the deepening shadows of fast-coming calamity. The auspicious signs which had greeted the eyes of men when he ascended the throne had all vanished before the close of his reign, and given place to omens of evil. The finances were embarrassed, the army was dispirited by repeated defeat, the court was a hot-bed of intrigue, and the nation, broken into factions, was on the brink of civil war. So rapid had been the decline of a kingdom which in the preceding reign was the most flourishing in Christendom.

Henry II. was succeeded on the throne by the eldest of his four sons, under the title of Francis II. The blood of the Valois and the blood of the Medici—two corrupt streams—were now for the first time united on the throne of France. With the new monarch came a shifting of parties in the Louvre; for of all slippery places in the world those near a throne are the most slippery. The star of Diana of Poictiers, as a matter of course, vanished from the firmament where it had shone with bright but baleful splendour. The Constable Montmorency had a hint given him that his health would be benefited by the air of his country-seat. The king knew not, so he said to him, how to reward his great merits, and recompense him for the toil he had undergone in his service, save by relieving him of the burden of affairs, in order that he might enjoy his age in quiet, being resolved not to wear him out as a vassal or servant, but always to honour him as a father.[2539] The proud Constable, grumbling a little, strode off to his Castle of Chantilly, ten leagues from Paris. The field cleared of these parties, the contest for power henceforward lay between the Guises and the Queen-mother.

Francis II. was a lad of sixteen, and when we think who had had the rearing of him, we are not surprised to learn that he was without principles and without morals. Feeble in mind and body, he was a tool all the more fit for the hand of a bold intriguer. At the foot of the throne from which she had just descended stood the crafty Italian woman, his mother, Catherine de Medici: might she not hope to be the sovereign-counsellor of her weak-minded son? During the lifetime of her husband, Henry II., her just influence as the wife had been baulked by the ascendance of the mistress, Diana of Poictiers. That rival had been swept from her path, but another and more legitimate competitor had come in the room of the fallen favourite. By the side of Francis II., on the throne of France, sat Mary Stuart, the heir of the Scottish crown, and the niece of the Guises. The king doted upon her beauty,[2540] and thus the niece was able to keep open the door of the royal closet, and the ear of her husband, to her uncles. This gave the Guises a prodigious advantage in the game that was now being played round the person of the king. And when we think how truculent they were, and how skilled they had now become in the arts by which princes' favour is to be won, it does not surprise us to learn that in the end of the day they were foremost in the race. Catherine de Medici was a match for them any day in craft and ambition, but with the niece of her rivals by the king's side, she found it expedient still to dissemble, and to go on a little while longer disciplining herself in those arts in which nature had fitted her to excel, and in which long practice would at last make her an expert, and then would she grasp the government of France.

The question which the Queen-mother now put, "What shall be my policy?" was to be determined by the consideration of who were her rivals, and what the tactics to which they were committed. Her rivals, we have just said, were the Guises, the heads of the Roman Catholic party. This threw Catherine somewhat on the other side. She was nearly as much the bigot as the Cardinal of Lorraine himself, but if she loved the Pope, still more did she love power, and in order to grasp it she stooped to caress what she mortally hated, and feigned to protect what she secretly wished to root out. Thus did God divide the counsels and the arms of these two powerful enemies of the Church. Had the Guises stood alone, the Reformation would have been crushed in France; or had Catherine de Medici stood alone, a like fate would have befallen it; but Providence brought both sides upon the scene together, and made their rivalry a shield over the little Protestant flock. The Queen-mother now threw herself between the leaders of the Reformed, and the Guises who were for striking them down without mercy. The new relation of Catherine brings certain personages upon the stage whom we have not yet met, but whom it is fitting, seeing they are to be conspicuous actors in what is to follow, we should now introduce.

The first is Anthony de Bourbon, Duke of Vendôme, and first prince of the blood. From the same parent stock sprang the two royal branches of France, the Valois and the Bourbon. Louis IX (St. Louis) had four sons, of whom one was named Philip and another Robert. From Philip came the line of the Valois, in which the succession was continued for upwards of 300 years. From Robert, through his son's marriage with the heiress of the Duchy of Bourbon, came the house of that name, which has come to fill so large a space in history, and has placed its members upon the thrones of France, and Spain, and Naples. Princes of the blood, and adding to that dignity vast possessions, a genius for war, and generous dispositions, the Bourbons aspired to fill the first posts in the kingdom. Their pretensions were often troublesome to the reigning monarch, who found it necessary at times to visit their haughty bearing with temporary banishment from court. They were under this cloud at the time when Henry II. died. On the accession of Francis II. they resolved on returning to court and resuming their old influence in the government; but to their chagrin they found those places which they thought they, as princes of the blood, should have held, already possessed by the Guises. The latter united with the Queen-mother in repelling their advances, and the Bourbons had again to retire, and to seek amid the parties of the country that influence which they were denied in the administration.

Anthony de Bourbon had married Jeanne d'Albret, who was the most illustrious woman of her time, and one of the most illustrious women in all history. She was the daughter of Margaret of Valois, Queen of Navarre, whose genius she inherited, and whom she surpassed in her gifts of governing, and in her more consistent attachment to the Reformation. Her fine intellect, elevated soul, and deep piety were unequally yoked with Anthony de Bourbon, who was a man of humane dispositions, but of low tastes, indolent habits, and of paltry character. His marriage with Jeanne d'Albret brought him the title of King of Navarre; but his wife was a woman of too much sense, and cherished too enlightened a regard for the welfare of her subjects, to give him more than the title. She took care not to entrust him with the reins of government. Today, so zealous was he for the Gospel, that he exerted himself to have the new opinions preached in his wife's dominions; and tomorrow would he be so zealous for Rome, that he would persecute those who had embraced the opinions he had appeared, but a little before, so desirous to have propagated. "Unstable as water," he spent his life in travelling between the two camps, the Protestant and the Popish, unable long to adhere to either, and heartily despised by both.[2542] The Romanists, knowing the vulgar ambition that actuated him, promised him a territory which he might govern in his own right, and he kept pursuing this imaginary princedom. It was a mere lure to draw him over to their side; and his life ended without his ever attaining the power he was as eager to grasp as he was unable to wield. He died fighting in the ranks of the Romanists before the walls of Rouen; and, true to his character for inconsistency to the last, he is said to have requested in his dying moments to be readmitted into the Protestant Church.

His brother, the Prince of Condé, was a person of greater talent, and more manly character. He had a somewhat diminutive figure, but this defect was counterbalanced by the graces of his manner, the wit of his discourse, and the gallantry of his spirit.[2543] He shone equally among the ladies of the court and the soldiers of the camp. He could be gay with the one, and unaffectedly frank and open with the other. The Prince of Condé attached himself to the Protestant side, from a sincere conviction that the doctrines of the Reformation were true, that they were favourable to liberty, and that their triumph would contribute to the greatness of France. But the Prince of Condé was not a great man. He did not rise to the true height of the cause he had espoused, nor did he bring to it that large sagacity, that entire devotion of soul, and that singleness of purpose which were required of one who would lead in such a cause. But what was worse, the Prince of Condé had not wholly escaped the blight of the profligacy of the age; although he had not suffered by any means to the same extent as his brother, the King of Navarre. A holy cause cannot be effectually succoured save by holy hands. "It may be asked whether the Bourbons, including even Henry IV., did not do as much damage as service to the Reformation. They mixed it up with politics, thrust it into the field of battle, dragged it into their private quarrels, and then when it had won for them the crown, they deserted it.[2544]

The next figure that comes before us is a truly commanding one. It is that of Gaspard de Coligny, better known as Admiral de Coligny. He towers above the Bourbon princes, and illustrates the fact that greatness of soul is a much more enviable possession than mere greatness of rank. Coligny, perhaps the greatest layman of the French Reformation, was descended from an ancient and honourable house, that of Chatillon. He was born in the same year in which Luther commenced the Reformation by the publication of his Theses, 1517. He lost his father on the 24th of August, 1522, being then only five years of age. The 24th of August was a fatal day to Coligny, for on that day, fifty years afterwards, he fell by the poignard of an assassin in the St. Bartholomew Massacre. His mother, Louise de Montmorency, a lady of lofty virtue and sincere piety, was happily spared to him, and by her instructions and example those seeds were sown in his youthful mind which afterwards bore so noble fruit in the cause of his country's religion and liberty. He was offered a cardinal's hat if he would enter the Church. He chose instead the profession of arms. He served with great distinction in the wars of Flanders and Italy, was knighted on the field of battle, and returning home in 1547 he married the daughter of the illustrious house of Laval—a woman of magnanimous soul and enlightened piety, worthy of being the wife of such a man, and by whose prompt and wise counsel he was guided at more than one critical moment of his life. What he might have been as a cardinal we do not know, but in his own profession as a soldier he showed himself a great reformer and administrator. Brantôme says of the military ordinances which he introduced into the French army, "They were the best and most politic that have ever been made in France, and, I believe, have preserved the lives of a million of persons; for, till then, there was nothing but pillage, brigandage, murders, and quarrels, so that the companies resembled hordes of wild Arabs rather than noble soldiers."[2545]

At an early age Coligny was taken prisoner by the Spaniards, and to beguile the solitary hours of his confinement, he asked for a Bible and some religious books. His request was complied with, and from that incident dates his attachment to the Reformed doctrines. But he was slow to declare himself. He must be fully persuaded in his own mind before openly professing the truth, and he must needs count the cost. With Coligny, Protestantism was no affair of politics or of party, which he might cast aside if on trial he found it did not suit. Having put his hand to the plough, he must not withdraw it, even though, leaving castle and titles, he should go forth an outcast and a beggar. For these same doctrines men were being every day burned at the stake. Before making profession of them, Coligny paused, that by reading, and converse with the Reformed pastors, he might arrive at a full resolution of all his doubts. But the step was all the more decisive when at last it was taken. As men receive the tidings of some great victory or of some national blessing, so did the Protestants of France receive the news that Coligny had cast in his lot with the Reformation. They knew that he must have acted from deep conviction, that his choice would never be reversed, and that it had brought a mighty accession of intellectual and moral power to the Protestant cause. They saw in Coligny's adherence an additional proof of its truth, and a new pledge of its final triumph. Protestantism in France, just entering on times of awful struggles, had now a leader worthy of it. A captain had risen up to march before its consecrated hosts, and fight its holy battles.

From the moment he espoused the Protestant cause, Coligny's character acquired a new grandeur. The arrangements of his household were a model of order. He rose early, and having dressed himself, he summoned his household to prayers, himself leading their devotions. Business filled up the day and not a few of its hours were devoted to the affairs of the Church; for deputies were continually arriving at the Castle of Chatillon from distant congregations, craving the advice or aid of the admiral. Every other day a sermon was preached before dinner when it chanced, as often happened, that a minister was living under his roof. At table a psalm was sung, and a prayer offered. After an early supper came family devotions, and then the household were dismissed to rest. It mattered not where Coligny was, or how occupied—in the Castle of Chatillon surrounded by his children and servants, or in the camp amid the throng of captains and soldiers—this was ever the God-fearing manner of his life. Not a few of the nobles of France felt the power of his example, and in many a castle the chant of psalms began to be heard, where aforetime there had reigned only worldly merriment and boisterous revelry.

To the graces of Christianity there were added, in the character of Coligny, the gifts of human genius. He excelled in military tactics, and much of his life was passed on the battle-field; but he was no less fitted to shine in senates, and to guide in matters of State. His foresight, sagacity, and patriotism would, had he lived in happier times, have been the source of manifold blessings to his native country. As it was, these great qualities were mainly shown in arranging campaigns and fighting battles. Protestantism in France, so at least Coligny judged, had nothing for it but to stand to its defence. A tyranny, exercised in the king's name, but none the less an audacious usurpation, was trampling on law, outraging all rights, and daily destroying by horrible deaths the noblest men in France, and the Protestants felt that they owed it to their faith, to their country, to the generations to come, and to the public liberties and Reformation of Christendom, to repel force by force, seeing all other means of redress were denied them. This alone made Coligny unsheathe the sword. The grand object of his life was freedom of worship for the Reformed in France. Could he have secured that object, most gladly would he have bidden adieu for ever to camps and battle-fields, and, casting honours and titles behind him, been content to live unknown in the privacy of Chatillon. This, however, was denied him. He was opposed by men who "hated peace," and so he had to fight on, almost without intermission, till the hour came when he was called to seal with his blood the cause he had so often defended with his sword.

Before quitting this gallery of portraits, there is one other figure which must detain us a little. Her name we have already mentioned incidentally, but her great qualities make her worthy of more lengthened observation. Jeanne d'Albret was the daughter of the accomplished and pious Margaret of Valois; but the daughter was greater than the mother. She had a finer genius, a stronger character, and she displayed the graces of a more consistent piety. The study of the Bible drew her thoughts in her early years to the Reformation, and her convictions ripening into a full belief of its truth, although untoward circumstances made her long conceal them, she at last, in 1560, made open profession of Protestantism. At that time not only did the Protestant cause underlie the anathemas of Popes, but the Parliament of Paris had put it beyond the pale of law, and having set a price upon the heads of its adherents, it left them to be hunted down like wild beasts. Jeanne d'Albret, having made her choice, was as resolute as her husband, Anthony de Bourbon, was vacillating. Emulating the noble steadfastness of Coligny, she never repented of her resolution. Whether victory shone or defeat lowered on the Reformed cause, Jeanne d'Albret was ever by its side. When overtaken by disaster, she was ever the first to rally its dispirited adherents, and to bring them succour. Her husband forsook her; her son was taken from her; nothing daunted, she withdrew to her own principality of Bearn, and there devised, with equal wisdom and spirit, measures for the Reformation of her own subjects, at the same time that she was aiding, by her counsels and her resources, the Protestants in all parts of France.

Her little kingdom lay on the slope of the Pyrenees, looking toward France, which it touched on its northern frontier. In former times it was divided into Lower Navarre, of which we have spoken above, and Upper Navarre, which lay on the southern slope of the Pyrenees, and was coterminous with Old Castile. Though but a small territory, its position gave Navarre great importance. Seated on the Pyrenees, it held in the one hand the keys of France, and in the other those of Spain. It was an object of jealousy to the sovereigns of both countries. It was coveted especially by the King of Spain, and in the days of Jeanne's grandfather Upper Navarre was torn from its rightful sovereigns by Ferdinand, King of Arragon, whose usurpation was confirmed by Pope Julius II. The loss of Upper Navarre inferred the loss of the capital of the kingdom, Pampeluna, which contained the tombs of its kings. Henceforward it became a leading object with Jean d'Albret to recover the place of his fathers' sepulchres, that his own ashes might sleep with theirs, but in this he failed; and when his granddaughter came to the throne, her dominions were restricted to that portion of the ancient Navarre which lay on the French side of the Pyrenees.

In 1560, we have said, Jeanne d'Albret made open profession of the Protestant faith. In 1563 came her famous edict, dated from her castle at Pau, abolishing the Popish service throughout Bearn, and introducing the Protestant worship. The majority of her subjects were already prepared for this change, and the priests, though powerful, did not venture openly to oppose the public sentiment. A second royal edict confiscated a great part of the temporalities of the Church, but without adding them to the crown. They were divided into three parts. One-third was devoted to the education of the youth, another third to the relief of the poor, and the remaining third to the support of the Protestant worship. The private opinion of the Roman Catholic was respected, and only the public celebration of his worship forbidden. All trials and punishment for differences of religious opinions were abolished. Where the majority of the inhabitants were Protestant, the cathedrals were made over to them for their use, the images, crucifixes, and relics being removed. Where the inhabitants were equally divided, or nearly so, the two faiths were permitted the alternate use of the churches. The monasteries were converted into schools, thus anticipating by three centuries a measure long afterwards adopted by the Italian and other Continental Governments. Colleges were founded for the higher education. Jeanne caused the Bible to be translated into the dialects of her dominions. She sent to Geneva for ministers, and recalled the native evangelists who had been driven out of Navarre, in order to the more perfect instruction of her subjects in the doctrines of the Word of God. Thus did she labour for the Reformation of her kingdom. The courage she displayed may be judged of, when we say that the Pope was all the while thundering his excommunications against her; and that the powerful Kings of Spain and France, affronted by the erection of an heretical establishment on the frontiers of their dominions, were threatening to overrun her territory, imprison her person in the dungeons of the Inquisition, and raze her kingdom from the map of Europe.

In the midst of these distractions the Queen of Navarre gave herself to the study of the principles of jurisprudence. Comparing together the most famous codes of ancient and modern times, she produced, after the labour of seven years, a body of laws for the government of her kingdom, which was far in advance of her times. She entertained the most enlightened views on matters then little cared for by kings or parliaments. By her wise legislation she encouraged husbandry, improved the arts, fostered intelligence, and in a short time the beautiful order and amazing prosperity of her principality attracted universal admiration, and formed a striking contrast to the disorder, the violence, and misery that overspread the lands around it. In her dominions not a child was permitted to grow up uneducated, nor could a beggar be seen. The flourishing condition of Bearn showed what the mightier realms of Spain and France would have become, had their peoples been so wise as to welcome the Reformation. The code of the wise queen continued in operation in the territories of the House of D'Albret down to almost our own times. She is still remembered in those parts, where she is spoken of as the "good queen."

We have dwelt the longer upon these portraits because one main end of history is to present us with such. The very contemplation of them is ennobling. In a recital like the present, which brings before us some of the worst of men that have ever lived, and portrays some of the darkest scenes that have ever been enacted, to meet at times grand characters, like those we have just passed in review, helps to make us forget the wickedness and worthlessness on which the mind is apt to dwell disproportionately, if not exclusively. All is not dark in the scene we are surveying; beams of glory break in through the deep shadows. Majestic and kingly spirits pass across the stage, whose deeds and renown shall live when the little and the base among their fellows, who laboured to defame their character and to extinguish their fame, have passed for ever from the knowledge of the world. Thus it is that the good overcomes the evil, and that the heroic long survives the worthless. The example of great men has a creative power: they reproduce, in the ages that come after, their own likeness, and enrich the world with men cast in their own lofty and heroic mould. Humanity is thus continually receiving seeds of greatness into its bosom, and the world is being led onwards to that high platform where its Maker has destined that it shall ultimately stand.

CHAPTER V
THE GUISES, AND THE INSURRECTION OF AMBOISE

HENRY II, smitten by a sudden blow, has disappeared from the scene. Francis II. is on the throne of France. The Protestants are fondly cherishing the hope that with a change of men will come a change of measures, and that they have seen the dawn of better times. "Alas! under the reign of this monarch," says Beza, "the rage of Satan broke out beyond all former bounds."[2546] No sooner had Henry breathed his last, than the Queen-mother and the two Guises carried the young king to the Louvre, and, installing him there, admitted only their own partisans to his presence. Now it was that the star of the Guises rose proudly into the ascendant. The duke assumed the command of the army; the cardinal, head of the Church, took also upon him the charge of the finances—thus the two brothers parted between them the government of France. Francis wore the crown; a sort of general superintendence was allowed to the Queen-mother; but it was the Guise and not the Valois that governed the country.[2547]

One of the last acts of Henry II. had been to arrest Councillor Du Bourg and issue a commission for his trial. Du Bourg, shut up in his iron cage, and fed on bread and water, was nevertheless continually singing psalms, which he sometimes accompanied on the lute. His trial ended in his condemnation as a heretic, and he was first strangled and them burned in the Place de Grève. His high rank, his many accomplishments, and his great character for uprightness fixed the eyes of all upon his stake, and made his death serviceable in no ordinary degree to the cause of Protestantism.[2548]

The power of the Guises, now in full blossom, was wholly put forth in the extirpation of heresy. Their zeal in this good work was not altogether without alloy. "Those of the religion," as the Protestants were termed, were not less the enemies of the House of Guise than of the Pope, and to cut them off was to consolidate their own power at the same time that they strengthened the foundations of the Papacy. To reclaim by argument men who had fallen into deadly error was not consonant with the habits of the Guises, scarcely with the habits of the age. The sword and the fanatical mob were their quickest and readiest weapons, and the only ones in which they had any confidence. They were the masters of the king's person; they carried him about from castle to castle; they took care to gratify his tastes; and they relieved him of all the cares of government, for which his sickly body, indolent disposition, and weak intellect so thoroughly indisposed him.

While the monarch lived in this inglorious pupilage, the Guises appended his seal to whatever edict it pleased them to indite. In the Treaty of Cateau Cambrésis, our readers will remember, there was a special clause binding the late king to exert himself to the utmost of his power to extirpate heresy. Under pretence of executing that treaty, the Guises fulminated several new and severe edicts against the Reformed. Their meetings were forbidden on pain of death, without any other form of judgment, and informers were promised half the forfeitures. Other rewards were added to quicken their diligence. The commissaries of the various wards of Paris were commanded to pay instant attention to the informations lodged before them by the spies, who were continually on the search, and the Lieutenant-Criminal was empowered by letters patent to judge without appeal, and execute without delay, those brought before him. And the vicars and curés were set to work to thunder excommunication and anathema in their parishes against all who, knowing who among their neighbours were Lutherans, should yet refrain from denouncing them to the authorities.[2549]

The Protestant Church in Paris in this extremity addressed the Queen-mother, Catherine de Medici. A former interview had inspired the members of that Church with the hope that she was disposed to pursue a moderate policy. They had not yet learned with what an air of sincerity, and even graciousness, the niece of Clement VII. could cover her designs—how bland she could look while cherishing the most deadly purpose. They implored Catherine to interpose and stay the rigour of the government, and, with a just and sagacious foresight, which the centuries since have amply justified, they warned her that "if a stop was not speedily put to those cruel proceedings, there was reason to fear lest people, provoked by such violences, should fall into despair, and break forth into civil commotions, which of course would prove the ruin of the kingdom: that these evils would not come from those who lived under their direction, from whom she might expect a perfect submission and obedience; but that the far greater number were of those who, knowing only the abuses of Popery, and having not as yet submitted to any ecclesiastical discipline, could not or would not bear persecution: that they had thought proper to give this warning to her Majesty, that if any mischief should happen it might not be put to their account."[2550] It suited the Queen-mother to interpret the warning of the Protestants, among whom were Coligny and other nobles, as a threat; and the persecution, instead of abating, grew hotter every day.[2551]

We have already related the failure of the priests and the Sorbonne to establish the Inquisition in Paris. Paul IV., whose fanaticism had grown in his old age into frenzy, had forwarded a bull for that purpose, but the Parliament put it quietly aside. The project was renewed by the Guises, and if the identical forms of the Spanish tribunal were not copied in the courts which they succeeded in erecting, a procedure was adopted which gained their end quite as effectually. These courts were styled *Chambres Ardentes*, nor did their name belie their terrible office, which was to dispatch to the flames all who appeared before them accused of the crime of heresy. They were presided over by three judges or inquisitors, and, like the Spanish Court, they had a body of spies or familiars in their employment, who were continually on the hunt for victims. The sergeants of the Châtelet, the commissaries of the various quarters of Paris, the officers of the watch, the city guard, and the vergers and beadles of the several ecclesiastical jurisdictions—a vast body of men—were all joined to aid the spies of the *Chambres Ardentes*, by day or night.[2552] These ruffians made domiciliary visits, pried into all secrets, and especially put their ingenuity on the rack to discover the Conventicle. When they succeeded in surprising a religious meeting, they fell on its members with terrible violence, maltreating and sometimes murdering them, and those unable to escape they dragged to prison. These miscreants were by no means discriminating in their seizures; they must approve their diligence to their masters by furnishing their daily tale of victims. Besides, they had grudges to feed, and enmities to avenge, and their net was thrown at times over some who had but small acquaintance with the Gospel. A certain Mouchares, or Mouchy, became the head of a band who made it their business to apprehend men in the act of eating flesh on Friday, or violating some other equally important command of the Church. This man has transmitted his name and office to our day in the term *mouchard*, a spy of the police. The surveillance of Mouchares' band was specially exercised over the Faubourg St. Germain, called from the number of the Reformed that lived in it, "the Little Geneva." A hostelry in this quarter, at which the Protestants from Geneva and Germany commonly put up, was assailed one Friday by Mouchares' men. They found the guests to the number of sixteen at table. The Protestants drew their swords, and a scuffle ensued. Mouchares' crew was driven off, but returning reinforced, they sacked the house, dragged the landlord and his family to prison, and in order to render them odious to the mob, they carried before them a larded capon and a piece of raw meat.[2553]

The footsteps of these wretches might be traced in the wreckings of furniture, in the pillage and ruins which they left behind them, in those quarters of Paris which were so unfortunate as to be visited by them. "Nothing was to be seen in the streets," says Beza, describing the violences of those days, "but soldiers carrying men and women, and persons of all ages and every rank, to prison. The streets were so encumbered with carts loaded with household furniture, that it was hardly possible to pass. The houses were abandoned, having been pillaged and sacked, so that Paris looked like a city taken by storm. The poor had become rich, and the rich poor. What was more pitiable still was to see the little children, whose parents had been imprisoned, famishing at the doors of their former homes, or wandering through the streets crying piteously for bread, and no man giving it to them, so odious had Protestantism become to the Parisians. Still more to inflame the populace, at the street-corners certain persons in priests' habits harangued the crowd, telling them that those heretics met together to feast upon children's flesh, and to commit all kinds of impurity after they had eaten a pig instead of the Paschal lamb. The Parliament made no attempt to stop these outrages and crimes."[2554] Nor were these violences confined to the capital; the same scenes were enacted in many other cities, as Poictiers, Toulouse, Dijon, Bordeaux, Lyons, Aix, and other places of Languedoc.[2555]

This terror, which had so suddenly risen up in France, struck many Romanists as well as Protestants with affright. Some Popish voices joined in the cry that was now raised for a moderate Reform; but instead of Reform came new superstitions. Images of the Virgin were set up at the corners of streets, tapers were lighted, and persons stationed near on pretence of singing hymns, but in reality to watch the countenances of the passers-by. If one looked displeased, or if he refused to uncover to the Virgin, or if he did not drop a coin into the box for defraying the cost of the holy candle that was kept burning before "our Lady," the cry of heretic was raised, and the obnoxious individual was straightway surrounded by the mob, and if not torn to pieces on the spot, was carried off to the prison of the Châtelet. The apprehensions were so numerous that the prisons were filled to overflow, and the trials of the incarcerated had to be hurried through to make room for fresh victims. The cells emptied in the morning were filled before night. "It was one vast system of terror," says Félice, "in which even the shadow of justice was no longer visible."[2556]

No arts were neglected by the Guises and the priests to maintain at a white heat the fanaticism of the masses, on which their power to a large extent was based. If any public calamity happened—if a battle was lost, if the crops were destroyed by hail-storms, or if a province or city was ravaged by disease—"Ah!" it was said, "see what judgments these heretics are bringing on France!" Odious calumnies were put in circulation against those of the "religion." To escape the pursuit of the spies by whom on all sides they were beset, the Reformed sought for retreats yet more secret in which to assemble—the darkest alley in the city, the gloomiest recess of forest, the most savage ravine of wilderness. "Ah!" said their enemies, "they seek the darkness to veil their monstrous and unnatural wickedness from the light of heaven and from the eyes of men." It was the story of pagan times over again. The long-buried calumny of the early persecutor was raked up from old histories, and flung at the French Protestant. Even the Cardinal of Lorraine was mean enough to have recourse to these arts. His own unchaste life was no secret, yet he had the effrontery to advance, not insinuations merely, but open charges against ladies of illustrious rank, and of still more illustrious virtue—ladies whose lives were a rebuke of the profligacy with which his lawn was bespotted and bemired. The cardinal knew how pure was the virtue which he laboured to blacken. Not so the populace. They believed these men and women to be the atheists and monsters which they had been painted as being, and they thought that in massacring and exterminating them, they were cleansing France from what was at once a defilement of the earth, and a provocation of Heaven.

Avarice came to the aid of bigotry. Not a few of the Reformed were persons of position and property, and in their case confiscation of goods was added to loss of life. Their persecutors shared their estates among them, deeming them doubtless a lawful prize for their orthodox zeal; and thus the purification of the kingdom, and the enriching of the court and its myrmidons, went on by equal stages. The history of these manors and lands cannot in every case be traced, but it is known that many of them remained in possession of the families which now appropriated them till the great day of reckoning in 1789, and then the wealth that had been got by confiscation and injustice went as it had come. Indeed, in perusing the era of Francis II. we seem to be reading beforehand the history of the times of the Great Revolution. The names of persons and parties changed, the same harrowing tale will suit both periods. The machinery of injustice and oppression, first constructed by the Guises, was a second time set a-working under Danton and Robespierre. Again is seen a Reign of Terror; again are crowds of spies; again are numberless denunciations, with all their terrible accompaniments—prison cells emptied in the morning to be filled before night, tribunals condemning wholesale, the axe incessantly at work, a triumphant tyranny wielding the mob as its tool, confiscations on a vast scale, and a furious political fanaticism madly driving the nation into civil war.

It was evident that a crisis was approaching. The king was a captive in the hands of the Guises. The laws were not administered—wrong and outrage stalked defiantly through the kingdom; and to complain was to draw upon oneself the punishment which ought to have visited the acts of which one complained. None were safe except the more bigoted of the Roman Catholics, and the rabble of the great cities, the pliant tools of the oppressor. Men began to ask one another, "What right have these strangers from Lorraine to keep the king a captive, and to treat France like a conquered country? Let us hurl the usurpers from power, and restore the government to its legitimate channels." This led to what has been called the "Conspiracy of Amboise."

This movement, in its first origin, was entirely political. It was no more formed in the interest of the Reformed religion than of the Popish faith. It was devised in the interests of France, the emancipation of which from a tyrannous usurpation was its sole aim. It was promoted by both Roman Catholics and Protestants, because both were smarting from the oppression of the Guises. The testimony of Davila, which is beyond suspicion, is full to this effect, that the plot was not for the overthrow of the royal house, but for the liberation of the king and the authority of the laws.[2557] The judgment of the German and Swiss pastors was asked touching the lawfulness of the enterprise. Calvin gave his voice against it, foreseeing "that the Reformation might lose, even if victorious, by becoming in France a military and political party."[2558] Nevertheless, the majority of the pastors approved the project, provided a prince of the blood were willing to take the lead, and that a majority of the estates of the nation gave it their sanction. Admiral de Coligny stood aloof from it.

It was resolved to proceed in the attempt. The first question was, Who should be placed at the head of the movement? The King of Navarre was the first prince of the blood; but he was too apathetic and too inconstant to bear the weight of so great an affair. His brother, the Prince of Condé, was believed to have the requisite talents, and he was accordingly chosen as the chief of the enterprise. It was judged advisable, however, that he should meanwhile keep himself out of sight, and permit Godfrey du Barry, Lord of La Renaudie, to be the ostensible leader.[2559] Renaudie was a Protestant gentleman of broken fortunes, but brave, energetic, and able. Entering with prodigious zeal into the affair, Renaudie, besides travelling over France, visited England,[2560] and by his activity and organising skill, raised a little army of 400 horse and a body of foot, and enlisted not fewer than 200 Protestant gentlemen in the business. The confederates met at Nantes, and the 10th of March, 1560, was chosen as the day to begin the execution of their project. On that day they were to march to the Castle of Blois, where the king was then residing, and posting their soldiers in the woods around the castle, an unarmed deputation was to crave an audience of the king, and present, on being admitted to his presence, two requests, one for liberty of worship, and the other for the dismissal of the Guises. If these demands were rejected, as they anticipated they would be, they would give the signal, their men-at-arms would rush in, they would arrest the Guises, and place the Prince of Condé at the head of the government. The confederates had taken an oath to hold inviolable the person of the king. The secret, though entrusted to thousands, was religiously kept till it was on the very eve of execution. A timorous Protestant, M. d'Avenelles, an attorney in Paris, revealed it to the court just at the last moment.[2561]

The Guises, having come to the knowledge of the plot, removed to the stronger Castle of Amboise, carrying the king thither also. This castle stood upon a lofty rock, which was washed by the broad stream of the Loire. The insurgents, though disconcerted by the betrayal of their enterprise, did not abandon it, nevertheless they postponed the day of execution from the 10th to the 16th of March.

Renaudie was to arrive in the neighbourhood of Amboise on the eve of the appointed day. Next morning he was to send his troops into the town, in small bodies, so as not to attract notice; he himself was to enter at noon. One party of the soldiers were to seize the gates of the citadel, and arrest the duke and the cardinal; this done, they were to hoist a signal on the top of the tower, and the men-at-arms, hidden in the neighbouring woods, would rush in and complete the revolution.[2562]

But what of the king while these strange events were in progress? Glimpses of his true condition, which was more that of a captive than a monarch, at times dawned upon him. One day, bursting into tears, he said to his wife's uncles, "What have I done to my people that they hate me so? I would like to hear their complaints and their reasons. I hear it said that people are against you only. I wish you could be away from here for a time, that we might see whether it is you or I that they are against." The men to whom he had made this touching appeal gruffly replied, "Do you then wish that the Bourbon should triumph over the Valois? Should we do as you desire, your house would speedily be rooted out."[2563]

We return to affairs outside the walls of Amboise. Among those to whom the secret was entrusted was a Captain Lignières, who repairing to Amboise revealed the whole matter to the Queen-mother. He made known the names of the confederates, the inns at which they were to lodge, the roads by which they were to march on Amboise—in short, the whole plan of the assault. The Guises instantly took their measures for the security of the town. They changed the king's guards, built up the gate of the city-wall, and dispatched troops to occupy the neighbouring towns. Renaudie, surrounded as he was advancing by forced marches to Amboise, fell, fighting bravely, while his followers were cut in pieces, or taken prisoners. Another body of troops under Baron de Castelnau was overpowered, and their leader, deeming farther resistance useless, surrendered on a written promise that his own life and that of his soldiers should be spared.

The insurgents were now in the power of the Guises, and their revenge was in proportion to their former terror, and that had been great. The market-place of the town of Amboise was covered with scaffolds. Fast as the axe and the gallows could devour one batch of victims, another batch was brought out to be dispatched in like manner. Crowding the windows of the palace were the Cardinal of Lorraine and the duke, radiant with victory; the ladies of the court, including the Scottish Mary Stuart, in their gayest attire; the young king and his lords, all feasting their eyes on the terrible scenes which were being enacted in front of the palace. The blood of those that fell by the axe overflowed the scaffolds, filled the kennels, and poured in rushing torrents to the Loire.[2564] That generous blood, now shed like water, would in after-years have enriched France with chivalry and virtue. Not fewer than 1,200 persons perished at this time. Four dismal weeks these tragedies were continued. At last the executioners grew weary, and bethought them of a more summary way of dispatching their victims. They tied their hands and feet, and flung them into the Loire. The stream went on its way with its ghastly freight, and as it rolled past corn-field and vineyard, village and city, it carried to Tours and Nantes, and other towns, the first horrifying news of the awful tragedies proceeding at Amboise. Castelnau and his companions, despite the promises on which they had surrendered, shared the fate of the other prisoners. One of the gentlemen of his company, before bowing his head to the axe, dipped his hands in the blood of his already butchered comrades, and holding them up to heaven, exclaimed, "Lord, behold the blood of thy children unjustly slain; thou wilt avenge it."[2565] That appeal went up to the bar of the great Judge; but the answer stood over for 230 years. With the Revolution of 1789, came Carrier of Nantes, a worthy successor of the Cardinal of Lorraine, and then it was seen that the cry had been heard at the great bar to which it ascended. On the banks of the same river did this man enact, in the name of liberty, the same horrible butcheries which the cardinal had perpetrated in the name of religion. A second time did the Loire roll onward a river of blood, bearing on its bosom a ghastly burden of corpses. When we look down on France in 1560, and see her rivers reddening the seas around her coasts, and when again we look down upon her in 1790, and see the same portentous spectacle renewed, we seem to hear the angel of the waters saying, "Thou art righteous, O Lord, who art, and wast, and shalt be, because thou hast judged thus: for they have shed the blood of saints and prophets, and thou hast given them blood to drink for they are worthy. And I heard another angel out of the altar say, Even so, Lord God Almighty, true and righteous are thy judgments."[2566]

The Reformation continued to advance in the face of all this violence.[2567] "There were many even among the prelates," Davila tells us, "that inclined to Calvin's doctrine."[2568] The same year that witnessed the bloody tragedy we have just recorded, witnessed also the establishment of the public celebration of Protestant worship in France. Up till this time the Reformed had held their assemblies for worship in secret; they met over-night, and in lonely and hidden places; but now the very increase of their numbers forced them into the light of day. When whole cities, and well-nigh entire provinces, had embraced the Reformation, it was no longer possible for the confessors of Protestant truth to bury themselves in dens and forests. Why should the population of a whole town go out of its gates to worship? why not assemble in its own cathedrals, seeing in many places there were not now Papists to occupy them? The very calumnies which their enemies invented and circulated against them compelled them to this course. They would worship in open day, and with open doors, and see who should dare accuse them of seeking occasion for unnatural and abominable crimes. But this courageous course on the part of the Reformed stung the Guises to madness, and their measures became still more violent. They got together bands of ruffians, and sent them into the provinces where the Calvinists abounded, with a commission to slay and burn at their pleasure. The city of Tours was almost entirely Protestant. So, too, were Valence and Romans. The latter towns were surprised, the principal inhabitants hanged, and the Protestant pastors beheaded with a label on their breasts, "These are the chiefs of the rebels."[2569] These barbarities, as might have been expected, provoked reprisals. Some of the less discreet of the Protestants made incursions, at the head of armed bands, into Provence and Dauphiné. Entering the cathedrals, and turning the images and priests to the door, they celebrated Protestant worship in them, sword in hand; and when they took their departure, they carried with them the gold and silver utensils which had been used in the Romish service.

Such was now the unhappy condition of France. The laws were no longer administered. The land, scoured by armed bands, was full of violence and terror, of rapine and blood. The anarchy was complete; the cup of the ruler's oppression, and the people's suffering, was full and running over.

The Guises, intent on profiting to the utmost from the suppression of the "Conspiracy of Amboise," pushed hard to crush their rivals before they had time to rally, or set on foot a second and, it might be, more formidable insurrection. In order to this, they resolved on two measures—first, to dispatch the Prince of Condé, the head of the Protestant party; and, secondly, to compel every man and woman in the kingdom to abjure Protestantism. In prosecution of the first, having lured the prince to Orleans, they placed him under arrest, and brought him to trial for complicity in the Amboise Conspiracy. As a matter of course he was condemned, and the Guises were now importuning the king to sign the death-warrant and have him executed. The moment Condé's head had fallen on the scaffold, they would put in force the second measure—the abjuration, namely. A form of abjuration was already drawn up, and it was resolved that on Christmas Day the king should present it to all the princes and officers of the court for their signature; that the queen, in like manner, should present it to all her ladies and maids of honour; the chancellor to all the deputies of Parliament and judges; the governors of provinces to all the gentry; the curés to all their parishioners; and the heads of families to all their dependents. The alternative of refusing to subscribe the abjuration oath was to be immediate execution. The cardinal, who loved to mingle a little grim pleasantry with his bloody work, called this cunning device of his "the Huguenot's rat-trap."[2570]

All was prospering according to the wish of the government. The scaffold was already erected on which Condé was to die. The executioner had been summoned, and was even now in Orleans. The abjuration formula was ready to be presented to all ranks and every individual the moment the prince had breathed his last; the year would not close without seeing France covered with apostasies or with martyrdoms. Verily, it seemed as if the grave of the French Reformation was dug.

When all was lost, as it appeared, an unseen finger touched this complicated web, woven with equal cruelty and cunning, and in an instant its threads were rent—the snare was broken. The king was smitten with a sudden malady in the head, which defied the skill of all his physicians. The Guises were thrown into great alarm by the illness of the king. "Surely," said the duke to the physicians, "your art can save one who is only in the flower of his age." And when told that the royal patient would not live till Easter, he stormed exceedingly, and accused the physicians of killing the king, and of having taken the money of the heretics for murdering him. His brother, the cardinal, betook him to the saints of Paradise. He ordered prayers and processions for his recovery. But, despite the prayers that ascended in the temples—despite the images and relics that were carried in solemn procession through the streets—the king rapidly sank, and before Condé's death-warrant could be signed, or the abjuration test presented for subscription, Francis II. had breathed his last.[2571]

The king died (5th December, 1560) at the age of seventeen, after a reign of only as many months. The courtiers were too busy making suit for their places, or providing for their safety, to care for the lifeless body of the king. It lay neglected on the bed on which he had expired. Yesterday they had cringed and bowed before him, today he was nothing more to them than so much carrion. A few days thereafter we see a funeral procession issuing from the gates of Orleans, and proceeding along the road to the royal vaults at St. Dénis. But what a poor show! What a meagre following! We see none of the usual pageantry of grief—no heralds; no nodding plumes; no grandees of State in robes of mourning; we hear no boom of cannon, no tolling of passing bell—in short, nothing to tell us that it is a king who is being borne to the tomb. A blind bishop and two aged domestics make up the entire train behind the funeral car.[2572] It was in this fashion that Francis II. was carried to his grave.

CHAPTER VI

CHARLES IX—THE TRIUMVIRATE—COLLOQUY AT POISSY

WE have seen Francis II. carried to the tomb with no more pomp or decency than if, instead of the obsequies of a king, it had been the funeral of a pauper. There followed a sudden shifting of the scenes at court. The day of splendour that seemed to be opening to Mary Stuart was suddenly overcast. From the throne of France she returned to her native country, carrying with her to the Scottish shore her peerless beauty, her almost unrivalled power of dissembling, and her hereditary and deeply cherished hatred of the Reformation. To her uncles, the Guises, the death of the king brought a not less sad reverse of fortune. Though they still retained their offices and dignities, they were no longer the uncontrolled masters of the State, as when Francis occupied the throne and their niece sat by his side. But in the room of the Guises there stood up one not less the enemy of the Gospel, and whose rule was not less prolific of woes to France.

Catherine de Medici was now supreme in the government; her day had at last arrived. If her measures were less precipitate, and her violence less open, her craft was deeper than that of the Guises, and her stroke, if longer delayed, was the more deadly when it fell. Her son, Charles IX., who now occupied the throne, was a lad of only nine and a half years; and, as might have been expected in the case of such a mother and such a son, Charles wore the crown, but Catherine governed the kingdom. The sudden demise of Francis had opened the prison doors to Condé. Snatching him from a scaffold, it restored him to liberty. As a prince of the blood, the Regency of France, during the minority of Charles, by right belonged to him; but Catherine boldly put him aside, and made herself be installed in that high office. In this act she gave a taste of the vigour with which she meant to rule. Still she did not proceed in too great haste. Her caution, which was great, served as a bridle to her ambition, and the Huguenots,[2573] as they began to be called, had now a breathing-space.

The Queen-mother fortified herself on the side of the Guises by recalling the Constable Montmorency, and installing him in all his dignities and offices. The next event of importance was the meeting of the States-General at Orleans (December 13th, 1560), a few days after Charles IX. had ascended the throne. The assembly was presided over by the Chancellor Michel de l'Hôpital, a man learned in the law, revered on the judgment-seat for the wisdom and equity of his decisions, and tolerant beyond the measure of his times. The words, few but weighty, with which he opened the proceedings, implied a great deal more than they expressed. The Church, he said, that great fountain of health or of disease to a nation, had become corrupt. Reformation was needed. "Adorn yourselves," said he to the clergy, "but let it be with virtues and morality. Attack your foes, by all means, but let it be with the weapons of charity, prayer, and persuasion."[2574] Enlightened counsels these, which needed only wisdom in those to whom they were addressed, to work the cure of many of the evils which afflicted France.

The city of Bordeaux had sent an orator to the Parliament. Lying remote from the court, and not domineered over by the Popish rabble as Paris was,

Bordeaux breathed a spirit more friendly to liberty and the Reformation than did the capital, and its deputy was careful to express the sentiments entertained by those who had commissioned him to represent them in this great assembly of the nation. "Three great vices," he said, "disfigure the clergy—ignorance, avarice, and luxury;" and after dwelling at some length on each, he concluded by saying that if the ministers of religion would undertake to reform themselves, he would undertake to reform the nation. The spokesman of the nobility, the Lord of Rochefort, next rose to express the sentiments of the body he represented. His words were not more palatable to the clergy than had been those of the speakers who preceded him. He complained that the course of justice was obstructed by the interference of the priests. He did not know which was the greater scandal, or the source of greater misery to the country—the prodigious wealth of the clergy, or the astounding ignorance of their flocks. And he concluded by demanding "churches" for the "gentlemen of the religion." Thus all the lay speakers in the States-General united as one man in arraigning the Roman Church as pre-eminently the source of the many evils which afflicted France. They all with one voice demanded that the clergy should reform their doctrine, amend their lives, moderate the magnificence in which they lived, and laying aside their arrogance and bigotry, should labour to instruct their flocks, and to reclaim those who had gone astray, not with the knife and the faggot, but with the weapons of truth and reason.

It was now the turn of the clergy to be heard through the oracle whom they had selected—Jean Quintin, Professor of Canon Law. He had undertaken the cause of an institution laden with abuses, and now arraigned at the bar of the nation, as the cause of the manifold distractions and oppressions under which the country groaned. He began by expressing his regret—a regret, we doubt not, perfectly sincere—that a most unwonted and dangerous innovation had been practised in permitting the nobility and commons to address the assembly. The Church, he said, was the mouth of the States-General; and had that mouth, and no other, been permitted to address them, they would have been spared the pain of listening to so many hard things of the Church, and so many smooth things of heresy. The heretics, said the orator, had no other Gospel than revolution; and this pestiferous Gospel admitted of no remedy but the sword. Were not all the men who had embraced this Gospel under the excommunication of the Church? and for what end had the sword been put in the hand of the king, if not to execute the deserved vengeance to which the Church had adjudged those who had so fatally strayed? And, turning to the young king, he told him that his first and most sacred duty, as a magistrate, was to defend the Church, and to root out her enemies. Coligny, who sat facing the speaker, started to his feet on hearing this atrocious proposal, which doomed to extermination a third of the population of France. He demanded an apology from the speaker. Quintin could doubtless plead the authority of canon law, and many a melancholy precedent to boot, for what he had said; but he had overshot the mark. He found no response in that assembly; even Catherine de Medici felt the speech to be an imprudent one, and the priests, whatever their secret wishes, durst not openly support their orator; and so Quintin was compelled to apologise. Sickening under his mortification, he died three days thereafter.

Something had been gained by the meeting of the States-General. The priest-party had suffered a rebuff; Catherine de Medici had felt the pulse of the nation, and was more convinced than ever that the course she had resolved to steer was the wise one. Her supreme object was power; and she would best attain it by being on good terms with both parties. She opened the halls of Fontainebleau to the Protestant preachers, and she and her maids of honour were to be seen at times waiting with edifying seriousness upon the sermons of the Reformed pastors. So far did the Queen Regent carry her favours to the Protestants, that the Roman Catholics took alarm, fearing that she had gone over, not in seeming only, but in reality, to the "religion." There was little cause for their alarm. Catherine had no intention of becoming a Huguenot. She was merely holding the balance between the two parties—making each weaken the other—judging this to be the most effectual way of strengthening herself.

These favours to the Protestants roused the slumbering zeal of the Romanists. Now arose the Triumvirate. The party so named, which makes some figure in the history of the times, was formed for the defence of the old religion, its members being the Duke of Guise, the Constable Montmorency, and the Marshal St. André. These three men had little in common. The bond which held them together was hatred of the new faith, the triumph of which, they foresaw, would strip them of their influence and possessions. There had been a prodigal waste of the public money, and a large confiscation of the estates of the Protestants under the two former reigns; these three men had carried off the lion's share of the spoil; and should Protestantism win the day, they would, in modern phrase, have to *recoup*, and this touched at once their honour and their purses. As regards the Guises, their whole influence hung upon the Roman Church; her destruction, therefore, would be their destruction. As respects the Constable Montmorency, he prided himself on being the first Christian in France. He was descended in a direct line from St. Louis; and a birth so illustrious—not to speak of the fair fame of his saintly ancestors—imposed upon him the duty of defending the old faith, or if that were impossible, of perishing with it. He was incapable of defending it by argument; but he had a sword, and it would ill become him to let it rust in its scabbard, when the Church needed its service. As regards Marshal St. André, the least influential member of the Triumvirate, he was a noted gourmand, a veritable Lucullus, to whom there was nothing in life half so good as a well-furnished table. Marshal St. André foresaw that should Roman Catholicism go down in France, he would not only lose his Church—he would lose his dinner. The first might be borne, but the latter was not to be thought of. These men had formerly been at deadly feud among themselves; but now they resolved to sacrifice their differences upon the altar of the country, and to unite together in this holy league for the defence of their religion and their estates. The Triumvirate will again come before us: it has left its mark on the history of France.

The States-General again assembled in the end of 1561. The first thing that came under its notice was the financial state of the kingdom. The national debt amounted to £48,000,000, and bade fair greatly to exceed that sum in a short time, for the expenditure was a long way in excess of the revenue. What was to be done? A proposal was made that anticipated the measure which was carried out in France in 1789, and adopted long after that date in all the countries in which Roman Catholicism is the established religion. The speaker who made the proposal in question, laid down the principle that the ecclesiastical property belongs to the nation; that the clergy are merely its administrators; and founding on that principle, he proposed that the estates of the Church should be put up for sale, and the proceeds divided as follows:—one-third to go to the support of the Church; one-third to the payment of the national debt; and one-third to the revenues of the crown, to be applied, of course, to national uses. In this way it was hoped the financial difficulty would be got over; but the great difficulty—the religious one—lay behind; how was it to be got over?

It was agreed that a Council should be summoned; but it augured ill for the era of peace it was to inaugurate, that men disputed regarding its name before it had assembled. The priests strongly objected to its being called a Council. That would imply that the Protestant pastors were Christian ministers as well as themselves, entitled to meet them on terms of equality, and that the Reformed bodies were part of the Church as well as the Roman Catholics. The difficulty was got over by the device of styling the approaching assembly a Colloquy. The two parties had a different ideal before their mind. That of the Romanists was, that the Protestants came to the bar to plead, and to have their cause judged by the Church. That of the Protestants was, that the two parties were to debate on equal terms, that the Bible should be the supreme standard, and that the State's authorities should decide without appeal. Knox, in Scotland, drew the line more justly; framing his creed from the Bible, he presented it to the Parliament, just a year before this, and asked the authorities to judge of it, but only for themselves, in order to the withdrawal from the Roman hierarchy of that secular jurisdiction in which it was vested, and which it was exercising for the hindrance of the evangel, and for the destruction of its disciples. The Protestant Church of France had no Knox.

On September 9th, 1561, this Colloquy—for we must not call it a Council—assembled at Poissy. On this little town, which lay a few leagues to the west of Paris, were the eyes of Christendom for the moment fixed. Will the conference now assembling there unite the two religions, and give peace to France? This issue was as earnestly desired by the Protestant States of Germany and England, as it was dreaded by the Pope and the King of Spain.

Nothing was wanting which pomp could give to make the conference a success. The hall in which it was held was the refectory of the convent at Poissy. There was set a throne, and on that throne sat the youthful sovereign of France, Charles IX. Right and left of him were ranged the princes and princesses of the blood, the great ministers of the crown, and the high lords of the court.[2575] Along two sides of the hall ran a row of benches, and on these sat the cardinals in their scarlet robes. On the seats below them were a crowd of bishops, priests, and doctors. The assembly was a brilliant one. Wherever the eye turned, it fell upon the splendour of official robes, upon the brilliance of rank, upon stars, crosses, and other insignia of academic distinction or of military achievement. It lacked the moral majesty, however, which a great purpose, earnestly and sincerely entertained, only can give. No affluence of embroidered and jewelled attire can compensate for the absence of a great moral end.

The king rose and said a few words. Much could not be looked for from a lad of only ten years. The chancellor, Michel de l'Hôpital, followed in a long speech, abounding in the most liberal and noble sentiments; and had the members of the assembly opened their ears to these wise counsels, they would have guided its deliberations to a worthy issue, and made the future of France a happy and glorious one. "Let us not pre-judge the cause we are met to discuss," said in effect the chancellor, "let us receive these men as brethren—they are Christians as well as ourselves; let us not waste time in subtleties, but with all humility proceed to the Reformation of the doctrine of the Church, taking the Bible as the arbiter of all our differences." L'Hôpital aimed at striking the key-note of the discussions; but so little were his words in harmony with the sentiments of those to whom they were addressed, that the speech very nearly broke up the conference before it had well begun. It called for Reform according to the Bible. "The Bible is enough," said he; "to this, as to the true rule, we must appeal for the decision of the doctrine. Neither must we be so averse to the Reformed, for they are our brethren, regenerated by the same baptism, and worshipping the same Christ as we do."[2576] Straightway there arose a great commotion among the cardinals and bishops; angry words and violent gestures bespoke the irritation of their minds; but the firmness of the chancellor succeeded in calming the storm, and the business was proceeded with.

The Protestant deputies had not yet been introduced to the conference. This showed that here all did not meet on equal terms. But now, the Papal members having taken their seats, and the preliminary speeches being ended, there was no excuse for longer delaying the admission of the Protestants. The doors were thrown open, and Theodore Beza, followed by ten Protestant pastors and twenty-two lay deputies, entered the hall. There was a general desire that Calvin, then in the zenith of his fame, should have taken part in the discussions. The occasion was not unworthy of him, and Catherine de Medici had invited him by letter; but the magistrates of Geneva, unable to obtain hostages of high rank as pledges of his safety, refused to let him come, and Theodore Beza was sent in his room. No better substitute could have been found for the illustrious chief of the Reformation than his distinguished disciple and fellow-labourer. Beza was a native of Burgundy, of noble birth; learned, eloquent, courtly, and of a dignified presence. We possess a sketch of the personal appearance of this remarkable man by the traveller Fynes Moryson, who chanced to pass through Geneva in the end of that century. "Here," says he, "I had the great contentment to speak and converse with the reverend Father Theodore Beza, who was of stature something tall and corpulent, or big-boned, and had a long thick beard white as snow. He had a grave senator's countenance, and was broad-faced, but not fat, and in general, by his comely person, sweet affability, and gravity, he would have extorted reverence from those that least loved him."[2577]

The Reformed pastors entered, gravely and simply attired. They wore the usual habits of the Geneva Church, which offered a striking contrast to the State robes and clerical vestments in which courtier and cardinal were arrayed. Unawed by the blaze of stars, crosses, and various insignia of rank and office which met their gaze, the deputies bore themselves with a calm dignity, as men who had come to plead a great cause before a great assembly. They essayed to pass the barrier, and mingle on equal terms with those with whom they were to confer. But, no; their place was outside. The Huguenot pastor could not sit side by side with the Roman bishop. The Reformation must not come nigh the throne of Charles IX. and the hierarchy of the Church. It must be made to appear as if it stood at the bar to be judged. The pastors, though they saw, were too magnanimous to complain of this studied affront; nor did they refuse on that account to plead a cause which did not rest on such supports as lofty looks and gorgeous robes.

The moral majesty of Beza asserted its supremacy, and carried it over all the mock magnificence of the men who said to him, "Stand afar off, we are holier than thou." Immediately on entering he fell on his knees, the other deputies kneeling around him, and in the presence of the assembly, which remained mute and awed, he offered a short but most impressive prayer that Divine assistance might be vouchsafed in the discussions now to commence and that these discussions might be guided to an issue profitable to the Church of God. Then rising up he made obeisance to the young monarch, thanking him for this opportunity of defending the Reformation; and next, turning to the prelates, he besought them to seek only to arrive at truth. Having thus introduced himself and his cause, he proceeded to unfold the leading doctrines of the Reformation. He took care to dwell on the spirit of loyalty that animated its disciples, well knowing that the Romanists charged it with being the enemy of princes; he touched feelingly on the rigours to which his co-religionists had been subjected, though no fault had been found in them, save in the matters of their God; and then launching out on the great question which had brought the conference together, he proceeded with much clearness and beauty of statement, and also with great depth of argument, to discuss the great outstanding points between the two Churches. The speech took the Roman portion of the assembly by surprise. Such erudition and eloquence they had not expected to find in the advocates of the Reform; they were not quite the contemptible opponents they had expected to meet, and they felt that they would do well to look to their own armour. Beza, having ended, presented on bended knee a copy of the Confession of the French Protestant Church to the king.

But the orator had not been permitted to pursue uninterruptedly his argument to its close. In dealing with the controverted points, Beza had occasion to touch on the Sacrament of the Eucharist. It was the centre of the controversy. The doctrine he maintained on this head was, in brief that Christ is spiritually present in the Sacrament, and spiritually partaken of by the faith of the recipient; but that his body is not in the elements, but in heaven. If the modest proposal of the Chancellor de l'Hôpital, that the Bible should rule in the discussion, had raised a commotion, the words of Beza, asserting the Protestant doctrine on the great point at issue between Rome and the Reformation, evoked quite a storm. First, murmurs were heard; these speedily grew into a tempest of voices. "He has spoken blasphemy! cried some. Cardinal Tournon demanded, anger almost choking his utterance, that the king should instantly silence Beza, and expel from France men whose very presence was polluting its soil and imperilling the faith of the "most Christian king." All eyes were turned upon Catherine de Medici. She sat unmoved amid the clamour that surrounded her. Her son, Charles IX., was equally imperturbable. The *ruse* of the Roman bishops had failed—for nothing else than a *ruse* could it be, if the Romanists did not expect the Protestant deputies quietly and without striking a blow to surrender their whole case to Rome—and the assembly by-and-by subsiding into calm, Beza went on with his speech, which he now pursued without interruption to its close.

The feeling among the bishops was that of discomfiture, though they strove to hide it under an air of affected contempt. Beza had displayed an argumentative power, and a range of learning and eloquence, which convinced them that they had found in him a more formidable opponent than they had expected to encounter. They regretted that the conference had ever met; they dreaded, above all things, the effect which the reasonings of Beza might have on the mind of the king. "Would to God," said the Cardinal of Lorraine, "that Beza had been dumb, or we deaf." But regrets were vain. The conference had met, Beza had spoken, and there was but one course—Beza must be answered. They promised a refutation of all he had advanced, in a few days.

The onerous task was committed to the hands of the Cardinal of Lorraine. The choice was a happy one. The cardinal was not lacking in ingenuity; he was, moreover, possessed of some little learning, and a master in address. Claude d'Espence, accounted one of the most learned of their doctors, was appointed to assist him in the way of collecting materials for his answer. On the 16th of September the Colloquy again met, and the cardinal stood forth before the assembly and delivered an eloquent oration. He confined himself to two points—the Church and the Sacrament. "The Church," he said, "was infallibly guarded from error by the special promise of Christ. True," he said, glancing at the Protestant members of the Colloquy, "individual Christians might err and fall out of the communion of the Church, but the Church herself cannot err, and when any of her children wander they ought to submit themselves to the Pontiff, who cannot fail to bring them back to the right path, and never can lose it himself." In proof of this indefectibility of the Church, the cardinal cast himself upon history, expatiating, as is the wont of Romish controversialists, upon her antiquity and her advance, *pari passu*, with the ages in power and splendour. He painted her as surviving all changes, withstanding the shock of all revolutions, outlasting dynasties and nations, triumphing over all her enemies, remaining unbroken by division within, unsubdued by violence without, and apparently as imperishable as the throne of her Divine Founder. So spoke the cardinal. The prestige that encompasses Rome has dazzled others besides Romanists, and we may be sure the picture, in the hands of the cardinal, would lose none of its attractions and illusions. The second point, the Sacrament, did not admit of the same dramatic handling, and the cardinal contented himself with a summary of the usual arguments of his Church in favour of transubstantiation. The orator had not disappointed the expectations formed of him; even a less able speech would have been listened to with applause by an audience so partial; but the cheers that greeted Lorraine when he had ended were deafening. "He has refuted, nay, extinguished Beza," shouted a dozen voices. Gathering round the king, "That, sire," said they, "is the true faith, which has been handed down from Clovis: abide in it."

When the noise had a little subsided, Beza rose and requested permission to reply on the spot. This renewed the confusion. "The deputies had but one course," insisted the prelates, "they ought to confess that they are vanquished; and, if they refused, they must be compelled, or banished the kingdom." But the hour was late; the lay members of the council were in favour of hearing Beza, and the bishops, being resolved at all hazards that he should not be heard, broke up the assembly. This may be said to have been the end of the conferences; for though the sittings were continued, they were held in a small chamber belonging to the prior; the king was not permitted to come any more to them; the lay deputies were also excluded; and the debates degenerated into mere devices on the part of the Romanist clergy to entrap the Protestants into signing articles craftily drafted and embodying the leading tenets of the Roman creed. Failing in this, the Cardinal of Lorraine attempted a characteristic *ruse*. He wrote to the Governor of Metz, desiring him to send to him a few divines of the Augsburg Confession, "holding their opinions with great obstinacy," his design being to set them a-wrangling with the Calvinists on the points of difference. Arriving at Paris, one of them died of the plague, and the rest could not be presented in public. The cardinal consequently was left to manage his little affair himself as best he could. "Do you," said he to Beza, "like the Lutherans of Germany, admit consubstantiation?" "And do you," rejoined Beza, "like them, deny transubstantiation?" The cardinal thought to create a little bad blood between the Protestants of Germany and the Protestants of France, and so deprive the latter of the assistance which he feared might be sent them from their co-religionists of the Fatherland. But his policy of "divide and conquer" did not prosper.[2578]

It was clear that no fair discussion, and no honest adjustment of the controversy on the basis of truth, had from the first been intended. Nevertheless, the Colloquy had prompted the inquiry, "Is Romanism simply a corruption of the Gospel, or rather, has it not changed in the course of the ages into a system alien from and antagonistic to Christianity, and can there in that case be a possibility of reconciling the two faiths?" The conference bore fruit also in another direction. It set the great Chancellor de l'Hôpital to work to solve the problem, how the two parties could live in one country. To unite them was impossible; to exterminate one of them—Rome's short and easy way—was abhorrent to him. There remained but one other device—namely, that each should tolerate the other. Simple as this way seems to us, to the men of the times of L'Hôpital, with a few rare exceptions, it was unthought of and untried, and appeared impossible. But, soon after the breakdown of Poissy, we find the chancellor beginning to air, though in ungenial times, his favourite theory—that men might be loyal subjects of the king, though not of the king's faith, and good members of the nation, though not of the nation's Church; in short, that difference of religious opinions ought not to infer exclusion from civil privileges, much less ought it to subject men to civil penalties.

Another important result of the Colloquy at Poissy, was that the Reformation stood higher in public estimation. It had been allowed to justify itself on a very conspicuous stage, and all to whom prejudice had left the power of judging, were beginning to see that it was not the disloyal and immoral system its enemies had accused it of being, nor were its disciples the vicious and monstrous characters which the priests had painted them. A fresh impulse was given to the movement. Some important towns, and hundreds of villages, after the holding of the Colloquy, left the communion of Rome. Farel was told by a pastor "that 300 parishes in the Agenois had put down the mass." From all quarters came the cry, "Send us preachers!" Farel made occasional tours into his native France. There arrived from Switzerland another remarkable man to take part in the work which had received so sudden a development. In October, 1561, Pierre Viret came to Nismes. He had been way-laid on the road, and beaten almost to death, by those who guessed on what errand he was travelling; and when he appeared on the scene of his labours, "he seemed," to use his own words, "to be nothing but a dry skeleton covered with skin, who had brought his bones thither to be buried." Nevertheless, on the day after his arrival, he preached to 8,000 hearers. When he showed himself in the pulpit, many among his audience asked, "What has this poor man come to do in our country? Is he not come to die?" But when the clear, silvery tones of his voice rang out upon the ear, they forgot the meagre look and diminutive figure of the man before them, and thought only of what he said. There were an unction and sweetness in his address, that carried captive their hearts. All over the south of France, and more particularly in the towns of Nismes, Lyons, Montpelier, and Orthez, he preached the Gospel; and the memory of this eloquent evangelist lingers in those parts to this day.[2579]

Nor was Beza in any haste to depart, although the conferences which brought him to Paris were at an end. Catherine de Medici, on whom his learning, address, and courtly bearing had not failed to make an impression, showed him some countenance, and he preached frequently in the neighbourhood of the capital. These gatherings took place outside the walls of Paris; the people, to avoid all confusion, going and returning by several gates. In the centre were the women; next came the men, massed in a broad circular column; while a line of sentinels stationed at intervals kept watch on the outside, lest the fanatical mob of Paris should throw itself upon the congregation of worshippers.

It was impossible that a great movement like this, obstructed by so many and so irritating hindrances, should pursue its course without breaking into occasional violences. In those parts of France where the whole population had passed over to Protestantism, the people took possession of the cathedrals, and, as a matter of course, they cleared out the crucifixes, images, and relics which they contained. In the eyes of the Protestants these things were the symbols of idolatry, and they felt that they had only half renounced Romanism while they retained the signs and symbols of its dogmas. They felt that they had not honestly put away the doctrine while they retained its exponent. A nation of philosophers might have been able to distinguish between the idea and its symbol, and completely to emancipate themselves from the former without destroying the latter. They might have said, These things are nothing to us but so much wood and metal; it is in the idea that the mischief lies, and we have effectually separated ourselves from it, and the daily sight of these things cannot bring it back or restore its dominancy over us. But the great mass of mankind are too little abstract to feel or reason in this way. They cannot fully emancipate themselves from the idea till its sign has been put away. The Bible has recognised this feebleness, if one may term it so, of the popular mind, when it condemned, as in the second commandment, worship *by* an image, as the worship *of* the image of the false gods, stringently commanded that both should be put away. And the distinctive feeling of the masses in all revolutions, political as well as religious, has recognised this principle. Nations, in all such cases, have destroyed the symbols as well as exploded the idea these symbols represented. The early Christians broke the idols and demolished the temples of paganism. In the revolution of 1789, and in every succeeding revolution in France, the populace demolished the monuments and tore down the insignia of the former *régime*. If this is too great a price to pay for Reformation, that is another thing; but we cannot have a Reformation without it. We cannot have liberty without the loss, not of tyranny only, but its symbols also; nor the Gospel without the loss of idolatry, substance and symbol. Nor can these symbols return without the old ideas returning too. Hence Ranke tells us that the first indication of a reaction against the Reformation in Germany was "the wearing of rosaries." This may enable us to understand the ardour of the French iconoclasts of the sixteenth century. Of that ardour we select, from a multitude of illustrative incidents, the following:—On one occasion, during the first war of religion, news was brought to Condé and Coligny that the great Church of St. Croix in Orleans was being sacked. Hurrying to the spot, they found a soldier mounted on a ladder, busied in breaking an image. The prince pointed an arquebuse at him. "Monseigneur," said the Huguenot, "have patience till I have knocked down this idol, and then I will die, if you please."

CHAPTER VII
MASSACRE AT VASSY AND COMMENCEMENT OF THE CIVIL WARS

THE failure of the Colloquy of Poissy was no calamity to either Protestantism or the world. Had the young Reform thrown itself into the arms of the old Papacy, it would have been strangled in the embrace. The great movement of the sixteenth century, like those of preceding ages, after illuminating the horizon for a little while, would again have faded into darkness.

By what means and by what persons the Gospel was spread in France at this era is difficult to say. A little company of disciples would start up in this town, and in that village, and their numbers would go on increasing, till at last the mass was forsaken, and instead of the priest's chant there was heard the Huguenot's psalm. The famous potter, Palissy, has given us in his *Memoirs* some interesting details concerning the way in which many of these congregations arose. Some poor but honest citizen would learn the way of peace in the Bible; he would tell it to his next neighbour; that neighbour would tell it in his turn; and in a little while a small company of simple but fervent disciples would be formed, who would meet regularly at the midnight hour to pray and converse together. Ere their enemies were aware, half the town had embraced "the religion;" and then, taking courage, they would avow their faith, and hold their worship in public. As the rich verdure spreads over the earth in spring, adding day by day a new brightness to the landscape, and mounting ever higher on the mountain's side, so with the same silence, and the same beauty, did the new life diffuse itself throughout France. The sweetness and joy of this new creation, the inspired Idyll alone can adequately depict—"Lo, the winter is past, the rain is over and gone: the flowers appear on the earth; the time of the singing of birds is come, and the voice of the turtle is heard in our land. The fig-tree putteth forth her green figs, and the vines with the grape give a good smell."

Like that balmy morning, so exquisitely painted in these words, that broke on the heathen world after the pagan night, so was the morning that was now opening on France. Let the words of an eyewitness bear testimony:—"The progress made by us was such," says Palissy, "that in the course of a few years, by the time that our enemies rose up to pillage and persecute us, lewd plays, dances, ballads, gourmandisings, and superfluities of dress and head-gear had almost entirely ceased. Scarcely was there any more bad language to be heard on any side, nor were there any more crimes and scandals. Law-suits greatly diminished. . . . Indeed, the Religion made such progress that even the magistrates began to prohibit things that had grown up under their authority. Thus they forbade innkeepers to permit gambling or dissipation to be carried on within their premises, to the enticement of men away from their own homes and families.

"In those days might be seen on Sundays bands of workpeople abroad in the meadows, in the groves, in the fields, singing psalms and spiritual songs, and reading to and instructing one another. There might also be seen girls and maidens seated in groups in the gardens and pleasant places, singing songs or sacred themes; or boys, accompanied by their teachers, the effects of whose instructions had already been so salutary that those young persons not only exhibited a manly bearing, but a manful steadfastness of conduct. Indeed, these various influences, working one with another, had already effected so much good that not only had the habits and modes of life of the people been reformed, but their very countenances seemed to be changed and improved."[2580]

On the 17th of January, 1562, an Assembly of Notables was convened at St. Germain.[2581] This gave the Chancellor de l'Hôpital another opportunity of ventilating his great idea of toleration, so new to the men of that age. If, said the chancellor, we cannot unite the two creeds, does it therefore follow that the adherents of the one must exterminate those of the other? May not both live together on terms of mutual forbearance? An excommunicated man does not cease to be a citizen. The chancellor, unhappily, was not able to persuade the Assembly to adopt his wise principle; but though it did not go all lengths with L'Hôpital, it took a step on the road to toleration. It passed an edict, commonly known as the "Edict of January," "by which was granted to the Huguenots," says Davila, "a free exercise of their religion, and the right to assemble at sermons, but unarmed, outside of the cities in open places, the officers of the place being present and assistant."[2582] Till this edict was granted the Protestants could build no church within the walls of a city, nor meet for worship even in the open country. Doubtless they sometimes appropriated a deserted Popish chapel, or gathered in the fields in hundreds and thousands to hear sermons, but they could plead no statute for this: it was their numbers solely that made them adventure on what the law did not allow. Now, however, they could worship in public under legal sanction.

But even this small scrap of liberty was bestowed with the worst grace, and was fettered by qualifications and restrictions which were fitted, perhaps intended, to annul the privilege it professed to grant. The Protestants might indeed worship in public, but in order to do so they must go outside the gates of the city. In many towns they were the overwhelming majority: could anything be more absurd than that a whole population should go outside the walls of its own town to worship? The edict, in truth, pleased neither party. It conferred too small a measure of grace to awaken the lively gratitude of the Protestants; and as regards the Romanists, they grudged the Reformed even this poor crumb of favour.

Nevertheless, paltry though the edict was, it favoured the rapid permeation of France with the Protestant doctrines. The growth of the Reformed Church since the death of Henry II. was prodigious. At the request of Catherine de Medici, Beza addressed circular letters at this time to all the Protestant pastors in France, desiring them to send in returns of the number of their congregations. The report of Beza, founded on these returns, was that there were then upwards of 2,150 congregations of the Reformed faith in the kingdom. Several of these, especially in the great cities, were composed of from 4,000 to 8,000 communicants. The Church at Paris had no less than 20,000 members. As many as 40,000 would at times convene for sermon outside the gates of the capital. This multitude of worshippers would divide itself into three congregations, to which as many ministers preached; with a line of horse and foot, by orders from Catherine de Medici, drawn round the assembly to protect it from the insults of the mob.[2583] The number of the Reformed in the provincial cities was in proportion to those of Paris. According to contemporary estimates of the respective numbers of the two communions, the Reformed Church had gathered into its bosom from one fourth to one half the nation—the former is the probable estimate; but that fourth embraced the flower of the population in respect of rank, intelligence, and wealth.

The chiefs of Romanism beheld, with an alarm that bordered on panic, all France on the point of becoming Lutheran. The secession of so great a kingdom from Rome would tarnish the glory of the Church, dry up her revenues, and paralyse her political arm. Nothing must be left undone that could avert a calamity so overwhelming. The Pope, Philip II. of Spain, and the Triumvirate at Paris took counsel as to the plan to be pursued, and began from this hour to prosecute each his part, in the great task of rolling back the tide of a triumphant Huguenotism. They must do so at all costs, or surrender the battle. The Pope wrote to Catherine de Medici, exhorting her as a daughter of Italy to rekindle her dying zeal—not so near extinction as the Pope feared—and defend the faith of her country and her house. The wily Catherine replied, thanking her spiritual father, but saying that the Huguenots were, meanwhile, too powerful to permit her to follow his advice, and to break openly with Coligny. The King of Navarre, the first prince of the blood, was next tampered with. The Romanists knew his weak point, which was an inordinate ambition to be what nature—by denying him the requisite talents—had ordained he should not be, a king in his own right, and not a titular sovereign merely. They offered him a kingdom whose geographical position was a movable one, lying sometimes in Africa, sometimes in the island of Sardinia, seeing the kingdom itself was wholly imaginary. They even flattered him with hopes that he might come to wear the crown of Scotland. The Pope would dissolve his marriage with Jeanne d'Albret, on the ground of heresy, and he would then secure him the hand of the young and beautiful Mary Stuart. Dazzled by these illusions, which he took for realities, the weak, unstable, unprincipled Antoine de Bourbon passed over to the Roman camp, amid the loud vauntings of those who knew how worthless, yet how handy, the prize was.[2584]

The way was thus prepared so far for the execution of bolder measures. The Duke of Guise, quitting Paris, spent the winter on his family estates in Lorraine, and there, unobserved, began to collect an army, to co-operate with the troops which the King of Spain had promised to send him. He hoped to take the field in spring with such a force as would enable him to root out Huguenotism from the soil of France, and restore the supremacy of the old faith.

But matters so fell out that the duke was obliged to begin his campaign sooner than he had intended. All that winter (1562) the populace of Paris had been kept in a state of great excitement. The Romanists believed that they were being betrayed. They saw the Queen-mother, whose present policy it was to play off the Huguenots against the Triumvirate, favouring the "religion." Then there was the Edict of January, permitting the free exercise of the Protestant worship. In the eyes of every Roman Catholic this edict was abomination—a disgrace to the statute book—a bulwark to the Huguenots, whom it protected in their psalm-singing and sermonising. The pulpits of Paris thundered against the edict. The preachers expatiated on the miseries, temporal and eternal, into which it was dragging down France. They told how they were nightly besieged by souls from purgatory, dolefully lamenting the cruelty of their relations who no longer cared to say mass for their deliverance. Visions of hell, moreover, had been made to them, and they saw it filled with Huguenots. They turned their churches into arsenals, and provided the mob with arms.[2585] The Duke of Guise had been heard to say that he "would cut the knot of the edict with his sword,"[2586] and when the Parisians saw the Huguenots, in thousands, crowding out at the city gates to sermon, and when they heard their psalm borne back on the breeze, they said, "Would that the duke were here, we would make these men pipe to another tune." These were unmistakable signs that the moment for action was come. The duke was sent for.

The message found him at his Château of Joinville. He lost no time in obeying the summons. He set out on Saturday, the 28th of February, 1562, accompanied by his brother the cardinal, 200 gentlemen, and a body of horse. Three leagues on the road to Paris is the town of Vassy. It contained in those days 3,000 inhabitants, about a third of whom had embraced the Reformed faith. It stood on lands which belonged to the duke's niece, Mary Stuart of Scotland, and its Protestant congregation gave special umbrage to the Dowager-Duchess of Guise, who could not brook the idea that the vassals of her granddaughter should profess a different faith from that of their feudal superior. The duke, on his way to this little town, recruited his troop at one of the villages through which he passed, with a muster of foot-soldiers and archers. "The Saturday before the slaughter," says Crespin, "they were seen to make ready their weapons—arquebuses and pistols."[2587]

On Sunday morning, the 1st of March, the duke, after an early mass, resumed his march. "Urged by the importunities of his mother," says Thaunus, "he came with intention to dissolve these conventicles by his presence."[2588] He was yet a little way from Vassy when a bell began to ring. On inquiring what it meant, seeing the hour was early, he was told that it was the Huguenot bell ringing for sermon. Plucking at his beard, as his wont was when he was choleric, he swore that he would Huguenot them after another fashion.[2589] Entering the town, he met the provost, the prior, and the curate in the market-place, who entreated him to go to the spot where the Protestants were assembled.[2590] The Huguenot meeting-house was a barn, about 100 yards distant, on the city wall. A portion of the duke's troop marched on before, and arrived at the building. The Protestants were assembled to the number of 1,200; the psalm and the prayer were ended, and the sermon had begun. The congregation were suddenly startled by persons outside throwing stones at the windows, and shouting out, "Heretics! rebels! dogs!" Presently the discharge of fire-arms told them that they were surrounded by armed men. The Protestants endeavoured to close the door, but were unable for the crowd of soldiers pressing in, with oaths and shouts of "Kill, kill!" "Those within," says Crespin, "were so astonied that they knew not which way to turn them, but running hither and thither fell one upon another, flying as poor sheep before a company of ravening wolves. Some of the murderers shot off their pieces at those that were in the galleries; others cut in pieces such as they lighted upon; others had their heads cleft in twain, their arms and hands cut off, and thus did they what they could to hew them all in pieces, so as many of them gave up the ghost even in the place. The walls and galleries of the said barn were dyed with the blood of those who were everywhere murdered."

Hearing the tumult, the duke hastened to the spot. On coming up he was hit with a stone in the face. On seeing him bleeding, the rage of his soldiers was redoubled, and the butchery became more horrible. Seeing escape impossible by the door or window, many of the congregation attempted to break through the roof, but they were shot down as they climbed up on the rafters. One soldier savagely boasted that he had brought down a dozen of these pigeons. Some who escaped in this way leaped down from the city walls, and escaped into the woods and vineyards. The pastor, M. Morel, on his knees in the pulpit invoking God, was fired at. Throwing off his gown, he attempted to escape, but stumbling over a dead body, he received two sabre-cuts, one on the shoulder, another on the head. A soldier raised his weapon to hough him, but his sword broke at the hilt. Supported by two men, the pastor was led before the duke. "Who made you so bold as to seduce this people?" demanded the duke. "Sir," replied M. Morel, "I am no seducer, for I have preached to them the Gospel of Jesus Christ." "Go," said the duke to the provost, "and get ready a gibbet, and hang this rogue." These orders were not executed. The duke's soldiers were too busy sabreing the unarmed multitude, and collecting the booty, to hang the pastor, and none of the town's-people had the heart to do so cruel a deed.[2591]

When the dreadful work was over, it was found that from sixty to eighty persons had been killed, and 250 wounded, many of them mortally. The streets were filled with the most piteous spectacles. Women were seen with disheveled hair, and faces besmeared with blood from their streaming wounds, dragging themselves along, and filling the air with their cries and lamentations. The soldiers signalised their triumph by pulling down the pulpit, burning the bibles and Psalters, plundering the poor's-box, spoiling the killed of their raiment, and wrecking the place. The large pulpit Bible was taken to the duke. He examined the title page, and his learning enabled him to make out that it had been printed the year before. He carried it to his brother the cardinal, who all the time of the massacre had been loitering by the wall of the church-yard, and presented the Bible to him as a sample of the pestiferous tenets of the Huguenots. "Why, brother," said the cardinal, after scanning its title-page a moment, "there is no harm in this book, for it is the Bible—the Holy Scripture." "The duke being offended at that answer," says Crespin, "grew into a greater rage than before, saying, 'Blood of God!—what!—how now!—the Holy Scripture! It is a thousand and five hundred years ago since Jesus Christ suffered his death and passion, and it is but a year ago since these books were imprinted; how, then, say you that this is the Gospel?'"[2592]

The massacre at Vassy was the first blow struck in the civil wars of France, and it is important to note that it was the act of the Romanists. Being done in violation of the Edict of January, which covered the Protestants of Vassy, and never disowned or punished by any constituted authority of the nation, it proclaimed that the rule of law had ceased, and that the reign of force had begun. A few days afterwards the duke entered Paris, more like a conqueror who had routed the enemies of France, than a man dripping with the blood of his fellow-subjects. Right and left of him rode the Constable and the Marshal St. André, the other two members of the Triumvirate, while the nobles, burgesses, and whole populace of the capital turned out to grace his entry, and by their enthusiastic cheers proclaim his welcome. As if he had been king, they shouted, "Long life to Guise!"[2593] The blood of Vassy, said the mob of Paris, be on us, and on our children.

The Protestants of France had for some time back been revolving the question of taking up arms and standing to their defence, and this deplorable massacre helped to clear their minds. The reverence, approaching to a superstition, which in those days hedged round the person of a king, made the Huguenots shrink with horror from what looked like rebellion. But the question was no longer, Shall we oppose the king? The Triumvirate had, in effect, set aside both king and regent, and the duke and the mob were masters of the State. The question was, Shall we oppose the Triumvirate which has made itself supreme over throne and Parliament? Long did the Huguenots hesitate, most unwilling were they to draw the sword; especially so was the greatest Huguenot that France then contained, Coligny. Ever as he put his hand upon the sword's hilt, there would rise before him the long and dismal vista of battle and siege and woe through which France must pass before that sword, once unsheathed, could be returned into its scabbard. He, therefore, long forbore to take the irrevocable step, when one less brave or less foreseeing would have rushed to the battlefield. But even Coligny was at last convinced that farther delay would be cowardice, and that the curse of liberty would rest on every sword of Huguenot that remained longer in its scabbard.

Had the Edict of January, which gave a qualified permission for the open celebration of the Reformed worship, been maintained, the Protestants of France never would have thought of carrying their appeal to the battle-field. Had argument been the only weapon with which they were assailed, argument would have been the only weapon with which they would have sought to defend themselves; but when a lawless power stood up, which trampled on royal authority, annulled laws, tore up treaties, and massacred Protestant congregations wholesale; when to them there no longer existed a throne, or laws, or tribunals, or rights of citizenship; when their estates were confiscated, their castles burned, the blood of their wives and children spilt, their names branded with infamy, and a price put upon their heads, why, surely, if ever resistance was lawful in the case of any people, and if circumstances could be imagined in which it was dutiful to repel force by force, they were those of the French Protestants at that hour. Even when it is the civil liberties only of a nation that are menaced by the tyrant or the invader, it is held the first duty of the subject to gird on his sword, and to maintain them with his blood; and we are altogether unable to understand why it should be less his duty to do so when, in addition to civil liberty, the battle is for the sanctity of the home, the freedom of conscience, and the lives and religion of half a nation. So stood the case in France at that hour. Every end for which government is ordained, and society exists, was attacked and overthrown. If the Huguenots had not met their foes on the battle-field, their name, their race, their faith would have been trodden out in France.

Far and wide over the kingdom flew the news of the Massacre at Vassy. One party whispered the dreadful tale in accents of horror; another party proclaimed it in a tone of exultation and triumph. The impunity, or rather applause, accorded to its author emboldened the Romanists to proceed to even greater excesses. In a few weeks the terrible scenes of Vassy were repeated in many of the towns of France. At Paris, at Senlis, at Meaux, at Amiens, at Chalons, at Tours, at Toulouse, and many other towns, the fanatic mob rose upon the Protestants and massacred them, pillaging and burning their dwellings. All the while the cathedral bells would be tolled, and the populace would sing songs of triumph in the streets. At Tours 300 Protestants were shut up in their church, where they were kept three days without food, and then brought out, tied two and two, led to the river's brink, and butchered like sheep. Children were sold for a crown a-piece. The President of Tours was tied to two willow-trees, and disembowelled alive.[2594] At Toulouse the same horrible scenes were enacted on a larger scale. That city contained at this time between 30,000 and 40,000 Protestants—magistrates, students, and men of letters and refinement. The tocsin was rung in all the churches, the peasantry for miles around the city was raised *en masse;* the Huguenots took refuge in the Capitol of Toulouse, where they were besieged, and finally compelled to surrender. Then followed a revolting massacre of from 3,000 to 4,000 Protestants.[2595] The Seine, the Loire, and the Garonne were dyed with Protestant blood, and ghastly corpses, borne on the bosom of the stream, startled the dwellers in distant cities and castles, and seemed to cry for justice, as they floated away to find burial in the ocean.

The Duke of Guise now repaired to Fontainebleau, whither the King and the Queen-mother had fled, and compelled them to return to Paris. Catherine de Medici and her son were now wholly in the hands of the duke, and when they entered the Castle of Vincennes, about a mile from Paris, "the queen bore a doleful countenance, not able to refrain from tears; and the young king crying like a child, as if they had been both led into captivity."[2596] The Parliament was not less obsequious. Its humble office was to register *arrêts* at the duke's bidding. These persecuting edicts followed each other with alarming rapidity during the terrible summer of 1562, than which there is no more doleful year in the French annals, not even excepting perhaps the outstanding horror of 1572—the Massacre of St. Bartholomew. The Popish mob was supplied with arms and formed into regiments. The churches served as club-houses. When the tocsin sounded, 50,000 men would turn out at the summons. All Huguenots were ordered to quit Paris within twenty-four hours;[2597] after this, any one seen in the streets, and suspected of being a Huguenot, was mobbed and dispatched. Advantage was in some cases taken of this to gratify private revenge. One had only to raise the cry of Huguenot against those at whom one happened to have a spite, or to whom one owed money, and the bystanders did the rest. On the 8th of June the Parliament passed a law empowering any one who should meet a Huguenot to kill him on the spot. The edict was to be read by the curés every Sunday after the sermon that follows high mass.[2598] The peasantry provided themselves with scythes, pikes, cutlasses, knives, and other cruel weapons, and scoured the country as if they had been ridding it of wild beasts. The priests facetiously called this "letting slip the big hound."[2599] They selected as captain, sometimes a monk, sometimes a brigand; and on one occasion, at least, a bishop was seen marching at their head. Their progress over the country, especially in the south, where the Protestants were numerous, could be traced in the frightful memorials they left on their track—corpses strewed along the roads, bodies dangling from the trees, mangled victims dying the verdure of the fields with their blood, and spending their last breath in cries and supplications to Heaven.

On the 18th of August, 1562, the Parliament issued yet another decree, declaring all the gentlemen of "the religion" traitors to God and the king. From this time the conflict became a war of province against province, and city against city, for the frightful outrages to which the Protestants were subjected provoked them into reprisals. Yet the violence of the Huguenot greatly differed from the violence of the Romanist. The former gutted Popish cathedrals and churches, broke down the images, drove away the priests. The latter burned houses, tore up vines and fruit-trees, and slaughtered men and women, often with such diabolical and disgusting cruelty as forbids us to describe their acts. In some places rivulets of Huguenot blood, a foot in depth, were seen flowing. Those who wish to read the details of the crimes and woes that then overwhelmed France will find the dreadful recital, if they have courage to peruse it, in the pages of Agrippa d'Aubigné, De Thou, Beza, Crespin, and other historians.[2600]

But before these latter edicts were issued the Huguenots had come to a decision. While Coligny, shut up in his Castle of Chatillon, was revolving the question of civil war, events were solving that question for him. Wherever he looked he saw cities sacked, castles in flames, and men and women slaughtered in thousands; what was this but civil war? The tidings of today were ever sadder than those of yesterday, and the tidings of tomorrow would, he but too surely guessed, be sadder than those of today. The heart of his wife, the magnanimous Charlotte Laval, was torn with anguish at the thought of the sufferings her brethren and sisters in the faith were enduring. One night she awoke her husband from sleep by her tears and sobs. "We lie here softly," said she, "while our brethren's bodies, who are flesh of our flesh and bone of our bone, are some of them in dungeons, and others lying in the open fields, food for dogs and ravens. This bed is a tomb for me, seeing they are not buried. Can we sleep in peace, without hearing our brethren's last groanings?" "Are you prepared," asked the admiral in reply, "to hear of my defeat, to see me dragged to a scaffold and put to death by the common hangman? are you prepared to see our name branded, our estates confiscated, and our children made beggars? I will give you," he continued, "three weeks to think on these things, and when you have fortified yourself against them, I will go forth to perish with my brethren." "The three weeks are gone already," was the prompt and noble reply of Charlotte Laval. "Go in God's name and he will not suffer you to be defeated."[2601]

A few mornings only had passed when Admiral Coligny was seen on his way to open the first campaign of the civil wars.

CHAPTER VIII
COMMENCEMENT OF THE HUGUENOT WARS

THE Protestant chiefs having resolved to take up the gage which the Triumvirate had thrown down, the Prince of Condé struck the first blow by dispatching Coligny's brother D'Andelot, with 5,000 men, to make himself master of Orleans. In a few days thereafter (April 2nd, 1562), the prince himself entered that city, amid the acclamations of the inhabitants, who accompanied him through the streets chanting grandly the 124th Psalm, in Marot's metre.[2602] Admiral Coligny, on arriving at headquarters, found a brilliant assemblage gathered round Condé. Among those already arrived or daily expected was Anthony of Croy, Prince of Porcian. Though related to the House of Lorraine, the Prince of Porcian was a firm opponent of the policy of the Guises, and one of the best captains of his time. He was married to Catherine of Cleves, Countess of Eu, niece to the Prince of Condé, by whom he was greatly beloved for his amiable qualities as well as for his soldierly accomplishments. And there was also Francis, Count of La Rochefoucault, Prince of Marcillac. He was by birth and dignity the first noble of Guienne, and the richest and most potent man in all Poitou. He could have raised an army among his relations, friends, and vassals alone. He was an experienced soldier: valiant, courageous, generous, and much beloved by Henry II., in whose wars he had greatly distinguished himself. It was his fate to be inhumanly slaughtered, as we shall see, in the St. Bartholomew Massacre. There was René, Viscount of Rohan. He was by the mother's side related to the family of Navarre, being cousin-german to Jeanne d'Albret. Being by her means instructed in the Reformed faith, that queen made him her lieutenant-general during the minority of her son Henry, afterwards King of France, whom he served with inviolable fidelity. There was Anthony, Count of Grammont, who was in great esteem among the Reformed on account of his valour and his high character. Having embraced the Protestant faith, he opposed uncompromisingly the Guises, and bore himself with great distinction and gallantry among the Huguenot chiefs in the civil wars. No less considerable was Gabriel, Count of Montgomery, also one of the group around the prince. His valour, prudence, and sagacity enabled him, in the absence of large estates or family connections, to uphold the credit of the Protestant party and the lustre of the Protestant arms after the fall of Condé, of Coligny, and of other leaders. It was from his hand that Henry II. had received his death-blow in the fatal tournament—as fatal in the end to Montgomery as to Henry, for Catherine de Medici never forgave him the unhappy accident of slaying her husband; and when at last Montgomery fell into her hands, she had him executed on the scaffold. And there was John, Lord of Soubise, of the illustrious House of Partenay of Poitou, and the last who bore the name and title. Soubise had borne arms under Henry II., being commander-in-chief in the army of Tuscany. This gave him an opportunity of visiting the court of René at Ferrara, where he was instructed in the Reformed doctrine. On his return to France he displayed great zeal in propagating the Protestant faith, and when the civil wars broke out the Prince de Condé sent him to command at Lyons, where, acquitting himself with equal activity and prudence, he fully answered the expectations of his chief. Louis of Vadray, known in history by the name of Lord of Mouy St. Phale, was one of the more considerable of the patriot-heroes that followed the banners of Condé. Of great intrepidity and daring, his achievements are amongst the most brilliant feats of the civil wars. He was assassinated in 1569 by the same person—Maurevel of Brie—who wounded the Admiral Coligny in Paris in 1572. Nor must we omit to mention Anthony Raguier, Lord of Esternay and of La Mothe de Tilly. Not only did he place his own sword at the service of Condé, he brought over to the standard of the prince and the profession of the Protestant faith, his brother-in-law Francis of Bethune, Baron of Rosny, father of the Duke of Sully. And there was the head of the ancient and illustrious House of Picardy, Adrian de Hangest, Lord of Genlis, who was the father of thirty-two children by his wife Frances du Maz. Like another Hamilcar leading his numerous sons to the altar, he devoted them to the defence of their country's laws, and the maintenance of its Protestant faith. The enthusiasm and bravery of the sons, as displayed under the banners of Condé, amply rewarded the devotion and patriotism of the father. All of them became distinguished in the campaigns that followed.[2603]

Nothing could more conclusively attest the strength of the position which Protestantism had conquered for itself in France than this brilliant list. The men whom we see round the Huguenot chief are the flower of a glorious land. They are no greedy adventurers, whom the love of excitement, or the hope of spoil, or the thirst for distinction has driven to the battle-field. Their castles adorn the soil, and their names illustrate the annals of their country; yet here we see them coming forward, at this supreme hour, and deliberately staking the honour of their houses, the revenues of their estates, the glory of their names, and even life itself! What could have moved them to this but their loyalty to the Gospel—their deep, thorough, and most intelligent conviction that the Reformed doctrine was based on Scripture, and that it had bound up with it not more their own personal salvation than the order, the prosperity, and the glory of their country?

The Protestant cause had attractions not alone for the patricians of France; it was embraced by the intelligence and furthered by the energy of the middle classes. It is well to remember this. Bankers and men of commerce; lawyers and men of letters; magistrates and artists; in short, the staple of the nation, the guides of its opinion, the creators of its wealth, and the pillars of its order, rallied to the Protestant standard. In every part of France the Reformed faith spread with astonishing rapidity during the reign of Francis II. and Charles IX. It was embraced by the villages scattered along at the foot of the Alps and the base of the Pyrenees. It established itself in the powerful city of Grenoble. The Parliament and magistracy of that prosperous community took special interest in the preaching of the Protestant doctrine in their town; and the example of Grenoble had a great influence on the whole of that rich region of which it was the capital. The city of Marseilles on the Mediterranean shore; the flourishing seaports on the western coast; the fertile and lovely valleys of central France; the vine-clad plains on the east; the rich and populous Picardy and Normandy on the north—all were covered with the churches and congregations of the Reformed faith. "Climate, custom, prejudice, superstition," says Gaberel, "seemed to have no power to resist or modify the spread of the Protestant doctrines. No sooner was a church provided with a pastor, than the inhabitants of the villages and towns in the neighbourhood demolished their Popish altars, and flocked to hear the preaching of the Protestant doctrine. The occupants of the castles and rich houses followed the example of their tenantry, and opened their mansions for worship when the church stood at too great a distance."[2604] Many of the prelates, even, had perused the writings of Calvin, and were favourable to the Reformed doctrine, although, for obvious reasons, they had to be careful in avowing their convictions and preferences.

When we turn from the grand phalanx of nobles, warriors, jurists, literary men, merchants, and cities around the Protestant standard, to contemplate the opposing ranks which still remained loyal to Rome, and were now challenging the Reformed to do battle for their faith, we are forcibly struck with the vast inferiority, in all the elements of real power, on the Popish side. First on that side came the crown. We say the crown, for apart from it Charles IX. had no power. Next to the crown came the Queen-mother, who, despite certain caprices which at times excited the hopes of the Protestants and awakened the fears of the Pope, remained staunchly loyal at heart to the cause of Rome—for what else could be expected of the niece of Clement VII.? After the Queen-mother came the Triumvirate. It embraced one grand figure—the bluff, honest, wilful Constable, so proud of his ancient blood and his ancient Christianity! Over against him we may set the weak and wicked St. André, who was continually enriching himself with plunder, and continually sinking deeper in debt. Then came the Guises—truculent, thoroughly able, and as athirst for blood as the Marshal St. André for money. These strangers in France seem to have taken kindly to the soil, if one may judge from the amazing rapidity with which their power and their honours had flourished since their arrival in it. We assign the last place here to the King of Navarre, though as a prince of the blood he ought to have had the first place after the crown, but for his utter insignificance, which made him be fully more contemned even by the Papists than by the Protestants.

The Popish party were numerically the majority of the nation, but in respect of intelligence and virtue they were by much the smaller portion of it. There was, of course, a moiety of the nobility, of professional men, and of the middle orders still attached to the Roman worship, and more or less zealous in its behalf; but the great strength of the Triumvirate lay in another quarter. The Sorbonne, the secular priests, and the cloistered orders continued unwavering in their attachment to the Pope. And behind was a yet greater force—without which, the zeal of the Triumvirate, of curé, and of friar would have effected but little— the rabble, namely, of Paris and many of the great cities. This was a very multifarious host, more formidable in numbers than in power, if names are to be weighed and not counted. Protestantism in France was not merely on the road to victory, morally it had already achieved it.

And further, to form a true estimate of the strength of the position which Protestantism had now won, we must take account of the situation of the country, and the endowments of the people in which it had so deeply rooted itself. Placed in the centre of Christendom, France acted powerfully on all the nations around it. It was, or till a few years ago had been, the first of the European kingdoms in letters, in arts, in arms. Its people possessed a beautiful genius. Since the intellect of classic days there had appeared, perhaps, no finer mental development than the French mind; none that came so near the old Roman type. Without apparent labour the French genius could lay open with a touch the depths of an abstruse question, or soar to the heights of a sublime one. Protestantism had begun to quicken the French intellect into a marvellous development of strength and beauty, and but for the sudden and unexpected blight that overtook it, its efflorescence would have rivalled, it may be eclipsed, in power and splendour that extraordinary outburst of intellect that followed the Reformation in England, and which has made the era of Elizabeth for ever famous.

Nor was it the least of the advantages of French Protestantism that its headquarters were not within, but outside the kingdom. By a marvellous Providence a little territory, invisibly yet inviolably guarded, had been called into existence as an asylum where, with the thunders of the mighty tempests resounding on every side of it, the great chief of the movement might watch the execution of his plans in every part of the field, but especially in France. Calvin was sufficiently distant from his native land to be undisturbed by its convulsions, and yet sufficiently near to send daily assistance and succour to it, to commission evangelists, to advise, to encourage—in short, to do whatever could tend to maintain and advance the work. The Reformer was now giving the last touches to his mighty task before retiring from the view of men, but Geneva, through her Church, through her schools, and through her printing-presses, would, it was thought, continue to flood France with those instrumentalities for the regeneration of Christendom, which the prodigious industry and mighty genius of Calvin had prepared.

But the very strength of Protestantism in France at this era awakens doubts touching the step which the Protestants of that country were now about to take, and compels us to pause and review a decision at which we have already arrived. How had Protestantism come to occupy this position, and what were the weapons which had conquered for it so large a place in the national mind? This question admits of but one answer: it was the teachings of evangelists, the blood of martyrs, and the holy lives of confessors. Then why not permit the same weapons to consummate the victory? Does it not argue a criminal impatience to exchange evangelists for soldiers? Does it not manifest a sinful mistrust of those holy instrumentalities which have already proved their omnipotency by all but converting France, to supersede them by the rude appliances of armies and battle-fields? In truth, so long as the Protestants had it in their power to avoid the dire necessity of taking up arms, so long, in short, as the certain ruin of the cause did not stare them in the face in the way of their sitting still, they were not justified in making their appeal to arms. But they judged, and we think rightly, that they had now no alternative; that the Triumvirate had decided this question for them; and that nothing remained, if the last remnants of conscience and liberty were not to be trodden out, but to take their place on the battle-field. The legitimate rule of the king had been superseded by the usurpation of a junto, the leading spirits of which were foreigners. The Protestants saw treaties torn up, and soldiers enrolled for the work of murder. They saw their brethren slaughtered like sheep, not in hundreds only, but literally in thousands. They saw the smoke of burning cities and castles darkening the firmament, unburied corpses tainting the air, and the blood of men and women dyeing their rivers, and tinting the seas around their coasts. They saw groups of orphans wandering about, crying for bread, or laying themselves down to die of hunger. The touching words of Charlotte Laval addressed to her husband, which we have already quoted, show us how the noblest minds in France felt and reasoned in the presence of these awful tragedies. To remain in peace in their houses, while these oppressions and crimes were being enacted around them—were being done, so to speak, in their very sight—was not only to act a cowardly part, it was to act an inhuman part. It was to abnegate the right, not of citizens only, but of men. If they should longer refuse to stand to their defence, posterity, they felt, would hold them guilty of their brethren's blood, and their names would be coupled with those of the persecutors in the cry of that blood for vengeance.

The pre-eminence of France completes the justification of the Huguenots, by completing the necessity for the step to which they now had recourse. Rome could not possibly permit Protestantism to triumph in a country so central, and whose influence was so powerfully felt all over Europe. The Pope must needs suppress the Reformation in France at all costs. The Popish Powers, and especially Spain, felt equally with the Pope the greatness of the crisis, and willingly contributed the aid of their arms to extinguish Huguenotism. Its triumph in France would have revolutionised their kingdoms, and shaken their thrones. It was a life-and-death struggle; and but for the stand which the Protestant chiefs made, the soldiers of the Triumvirate, and the armies of Spain, would have marched from the Seine to the Mediterranean, from the frontier of Lorraine to the western seaboard, slaughtering the Huguenots like sheep, and Protestantism would have been as completely trampled out in France as it was in Spain.

Both sides now began to prepare with vigour for the inevitable conflict. On the Huguenot banner was inscribed "Liberty of Worship," and the special grievance which compelled the unfurling of that banner was the flagrant violation of the Edict of January—which guaranteed them that liberty—in the dreadful massacre of the Protestants as they were worshipping at Vassy under the supposed protection of that edict. This was specially mentioned in the manifesto which the Huguenots now put forth, but neither was regret expressed by the Triumvirate for the violation of the edict, nor promise given that it would be observed in time to come, which made the Protestant princes conclude that the Massacre of Vassy would be repeated again and again, till not a Huguenot was left to charge the Government with its shameful breach of faith. "To arms!" must therefore be their watchword.

Wars, although styled religious, must be gone about in the ordinary way; soldiers must be enrolled, and money collected, without which it is impossible to fight battles. The Prince of Condé wrote circular letters to the Reformed Churches in France, craving their aid in men and money to carry on the war about to be commenced.[2605] Several of the Churches, before voting the desired assistance, sent deputies to Paris to ascertain the real state of matters, and whether any alternative was left them save the grave one of taking up arms. As a consequence, funds and fighting men came in slowly. From La Rochelle came neither men nor money, till after the campaign had been commenced; but that Church, and others, finding on careful inquiry that the state of matters was such as the Huguenot manifesto had set forth, threw themselves afterwards with zeal into the conflict, and liberally supported it.

The Huguenot chiefs, before unsheathing the sword, sat down together and partook of the Lord's Supper. After communion they subscribed a bond, or "Act of Association," in which they pledged themselves to fidelity to God and to one another, and obedience to Condé as head of the Protestant League, and promised to assist him with "money, arms, horses, and all other warlike equipages." They declared themselves in arms for "the defence of the king's honour and liberty, the maintenance of the pure worship of God, and the due observance of the edicts."[2606] They swore also to promote reformation of manners and true piety among themselves and followers, to punish blasphemy, profanation, and vice, and to maintain the preaching of the Gospel in their camp.[2607] This deed, by which the Huguenot wars were inaugurated, tended to promote confidence among the confederates, and to keep them united in the presence of a crafty enemy, who continually laboured to sow jealousies and divisions among them; and further, it sanctified and sublimed the war by keeping its sacred and holy object in the eye of those who were in arms.

Another matter which the Calvinist lords deemed it prudent to arrange before coming to blows, was the important one of succours from abroad. On this point their opponents enjoyed great advantages. Not only could they draw upon the national treasury for the support of the war, having the use of the king's name, but they had powerful and zealous friends abroad who, they knew, would hasten to their aid. The Triumvirate had promises of large succours from the then wealthy governments of Spain, Italy, and Savoy; and they had perfect confidence in these promises being kept, for the cause for which the Triumvirate was in arms was the cause of the Pope and Philip of Spain quite as much as it was that of the Guises. The Huguenots, in like manner, cast their eyes abroad, if haply they might find allies and succourers in those countries where the Protestant faith was professed. The war now commencing was not one of race or nationality; it was no war of creed in a narrow sense; it was a war for the great principle of Protestantism in both its Lutheran and Reformed aspects, and which was creating a new commonwealth, which the Rhine could not divide, nor the Alps bound. That was not a Gallic commonwealth, or a Teutonic commonwealth, but a great spiritual empire, which was blending in sympathy and in interest every kindred and tribe that entered its holy brotherhood. Therefore, in the war now beginning neither Germany nor England could, with due regard to themselves, be neutral, for every victory of the Roman Catholic powers, now confederate for the suppression of the Reformation, not in France only, but in all countries, was a step in the triumphant march of these powers towards the frontiers of the other Reformed countries. The true policy of England and Germany was clearly to fight the battle at as great a distance as possible from their own doors.

To Coligny the project of bringing foreign soldiers into France was one the wisdom of which he extremely doubted. He feared the effect which such a step might have on a people naturally jealous and proud, and to whom he knew it would be distasteful. For every foreign auxiliary he might obtain he might lose a home soldier. But again events decided the matter for him. He saw the

Savoyards, the Swiss, and the Spaniards daily arriving to swell the royalist ranks, and slaughter the children of France, and if he would meet the enemy, not in equal numbers—for he saw no likelihood of being able to bring man for man into the field—but if he would meet him at the head of such a force as should enable him to fight with some chance of success, he must do as his opponents were doing, and accept help from those who were willing to give it. Accordingly two ambassadors were dispatched on the errand of foreign aid, the one to Germany and the other to England, and both found a favourable reception for their overtures. The one succeeded in negotiating a treaty for some thousands of German Reiter, or heavy cavalry—so well known in those days for the execution they did on the field, where often they trampled down whole ranks of the lighter troops of France; and the other ambassador was able to persuade Queen Elizabeth—so careful both of her money and her subjects, for England was not then so rich in either as she long years afterwards became—to aid the Huguenots with 140,000 crowns and 6,000 soldiers, in return for which the town of Havre was put in her keeping.

CHAPTER IX
THE FIRST HUGUENOT WAR, AND DEATH OF THE DUKE OF GUISE

UNWILLING to commit himself irrevocably to war, the Prince of Condé made yet another overture to the court, before unsheathing the sword and joining battle. He was willing to furl his banner and dismiss his soldiers, provided a guarantee were given him that the Edict of January would be observed till the king attained his majority, and if then his majesty should be pleased no longer to grant liberty of conscience to his subjects, the prince and his confederates were to have liberty to retire into some other country, without prejudice to their estates and goods. And further, he demanded that the Triumvirs meanwhile should withdraw from court, adding that if the Government did not accept these reasonable terms, it would be answerable for all the calamities that might befall the kingdom.[2608] These terms were not accepted; and all efforts in the interest of peace having now been exhausted, the several provinces and cities of the kingdom made haste to rally, each under its respective standard. Once again France pronounces upon the question of its future: it confirms the choice it had made under Francis I. A second time it takes the downward road—that leading to revolution and the abyss. France is not unanimous, however; it is nearly equally divided. Speaking generally, all France south of the Loire declared for the Protestant cause. All the great cities of the Orleanois—Tours, Poictiers, Bourges, Nismes, Montauban, Valence, Lyons, Toulouse, Bordeaux—opened their gates to the soldiers of Condé, and cordially joined his standard: as did also the fortified castles of Languedoc and Dauphiné. In the north, Normandy, with its towns and castles, declared for the same side.[2609] The cities and provinces just enumerated were the most populous and flourishing in France. It was in these parts that the Reformation had struck its roots the most deeply, and hence the unanimity and alacrity with which their inhabitants enrolled themselves on the Protestant side.

Coligny, though serving as Condé's lieutenant, was the master-genius and director of the campaign. His strength of character, his long training in military affairs, his resource, his prudence, his indomitable resolution, all marked him out as the man pre-eminently qualified to lead, although the notions of the age required that such an enterprise should be graced by having as its ostensible head a prince of the blood. Coligny, towering above the other princes and nobles around Condé, inspired the soldiers with confidence, for they knew that he would lead them to victory, or if that were denied, that he could do what may seem more difficult, turn defeat into triumph. His sagacious eye it was that indicated Orleans as the true centre of the Huguenot strategy. Here, with the broad stream of the Loire rolling in front of their position, and the friendly provinces of the south lying behind it, they would lack neither provisions nor soldiers. Supplies to any amount would be poured into their camp by the great highway of the river, and they could recruit their army from the enthusiastic populations in their rear. But further, the Huguenots made themselves masters of Rouen in Normandy, which commands the Seine; this enabled them to isolate Paris, the camp of the enemy; they could close the gates of the two main arteries through which the capital procured its supplies, and afflict it with famine: by shutting the Loire they could cut off from it the wine and fruits of the fertile south; and their command of the Seine enabled them to stop at their pleasure the transportation of the corn and cattle of the north.

With these two strong positions, the one in the south and the other in the north of the capital, it seemed as if it needed only that the Huguenots should make themselves masters of Paris in order to end the campaign. "Paris," says Davila, "alone gave more credit to its party than half the kingdom would have done." It was a stronghold of Romanism, and its fanatical population furnished an unrivalled recruiting-field for the Triumvirate. The advantage which the possession of Paris would give the Huguenots, did not escape the sagacious glance of Coligny, and he counselled Condé to march upon it at once, and strike before the Guises had had time to complete their preparations for its defence. The Prince unhappily delayed till the golden opportunity had passed.[2610]

In the end of June, Condé and Coligny set out from Orleans to attack Paris, and almost at the same moment the Triumvirs began their march from Paris to besiege the Huguenots in Orleans. The two armies, which consisted of about 10,000 each, met half-way between the two cities. A battle was imminent, and if fought at that moment would probably have been advantageous to the Huguenot arms. But the Queen-mother, feigning a horror of bloodshed, came forward with a proposal for a conference between the leaders on both sides. Catherine de Medici vaunted that she could do more with her pen than twenty generals with their swords, and her success on this occasion went far to justify her boast. Her proposal entangled the Protestants in the meshes of diplomacy. The expedient which Catherine's genius had hit upon for securing peace was that the leaders of the two parties should go into exile till the king had attained his majority, and the troubles of the nation had subsided. But the proposed exile was not equal. Coligny and his confederates were to quit France, the Guises and their friends were only to retire from court.[2611] One obvious consequence of this arrangement was that Catherine would remain within call, should the Queen-mother desire their presence; Condé and Coligny, on the other hand, were to remove beyond the frontier; and once gone, a long time would elapse before they should be told that their services were needed, or that the soil of France was able to bear their steps. The trap was too obvious for the Huguenot chiefs to fall into it. The Queen had gained her end, however; her adroitness had shielded Paris, and it had wasted time in favour of the Government, for the weeks as they sped past increased the forces of the royalists and diminished those of the Huguenots.

It was the Triumvirs that made the next move in the campaign, by resolving to attack Rouen. Masters of this town, the Huguenots, as we have said, held the keys of the Seine, and having cut off the supplies from Paris, the Triumvirs were greatly alarmed, for it was hard to say how long the fanaticism and loyalty of the Parisians would withstand the sobering influences of starvation. The Seine must be kept open at all costs; the Government, moreover, was not free from fear that the Queen of England would send troops into Normandy, and occupy that province, with the help of the Huguenots. Should this happen, Paris itself would be in danger. Accordingly the Duke of Guise was dispatched with his army to besiege Rouen. While he is digging his trenches, posting his forces, and preparing the assault, let us observe the state of discipline and sobriety in the two camps.

We are all familiar with the pictures of Cromwell's army. We have read how his camp resounded with the unwonted sounds of psalms and prayers, and how his soldiers were animated by a devotion that made them respond as alertly to a summons to a sermon, which they knew would be of two hours' length, as to a summons to scale the breach, or join battle. A century before the great English Puritan, similar pictures might be witnessed in the camp of the French Huguenots. The *morale* of their armies was high, and the discipline of their camp strict, especially in their early campaigns. The soldier carried the Bible afield, and this did more than the strictest code or severest penalty to check disorder and excess. The Huguenots had written up on their banners, "For God and the Prince," and they felt bound to live the Gospel as well as fight for it. Their troops were guilty of no acts of pillage, the barn of the farmer and the store of the merchant were perfectly safe in their neighbourhood, and everything which they obtained from the inhabitants they paid for. Cards and dice were banished their camp; oaths and blasphemies were never heard; acts of immorality and lewdness were prohibited under very severe penalties, and were of rare occurrence. One officer of high rank, who brought disgrace upon the Huguenot army by an act of libertinism, was hanged.[2612]

Inside the town of Rouen, round which there now rose a bristling wall of hostile standards and redoubts, the same beautiful order prevailed. Besides the inhabitants, there were 12,000 choice foot-soldiers from Condé's army, four squadrons of horse, and 2,000 English in the place, with 100 gentlemen who had volunteered to perish in the defence of the town.[2613] The theatres were closed. There needed no imaginary drama, when one so real was passing before the inhabitants. The churches were opened, and every day there was sermon in them. In their houses the citizens chanted their daily psalm, just as if battle had been far distant from their gates. On the ramparts, the inspired odes of Hebrew times were thundered forth with a chorus of voices that rose loud above the shouting of the captains, and the booming of the cannon.

The enthusiasm for the defence pervaded all ranks, and both sexes. The daughters and wives of the citizen-soldiers hastened to the walls, and regardless of the deadly shot falling thick around them, they kept their fathers and husbands supplied with ammunition and weapons.[2614] They would maintain their liberties or die. The town was under the command of the Count Montgomery.[2615] Pursued by the implacable resentment of Catherine de Medici, he had fled to England, where he embraced the Reformed religion, and whence he returned to France to aid the Huguenots in their great struggle. He was a skilful and courageous general, and knowing that he would receive no quarter, he was resolved rather than surrender to make Rouen his grave.

Let us turn to the royalist camp. The picture presented to us there is the reverse of that which we have been contemplating. "There," says Félice, "the grossest licentiousness prevailed." Catherine de Medici was present with her maids of honour, who did not feel themselves under any necessity to practise severer virtues in the trenches than they usually observed in the Louvre. Games and carousals filled up the leisure hours of the common soldiers, while tournaments and intrigues occupied the captains and knights. These two widely different pictures are parted not by an age, but simply by the city walls of Rouen.

The King of Navarre commanded in the royalist camp. The besiegers assaulted the town not less than six times, and each time were repulsed. At the end of the fifth week a mine was sprung, great part of the wall was laid in ruins, and the soldiers scaling the breach, Rouen was taken. It was the first to drink that bitter cup which so many of the cities of France were afterwards called to drain. For a whole week it was given up to the soldiers. They did their pleasure in it, and what that pleasure was can be conceived without our describing it. Permitting the veil to rest on the other horrors, we shall select for description two deaths of very different character. The first is that of Pastor Augustin Marlorat. Of deep piety and great erudition, he had figured conspicuously in the Colloquy of Poissy, where the Reformation had vindicated itself before the civil and ecclesiastical grandees of France. Present in the city during the five memorable weeks of the siege, his heroic words, daily addressed to the citizens from the pulpit, had been translated by the combatants into heroic deeds on the wall. "You have seduced the people," said Constable de Montmorency to him, when he was brought before him after the capture of the town. "If so," calmly replied Marlorat, "God first seduced me, for I have preached nothing to them but the Gospel of his Son." Placed on a hurdle, he was straightway dragged to the gallows and hanged, sustaining with meekness and Christian courage the indignities and cruelties inflicted on him at the place of execution.[2616]

The other death-scene is that of Antoine de Bourbon, King of Navarre. Ensnared, as we have already said, by the brilliant but altogether delusive promises of the King of Spain, he had deserted the Protestants, and consented to be the ornamental head of the Romanist party. He was mortally wounded in the siege, and seeing death approaching, he was visited with a bitter but a late repentance. He implored his physician, who strove in vain to cure his wound, to read to him out of the Scriptures; and he protested, the tears streaming down his face, that if his life were spared he would cause the Gospel to be preached all throughout his dominions.[2617] He died at the age of forty-four, regretted by neither party.

After the fall and sack of Rouen, seven weeks passed away, and then the two armies met (19th December) near the town of Dreux. This was the first pitched battle of the civil wars, and the only regular engagement in the first campaign. The disparity of forces was considerable, the Huguenots having only 10,000 of all arms, while the royalists had 20,000, horse and foot, on the field. Battle being joined, the Huguenots had won the day when a stratagem of the Duke of Guise snatched victory from their grasp. All the time that the battle was raging—that is, from noon till five in the afternoon —Guise sat in the rear, surrounded by a chosen body of men-at-arms, intently watching the progress of the action, and at times sending forward the other Triumvirs with succours. At last the moment he had waited for came. The duke rode out to the front, rose in his stirrups, cast a glance over the field, and bidding his reserves follow, for the day was theirs, dashed forward. The Huguenots had broken their ranks and were pursuing the routed royalists all over the field. The duke was upon them before they had time to re-form, and wearied with fighting, and unable to sustain this onset of fresh troops, they went down before the cavalry of the duke.[2618] Guise's stratagem had succeeded. Victory passed over from the Huguenot to the royalist side.

The carnage was great. Eight thousand dead covered the field, among whom was La Brosse, who had begun the massacre at Vassy. The rank not less than the numbers of the slain gave great political consequences to the battle. The Marshal St. André was killed; Montmorency, severely wounded, had surrendered himself prisoner; and thus, of the three Triumvirs, Guise alone remained. The battle of Dreux had crowned him with a double victory, for his immediate appointment as lieutenant-general of the kingdom, and commander-in-chief of the army, placed France in his hands.

This battle left its mark on the Huguenot side also. The Prince of Condé was taken prisoner at the very close of the action. Being led to the headquarters of Guise, the duke and the prince passed the night in the same bed;[2619] the duke, it is said, sleeping soundly, and Condé lying awake, ruminating on the strange fortune of war which had so suddenly changed him from a conqueror into a captive. The prince being now a prisoner, Coligny was appointed generalissimo of the Huguenots. The two Bourbons were removed, and Guise and Coligny stood face to face.

It chanced that a messenger who had left the field at the moment that the battle was going against the Government, brought to the Louvre the news that the Huguenots had won the day. The remark of Catherine de Medici, who foresaw that the triumph of Coligny would diminish the power of Guise—whose authority had begun to overshadow her own—was imperturbably cool, and shows how little effort it cost her to be on either side, if only she could retain power. "Well, then," she said, on hearing the messenger's report, "Well, then, we shall have to say our prayers in French."[2620]

The war went on, although it had to be waged on a frozen earth, and beneath skies often dark with tempest; for it was winter. All France was at this hour a battle-field. Not a province was there, scarce even a city, in which the Roman Catholics and Huguenots were not arrayed in arms against each other. We must follow the march of the main army, however, without turning aside to chronicle provincial conflicts. After the defeat at Dreux, Coligny—now commander-in-chief—formed the Huguenot forces into two armies, and with the one he marched into Normandy, and sent his brother D'Andelot at the head of the other to occupy Orleans—that great centre and stronghold of the Huguenot cause. The Duke of Guise followed close on the steps of the latter, in order to besiege Orleans. Having sat down before the town on the 5th of February, 1563, the siege was prosecuted with great vigour. The bridge of the Loire was taken. Next two important suburbs fell into the hands of the duke. On the 18th all was ready for the capture of Orleans on the morrow. He wrote to the Queen-mother, telling her that his purpose was to put every man and woman in Orleans to the sword, and sow its foundations with salt.[2621] This good beginning he would follow up by summoning all the nobles of France, with their retainers, to his standard, and with this mighty host he would pursue the admiral into Normandy, and drive him and all his followers into the sea, and so stamp out the Huguenot insurrection. "Once unearth the foxes," said he, "and we will hunt them all over France."[2622]

Such was the brief and terrible programme of the duke for purging France of the Huguenot heresy. Where today stood the fair city of Orleans, tomorrow would be seen only a blackened heap; and wherever this leprosy had spread, thither, all over France, would the duke pursue it with fire and sword, and never rest till it was burned out. A whole hecatomb of cities, provinces, and men would grace the obsequies of Huguenotism.

The duke had gone to the trenches to see that all was ready for the assault that was to give Orleans to him on the morrow. Of all that he had ordered to be done, nothing had been omitted. Well pleased the duke was returning along the road to his château in the evening twilight. Behind him was the city of Orleans, the broad and deep Loire rolling beneath its walls, and the peaceful darkness gathering round its towers. Alas! before another sun shall set, there will not be left in that city anything in which is the breath of life. The blood of mother and helpless babe, of stern warrior, grey patriarch, and blooming maiden, will be blent in one red torrent, which shall rival the Loire in depth. It is a great sacrifice, but one demanded for the salvation of France. By the side of the road, partly hidden by two walnut-trees that grow on the spot, sits a figure on horseback, waiting for the approach of some one. He hears the sound of horses' hoofs. It is the duke that is coming; he knows him by his white plume; he permits him to pass, then slipping up close behind him, discharges his pistol. The ball entered the right shoulder of the duke—for he wore no cuirass—and passed through the chest. The duke bent for a moment upon his horse's mane, but instantly resuming his erect position in the saddle, he declared his belief that the wound was slight, and added good-humouredly, "They owed me this." It was soon seen, however, that the wound was mortal, and his attendants crowding round him, carried him to his house, and laid him on the bed from which he was to rise no more.

The assassin was John Poltrot, a petty nobleman of Angoumois, whom the duke's butcheries, and his own privations, had worked up into a fanaticism as sincere and as criminal as that of the duke himself. The horror of the crime seems to have bewildered him, for instead of making his escape on his fine Spanish horse, he rode round and round the spot where the deed had been done, all night,[2623] and when morning broke he was apprehended. He at first charged Coligny with being privy to the murder, and afterwards denied it. The admiral indignantly repudiated the accusation, and demanded to be confronted with Poltrot.[2624] The Government hurried on the execution of the assassin, and thus showed its disbelief in the charge he had advanced against Coligny, by preventing the opportunity of authenticating an allegation, which, had they been able to substantiate it, would have done much to bring strength and credit to their cause, and in the same proportion to disgrace and damage that of the Huguenots.

We return to the duke, who was now fast approaching his latter end. Death set some things in a new light. His belief in Roman Catholicism it did not shake, but it filled him with remorse for the cruel measures by which he had endeavoured to support it. He forgave his enemies, he asked that his blood might not be revenged, he confessed his infidelities to his duchess,[2625] who stood beside him dissolved in tears, and he earnestly counselled Catherine de Medici to make peace with the Huguenots, saying "that it was so necessary, that whoever should oppose it ought to be deemed an impious man, and an enemy to the king and the kingdom."[2626] The death of the Duke of Guise redeems somewhat the many dark passages in his life, and the sorrow into which he was melted at his latter end moderates the horror we feel at his bigotry and the cruel excesses into which it hurried him. But it more concerns us to note that he died at the moment when he had attained that proud summit he had long striven to reach. He was the sole Triumvir: he was at the head of the army: all the powers of government were gathered in his single hand: Huguenotism was at his feet: his arm was raised to crush it, when, in the words of Pasquier, his "horn was lowered."

The death of the Duke of Guise threw the government into the hands of Catherine de Medici. It was now that this woman, whom death seemed ever to serve, reached the summit of her wishes. Her son, Charles IX., reigned, but the mother governed. In presence of the duke's bier, Catherine was not indisposed to peace with the Protestants, but it was of her nature to work crookedly in all that she undertook. She had the Prince of Condé in the Louvre with her, and she set herself to weave her toils around him. Taken prisoner on the battle-field, as we have already said, "he was breathing," says Mezeray, "the soft air of the court," and the Queen-mother made haste to conclude the negotiations for peace before Coligny should arrive, who might not be so pliant as Condé. The prince had a conference with several of the Protestant ministers, who were unanimously of opinion that no peace could be satisfactory or honourable unless it restored, without restriction or modification, the Edict of January, which gave to all the Reformed in France the liberty of public worship. The Queen-mother and Condé, however, patched up a Pacification of a different kind. They agreed on a treaty, of which the leading provisions were that the nobles should have liberty to celebrate the Reformed worship in their castles, that the same privilege should be granted to certain of the gentry, and that a place should be set apart in certain *only* of the towns, where the Protestants might meet for worship. This arrangement came far short of the Edict of January, which knew no restriction of class or place in the matter of worship, but extended toleration to all the subjects of the realm. This new treaty did nothing for the pastors: it did nothing for the great body of the people, save that it did not hinder them from holding opinions in their own breasts, and celebrating, it might be, their worship at their own firesides. This peace was signed by the king at Amboise on the 19th of April, 1563; it was published before the camp at Orleans on the 22nd, amid the murmurs of the soldiers, who gave vent to their displeasure by the demolition of some images which, till that time, had been permitted to repose quietly in their niches.[2627] This edict was termed the "Pacification of Amboise." When the Admiral de Coligny was told of it he said indignantly, "This stroke of the pen has ruined more churches than our enemies could have knocked down in ten years."[2628] Returning by forced marches to Orleans in the hope of finding better terms, Coligny arrived just the day after the treaty had been signed and sealed.

Such was the issue of the first Huguenot war. If the Protestants had won no victory on the battlefield, their cause nevertheless was in a far stronger position now than when the campaign opened. The Triumvirs were gone; the Roman Catholic armies were without a leader, and the national exchequer was empty; while, on the other side, at the head of the Huguenot host was now the most skilful captain of his age. If the Huguenot nobles had had the wisdom and the courage to demand full toleration of their worship, the Government would not have dared to refuse it, seeing they were not in circumstances at the time to do so; but the Protestants were not true to themselves at this crisis, and so the hour passed, and with it all the golden opportunities it had brought. New enemies stood up, and new tempests darkened the sky of France.

CHAPTER X
CATHERINE DE MEDICI AND HER SON, CHARLES IX.—CONFERENCE AT BAYONNE—THE ST. BARTHOLOMEW MASSACRE PLOTTED

THE Pacification of Amboise (1563) closed the first Huguenot war. That arrangement was satisfactory to neither party. The Protestants it did not content; for manifestly it was not an advance but a retrogression. That toleration which the previous Edict of January had extended over the whole kingdom, the Pacification of Amboise restricted to certain bodies, and to particular localities. The Huguenots could not understand the principle on which such an arrangement was based. If liberty of worship was wrong, they reasoned, why permit it in any part of France? but if right, as the edict seemed to grant, it ought to be declared lawful, not in a few cities only, but in all the towns of the kingdom.

Besides, the observance of the Amboise edict was obviously impracticable. Were nine-tenths of the Protestants to abstain altogether from public worship? This they must do under the present law, or undertake a journey of fifty, or, it might be, a hundred miles to the nearest privileged city. A law that makes itself ridiculous courts contempt, and provokes to disobedience.

Moreover, the Pacification of Amboise was scarcely more to the taste of the Romanists. The concessions it made to the Huguenots, although miserable in the extreme, and accompanied by restrictions that made them a mockery, were yet, in the opinion of zealous Papists, far too great to be made to men to whom it was sinful to make any concession at all. On both sides, therefore, the measure was simply unworkable; perhaps it never was intended by its devisers to be anything else. In places where they were numerous, the Protestants altogether disregarded it, assembling in thousands and worshipping openly, just as though no Pacification existed. And the Roman Catholics on their part assailed with violence the assemblies of the Reformed, even in those places which had been set apart by law for the celebration of their worship; thus neither party accepted the arrangement as a final one. Both felt that they must yet look one another in the face on the battlefield; but the Roman Catholics were not ready to unsheathe the sword, and so for a brief space there was quiet—a suspension of hostilities if not peace.

It was now that the star of Catherine de Medici rose so triumphantly into the ascendant. The clouds which had obscured its lustre hitherto were all dispelled, and it blazed forth in baleful splendour in the firmament of France. It was thirty years since Catherine, borne over the waters of the Mediterranean in the gaily-decked galleys of Pisa, entered the port of Marseilles, amid the roar of cannon and the shouts of assembled thousands, to give her hand in marriage to the second son of the King of France. She was then a girl of sixteen, radiant as the country from which she came, her eyes all fire, her face all smiles, a strange witchery in her every look and movement; but in contrast with these fascinations of person was her soul, which was encompassed with a gloomy superstition, that might more fittingly be styled a necromancy than a faith. She came with a determined purpose of making the proud realm on which she had just stepped bow to her will, and minister to her pleasures, although it should be by sinking it into a gulf of pollution or drowning it in an ocean of blood. Thirty years had she waited, foreseeing the goal afar off, and patiently bending to obstacles she had not the power summarily to annihilate.

Death had been the steady and faithful ally of this extraordinary woman. Often had he visited the Louvre since the daughter of the House of Medici came to live under its roof; and each visit had advanced the Florentine a stage on her way to power. First, the death of the Dauphin—who left no child—opened her way to the throne. Then the death of her father-in-law, Francis I., placed her on that throne by the side of Henry II. She had the crown, but not yet the kingdom; for Diana of Poictiers, as the mistress, more than divided the influence which ought to have been Catherine's as the wife. The death of her husband took that humiliating impediment out of her way. But Mary Stuart, the niece of the Guises, and the wife of the weak-minded Francis II., profited by the imbecility through which Catherine had hoped to govern. Death, however, removed this obstacle, as he had done every previous one, by striking down Francis II. only seventeen short months after he had ascended the throne. Once more there stood up another rival, and Catherine had still to wait. Now it was that the Triumvirate rose and grasped with powerful hand the direction of France. Was the patience of the Italian woman to be always baulked? No: Death came again to her help. The fortune of battle and the pistol of the assassin rid her of the Triumvirate. The Duke of Guise was dead: rival to her power there no longer existed. The way so long barred was open now, and Catherine boldly placed herself at the head of affairs; and this position she continued to hold, with increasing calamity to France and deepening infamy to herself, till almost her last hour. This long delay, although it appeared to be adverse, was in reality in favour of the Queen-mother. If it gave her power late, it gave it her all the more securely. When her hour at last came, it found her in the full maturity of her faculties. She had had time to study, not only individual men, but all the parties into which France was divided. She had a perfect comprehension of the genius and temper of the nation. Consummate mistress of an art not difficult of attainment to an Italian—the art of dissembling—with an admirable intellect for intrigue, with sense enough not to scheme too finely, and with a patience long trained in the school of waiting, and not so likely to hurry on measures till they were fully ripened, it was hardly possible but that the daughter of the Medici would show herself equal to any emergency, and would leave behind her a monument which should tell the France of after times that Catherine de Medici had once governed it.

Standing as she now did on the summit, it was natural that Catherine should look around her, and warily choose the part she was to play. She had outlived all her rivals at court, and the Huguenots were now the only party she had to fear. Should she, after the examples of the Guises, continue to pursue them with the sword, or should she hold out to them the olive-branch? Catherine felt that she never could be one with the Huguenots. That would imply a breach with all the traditions of her house, and a change in the whole habits of her life, which was not to be thought of. Nor could she permit France to embrace the Protestant creed, for the country would thus descend in the scale of nations, and would embroil itself in a war with Italy and Spain. But, on the other side, there were several serious considerations which had to be looked at. The Huguenots were a powerful party; their faith was spreading in France; their counsels were guided and their armies were led by the men of the greatest character and intellect in the nation. Moreover, they had friends in Germany and England, who were not likely to look quietly on while they were being crushed by arms. To continue the war seemed very unadvisable. Catherine had no general able to cope with Coligny, and it was uncertain on which side victory might ultimately declare itself. The Huguenot army was inferior in numbers to that of the Roman Catholics, but it surpassed it in bravery, in devotion, and discipline; and the longer the conflict lasted, the more numerous the soldiers that flocked to the Huguenot standard.

It was tolerably clear that Catherine must conciliate the Protestants, yet all the while she must labour to diminish their numbers, to weaken their influence, and curtail their privileges, in the hope that at some convenient moment, which future years might bring, she might be able to fall upon them and cut them off, either by sudden war or by secret massacre. Doubtless what she now sketched was a policy of a general kind: content to fix its great outlines, and leave its details to be filled in afterwards, as circumstances might arise and opportunity offer. Accordingly, the Huguenots had gracious looks and soft words, but no substantial benefits, from the Queen-mother. There was a truce to open hostilities; but blood was flowing all the time. Private murder stalked through France; and short as the period was since the Pacification had been signed, not fewer than three thousand Huguenots had fallen by the poignard of the assassin. In truth, there was no longer in France only one nation. There were now two nations on its soil. The perfidy and wrong which had marked the whole policy of the court had so deeply parted the Huguenot and Romanist, that not the hope only, but the wish for conciliation had passed away. The part Catherine de Medici had imposed upon herself—of standing well with both, and holding the poise between the two, yet ever making the preponderance of encouragement and favour to fall on the Roman Catholic side—was an extremely difficult one; but her Italian nature and her discipline of thirty years made the task, which to another would have been impossible, to her comparatively easy.

Her first care was to mould her son, Charles IX., into her own likeness, and fit him for being an instrument, pliant and expert, for her purposes. Intellectually he was superior to his brother Francis II., who during his short reign had been treated by both wife and mother as an imbecile, and when dead was buried like a pauper. Charles IX. is said to have discovered something of the literary taste and aesthetic appreciation which were the redeeming features in the character of his grandfather Francis I. In happier circumstances he might have become a patron of the arts, and have found scope for his fitful energy in the hunting-field; but what manly grace or noble quality could flourish in an air so fetid as that of the Louvre? The atmosphere in which he grew up was foul with corruption, impiety, and blood. To fawn on those he mortally disliked, to cover bitter thoughts with sweet smiles and to caress till ready to strike, were the unmanly and unkingly virtues in which Charles was trained. His mother sent all the way to her own native city of Florence for a man to superintend the education of the prince—Albert Gondi, afterwards created Duke of Retz. Of this man, the historian Brantôme has drawn the following character:—"Cunning, corrupt, a liar, a great dissembler, swearing and denying God like a sergeant." Under such a teacher, it is not difficult to conceive what the pupil would become; by no chance could he contract the slightest acquaintance with virtue or honour. What a spectacle we are contemplating! At the head of a great nation is a woman without moral principle, without human pity, without shame; a very tigress, and she is rearing her son as the tigress rears her cubs. Unhappy France, what a dark future begins to project its shadow across thee!

In the summer of 1565, Catherine and her son made a royal progress through France. A brilliant retinue, composed of the princes of the blood, the great officers of state, the lords and ladies of the court—the dimness of their virtues concealed beneath the splendour of their robes—followed in the train of the Queen-mother and the royal scion. The wondering provinces sent out their inhabitants in thousands to gaze on the splendid cavalcade, as it swept comet-like past them. This progress enabled Catherine to judge for herself of the relative strength of the two parties in her dominions, and to shape her measures accordingly. Onward she went from province to province, and from city to city, scattering around her prodigally, yet judiciously, smiles, promises, and frowns; and who knew so well as she when to be gracious, and when to affect a stern displeasure? In those places where the Protestants had avenged upon the stone images the outrages which the Roman Catholics had committed upon living men, Catherine took care to intimate emphatically her disapproval. Her piety was hurt at the sight of the demolition of objects elevated to sacred uses. She took special care that her son's attention should be drawn to those affecting mementoes of Huguenot iconoclast zeal. In some parts monasteries demolished, crosses overturned, images mutilated, offered a spectacle exceedingly depressing to pious souls, and over which the devout and tender-hearted daughter of the Medici could scarcely refrain from shedding tears. How detestable the nature of that religion—so was the king taught to view the matter—which could prompt to acts so atrocious and impious! He felt that his kingdom had been polluted, and he trembled—not with a well-feigned terror like his mother, but a real dread—lest God, who had been affronted by these daring acts of sacrilege, should smite France with judgment; for in that age stone statues and crosses, and not divine precepts or moral virtues, were religion. The impression made upon the mind of the young king, especially in the southern provinces, where it seemed as if this impiety had reached its climax in a general sack of holy buildings and sacred furniture, was never, it is said, forgotten by him. It is believed to have inspired his policy in after-years.[2629]

The Queen-mother had another object in view in the progress she was now making. It enabled her, without attracting observation, to gather the sentiments of the neighbouring sovereigns on the great question of the age—namely, Protestantism—and to come to a common understanding with them respecting the measures to be adopted for its suppression. The kings of the earth were "plotting against the Lord and his anointed," and although willingly submitting to the cords with which the chief ruler of the Seven-hilled City had bound them, they were seeking how they might break the bands of that king whom God hath set upon the holy hill of Zion. The great ones of the earth did not understand the Reformation, and trembled before it. A power which the sword could slay would have caused them little uneasiness; but a power which had been smitten with the sword, which had been trodden down by armies, which had been burned at the stake, but which refused to die—a power which the oftener it was defeated the mightier it became, which started up anew to the confusion of its enemies from what appeared to be its grave, was a new thing in the earth. There was a mystery about it which made it a terror to them. They knew not whence it came, nor whereunto it might grow, nor how it was "to be met." Still the sword was the only weapon they knew to wield, and this caused them to meet often together to consult and plot. The Council of Trent, which had just closed its sittings, had recommended—indeed enjoined—a league among the Roman Catholic sovereigns and States for the forcible suppression of the Reformed opinions; and Philip II. of Spain took the lead in the matter, as became his position. His morose and fanatical genius scarcely needed the prompting of the Council. Catherine de Medici was now on her way to meet the envoy of this man, and to agree on a policy which should bind together in a common action the two crowns of Spain and France. Her steps were directed to Bayonne, the south-western extremity of her dominions; but her route thither was circuitous—being so on purpose that she might, under show of mutual congratulations, collect the sentiments of neighbouring rulers. As she skirted along by the Savoy Alps, she had an interview with the ambassador of the Duke of Savoy, who carried back Catherine's good wishes, and other things besides, to his master. At Avignon, the capital of the Papacy when Rome was too turbulent to afford safe residence to her Popes, Catherine halted to give audience to the Papal legate. She then pushed forward to Bayonne, where she was to meet the Duke of Alva, who, as the spokesman of the then mightiest monarch in Christendom, was a more important personage than the other ambassadors to whom she had already given audience. There a final decision was to be come to.

The royal cavalcade now drew nigh that quiet spot on the shores of the Bay of Biscay where, amid flourishing plantations and shrubs of almost tropical luxuriance, and lines of strong forts, nestles the little town of Bayonne—the "good bay"—a name its history has sadly belied. A narrow firth, which terminates in a little bay, admits the waters of the Atlantic within the walls of the town, and permits the ships of friendly Powers to lie under the shelter of its guns. The azure tops of the Pyrenees appearing in the south notify to the traveller that he has almost touched the frontier of Spain. Here, in the château which still stands crowning the height on the right of the harbour, Catherine de Medici met the plenipotentiary of Philip II.[2630] The King of Spain did not come in person, but sent his wife Elizabeth, the daughter of this same Catherine de Medici, and sister of Charles IX. Along with his queen came Philip's general, the well-known Duke of Alva. This man was inspired with an insane fury against Protestantism, which, meeting a fanaticism equally ferocious on the part of his master, was a link between the two. Alva was the right hand of Philip; he was his counsellor in all evil; and by the sword of Alva it was that Philip shed those oceans of blood in which he sought to drown Protestantism. Here, in this château, the dark sententious Spaniard met the crafty and eloquent Italian woman. Catherine made a covered gallery be constructed in it, that she might visit the duke whenever it suited her without being observed.[2631] Their meetings were mostly nocturnal, but as no one was admitted to them, the precise schemes discussed at them, and the plots hatched, must, unless the oaken walls shall speak out, remain secrets till the dread Judgment-day, save in so far as they may be guessed at from the events which flowed from them, and which have found a place on the page of history. It is certain from an expression of Alva's, caught up by the young son of the Queen of Navarre, the future Henry IV.—whose sprightliness had won for him a large place in Catherine's affections, and whom she at times permitted to go with her to the duke's apartments, thinking the matters talked of there altogether beyond the boy's capacity—that massacre was mooted at these interviews, and was relied upon as one of the main methods for cleansing Christendom from the heresy of Calvin. The expression has been recorded by all historians with slight verbal differences, but substantial identity. The idea was embodied by the duke in a vulgar but most expressive metaphor—namely, "The head of one salmon is worth that of ten thousand frogs." This expression, occurring as it did in a conversation in which the names of the Protestant leaders figured prominently, explained its meaning sufficiently to the young but precocious Henry of Navarre. He communicated it to the lord who waited upon him. This nobleman sent it in cipher to the prince's mother, Jeanne d'Albret, and by her it was communicated to the heads of Protestantism. All the Protestant chiefs, both in France and Germany, looked upon it as the foreshadowing of some terrible tragedy, hatched in this château, between the daughter of the fanatical House of Medici and the sanguinary lieutenant of Philip II. Retained meanwhile in the darkness of these two bosoms, and it might be of one or two others, the secret was destined to write itself one day on the face of Europe in characters of blood; whispered in the deep stillness of these oaken chambers, it was soon to break in a thunder-crash upon the world, and roll its dread reverberations along history's page till the end of time. This, in all probability, was what was resolved upon at these conferences at Bayonne. The conspirators did not plan a particular massacre, to come off on a particular day of a particular year; what they agreed upon was rather a policy towards the Protestants of treachery and murder, which however, should circumstances favour, might any day explode in a catastrophe of European dimensions.

"The Queen of Spain," says Davila, narrating the meeting at Bayonne, "being come to this place, accompanied with the Duke of Alva and the Count de Beneventa, whilst they made show with triumphs, tournaments, and several kinds of pastimes, as if they had in eye nothing but amusement and feasting, there was held a secret conference in order to arrive at a mutual understanding between the two crowns. Their common interest being weighed and considered, they agreed in this, that it was expedient for one king to aid and assist the other in pacifying their States and purging them from diversity of religions. But they were not of the same opinion as to the way that was most expeditious and secure for arriving at this end. . . . The duke said that a prince could not do a thing more unworthy or prejudicial to himself than to permit liberty of conscience to his people, bringing as many varieties of religion into a State as there are fancies in the minds of men; that diversities of opinion never failed to put subjects in arms, and stir up grievous treacheries and rebellions; therefore, he concluded that they ought by severe remedies, no matter whether by fire or sword, to cut away the roots of that evil."[2632]

The historian says that the Queen-mother was inclined to milder measures, in the first place, being indisposed to embrue her hands in the blood of the royal family, and of the great lords of the kingdom, and that she would reserve this as the last resort. "Both parties," says he, "aimed at the destruction of the Huguenots, and the establishment of obedience. Wherefore, at last they came to this conclusion, that the one king should aid the other either covertly or openly, as might be thought most conducive to the execution of so difficult and so weighty an enterprise, but that both of them should be free to work by such means and counsels as appeared to them most proper and seasonable."[2633] Tavannes, whose testimony is above suspicion, confirms the statement of Davila. "The Kings of France and Spain at Bayonne," says he in his *Mémoires*, "through the instrumentality of the Duke of Alva, resolved on the destruction of the Huguenots of France and Spain."[2634] Maimbourg reiterates the same thing. "The two kings came to an agreement," says he, "to exterminate all the Protestants in their dominions."[2637]

The massacre, it is now believed, was to have been executed in the year following (1566) at the Assembly of Notables at Moulins. But meanwhile the dark secret of Bayonne had oozed out in so many quarters, that Condé and Coligny could not with prudence disregard it, and though they came, with their confederates, to Moulins, in obedience to the royal summons, they were so well armed that Catherine de Medici durst not attempt her grand stroke.

CHAPTER XI
SECOND AND THIRD HUGUENOT WARS

WE return to the consideration of the condition of the Protestants of France. The Pacification of Amboise, imperfect from the first, was now flagrantly violated. The worshipping assemblies of the Protestants were dispersed, their persons murdered, their ministers banished or silenced; and for these wrongs they could obtain no redress. The iron circle was continually narrowing around them. Were they to sit still until they were inextricably enfolded and crushed? No; they must again draw the sword.

The court brought matters to extremity by hiring 6,000 Swiss mercenaries. On hearing of this, the Prince de Condé held a consultation with the Huguenot chiefs. Opinions were divided. Coligny advised a little longer delay. "I see perfectly well," said he, "how we may light the fire, but I do not see the water to put it out." His brother D'Andelot counselled instant action. "If you wait," he exclaimed, "till you are driven into banishment in foreign countries, bound in prisons, hunted down by the mob, of what avail will our patience be? Those who have brought 6,000 foreign soldiers to our very hearths have thereby declared war already." Condé and Coligny went to the Queen to entreat that justice might be done the Reformed. Catherine was deaf to their appeal. They next—acting on a precedent set them by the Duke of Guise five years before—attempted to seize the persons of the King and Queen-mother, at their Castle of Monceaux, in Brie. The plot being discovered, the court saved itself by a hasty flight. The Swiss had not yet arrived, and Catherine, safe again in Paris, amused the Protestants with negotiations. "The free exercise of their religion" was the one ever-reiterated demand of the Huguenots. At last the Swiss arrived, the negotiations were broken off, and now nothing remained but an appeal to arms.

This brings us to the second civil war, which we shall dispatch in a few sentences. The second Huguenot war was a campaign of but one battle, which lasted barely an hour. This affair, styled the Battle of St. Dénis, was fought under the walls of Paris, and the field was left in possession of the Huguenots,[2636] who offered the royalists battle on the following day, but they declined it, so giving the Protestants the right of claiming the victory. The veteran Montmorency, who had held the high office of Constable of France during four reigns, was among the slain. The Duke of Anjou, the favourite son of Catherine, succeeded him as generalissimo of the French army, and thus the chief authority was still more completely centred in the hands of the Queen-mother. The winter months passed without fighting. When the spring opened, the Protestant forces were so greatly reinforced by auxiliaries from Germany, that the court judged it the wiser part to come to terms with them, and on March 20th, 1568, the short-lived Peace of Longjumeau was signed. "This peace," says Mezeray, "left the Huguenots at the mercy of their enemies, with no other security than the word of an Italian woman."[2637]

The army under Condé melted away, and then Catherine forgot her promise. All the while the peace lasted, which was only six short months, the Protestants had to endure even greater miseries than if they had been in the field with arms in their hands. Again the pulpits thundered against heresy, again the passions of the mob broke out, again the dagger of the assassin was set to work, and the blood of the Huguenots ceased not to flow in all the cities and provinces of France. It is estimated that not fewer than ten thousand persons perished during this short period. The court did nothing to restrain, but much, it is believed, to instigate to these murders. One gets weary of writing so monotonous a recital of outrage and massacre. This bloodshed, it must be acknowledged, was not all confined to one side. Some two hundred Roman Catholics, including several priests, were massacred by the Protestants. This is to be deplored, but it need surprise no one. Of the hundreds of thousands of Huguenots in France, all were not pious men; and further, while these two hundred or so of Romanists were murdered, the Huguenots were perishing in tens of thousands by every variety of cruel death, and of shocking and shameful outrage. There was no justice in the land. The crew that occupied the Louvre, and styled themselves the Government, were there, as the Thug is in his den, to entrap and dispatch his victim. There were men in France doubtless who reasoned that, although the laws of society had fallen, the laws of nature were still in force.

Matters were brought to a head by the discovery of a plot which was to be immediately executed. At a council in the Louvre, it was resolved to seize the two Protestant chiefs—the Prince of Condé and Admiral Coligny—and put them out of the way, by consigning the first to a dungeon for life, and sending the second to the scaffold. The moment they were informed of the plot, the prince and the admiral fled with their wives and children to La Rochelle. The road was long and the journey toilsome. They had to traverse three hundred miles of rough country, obstructed by rivers, and beset by the worse dangers of numerous foes. An incident which befell them by the way touched their hearts deeply, as showing the hand of God. Before them was the Loire—a broad and rapid river. The bridges were watched. How were they to cross? A friendly guide, to whom the by-paths and fords were known, conducted them to the river's banks opposite Sancerre, and at that point the company, amounting to nearly two hundred persons, crossed without inconvenience or risk. They all went over singing the psalm, *When Israel went out of Egypt*. Two hours after, the heavens blackened, and the rain falling in torrents, the waters of the Loire, which a little before had risen only to their horses' knees, were now swollen, and had become impassable. In a little while they saw their pursuers arrive on the further side of the river; but their progress was stayed by the deep and angry flood, to which they dared not commit themselves. "Escaped as a bird out of the snare of the fowlers," the company of Coligny exchanged looks of silent gratitude with one another.[2638] What remained of their way was gone with lighter heart and nimbler foot; they felt, although they could not see, the Almighty escort that covered them; and so, journeying on, they came at last safely to La Rochelle.

La Rochelle was at this period a great mart of trade. Its inhabitants shared the independence of sentiment which commerce commonly brings in its train. Having early embraced the Reformation, the bulk of its inhabitants were by this time Protestants. An impression was abroad that another great crisis impended; and under this belief, too well founded, all the chiefs and captains of the army were repairing with their followers to this stronghold of Huguenotism. We have seen Condé and Coligny arrive here; and soon thereafter came another illustrious visitor—Jeanne d'Albret. The Queen of Navarre did not come alone; she brought with her, her son Henry, prince of Bearn, whose heroic character was just then beginning to open, and whom his mother, in that dark hour, dedicated to the service of the Protestant cause. This arrival awakened the utmost enthusiasm in La Rochelle among both citizens and soldiers. Condé laid his command of the Huguenot army at the feet of the young Prince of Bearn—magnanimously performing an act which the conventional notions of the age exacted of him, for Henry was nearer the throne than himself. The magnanimity of Condé evoked an equal magnanimity. "No," said Jeanne d'Albret; "I and my son are here to promote the success of this great enterprise, or to share its disaster. We will joyfully unite beneath the standard of Condé. The cause of God is dearer to me than my son."

At this juncture the Queen-mother published an edict, revoking the Edict of January, forbidding, on pain of death, the profession of Protestantism, and commanding all ministers to leave the kingdom within a fortnight.[2639] If anything was wanting to complete the justification of the Protestants, in this their third war, it was now supplied. During the winter of 1569, the two armies were frequently in presence of one another; but as often as they essayed to join battle, storms of unprecedented violence broke out, and the assailants had to bow to the superior force of the elements. At last, on the 15th of March, they met on the field of Jarnac. The day was a disastrous one for the Protestants. Taken at unawares, the Huguenot regiments arrived one after the other on the field, and were butchered in detail, the enemy assailing in overwhelming numbers. The Prince of Condé, after performing prodigies of valour, wounded, unhorsed, and fighting desperately on his knees, was slain.[2640] Coligny, judging it hopeless to prolong the carnage, retired with his soldiers from the field; and the result of the day as much elated the court and the Roman Catholics, as it engendered despondency and despair in the hearts of the Protestants.

While the Huguenot army was in this mood—beaten by their adversaries, and in danger of being worse beaten by their fears—the Queen of Navarre suddenly appeared amongst them. Attended by Coligny, she rode along their ranks, having on one hand her son, the Prince of Bearn, and on the other her nephew, Henry, son of the fallen Condé. "Children of God and of France," said she, addressing the soldiers, "Condé is dead; but is all therefore lost? No; the God who gave him courage and strength to fight for this cause, has raised up others worthy to succeed him. To those brave warriors I add my son. Make proof of his valour. Soldiers! I offer you everything I have to give—my dominions, my treasures, my life, and what is dearer to me than all, my children. I swear to defend to my last sigh the holy cause that now unites us!" With these heroic words she breathed her own spirit into the soldiers. They looked up; they stood erect; the fire returned to their eyes. Henry of Navarre was proclaimed general of the army, amid the plaudits of the soldiers; and Coligny and the other chiefs were the first to swear fidelity to the hero, to whom the whole realm was one day to vow allegiance.

Thus the disaster of Jarnac was so far repaired; but a yet deeper reverse awaited the Huguenot arms. The summer which opened so ominously passed without any affair of consequence till the 3rd of October, and then came the fatal battle of Montcontour. It was an inconvenient moment for Coligny to fight, for his German auxiliaries had just mutinied; but no alternative was left him. The Huguenots rushed with fury into action; but their ranks were broken by the firm phalanxes on which they threw themselves, and before they could rally, a tremendous slaughter had begun, which caused something like a panic amongst them. Coligny was wounded at the very commencement; his lower jaw was broken, and the blood, oozing from the wound and trickling down his throat, all but choked him. Being unable to give the word of command, he was carried out of the battle. A short hour only did the fight rage; but what disasters were crowded into that space of time! Of the 25,000 men whom Coligny had led into action, only 8,000 stood around their standards when it was ended. Ammunition, cannon, baggage, and numerous colours were lost. Again the dark night was closing in around French Protestantism.

As Coligny was being carried out of the field, another litter in which lay a wounded soldier passed him by. The occupant of that other litter was Lestrange, an old gentleman, and one of the admiral's chief counsellors. Lestrange, happening to draw aside the curtains and look out, recognised his general. "Yes," said he, brushing away a tear that dimmed his eye— "Yes, God is very sweet." This was all he spoke. It was as if a Divine hand had dropped a cordial into the soul of Coligny. Speaking afterwards to his friends of the incident, he said that these words were as balm to his spirit, then more bruised than his body. There is here a lesson for us—nay, many lessons, though we can particularise only one. We are apt to suppose that those exemplify the highest style of piety, and enjoy most of the Spirit's presence, who are oftenest in the closet engaged in acts of devotion, and that controversy and fighting belong to a lower type of Christianity. There are exceptions, of course; but the rule, we believe, is the opposite. We must distinguish between a contentious lot and a contentious spirit; the former has been assigned to some of the most loving natures, and the most spiritual of men. That is the healthiest piety that best endures the wear and tear of hard work, just as those are the healthiest plants which, in no danger of pining away without the shelter of a hot-house, flourish in the outer air, and grow tall, and strong, and beautiful amid the rains and tempests of the open firmament. So now: breaking through the clouds and dust of the battlefield, a ray from heaven shot into the soul of Coligny.

The admiral had now touched the lowest point of his misfortunes. We have seen him borne out of the battle, vanquished and wounded almost to death. His army lay stretched on the field. The few who had escaped the fate of their comrades were dispirited and mutinous. Death had narrowed the circle of his friends, and of those who remained, some forsook him, and others even blamed him. To crown these multiplied calamities, Catherine de Medici came forward to deal him the *coup de grâce*. At her direction the Parliament of Paris proclaimed him an outlaw, and set a price of 30,000 crowns upon his head. His estates were confiscated, his Castle of Châtillon was burned to the ground, and he was driven forth homeless and friendless. Were his miseries now complete? Not yet. Pius V. cursed him as "an infamous, execrable man." It was now that Coligny appeared greatest. Furious tempests assailed him from all quarters at once, but he did not bow to their violence. In the presence of defeat, desertion, outlawry, and the bitter taunts and curses of his enemies, his magnanimity remained unsubdued, and his confidence in God unshaken. A glorious triumph yet awaited the cause that was now so low. Perish it could not, and with it he knew would revive his now sore-tarnished name and fame.

He stood upon a rock, and the serenity of soul which he enjoyed, while these tempests were raging at his feet, is finely shown in the letters which at that time he addressed to his children—for his wife, the heroic Charlotte Laval, was dead two years, and saw not the evil that came upon her house. "We must follow Jesus Christ," wrote Coligny (October 16th, 1569), "our Captain, who has marched before us. Men have stripped us of all they could; and if this is still the will of God, we shall be happy, and our condition good, seeing this loss has not happened through any injury we have done to those who have inflicted it, but solely through the hatred they bear toward me, because it has pleased God to make use of me to aid his Church. For the present, it suffices that I admonish and conjure you, in the name of God, to persevere courageously in the study of virtue."

CHAPTER XII
SYNOD OF LA ROCHELLE

WE left Protestantism in France, and its greatest champion, Admiral de Coligny, reeling under what seemed to be a mortal blow. The Prince of Condé was dead; the battle of Montcontour had been lost; the army mostly lay rotting on the field; and a mere handful of soldiers only remained around the standard of their chief. Many who had befriended his cause till now abandoned it in despair, and such as still remained faithful were greatly disheartened, and counselled submission. Catherine de Medici, as we have seen, thinking that now was the hour of opportunity, hastened to deal what she did not doubt would be the finishing blow to the Protestant cause, and to the man who was pre-eminently its chief. It was now, in the midst of these misfortunes, that Coligny towered up, and reached the full stature of his moral greatness; and with him, rising from its ashes, soared up anew the Protestant cause.

Success in the eye of the world is one thing; success in the eye of God is another and a different thing. When men are winning battles, and every day adding to the number of their friends, and the greatness of their honours—These men," says the world, "are marching on to victory." But when to a cause or to a party there comes defeat after defeat, when friends forsake, and calamities thicken, the world sees nothing but disaster, and prognosticates only ruin. Yet these things may be but the necessary steps to success.

Chastened by these sore dispensations, they who are engaged in the work of God are compelled to turn from man, and to fortify themselves by a yet more entire and exclusive reliance on the Almighty. They cleanse themselves from the vitiating stains of flattery and human praise; they purge out the remaining leaven of selfishness; God's Spirit descends in richer influences upon them; the calm of the celestial power fills their souls; they find that they have been cast down in order that they may be lifted up, and that, instead of ruin, which the world's wise men and their own fears had foretold, they are now nearing the goal, and that it is triumph that awaits them. So was it with Protestantism in France at this hour. The disaster which had overtaken it, and in which its enemies saw only ruin, was but the prelude to its vindicating for itself a higher position than it had ever before attained in that nation.

The heads of the Protestant cause and the captains of the army gathered round Admiral de Coligny, after the battle, but with looks so crestfallen, and speaking in terms so desponding, that it was plain they had given up all as lost. Not so Coligny. The last to unsheathe the sword, he would be the last to return it to its scabbard, nor would he abandon the enterprise so long as a single friend was by his side.

"No," said Coligny, in answer to the desponding utterances of the men around him, "all is not lost; nothing is lost; we have lost a battle, it is true; but the burial trenches of Montcontour do not contain all the Huguenots; the Protestants of France have not been conquered; those provinces of the kingdom in which Protestantism has taken the deepest root, and which have but slightly felt the recent reverses, will give us another army." The Protestants of Germany and England, he reminded them, were their friends, and would send them succours; they must not confine their eye to one point, nor permit their imagination to dwell on one defeat; they must embrace in their survey the whole field; they must not count the soldiers of Protestantism, they must weigh its moral and spiritual forces, and, when they had done so, they would see that there was no cause to despair of its triumph. By these magnanimous words Coligny raised the spirit of his friends, and they resolved to continue the struggle.[2641]

The result justified the wisdom as well as the courage of the admiral. He made his appeal to the provinces beyond the Loire, where the friends of Protestantism were the most numerous. Kindling into enthusiasm at his call, there flocked to his standard from the mountains of Bearn, from the cities of Dauphiné, and the region of the Cevennes, young and stalwart warriors, who promised to defend their faith and liberties till death.[2642] When the spring opened the brave patriot-chief had another army, more numerous and better disciplined than the one he had lost, ready to take the field and strike another blow. The fatal fields of Jarnac and Montcontour were not to be the grave of French Huguenotism.

When the winter had passed, and after some encounters with the enemy, which tested the spirit of his army, Coligny judged it best to march direct on Paris, and make terms under the walls of the capital. The bold project was put in instant execution. The tidings that Coligny was approaching struck the Government with consternation. The court, surrendering itself to the pleasant dream that Protestantism lay buried in the gory mounds of its recent battlefields, had given itself up to those pleasures which ruin, body and soul, those who indulge in them. The court was at its wits' end. Not only was the redoubtable Huguenot chief again in the field, he was on his road to Paris, to demand a reckoning for so many Pacifications broken, and so much blood spilt. The measure which the court adopted to ward off the impending danger was a weak one. They sent the Duke of Anjou—the third son of Catherine de Medici, the same who afterwards ascended the throne under the title of Henry III.—with an army of gallants, to stop Coligny's march. The stern faces and heavy blows of the mountain Huguenots drove back the emasculated recruits of Anjou. Coligny continued his advance. A few days more and Paris, surrounded by his Huguenots, would be enduring siege. A council of war was immediately held, attended by the King, the Queen-mother, the Duke of Anjou, and the Cardinal of Lorraine. It was resolved, says Davila, to have recourse to the old shift, that namely of offering peace to the Huguenots.

The peace was granted, Davila tells us—and he well knew the secrets of the court—in the hope "that the foreign troops would be sent out of France, and that artifice and opportunity would enable them to take off the heads of the Protestant faction, when the common people would yield, and return to their obedience."[2643] This ending of the matter, by "artifice and opportunity," the historian goes on to remark, had been long kept in view. Catherine de Medici now came to terms with Coligny, the man whom a little time ago she had proclaimed an outlaw, setting a price upon his head; and on the 8th of August, 1570, the Peace of St. Germain-en-Laye was signed.

The terms of that treaty were unexpectedly favourable. Its general basis was an amnesty for all past offences; the right of the Huguenots to reside in any part of France without being called in question for their religious opinions; liberty of worship in the suburbs of two towns in each province; admissibility of the Protestants to most of the offices of state, and the restoration of all confiscated property. As a guarantee for the faithful execution of the treaty, four cities were put into the hands of the Protestants—La Rochelle, La Charité, Cognac, and Montauban. The torn country had now a little rest; sweet it was for the Huguenots to exchange camps and battlefields for their peaceful homes. There was one drawback, however, the remembrance of the many Pacifications that had been made only to be broken. This was the third in the space of seven years. Meanwhile the daughter of the Medici held out the olive-branch: but so little was she trusted that none of the Huguenot chiefs presented themselves at court, nor did they even deem themselves secure in their own castles; they retired in a body within the strongly fortified city of La Rochelle.

Davila admits that the Protestants had good grounds for these suspicions. The peace was the gift of the Trojans; and from this time the shadow of the St. Bartholomew massacre begins to darken the historian's page. "The peace having been concluded and established," says he, "the stratagem formed in the minds of the king and queen for bringing the principal Huguenots into the net began now to be carried out, and they sought to compass by policy that which had so often been attempted by war, but which had been always found fruitless and dangerous."[2644] Davila favours us with a glimpse of that policy, which it was hoped would gain what force had not effected. The king "being now come to the age of two-and-twenty, of a resolute nature, a spirit full of resentment, and above all, an absolute dissembler," scrupulously observed the treaty, and punished the Roman Catholic mobs for their infractions of it in various places, and strove by "other artifices to lull to sleep the suspicions of Coligny and his friends, to gain their entire confidence, and so draw them to court." Maimbourg's testimony, which on this head may be entirely trusted, is to the same effect. "But not to dissemble," says he, "as the queen did in this treaty, there is every appearance that a peace of this kind was not made in good faith on the part of this princess, who had her concealed design, and who granted such things to the Huguenots only to disarm them, and afterwards to surprise those upon whom she wished to be revenged, and especially the admiral, at the first favourable opportunity she should have for it."[2645]

When from the stormy era at which we are now arrived—the eighth year of the civil wars—we look back to the calm day-break under Lefevre, we are touched with a tender sorrow, and recall, with the din of battle in our ears, the psalms that the reapers, as they rested at mid-day, were wont to sing on the harvest-field of Meaux. The light of that day-break continued to wax till the morning had passed into almost noon-day. But with the war came an arrest of this most auspicious progress. Piety decayed on the battlefield, and the evangelisation began to retrograde. "Before the wars," says Félice, "proselytism was conducted on a large scale, and embraced whole cities and provinces; peace and freedom allowed of this; afterwards proselytes were few in number, and obtained with difficulty. How many corpses were there heaped up as barriers between the two communions; how many bitter enmities, and cruel remembrances, watched around the two camps to forbid approach."[2646] Still, if the root of that once noble vine which stretched its branches on the one side of the Pyrenees, and on the other to the English sea, is still in the soil of France, we owe it to the heroes of the Huguenot wars. Different circumstances demand the display of different graces. Psalms and hymns became the first Protestants of France. Strong cries to God, trust in his arm, and strivings unto blood formed the worship of the Huguenots. They were martyrs, though they died in armour. The former is the lovelier picture, the latter is the grander. In truth, times like those in which Coligny lived, act on the spiritual constitution much as a stern climate acts on the physical. The sickly are dwarfed by it, the robust are nourished into yet greater robustness. The oak, that battles with the winds, shows its boughs sorely gnarled, and its trunk sheathed in a bark of iron, but within there flows a current of living sap, which enables it to live and ripen its acorns through a thousand years. And so of the Christian who is exposed to such tempests as those amid which Coligny moved; what his piety loses in point of external grace, it acquires in respect of an internal strength, which is put forth in acts of faith in God, and in deeds of sacrifice and service to man.

Meanwhile the great winds were holden that they might not blow on the vine of France, and during those two tranquil years a synod of the Reformed Church was held at La Rochelle (1571). This synod marks the acme of Protestantism in France. To borrow a figure from classic times, the doors of the temple of Janus were closed; war's banner was furled; and the Huguenots went up to their strong city of La Rochelle, and held their great convocation within its gates. The synod was presided over by Theodore Beza. Calvin was dead, having gone to the grave just as these troubles were darkening over France; but his place was not unworthily filled by his great successor, the learned and eloquent Beza. The synod was attended by the Queen of Navarre, Jeanne d'Albret, who was accompanied by her son, the Prince of Bearn, the future Henry IV. There were present also Henry, the young Prince of Condé; Gaspard de Coligny, Admiral of France; the Count of Nassau; the flower of the French *noblesse*; the pastors, now a numerous body; the captains of the army, a great many lay deputies, together with a miscellaneous assemblage composed of the city burghers, the vine-dressers of the plains, and the herdsmen of the hills. They sat day by day to receive accounts of the state of Protestantism in the various provinces, and to concert measures for the building up of the Reformed Church in their native land.

We have already related the meeting of the first synod of the French Protestant Church at Paris, 1559. At that synod were laid the foundations of the Church's polity; her confession of faith was compiled, and her whole order and organisation were settled. Five national synods had assembled in the interval, and this at La Rochelle was the seventh; but neither at this, or at the five that preceded it, had any alteration of the least importance been made in the creed or in the constitution of the French Church, as agreed on at its first national synod, in 1559. This assembly, so illustrious for the learning, the rank, and the numbers of its members, set the seal of approval on what the eleven pastors had done at Paris twelve years before. There is no synod like this at La Rochelle, before or since, in the history of the French Protestant Church. It was a breathing-time, short, but beyond measure refreshing. "The French Church," says one, "now sat under the apple-tree; God spread a table for her in the presence of her enemies."

CHAPTER XIII

THE PROMOTERS OF THE ST. BARTHOLOMEW MASSACRE

THE ever-memorable Synod of La Rochelle has closed its sittings; the noon of Protestantism in France has been reached; and now we have sadly to chronicle the premature decline of a day that promised to be long and brilliant. Already we are within the dark shadow of a great coming catastrophe.

The springs and causes of the St. Bartholomew Massacre are to be sought for outside the limits of the country in which it was enacted. A great conjunction of principles and politics conspired to give birth to a tragedy which yields in horror to no crime that ever startled the world. The first and primary root of this, as of all similar massacres in Christendom, is the divine vicegerency of the Pope. So long as Christendom is held to be a theocracy, rebellion against the law of its divine monarch, in other words, heresy, is and must be justly punishable with death.

But, over and above, action in this special direction had been plotted and solemnly enjoined by the Council of Trent. "Roman Catholic Europe," says Gaberel, "was to erase Reformed Europe, and proclaim the two principles—the sovereign authority of the kings in political affairs, and the infallibility of the Pope in religious questions. The right of resisting the temporal, and the right of inquiring into the spiritual, were held to be detestable crimes, which the League wished to banish from the world."[2647] At the head of the League was Philip II.; and the sanguinary ferocity of the King of Spain made the vast zeal of the French court look but as lukewarmness. A massacre was then in progress in the Low Countries, which took doubtless the form of war, but yielded its heaps of corpses almost daily, and which thrills us less than the St. Bartholomew only because, instead of consummating its horrors in one terrible week, it extended them over many dismal years. Philip never ceased to urge on Catherine de Medici and Charles IX. to do in France as he was doing in Flanders. These reiterated exhortations were doubtless the more effectual inasmuch as they entirely coincided with what Catherine deemed her truest policy. The hopelessness of overcoming the Huguenots in the field was now becoming very apparent. Three campaigns had been fought, and the position of the Protestants was stronger than at the beginning of the war. No sooner was one Huguenot army defeated and dispersed, than another and a more powerful took the field. The Prince of Condé had fallen, but his place was filled by a chief of equal rank. The court of France had indulged the hope that if the leaders were cut off the people would grow disheartened, and the contest would languish and die out; but the rapidity with which vacancies were supplied, and disasters repaired, at last convinced the King and Queen-mother that these hopes were futile. They must lay their account with a Huguenot ascendance at an early day, unless they followed the counsels of Philip of Spain, and by a sudden and sweeping stroke cut off the whole Huguenot race. But the time and the way, as Catherine told Philip, must be left to herself.

At this great crisis of Papal affairs—for if Huguenotism had triumphed in France it would have carried its victorious arms over Spain and Italy—a higher authority than even Philip of Spain came forward to counsel the steps to be taken—nay, not to counsel only, but to *teach authoritatively* what was DUTY in the matter, and enjoin the performance of that duty under the highest sanctions. This brings the reigning Pontiff upon the scene, and we shall try and make clear Pope Pius V.'s connection with the terrible event we are approaching. It will assist us in understanding this part of history, if we permit his biographers to bring before us the man who bore no inconspicuous part in it.

The St. Bartholomew Massacre was plotted under the Pontificate of Pius V., and enacted under that of his immediate successor, Gregory XIII. Michael Ghisliere (Pius V.) was born in the little town of Bosco, on the plain of Piedmont, in the year 1504. His parents were in humble station. "The genius of the son," says his biographer Gabutius, "fitted him for higher things than the manual labours that occupied his parents. The spirit of God excited him to that mode of life by which he might the more signally serve God and, escaping the snares of earth, attain the heavenly felicity.[2648] He was marked from his earliest years by an austere piety. Making St. Dominic, the founder of the Inquisition, his model, and having, it would seem, a natural predilection for this terrible business, he entered a Dominican convent at the age of fourteen. He obeyed, body and soul, the laws of his order. The poverty which his vow enjoined he rigidly practised. Of the alms which he collected he did not retain so much as would buy him a cloak for the winter; and he fortified himself against the heats of summer by practising a severe abstinence. He laboured to make his fellow-monks renounce their slothful habits, their luxurious meals, and their gay attire, and follow the same severe, mortified, and pious life with himself. If not very successful with them, he continued nevertheless to pursue these austerities himself, and soon his fame spread far and near. He was appointed confessor to the Governor of Milan, and this necessitated an occasional journey of twenty miles, which was always performed on foot, with his wallet on his back.[2649] On the road he seldom spoke to his companions, "employing the time," says the biographer, "in reciting prayers or meditating on holy things."[2650] His devotion to the Roman See, and the zeal with which he combated Protestantism, recommended him to his superiors, and his advancement was rapid. Of several offices which were now in his choice, he gave his decided preference to that of inquisitor, "from his ardent desire," his biographer tells us, "to exterminate heretics, and extend the Roman Catholic faith." The district including Como and the neighbouring towns was committed to his care, and he discharged the duties of this fearful office with such indefatigable, and indeed ferocious zeal, as often to imperil his own life. The Duchy of Milan was then being inoculated with "the pernicious and diabolical doctrines," as Gabutius styles them, of Protestantism; and Michael Ghislieri was pitched upon as the only man fit to cope with the evil. Day and night he perambulated his diocese on the quest for heretics. This was judged too narrow a sphere for an activity so prodigious, and Paul IV., himself one of the greatest of persecutors, nominated Ghislieri to the office of supreme inquisitor. This brought him to Rome; and here, at last, he found a sphere commensurate with the greatness of his zeal. He continued to serve under Pius IV., adding to the congenial office of inquisitor, the scarlet of the cardinalate.[2651] On the death of Pius IV., Ghislieri was elevated to the Popedom, his chief recommendation in the eyes of his supporters, including Cardinal Borromeo and Philip II., being his inextinguishable zeal for the suppression of heresy. Rome was then in the thick of her battle, and Ghislieri was selected as the fittest man to preside over and infuse new vigour into that institution on which she mainly relied for victory. The future life of Pius V. justified his elevation. His daily fare was as humble, his clothing as mean, his fasts as frequent, and his household arrangements as economical, now that he wore the tiara, as when he was a simple monk. He rose with the first light, he kneeled long in prayer, and often would he mingle his tears with his supplications; he abounded in alms, he forgot injuries, he was kind to his domestics; he might often be seen with naked feet, and head uncovered, his white beard sweeping his breast, walking in procession, and receiving the reverence of the populace as one of the holiest Popes that had ever trodden the streets of Rome.[2652] But one formidable quality did Pius V. conjoin with all this—even an intense, unmitigated detestation of Protestantism, and a fixed, inexorable determination to root it out. In his rapid ascent from post to post, he saw the hand of God conducting him to the summit, that there, wielding all the arms, temporal and spiritual, of Christendom, he might discharge, in one terrible stroke, the concentrated vengeance of the Popedom on the hydra of heresy. Every hour of every day he occupied in the execution of what he believed to be his predestined work. He sent money and soldiers to France to carry on the war against the Huguenots; he addressed continual letters to the kings and bishops of the Popish world, inciting them to yet greater zeal in the slaughter of heretics; ever and anon the cry "To massacre!" was sounded forth from the Vatican; but not a doubt had Pius V. that this butchery was well-pleasing to God, and that he himself was the appointed instrument for emptying the vials of wrath upon a system which he regarded as accursed, and believed to be doomed to destruction.

Such was the man who at this era filled the Papal throne. But let us permit Pius V. himself to speak. In 1569, the Pope, despairing of overcoming the French heretics in open war, darkly suggests a way more secret and more sure. "Our zeal," says he, in his letter to the Cardinal of Lorraine, "gives us the right of earnestly exhorting and exciting you to use all your influence for procuring a definite and serious adoption of the measure most proper for bringing about the destruction of the implacable enemies of God and the king."[2653] After the victory of Jarnac the French Government acknowledged the help the Pope had given them in winning it, by sending to Rome some Huguenot standards taken on the field, to be displayed in the Lateran. Pius V. replied in a strain of exultation, and laboured to stimulate the court to immediate and remorseless massacre. "The more the Lord has treated you and me with kindness," so wrote he to Charles IX., "the more you ought to take advantage of the opportunity this victory offers you, for pursuing and destroying all the enemies that still remain; for tearing up entirely all the roots, and even the smallest fibres of the roots, of so terrible and confirmed an evil. For unless they are radically extirpated, they will be found to shoot up again; and, as it has already happened several times, the mischief will reappear when your majesty least expects it. You will bring this about if no consideration for persons, or worldly things, induces you to spare the enemies of God—who have never spared yourself. For you will not succeed in turning away the wrath of God, except by avenging him rigorously on the wretches who have offended him, by inflicting on them the punishment they have deserved."[2654]

These advices, coming from such a quarter, were commands, and they could take no practical shape but that of massacre; and to make it unmistakable that this was the shape the Pope meant his counsels to take, he proceeds to cite a case in point from Old Testament history.

"Let your majesty take for example, and never lose sight of, what happened to Saul, King of Israel. He had received the orders of God, by the mouth of the prophet Samuel, to fight and to exterminate the Amalekites, in such a way that he should not spare one in any case, or under any pretext. But he did not obey the will and voice of God . . . therefore he was deprived of his throne and his life." If for Saul we read Charles IX., and for the prophet Samuel we substitute Pius V., as the writer clearly intended should be done, what is this but a command addressed to the King of France, on peril of his throne, to massacre all the Huguenots in his realm, without sparing even one? "By this example," continues the Pope, "God has wished to teach all kings that to neglect the vengeance of outrages done to him is to provoke his wrath and indignation against themselves."

To Catherine de Medici, Pius V. writes in still plainer terms, as if he knew her wolfish nature, as well as her power over her son, promising her the assistance of Heaven if she would pursue the enemies of the Roman Catholic religion "till they are all massacred,[2655] for it is only by the entire extermination of heretics[2656] that the Roman Catholic worship can be restored."[2657]

There follow letters to the Duke of Anjou, and the Cardinal of Lorraine, and another to the king, all breathing the same sanguinary spirit, and enjoining the same inexorability towards the vanquished heretics.[2658]

At Bayonne, in 1565, Catherine met the Duke of Alva, as we have already seen, to consult as to the means of ridding France of heretics. "They agreed at last," says the contemporary historian Adriani, "in the opinion of the Catholic King, that this great blessing could not have accomplishment save by the death of all the chiefs of the Huguenots, and by a new edition, as the saying was, of *the Sicilian Vespers*.[2659] "They decided," says Guizot, "that the deed should be done at Moulins, in Bourbonnes, whither the king was to return. The execution of it was afterwards deferred to the date of the St. Bartholomew, in 1572, at Paris, because of certain suspicions which had been manifested by the Huguenots, and because it was considered easier and more certain to get them all together at Paris than at Moulins." This is confirmed by Tavannes, who says: "The Kings of France and of Spain, at Bayonne, assisted by the Duke of Alva, resolved on the destruction of the heretics in France and Flanders."[2660] La Nouë in his *Mémoires* bears witness to the "resolution taken at Bayonne with the Duke of Alva, to extirpate the Huguenots of France and the *beggars* of Flanders, which was brought to light by intercepted letters coming from Rome to Spain."[2261]

"Catherine de Medici," says Guizot, "charged Cardinal Santa Croce to assure Pope Pius V. 'that she and her son had nothing more at heart than to get the admiral and all his confidants together some day, and make a massacre [un macello] of them; but the matter,' she said, 'was so difficult, that there was no possibility of promising to do it at one time more than at another.'" "De Thou," adds the historian, "regards all these facts as certain, and after having added some details, he sums them all up in the words, 'This is what passed at Bayonne in 1565.'"[2662]

We have it, thus, under the Pope's own hand, that he enjoined on Charles IX. and Catherine de Medici the entire extermination of the French Protestants, on the battlefield if possible; if not, by means more secret and more sure; we have it on contemporary testimony, Popish and Protestant, that this was what was agreed on between Catherine and Alva at Bayonne; and we also find the Queen-mother, through Santa Croce, promising to the Pope, for herself and for her son, to make a massacre of the Huguenots, although, for obvious reasons, she refuses to bind herself to a day. From this time that policy was entered on which was designed to lead up to the grand *dénouement* so unmistakably shadowed forth in the letters of the Pope, and in the agreement between Alva and Catherine.

CHAPTER XIV
NEGOTIATIONS OF THE COURT WITH THE HUGUENOTS

GREAT difficulties, however, lay in the path of the policy arranged between the Queen-mother and Alva. The first was the deep mistrust which the Protestants cherished of Catherine and Charles IX. Not one honest peace had the French court ever made with them. Far more Protestants had perished by massacre during the currency of the various Pacifications, than had fallen by the sword in times of war. Accordingly, when the Peace of St. Germain-en-Laye was made, the Huguenot chiefs, instead of repairing to court, retired within the strongly fortified town of La Rochelle. They must be drawn out; their suspicions must be lulled to sleep, and their chief men assembled in Paris. This was the point to be first effected, and nothing but patience and consummate craft could achieve it.

No ordinary illusion could blind men who had been so often and so deeply duped already. This the French court saw. A new and grander style of stratagem than any heretofore employed was adopted. Professions, promises, and dignities were profusely lavished upon the Huguenots, but, over and above, great schemes of national policy were projected, reaching into the future, embracing the aggrandisement of France, coinciding with the views of the Huguenot chiefs, and requiring their co-operation in order to their successful execution. This gave an air of sincerity to the professions of the court which nothing else could have done, for it was thought impossible that men who were cogitating plans so enlightened, were merely contriving a cunning scheme, and weaving a web of guile. But Catherine was aware that she was too well known for anything less astute to deceive the Huguenot leaders. The proposal of the court was that the young King of Navarre should marry Margaret de Valois, the sister of Charles IX., and that an armed intervention should be made in the Low Countries in aid of the Prince of Orange against Philip of Spain, and that Coligny should be placed at the head of the expedition. These were not new ideas. The marriage had been talked of in Henry II.'s time, while Margaret and Henry of Navarre were yet children; and as regards the intervention in behalf of the Protestants of the Low Countries, that was a project which the Liberal party, headed by Chancellor l'Hôpital, had thrown out. They were revived by Catherine as by far her best stratagem: "the King and Queen-mother," says Davila, "imparting their private thoughts only to the Duke of Anjou, the Cardinal of Lorraine, the Duke of Guise, and Alberto Gondi, Count of Retz."[2663]

Charles IX. instantly dispatched Marshal de Biron to La Rochelle, to negotiate the marriage of his sister with the Prince of Bearn, and to induce his mother, the Queen of Navarre, to repair to court, that the matter might be concluded. The king sent at the same time the Marshal de Cosse to La Rochelle, to broach the project of the Flanders expedition to Admiral de Coligny, "but in reality," says Sully, "to observe the proceedings of the Calvinists, to sound their thoughts, and to beget in them that confidence which was absolutely necessary for his own designs."[2664] After the repeated violations of treaties, Pacifications, and oaths on the part of Catherine and her son, it was no easy matter to overcome the deeply-rooted suspicions of men who had so often smarted from the perfidy of the king and his mother. But Catherine and Charles dissembled on this occasion with an adroitness which even they had never shown before. Admiral de Coligny was the first to be won. He was proverbial for his wariness, but, as sometimes happens, he was now conquered on the point where he was strongest. Setting out from La Rochelle, in despite of the tears and entreaties of his wife, he repaired to Blois (September, 1571), where the court was residing. On entering the presence of the king, Coligny went on his knee, but Charles raised and embraced him, calling him his father. The return of the warrior to court put him into a transport of joy. "I hold you now," exclaimed the king; "yes, I hold you, and you shall not leave me again; this is the happiest day of my life." "It is remarkable," says the Popish historian Davila, after relating this, "that a king so young should know so perfectly how to dissemble."[2665] The Queen-mother, the Dukes of Anjou and Alençon, and all the chief nobles of the court, testified the same joy at the admiral's return. The king restored him to his pensions and dignities, admitted him of his council, and on each succeeding visit to the Louvre, loaded him with new and more condescending caresses and flatteries.

Charles IX. was at this time often closeted with the admiral. The topic discussed was the expedition to Flanders in aid of William of Orange in his war with Spain. The king listened with great seeming respect to the admiral, and this deference to his sentiments and views, in a matter that lay so near his heart, inspired Coligny doubtless with the confidence he now began to feel in Charles, and the hopes he cherished that the king was beginning to see that there was something nobler for himself than the profligacies in which his mother, for her own vile ends, had reared him, and nobler for France than to be dragged, for the Pope's pleasure, at the chariot-wheel of Spain. The admiral would thus be able to render signal service to Protestantism in all the countries of Europe, as well as rescue France from the gulf into which it was fast descending; and this hope made him deaf to the warnings, which every day he was receiving from friends, that a great treachery was meditated. And when these warnings were reiterated, louder and plainer, they only drew forth from Coligny, who longed for peace as they only long for it who have often gazed upon the horrors of the stricken field, protestations that rather would he risk massacre—rather would he be dragged as a corpse through the streets of Paris, thank rekindle the flames of civil war, and forego the hope of detaching his country from the Spanish alliance.

The admiral, having been completely gained over, used his influence to win Jeanne d'Albret to a like confidence. Ever as the marriage of her son to the daughter of Catherine de Medici was spoken of, a vague but dreadful foreboding oppressed her. She knew how brilliant was the match, and what important consequences might flow from it. It might lead her son up the steps of the throne of France, and that would be tantamount to the establishment of Protestantism in that great kingdom; nevertheless she could not conquer her instinctive recoil from the union. It was a dreadful family to marry into, and she trembled for the principles and the morals of her son. Perefixe, afterwards Archbishop of Paris, who cannot be suspected of having made the picture darker than the reality, paints the condition of the French court in one brief but terrible sentence. He says that "impiety, atheism, necromancy, most horrible pollutions, black cowardice, perfidy, poisonings, and assassinations reigned there in a supreme degree." But Catherine de Medici urged and re-urged her invitations. "Satisfy," she wrote to the Queen of Navarre, "the extreme desire we have to see you in this company; you will be loved and honoured therein as accords with reason, and what you are." At last Jeanne d'Albret gave her consent to the marriage, and visited the court at Blois in March, 1572, to arrange preliminaries. The Queen-mother but trifled with and insulted her after she did come. Jeanne wrote to her son that she could make no progress in the affair which had brought her to court. She returned to Paris in the beginning of June. She had not been more than ten days at court, when she sickened and died. The general belief, in which Davila and other Popish historians concur, was that she died of a subtle poison, which acted on the brain alone, and which exuded from certain gloves that had been presented to her. This suspicion was but natural, nevertheless we are inclined to think that a more likely cause was the anxiety and agitation of mind she was then enduring, and which brought on a fever, of which she died on the fifth day.[2666] She was but little cared for during her illness, and after death her corpse was treated with studied neglect. "This," says Davila, "was the first thunderbolt of the great tempest."

The king was dissembling so perfectly that he awakened the suspicions of the Papists. Profound secrecy was absolutely necessary to the success of the plot, and accordingly it was disclosed, in its details, to only two or three whose help was essential to its execution. Meanwhile the admirable acting of the king stumbled the Romanists: it was so like sincerity that they thought it not impossible that themselves and not the Huguenots would be the victims of the drama now in progress. The courtiers murmured, the priests were indignant, the populace expected every day to see Charles go over to the "religion;" and neither the Pope nor the King of Spain could comprehend why the king was so bent on marrying his sister to the son of the Protestant Queen of Navarre. That, said the direct and terrible Pius V., was to unite light and darkness, and to join in concord God and Belial. Meanwhile, Charles IX., who could not drop the mask but at the risk of spoiling all, contemplated with a certain pride the perfection of his own dissimulation. "Ah, well," said he one evening to his mother, "do I not play my *rôle* well?" "Yes, very well, my son," replied Catherine, "but it is nothing if it is not maintained to the end."[2667] And Charles did maintain it to the end, and even after the St. Bartholomew, for he was fond of saying with a laugh, "My big sister Margot caught all these Huguenot rebels in the bird-catching style. What has grieved me most is being obliged to dissimulate so long."[2668]

The marriage, we have said, was the hinge on which the whole plot turned; for ordinary artifices would never have enabled Catherine and Charles to deceive on a great scale. But Pius V. either did not quite comprehend this, or he disapproved of it as a means of bringing about the massacre, for he sent his legate, Cardinal Alexandrino, to Paris to protest against the union. At his interview with the legate, Charles IX. pleaded the distractions of his kingdom, and the exhaustion of his treasury, as his reasons for resorting to the marriage rather than continuing the civil wars. But these excuses the legate would not accept as sufficient. "You are in the right," replied Charles. "And if I had any other means of taking vengeance on my enemies, I would never consent to this marriage; but I can find no other way." And he concluded by bidding the legate assure the Pope that all he was doing was with the best intention, and for the aggrandisement of the Roman Catholic religion; and taking a valuable ring from his finger he offered it to Alexandrino as "a pledge of his indefectible obedience to the 'Holy See,' and his resolution to implement whatever he had promised to do in opposition to the impiety of these wicked men."[2669] The legate declined the ring on the pretext that the word of so great a king was enough. Nevertheless, after the massacre, Charles IX. sent the ring to Rome, with the words NE PIETAS POSSIT MEA SANGUINE SALVI engraven upon it. Clement VIII., who was auditor and companion to Alexandrino on his mission to France, afterwards told Cardinal d'Ossat that when the news of the St. Bartholomew Massacre reached Rome, the cardinal exclaimed in a transport of joy, "Praise be to God, the King of France has kept his word with me!"[2670]

Action was at the same time taken in the matter of supporting the Protestant war in the Low Countries, for the dissimulation had to be maintained in both its branches. A body of Huguenot soldiers, in which a few Papists were mingled, was raised, placed under Senlis, a comrade of Coligny's in faith and arms, and dispatched to the aid of William of Orange. Senlis had an interview with Charles IX. before setting out, and received from him money and encouragement. But the same court that sent this regiment to fight against the Duke of Alva, sent secret information to the duke which enabled him to surprise the Protestant soldiers on the march, and cut them in pieces. "I have in my hands," wrote the Duke of Alva to his master, Philip II., "a letter from the King of France, which would strike you dumb if you were to see it; for the moment it is expedient to say nothing about it."[2671] Another piece of equal dissimulation did Charles IX. practise about this time. The little party at the French court which was opposed to the Spanish alliance, and in the same measure favoured the success of William of Orange in Flanders, was headed by the Chancellor l'Hôpital. At the very time that Charles IX. was making Coligny believe that he had become a convert to that plan, Chancellor l'Hôpital was deprived of the seals, and banished from court.[2672]

The inconsistencies and doublings of Charles IX. are just enough to give some little colour to a theory which has found some advocates—namely, that the St. Bartholomew Massacre was unpremeditated, and that it was a sudden and violent resolve on the part of Catherine de Medici and the Guises, to prevent the king yielding to the influence of Admiral de Coligny, and putting himself at the head of a Huguenot crusade in favour of Protestantism.[2673] Verily there never was much danger of this; but though the hesitations of Charles impart some feasibility to the theory, they give it no solid weight whatever. All the historians, Popish and Protestant, who lived nearest the time, and who took every care to inform themselves, with one consent declare that the massacre was premeditated and arranged. It had its origination in the courts of Paris, Madrid, and the Vatican. A chain of well-established facts conduces us to this conclusion. Most of these have already come before us, but some of them yet remain to be told. But even irrespective of these facts, looking at the age, at Charles IX., and at the state of Christendom, can any man believe that the King of France should have seriously contemplated, as he must have done if his professions to the Huguenots were sincere, not only proclaiming toleration in France, but becoming the head of an armed European confederation in behalf of Protestantism? This is wholly inconceivable.

CHAPTER XV

THE MARRIAGE, AND PREPARATIONS FOR THE MASSACRE

THE Queen of Navarre, the magnanimous Jeanne d'Albret, was dead; moreover, news had reached Paris that the Protestant troop which had set out to assist the Prince of Orange had been overpowered and slain on the road; and further, the great advocate of toleration, L'Hôpital, dismissed from office, had been banished to his country-seat of Vignay. All was going amiss, save the promises and protests of the King and the Queen-mother, and these were growing louder and more emphatic every day. Some of the Huguenots, alarmed by these suspicious occurrences, were escaping from the city, others were giving expression to their fears in prognostications of evil. The Baron de Rosny, father of the celebrated Duke of Sully, said that "if the marriage took place at Paris the wedding favours would be crimson."[2674] In the midst of all this the preparations for the marriage went rapidly on.

The King of Navarre arrived at Paris in deep mourning, "attended by eight hundred gentlemen all likewise in mourning." "But," says Margaret de Valois herself, "the nuptials took place a few days afterwards, with such triumph and magnificence as none others of my quality; the King of Navarre and his troop having changed their mourning for very rich and fine clothes, and I being dressed royally, with crown and corset of tufted ermine, all blazing with crown jewels, and the grand blue mantle with a train four ells long, borne by three princesses, the people choking one another down below to see us pass."[2675] The marriage was celebrated on the 18th of August by the Cardinal of Bourbon, in a pavilion erected in front of the principal entrance of Notre Dame. When asked if she accepted Henry of Navarre as her husband, Margaret, it is said, remained silent;[2676] whereupon the king, putting his hand upon her head, bent it downward, which being interpreted as consent, the ceremony went on. When it was over, the bride and her party entered Notre Dame, and heard mass; meanwhile the bridegroom with Coligny and other friends amused themselves by strolling through the aisles of the cathedral. Gazing up at the flags suspended from the roof, the admiral remarked that one day soon these would be replaced by others more appropriate; he referred, of course, to the Spanish standards to be taken, as he hoped, in the approaching war. The four following days all Paris was occupied with fêtes, ballets, and other public rejoicings. It was during these festivities that the final arrangements were made for striking the great meditated blow.

Before this, however, one of the chief actors passed away, and saw not the work completed which he had so largely helped to bring to pass. On the 5th of May, 1572, Pope Pius V. died. There was scarcely a stormier Pontificate in the history of the Popes than that of the man who descended into the tomb at the very moment when he most wished to live. From the day he ascended the Papal throne till he breathed his last, neither Asia nor Europe had rest. His Pontificate of seven years was spent in raising armaments, organising expeditions, giving orders for battles, and writing letters to sovereigns inciting them to slay to the last man those whom he was pleased to account the enemies of God and of himself. Now it was against the Turk that he hurled his armed legionaries, and now it was against the Lutherans of Germany, the Huguenots of France, and the Calvinists of England and Scotland that he thundered in his character of Vicar of God. Well it was for Christendom that so much of the military *furor* of Pius was discharged in an eastern direction. The Turk became the conducting-rod that drew off the lightnings of the Vatican and helped to shield Europe. Pius' exit from the world was a dreadful one, and bore a striking resemblance to the bloody malady of which the King of France expired so soon thereafter.[2677] The Pontiff, however, bore up wonderfully under his disease, which was as painful as it was loathsome.

The death of the Pope opened a free path to the marriage which we have just seen take place. The dispensation from Rome, which Pius V. had refused, his successor Gregory XIII. conceded. Four days after the ceremony—Friday, the 22nd of August—as Coligny was returning on foot from the Louvre, occupied in reading a letter, he was fired at from the window of a house in the Rue des Fossés, St. Germain. One of the three balls with which the assassin loaded his piece, to make sure of his victim, smashed the two fore-fingers of his right hand, while another lodged in his left arm. The admiral, raising his wounded hand, pointed to the house whence the shot had come. It belonged to an old canon, who had been tutor to Henry, Duke of Guise; but before it could be entered, the assassin had escaped on a horse from the king's stables, which was waiting for him by the cloisters of the Church of L'Auxerrois.[2678] It was Maurevel who had fired the shot, the same who was known as the king's assassin. He had posted himself in one of the lower rooms of the house, and covering the iron bars of the window with an old cloak, he waited three days for his victim.

The king was playing tennis with the Duke of Guise and Téligny, the admiral's son-in-law, when told of what had happened; Charles threw down his stick, and exclaiming with an oath, "Am I never to have peace?" rushed to his apartment. Guise slunk away, and Téligny went straight to the admiral's house in the adjacent Rue de Bétizy.

Meanwhile Ambrose Paré had amputated the two broken fingers of Coligny. Turning to Merlin, his chaplain, who stood by his bedside, the admiral said, "Pray that God may grant me the gift of patience." Seeing Merlin and other friends in tears, he said, "Why do you weep for me, my friends? I reckon myself happy to have received these wounds in the cause of God." Toward midday Marshals de Damville and de Cossé came to see him. To them he protested, "Death affrights me not; but I should like very much to see the king before I die." Damville went to inform his majesty.

About two of the afternoon the King, the Queen-mother, the Duke of Anjou, and a number of the gentlemen of the court entered the apartments of the wounded man. "My dear father," exclaimed Charles, "the hurt is yours, the grief and the outrage mine; but," added he, with his usual oaths, "I will take such vengeance that it shall never be effaced from the memory of man." Coligny drew the king towards him, and commenced an earnest conversation with him, in a low voice, urging the policy he had so often recommended to Charles, that namely of assisting the Prince of Orange, and so lowering Spain and elevating France in the councils of Europe. Catherine de Medici, who did not hear what the admiral was saying to the king, abruptly terminated the interview on pretence that to prolong it would be to exhaust the strength and endanger the life of Coligny. The King and Queen-mother now returned to the Louvre at so rapid a pace that they were unobservant of the salutations of the populace, and even omitted the usual devotions to the Virgin at the corners of the streets. On arriving at the palace a secret consultation was held, after which the king was busied in giving orders, and making up dispatches, with which couriers were sent off to the provinces. When Charles and his suite had left Coligny's hotel, the admiral's friends expressed their surprise and pleasure at the king's affability, and the desire he showed to bring the criminal to justice. "But all these fine appearances," says Brantôme, "afterwards turned to ill, which amazed every one very much how their majesties could perform so counterfeit a part, unless they had previously resolved on this massacre."[2679]

They began with the admiral, says Davila, "from the apprehension they had of his fierceness, wisdom, and power, fearing that were he alive he would concert some means for the safety of himself and his confederates."[2680] But as the Popish historian goes on to explain, there was a deeper design in selecting Coligny as the first victim. The Huguenots, they reasoned, would impute the murder of the admiral to the Duke of Guise and his faction, and so would avenge it upon the Guises. This attack upon the Guises would, in its turn, excite the fury of the Roman Catholic mob against the Huguenots. The population would rise *en masse*, and slaughter the Protestants; and in this saturnalia of blood the enemies of Charles and Catherine would be got rid of, and yet the hand of the court would not be seen in the affair. The notorious Retz, the Florentine tutor of Charles, is credited with the authorship of this diabolically ingenious plan. But the matter had not gone as it was calculated it would. Coligny lived, and so the general *mêlée* of assassination did not come off. The train had been fired, but the mine did not explode.

The king had already given orders to close all the gates of Paris, save two, which were left open to admit provisions. The pretence was to cut off the escape of Maurevel. If this order could not arrest the flight of the assassin, who was already far away on his fleet steed, it effectually prevented the departure of the Huguenots. Troops were now introduced into the city. The admiral had earnestly asked leave to retire to Chatillon, in the quiet of which place he hoped sooner to recover from his wounds; but the king would not hear of his leaving Paris. He feared the irritation of the wounds that might arise from the journey; he would take care that neither Cologny nor his friends should suffer molestation from the populace. Accordingly, bidding the Protestants lodge all together in Coligny's quarter,[2681] he appointed a regiment of the Duke of Anjou to guard that part of Paris.[2682] Thus closely was the net drawn around the Huguenots. These soldiers were afterwards the most zealous and cruel of their murderers.[2685]

Friday night and Saturday were spent in consultations on both sides. To a few of the Protestants the designs of the court were now transparent, and they advised an instant and forcible departure from Paris, carrying with them their wounded chief. Their advice was over-ruled mainly through the over-confidence of Téligny in the king's honour, and only a few of the Huguenots left the city. The deliberations in the Louvre were more anxious still. The blow, it was considered, should be struck immediately, else the Huguenots would escape, or they would betake them to arms. But as the hour drew near the king appears to have wavered. Nature or conscience momentarily awoke. Now that he stood on the precincts of the colossal crime, he seems to have felt a shudder at the thought of going on; as well he might, fierce, cruel, vindictive though he was. To wade through a sea of blood so deep as that which was about to flow, might well appall even one who had been trained, as Charles had been, to look on blood. It is possible even that the nobleness of Coligny had not been without its effect upon him. The Queen-mother, who had doubtless foreseen this moment of irresolution on the part of her son when the crisis should arrive, was prepared for it. She instantly combated the indecision of Charles with the arguments most fitted to influence his weak mind. She told him that it was now too late to retreat; that the attempt on the admiral's life had aroused the Protestants, that the plans of the court were known to them, and that already messengers from the Huguenots were on their way to Switzerland and Germany, for assistance, and that to hesitate was to be lost. If he had a care for his throne and house he must act; and with a well-feigned dread of the calamities she had so vividly depicted, she is said to have craved leave for herself and her son, the Duke of Anjou, to retire to some place of safety before the storm should burst. This was enough. The idea of being left alone in the midst of all these dangers, without his mother's strong arm to lean upon, was frightful to Charles. He forgot the greatness of the crime in the imminency of his own danger. His vulpine and cowardly nature, incapable of a brave course, was yet capable of a sudden and deadly spring. "He was seized with an eager desire," says Maimbourg, "to execute the resolution already taken in the secret council to massacre all the Huguenots."[2685] "Then let Coligny be killed," said Charles, with an oath, "and let not one Huguenot in all Paris be left to reproach me with the deed."

One other point yet occasioned keen debates in the council. Shall the King of Navarre and the Prince of Condé be slain with the rest of the Huguenots? "The Duke of Guise," says Davila, "was urgent for their death; but the King and the Queen-mother had a horror at embruing their hands in royal blood;"[2686] but it would seem that the resolution of the council was for putting them to death. The Archbishop of Paris, Perefixe, and Brantôme inform us that "they were down on the red list" on the ground of its being necessary "to dig up the roots," but were afterwards saved, "as by miracle." Queen Margaret, the newly-married wife of Navarre, throwing herself on her knees before the king and earnestly begging the life of her husband, "the King granted it to her with great difficulty, although she was his good sister."[2687] Meanwhile, to keep up the delusion to the last, the king rode out on horseback in the afternoon, and the queen had her court circle as usual.

CHAPTER XVI

THE MASSACRE OF ST. BARTHOLOMEW

*I*T was now eleven o'clock of Saturday night, and the massacre was to begin at daybreak. Tavannes was sent to bid the Mayor of Paris assemble the citizens, who for some days before had been provided with arms, which they had stored in their houses. To exasperate them, and put them in a mood for this unlimited butchery of their countrymen, in which at first they were somewhat reluctant to engage, they were told that a horrible conspiracy had been discovered, on the part of the Huguenots, to cut off the king and the royal family, and destroy the monarchy and the Roman Catholic religion.[2684] The signal for the massacre was to be the tolling of the great bell of the Palace of Justice. As soon as the tocsin should have flung its ominous peal upon the city, they were to hasten to draw chains across the streets, place pickets in the open spaces, and sentinels on the bridges. Orders were also given that at the first sound of the bell torches should be placed in all the windows, and that the Roman Catholics, for distinction, should wear a white scarf on the left arm, and affix a white cross on their hats.

"All was now arranged," says Maimbourg, "for the carnage;" and they waited with impatience for the break of day, when the tocsin was to sound. In the royal chamber sat Charles IX., the Queen-mother, and the Duke of Anjou. Catherine's fears lest the king should change his mind at the last minute would not permit her to leave him for one moment. Few words, we may well believe, would pass between the royal personages. The great event that impended could not but weigh heavily upon them. A deep stillness reigned in the apartment; the hours wore wearily away; and the Queen-mother feeling the suspense unbearable, or else afraid, as Maimbourg suggests, that Charles, "greatly disturbed by the idea of the horrible butchery, would revoke the order he had given for it," anticipated the signal by sending one at two o'clock of the morning to ring the bell of St. Germain l'Auxerois, which was nearer than that of the Palace of Justice. Scarcely had its first peal startled the silence of the night when a pistol shot was heard. The king started to his feet, and summoning an attendant he bade him go and stop the massacre.[2689] It was too late; the bloody work had begun. The great bell of the Palace had now begun to toll; another moment and every steeple in Paris was sending forth its peal; a hundred tocsins sounded at once; and with the tempest of their clamour there mingled the shouts, oaths, and howlings of the assassins. "I was awakened," says Sully, "three hours after midnight with the ringing of all the bells, and the confused cries of the populace."[2690] Above all were heard the terrible words, "Kill, kill!"

The massacre was to begin with the assassination of Coligny, and that part of the dreadful work had been assigned to the Duke of Guise. The moment he heard the signal, the duke mounted his horse and, accompanied by his brother and 300 gentlemen and soldiers, galloped off for the admiral's lodgings. He found Anjou's guards with their red cloaks, and their lighted matches, posted round it; they gave the duke and his armed retinue instant admission into the courtyard. To slaughter the halberdiers of Navarre, and force open the inner entrance of the admiral's lodgings, was the work of but a few minutes. They next mounted the stairs, while the duke and his gentlemen remained below. Awakened by the noise, the admiral got out of bed, and wrapping his dressing-gown round him and leaning against the wall, he bade Merlin, his minister, join with him in prayer. One of his gentlemen at that moment rushed into the room. "My lord," said he, "God calls us to himself!" "I am prepared to die," replied the admiral; "I need no more the help of men; therefore, farewell, my friends; save yourselves, if it is still possible." They all left him and escaped by the roof of the house. Téligny, his son-in-law, fleeing in this way was shot, and rolled into the street. A German servant alone remained behind with his master. The door of the chamber was now forced open, and seven of the murderers entered, headed by Behme of Lorraine, and Achile Petrucci of Sienna, creatures of the Duke of Guise. "Art thou Coligny?" said Behme, presenting himself before his victim, and awed by the perfect composure and venerable aspect of the admiral. "I am," replied Coligny; "young man, you ought to respect my gray hairs; but do what you will, you can shorten my life only by a few days." The villain replied by plunging his weapon into the admiral's breast; the rest closing round struck their daggers into him. "Behme," shouted the duke from below, "hast done?" " 'Tis all over," cried the assassin from the window. "But M. d'Angoulême," replied the duke, "will not believe it till he see him at his feet." Taking up the corpse, Behme threw it over the window, and as it fell on the pavement, blood spurted on the faces and clothes of the two lords. The duke, taking out his handkerchief and wiping the face of the murdered man, said," 'Tis he sure enough," and kicked the corpse in its face. A servant of the Duke of Nevers cut off the head, and carried it to Catherine de Medici and the king. The trunk was exposed for some days to disgusting indignities; the head was embalmed, to be sent to Rome; the bloody trophy was carried as far as Lyons, but there all trace of it disappears.[2691]

The authors of the plot having respect to the maxim attributed to Alaric, that "thick grass is more easily mown than thin," had gathered the leading Protestants that night, as we have already narrated, into the same quarter where Coligny lodged. The Duke of Guise had kept this quarter as his special preserve; and now, the admiral being dispatched, the guards of Anjou, with a creature of the duke's for their captain, were let loose upon the *battue* of ensnared Huguenots. Their work was done with a summary vengeance, to which the flooded state of the kennels, and the piles of corpses, growing ever larger, bore terrible witness. Over all Paris did the work of massacre by this time extend. Furious bands, armed with guns, pistols, swords, pikes, knives, and all kinds of cruel weapons, rushed through the streets murdering all they met. They began to thunder at the doors of Protestants, and the terrified inmates, stunned by the uproar, came forth in their night-clothes, and were murdered on their own thresholds. Those who were too affrighted to come abroad, were slaughtered in their bedrooms and closets, the assassins bursting open all places of concealment, and massacring all who opposed their entrance, and throwing their mangled bodies into the street. The darkness would have been a cover to some, but the lights that blazed in the windows denied even this poor chance of escape to the miserable victims. The Huguenot as he fled through the street, with agonised features, and lacking the protection of the white scarf, was easily recognised, and dispatched without mercy.

The Louvre was that night the scene of a great butchery. Some 200 Protestant noblemen and gentlemen from the provinces had been accommodated with beds in the palace; and although the guests of the king, they had no exemption, but were doomed that night to die with others. They were aroused after midnight, taken out one by one, and made to pass between two rows of halberdiers, who were stationed in the underground galleries. They were hacked in pieces or poniarded on their way, and their corpses being carried forth were, horrible to relate, piled in heaps at the gates of the Louvre. Among those who thus perished were the Count de la Rochefoucault, the Marquis de Renel, the brave Piles—who had so gallantly defended St. Jean D'Angely—Francourt, chancellor to the King of Navarre, and others of nearly equal distinction. An appeal to the God of Justice was their only protest against their fate.[2692]

By-and-by the sun rose; but, alas! who can describe the horrors which the broad light of day disclosed to view? The entire population of the French capital was seen maddened with rage, or aghast with terror. On its wretched streets what tragedies of horror and crime were being enacted! Some were fleeing, others were pursuing; some were supplicating for life, others were responding by the murderous blow, which, if it silenced the cry for mercy, awoke the cry for justice. Old men, and infants in their swaddling clothes, were alike butchered on that awful night. Our very page would weep, were we to record all the atrocities now enacted. Corpses were being precipitated from the roofs and windows, others were being dragged through the streets by the foot, or were piled up in carts, and driven away to be shot into the river. The kennels were running with blood. Guise, Tavannes, and D'Angoulême—traversing the streets on horseback, and raising their voices to their highest pitch, to be audible above the tolling of the bells, the yells of the murderers, and the cries and moanings of the wounded and the dying—were inciting to yet greater fury those whom hate and blood had already transformed into demons. "It is the king's orders!" cried Guise. "Blood, blood!" shouted out Tavannes. Blood! every kennel was full; the Seine as it rolled through Paris, seemed but a river of blood; and the corpses which it was bearing to the ocean were so numerous that the bridges had difficulty in giving them passage, and were in some danger of becoming choked and turning back the stream, and drowning Paris in the blood of its own shedding. Such was the gigantic horror on which the sun of that Sunday morning, the 24th of August, 1572—St. Bartholomew's Day—looked down.

We have seen how Charles IX. stood shuddering for some moments on the brink of his great crime, and that, had it not been for the stronger will and more daring wickedness of his mother, he might after all have turned back. But when the massacre had commenced, and he had tasted of blood, Charles shuddered no longer—he became as ravenous for slaughter as the lowest of the mob. He and his mother, when it was day, went out on the palace balcony to feast their eyes upon the scene. Some Huguenots were seen struggling in the river, in their efforts to swim across, the boats having been removed. Seizing an arquebus, the king fired on them. "Kill, kill!" he shouted; and making a page sit beside him and load his piece,[2693] he continued the horrible pastime of murdering his subjects, who were attempting to escape across the Seine, or were seeking refuge at the pitiless gates of his palace.[2694]

The same night, while the massacres were in progress, Charles sent for the King of Navarre and the Prince de Condé. Receiving them in great anger, he commanded them with oaths to renounce the Protestant faith, threatening them with death as the alternative of refusal. They demurred: whereupon the king gave them three days to make their choice.[2695] His physician, Ambrose Paré, a Protestant, he kept all night in his cabinet, so selfishly careful was he of his own miserable life at the very moment when he was murdering in thousands the flower of his subjects. Paré he also attempted to terrify by oaths and threats into embracing Romanism, telling him that the time was now come when every man in France must become Roman Catholic. So apparent was it that the leading motive of Charles IX. in these great crimes was the dominancy of the Roman faith and the entire extinction of Protestantism.

For seven days the massacres were continued in Paris, and the first three especially with unabating fury. Nor were they confined within the walls of the city. In pursuance of orders sent from the court,[2696] they were extended to all provinces and cities where Protestants were found. Even villages and châteaux became scenes of carnage. For two months these butcheries were continued throughout the kingdom. Every day during that fearful time the poniard reaped a fresh harvest of victims, and the rivers bore to the sea a new and ghastly burden of corpses. In Rouen above 6,000 perished; at Toulouse some hundreds were hewn to pieces with axes; at Orleans the Papists themselves confessed that they had destroyed 12,000; some said 18,000; and at Lyons not a Protestant escaped. After the gates were closed they fell upon them without mercy; 150 of them were shut up in the archbishop's house, and were cut to pieces in the space of one hour and a half. Some Roman Catholic, more humane than the rest, when he saw the heaps of corpses, exclaimed, "They surely were not men, but devils in the shape of men, who had done this."

The whole number that perished in the massacre cannot be precisely ascertained. According to De Thou there were 2,000 victims in Paris the first day; Agrippa d'Aubigné says 3,000. Brantôme speaks of 4,000 bodies that Charles IX. might have seen floating down the Seine. La Popelinière reduced them to 1,000. "There is to be found, in the account-books of the city of Paris, a payment to the grave-diggers of the Cemetery of the Innocents, for having interred 1,100 dead bodies stranded at the turns of the Seine near Challot, Auteuil, and St. Cloud; it is probable that many corpses were carried still further, and the corpses were not all thrown into the river."[2697] There is a still greater uncertainty touching the number of victims throughout the whole of France. Mezeray computes it at 25,000; De Thou at 30,000; Sully at 70,000; and Perefixe, Archbishop of Paris in the seventeenth century, raises it to 100,000; Davila reduces it to 10,000. Sully, from his access to official documents, and his unimpeachable honour, has been commonly reckoned the highest authority. Not a few municipalities and governors, to their honour, refused to execute the orders of the king. The reply of the Vicompte d'Orte has become famous. "Sire," wrote he to Charles IX., "among the citizens and garrison of Bayonne, you have many brave soldiers, and loyal subjects, but not one hangman."[2698]

Blood and falsehood are never far apart. The great crime had been acted and could not be recalled; how was it to be justified? The poor unhappy king had recourse to one dodge after another, verifying the French saying that "to excuse is to accuse one's self." On the evening of the first day of the massacre, he dispatched messengers to the provinces to announce the death of Coligny, and the slaughters in Paris, attributing everything to the feud which had so long subsisted between Guise and the admiral. A day's reflection convinced the king that the duke would force him to acknowledge his own share in the massacre, and he saw that he must concoct another excuse; he would plead a political necessity. Putting his lie in the form of an appeal to the Almighty, he went, attended by the whole court, to mass, solemnly to thank God for having delivered him from the Protestants; and on his return, holding "a bed of justice," he professed to unveil to the Parliament, a terrible plot which Coligny and the Huguenots had contrived for destroying the king and the royal house, which had left him no alternative but to order the massacre. Although the king's story was not supported by one atom of solid truth, but on the other hand was contradicted by a hundred facts, of which the Parliament was cognisant, the obsequious members sustained the king's accusation, and branded with outlawry and forfeiture the name, the titles, the family, and the estates of Admiral de Coligny. The notorious and brazen-faced Retz was instructed to tell England yet another falsehood, namely, that Coligny was meditating playing the part of Pepin, mayor of the palace, and that the king did a wise and politic thing in nipping the admiral's treason in the bud. To the court of Poland, Charles sent, by his ambassador Montluc, another version of the affair; and to the Swiss yet another; in short, the inconsistencies, prevarications, and contradictions of the unhappy monarch were endless, and attest his guilt not less conclusively than if he had confessed the deed.

Meanwhile, the tidings were travelling over Europe, petrifying some nations with horror, awakening others into delirious and savage joy. When the news of the massacre reached the Spanish army in the Netherlands the exultation was great. The skies resounded with salvoes of cannon; the drums were beat, the trumpets blared, and at night bonfires blazed all round the camp. The reception which England gave the French ambassador was dignified and most significant. Fénelon's description of his first audience after the news of the massacre had arrived is striking. "A gloomy sorrow," says he, "sat on every face; silence, as in the dead of night, reigned through all the chambers of the royal residence. The ladies and courtiers, clad in deep mourning, were ranged on each side; and as I passed by them, in my approach to the queen, not one bestowed on me a favourable look, or made the least return to my salutations."[2699] Thus did England show that she held those whom the King of France had barbarously murdered as her brethren.

We turn to Geneva. Geneva was yet more tenderly related to the seventy thousand victims whose bodies covered the plains of France, or lay stranded on the banks of its rivers. It is the 30th of August, 1572. Certain merchants have just arrived at Geneva from Lyons; leaving their pack-horses and bales in charge of the master of their hotel, they mount with all speed the street leading to the Hôtel de Ville, anxiety and grief painted on their faces; "Messieurs," said they to the councillors, "a horrible massacre of our brethren has just taken place at

Lyons. In all the villages on our route we have seen the gibbets erected, and blood flowing; it seems that it is the same all over France. Tomorrow, or the day after, you will see those who have escaped the butchery arrive on your frontier." The distressing news spread like lightning through the town; shops were closed, and the citizens met in companies in the squares. Their experience of the past had taught them the demands which this sad occurrence would make on their benevolence. Indoors the women busied themselves providing clothes, medicines, and abundance of viands for those whom they expected soon to see arrive in hunger and sickness. The magistrates dispatched carriages and litters to the villages in the Pays de Gex; the peasants and the pastors were on the outlook on the frontier to obtain news, and to be ready to succour the first arrivals. Nor had they long to wait. On the 1st of September they beheld certain travellers approaching, pale, exhausted by fatigue, and responding with difficulty to the caresses with which they were overwhelmed. They could hardly believe their own safety, seeing that days before, in every village through which they passed, they had been in imminent danger of death. The number of these arrivals rapidly increased; they now showed their wounds, which they had carefully concealed, lest they should thereby be known to belong to the Reformed. They declared that since the 26th of August the fields and villages had been deluged with the blood of their brethren. All of them gave thanks to God that they had been permitted to reach a "land of liberty." Their hearts were full of heaviness, for not one family was complete; when they mustered on the frontier, alas! how many parents, children, and friends were missing! By-and-by this sorrowful group reached the gates of Geneva, and as they advanced along the streets, the citizens contended with each other for the privilege of entertaining those of the travellers who appeared the greatest sufferers. The wounded were conveyed to the houses of the best families, where they were nursed with the most tender care. So ample was the hospitality of the citizens, that the magistrates found it unnecessary to make any public distribution of clothes or victuals.[2700]

On the suggestion of Theodore Beza, a day of general fasting was observed, and appointed to be repeated every year on St. Bartholomew's Day. On the arrival of the news in Scotland, Knox, now old and worn out with labours, made himself be borne to his pulpit, and "summoning up the remainder of his strength," says McCrie, "he thundered the vengeance of Heaven against 'that cruel murderer and false traitor, the King of France,' and desired Le Croc, the French ambassador, to tell his master that sentence was pronounced against him in Scotland; that the Divine vengeance would never depart from him, nor from his house, if repentance did not ensue; but his name would remain an execration to posterity, and none proceeding from his loins would enjoy his kingdom in peace."[2701]

At Rome, when the news arrived, the joy was boundless. The messenger who carried the despatch was rewarded like one who brings tidings of some great victory,[2702] and the triumph that followed was such as old pagan Rome might have been proud to celebrate. The news was thundered forth to the inhabitants of the Seven-hilled City by the cannon of St. Angelo, and at night bonfires blazed on the street. Before this great day, Pius V., as we have already seen, slept with the Popes of former times, and his ashes consigned to the vaults of St. Peter's, waited the more gorgeous tomb that was preparing for them in Santa Maria Maggiore;

but Gregory XIII. conducted the rejoicings with even greater splendour than the austere Pius would probably have done. Through the streets of the Eternal City swept, in the full blaze of Pontifical pomp, Gregory and his attendant train of cardinals, bishops, and monks, to the Church of St. Mark, there to offer up prayers and thanksgivings to the God of heaven for this great blessing to the See of Rome and the Roman Catholic Church. Over the portico of the church was hung a cloth of purple, on which was a Latin inscription most elegantly embroidered in letters of gold, in which it was distinctly stated that the massacre had occurred after "counsels had been given."[2703] On the following day the Pontiff went in procession to the Church of Minerva, where, after mass, a jubilee was published to all Christendom, "that they might thank God for the slaughter of the enemies of the Church, lately executed in France." A third time did the Pope go in procession, with his cardinals and all the foreign ambassadors then resident at his court, and after mass in the Church of St. Louis, he accepted homage from the Cardinal of Lorraine, and thanks in the name of the King of France, "for the counsel and help he had given him by his prayers, of which he had found the most wonderful effects."

But as if all this had not been enough, the Pope caused certain more enduring monuments of the St. Bartholomew to be set up, that not only might the event be held in everlasting remembrance, but his own approval of it be proclaimed to the ages to come. The Pope, says Bonanni, "gave orders for a painting, descriptive of the slaughter of the admiral and his companions, to be made in the hall of the Vatican by Georgio Vasari, as a monument of vindicated religion, and a trophy of exterminated heresy." These representations form three different frescoes.[2704] The first, in which the admiral is represented as wounded by Maurevel, and carried home, has this inscription—*Gaspar Colignius Amirallius accept vulnere domum refertur. Greg. XIII., Pontif. Max.*, 1572.[2705] The second, which exhibits Coligny murdered in his own house, with Téligny and others, has these words below it—*Cædes Coligni et sociorum ejus.*[2706] The third, in which the king is represented as hearing the news, is thus entitled—*Rex necem Colignii probat.*[2707]

The better to perpetuate the memory of the massacre, Gregory caused a medal to be struck, the device on which, as Bonanni interprets it, inculcates that the St. Bartholomew was the joint result of the Papal counsel and God's instrumentality. On the one side is a profile of the Pope, surrounded by the words—*Gregorius XIII., Pont. Max., an. I.* On the obverse is seen an angel bearing in one hand a cross, in the other a drawn sword, with which he is smiting a prostrate host of Protestants; and to make all clear, above is the motto—*Ugonotorum strages*, 1572.[2708]

CHAPTER XVII
RESURRECTION OF HUGUENOTISM—DEATH OF CHARLES IX

WHEN the terrible storm of the St. Bartholomew Day had passed, men expected to open their eyes on only ruins. The noble vine that had struck its roots so deep in the soil of France, and with a growth so marvellous was sending out its boughs on every side, and promising to fill the land, had been felled to earth by a cruel and sudden blow, and never again would it lift its branches on high. So thought Charles IX. and the court of France. They had closed the civil wars in the blood of Coligny and his 70,000 fellow-victims. The governments of Spain and Rome did not doubt that Huguenotism had received its death-blow. Congratulations were exchanged between the courts of the Louvre, the Escorial, and the Vatican on the success which had crowned their projects. The Pope, to give enduring expression to these felicitations, struck, as we have seen, a commemorative medal. That medal said, in effect, that Protestantism *had been!* No second medal, of like import, would Gregory XIII., or any of his successors, ever need to issue; for the work had been done once for all; the revolt of Wittemberg and Geneva had been quelled in a common overthrow, and a new era of splendour had dawned on the Popedom.

In proportion to the joy that reigned in the Romanist camp, so was the despondency that weighed upon the spirits of the Reformed. They too, in the first access of their consternation and grief, believed that Protestantism had been fatally smitten. Indeed, the loss which the cause had sustained was tremendous, and seemed irretrievable. The wise counsellors, the valiant warriors, the learned and pious pastors—in short, that whole array of genius, and learning, and influence that adorned Protestantism in France, and which, humanly speaking, were the bulwarks around it—had been swept away by this one terrible blow.

And truly, had French Protestantism been a mere political association, with only earthly bonds to hold its members together, and only earthly motives to inspire them with hope and urge them to action, the St. Bartholomew Massacre would have terminated its career. But the cause was Divine; it drew its life from hidden sources, and so, flourishing from what both friend and foe believed to be its grave, it stood up anew, prepared to fight ever so many battles and mount ever so many scaffolds, in the faith that it would yet triumph in that land which had been so profusely watered with its blood.

The massacre swept the cities and villages on the plains of France with so unsparing a fury, that in many of these not a Protestant was left breathing; but the mountainous districts were less terribly visited, and those now became the stronghold of Huguenotism. Some fifty towns situated in these parts closed their gates, and stood to their defence. Their inhabitants knew that to admit the agents of the government was simply to offer their throats to the assassins of Charles; and rather than court wholesale butchery, or ignominiously yield, they resolved to fight like men. Some of these cities were hard put to it in the carrying out of this resolution. The sieges of La Rochelle and Sancerre have a terribly tragic interest. The latter, though a small town, held out against the royal forces for more than ten months. Greatly inferior to the enemy in numbers, the citizens laboured under the further disadvantage of lacking arms. They appeared on the ramparts with slings instead of fire-arms; but, unlike their assailants, they defended their cause with hands untainted with murder. "We fight here," was the withering taunt which they flung down upon the myrmidons of Catherine—"We fight here: go and assassinate elsewhere." Famine was more fatal to them than the sword; for while the battle slew only eighty-four of their number, the famine killed not fewer than 500. The straits now endured by the inhabitants of Sancerre recall the miseries of the siege of Jerusalem, or the horrors of Paris in the winter of 1870–71. An eye-witness, Pastor Jean de Lery, has recorded in his Journal the incidents of the siege, and his tale is truly a harrowing one. "The poor people had to feed on dogs, cats, mice, snails, moles, grass, bread made of straw, ground into powder and mixed with pounded slate; they had to consume harness, leather, the parchment of old books, title-deeds, and letters, which they softened by soaking in water." These were the revolting horrors of their *cuisine*. "I have seen on a table," says Lery, "food on which the printed characters were still legible, and you might even read from the pieces lying on the dishes ready to be eaten." The mortality of the young by the famine was frightful; scarce a child under twelve years survived. Their faces grew to be like parchment; their skeleton figures and withered limbs; their glazed eye and dried tongue, which could not even wail, were too horrible for the mother to look on, and thankful she was when death came to terminate the sufferings of her offspring. Even grown men were reduced to skeletons, and wandered like phantoms in the street, where often they dropped down and expired of sheer hunger.[2709] Yet that famine could not subdue their resolution. The defence of the town went on, the inhabitants choosing to brave the horrors which they knew rather than, by surrendering to such a foe, expose themselves to horrors which they knew not. A helping hand was at length stretched out to them from the distant Poland. The Protestantism of that country was then in its most flourishing condition, and the Duke of Anjou, Catherine's third son, being a candidate for the vacant throne, the Poles made it a condition that he should ameliorate the state of the French Huguenots, and accordingly the siege of Sancerre was raised.

It was around La Rochelle that the main body of the royal army was drawn. The town was the capital of French Protestantism, and the usual rendezvous of its chiefs. It was a large and opulent city, "fortified after the modern way with moats, walls, bulwarks, and ramparts."[2710] It was open to the sea, and the crowd of ships that filled its harbour, and which rivalled in numbers the royal navy, gave token of the enriching commerce of which it was the seat. Its citizens were distinguished by their intelligence, their liberality, and above all, their public spirit. When the massacre broke out, crowds of Protestant gentlemen, as well as of peasants, together with some fifty pastors, fleeing from the sword of the murderers, found refuge within its walls. Thither did the royal forces follow them, shutting in La Rochelle on the land side, while the navy blockaded it by the sea. Nothing dismayed, the citizens closed their gates, hoisted the flag of defiance on their walls, and gave Anjou, who conducted the siege, to understand that the task he had now on hand would not be of so easy execution as a cowardly massacre planned in the darkness, like that which had so recently crimsoned all France, and of which he had the credit of being one of the chief instigators.

Here he must fight in open day, and with men who were determined that he should enter their city only when it was a mass of ruins. He began to thunder against it with his cannon; the Rochellese were not slow to reply. Devout as well as heroic, before forming on the ramparts they knelt before the God of battles in their churches, and then with a firm step, and singing the Psalms of David as they marched onward, they mounted the wall, and looked down with faces undismayed upon the long lines of the enemy. The ships thundered from the sea, the troops assailed on land; but despite this double tempest, there was the flag of defiance still waving on the walls of the beleaguered city. They might have capitulated to brave men and soldiers, but to sue for peace from an army of assassins, from the train-bands of a monarch who knew not how to reward men who were the glory of his realm, save by devoting them to the dagger, rather would they die a hundred times. Four long months the battle raged; innumerable mines were dug and exploded; portions of he wall fell in, and the soldiers of Anjou hurried to the breach in the hope of taking the city. It was now only that they realised the full extent of the difficulty. The forest of pikes on which they were received, and the deadly volleys poured into them, sent them staggering down the breach and back to the camp. Not fewer than twenty-nine times did the besiegers attempt to carry La Rochelle by storm; but each time they were repulsed,[2711] and forced to retreat, leaving a thick trail of dead and wounded to mark their track. Thus did this single town heroically withstand the entire military power of the government. The Duke of Anjou saw his army dwindling away. Twenty-nine fatal repulses had greatly thinned its ranks. The siege made no progress. The Rochellese still scowled defiance from the summit of their ruined defences. What was to be done?

At that moment a messenger arrived in the camp with tidings that the Duke of Anjou had been elected to the throne of Poland. One cannot but wonder that a nation so brave, and so favourably disposed as the Poles then were towards Protestantism, should have made choice of a creature so paltry, cowardly, and vicious to reign over them. But the occurrence furnished the duke with a pretext of which he was but too glad to avail himself for quitting a city which he was now convinced he never would be able to take. The blood spilt in its defence had not been shed in vain. The Rochellese had maintained their independence; they had rendered a service to the Protestantism of Europe; they had avenged in part the St. Bartholomew; they had raised the renown of the Huguenot arms; and now that the besiegers were gone, they set about rebuilding their fallen ramparts, and repairing the injuries their city had sustained; and they had the satisfaction of seeing the flow of political and commercial prosperity, which had been so rudely interrupted, gradually return.

By the time these transaction were terminated, a year well-nigh had elapsed since the great massacre. Catherine and Charles could now calculate what they had gained by this enormous crime. Much had France lost abroad, for though Catherine strove by enormous lying to persuade the world that she had not done the deed, or at least that the government had been forced in self-defence to do it, she could get no one to believe her. To compensate for the loss of prestige and influence abroad, what had she gained at home? Literally nothing. The Huguenots in all parts of France were coming forth from their hiding-places;

important towns were defying the royal arms; whole districts were Protestant; and the demands of the Huguenots were once more beginning to be heard, loud and firm as ever. What did all this mean? Had not Alva and Catherine dug the grave of Huguenotism? Had not Charles assisted at its burial? and had not the Pope set up its gravestone? What right then had the Huguenots to be seen any more in France? Had Coligny risen from the dead, with his mountain Huguenots, who had chased Anjou back to Paris, and compelled Charles to sign the Peace of St. Germain? Verily it seemed as if it were so.

A yet greater humiliation awaited the court. When the 24th of August, 1573—the anniversary of the massacre—came round, the Huguenots selected the day to meet and draw up new demands, which they were to present to the government.

Obtaining an interview with Charles and his mother, the delegates boldly demanded, in the name of the whole body of the Protestants, to be replaced in the position they had occupied before St. Bartholomew's Day, and to have back all the privileges of the Pacification of 1570. The king listened in mute stupefaction. Catherine, pale with anger, made answer with a haughtiness that ill became her position. "What!" said she, "although the Prince of Condé had been still alive, and in the field with 20,000 horse and 50,000 foot, he would not have dared to ask half of what you now demand." But the Queen-mother had to digest her mortification as best she could. Her troops had been worsted; her kingdom was full of anarchy; discord reigned in the very palace; her third son, the only one she loved, was on the point of leaving her for Poland; there were none around her whom she could trust; and certainly there was no one who trusted her; the only policy open to her, therefore, was one of conciliation. Hedged in, she was made to feel that her way was a hard one. The St. Bartholomew Massacre was becoming bitter even to its authors, and Catherine now saw that she would have to repeat it not once, but many times, before she could erase the "religion," restore the glories of the Roman Catholic worship in France, and feel herself firmly seated in the government of the country.

To the still further dismay of the court, the Protestants took a step in advance. Portentous theories of a social kind began at this time to lift up their heads in France. The infatuated daughter of the Medici thought that, could she extirpate Protestantism, Roman Catholicism would be left in quiet possession of the land; little did she foresee the strange doctrines—foreshadowings of those of 1789, and of the Commune of still later days—that were so soon to start up and fiercely claim to share supremacy with the Church.

The Huguenots of the sixteenth century did not indeed espouse the new opinions which struck at the basis of government as it was then settled, but they acted upon them so far as to set up a distinct politico-ecclesiastical confederation. The objects aimed at in this new association were those of self-government and mutual defence. A certain number of citizens were selected in each of the Huguenot towns. These formed a governing body in all matters appertaining to Protestants. They were, in short, so many Protestant municipalities, analogous to those cities of the Middle Ages which, although subject to the sway of the feudal lord, had their own independent municipal government. Every six months, delegates from these several municipalities met together, and constituted a supreme council. This council had power to impose taxes, to administer justice, and, when threatened with violence by the government, to raise soldiers and carry on war. This was a State within a State. The propriety of the step is open to question, but it is not to be hastily condemned. The French Government had abdicated its functions. It neither respected the property nor defended the lives of the Huguenots. It neither executed the laws of the State in their behalf, nor fulfilled a moment longer than it had the power to break them the special treaties into which it had entered. So far from redressing their wrongs, it was the foremost party to inflict wrong and outrage upon them. In short, society in that unhappy country was dissolved, and in so unusual a state of things, it were hard to deny the Protestants the right to make the best arrangements they could for the defence of their natural and social rights.

At the court even there now arose a party that threw its shield over the Huguenots. That party was known as the *Politiques* or *Tiers Parti*.[2712] It was composed mostly of men who were the disciples of the great Chancellor de l'Hôpital, whose views were so far in advance of the age in which he lived, and whose reforms in law and the administration of justice made him one of the pioneers of better and more tolerant times. The chancellor was now dead—happily for himself, before the extinction of so many names which were the glory of his country—but his liberal opinions survived in a small party which was headed by the three sons of the Constable Montmorency, and the Marshals Cosé and Biron. These men were not Huguenots; on the contrary, they were Romanists, but they abhorred the policy of extermination pursued toward the Protestants, and they lamented the strifes which were wasting the strength, lowering the character, and extinguishing the glory of France. Though living in an age not by any means fastidious, the spectacle of the court—now become a horde of poisoners, murderers, and harlots—filled them with disgust. They wished to bring back something like national feeling and decency of manners to their country. Casting about if haply there were any left who might aid them in their schemes, they offered their alliance to the Huguenots. They meant to make a beginning by expelling the swarm of foreigners which Catherine had gathered round her. Italians and Spaniards filled the offices at court, and in return for their rich pensions rendered no service but flattery, and taught no arts but those of magic and assassination. The leaders of the *Tiers Parti* hoped by the assistance of the Huguenots to expel these creatures from the government which they had monopolised, and to restore a national *régime*, liberal and tolerant, and such as might heal the deep wounds of their country, and recover for France the place she had lost in Europe. The existence of this party was known to Catherine, and she had divined, too, the cleansing they meant to make in the Augean stable of the Louvre. Such a reformation not being at all to her taste, she began again to draw toward the Huguenots. Thus wonderfully were they shielded.

There followed a few years of dubious policy on the part of Catherine, of fruitless schemes on the part of the *Politiques*, and of uncertain prospects to all parties. While matters were hanging thus in the balance, Charles IX. died. His life had been full of excitement, of base pleasures, and of bloody crimes, and his death was full of horrors. But as the curtain is about to drop, a ray—a solitary ray—is seen to shoot across the darkness. No long time after the perpetration of the massacre, Charles IX. began to be visited with remorse. The awful scene would not quit his memory. By day, whether engaged in business or mingling in the gaieties of the court, the sights and sounds of the massacre would rise unbidden before his imagination; and at night its terrors would return in his dreams. As he lay in his bed, he would start up from broken slumber, crying out, "Blood, blood!" Not many days after the massacre, there came a flock of ravens and alighted upon the roof of the Louvre. As they flitted to and fro they filled the air with their dismal croakings. This would have given no uneasiness to most people; but the occupants of the Louvre had guilty consciences. The impieties and witchcrafts in which they lived had made them extremely superstitious, and they saw in the ravens other creatures than they seemed, and heard in their screams more terrible sounds than merely earthly ones. The ravens were driven away; the next day, at the same hour, they returned, and so did they for many days in succession. There, duly at the appointed time, were the sable visitants of the Louvre, performing their gyrations round the roofs and chimneys of the ill-omened palace, and making its courts resound with the echoes of their horrid cawings. This did not tend to lighten the melancholy of the king.

One night he awoke with fearful sounds in his ears. It seemed—so he thought—that a dreadful fight was going on in the city. There were shoutings and shrieks and curses, and mingling with these were the tocsin's knell and the sharp ring of fire-arms—in short, all those dismal noises which had filled Paris on the night of the massacre. A messenger was dispatched to ascertain the cause of the uproar. He returned to say that all was at peace in the city, and that the sounds which had so terrified the king were wholly imaginary. These incessant apprehensions brought on at last an illness. The king's constitution, sickly from the first, had been drained of any original vigour it ever possessed by the vicious indulgences in which he lived, and into which his mother, for her own vile ends, had drawn him; and now his decline was accelerated by the agonies of remorse—the Nemesis of the St. Bartholomew. Charles was rapidly approaching the grave. It was now that a malady of a strange and frightful kind seized upon him. Blood began to ooze from all the pores of his body. On awakening in the morning his person would be wet all over with what appeared a sweat of blood, and a crimson mark on the bed-clothes would show where he had lain. Mignet and other historians have given us most affecting accounts of the king's last hours, but we content ourselves with an extract from the old historian Estoile. And be it known that the man who stipulated, when giving orders for the St. Bartholomew Massacre, that not a single Huguenot should be left alive to reproach him with the deed, was waited upon on his death bed by a Huguenot nurse! "As she seated herself on a chest," says Estoile, "and was beginning to doze, she heard the king moan and weep and sigh. She came gently to his bedside, and adjusting the bed-clothes, the king began to speak to her; and heaving a deep sigh, and while the tears poured down, and sobs choked his utterance, he said, 'Ah, nurse, dear nurse, what blood, what murders! Ah, I have followed bad advice. Oh, my God, forgive me! Have pity on me, if it please thee. I do not know what will become of me. What shall I do? I am lost; I see it plainly.' Then the nurse said to him, 'Sire, may the murders be on those who made you do them; and since you do not consent to them, and are sorry for them, believe that God will not impute them to you, but will cover them with the robe of his Son's justice. To him alone you must address yourself.'"

Charles IX. died on the 30th of May, 1574, just twenty-one months after the St. Bartholomew Massacre, having lived twenty-five years and reigned fourteen.[2713]

CHAPTER XVIII

NEW PERSECUTIONS—REIGN AND DEATH OF HENRY III

THE Duke of Anjou, the heir to the throne, was in Poland when Charles IX. died. He had been elected king of that country, as we have stated, but he had already brought it to the brink of civil war by the violations of his coronation oath. When he heard that his brother was dead, he stole out of Poland, hurried back to Paris, and became King of France under the title of Henry III. This prince was shamelessly vicious, and beyond measure effeminate. Neglecting business, he would shut himself up for days together with a select band of youths, debauchees like himself, and pass the time in orgies which shocked even the men of that age. He was the tyrant and the bigot, as well as the voluptuary, and the ascetic fit usually alternated at short intervals with the sensual one. He passed from the beast to the monk, and from the monk to the beast, but never by any chance was he the man. It is true we find no St. Bartholomew in this reign, but that was because the first had made a second impossible. That the will was not wanting is attested by the edict with which Henry opened his reign, and which commanded all his subjects to conform to the religion of Rome or quit the kingdom. His mother, Catherine de Medici, still held the regency; and we trace her hand in this tyrannous decree, which happily the government had not the power to enforce. Its impolicy was great, and it instantly recoiled upon the king, for it advertised the Huguenots that the dagger of the St. Bartholomew was still suspended above their heads, and that they should commit a great mistake if they did not take effectual measures against a second surprise. Accordingly, they were careful not to let the hour of weakness to the court pass without strengthening their own position.

Coligny had fallen, but Henry of Navarre now came to the front. He lacked the ripened wisdom, the steady persistency, and deep religious convictions of the great admiral; but he was young, chivalrous, heartily with the Protestants, and full of dash in the field. His soldiers never feared to follow wherever they saw his white plume waving "amidst the ranks of war." The Protestants were further reinforced by the accession of the *Politiques*. These men cared nothing for the "religion," but they cared something for the honour of France, and they were resolved to spare no pains to lift it out of the mire into which Catherine and her allies had dragged it. At the head of this party was the young Duke of Alençon, the youngest brother of the king. This combination of parties, formed in the spring of 1575, brought fresh courage to the Huguenots. They now saw their cause espoused by two princes of the blood, and their attitude was such as thoroughly to intimidate the King and Queen-mother. Never before had the Protestants presented a bolder front or made larger demands, and bitter as the mortification must have been, the court had nothing for it but to grant all the concessions asked. Passing over certain matters of a political nature, it was agreed that the public exercise of the Reformed religion should be authorised throughout the kingdom; that the provincial Parliaments should consist of an equal number of Roman Catholics and Protestants; that all sentences passed against the Huguenots should be annulled; that eight towns should be placed in their hands as a material guarantee; that they should have a right to open schools, and to hold synods; and that the States-General should meet within six months to ratify this agreement. This treaty was signed May 6th, 1576. Thus within four years after the St. Bartholomew Massacre, the Protestants, whom it was supposed that that massacre had exterminated, had all their former rights conceded to them, and in ampler measure.

The Roman Catholics opened their eyes in astonishment. Protestant schools; Protestant congregations; Protestant synods! They already saw all France Protestant. Taking the alarm, they promptly formed themselves into an organisation, which has since become famous in history under the name of "The League." The immediate aim of the League was the prevention of the treaty just signed; its ulterior and main object was the extirpation, root and branch, of the Huguenots. Those who were enrolled in it bound themselves by oath to support it with their goods and lives. Its foremost man was the Duke of Guise; its backbone was the ferocious rabble of Paris; it found zealous and powerful advocates in the numerous Jesuit fraternities of France; the duty of adhesion to it was vociferously preached from the Roman Catholic pulpits, and still more persuasively, if less noisily, urged in all the confessionals; and we do not wonder that, with such a variety of agency to give it importance, the League before many months had passed numbered not fewer than 30,000 members, and from being restricted to one province, as at the beginning, it extended over all the kingdom. A clause was afterwards added to the effect that no one should be suffered to ascend the throne of France who professed or tolerated the detestable opinions of the Huguenots, and that they should have recourse to arms to carry out the ends of the League. Thus were the flames of war again lighted in France.

The north and east of the kingdom declared in favour of the League, the towns in the south and west ranged themselves beneath the standard of Navarre. The king was uncertain which of the two parties he should join.

Roused suddenly from his sensualities, craven in spirit, clouded in understanding, the unhappy Henry saw but few followers around him. Navarre offered to rally the Huguenots round him, and support the crown, would he only declare on their side. Henry hesitated; at last he threw himself into the arms of the League, and, to cement the union between himself and them, he revoked all the privileges of the Protestants, and commanded them to abjure their religion or leave the kingdom. The treaty so recently formed was swept away. The war was resumed with more bitterness than ever. It was now that the brilliant military genius of Navarre, "Henry of the White Plume," began to blaze forth. Skilful to plan, cool and prompt to execute, never hesitating to carry his white plume into the thick of the fight, and never failing to bring it out victoriously, Henry held his own in the presence of the armies of the king and Guise. The war watered afresh with blood the soil so often and so profusely watered before, but it was without decisive results on either side. One thing it made evident, namely, that the main object of the League was to wrest the sceptre from the hands of Henry III., to bar the succession of Henry of Navarre, the next heir, and place the Duke of Guise upon the throne, and so grasp the destinies of France.

The unhappy country did not yet know rest; for if there was now a cessation of hostilities between the Roman Catholics and the Huguenots, a bitter strife broke out between the king and Guise. The duke aspired to the crown. He was the popular idol; the mob and the army were on his side, and knowing this, he was demeaning himself with great haughtiness. The contempt he felt for the effeminacy and essential baseness of Henry III., he did not fail to express. The king was every day losing ground, and the prospects of the duke were in the same proportion brightening. The duke at last ventured to come to Paris with an army, and Henry narrowly escaped being imprisoned and slain in his own capital. Delaying the entrance of the duke's soldiers by barricades, the first ever seen in Paris, he found time to flee, and taking refuge in the Castle of Blois, he left Guise in possession of the capital. The duke did not at once proclaim himself king; he thought good to do the thing by halves; he got himself made lieutenant of the kingdom, holding himself, at the same time, on excellent terms of friendship with Henry. Henry on his part met the duke's hypocrisy with cool premeditated treachery. He pressed him warmly to visit him at his Castle of Blois. His friends told him that if he went he would never return; but he made light of all warnings, saying, with an air that expressed his opinion of the king's courage, "He dare not." To the Castle of Blois he went.

The king had summoned a council at the early hour of eight o'clock to meet the duke. While the members were assembling, Guise had arrived, and was sauntering carelessly in the hall, when a servant entered with a message that the king wished to see him in his bed-room. To reach the apartment in question the duke had to pass through an ante-chamber. In this apartment had previously been posted a strong body of men-at-arms. The duke started when his eye fell on the glittering halberds and the scowling faces of the men; but disdaining retreat he passed on. His hand was already on the curtain which separated the ante-chamber from the royal bed-room, with intent to draw it aside to enter, when a soldier struck his dagger into him. The duke sharply faced his assailants, but only to receive another and another stroke. He grappled with the men, and so great was his strength that he bore them with himself to the floor, where, after struggling a few minutes, he extricated himself, though covered with wounds. He was able to lift the curtain, and stagger into the room, where, falling at the foot of the bed, he expired in the presence of the king. Henry, getting up, looked at the corpse, and kicked it with his foot.

The Queen-mother was also at the Castle of Blois. Sick and dying, she lay in one of the lower apartments. The king instantly descended to visit her. "Madam," he said, "congratulate me, for I am again King of France, seeing I have this morning slain the King of Paris." The tidings pleased Catherine, but she reminded her son that the old fox, the uncle of the duke, still lived, and that the morning's work could not be considered complete till he too was dispatched. The Cardinal of Lorraine, who had lived through all these bloody transactions, was by the royal orders speedily apprehended and slain. To prevent the superstitious respect of the populace to the bodies of the cardinal and the duke, their corpses were tied by a rope, let down through a window into a heap of quicklime, and when consumed, their ashes were scattered to the winds. Such was the end of these ambitious men.[2714] Father, son, and uncle had been bloody men, and their grey hairs were brought down to the grave in blood.

These deeds brought no stability to Henry's power. Calamity after calamity came upon him in rapid succession. The news of his crime spread horror through France. The Roman Catholic population of the towns rose in insurrection, enraged at the death of their favourite, and the League took care to fan their fury. The Sorbonne released the subjects of the kingdom from allegiance to Henry. The Parliament of Paris declared him deposed from the throne. The Pope, dealing him the unkindest cut of all, excommunicated him. Within a year of the duke's death, a provisional government, with a younger brother of Guise's at its head, was installed at the Hôtel de Ville. Henry, appalled by this outburst of indignation, fled to Tours, where such of the nobility as adhered to the royalist cause, with 2,000 soldiers, gathered round him.

This force was not at all adequate to cope with the army of the League, and the king had nothing for it but to accept the hand which Henry of Navarre held out to him, and which he had aforetime rejected. Considering that Henry, as Duke of Anjou, had been one of the chief instigators of the St. Bartholomew Massacre, it must have cost him one would imagine, a severe struggle of feeling to accept the aid of the Huguenots; and not less must they have felt it, we should think, unseemly and anomalous to ally their cause with that of the murderer of their brethren. But the flower of the Huguenots were in their grave; the King of Navarre was not the high-minded hero that Coligny had been. We find now a lower type of Huguenotism than before the St. Bartholomew Massacre; so the alliance was struck, and the two armies, the royalist and the Huguenot, were now under the same standard. Here was a new and strange arrangement of parties in France. The League had become the champion of the democracy against the throne, and the Huguenots rallied for the throne against the democracy. The united army, with the two Henries at its head, now began its march upon Paris; the forces of the League, now inferior to the enemy, retreating before them. While on their march the king and Navarre learned that the Pope had fulminated excommunication against them, designating them "the two sons of wrath," and consigning them, "in the name of the Eternal King," to "the company of Korah, Dathan, and Abiram," and "to the devil and his angels." The weak superstitious Henry III. was so terrified that for two days he ate no food. "Cheer up, brother," said the more valorous Henry of Navarre, "Rome's bolts don't hurt kings when they conquer." Despite the Papal bull, the march to Paris was continued. King Henry, with his soldiers, was now encamped in St. Cloud; and Navarre, with his Huguenots, had taken up his position at Meudon. It seemed as if the last hour of the League had come, and that Paris must surrender. The Protestants were overjoyed. But the alliance between the royalist and Huguenot arms was not to prosper. The bull of the Pope was, after all, destined to bear fruit. It awoke all the pulpits in Paris, which began to thunder against excommunicated tyrants, and to urge the sacred duty of taking them off; and not in vain, for a monk of the name of Jacques Clement offered himself to perform the holy yet perilous deed. Having prepared himself by fasting and absolution, this man, under pretence of carrying a letter, which he would give into no hands but those of the king himself, penetrated into the royal tent, and plunged his dagger into Henry. The League was saved, the illusions of the Huguenots were dispelled, and there followed a sudden shifting of the scenes in France. With Henry III. the line of Valois became extinct. The race had given thirteen sovereigns to France, and filled the throne during 261 years.

The last Valois has fallen by the dagger. Only seventeen years have elapsed since the St. Bartholomew Massacre, and yet the authors of that terrible tragedy are all dead, and all of them, with one exception, have died by violence. Charles IX., smitten with a strange and fearful malady, expired in torments. The Duke of Guise was massacred in the Castle of Blois, the king kicking his dead body as he had done the corpse of Coligny. The Cardinal of Lorraine was assassinated in prison; and Henry III. met his death in his own tent as we have just narrated, by the hand of a monk. The two greatest criminals in this band of great criminals were the last to be overtaken by vengeance. Catherine de Medici died at the Castle of Blois twelve days after the murder of the Duke of Guise, as little cared for in her last hours as if she had been the poorest peasant in all France; and when she had breathed her last, "they took no more heed of her," says Estoile, "than of a dead goat." She lived to witness the failure of all her schemes, the punishment of all her partners in guilt, and to see her dynasty, which she had laboured to prop up by so many dark intrigues and bloody crimes, on the eve of extinction. And when at last she went to the grave, it was amid the execrations of all parties. "We are in a great strait about this bad woman," said a Romanist preacher when announcing her death to his congregation; "if any of you by chance wish, out of charity, to give her a *pater* or an *ave*, it may perhaps do her some good." Catherine de Medici died in the seventieth year of her age; during thirty of which she held the regency of France. Her estates and legacies were all swallowed up by her debts.[2715]

CHAPTER XIX
HENRY IV. AND THE EDICT OF NANTES

THE dagger of Jacques Clement had transferred the crown of France from the House of Valois to that of Bourbon. Henry III. being now dead, Henry of Navarre, the Knight of the White Plume, ascended the throne by succession. The French historians paint in glowing colours the manly grace of his person, his feats of valour in the field, and his acts of statesmanship in the cabinet. They pronounce him the greatest of their monarchs, and his reign the most glorious in their annals. We must advance a little further into our subject before we can explain the difficulty we feel in accepting this eulogium as fully warranted.

Henry was born in the old Castle of Pau, in Bearn, and was descended in a direct line from Robert, the sixth son of Saint Louis. The boy, the instant of his birth, was carried to his grandfather, who rubbed his lips with a clove of garlic, and made him drink a little wine; and the rearing begun thus was continued in the same hardy fashion.

The young Henry lived on the plainest food, and wore the homeliest dress; he differed little or nothing, in these particulars, from the peasant boys who were his associates in his hours of play. His delight was to climb the great rocks of the Pyrenees around his birthplace, and in these sports he hardened his constitution, familiarised himself with peril and toil, and nurtured that love of adventure which characterised him all his days. But especially was his education attended to. It was conducted under the eye of his mother, one of the first women of her age, or indeed of any age. He was carefully instructed in the doctrines of Protestantism, that in after-life his religion might be not an ancestral tradition, but a living faith. In the example of his mother he had a pattern of the loftiest virtue. Her prayers seemed the sacred pledges that the virtues of the mother would flourish in the son, and that after she was gone he would follow the with the same devotion, and defend with a yet stronger arm, the cause for which she had lived. As Henry grew up he displayed a character in many points corresponding to these advantages of birth and training. To a robust and manly frame he added a vigorous mind. His judgment was sound, his wit was quick, his resource was ready. In disposition he was brave, generous, confiding. He despised danger; he courted toil; he was fired with the love of glory. But with these great qualities he blended an inconvenient waywardness, and a decided inclination to sensual pleasure.

The king had breathed his last but a few moments, when Henry entered the royal apartment to receive the homage of the lords who were there in waiting. The Huguenot chiefs readily hailed him as their sovereign, but the Roman Catholic lords demanded, before swearing the oath of allegiance, that he should declare himself of the communion of the Church of Rome. "Would it be more agreeable to you," asked Henry of those who were demanding of him a renunciation of his Protestantism upon the spot, "Would it be more agreeable to you to have a godless king? Could you confide in the faith of an atheist? and in the day of battle would it add to your courage to think that you followed the banner of a perjured apostate? Brave words spoken like a man who had made up his mind to ascend the throne with a good conscience or not at all. But the words were not followed up by a conduct equally brave and high-principled. The Roman Catholic lords were obstinate. Henry's difficulties increased. The dissentients were withdrawing from his camp; his army was melting away, and every new day appeared to be putting the throne beyond his reach. Now was the crisis of his fate. Had Henry of Navarre esteemed the reproach of being a Huguenot greater riches than the crown of France, he would have worn that crown, and worn it with honour. His mother's God, who, by a marvellous course of Providence, had brought him to the foot of the throne, was able to place him upon it, had he had faith in him. But Henry's faith began to fail. He temporised. He neither renounced Protestantism nor embraced Romanism, but aimed at being both Protestant and Romanist at once. He concluded an arrangement with the Roman Catholics, the main stipulation in which was that he would submit to a six months' instruction in the two creeds—just as if he were or could be in doubt—and at the end of that period he would make his choice, and his subjects would then know whether they had a Protestant or a Roman Catholic for their sovereign. Henry, doubtless, deemed his policy a masterly one; but his mother would not have adopted it. She had risked her kingdom for her religion, and God gave her back her kingdom after it was as good as lost. What the son risked was his religion, that he might secure the throne. The throne he did secure in the first instance, but at the cost of losing in the end all that made it worth having. "There is a way that seemeth right in a man's own eyes, but the end thereof is death."

Henry had tided over the initial difficulty, but at what a cost!—a virtual betrayal of his great cause. Was his way now smooth? The Roman Catholics he had not really conciliated, and the Protestants stood in doubt of him. He had two manner of peoples around his standard, but neither was enthusiastic in his support, nor could strike other than feeble blows. He had assumed the crown, but had to conquer the kingdom. The League, whose soldiers were in possession of Paris, still held out against him. To have gained the capital and displayed his standard on its walls would have been a great matter, but with an army dwindled down to a few thousands, and the Roman Catholic portion but halfhearted in his cause, Henry dared not venture on the siege of Paris. Making up his mind to go without the prestige of the capital meanwhile, he retreated with his little host into Normandy, the army of the League in overwhelming numbers pressing on his steps and hemming him in, so that he was compelled to give battle to them in the neighbourhood of Dieppe. Here, with the waters of the English Channel behind him, into which the foe hoped to drive him, God wrought a great deliverance for him. With only 6,000 soldiers, Henry discomfited the entire army of the League, 30,000 strong, and won a great victory.

This affair brought substantial advantages to Henry. It added to his renown in arms, already great. Soldiers began to flock to his standard, and he now saw himself at the head of 20,000 men. Many of the provinces of France which had hung back till this time recognised him as king. The Protestant States abroad did the same thing; and thus strengthened, Henry led his army southward, crossed the Loire, and took up his winter quarters at Tours, the old capital of Clovis.

Early next spring (1590) the king was again in the field. Many of the old Huguenot chiefs, who had left him when he entered into engagements with the Roman Catholics, now returned, attracted by the vigour of his administration and the success of his arms. With this accession he deemed himself strong enough to take Paris, the possession of which would probably decide the contest. He began his march upon the capital, but was met by the army of the League (March 14, 1590) on the plains of Ivry. His opponents were in greatly superior numbers, having been reinforced by Spanish auxiliaries and German *reiter*. Here a second great victory crowned the cause of Henry of Navarre; in fact, the battle of Ivry is one of the most brilliant on record. Before going into action, Henry made a solemn appeal to Heaven touching the justice of his cause. "If thou seest," said he, "that I shall be one of those kings whom thou givest in thine anger, take from me my life and crown together, and may my blood be the last that shall be shed in this quarrel." The battle was not to be joined, but first the Huguenots knelt in prayer. "They are begging for mercy," cried some one. "No," it was answered, "they never fight so terribly as after they have prayed." A few moments, and the soldiers arose, and Henry addressed some stirring words to them. "Yonder," said he, as he fastened on his helmet, over which waved his white plume, "Yonder is the enemy: here is your king. God is on our side. Should you lose your standards in the battle, rally round my plume; you will always find it on the path of victory and honour." Into the midst of the enemy advanced that white plume; where raged the thickest of the fight, there it was seen to wave, and thither did the soldiers follow. After a terrible combat of two hours, the day declared decisively in favour of the king. The army of the League was totally routed, and fled from the field, leaving its cannon and standards behind it to become the trophies of the victors.[2716]

This victory, won over great odds, was a second lesson to Henry of the same import as the first. But he was trying to profess two creeds, and "a double-minded man is unstable in all his ways." This fatal instability caused Henry to falter when he was on the point of winning all. Had he marched direct on Paris, the League, stunned by the blow he had just dealt it, would have been easily crushed; the fall of the capital would have followed, and, with Paris as the seat of his government, his cause would have been completely triumphant. He hesitated—he halted; his enthusiasm seemed to have spent itself on the battlefield. He had won a victory, but his indecision permitted its fruits to escape him. All that year was spent in small affairs—in the sieges of towns which contributed nothing to his main object. The Duke of Parma—the most illustrious general of his age—came to its help. Henry's affairs made no progress; and thus the following year (1591) was as uselessly spent as its predecessor. Meanwhile, the unhappy country of France—divided into factions, traversed by armies, devastated by battles—groaned under a combination of miseries. Henry's great qualities remained with him; his bravery and dash were shown on many a bloody field; victories crowded in upon him; fame gathered round the white plume; nevertheless, his cause stood still. An eclipse seemed to rest upon the king, and a Nemesis appeared to dog his triumphal car.

With a professed Protestant upon the throne, one would have expected the condition of the Huguenots to be greatly alleviated; but it was not so. The concessions which might have been expected from even a Roman Catholic sovereign were withheld by one who was professedly a Protestant. The Huguenots as yet had no legal security for their civil and religious liberties. The laws denouncing confiscation and death for the profession of the Protestant religion, re-enacted by Henry III., remained unrepealed, and were at times put in force by country magistrates and provincial Parliaments. It sometimes happened that while in the camp of the king the Protestant worship was celebrated, a few leagues off the same worship was forbidden to a Huguenot congregation under severe penalties. The celebrated Mornay Duplessis well described the situation of the Protestants in these few words: "They had the halter always about their necks." Stung by the temporising and heartless policy of Henry, the Huguenots proposed to disown him as their chief, and to elect another protector of their Churches. Had they abandoned him, his cause would have been ruined. To the Protestants the safety of the Reformed faith was the first thing. To Henry the possession of the throne was the first thing, and the Huguenots and their cause must wait. The question was, How long?

It was now four years since Henry after a sort had been King of France; but the peaceful possession of the throne was becoming less likely than ever. Every day the difficulties around him, instead of diminishing, were thickening. Even the success which had formerly attended his arms appeared to be deserting him. Shorn of his locks, like Samson, he was winning brilliant victories no longer. What was to be done? this had now come to be the question with the king. Henry, to use a familiar expression, was "falling between two stools." The time had come for him to declare himself, and say whether he was to be a Roman Catholic, or whether he was to be a Protestant. There were not wanting weighty reasons, as they seemed, why the king should be the former. The bulk of his subjects were Roman Catholics, and by being of their religion he would conciliate the majority, put an end to the wars between the two rival parties, and relieve the country from all its troubles. By this step only could he ever hope to make himself King of all France. So did many around him counsel. His recantation would, to a large extent, be a matter of form, and by that form how many great ends of State would be served!

But on the other side there were sacred memories which Henry could not erase, and deep convictions which he could not smother. The instructions and prayers of a mother, the ripened beliefs of a lifetime, the obligations he owed to the Protestants, all must have presented themselves in opposition to the step he now meditated. Were all these pledges to be profaned? were all these hallowed bonds to be rent asunder? With the Huguenots how often had he deliberated in council; how often worshipped in the same sanctuary; how often fought on the same battlefield; their arms mainly it was that raised him to the throne; was he now to forsake them? Great must have been the conflict in the mind of the king. But the fatal step had been taken four years before, when, in the hope of disarming the hostility of the Roman Catholic lords, he consented to receive instruction in the Romish faith. To hesitate in a matter of this importance was to surrender—was to be lost; and the choice which Henry now made is just the choice which it was expected he would make. There is reason to fear that he had never felt the power of the Gospel upon his heart. His hours of leisure were often spent in adulterous pleasures. One of his mistresses was among the chief advisers of the step he was now revolving. What good would this Huguenotism do him? Would he be so great a fool as to sacrifice a kingdom for it? Listening to such counsels as these, he laid his birth-right, where so many kings before and since have laid theirs, at the feet of Rome.

It had been arranged that a conference composed of an equal number of Roman Catholic bishops and Protestant pastors should be held, and that the point of difference between the two Churches should be debated in the presence of the king. This was simply a device to save appearances, for Henry's mind was already made up. When the day came, the king forbade the attendance of the Protestants, assigning as a reason that he would not put it in the power of the bishops to say that they had vanquished them in the argument. The king's conduct throughout was marked by consummate duplicity. He invited the Reformed to fast, in prospect of the coming conference, and pray for a blessing upon it; and only three months before his abjuration, he wrote to the pastors assembled at Samur, saying that he would die rather than renounce his religion; and when the conference was about to be held, we find him speaking of it to Gabrielle d'Estrées, with whom he spent the soft hours of dalliance, as an ecclesiastical tilt from which he expected no little amusement, and the *dénouement* of which was fixed already. "This morning I begin talking with the bishops. On Sunday I am to take the perilous leap."[2717]

Henry IV. had the happiness to possess as counsellors two men of commanding talent. The first was the Baron Rosny, better known as the illustrious Sully. He was a statesman of rare genius. Like Henry, he was a Protestant; and he bore this further resemblance to his royal master, that his Protestantism was purely political. The other, Mornay Duplessis, was the equal of Sully in talent, but his superior in character. He was inflexibly upright. These two men were much about the king at this hour; both felt the gravity of the crisis, but differed widely in the advice which they gave. "I can find," said Sully, addressing the king," but two ways out of your present embarrassments. By the one you may pass through a million of difficulties, fatigues, pains, perils, and labours. You must be always in the saddle; you must always have the corselet on your back, the helmet on your head, and the sword in your hand. Nay, what is more, farewell to repose, to pleasure, to love, to mistresses, to games, to dogs, to hawking, to building; for you cannot come out through these affairs but by a multitude of combats, taking of cities, great victories, a great shedding of blood. Instead of all this, by the other way—that is, changing your religion—you escape all those pains and difficulties in this world," said the courtier with a smile, to which the king responded by a laugh: "as for the other world, I cannot answer for that."

Mornay Duplessis counselled after another fashion. The side at which Sully refused to look—the other world—was the side which Duplessis mainly considered. He charged the king to serve God with a good conscience; to keep Him before his eyes in all his actions; to attempt the union of the kingdom by the Reformation of the Church, and so to set an example to all Christendom and posterity. "With what conscience," said he, "can I advise you to go to mass if I do not first go myself? and what kind of religion can that be which is taken off as easily as one's coat?" So did this great patriot and Christian advise.

But Henry was only playing with both his counsellors. His course was already irrevocably taken; he had set his face toward Rome. On Thursday, July 22, 1593, he met the bishops, with whom he was to confer on the points of difference between the two religions. With a half-malicious humour he would occasionally interrupt their harangues with a few puzzling questions. On the following Sunday morning, the 25th, he repaired with a sumptuous following of men-at-arms to the Church of St. Dénis. On the king's knocking the cathedral door was immediately opened. The Bishop of Bourges met him at the head of a train of prelates and priests, and demanded to know the errand on which the king had come. Henry made answer, "To be admitted into the Church of Rome." He was straightway led to the altar, and kneeling on its steps, he swore to live and die in the Romish faith. The organ pealed, the cannon thundered, the warriors that thronged the nave and aisle clashed their arms; high mass was performed, the king, as he partook, bowing down till his brow touched the floor; and a solemn *Te Deum* concluded and crowned this grand jubilation.[2718]

The abjuration of Henry was viewed by the Protestants with mingled sorrow, astonishment, and apprehension. The son of Jeanne d'Albret, the foremost of the Huguenot chiefs, the Knight of the White Plume, to renounce his faith and go to mass! How fallen! But Protestantism could survive apostasies as well as defeats on the battlefield; and the Huguenots felt that they must look higher than the throne of Henry IV., and trusting in God, they took measures for the protection and advancement of their great cause. From their former compatriot and co-religionist, ever since, by the help of their arms, he had come to the throne, they had received little save promises. Their religion was proscribed, their worship was in many instances forbidden, their children were often compulsorily educated in the Romish faith, their last wills made void, and even their corpses dug out of the grave and thrown like carrion on the fields. When they craved redress, the were bidden be patient till Henry should be stronger on the throne. His apostasy had brought matters to a head, and convinced the Huguenots that they must look to themselves. The bishops had made Henry swear, "I will endeavour to the utmost of my power, and in good faith, to drive out of my jurisdiction, and from the lands under my sway, all heretics denounced by the Church." Thus the sword was again hung over their heads; and can we blame them if now they formed themselves into a political organisation, with a General Council, or Parliament, which met every year to concert measures of safety, promote unity of action, and keep watch over the affairs of the general body? To Henry's honour it must be acknowledged that he secretly encouraged this Protestant League. An apostate, he yet escaped the infamy of the persecutor.

The Huguenot council applied to Henry's government for the redress of their wrongs, and the restoration of Protestant rights and privileges. Four years passed away in these negotiations, which often degenerated into acrimonious disputes, and the course of which was marked (1595) by an atrocious massacre—a repetition, in short, of the affair of Vassy. At length Henry, sore pressed in his war with Spain, and much needing the swords of the Huguenots, granted an edict in their favour, styled, from the town from which it was issued, the Edict of Nantes, which was the glory of his reign. It was a tardy concession to justice, and a late response to complaints long and most touchingly urged. "And yet, sire," so their remonstrances ran, "among us we have neither Jacobins nor Jesuits who aim at your life, nor Leagues who aim at your crown. We have never presented the points of our swords instead of petitions. We are paid with considerations of State policy. It is not time yet, we are told, to grant us an edict,—yet, O merciful God, after thirty-five years of persecution, ten years of banishment by the edicts of the League, eight years of the present king's reign, and four of persecutions. We ask your majesty for an edict by which we may enjoy that which is common to all your subjects. The glory of God alone, liberty of conscience, repose to the State, security for our lives and property—this is the summit of our wishes, and the end of our requests."

The king still thought to temporise; but new successes on the part of the Spaniards admonished him that he had done so too long, and that the policy of delay was exhausted. The League hailed the Spanish advances, and the throne which Henry had secured by his abjuration he must save by Protestant swords. Accordingly, on the 15th April, 1598, was this famous decree, the Edict of Nantes, styled "perpetual and irrevocable," issued.

"This *Magna Charta*," says Félice, "of the French Reformation, under the ancient *régime*, granted the following concessions in brief:—Full liberty of conscience to all; the public exercise of the 'religion' in all those places in which it was established in 1577, and in the suburbs of the cities; permission to the lords' high justiciary to celebrate Divine worship in their castles, and to the inferior gentry to admit thirty persons to their domestic worship; admission of the Reformed to office in the State, their children to be received into the schools, their sick into the hospitals, and their poor to share in the alms; and the concession of a right to print their books in certain cities." This edict further provided for the erection of courts composed of an equal number of Protestants and Roman Catholics for the protection of Protestant interests, four Protestant colleges or institutions, and the right of holding a National Synod, according to the rules of the Reformed faith, once every three years.[2719] The State was charged with the duty of providing the salaries of the Protestant ministers and rectors, and a sum of 165,000 livres of those times (495,000 francs of the present day) was appropriated to that purpose. The edict does not come fully up to our idea of liberty of conscience, but it was a liberal measure for the time. As a guarantee it put 200 towns into the hands of the Protestants. It was the Edict of Nantes much more than the abjuration of Henry which conciliated the two parties in the kingdom, and gave him the peaceful possession of the throne during the few years he was yet to occupy it.

The signing of this edict inaugurated an era of tranquility and great prosperity to France. The twelve years that followed are perhaps the most glorious in the annals of that country since the opening of the sixteenth century. Spain immediately offered terms of peace, and France, weary of civil war, sheathed the sword with joy.

Now that Henry had rest from war, he gave himself to the not less glorious and more fruitful labours of peace. France in all departments of her organisation was in a state of frightful disorder—was, in fact, on the verge of ruin. Castles burned to the ground, cities half in ruins, lands reverting into a desert, roads unused, marts and harbours forsaken, were the melancholy memorials which presented themselves to one's eye wherever one journeyed. The national exchequer was empty; the inhabitants were becoming few, for those who should have enriched their country with their labour, or adorned it with their intellect, were watering its soil with their blood. Summoning all his powers, Henry set himself to repair this vast ruin. In this arduous labour he displayed talents of a higher order and a more valuable kind than any he had shown in war, and proved himself not less great as a statesman than he was as a soldier. There was a debt of three hundred millions of francs pressing on the kingdom. The annual expenditure exceeded the revenue by upwards of one hundred millions of francs. The taxes paid by the people amounted to two hundred millions of francs; but, owing to the abuses of collection, not more than thirty millions found their way into the treasury. Calling Sully to his aid, the king set himself to grapple with these gigantic evils, and displayed in the cabinet no less fertility of resource and comprehensiveness of genius than in the field. He cleared off the national debt in ten years. He found means of making the income not only balance the expenditure, but of exceeding it by many millions. He accomplished all this without adding to the burdens of the people. He understood the springs of the nation's prosperity, and taught them to flow again. He encouraged agriculture, promoted industry and commerce, constructed roads, bridges, and canals. The lands were tilled, herds were reared, the silkworm was introduced, the ports were opened for the free export of corn and wine, commercial treaties were framed with foreign countries; and France, during these ten years, showed as conclusively as it did after the war of 1870–71, how speedily it can recover from the effects of the most terrible disasters, when the passions of its children permit the boundless resources which nature has stored up in its soil and climate to develop themselves.

Henry's views in the field of foreign politics were equally comprehensive. He clearly saw that the great menace to the peace of Europe, and the independence of its several nations, was the Austrian power in its two branches—the German and Spanish. Philip II. was dead; Spain was waning; nevertheless that ambitious Power waited an opportunity to employ the one half of Christendom of which she was still mistress, in crushing the other half. Henry's project, formed in concert with Elizabeth of England, for humbling that Power was a vast one, and he had made such progress in it that twenty European States had promised to take part in the campaign which Henry was to lead against Austria. The moment for launching that great force was come, and Henry's contingent had been sent off, and was already on German soil. He was to follow his soldiers in a few days and open the campaign. But this deliverance for Christendom he was fated not to achieve. His queen, Marie de Medici, to whom he was recently married, importuned him for a public coronation, and Henry resolved to gratify her. The ceremony, which was gone about with great splendour, was over, and he was now ready to set out, when a melancholy seized him, which he could neither account for nor shake off. This pensiveness was all the more remarkable that his disposition was naturally gay and sprightly. In the words of Schiller, in his drama of "Wallenstein"—

"The king
Felt in his heart the phantom of the knife
Long ere Ravaillac armed himself therewith.
His quiet mind forsook him; the phantasma
Startled him in his Louvre, chased him forth
Into the open air: like funeral knells
Sounded that coronation festival;
And still, with boding sense, he heard the tread
Of those feet that even then were seeking him
Throughout the streets of Paris."

When the coming campaign was referred to, he told the queen and the nobles of his court that Germany he would never see—that he would die soon, and in a carriage. They tried to laugh away these gloomy fancies, as they accounted them. "Go to Germany instantly," said his minister, Sully, "and go on horseback." The 19th of May, 1610, was fixed for the departure of the king. On the 16th, Henry was so distressed as to move the compassion of his attendants. After dinner he retired to his cabinet, but could not write; he threw himself on his bed, but could not sleep. He was overheard in prayer. He asked, "What o'clock is it?" and was answered, "Four of the afternoon. Would not your Majesty be the better of a little fresh air?" The king ordered his carriage, and, kissing the queen, he set out, accompanied by two of his nobles, to go to the arsenal.[2720]

He was talking with one of them, the Duke d'Epernon, his left hand resting upon the shoulder of the other, and thus leaving his side exposed. The carriage, after traversing the Rue St. Honoré, turned into the narrow Rue de la Ferronière, where it was met by a cart, which compelled it to pass at a slow pace, close to the kerbstone. A monk, François Ravaillac, who had followed the royal *cortége* unobserved, stole up, and mounting on the wheel, and leaning over the carriage, struck his knife into the side of Henry, which it only grazed. The monk struck again, and this time the dagger took the direction of the heart. The king fell forward in his carriage, and uttered a low cry. "What is the matter, sire?" asked one of his lords. "It is nothing," replied the king twice, but the second time so low as to be barely audible. Dark blood began to ooze from the wound, and also from the mouth. The carriage was instantly turned in the direction of the Louvre. As he was being carried into the palace, Sieur de Cerisy raised his head; his eyes moved, but he spoke not. The king closed his eyes to open them not again any more. He was carried upstairs, and laid on his bed in his closet, where he expired.[2721]

Ravaillac made no attempt to escape: he stood with his bloody knife in his hand till he was apprehended; and when brought before his judges and subjected to the torture he justified the deed, saying the king was too favourable to heretics, and that he purposed making war on the Pope, which was to make war on God.[2722] Years before, Rome had launched her excommunications against the "two Henries," and now both had fallen by her dagger.

On the character of Henry IV. we cannot dwell. It was a combination of great qualities and great faults. He was a brave soldier and an able ruler; but we must not confound military brilliance or political genius with moral greatness. Entire devotion to a noble cause—the cornerstone of greatness—he lacked. France—in other words, the glory and dominion of himself and house—was the supreme aim and end of all his toils, talents, and manœuvrings. The great error of his life was his abjuration. The Roman Catholics it did not conciliate, and the Protestants it alienated. It was the Edict of Nantes that made him strong, and gave to France almost the only ten years of real prosperity and glory which it has seen since the reign of Francis I. Had Henry nobly resolved to ascend the throne with a good conscience, or not at all—had he not paltered with the Jesuits—had he said, "I will give toleration to all, but will myself abide in the faith my mother taught me"—his own heart would have been stronger, his life purer, his course less vacillating and halting; the Huguenots, the flower of French valour and intelligence, would have rallied round him and borne him to the throne, and kept him on it, in spite of all his enemies. On what different foundations would his throne in that case have rested, and what a different glory would have encircled his memory! He set up a throne by abjuration in 1593, to be cast down on the scaffold of 1793!

We have traced the great drama of the sixteenth century to its culmination, first in Germany, and next in Geneva and France, and we now propose to follow it to its new stage in other countries of Europe.

THE HISTORY OF PROTESTANTISM

Book Eighteenth
HISTORY OF PROTESTANTISM IN THE NETHERLANDS

CHAPTER I
THE NETHERLANDS AND THEIR INHABITANTS

DESCENDING from the summits of the Alps, and rolling its floods along the vast plain which extends from the Ural Mountains to the shores of the German Ocean, the Rhine, before finally falling into the sea, is parted into two streams which enclose between them an island of goodly dimensions. This island is the heart of the Low Countries. Its soil spongy, its air humid, it had no attractions to induce man to make it his dwelling, save indeed that nature had strongly fortified it by enclosing it on two of its sides with the broad arms of the disparted river, and on the third and remaining one with the waves of the North Sea. Its earliest inhabitants, it is believed, were Celts. About a century before our era it was left uninhabited; its first settlers being carried away, partly in the rush southward of the first horde of warriors that set out to assail the Roman Empire, and partly by a tremendous inundation of the ocean, which submerged many of the huts which dotted its forlorn surface, and drowned many of its miserable inhabitants. Finding it empty, a German tribe from the Hercynian forest took possession of it, and called it *Betauw*, that is, the "Good Meadow," a name that has descended to our day in the appellative Batavia.

North and south of the "Good Meadow" the land is similar in character and origin. It owes its place on the surface of the earth to the joint action of two forces—the powerful current of the Rhine on the one side, continually bringing down vast quantities of materials from the mountains and higher plains, and the tides of the restless ocean on the other, casting up sand and mud from its bed. Thus, in the course of ages, slowly rose the land which was destined in the sixteenth century to be the seat of so many proud cities, and the theatre of so many sublime actions.

An expanse of shallows and lagoons, neither land nor water, but a thin consistency, quaking beneath the foot, and liable every spring and winter to the terrible calamities of being drowned by waves, when the high tides or the fierce tempests heaped up the waters of the North Sea, and to be overflown by the Rhine, when its floods were swollen by the long-continued rains, what, one asks, tempted the first inhabitants to occupy a country whose conditions were so wretched, and which was liable moreover to be overwhelmed by catastrophe so tremendous? Perhaps they saw in this oozy and herbless expanse the elements of future fertility. Perhaps they deemed it a safe retreat, from which they might issue forth to spoil and ravage, and to which they might retire and defy pursuit. But from whatever cause, both the centre island and the whole adjoining coast soon found inhabitants. The Germans occupied the centre; the Belgæ took possession of the strip of coast stretching to the south, now known as Belgium. The similar strip running off to the north, Holland namely, was possessed by the

Frisians, who formed a population in which German and Celtic elements were blended without uniting.

The youth of these three tribes was a severe one. Their first struggle was with the soil; for while other nations choose their country, the Netherlanders had to create theirs. They began by converting the swamps and quicksands of which they had taken possession into grazing-lands and corn-fields. Nor could they rest even after this task had been accomplished: they had to be continually on the watch against the two great calamities that were ever ready to spring upon them, and rob them of the country which their industry had enriched and their skill embellished, by rearing and maintaining great dykes to defend themselves on the one side from the sea, and on the other from the river.

Their second great struggle was with the Roman power. The mistress of the world, in her onward march over the West, was embracing within her limits the forests of Germany, and the warlike tribes that dwelt in them. It is the pen of Julius Cæsar, recording his victorious advance, that first touches the darkness that shrouded this land. When the curtain rises, the tribe of the Nervii is seen drawn up on the banks of the Sambre, awaiting the approach of the master of the world. We see them closing in terrific battle with his legions, and maintaining the fight till a ghastly bank of corpses proclaimed that they had been exterminated rather than subdued.[2723] The tribes of Batavia now passed under the yoke of Rome, to which they submitted with great impatience. When the empire began to totter they rose in revolt, being joined by their neighbours, the Frisians and the Belgæ, in the hope of achieving their liberty; but the Roman power, though in decay, was still too strong to be shaken by the assault of these tribes, however brave; and it was not till the whole German race, moved by an all-pervading impulse, rose and began their march upon Rome, that they were able, in common with all the peoples of the North, to throw off the yoke of the oppressor.

After four centuries of chequered fortunes, during which the Batavian element was inextricably blended with the Frisian, the Belgic, and the Frank, the Netherlanders, for so we may now call the mixed population, in which however the German element predominated, came under the empire of Charlemagne. They continued under his sway and that of his successors for some time. The empire whose greatness had severely taxed the energies of the father was too heavy for the shoulders of his degenerate sons, and they contrived to lighten the burden by dividing it. Germany was finally severed from France, and in A.D. 922 Charles the Simple, the last of the Carlovingian line, presented to Count Dirk the northern horn of this territory, the portion now known as Holland, which henceforth became the inheritance of his descendants; and about the same time, Henry the Fowler, of Germany, acquired the sovereignty of the southern portion, together with that of Lotharinga, the modern Lorrain, and thus the territory was broken into two, each part remaining connected with the German Empire; but loosely so, its rulers yielding only a nominal homage to the head of the empire, while they exercised sovereign rights in their own special domain.[2724]

The reign of Charlemagne had effaced the last traces of free institutions and government by law which had lingered in Holland and Belgium since the Roman era, and substituted feudalism, or the government of the sword. Commerce began to flow, and from the thirteenth century its elevating influence was felt in the Netherlands. Confederations of trading towns arose, with their charters of freedom and their leagues of mutual defence, which greatly modified the state of society in Europe. These confederated cities were, in fact, free republics flourishing in the heart of despotic empires. The cities which were among the first to rise into eminence were Ghent and Bruges. The latter became a main *entrepôt* of the trade carried on with the East by way of the Mediterranean. "The wives and daughters of the citizens outvied, in the richness of their dress, that of a queen of France. . . . At Mechlin, a single individual possessed counting-houses and commercial establishments at Damascus and Grand Cairo."[2725] To Bruges the merchants of Lombardy brought the wares of Asia, and thence were they dispersed among the towns of Northern Europe, and along the shores of the German Sea. "A century later, Antwerp, the successful rival of Venice, could, it is said, boast of almost five hundred vessels daily entering her ports, and two thousand carriages lade with merchandise passing through her gates every week."[2726] Venice, Verona, Nuremberg, and Bruges were the chief links of the golden chain that united the civilised and fertile East with the comparatively rude and unskilful West. In the former the arts had long flourished. There men were expert in all that is woven on the loom or embroidered by the needle; they were able to engrave on iron, and to set precious jewels in cunningly-wrought frames of gold and silver and brass. There, too, the skilful use of the plough and the pruning-hook, combined with a vigorous soil, produced in abundance all kinds of luxuries; and along the channel we have indicated were all these various products poured into countries where arts and husbandry were yet in their infancy.[2727]

Such was the condition of Holland and Flanders at the end of the fifteenth and the beginning of the sixteenth centuries. They had come to rival the East, with which they traded. The surface of their country was richly cultivated. Their cities were numerous; they were enclosed within strong ramparts, and adorned with superb public buildings and sumptuous churches. Their rights and privileges were guaranteed by ancient charters, which they jealously guarded and knew how to defend. They were governed by a senate, which possessed legislative, judicial, and administrative powers, subject to the Supreme Council at Mechlin—as that was to the sovereign authority. The population was numerous, skilful, thriving, and equally expert at handling the tool or wielding the sword. These artisans and weavers were divided into guilds, which elected their own deans or rulers. They were brave, and not a little turbulent. When the bell tolled to arms, the inmate of the workshop could, in a few minutes, transform himself into a soldier; and these bands of artificers and weavers would present the appearance as well as the reality of an army. "Nations at the present day scarcely named," says Müller, "supported their struggle against great armies with a heroism that reminds us of the valour of the Swiss."[2728]

Holland, lying farther to the north, did not so largely share in the benefits of trade and commerce as the cities of Flanders. Giving itself to the development of its internal resources, it clothed its soil with a fertility and beauty which more southern lands might have envied. Turning to its seas, it reared a race of fishermen, who in process of time developed into the most skilful and adventurous seamen of Europe. Thus were laid the foundations of that naval ascendancy which Holland for a time enjoyed, and that great colonial empire of which this dyke-encircled territory was the mother and the mistress. "The common opinion is," says Cardinal Bentivoglio, who was sent as Papal nuncio to the Low Countries in the beginning of the seventeenth century—"The common opinion is that the navy of Holland, in the number of vessels, is equal to all the rest of Europe together."[2729] Others have written that the United Provinces have more ships than houses.[2730] And Bentivoglio, speaking of the Exchange of Amsterdam, says that if its harbour was crowded with ships, its piazza was not less so with merchants, "so that the like was not to be seen in all Europe; nay, in all the world."[2731]

By the time the Reformation was on the eve of breaking out, the liberties of the Netherlanders had come to be in great peril. For a century past the Burgundo-Austrian monarchs had been steadily encroaching upon them. The charters under which their cities enjoyed municipal life had become little more than nominal. Their senates were entirely subject to the Supreme Court at Mechlin. The forms of their ancient liberties remained, but the spirit was fast ebbing. The Netherlanders were fighting a losing battle with the empire, which year after year was growing more powerful, and stretching its shadow over the independence of their towns. They had arrived at a crisis in their history. Commerce, trade, liberty, had done all for them they would ever do. This was becoming every day more clear. Decadence had set in, and the Netherlanders would have fallen under the power of the empire and been reduced to vassalage, had not a higher principle come in time to save them from this fate. It was at this moment that a celestial fire descended upon the nation: the country shook off the torpor which had begun to weigh upon it, and girding itself for a great fight, it contended for a higher liberty than any it had yet known.[2732]

CHAPTER II
INTRODUCTION OF PROTESTANTISM INTO THE NETHERLANDS

THE great struggle for religion and liberty, of which the Netherlands became the theatre in the middle of the sixteenth century, properly dates from 1555, when the Emperor Charles V. is seen elevating to the throne, from which he himself has just descended, his son Philip II. In order to the right perception of that momentous conflict, it is necessary that we should rapidly survey the three centuries that preceded it. The Church of Rome in the Netherlands is beheld, in the thirteenth century, flourishing in power and riches. The Bishops of Utrecht had become the Popes of the North. Favoured by the emperors, whose quarrel they espoused against the Popes in the Middle Ages, these ambitious prelates were now all but independent of Rome. "They gave place," says Brandt, the historian of the Netherlands' Reformation, "to neither kings nor emperors in the state and magnificence of their court; they reckoned the greatest princes in the Low Countries among their feudatories because they held some land of the bishopric in fee, and because they owed them homage. Accordingly, Baldwin, the second of that name and twenty-ninth bishop of the see, summoned several princes to Utrecht, to receive investiture of the lands that were so holden by them: the Duke of Brabant as the first steward; the Count of Flanders as second; the Count of Holland as marshal."[2733] The clergy regulated their rank by the spiritual princedom established at Utrecht. They were the grandees of the land. They monopolised all the privileges but bore none of the burdens of the State. They imposed taxes on others, but they themselves paid taxes to no one. Numberless dues and offerings had already swollen their possessions to an enormous amount, while new and ever-recurring exactions were continually enlarging their territorial domains. Their immoralities were restrained by no sense of shame and by no fear of punishment, seeing that to the opinion of their countrymen they paid no deference, and to the civil and criminal tribunals they owed no accountability. They framed a law, and forced it upon the government, that no charge should be received against a cardinal-bishop, unless supported by seventy-two witnesses; nor against a cardinal-priest, but by forty-four; nor against a cardinal-deacon, but by twenty-seven; nor against the lowest of the clergy, but by seven.[2734] If a voice was raised to hint that these servants of the Church would exalt themselves by being a little more humble, and enrich themselves by being a little less covetous, and that charity and meekness were greater ornaments than sumptuous apparel and gaily-caparisoned mules, instantly the ban of the Church was evoked to crush the audacious complainer; and the anathema in that age had terrors that made even those look pale who had never trembled on the battle-field.

But the power, affluence, and arrogance of the Church of Rome in the Low Countries had reached their height; and in the fourteenth century we find an ebb setting in, in that tide which till now had continued at flood. Numbers of the Waldenses and Albigenses, chased from Southern France of from the valleys of the Alps, sought refuge in the cities of the Netherlands, bringing with them the Romaunt version of the Bible, which was translated into Low Dutch rhymes.[2735]

The city of Antwerp occupies a most distinguished place in this great movement. So early as 1106, before the disciples of Peter Waldo had appeared in these parts, we find a celebrated preacher, Tanchelinus by name, endeavouring to purge out the leaven of the Papacy, and spread purer doctrine not only in Antwerp, but in the adjoining parts of Brabant and Flanders; and, although vehemently opposed by the priests and by Norbert, the first founder of the order of Premonstratensians, his opinions took a firm hold of some of the finest minds.[2736] In the following century, the thirteenth, William Cornelius, also of Antwerp, taught a purer doctrine than the common one on the Eucharistic Sacrament, which he is said to have received from the disciples of Tanchelinus. Nor must we omit to mention Nicolas, of Lyra, a town in the east of Brabant, who lived about 1322, and who impregnated his Commentary on the Bible with the seeds of Gospel truth. Hence the remark of Julius Pflugius, the celebrated Romish doctor[2737]—"Si Lyra non lirasset, Lutherus non saltasset."[2738] In the fourteenth century came another sower of the good seed of the Word in the countries of which we speak, Gerard of Groot. Nowhere, in short, had forerunners of the Reformation been so numerous as on this famous sea-board, a fact doubtless to be accounted for, in part at least, by the commerce, the intelligence, and the freedom which the Low Countries then enjoyed.

Voices began to be heard prophetic of greater ones to be raised in after-years. Whence came those voices? From the depths of the convents. The monks became the reprovers and accusers of one another. The veil was lifted upon the darkness that hid the holy places of the Roman Church. In 1290, Henry of Ghent, Archbishop of Tournay, published a book against the Papacy, in which he boldly questioned the Pope's power to transform what was evil into good. Guido, the forty-second Bishop of Utrecht, refused—rare modesty in those times—the red hat and scarlet mantle from the Pope. He contrasts with Wevelikhoven, the fiftieth bishop of that see, who in 1380 dug the bones of a Lollard out of the grave, and burned them before the gates of his episcopal palace, and cast the ashes into the town ditch. His successor, the fifty-first Bishop of Utrecht, cast into a dungeon a monk named Matthias Grabo, for writing a book in support of the thesis that "the clergy are subject to the civil powers." The terrified author recanted the doctrine of his book; but the magistrates of several cities esteemed it good and sound notwithstanding. As in the greater Papacy of Rome, so in the lesser Papacy at Utrecht, a schism took place, and rival Popes thundered anathemas at one another; this helped to lower the prestige of the Church in the eyes of the people. Henry Loeder, Prior of the Monastery of Fredesweel, near Northova, wrote to his brother in the following manner—"Dear brother, the love I bear your state, and welfare for the sake of the Blood of Christ, obliges me to take a rod instead of a pen into my hand. . . . I never saw those cloisters flourish and increase in godliness which daily increased in temporal estates and possessions. . . . The filth of your cloister greatly wants the broom and the mop. . . . Embrace the Cross and the Crucified Jesus; therein ye shall find full content." Near Haarlem was the cloister of "The Visitation of the Blessed Lady," of which John van Kempen was prior. We find him censuring the lives of the monks in these words—"We would be humble, but cannot bear contempt; patient, without oppressions or sufferings; obedient, without subjection; poor, without wanting anything, &c. Our Lord said the kingdom of heaven is to be entered by force." Henry Wilde, Prior of the Monastery of Bois le Duc, purged the hymn-books of the wanton songs which the monks had inserted with the anthems. "Let them pray for us," was the same prior wont to say when asked to sing masses for the dead; "our prayers will do them no good." We obtain a glimpse of the rigour of the ecclesiastical laws from the attempts that now began to be made to modify them. In 1434 we find Bishop Rudolph granting power to the Duke of Burgundy to arrest by his bailiffs all drunken and fighting priests, and deliver them up to the bishop, who promises not to discharge them till satisfaction shall have been given to the duke. He promises farther not to grant the protection of churches and church-yards to murderers and similar malefactors; and that no subject of Holland shall be summoned to appear in the bishop's court at Utrecht, upon any account whatsoever, if the person so summoned be willing to appear before the spiritual or temporal judge to whose jurisdiction he belongs.[2739]

There follow, as it comes nearer the Reformation, the greater names of Thomas à Kempis and John Wessel. We see them trim their lamp and go onward to show men the Way of Life. It was a feeble light that now began to break over these lands; still it was sufficient to reveal many things which had been unobserved or unthought of during the gross darkness that preceded it. It does not become Churchmen, the barons now began to say, to be so enormously rich, and so effeminately luxurious; these possessions are not less ours than they are theirs, we shall share them with them. These daring barons, moreover, learned to deem the spiritual authority not quite so impregnable as they had once believed it to be, and the consequence of this was that they held the persons of Churchmen in less reverence, and their excommunications in less awe than before. There was planted thus an incipient revolt. The movement received an impulse from the writings of Wicliffe, which began to be circulated in the Low Countries in the end of the fourteenth century.[2740] There followed, in the beginning of the next century, the martyrdoms of Huss and Jerome. The light which these two stakes shed over the plains of Bohemia was reflected as far as to the banks of the Rhine and the shores of the North Sea, and helped to deepen the inquiry which the teachings of the Waldenses and the writings of Wicliffe had awakened among the burghers and artisans of the Low Countries. The execution of Huss and Jerome was followed by the Bohemian campaign. The victories of Ziska spread the terror of the Hussite arms, and to some extent also the knowledge of the Hussite doctrines, over Western Europe. In the great armaments which were raised by the Pope to extinguish the heresy of Huss, numerous natives of Holland and Belgium enrolled themselves; and of these, some at least returned to their native land converts to the heresy they had gone forth to subdue.[2741] Their opinions, quietly disseminated among their countrymen, helped to prepare the way for that great struggle in the Netherlands which we are now to record, and which expanded into so much vaster dimensions than that which had shaken Bohemia in the fifteenth century.

To these causes, which conspired for the awakening of the Netherlands, is to be added the influence of trade and commerce. The tendency of commerce to engender activity of mind, and nourish independence of thought, is too obvious to require that we should dwell upon it. The tiller of the soil seldom permits his thoughts to stray beyond his native acres, the merchant and trader has a whole hemisphere for his mental domain. He is compelled to reflect, and calculate, and compare, otherwise he loses his ventures. He is thus lifted out of the slough in which the agriculturist or the herdsman is content to lie all his days. The Low Countries, as we have said in the previous chapter, were the heart of the commerce of the nations. They were the clearing-house of the world. This vast trade brought with it knowledge as well as riches; for the Fleming could not meet his customers on the wharf, or on the Bourse, without hearing things to him new and strange. He had to do with men of all nations, and he received from them not only foreign coin, but foreign ideas.

The new day was coming on apace. Already its signals stood displayed before the eyes of men. One powerful instrumentality after another stood up to give rapid and universal diffusion to the new agencies that were about to be called into existence. Nor have the nations long to wait. A crash is heard, the fall of an ancient empire shakes the earth, and the sacred languages, so long imprisoned within the walls of Constantinople, are liberated, and become again the inheritance of the race. The eyes of men begin to be turned on the sacred page, which may now be read in the very words in which the inspired men of old time wrote it. Not for a thousand years had so fair a morning visited the earth. Men felt after the long darkness that truly "light is sweet, and a pleasant thing it is for the eyes to behold the sun." The dawn was pale and chilly in Italy, but in the north of Europe it brought with it, not merely the light of pagan literature, but the warmth and brightness of Christian truth.

We have already seen with what fierce defiance Charles V. flung down the gage of battle to Protestantism. In manner the most public, and with vow the most solemn and awful, he bound himself to extirpate heresy, or to lose armies, treasures, kingdoms, body and soul, in the attempt. Germany, happily, was covered from the consequences of that mortal threat by the sovereign rights of its hereditary princes, who stood between their subjects and that terrible arm that was now uplifted to crush them. But the less fortunate Netherlands enjoyed no such protection. Charles was master there. He could enforce his will in his patrimonial estates, and his will was that no one in all the Netherlands should profess another than the Roman creed.

One furious edict was issued after another, and these were publicly read twice every year, that no one might pretend ignorance.[2742] These edicts did not remain a dead letter as in Germany; they were ruthlessly executed, and soon, alas! the Low Countries were blazing with stakes and swimming in blood. It is almost incredible, and yet the historian Meteren asserts that during the last thirty years of Charles's reign not fewer than 50,000 Protestants were put to death in the provinces of the Netherlands. Grotius, in his *Annals*, raises the number to 100,000.[2743] Even granting that these estimates are extravagant, still they are sufficient to convince us that the number of victims was great indeed. The bloody work did not slacken owing to Charles's many absences in Spain and other countries. His sister Margaret, Dowager-queen of Hungary, who was appointed regent of the provinces, was compelled to carry out all his cruel edicts. Men and women, whose crime was that they did not believe in the mass, were beheaded, hanged, burned, or buried alive. These proceedings were zealously seconded by the divines of Louvain, whom Luther styled "bloodthirsty heretics, who, teaching impious doctrines which they could make good neither by reason nor Scripture, betook themselves to force, and disputed with fire and sword.[2744] This terrible work went on from the 23rd of July, 1523, when the proto-martyrs of the provinces were burned in the great square of Brussels,[2745] to the day of the emperor's abdication. The Dowager-queen, in a letter to her brother, had given it as her opinion that the good work of purgation should stop only when to go farther would be to effect the entire depopulation of the country. The "Christian Widow," as Erasmus styled her, would not go the length of burning the last Netherlander; she would leave a few orthodox inhabitants to repeople the land.

Meanwhile the halter and the axe were gathering their victims so fast, that the limits traced by the regent—wide as they were—bade fair soon to be reached. The genius and activity of the Netherlanders were succumbing to the terrible blows that were being unremittingly dealt them. Agriculture was beginning to languish; life was departing from the great towns; the step of the artisan, as he went to and returned from his factory at the hours of meal, was less elastic, and his eye less bright; the workshops were being weeded of their more skilful workmen; foreign Protestant merchants were fleeing from the country; and the decline of the internal trade kept pace with that of the external commerce.

It was evident to all whom bigotry had not rendered incapable of reflection, that, though great progress had been made towards the ruin of the country, the extinction of heresy was still distant, and likely to be reached only when the land had become a desert, the harbours empty, and the cities silent. The blood with which the tyrant was so profusely watering the Netherlands, was but nourishing the heresy which he sought to drown.

CHAPTER III
ANTWERP: ITS CONFESSORS AND MARTYRS

NO city did the day that was now breaking over the Low Countries so often touch with its light as Antwerp. Within a year after Luther's appearance, Jacob Spreng, prior of the Augustinian convent in that town, confessed himself a disciple of the Wittemberg monk, and began to preach the same doctrine. He was not suffered to do so long. In 1519 he was seized in his own convent, carried to Brussels, and threatened with the punishment of the fire. Though his faith was genuine, he had not courage to be a martyr. Vanquished by the fear of death, he consented to read in public his recantation. Being let go, he repaired to Bremen, and there, "walking softly from the memory of his fall," he passed the remaining years of his life in preaching the Gospel as one of the pastors of that northern town.[2746]

The same city and the same convent furnished another Reformer yet more intrepid than Spreng. This was Henry of Zutphen. He, too, had sat at the feet of Luther, and along with his doctrine had carried away no small amount of Luther's dramatic power in setting it forth. Christ's office as a Saviour he finely put into the following antitheses:—"He became the servant of the law that he might be its master. He took all sin that he might take away sin.[2747] He is at once the victim and the vanquisher of death; the captive of hell, yet he it was by whom its gates were burst open." But though he refused to the sinner any share in the great work of expiating sin, reserving that entirely and exclusively to the Saviour, Zutphen strenuously insisted that the believer should be careful to maintain good works. "Away," he said, "with a dead faith." His career in Antwerp was brief. He was seized and thrown into prison. He did not deceive himself as to the fate that awaited him. He kept awake during the silent hours of the night, preparing for the death for which he looked on the coming day. Suddenly a great uproar arose round his prison. The noise was caused by his townsmen, who had come to rescue him. They broke open his gaol, penetrated to his cell, and bringing him forth, made him escape from the city. Henry of Zutphen, thus rescued from the fires of the Inquisition, visited in the course of his wanderings several provinces and cities, in which he preached the Gospel with great eloquence and success. Eventually he went to Holstein, where, after labouring for some time, a mob, instigated by the priests, set upon him and murdered him[2748] in the atrociously cruel and barbarous manner we have described in a previous part of our history.[2749]

It seemed as if the soil on which the convent of the Augustines in Antwerp stood produced heretics. It must be dug up. In October, 1522, the convent was dismantled. Such of the monks as had not caught the Lutheran disease had quarters provided for them elsewhere. The Host was solemnly removed from a place, the very air of which was loaded with deadly pravity, and the building, like the house of the leper of old, was razed to the ground.[2750] No man lodged under that roof any more for ever.

But the heresy was not driven away from Brabant, and the inquisitors began to wreak their vengeance on other objects besides the innocent stones and timbers of heretical monasteries. In the following year (1523) three monks, who had been inmates of that same monastery whose ruins now warned the citizens of Antwerp to eschew Lutheranism as they would the fire, were burned at Brussels.[2751] When the fire was kindled, they first recited the Creed; then they chanted the *Te Deum Laudamus*. This hymn they sang, each chanting the alternate verse, till the flames had deprived them of both voice and life.[2752]

In the following year the monks signalised their zeal by a cruel deed. The desire to hear the Gospel continuing to spread in Antwerp and the adjoining country, the pastor of Meltz, a little place near Antwerp, began to preach to the people. His church was often unable to contain the crowds that came to hear him, and he was obliged to retire with his congregation to the open fields. In one of his sermons, declaiming against the priests of his time, he said:—"We are worse than Judas, for he both sold and delivered the Lord; but we sell him to you, and do not deliver him." This was doctrine, the public preaching of which was not likely to be tolerated longer than the priests lacked power to stop it. Soon there appeared a placard or proclamation silencing the pastor, as well as a certain Augustinian monk, who preached at times in Antwerp. The assemblies of both were prohibited, and a reward of thirty gold *caroli* set upon their heads. Nevertheless, the desire for the Gospel was not extinguished, and one Sunday the people convened in great numbers in a ship-building yard on the banks of the Scheldt, in the hope that some one might minister to them the Word of Life. In that gathering was a young man, well versed in the Scriptures, named Nicolas, who seeing no one willing to act as preacher, rose himself to address the people. Entering into a boat that was moored by the river's brink, he read and expounded to the multitude the parable of the five loaves and the two small fishes. The thing was known all over the city. It was dangerous that such a man should be at large; and the monks took care that he should preach no second sermon. Hiring two butchers, they waylaid him next day, forced him into a sack, tied it with a cord, and hastily carrying him to the river, threw him in. When the murder was known a thrill of horror ran through the citizens of Antwerp.[2753]

Ever since the emperor's famous fulmination against Luther, in 1521, he had kept up a constant fire of placards, as they were termed—that is, of persecuting edicts—upon the Netherlands. They were posted up in the streets, read by all, and produced universal consternation and alarm. They succeeded each other at brief intervals; scarcely had the echoes of one fulmination died away when a new and more terrible peal was heard resounding over the startled and affrighted provinces. In April, 1524, came a placard forbidding the printing of any book without the consent of the officers who had charge of that matter.[2754] In 1525 came a circular letter from the regent Margaret, addressed to all the monasteries of Holland, enjoining them to send out none but discreet preachers, who would be careful to make no mention of Luther's name. In March, 1526, came another placard against Lutheranism, and in July of the same year yet another and severer. The preamble of this edict set forth that the "vulgar had been deceived and misled, partly by the contrivance of some ignorant fellows, who took upon them to preach the Gospel privately, without the leave of their superiors, explaining the same, together with other holy writings, after their own fancies, and not according to the orthodox sense of the doctors of the Church, racking their brains to produce new-fangled doctrines. Besides these, divers secular and regular priests presumed to ascend the pulpit, and there to relate the errors and sinister notions of Luther and his adherents, at the same time reviving the heresies of ancient times, and some that had likewise been propagated in these countries, recalling to men's memories the same, with other false and damnable opinions that had never till now been heard, thought of, or spoken of . . . Wherefore the edit forbids, in the emperor's name, all assemblies in order to read, speak, confer, or preach concerning the Gospel or other holy writings in Latin, Flemish, or in the Walloon languages—as likewise to preach, teach, or in any sort promote the doctrines of Martin Luther; especially such as related to the Sacrament of the altar, or to confession, and other Sacraments of the Church, or anything else that affected the honour of the holy mother Mary, and the saints and saintesses, and their images. . . . By this placard it was further ordained that, together with the books of Luther, &c., and all their adherents of the same sentiments, all the gospels, epistles, prophecies, and other books of the Holy Scriptures in High Dutch, Flemish, Walloon, or French, that had marginal notes, or expositions according to the doctrine of Luther, should be brought to some public place, and there burned; and that whoever should presume to keep any of the aforesaid books and writings by them after the promulgation of this placard should forfeit life and goods."[2755]

In 1528 a new placard was issued against prohibited books, as also against monks who had abandoned their cloister. There followed in 1529 another and more severe edict, condemning to death without pardon or reprieve all who had not brought their Lutheran books to be burned, or had otherwise contravened the former edicts. Those who had relapsed after having abjured their errors were to die by fire; as for others, the men were to die by the sword, and the women by the pit—that is, they were to be buried alive. To harbour or conceal a heretic was death and the forfeiture of goods. Informers were to have one-half of the estates of the accused on conviction; and those who were commissioned to put the placard in execution were to proceed, not with "the tedious formalities of trial," but by summary process.[2756]

It was about this time that Erasmus addressed a letter to the inhabitants of the Low Countries in which he advised them thus:—"Keep yourselves in the ark, that you do not perish in the deluge. Continue in the little ship of our Saviour, lest ye be swallowed by the waves. Remain in the fold of the Church, lest ye become a prey to the wolves or to Satan, who is always going to and fro, seeking whom he may devour. Stay and see what resolutions will be taken by the emperor, the princes, and afterwards by a General Council."[2757] It was thus that the man who was reposing in the shade exhorted the men who were in the fire. As regarded a "General Council," for which they were bidden to wait, the Reformers had had ample experience, and the result had been uniform—the mountain had in every case brought forth a mouse. They were able also by this time to guess, one should think, what the emperor was likely to do for them. Almost every year brought with it a new edict, and the space between each several fulmination was occupied in giving practical application to these decrees—that is, in working the axe, the halter, the stake, and the pit.

A new impetus was given about this time to the Reform movement, by the translation of Luther's version of the Scriptures into Low Dutch. It was not well executed; nevertheless, being read in their assemblies, the book instructed and comforted these young converts. Many of the priests who had been in office for years, but who had never read a single line of the Bible, good-naturedly taking it for granted that it amply authenticated all that the Church taught, dipped into it, and being much astonished at its contents, began to bring both their life and doctrine into greater accordance with it. One of the printers of this first edition of the Dutch Bible was condemned to death for his pains, and died by the axe. Soon after this, some one made a collection of certain passages from the Scriptures, and published them under the title of "The Well of Life." The little book, with neither note nor comment, contained but the words of Scripture itself; nevertheless it was very obnoxious to the zealous defenders of Popery. A "Well of Life" to others, it was a Well of Death to their Church and her rites, and they resolved on stopping it. A Franciscan friar of Brabant set out on purpose for Amsterdam, where the little book had been printed, and buying up the whole edition, he committed it to the flames. He had only half done his work, however. The book was printed in other towns. The Well would not be stopped; its waters would gush out; the journey and the expense which the friar had incurred had been in vain.

We pass over the edicts that were occasionally seeing the light during the ten following years, as well as the Anabaptist opinions and excesses, with the sanguinary wars to which they led. These we have fully related in a previous part of our history.[2758] In 1540 came a more atrocious edict than any that had yet been promulgated. The monks and doctors of Louvain, who spared no pains to root out the Protestant doctrine, instigated the monarch to issue a new placard, which not only contained the substance of all former edicts, but passed them into a perpetual law. It was dated from Brussels, the 22nd September, 1540, and was to the following effect:—That the heretic should be incapable of holding or disposing of property; that all gifts, donations, and legacies made by him should be null and void; that informers who themselves were heretics should be pardoned that once; and it especially revived and put in force against Lutherans an edict that had been promulgated in 1535, and specially directed against Anabaptists—namely, that those who abandoned their errors should have the privilege, if men, of dying by the sword; and if women, of being buried alive; such as should refuse to recant were to be burned.[2759]

It was an aggravation of these edicts that they were in violation of the rights of Holland. The emperor promulgated them in his character of the Count of Holland; but the ancient Counts of Holland could issue no decree or law till first they had obtained the consent of the nobility and Commons. Yet the emperor issued these placards on his own sole authority, and asked leave of no one. Besides, they were a virtual establishment of the Inquisition. They commanded that when evidence was lacking, the accused should themselves be put to the question—that is, by torture or other inquisitorial methods. Accordingly, in 1522, and while only at the beginning of the terrible array of edicts which we have recited, the emperor appointed Francis van Hulst to make strict inquiry into people's opinions in religious matters all throughout the Netherlands; and he gave him as his fellow-commissioner, Nicolas van Egmont, a Carmelite monk. These two worthies Erasmus happily and characteristically hit off thus:—"Hulst," said he, "is a wonderful enemy to learning," and "Egmont is a madman with a sword in his hand." "These men," says Brandt, "first threw men into prison, and then considered what they should lay to their charge."

Meanwhile the Reformed doctrine was spreading among the inhabitants of Holland, Brabant, and Flanders. At Bois-le-Duc all the Dominican monks were driven out of the city. At Antwerp, in spite of the edicts of the emperor, the conventicles were kept up. The learned Hollander, Dorpius, Professor of Divinity at Louvain, was thought to favour Luther's doctrine, and he, as well as Erasmus, was in some danger of the stake. Nor did the emperor's secretary at the Court of Brabant, Philip de Lens, escape the suspicion of heresy. At Naarden, Anthony Frederick became a convert to Protestantism, and was followed by many of the principal inhabitants—among others, Nicolas Quich, under-master of the school there. At Utrecht the Reformation was embraced by Rhodius, Principal of the College of St. Jerome, and in Holland by Cornelius Honius, a learned civilian, and counsellor to the Courts of Holland. Honius interpreted the text, "This is my body," by the words, "This signifies my body"—an interpretation which he is said to have found among the papers of Jacob Hook, sometime Dean of Naldwick, and which was believed to have been handed down from hand to hand for two hundred years.[2761] Among the disciples of Honius was William Gnaphæus, Rector of the Gymnasium at the Hague. To these we may add Cornelius Grapheus, Secretary of Antwerp, a most estimable man, and an enlightened friend of the Reformation.

The first martyr of the Reformation in Holland deserves more particular notice. He was John de Bakker, of Woerden, which is a little town between Utrecht and Leyden. He was a priest of the age of twenty-seven years, and had incurred the suspicion of heresy by speaking against the edicts of the emperor, and by marrying. Joost Laurence, a leading member of the Inquisition, presided at his trial. He declared before his judges that "he could submit to no rule of faith save Holy Writ, in the sense of the Holy Ghost, ascertained in the way of interpreting Scripture by Scripture." He held that "men were not to be forced to 'come in,' otherwise than God forces them, which is not by prisons, stripes, and death, but by gentleness, and by the strength of the Divine Word, a force as soft and lovely as it is powerful." Touching the celibacy of priests, concerning which he was accused, he did "not find it enjoined in Scripture, and an angel from heaven could not, he maintained, introduce a new article of faith, much less the Church, which was subordinate to the Word of God, but had no authority over it." His aged father, who was churchwarden—although after this expelled from his office—was able at times to approach his son, as he stood upon his trial, and at these moments the old man would whisper into his ear, "Be strong, and persevere in what is good; as for me, I am contented, after the example of Abraham, to offer up to God my dearest child, that never offended me."

The presiding judge condemned him to die. The next day, which was the 15th of September, 1525, he was led out upon a high scaffold, where he was divested of his clerical garments, and dressed in a short yellow coat. "They put on his head," says the Dutch Book of Martyrs, "a yellow hat, with flaps like a fool's cap. When they were leading him away to execution," continues the martyrologist, "as he passed by the prison where many more were shut up for the faith, he cried with a loud voice, 'Behold! my dear brethren, I have set my foot upon the threshold of martyrdom; have courage, like brave soldiers of Jesus Christ, and being stirred up by my example, defend the truths of the Gospel against all unrighteousness.' He had no sooner said this than he was answered by a shout of joy, triumph, and clapping of hands by the prisoners; and at the same time they honoured his martyrdom with ecclesiastical hymns, singing the *Te Deum Laudamus, Certamen Magnum*, and *O beata Martyrum Solemnia*. Nor did they cease till he had given up the ghost. When he was at the stake, he cried, 'O death! where is thy sting? O grave! where is thy victory?' And again, 'Death is swallowed up in the victory of Christ.' And last of all, 'Lord Jesus, forgive, them, for they know not what they do. O Son of God! remember me, and have mercy upon me.' And thus, after they had stopped his breath, he departed as in a sweet sleep, without any motions or convulsions of his head and body, or contortions of his eyes. This was the end of John de Bakker, the first martyr in Holland for the doctrine of Luther. The next day Bernard the monk, Gerard Wormer, William of Utrecht, and perhaps also Gnaphæus himself, were to have been put to death, had not the constancy of our proto-martyr softened a little the minds of his judges.[2762]

CHAPTER IV

ABDICATION OF CHARLES V AND ACCESSION OF PHILIP II

IN the midst of his cruel work, and, we may say, in the midst of his years, the emperor was overtaken by old age. The sixteenth century is waxing in might around him; its great forces are showing no sign of exhaustion or decay; on the contrary, their vigour is growing from one year to another; it is plain that they are only in the opening of their career, while in melancholy contrast Charles V. is closing his, and yielding to the decrepitude that is creeping over himself and his empire. The sceptre and the faggot—so closely united in his case, and to be still more closely united in that of his successor—he must hand over to his son Philip. Let us place ourselves in the hall where the act of abdication is about to take place, and be it ours not to record the common-places of imperial flattery, so lavishly bestowed on this occasion, nor to describe the pomps under which the greatest monarch of his age so adroitly hid his fall, but to sketch the portraits of some of those men who await a great part in the future, and whom we shall frequently meet in the scenes that are about to open.

We enter the great hall of the old palace of Brabant, in Brussels. It is the 25th of October, 1555, and this day the Estates of the Netherlands have met here, summoned by an imperial edict, to be the witnesses of the surrender of the sovereignty of his realms by Charles to his son. With the act of abdication one tragedy closes, and another and bloodier tragedy begins. No one in that glittering throng could forecast the calamitous future which was coming along with the new master of the Spanish monarchy. Charles V. enters the gorgeously tapestried hall, leaning his arm on the shoulder of William of Nassau. Twenty-five years before, we saw the emperor entering Augsburg, bestriding a steed of "brilliant whiteness," and exciting by his majestic port, his athletic frame, and manly countenance, the enthusiasm of the spectators, who, with a touch of exaggeration pardonable in the circumstances, pronounced him "the handsomest man in the empire." And now what a change in Charles! How sad the ravages which toil and care have, during these few years, made on this iron frame! The bulky mould in which the outer man of Charles was cast still remains to him—the ample brow, the broad chest, the muscular limbs; but the force that animated that powerful framework, and enabled it to do such feats in the tournament, the bull-ring, and the battlefield, has departed. His limbs totter, he has to support his steps with a crutch, his hair is white, his eyes have lost their brightness, his shoulders stoop—in short, age has withered and crippled him all over; and yet he has seen only fifty-five years. The toils that had worn him down he briefly and affectingly summarised in his address to the august assemblage before him. Resting this hand on his crutch, and that on the shoulder of the young noble by his side, he proceeds to count up forty expeditions undertaken by him since he was seventeen—nine to Germany, six to Spain, seven to Italy, four to France, ten to the Netherlands, two to England, and two to Africa. He had made eleven voyages by sea; he had fought four battles, won victories, held Diets, framed treaties—so ran the tale of his work. He had passed nights and nights in anxious deliberation over the growth of Protestantism, and he had sought to alleviate the mingled mortification and alarm its progress caused him, by fulminating one persecuting edict after another in the hope of arresting it. In addition to marches and battles, thousands of halters and stakes had he erected; but of these he is discreetly silent. He is silent too regarding the success which had crowned these mighty efforts and projects. Does he retire because he has succeeded? No; he retires because he has failed. His infirm frame is but the image of his once magnificent empire, over which decrepitude and disorder began to creep. One young in years, and alert in body, is needed to recruit those armies which battle has wasted, to replenish that exchequer which so many campaigns have made empty, to restore the military prestige which the flight from Innspruck and succeeding disasters have tarnished, to quell the revolts that are springing up in the various kingdoms which form his vast monarchy, and to dispel those dark clouds which his eye but too plainly sees to be gathering all round the horizon, and which, should he, with mind enfeebled and body crippled, continue to linger longer on the scene, will assuredly burst in ruin. Such is the true meaning of that stately ceremonial in which the actors played so adroitly, each his part, in the Brabant palace at Brussels, on the 25th of October, 1555. The tyrant apes the father; the murderer of his subjects would fain seem the paternal ruler; the disappointed, baffled, fleeing opponent of Protestantism puts on the airs of the conqueror, and strives to hide defeat under the pageantries of State, and the symbols of victory. The closing scene of Charles V. is but a repetition of Julian's confession of discomfiture— "Thou has overcome, O Galilean."

We turn to the son, who, in almost all outward respects, presents a complete contrast to the father. If Charles was prematurely old, Philip, on the other hand, looked as if he never had been young. He did not attain to middle height. His small body was mounted on thin legs. Nature had not fitted him to shine in either the sports of the tournament or the conflicts of the battlefield; and both he shunned. He had the ample brow, the blue eyes, and the aquiline nose of his father; but these agreeable features were forgotten in the ugliness of the under part of his face. His lower jaw protruded. It was a Burgundian deformity, but in Philip's case it had received a larger than the usual family development. To this disagreeable feature was added another repulsive one, also a family peculiarity, a heavy hanging under-lip, which enlarged the apparent size of his mouth, and strengthened the impression, which the unpleasant protrusion of the jaw made on the spectator, of animal voracity and savageness.

The puny, meager, sickly-looking man who stood beside the warlike and once robust form of Charles, was not more unlike his father in body than he was unlike him in mind. Not one of his father's great qualities did he possess. He lacked his statesmanship; he had no knowledge of men, he could not enter into their feelings, nor accommodate himself to their ways, nor manifest any sympathy in what engaged and engrossed them; he, therefore, shunned them. He had the shy, shrinking air of the valetudinarian, and looked around with something like the scowl of the misanthrope on his face. Charles moved about from province to province of his vast dominions, speaking the language and conforming to the manners of the people among whom he chanced for the time to be; he was at home in all places. Philip was a stranger everywhere, save in Spain. He spoke no language but his mother tongue. Amid the gay and witty Italians—

Book Eighteenth

amid the familiar and courteous Flemings—amid the frank and open Germans—Philip was still the Spaniard: austere, haughty, taciturn, unapproachable. Only one quality did he share with his father—the intense passion, namely, for extinguishing the Reformation.[2763]

From the two central figures we turn to glance at a third, the young noble on whose shoulder the emperor is leaning. He is tall and well-formed, with a lofty brow, a brown eye, and a peaked beard. His service in camps has bronzed his complexion, and given him more the look of a Spaniard than a Fleming. He is only in his twenty-third year, but the quick eye of Charles had discovered the capacity of the young soldier, and placed him in command of the army on the frontier, where resource and courage were specially needed, seeing he had there to confront some of the best generals in France. Could the emperor, who now leaned so confidently on his shoulder, have foreseen his future career, how suddenly would he have withdrawn his arm! The man on whom he reposed was destined to be the great antagonist of his son. Despotism and Liberty stood embodied in the two forms on either hand of the abdicating emperor—Philip, and William, Prince of Orange; for it was he on whom Charles leaned. The contest between them was to shake Christendom, bring down from its pinnacle of power that great monarchy which Charles was bequeathing to his son, raise the little Holland to a pitch of commercial prosperity and literary glory which Spain had never known, and leave to William a name in the wars of liberty far surpassing that which Charles had won by his many campaigns—a name which can perish only with the Netherlands themselves.

Besides the three principal figures there were others in that brilliant gathering, who were either then, or soon to be, celebrated throughout Europe, and whom we shall often meet in the stirring scenes that are about to open. In the glittering throng around the platform might be seen the bland face of the Bishop of Arras; the tall form of Lamoral of Egmont, with his long dark hair and soft eye, the representative of the ancient Frisian kings; the bold but sullen face, and fan-shaped beard, of Count Horn; the debauched Brederode; the infamous Noircarmes, on whose countenance played the blended lights of ferocity and greed; the small figure of the learned Viglius, with his yellow hair and his glittering eye, and round rosy face, from which depended an ample beard; and, to close our list, there was the slender form of the celebrated Spanish grandee, Ruy Gomez, whose coal-black hair and burning eye were finely set off by a face which intense application had rendered as colourless almost as the marble.

The pageant was at an end. Charles had handed over to another that vast possession of dominion which had so severely taxed his manhood, and which was crushing his age. The princes, knights, warriors, and counsellors have left the hall, and gone forth to betake them each to his own several road—Charles to the monastic cell which he had interposed between him and the grave; Philip to that throne from which he was to direct that fearful array of armies, inquisitors, and executioners, that was to make Europe swim in blood; William of Orange to prepare for that now not distant struggle, which he saw to be inevitable if bounds were to be set to the vast ambition and fanatical fury of Spain, and some remnants of liberty preserved in Christendom. Others went forth to humbler yet important tasks; some to win true glory by worthy deeds, others to leave behind them names which should be an execration to posterity; but nearly all of them to expire, not on the bed of peace, but on the battlefield, on the scaffold, or by the poignard of the assassin.

CHAPTER V

PHILIP ARRANGES THE GOVERNMENT OF THE NETHERLANDS, AND DEPARTS FOR SPAIN

SOME few years of comparative tranquillity were to intervene between the accession of Philip II., and the commencement of those terrible events which made his reign one long dark tragedy. But even now, though but recently seated on the throne, one startling and ominous act gave warning to the Netherlands and to Europe of what was in store for them under the austere, bigoted, priest-ridden man, whom half a world had the misfortune to call master. In 1559, four years after his accession, Philip renewed that atrociously inhuman edict which his father had promulgated in 1540. This edict had imported into the civilised Netherlands the disgusting spectacles of savage lands; it kept the gallows and the stake in constant operation, and made such havoc in the ranks of the friends of freedom of conscience, that the more moderate historians have estimated the number of its victims, as we have already said, at 50,000.

The commencement of this work, as our readers know, was in 1521, when the emperor issued at Worms his famous edict against "Martin," who was "not a man, but a devil under the form of a man." That bolt passed harmlessly over Luther's head, not because being "not a man," but a spirit, even the imperial sword could not slay him, but simply because he lived on German soil, where the emperor might issue as many edicts as he pleased, but could not execute one of them without the consent of the princes. But the shaft that missed Luther stuck deep into the unhappy subjects of Charles's Paternal Estates. "Death or forfeiture of goods" was the sentence decreed against all Lutherans in the Netherlands, and to effect the unsparing and vigorous execution of the decree, a new court was erected in Belgium, which bore a startling resemblance to the Inquisition of Spain. In Antwerp, in Brussels, and in other towns piles began straightway to blaze.

The fires once kindled, there followed similar edicts, which kept the flames from going out. These made it death to pray with a few friends in private; death to read a page of the Scriptures; death to discuss any article of the faith, not on the streets only, but in one's own house; death to mutilate an image; death to have in one's possession any of the writings of Luther, or Zwingle, or Œcolampadius; death to express doubt respecting the Sacraments of the Church, the authority of the Pope, or any similar dogma. After this, in 1535, came the edict of which we have just made mention, consigning to the horrors of a living grave even repentant heretics, and to the more dreadful horrors, as they were deemed, of the stake, obstinate ones. There was no danger of these cruel laws remaining inoperative, even had the emperor been less in earnest than he was. The Inquisition of Cologne, the canons of Louvain, and the monks of Mechlin saw to their execution; and the obsequiousness of Mary of Hungary, the regent of the kingdom, pushed on the bloody work, nor thought of pause till she should have reached the verge of "entire depopulation."

When Philip II. re-enacted the edict of 1540, he re-enacted the whole of that legislation which had disgraced the last thirty years of Charles's reign, and which, while it had not extinguished, nor even lessened the Lutheranism against which it was directed, had crippled the industry and commerce of the Low Countries. There had been a lull in the terrible work of beheading and burning men for conscience sake during the last few years of the emperor's reign; Charles's design, doubtless, being to smooth the way for his son. The fires were not extinguished, but they were lowered; the scaffolds were not taken down, but the blood that flooded them was less deep; and as during the last years of Charles, so also during the first years of Philip, the furies of persecution seemed to slumber. But now they awoke; and not only was the old condition of things brought back, but a new machinery, more sure, swift, and deadly than that in use under Charles, was constructed to carry out the edicts which Philip had published anew. The emperor had established a court in Flanders that sufficiently resembled the Inquisition; but Philip II. made a still nearer approach to that redoubtable institution, which has ever been the pet engine of the bigot and persecutor, and the execration of all free men. The court now established by Philip was, in fact, the Inquisition. It did not receive the name, it is true; but it was none the less the Inquisition, and lacked nothing which the "Holy Office" in Spain possessed. Like it, it had its dungeons and screws and racks. It had its apostolic inquisitors, its secretaries and sergeants. It had its familiars dispersed throughout the Provinces, and who acted as spies and informers. It apprehended men on suspicion, examined them by torture, and condemned them without confronting them with the witnesses, or permitting them to lead proof of their innocence. It permitted the civil judges to concern themselves with prosecutions for heresy no farther than merely to carry out the sentences the inquisitors had pronounced. The goods of the Victims were confiscated, and denunciations were encouraged by the promise of rewards, and also the assurance of impunity to informers who had been co-religionists of the accused.

Even among the submissive natives of Italy and Spain, the establishment of the Inquisition had encountered opposition; but among the spirited and wealthy citizens of the Netherlands, whose privileges had been expanding, and whose love of liberty had been growing, ever since the twelfth century, the introduction of a court like this was regarded with universal horror, and awakened no little indignation. One thing was certain, Papal Inquisition and Netherland freedom could not stand together. The citizens beheld, in long and terrible vista, calamity coming upon calamity; their dwellings entered at midnight by masked familiars, their parents and children dragged to secret prisons, the civic dignitaries led through the streets with halters round their necks, the foreign Protestant merchants fleeing from their country, their commerce dying, *autos da fé* blazing in all their cities, and liberty, in the end of the day, sinking under an odious and merciless tyranny.

There followed another measure which intensified the alarm and anger of the Netherlanders. The number of bishops was increased by Philip from four to seventeen. The existing sees were those of Arras, Cambray, Tournay, and Utrecht; to these thirteen new sees were added, making the number of bishoprics equal to that of the Provinces. The bull of Pius IV., ratified within a few months by that of Paul IV., stated that "the enemy of mankind being abroad, and the Netherlands, then under the sway of the beloved son of his Holiness, Philip the Catholic, being compassed about with heretic and schismatic nations, it was believed that the eternal welfare of the land was in great danger," hence the new labourers sent forth into the harvest. The object of the measure was transparent; nor did its authors affect to conceal that it was meant to strengthen the Papacy in Flanders, and extend the range of its right arm, the Inquisition. These thirteen new bishoprics were viewed by the citizens but as thirteen additional inquisitors.

These two tyrannical steps necessitated a third. Philip saw it advisable to retain a body of Spanish troops in the country to compel submission to the new arrangements. The number of Spanish soldiers at that moment in Flanders was not great: they amounted to only 4,000: but they were excellently disciplined: the citizens saw in them the sharp end of the wedge that was destined to introduce a Spanish army, and reduce their country under a despotism; and in truth such was Philip's design. Besides, these troops were insolent and rapacious to a degree. The inhabitants of Zealand refused to work on their dykes, saying they would rather that the ocean should swallow them up at once, than that they should be devoured piece-meal by the avarice and cruelty of the Spanish soldiers.[2764]

The measures adopted by Philip caused the citizens the more irritation and discontent, from the fact that they were subversive of the fundamental laws of the Provinces. At his accession Philip had taken an oath to uphold all the chartered rights of the Netherlanders; but the new edicts traversed every one of these rights. He had sworn to raise the clergy in the Provinces above the state in which he found them. In disregard of his solemn pledge, he had increased the ecclesiastical dioceses from four to seventeen. This was a formidable augmentation of the clerical force. The nobles looked askance on the new spiritual peers who had come to divide with them their influence; the middle classes regarded them as clogs on their industry, and the artisans detested them as spies on their freedom. The violation of faith on the part of their monarch rankled in their bosoms, and inspired them with gloomy forebodings as regarded the future. Another fundamental law, ever esteemed by the Netherlanders among the most valuable of their privileges, and which Philip had sworn to respect, did these new arrangements contravene. It was unlawful to bring a foreign soldier into the country. Philip, despite his oath, refused to withdraw his Spanish troops. So long as they remained, the Netherlanders well knew that the door stood open for the entrance of a much larger force. It was also provided in the ancient charters that the citizens should be tried before the ordinary courts and by the ordinary judges. But Philip had virtually swept all these courts away, and substituted in their room a tribunal that sat in darkness, that permitted those it dragged to its bar to plead no law, to defend themselves by no counsel, and that compelled the prisoner by torture to become his own accuser. Nor was this court required to assign, either to the prisoner himself or to the public, any reasons for the dreadful and horrible sentences it was in the habit of pronouncing. It was allowed the most unrestrained indulgence in a capricious and murderous tyranny. The ancient charters had farther provided that only natives should serve in the public offices, and that foreigners should be ineligible. Philip paid as little respect to this as to the rest of their ancient usages and rights. Introducing a body of foreign ecclesiastics and monks, he placed the lives and properties of his subjects of the Netherlands at the disposal of these strangers.

The ferment was great: a storm was gathering in the Low Countries: nor does one wonder when one reflects on the extent of the revolution which had been accomplished, and which outraged all classes. The hierarchy had been suddenly and portentously expanded: the tribunals had been placed in the hands of foreigners: in the destruction of their charters, the precious acquisitions of centuries had been swept away, and the citadel of their freedom razed. A foreign army was on their soil. The Netherlanders saw in all this a complete machinery framed and set up on purpose to carry out the despotism of the edicts.

The blame of the new arrangements was generally charged on the Bishop of Arras. He was a plausible, crafty, ambitious man, fertile in expedients, and even of temper. He was the ablest of the counsellors of Philip, who honoured him with his entire confidence, and consulted him on all occasions. Arras was by no means anxious to be thought the contriver, or even prompter, of that scheme of despotism which had supplanted the liberties of his native land; but the more he protested, the more did the nation credit him with the plan. To him had been assigned the place of chief authority among the new bishops, the Archbishopric of Mechlin. He was coy at first of the proffered dignity, and Philip had to urge him before he would accept the archiepiscopal mitre. "I only accepted it," we find him afterwards writing to the king, "that I might not live in idleness, doing nothing for God and your Majesty." If his See of Mechlin brought him labour, which he professed to wish, it brought him what he feigned not to wish, but which nevertheless he greedily coveted, enormous wealth and vast influence; and when the people saw him taking kindly to his new post, and working his way to the management of all affairs, and the control of the whole kingdom, they were but the more confirmed in their belief that the edicts, the new bishops the Inquisition, and the Spanish soldiers had all sprung from his fertile brain. The Netherlanders had undoubtedly to thank the Bishop of Arras for the first, the edicts namely, and these were the primal fountains of that whole tyranny that was fated to devastate the Low Countries. As regards the three last, it is not so clear that he had counselled their adoption. Nevertheless the nation persisted in regarding him as the chief conspirator against its liberties; and the odium in which he was held increased from day to day. Discontent was ripening into revolt.

Philip II. was probably the less concerned at this storm, which he could not but see was gathering, inasmuch as he contemplated an early retreat before it. He was soon to depart for Spain, and leave others to contend with the great winds he had unchained.

Before taking his departure, Philip looked round him for one whom he might appoint regent of this important part of his dominions in his absence. His choice lay between Christina, Duchess of Lorraine (his cousin), and Margaret, Duchess of Parma, a natural daughter of Charles V. He fixed at last on the latter, the Duchess of Parma. The Duchess of Lorraine would have been the wiser ruler; the Duchess of Parma, Philip knew, would be the more obsequious one. Her duchy was surrounded by Philip's Italian dominions, and she was willing, moreover, to send her son—afterwards the celebrated Alexander Farnese—on pretence of being educated at the court of Spain, but in reality as a pledge that she would execute to the letter the injunctions of Philip in her government of the Provinces. Though far away, the king took care to retain a direct and firm grasp of the Netherlands.[2765]

Under Margaret as regent, three Councils were organised—a Council of Finance, a Privy Council, and a Council of State, the last being the one of highest authority. These three Councils were appointed on the pretence of assisting the regent in her government of the Provinces, but in reality to mask her arbitrary administration by lending it the air of the popular will. It was meant that the government of the Provinces should possess all the simplicity of absolutism. Philip would order, Margaret would execute, and the Councils would consent; meanwhile the old charters of freedom would be sleeping their deep sleep in the tomb that Philip had dug for them; and woe to the man who should attempt to rouse them from their slumber!

Before setting sail, Philip convoked an assembly of the States at Ghent, in order to deliver to them his parting instructions. Attended by a splendid retinue, Philip presided at their opening meeting, but as he could not speak the tongue of the Flemings, the king addressed the convention by the mouth of the Bishop of Arras. The orator set forth, with that rhetorical grace of which he was a master, that "intense affection" which Philip bore to the Provinces; he next craved earnest attention to the three millions of gold florins which the king had asked of them; and these preliminaries dispatched, the bishop entered upon the great topic of his harangue, with a fervour that showed how much this matter lay on the heart of his master. The earnestness of the bishop, or rather of Philip, can be felt only by giving his words. "At this moment," said he, "many countries, and particularly the lands in my immediate neighbourhood, were greatly infested by various 'new, reprobate, and damnable sects;[2766] as these sects, proceeding from the foul fiend, father of discord, had not failed to keep those kingdoms in perpetual dissension and misery, to the manifest displeasure of God Almighty; as his Majesty was desirous to avert such terrible evils from his own realms, according to his duty to the Lord God, who would demand reckoning from him hereafter for the well-being of the Provinces; as all experience proved that change of religion ever brought desolation and confusion to the commonweal; as low persons, beggars, and vagabonds, under colour of religion, were accustomed to traverse the land for the purpose of plunder and disturbance; as his Majesty was most desirous of following in the footsteps of his lord and father; as it would be well remembered what the emperor had said to him on the memorable occasion of his abdication, therefore his Majesty had commanded the regent Margaret of Parma, for the sake of religion and the glory of God, accurately and exactly to cause to be enforced the edicts and decrees made by his Imperial Majesty, and renewed by his present Majesty, for the extirpation of all sects and heresies."[2766] The charge laid on the regent Margaret was extended to all governors, councillors, and others in authority, who were enjoined to trample heresy and heretics out of existence.

The Estates listened with intense anxiety, expecting every moment to hear Philip say that he would withdraw the Spanish troops, that he would lighten their heavy taxation, and that he would respect their ancient charters, which indeed he had sworn to observe. These were the things that lay near the hearts of the Netherlanders, but upon these matters Philip was profoundly silent. The convention begged till tomorrow to return its answer touching the levy of three millions which the king had asked for.

On the following day the Estates met in presence of the king, and each province made answer separately. The Estate of Artois was the first to read its address by its representative. They would cheerfully yield to the king, not only the remains of their property, but the last drop of their blood. At the hearing of these loyal words, a gleam of delight shot across the face of Philip. No ordinary satisfaction could have lighted up a face so habitually austere and morose. It was a burst of that "affection" which Philip boasted he bore the Netherlanders, and which showed them that it extended not only to them, but to theirs. But the deputy proceeded to append a condition to this apparently unbounded surrender; that condition was the withdrawal of the Spanish troops. Instantly Philip's countenance changed, and sinking into his chair of state, with gloomy and wrathful brow, the assembly saw how distasteful to Philip was the proposition to withdraw his soldiers from the Netherlands. The rest of the Estates followed; each, in its turn, making the same offer, but appending to it the same condition. Every florin of the three millions demanded would be forthcoming, but not a soldier must be left on the soil of the Provinces. The king's face grew darker still. Its rapid changes showed the tempest that was raging in his breast. To ask him to withdraw his soldiers was to ask him to give up the Netherlands. Without the soldiers how could he maintain the edicts and Inquisition? and these let go, the haughty and heretical Netherlands would again be their own masters, and would fill the Provinces with that rampant heresy which he had just cursed. The very idea of such a thing threw the king into a rage which he was at no pains to conceal.

But a still greater mortification awaited him before the convention broke up. A formal remonstrance on the subject of the Spanish soldiers was presented to Philip in the name of the States-General, signed by the Prince of Orange, Count Egmont, and many other nobles. The king was at the same time asked to annul, or at least to moderate, the edicts; and when one of his ministers represented, in the most delicate terms possible, that to persist in their execution would be to sow the seeds of rebellion, and thereby lose the sovereignty of the Provinces, Philip replied that "he had much rather be no king at all than have heretics for subjects."[2767]

So irritated was the king by these requests that he flung out of the hall in a rage, remarking that as he was a Spaniard it was perhaps expected that he, too, should withdraw himself. A day or two, however, sufficed for his passion to cool, and then he saw that his true policy was dissimulation till he should have tamed the stubbornness and pride of these Netherland nobles. He now made a feint of concession; he would have been glad, he said, to carry his soldiers with him in his fleet, had he been earlier made acquainted with the wishes of the Estates; he promised, however, to withdraw them in a few months. On the matter of Lutheranism he was inexorable, and could not even bring himself to dissemble. His parting injunction to the States was to pursue heresy with the halter, the axe, the stake, and other modes of death duly enacted and set forth in his own and his royal father's edicts.

On the 26th of August, Philip II., on the shore of Flushing, received the farewell salutations of the grandees of the Provinces, and then set sail for Spain, attended by a fleet of ninety vessels. He had quitted an angry land; around him was a yet angrier ocean. The skies blackened, the wind rose, and the tempest lay heavy upon the royal squadron. The ships were laden with the precious things of the Netherlands. Tapestries, silks, laces, paintings, marbles, and store of other articles which had been collected by his father, the emperor, in the course of thirty years, freighted the ships of Philip. He meant to fix his capital in Spain, and these products of the needles, the looms, and the pencils of his skilful and industrious subjects of the Low Countries were meant to adorn his palace. The greedy waves swallowed up nearly all that rich and various spoil. Some of the ships foundered outright; those that continued to float had to lighten themselves by casting their precious cargo into the sea. "Philip," as the historian Meteren remarks, "had robbed the land to enrich the ocean." The king's voyage, however, was safely ended, and on the 8th of September he disembarked at Loredo, on the Biscayan coast.

The gloomy and superstitious mind of Philip interpreted his deliverance from the storm that had burst over his fleet in accordance with his own fanatical notions. He saw in it an authentication of the grand mission with which he had been entrusted as the destroyer of heresy;[2768] and in token of thankfulness to that Power which had rescued him from the waves and landed him safely on Spanish earth, he made a vow, which found its fulfilment in the magnificent and colossal palace that rose in after-years on the savage and boulder-strewn slopes of the Sierra Guadarrama—the Escorial.

CHAPTER VI
STORMS IN THE COUNCIL, AND MARTYRS AT THE STAKE

THREE councils were organised, as we have said, to assist the Duchess of Parma in the government of the Provinces; the nobles selected to serve in these councils were those who were highest in rank, and who most fully enjoyed the confidence of their countrymen. This had very much the look of popular government. It did not seem exactly the machinery which a despot would set up. The administration of the Provinces appeared to be within the Provinces themselves, and the popular will, expressed through the members of the councils, must needs be an influential element in the decision of all affairs. And yet the administration which Philip had constructed was simply a despotism. He had so arranged it that the three councils were but one council; and the one council was but one man; and that one man was Philip's most obedient tool. Thus the government of the Netherlands was worked from Madrid, and the hand that directed it was that of the king.

A few words will enable us to explain in what way Philip contrived to convert this semblance of popular rule into a real autocracy. The affairs of the nation were managed neither by the Council of Finance, nor by the Privy Council, nor by the Council of State, but by a committee of the latter. That committee was formed of three members of the Council of State, namely, the Bishop of Arras, Viglius, and Berlaymont. These three men constituted a Consulta, or secret conclave, and it soon became apparent that in that secret committee was lodged the whole power of government. The three were in reality but one; for Viglius and Berlaymont were so thoroughly identified in sentiment and will with their chief, that in point of fact the Bishop of Arras was the Consulta. Arras was entirely devoted to Philip, and the regent, in turn, was instructed to take counsel with Arras, and to do as he should advise. Thus from the depths of the royal cabinet in Spain came the orders that ruled the Netherlands.

Margaret had been gifted by nature with great force of will. Her talents, like her person, were masculine. In happier circumstances, she would have made a humane as well as a vigorous ruler, but placed as she was between an astute despot, whom she dared not disobey, and an unscrupulous and cunning minister, whose tact she could not overrule, she had nothing for it but to carry out the high-handed measures of others, and so draw down upon herself the odium which of right belonged to guiltier parties. Educated in the school of Machiavelli, her statesmanship was expressed in a single word, *dissimulation*, and her religion taught her to regard thieves, robbers, and murderers as criminals less vile than Lutherans and Huguenots. Her spiritual guide had been Loyola.

Of Anthony Perrenot, Bishop of Arras, we have already spoken. He had been raised to the See of Mechlin, in the new scheme of the enlarged hierarchy; and was soon to be advanced to the purple, and to become known in history under the more celebrated title of Cardinal Granvelle. His learning was great, his wit was ready, his eloquence fluent, and his tact exquisite. His appreciation of men was so keen, penetrating, and perfect, that he clothed himself as it were with their feelings, and projects, and could be not so much *himself* as *them*. This rare power of sympathy, joined to his unscrupulousness, enabled him to inspire others with his own policy, in manner so natural and subtle that they never once suspected that it was his and not their own. By this masterly art—more real than the necromancy in which that age believed—he seated himself in Philip's cabinet—in Philip's breast—and dictated when he appeared only to obey. It is the fate of such men to be credited at times with sinister projects which have arisen not in their own brain, but in those of others, and thus it came to pass that the Bishop of Arras was believed to be the real projector, not only of the edicts, which Philip had republished at his suggestion, but also of that whole machinery which had been constructed for carrying them out—the new bishops, the Inquisition, and the Spanish soldiers. The idea refused to quit the popular mind, and as grievance followed grievance, and the nation saw one after another of its liberties invaded, the storm of indignation and wrath which was daily growing fiercer took at first the direction of the bishop rather than of Philip.

The new changes began to take effect. The bishops created by the recent bull for the extension of the hierarchy, began to arrive in the country, and claim possession of their several sees. Noble, abbot, and commoner with one consent opposed the entrance of these new dignitaries; the commoners because they were foreigners, the abbots because their abbacies had been partially despoiled to provide livings for them, and the nobles because they regarded them as rivals in power and influence. The regent Margaret, however, knowing how unalterable was Philip's will in the matter, braved the storm, and installed the new bishops. In one case she was compelled to yield. The populous and wealthy city of Antwerp emphatically refused to receive its new spiritual ruler. With the bishop they knew would come the Inquisition; and with secret denunciations, midnight apprehensions, and stakes blazing in their market-place they foresaw the flight of foreign merchants from their country, and the ruin of their commerce. They sent deputies to Madrid, who put the matter in this light before Philip; and the king, having respect to the state of his treasury, and the sums with which these wealthy merchants were accustomed to replenish his coffers, was graciously pleased meanwhile to tolerate their opposition.[2769]

At the State Council storms were of frequent occurrence. At that table sat men, some of whom were superior in rank to Arras, yet his equals in talent, and who moreover had claims on Philip's regard to which the bishop could make no pretensions, seeing they had laid him under great obligations by the brilliant services which they had rendered in the field. There were especially at that board the Prince of Orange and the Counts Egmont and Horn, who in addition to great wealth and distinguished merit, held high position in the State as the Stadtholders of important Provinces. Yet they were not consulted in the public business, nor was their judgment ever asked in State affairs; on the contrary, all matters were determined in secret by Granvelle. They were but puppets at the Council-board, while an arrogant and haughty ecclesiastic ruled the country.

Meanwhile the popular discontent was growing; Protestantism, which the regent and her ministers were doing all that the axe and the halter enabled them to do to extirpate, was spreading every day wider among the people. Granvelle ascribed this portentous growth to the negligence of the magistrates in not executing the "edicts." Orange and Egmont, on the other hand, threw the blame on the cardinal, who was replacing old Netherland liberty with Spanish despotism, and they demanded that a convention of the States should be summoned to devise a remedy for the commotions and evils that were distracting the kingdom.

This proposal was in the highest degree distasteful to Granvelle. He could tell beforehand the remedy which the convention would prescribe for the popular discontent. The convention, he felt assured, would demand the cancelling of the edicts, the suppression of the Inquisition, and the revival of those charters under which civil liberty and commercial enterprise had reached that palmy state in which the Emperor Charles had found them when he entered the Netherlands. Granvelle accordingly wrote to his master counselling him not to call a meeting of the States. The advice of the cardinal but too well accorded with the views of Philip. Instead of summoning a convention the king sent orders to the regent to see that the edicts were more vigorously executed. It was not gentleness but rigour, he said, that was needed for these turbulent subjects.

Things were taking an ominous turn. The king's letter showed plainly to the Prince of Orange, and Counts Egmont and Horn, that Philip was resolved at all hazards to carry out his grand scheme against the independence of the provinces. Not one of the edicts would he cancel; and so long as they continued in force Philip must have bishops to execute them, and Spanish soldiers to protect the bishops from the violence of an oppressed and indignant people. The regent, in obedience to the king's new missive, sent out fresh orders, urging upon the magistrates the yet hotter persecution of heresy. The executions were multiplied. The scaffolds made many victims, but not one convert. On the contrary, the Protestants increased, and every day furnished new evidence that sufferers for conscience sake were commanding the admiration of many who did not share their faith, and that their cause was attracting attention in quarters where before it had received no notice. The regent, and especially Granvelle, were daily becoming more odious. The meetings at the Council-board were stormier than ever. The bland insolence and supercilious haughtiness of the cardinal were no longer endurable by Egmont and Horn. Bluff, out-spoken, and irascible, they had come to an open quarrel with him. Orange could parry the thrust of Granvelle with a weapon as polished as his own, and so was able still to keep on terms of apparent friendliness with him; but his position in the Council, where he was denied all share in the government, and yet held responsible for its tyrannical proceedings, was becoming unbearable, and he resolved to bring it to an end. On the 23rd of July, 1561, Orange and Egmont addressed a joint letter to the king, stating how matters stood in Flanders, and craving leave to retire from the Council, or to be allowed a voice in those measures for which they were held to be responsible. The answer, which was far from satisfactory, was brought to Flanders by Count Horn, who had been on a visit to Madrid, and had parted from the king in a fume at the impertinence of the two Flemish noblemen. His majesty expected them to give attendance at the Council-board as aforetime, without, however, holding out to them any hope that they would be allowed a larger share than heretofore in the business transacted there.

The gulf between Orange and Cardinal Granvelle was widening. The cardinal did not abate a jot of his tyranny. He knew that Philip would support him in the policy he was pursuing; indeed, that he could not retain the favour of his master unless he gave rigorous execution to the edicts. He must go forward, it mattered not at what amount of odium to himself, and of hanging, burning, and burying alive of Philip's subjects of the Netherlands. Granvelle sat alone in his "smithy"—for so was his country house, a little outside the walls of Brussels, denominated—writing daily letters to Philip, insinuating or directly advancing accusations against the nobles, especially Orange and Egmont, and craftily suggesting to Philip the policy he ought to pursue. In reply to those letters would come fresh orders to himself and the regent, to adopt yet sterner measures toward the refractory and the heretical Netherlanders. He had suspended the glory of his reign on the trampling out of heresy in this deeply-infected portion of his dominions, and by what machinery could he do this unless by that which he had set up—the edicts, the bishops, and the Inquisition?— the triple wall within which he had enclosed the heretics of the Low Countries, so that not one of them should escape.

The Flemings are a patient and much-enduring people. Their patience has its limits, however, and these limits once passed, their determination and ire are in proportion to their former forbearance. As yet their submissiveness had not been exhausted; they permitted their houses to be entered at midnight, and themselves dragged from their beds and conducted to the Inquisition, with the meekness of a lamb that is being led to the slaughter; or if they opened their mouths it was only to sing one of Marot's psalms. The familiars of this abhorred tribunal, therefore, encountered hardly any resistance in executing their dreadful office. The nation as yet stood by in silence, and saw the agents of Granvelle and Philip hewing their victims in pieces with axes, or strangling them with halters, or drowning them in ponds, or digging graves for their living entombment, and gave no sign. But all the while these cruelties were writing on the nation's heart, in ineffaceable characters, an abhorrence of the Spanish tyrant, and a stern unconquerable resolve, when the hour came, to throw off his yoke. In the crowd of those monsters who were now revelling in the blood and lives of the Netherlanders, there stands out one conspicuous monster, Peter Titlemann by name; not that he was more cruel than the rest of the crew, but because his cruelty stands horridly out against a grim pleasantry that seems to have characterised the man. "Contemporary chroniclers," says Motley, "give a picture of him as of some grotesque yet terrible goblin, careering through the country by night or day, alone, on horseback, smiting the trembling peasants on the head with a great club, spreading dismay far and wide, dragging suspected persons from their firesides or their beds, and thrusting them into dungeons, arresting, torturing, strangling, burning, with hardly the shadow of a warrant, information, or process.[2770]

The whole face of the Low Countries during the years of which we write (1560–65), was crossed and recrossed with lines of blood, traced by the cruel feet of monsters like this man. It was death to pray to God in one's own closet; it was death not to bow when an image was carried past one in the street; it was death to copy a hymn from a Genevese psalter, or sing a psalm; it was death not to deny the heresy of which one was suspected when one was questioned, although one had never uttered it. The monster of whom we have made mention above one day arrested Robert Ogier of Ryssel, with his wife and two sons. The crime of which they were accused was that of not going to mass, and of practising worship at home. The civil judges before whom Titlemann brought them examined them touching the rites they practised in private. One of the sons answered, "We fall on our knees and pray that God may enlighten our minds and pardon our sins; we pray for our sovereign, that his reign may be prosperous, and his life happy; we pray for our magistrates, that God may preserve them." This artless answer, from a mere boy, touched some of the judges, even to tears. Nevertheless the father and the elder son were adjudged to the flames. "O God," prayed the youth at the stake, "Eternal Father, accept the sacrifice of our lives in the name of thy beloved Son!" "Thou liest, scoundrel!" fiercely interrupted a monk, who was lighting the fire. "God is not your father; ye are the devil's children." The flames rose; again the boy exclaimed, "Look, my father, all heaven is opening and I see ten hundred thousand angels rejoicing over us. Let us be glad, for we are dying for the truth." "Thou liest, thou liest," again screamed the monk; "I see hell opening, and ten thousand devils waiting to thrust you into eternal fire." The father and son were heard talking with one another in the midst of the flames, even when they were at the fiercest; and so they continued till both expired.[2771]

If the fury of the persecutor was great, not less was the heroism of the martyrs. They refused all communion with Rome, and worshipped in the Protestant forms, in the face of all the dreadful penalties with which they were menaced. Nor was it the men only who were thus courageous; women—nay, young girls— animated by an equal faith, displayed an equal fortitude. Some of them refused to flee when the means of escape from prison were offered to them. Wives would take their stand by their husband's stake, and while he was enduring the fire they would whisper words of solace, or sing psalms to cheer him; and so, in their own words, would they bear him company while "he was celebrating his last wedding feast." Young maidens would lie down in their living grave as if they were entering into their chamber of nightly sleep; or go forth to the scaffold and the fire, dressed in their best apparel, as if they were going to their marriage.[2772] In April, 1554, Galein de Mulere, schoolmaster at Oudenard, was arrested by Inquisitor Titlemann. The poor man was in great straits, for he had a wife and five young children, but he feared to deny God and the truth. He endeavoured to extricate himself from the dilemma by demanding to be tried before the magistrate, and not by the Inquisition. "You are my prisoner," replied Titlemann; "I am the Pope's and the emperor's plenipotentiary." The schoolmaster gave, at first, evasive answers to the questions put to him. "I adjure thee not to trifle with me," said Titlemann, and cited Scripture to enforce his adjuration; "St. Peter," said the terrible inquisitor, "commands us to be ready always to give to every man that asketh of us, a reason of the hope that is in us." On these words the schoolmaster's tongue broke loose. "My God, my God, assist me now according to thy promise," prayed he. Then turning to the inquisitors he said, "Ask me now what you please, I shall plainly answer." He then laid open to them his whole belief, concealing nothing of his abhorrence of Popery, and his love for the Saviour. They used all imaginable arts to induce him to recant; and finding that no argument would prevail with him, "Do you not love your wife and children?" said they to him as the last appeal. "You know," replied he, "that I love them from my heart; and I tell you truly, if the whole world were turned into gold, and given to me, I would freely resign it, so that I might keep these dear pledges with me in my confinement, though I should live upon bread and water." "Forsake, then," said Titlemann, "your heretical opinions, and then you may live with your wife and children as formerly." "I shall never," he replied, "for the sake of wife and children renounce my religion, and sin against God and my conscience, as God shall strengthen me with his grace." He was pronounced a heretic; and being delivered to the secular arm, he was strangled and burned.[2773]

The very idiots of the nation lifted up their voice in reproof of the tyrants, and in condemnation of the tyranny that was scourging the country. The following can hardly be read without horror. At Dixmuyde, in Flanders, lived one Walter Capel, who abounded in almsgiving, and was much beloved by the poor. Among others whom his bounty had fed was a poor simple creature, who hearing that his benefactor was being condemned to death (1553), forced his way into the presence of the judge, and cried out, "Ye are murderers, ye are murderers, ye spill innocent blood; the man has done no ill, but has given me bread." When Capel was burning at the stake, this man would have thrown himself into the flames and died with his patron, had he not been restrained by force. Nor did his gratitude die with his benefactor. He went daily to the gallows-field where the half-burned carcase was fastened to a stake, and gently stroking the flesh of the dead man with his hand, he said, "Ah, poor creature, you did no harm, and yet they have spilt your blood. You gave me my bellyful of victuals." When the flesh was all gone, and nothing but the bare skeleton remained, he took down the bones, and laying them upon his shoulders, he carried them to the house of one of the burgomasters, with whom it chanced that several of the magistrates were at that moment feasting. Throwing his ghastly burden at their feet, he cried out, "There, you murderers, first you have eaten his flesh, now eat his bones."[2773]

The following three martyrdoms connect themselves with England. Christian de Queker, Jacob Dienssart, and Joan Konings, of Stienwerk, in Flanders, had found an asylum in England, under Queen Elizabeth. In 1559, having visited their native country on private affairs, they fell into the hands of Peter Titlemann. Being brought before the inquisitors, they freely confessed their opinions. Meanwhile, the Dutch congregation in London procured letters from the Archbishop of Canterbury and other English prelates, which were forwarded to the magistrates of Furness, where they were confined in prison. The writers said that they had been informed of the apprehension of the three travellers; that they were the subjects of the Queen of England; that they had gone into the Low Countries to dispatch of their private affairs, with intent to return to England; that they had avoided disputes and contest by the way, and therefore could not be charged with the breach of any law of the land; that none of the Flemings had been meddled with in England, but that if now those who had put themselves under English jurisdiction, and were members of the English Church, were to be thus treated in other countries, they should be likewise obliged, though much against their wills, to deal out the same measure to foreigners. Nevertheless, they expected the magistrates of Furness to show prudence and justice, and abstain from the spilling of innocent blood.

The magistrates, on receipt of this letter, deputed two of their number to proceed to Brussels, and lay it before the Council. It was read at the Board, but that was all the attention it received. The Council resolved to proceed with the prisoners according to the edicts. A few days thereafter they were conducted to the court to receive their sentence, their brethren in the faith lining the way, and encouraging and comforting them. They were condemned to die. They went cheerfully to the stake. A voice addressing them from the crowd was heard, saying, "Joan, behave valiantly; the crown of glory is prepared for you." It was that of John Bels, a Carmelite friar. While the executioner was fastening them to the stake, with chains put round their necks and feet, they sang the 130th Psalm, "Out of the depths have I cried to thee, O Lord;" whereupon a Dominican, John Campo, cried out, "Now we perceive you are no Christians, for Christ went weeping to his death;" to which one of the bystanders immediately made answer, "That's a lie, you false prophet." The martyrs were then strangled and scorched, and their bodies publicly hung in chains in the gallows-field. Their remains were soon after taken down by the Protestants of Furness, and buried.[2775]

These men, although in number amounting to many thousands, were only the first rank of that greater army of martyrs which was to come after them. With the exception of a very few, we do not know even the names of the men who so willingly offered their lives to plant the Gospel in their native land. They were known only in the town, or village, or district in which they resided, and did not receive, as they did not seek, wider fame. But what matters it? They themselves are safe, and so too are their names. Not one of them but is inscribed in a record more lasting than the historian's page, and from which they can never be blotted out. They were mostly men in humble station—weavers, tapestry-workers, stone-cutters, tanners; for the nobles of the Netherlands, not even excepting the Prince of Orange, had not yet abjured the Popish faith, or embraced that of Protestantism. While the nobles were fuming at the pride of Granvelle, or humbly but uselessly petitioning Philip, or fighting wordy battles at the Council-board, they left it to the middle and lower classes to bear the brunt of the great war, and jeopardise their lives in the high places of the field. These humble men were the true nobles of the Netherlands. Their blood it was that broke the power of Spain, and redeemed their native land from vassalage. Their halters and stakes formed the basis of that glorious edifice of Dutch freedom which the next generation was to see rising proudly aloft, and which, but for them, would never have been raised.

CHAPTER VII
RETIREMENT OF GRANVELLE—BELGIC CONFESSION OF FAITH

THE murmurs of the popular discontent grew louder every day. In that land the storm is heard long to mutter before the sky blackens and the tempest bursts; but now there came, not indeed the hurricane—that was deferred for a few years—but a preliminary burst like the sudden wave which, while all as yet is calm, the ocean sends as the herald of the storm. At Valenciennes were two ministers, Faveau and Mallart, whose preaching attracted large congregations. They were condemned in the autumn of 1561 to be burned. When the news spread in Valenciennes that their favourite preachers had been ordered for execution, the inhabitants turned out upon the street, now chanting Clement Marot's psalms, and now hurling menaces at the magistrates should they dare to touch their preachers. The citizens crowded round the prison, encouraging the ministers, and promising to rescue them should an attempt be made to put them to death. These commotions were continued nightly for the space of six months. The magistrates were in a strait between two evils—the anger of the cardinal, who was daily sending them peremptory orders to have the heretics burned, and the wrath of the people, which was expressed in furious menaces should they do as Granvelle ordered. At last they made up their minds to brave what they took to be the lesser evil, for they trusted that the people would not dare openly to resist the law. The magistrates brought forth Faveau and Mallart one Monday morning, before sunrise, led them to the market-place, where preparations had been made, tied them to the stake, and were about to light the fires and consume them. At that moment a woman in the crowd threw her shoe at the stake; it was the preconcerted signal. The mob tore down the barriers, scattered the faggots, and chased away the executioners. The guard, however, had adroitly carried off the prisoners to their dungeon. But the people were not to be baulked; they kept possession of the street; and when night came they broke open the prison, and brought forth the two ministers, who made their escape from the city. This was called "The Day of the Ill-burned," one of the ministers having been scorched by the partially kindled faggots before he was rescued.[2776]

A terrible revenge was taken for the slur thus cast upon the Inquisition, and the affront offered to the authority of Granvelle. Troops were poured into the ill-fated city. The prisons were filled with men and women who had participated, or were suspected of having participated, in the riot. The magistrates who had trembled before were furious now. They beheaded and burned almost indiscriminately; the amount of blood spilt was truly frightful—to be remembered at a future day by the nation, and atonement demanded for it.

We return to the Council-board at Brussels, and the crafty tyrannical man who presided at it—and who, buried in the depths of his cabinet, edited his edicts of blood, and sent them forth to be executed by his agents. The bickerings still continued at the Council-table, much to the disgust of Granvelle. But besides the rough assaults of Egmont and Horn, and the delicate wit and ridicule of Orange, other assailants arose to embitter the cardinal's existence, and add to the difficulties of his position. The Duchess of Parma became alienated from him.

As regent, she was nominal head of the government, but the cardinal had reduced her to the position of a puppet, by grasping the whole power of the States, and leaving to her only an empty title. However, the cardinal consoled himself by reflecting that if he had lost the favour of Margaret, he could very thoroughly rely on that of Philip, who, he knew, placed before every earthly consideration the execution of his edicts against heresy. But what gave more concern to Granvelle was a class of foes that now arose outside the Council-chamber to annoy and sting him. These were the members of the "Rhetoric Clubs." We find similar societies springing up in other countries of the Reformation, especially in France and Scotland, and they owed their existence to the same cause that is said to make wit flourish under a despotism. These clubs were composed of authors, poetasters, and comedians; they wrote plays, pamphlets, pasquils, in which they lashed the vices and superstitions, and attacked the despotisms of the age. They not only assailed error, but in many instances they were also largely instrumental in the diffusion of truth. They discharged the same service to that age which the newspaper and the platform fulfil in ours. The literature of these poems and plays was not high; the wit was not delicate, nor the satire polished—the wood-carving that befits the interior of a cathedral would not suit for the sculpture-work of its front—but the writers were in earnest; they went straight to the mark, they expressed the pent-up feeling of thousands, and they created and intensified the feeling which they expressed.

Such was the battery that was now opened upon the minion of Spanish and Papal tyranny in the Low Countries. The intelligent, clever, and witty artisans of Ghent, Bruges, and other towns chastised Granvelle in their plays and lampoons, ridiculed him in their farces, laughed at him in their burlesques, and held him up to contempt and scorn in their caricatures. The weapon was rough, but the wound it inflicted was rankling. These farces were acted in the street, where all could see them, and the poem and pasquil were posted on the walls where all could read them. The members of these clubs were individually insignificant, but collectively they were most formidable. Neither the sacredness of his own purple, nor the dread of Philip's authority, could afford the cardinal any protection. As numerous as a crowd of insects, the annoyances of his enemies were ceaseless as their stings were countless. As a sample of the broad humour and rude but truculent satire with which Philip's unfortunate manager in the Netherlands was assailed, we take the following caricature. In it the worthy cardinal was seen occupied in the maternal labour of hatching a brood of bishops. The ecclesiastical chickens were in all stages of development. Some were only chipping the shell; some had thrust out their heads and legs; others, fairly disencumbered from their original envelopments, were running about with mitres on their heads. Each of these fledglings bore a whimsical resemblance to one or other of the new bishops. But the coarsest and most cutting part of the caricature remains to be noticed. Over the cardinal was seen to hover a dark figure, with certain appendages other than appertain to the human form, and that personage was made to say, "This is my beloved son, hear ye him."[2777]

Such continued for some years to be the unsatisfactory and eminently dangerous state of affairs in the Low Countries. The regent Margaret, humiliated by the ascendancy of Granvelle, and trembling at the catastrophe to which his rigour was driving matters, proposed that the States should be summoned, in order to concert measures for restoring the tranquillity of the nation. Philip would on no account permit such an assembly to be convoked. Margaret had to yield, but she resorted to the next most likely expedient. She summoned a meeting of the Knights of the Golden Fleece and the Stadtholders of the Provinces. Viglius, one of the members of Council, but less obnoxious than Granvelle, was chosen to address the knights. He was a learned man, and discoursed, with much plausibility and in the purest Latin, on the disturbed state of the country, and the causes which had brought it into its present condition. But it was not eloquence, but the abolition of the edicts and the suppression of the Inquisition, that was needed, and this was the very thing which Philip was determined not to grant. In vain had the Knights of the Fleece and the Stadtholders assembled. Still some good came of the gathering, although the result was one which Margaret had neither contemplated nor desired. The Prince of Orange called a meeting of the nobles at his own house, and the discussion that took place, although a stormy one, led to an understanding among them touching the course to be pursued in the future. The Lord of Montigny was sent as a deputy to Spain to lay the state of matters before Philip, and urge the necessity, if his principality of the Netherlands was to be saved, of stopping the persecution. Philip, who appeared to have devoted himself wholly to one object, the extirpation of heresy, was incapable of feeling the weight of the representations of Montigny. He said that he had never intended, and did not even now intend, establishing the Inquisition in the Low Countries in its Spanish form; and while he bade Montigny carry back this assurance—a poor one even had it been true—to those from whom he had come, he sent at the same time secret orders to Granvelle to carry out yet more rigorously the decrees against the heretics.

Orange, Egmont, and Horn, now utterly disgusted and enraged, retired from the Council-table. They wrote a joint letter to the king, stating the fact of their withdrawal, with the reasons which had led to it, and demanding the dismissal of the cardinal as the only condition on which they could resume their place at the Board. They also plainly avowed their belief that should Granvelle be continued in the administration, the Netherlands would be lost to Philip. The answer returned to this letter was meant simply to gain time. While Philip was musing on the steps to be taken, the fire was spreading. The three seigniors wrote again to the monarch. They begged to say, if the statement had any interest for him, that the country was on the road to ruin. The regent Margaret about the same time wrote also to her brother, the king. As she now heartily hated Granvelle, her representations confirmed those of Orange, although, reared as she had been in the school of Loyola, she still maintained the semblance of confidence in and affection for the cardinal. The king now began to deliberate in earnest. Pending the arrival of Philip's answer, the Flemish grandees, at a great feast where they all met, came to the resolution of adopting a livery avowedly in ridicule of the cardinal. Accordingly, in a few days, all their retainers appeared in worsted hose, and doublets of coarse grey, with hanging sleeves, but with no ornament whatever, except a fool's cap and bells embroidered upon each sleeve. The jest was understood, but the cardinal affected to laugh at it. In a little while the device was changed. The fool's cap and bells disappeared, and a sheaf of arrows came in the room of the former symbol.[2778] The sheaf of arrows, Granvelle, in writing to Philip, interpreted to mean "conspiracy." Meanwhile the king had made up his mind as to the course to be taken. He dispatched two sets of instructions to Brussels, one open and the other secret. According to the first, the Duchess Margaret was commanded to prosecute the heretics with more rigour than ever; the three lords were ordered to return to their posts at the Council-table; and the cardinal was told that the king, who was still deliberating, would make his resolution known through the regent. But by the secret letter, written at the same time, but sent from Madrid so as to arrive behind the others, Philip wrote to the cardinal, saying that it appeared to him that it *might be well* he should leave the Provinces for some days, in order to visit his mother, and bidding him ask permission to depart from the regent, whom he had secretly instructed to give such permission, without allowing it to be seen that these orders had come from the king.

The plan mystified all parties at the time, save Orange, who guessed how the matter really stood; but the examination of Philip's correspondence has since permitted this somewhat complicated affair to be unravelled. The king had, in fact, yielded to the storm and recalled Granvelle. All were delighted at the cardinal's new-sprung affection for his mother, and trusted that it would not cool as suddenly as it had arisen;[2779] in short, that "the red fellow," as they termed him, had taken a final leave of the country. Nor, indeed, did Granvelle ever return.

It is time that we should speak of the summary of doctrines, or Confession of Faith, which was put forth by these early Protestants of the Netherlands. About the year 1561, Guido de Bres, with the assistance of Adrian Saravia, and three other ministers, published a little treatise in French under the title of "A Confession of the Faith generally and unanimously maintained by the Believers dispersed throughout the Low Countries, who desire to live according to the purity of the holy Gospel of our Lord Jesus Christ."[2780] This treatise was afterwards translated into Dutch. Saravia, who assisted De Bres in the compilation of it, states in a letter which the historian Brandt says he had seen, that "Guido de Bres communicated this Confession to such ministers as he could find, desiring them to correct what they thought amiss in it, so that it was not to be considered as one man's work, but that none who were concerned in it ever designed it for a rule of faith to others, but only as a scriptural proof of what they themselves believed." In the year 1563, this Confession was published both in high and low Dutch. It consists of thirty-seven articles. Almost every one of these articles is formally and antithetically set over against some one dogma of Romanism. With the great stream of Reformation theology as set forth in the Confessions of the Protestant Churches, the Belgic Confession is in beautiful harmony. It differs from the Augsburg Confession under the head of the Lord's Supper, inasmuch as it repudiates the idea of consubstantiation, and teaches that the bread and wine are only symbols of Christ's presence, and signs and seals of the blessing. In respect of the true catholicity of the Church, the doctrine of human merit and good works, and the justification of sinners by faith alone, on the righteousness of Christ, and, in short, in all the fundamental doctrines of the Scriptures, the Belgic Confession is in agreement with the Augustine Creed, and very specially with the Confession of Helvetia, France, Bohemia, England, and Scotland. The Reformation, as we have seen, entered the Low Countries by the gate of Wittemberg, rather than by the gate of Geneva: nevertheless, the Belgic Confession has a closer resemblance to the theology of those countries termed *Reformed* than to that of those usually styled *Lutheran*. The proximity of Flanders to France, the asylum sought on the soil of the Low Countries by so many of the Huguenots, and the numbers of English merchants trading with the Netherlanders, or resident in their cities, naturally led to the greater prominence in the Belgic Confession of those doctrines which have been usually held to be peculiar to Calvinism; although we cannot help saying that a very general misapprehension prevails upon this point. With the one exception stated above, the difference on the Lord's Supper namely, the theology of Luther and the theology of Calvin set forth the same views of Divine truth, and as respects that class of questions confessedly in their full conception and reconcilement beyond the reach of the human faculties, God's sovereignty and man's free agency, the two great chiefs, whatever differences may have come to exist between their respective followers, were at one in their theology. Luther was quite as Calvinistic as Calvin himself.

The Belgic Creed is notable in another respect. It first saw the light, not in any synod or Church assembly, for as yet the Church of the Low Countries as an organised body did not exist; it had its beginning with a few private believers and preachers in the Netherlands. This is a very natural and very beautiful genesis of a creed, and it admirably illustrates the real object and end of the Reformers in framing their Confessions. They compiled them, as we see these few Flemish teachers doing, to be a help to themselves and to their fellow-believers in understanding the Scriptures, and to show the world what they believed to be the truth as set forth in the Bible. It did not enter into their minds that they were forging a yoke for the conscience, or a fetter for the understanding, and that they were setting up a barrier beyond which men were not to adventure in the inquiry after truth. Nothing was further from the thoughts of the Reformers than this; they claimed no lordship over the consciences of men. The documents which they compiled and presented to the world they styled not a decree, or a rule, must less a creation, but a Confession, and they issued their Confessions under this reservation, that the Bible alone possessed inherent authority, that it alone was complete and perfect, and that their confession was only an approximation, to be reviewed, altered, amended, enlarged, or abbreviated according as believers advanced in the more precise, full, and accurate understanding of the meaning of the Spirit speaking in the Word. We have nowhere found the views of the Reformers on this point so admirably set forth as in the celebrated John à Lasco's preface to his book on the Sacraments; and as this is a matter on which great misapprehension has been spread abroad, we shall here give his words. Speaking of the union of the Churches of Zurich and Geneva on the doctrine of the Lord's Supper, he says: "Our union is not so to be understood as if we designed to exclude the endeavours of all such as shall attempt to introduce a greater purity of doctrine. We perceive, indeed, that many things are now taught much better than formerly, and that many old ways of speaking, long before used in the Church, are now altered. In like manner it may hereafter happen, that some of our forms of speaking being changed, many things may be better explained. The Holy Ghost will doubtless be present with others, in the Church of Christ after us, as he has vouchsafed to be with us and our ancestors; for he proceeds gradually, or by steps, and gives an insensible increase of his gifts. And since we find that all things tend to farther perfection, I do not know, I own, whether it becomes us to endeavour to confine the gradual increase of his gifts within the compass of our forms of speaking, as within certain palisades and entrenchments; as if that same Spirit were not at liberty, like the wind, to blow how, and when, and where he listeth. I do not pretend to give a loose to the sowing of all kinds of new-fangled doctrines, but I contend for the liberty of adorning and explaining the foundations when once laid, and with design to show that the Spirit of God does not cease from daily imparting to us more and more light." How truly catholic! and how happily the mean is here struck between those who say that Confessions ought to be abolished because they tyrannically forbid progress, and those who hold that they are to be changed in not one iota, because they are already perfect!

This Confession of Faith, being revised by a synod that met in Antwerp in May, 1566, was in that year reprinted and published.[2781] Following the example of Calvin in his celebrated letter to the King of France, which accompanied his *Institutes*, the Reformed in the Netherlands prefaced their Confession of Faith with a letter to the King of Spain. Their Confession was their defence against the charges of heresy and disloyalty which had been preferred against them; it was their "protestation before God and his angels" that what they sought was "to enjoy the liberty of a pure conscience in serving God, and reforming themselves according to his Word and Holy Commandments;" and it was their appeal to be freed from "the excommunications, imprisonments, banishments, racks and tortures, and other numberless oppressions which they had undergone." They remind the king that it was not their weakness which prompted this appeal to his compassion; and that if they did not resist, it was not because they were few in number—"there being," say they, "above one hundred thousand souls in these Provinces who profess the same religion, of which they presented him the Confession"—but to prevent his "stretching out his hand to embrue and embathe it in the blood of so many poor innocent men," and thereby bringing calamity upon his kingdom and throne.

They appended to their Confession a "Representation" to the magistrates and higher powers throughout the Low Countries. In this Representation we see these Flemish Protestants taking their stand at the very threshold of the modern religious liberties. Nay, they so state the functions of the magistrate, and so define his jurisdiction, that fairly interpreted their words approximate very nearly, if not altogether, to our own idea of toleration. They indeed condemn those who taught that it is "unlawful for the magistrate to speak of the Scripture, or to judge of doctrines and matters of religion." But these words in their mouths have a very different meaning from that which they would have in ours. The Church of Rome said to the magistrates, You are not to speak of Scripture, nor to judge of doctrines; that belongs exclusively to us: you are to believe that whatever we call heresy, is heresy, and, without farther inquiry, are to punish it with the sword.

On the contrary, the Flemish Protestants vindicated the rights of princes and magistrates in this matter. They were not to be the blind tools of the Church in putting to death all whom she may choose to condemn as heretical. They must, for their own guidance, though not for the coercion of others, judge of doctrines and matters of religion. "They are not for going so far," they say, "as those good old fathers who say that our consciences are not to be molested, much less constrained or forced to believe, by any powers on earth, to whom the sword is only entrusted for the punishment of robbers, murderers, and the like disturbers of civil government." "We acknowledge," they add, "that the magistrate may take cognisance of heresies." But let us mark what sort of heresies they are of which the magistrate may take cognisance. They are heresies which involve "sedition and uproars against the government."[2782]

Thus again, when they explain themselves they come back to their grand idea of the freedom of conscience, as respects all human authority, in matters appertaining to God and his worship. Toleration had its birth in the same hour with Protestantism; and, like the twins of classic story, the two powers have flourished together and advanced by equal stages. Luther exhibited toleration in act; Calvin, ten years before the time of which we write, began to formulate it, when he took heresy, strictly so called, out of the jurisdiction of the magistrate, and left him to deal with blasphemy, "which unsettled the foundation of civil order;" and now we behold the Protestants of the Low Countries treading in the steps of the Reformer of Geneva, and permitting the magistrate to take cognisance of heresy only when it shows itself in disturbances and uproars. It is important to bear in mind that the Reformers had to fight two battles at once. They had to contend for the emancipation of the magistrate, and they had to contend for the emancipation of the conscience. When they challenged for the magistrate exemption from the authority of Rome, they had to be careful not to appear to exempt him from the authority of the law of God. The Papists were ever ready to accuse them of this, and to say that the Reformation had assigned an atheistic position to princes. If at times they appear to deny the toleration which at other times they teach, much, if not all, of this is owing to the double battle which the times imposed upon them—the emancipation of the magistrate from the enslavement of the Church, and the emancipation of the conscience from the enslavement of both the magistrate and the Church.

CHAPTER VIII
THE RISING STORM

THE cardinal had taken flight and was gone, but the Inquisition remained. So long as the edicts were in force, what could be expected but that the waves of popular tumult would continue to flow? Nevertheless, the three lords—Orange, Egmont, and Horn—came to the helm which Granvelle had been compelled to let go, and, along with the regent, worked hard, if haply the shipwreck that appeared to impend over the vessel of the State might be averted. The clear eye of Orange saw that there was a deeper evil at work in the country than the cardinal, and he demanded the removal of that evil. Two measures he deemed essential for the restoration of quiet, and he strenuously urged the instant adoption of these:—first, the assembling of the States-General; and secondly, the abolition of the edicts. The prince's proposition struck at the evil in both its roots. The States-General, if permitted to meet, would resume its government of the nation after the ancient Flemish fashion, and the abolition of the edicts would cut the ground from under the feet of the bishops and the inquisitors—in short, it would break in pieces that whole machinery by which the king was coercing the consciences and burning the bodies of his subjects. These two measures would have allayed all the ferment that was fast ripening into revolt. But what hope was there of their adoption? None whatever while Philip existed, or Spain had a single soldier at her service or a single ducat in her treasury. The Prince of Orange and his two fellow-councillors, however, let slip no opportunity at the Council-board of urging the expediency of these measures if the country was to be saved. "It was a thing altogether impracticable," they said, "to extirpate such a multitude of heretics by the methods of fire and sword. On the contrary, the more these means were employed, the faster would the heretics multiply."[2783] Did not facts attest the truth and wisdom of their observation? Neither cords nor stakes had been spared, and yet on every hand the complaint was heard that heresy was spreading.

Waxing yet bolder, at a meeting of Council held towards the end of the year (1564), the Prince of Orange energetically pleaded that, extinguishing their fires, they should give liberty to the people to exercise their religion in their own houses, and that in public the Sacrament should be administered under both kinds. "With commotions and reformations on every side of them," he said, "it was madness to think of maintaining the old state of matters by means of placards, inquisitions, and bishops. The king ought to be plainly informed what were the wishes of his subjects, and what a mistake it was to propose enforcing the decrees of the Council of Trent, while their neighbours in Germany, as well Roman Catholics as Protestants, had indignantly rejected them." "As for himself," he said, in conclusion, "although resolved to adhere to the Roman Catholic religion, he could not approve that princes should aim at any dominion over the souls of men, or deprive them of the freedom of their faith and religion."

The prince warmed as he spoke. His words flowed like a torrent. Hour passed after hour, and yet there were no signs of his oration drawing to a close. The councillors, who usually sat silent, or contented themselves with merely giving a decorous assent to the propositions of Granville, might well be astonished at the eloquence that now resounded through the Council-chamber. It was now seven o'clock of the evening, and the orator would not have ended even yet, had not the Duchess of Parma hinted that the dinner-hour had arrived, and that the debate must be adjourned for the day. Viglius, who had taken the place of the cardinal at the Council-table, went home to his house in a sort of stupefaction at what he had witnessed. He lay awake all night ruminating on the line of argument he should adopt in reply to Orange. He felt how necessary it was to efface the impression the prince's eloquence had made. The dawn found him still perturbed and perplexed. He got up, and was dressing himself, when a stroke of apoplexy laid him senseless upon the floor. The disease left him shattered in mind as in body, and his place at the Council-board had to be supplied by his friend Joachin Hopper, a professor of Louvain, but a man of very humble parts, and entirely subservient to the regent.[2784]

It was resolved to dispatch Count Egmont to Madrid, to petition Philip for permission to the States-General to meet, as also for some mitigation of the edicts. But first the terms of Egmont's instructions had to be adjusted. The people must not cry too loudly, lest their tyrant should heat their furnace seven-fold. But it was no easy matter to find mild epithets to designate burning wrongs. Words that might appear sufficiently humble and loyal on the comparatively free soil of the Low Countries, might sound almost like treason when uttered in the Palace of Spain. This delicate matter arranged, Egmont set out. A most courteous reception awaited the deputy of the Netherlands on his arrival at Madrid. He was caressed by the monarch, fêted and flattered by the nobles, loaded with rich gifts; and these blandishments and arts had the effect, which doubtless they were meant to produce, of cooling his ardour as the advocate of his country. If the terms of the remonstrance which Egmont was to lay at the foot of the throne had been studiously selected so as not to grate on the royal ear, before the ambassador left Flanders, they were still further softened by Egmont now that he stood on Spanish soil. Philip frequently admitted him to a private audience, and consulted with him touching the matters respecting which he had been deputed to his court. The king professed to defer much to Egmont's opinion; he gave no promise, however, that he would change his policy as regarded religious matters, or soften in aught the rigours of the edicts. But to show Egmont and the seigniors of the Netherlands through him, that in this he was impelled by no caprice of cruelty or bigotry, but on the contrary was acting from high and conscientious motives, Philip assembled a council of divines, at which Egmont assisted, and put to them the question, whether he was bound to grant that liberty of conscience which some of the Dutch towns so earnestly craved of him? The judgment of the majority was that, taking into account the present troubles in the Low Countries—which, unless means were found for allaying them, might result in the Provinces falling away from their obedience to the king's authority, and to their duty to the one true Church—his Majesty might accord them some freedom in matters of religion without sinning against God. On this judgment being intimated to Philip, he informed the Fathers that they had misapprehended the special point of conscience he wished to have resolved. What he desired to know was, whether he *must*, not whether he *might* grant the liberty his Flemish subjects desired. The ecclesiastics made answer plainly that they did not think that the king was bound in conscience to do so. Whereupon Philip, falling down before a crucifix, addressed it in these words:—"I beseech thee, O God and Lord of all things, that I may persevere all the days of my life in the same mind as I am now, never to be a king, nor called so of any country, where thou art not acknowledged for Lord."[2785]

Egmont's embassy to the court of Spain being now ended, he set out on his return to the Low Countries. He was accompanied on his journey by the young Prince Alexander of Parma, the nephew of Philip, and son of Margaret, Regent of the Netherlands, and whose destiny it was in after-years to be fatally mixed up with the tragic woes of that land on which he now set foot for the first time. The results of Egmont's mission were already known at Brussels by letters from Spain, which, although written after his departure from Madrid, had arrived before him; nevertheless, he appeared in the Council on the 5th of May, 1565, and gave in a report of the measures which the king had in contemplation for the pacification of the Provinces. The Prince of Orange clearly saw that the "holy water" of the court had been sprinkled on Egmont, and that the man who had gone forth a patriot had come back a courtier and apologist. The deputy informed the Council that on the matter of the edicts no relaxation was to be expected. Heresy must be rooted out. Touching the meeting of the States-General, the king would send his decision to the regent. This was all. Verily Egmont had gone far and brought back little. But he had a little codicil or postscript in reserve for the Council, to the effect that Philip graciously granted leave for a synod of ecclesiastics, with a few civilians, to convene and concert measures for the instruction of the people, the reformation of the schools, and the purgation of heresy. And further, if the penal laws now in use did not serve their end, they had Philip's permission to substitute others "more efficacious." The Prince of Orange and others were willing to believe that by the "more efficacious" methods against heresy, milder methods only could be intended, seeing that it would be hard to invent measures more rigorous than those now in use; such, however, was not the meaning of Philip.[2786]

During the absence of Egmont, the persecution did not slacken. In February, Joost de Cruel was beheaded at Rosen. He had been first drawn to the Reformed faith by a sermon by Peter Titlemann, Dean of Rosen, who had since become the furious persecutor we have described above. In the same month, John Disreneaux, a man of seventy years, was burned at Lisle. At the same time, John de Graef was strangled and burned at Hulst, with the New Testament hung around his neck. His persecutors had subjected him while in prison to the extremities of hunger, and thirst, and cold, in the hope of subduing him. Mortification had set in, and he went halting to death, his frost-bitten toes and feet refusing their office. Tranquil and courageous, notwithstanding, he exhorted the bystanders, if they had attained a knowledge of the truth, not to be deterred by the fear of death from confessing it. In the following month, two youths were discovered outside the town of Tournay reading the Scriptures. An intimacy of the closest kind, hallowed by their love of the Gospel, had knit them together all their lives; nor were they parted now. They were strangled and burned at the same stake.[2787] Considering the number and the barbarity of these executions, it does not surprise one that Orange and his associates believed that if the methods of extirpating heresy were to be changed, it could only be for milder inflictions. They had yet to learn the fertility of Philip's inventive genius.

Scarcely had Egmont given in his report of his mission, when new instructions arrived from Philip, to the effect that not only were the old placards to be rigorously enforced, but, over and above, the canons of the Council of Trent were to be promulgated as law throughout the Netherlands. These canons gave the entire power of trying and punishing heretics to the clergy. In short, they delivered over the inhabitants of the Netherlands in all matters of opinion to the sole irresponsible and merciless jurisdiction of the Inquisition. Alarm, terror, and consternation overspread the Provinces. The nobles, states, and cities sent deputies to the governor to remonstrate against the outrage on their ancient rights about to be perpetrated, and the destruction into which such a policy was sure to drag the country. "There could be no viler slavery," they said, "than to lead a trembling life in the midst of spies and informers, who registered every word, action, look, and even every thought which they pretended to read from thence.' The four chief cities of Brabant, Louvain, Brussels, Antwerp, and Bois le Duc sent deputies to the Chancellor and Council of that Province, to say plainly that the orders of Philip were sounding the death-knell of the Province; the foreign merchants were making haste to get away, the commerce of their States was hastening to extinction, and soon their now-flourishing country would be a "mere wilderness." The Prince of Orange wrote to the Duchess of Parma to the effect that if this business of burning, beheading, and drowning was to go on, he begged that some other might be invested with the functions with which his sovereign had clothed him, for he would be no party to the ruin of his country, which he as clearly foresaw as he was powerless to avert. Other Stadtholders wrote to the Duchess of Parma, in reply to her earnest exhortations to assist in carrying out the edicts, saying that they were not inclined to be the lifeguards of the Inquisition. One of the chief magistrates of Amsterdam, a Roman Catholic, happening one day to meet a sheriff who was very zealous in the work of persecution, thus addressed him: "You would do well, when called to appear before the tribunal of God, to have the emperor's placards in your hand, and observer how far they will bear you out." Papers were being daily scattered in the streets and posted on the gates of the palace of Orange, and of other nobles, calling on them to come to their country's help in its hour of need, to the end that, the axe and the halter being abolished in the affairs of religions, every one might be able to live and die according to his conscience.

On the other hand, the governor was besieged by remonstrances and outcries from the bishops and monks, who complained that they were withstood in carrying out their sovereign's wish in the matter of the execution of the edicts. The aid they had been encouraged to expect in the work of the extirpation of heresy was withheld from them. The tribunals, prisons, and scaffolds of the country had been made over to them, and all magistrates, constables, and gaolers had been constituted their servants; nevertheless, they were often denied the use of that machinery which was altogether indispensable if their work was to be done, not by halves, but effectually. They had to bear odium and calumny, nay, sometimes they were in danger of their lives, in their zeal for the king's service and the Church's glory. On all sides is heard the cry that heresy is increasing, continued these much-injured men; but how can it be that heretics should not multiply, they asked, when they were denied the use of prisons in which to shut them up, and fires in which to burn them? The position of the Duchess of Parma was anything but pleasant. On the one side she was assailed by the screams and hootings of this brood of Inquisitors; and on the other was heard the muttered thunder of a nation's wrath.[2788]

Rocked thus on the great billows, the Duchess of Parma wrote to her brother, letting him know how difficult and dangerous her position had become, and craving his advice as to how she ought to steer amid tempests so fierce, and every hour growing fiercer. Philip replied that the edicts must ever be her beacon-lights. Philip's will was unalterably fixed on the extirpation of heresy in his kingdom of the Netherlands, and that will must be the duchess's pole-star. Nevertheless, the tyrant was pleased to set his wits to work, and to devise a method by which the flagrancy, but not the cruelty, of the persecution might be abated. Instead of bringing forth the heretic, and beheading or burning him at midday, he was to be put to death in his prison at midnight. The mode of execution was as simple as it was barbarous. The head of the prisoner was tied between his knees with a rope, and he was then thrown into a large tub full of water, kept in the prison for that use. This Christian invention is said to have been the original device of the "most Catholic king." The plea which Bishop Biro of Wesprim set up in defence of the clemency of the Church of Rome, would have been more appropriate in Philip's mouth, its terms slightly altered, than it was in the mouth of the bishop. "It is a calumny to say that the Church of Rome is bloodthirsty," said the worthy prelate, Biro; "that Church has always been content if heretics were burned."

A new and dreadful rumour which began to circulate through the Netherlands, added to the alarm and terrors of the nation. It was during this same summer that Catherine de Medici and the Duke of Alva held their celebrated conference at Bayonne. Soon thereafter, whispers which passed from land to land, and from mouth to mouth, reached the Low Countries, that a dark plot had been concocted between these two personages, having for its object the utter extirpation of the new opinions. These rumours corresponded with what was said to have been agreed upon at one of the last sessions of the Council of Trent, which had closed its sittings the year before, and on that account greater stress was laid on these whispers. They appeared to receive still further authentication, at least in the eyes of William, Prince of Orange, from the circumstance that a plot precisely identical had been disclosed to him six years before, by Henry II., when the king and the prince were hunting together in the Wood of Vincennes. The rest of the hunting-party had left them, Henry and William were alone, and the mind of the French king being full of the project, and deeming the prince, then the intimate friend of both Philip II. and the Duke of Alva, a safe depositary of the great secret, he unhappily for himself, but most happily for humanity, communicated to the prince the details of the plan.[2789] Henry II. told him how apprehensive he was of his throne being swept away in the flood of Protestantism, but he hoped, with the help of his son-in-law Philip II., soon to rid France of the last Huguenot. The monarch went on to explain to the prince how this was to be done, by entrapping the Protestants at the first convenient moment, destroying them at a single blow; and extending the same thorough purgation to all countries to which heresy had spread. William could not have been more astounded although the earth had suddenly yawned at his feet; however, he carried the secret in his breast from that dark wood, without permitting the French king to read, by word or look of his, the shock the disclosure had given him. And he retained it in his breast for years, without speaking of it to any one, although from the moment of his coming to the knowledge of it, it began to shape his conduct. It is from this circumstance that he received the significant name of "William the Silent."

All three—the rumours from Bayonne, the tidings from the Council of Trent, and the dark secret imparted to William in the Forest of Vincennes—pointed to a storm now gathering, of more than usual severity, and which should burst over all Christendom, in which the Netherlands could not miss having their full share. But what had been plotted at Trent among the Fathers was nearly as little known as what had been agreed on at Bayonne, between Catherine and Alva. The full truth—the definite plan—was locked up in the archives of the Vatican, whence it is probable its first suggestion had come, and in the breasts of the little coterie that met at the closing sessions of the Council. But a paper by one of the secretaries of Cardinal Boromeo, since given to the world, has published on the housetops what was then spoken in whispers in the cabinets of kings or the conclaves of ecclesiastical synods. "First, in order that the business may be conducted with the greater authority, they" (the Fathers of the Council) "advise to commit the superintendence of the whole affair to Philip the Catholic king, who ought to be appointed with common consent the head and conductor of the whole enterprise." The Catholic king was to begin by preferring a complaint to his neighbour, Anthony Bourbon, King of Navarre, "that, contrary to the institutions of his predecessors, he entertains and nourishes a new religion." Should the King of Navarre turn a deaf ear to this remonstrance, Philip was to essay him "by fair promises to draw him off from his wicked and unhappy design." He was to hold out to him the hope of having that portion of his ancestral dominions of which he had been stripped, restored, or an equivalent given him in some other part of Europe. Should Philip succeed in soothing him, "the operations of the future war will then be rendered more easy, short, and expeditious." If he still continued obstinate, the King of Spain was to "intermix some threatenings with his promises and flatteries." Meanwhile Philip was to be collecting an army "as privily as possible;" and in the event of the King of Navarre continuing obdurate, the Spanish king was to fall upon him suddenly and unawares, and chase him from his kingdom, which the leaguers were to occupy.

From the mountains of Navarre, the war was to be moved down to the plains. The Huguenots of France were to be extirpated root and branch. For the execution of this part of the programme, the main stress was rested on the zeal of the Duke of Guise, aided by reinforcements from Spain. While the sword was busy drowning the plains of that country in Protestant blood, such of the German princes as were Roman Catholic were to stop the passes into France, lest the Protestant princes should send succour to their brethren. Shut in, and left to contend unaided with two powerful armies, the fall of French Protestantism could not be doubtful. France, chastised and restored to obedience to the Roman See, would regain her pristine purity and glory.

Matters being thus "ordered in France," Germany was next to be undertaken. "Luther and his era"—that hour of portentous eclipse which had thrust itself into Germany's golden day—must be razed from the tablets and chronicles of the Fatherland, nor ever be once remembered or spoken of by the generations to come. "It will be necessary," says the document from which we quote, "with men collected from all quarters, to invade Germany, and with the aid of the emperor and the bishops, to render and restore it again to the Holy Apostolic See." It was arranged that this war of purgation should support itself. "The Duke of Guise shall lend to the emperor and the other princes of Germany, and the ecclesiastical lords, all the money that shall be gathered from the spoils and confiscations of so many noble, powerful, and wealthy citizens as shall be killed in France on account of the new religion, which will amount to a very great sum; the said Lord of Guise taking sufficient caution and security, that so he may, after the conclusion of the war, be reimbursed of all the money employed for that purpose, from the spoils of the Lutherans and others who shall, on account of religion, be slain in Germany."

What of Helvetia while this great conflagration should be raging all round it? At the cry of their brethren the Reformed Swiss would rush from their mountains to aid their co-religionists. To prevent their doing so, work was to be found for them at home. "For fear," says the document, "that the cantons of Switzerland should lend aids, it is necessary that the cantons which continue still obedient to the Roman Church declare war against the rest, and that the Pope assist these cantons that are of his religion to the utmost of his power."

The branches cut off in France and Germany, a last and finishing blow was to be dealt at the root of the tree in Geneva. "The Duke of Savoy, whilst the war thus embroils France and the Swiss, shall rush suddenly and unexpectedly with all his forces upon the city of Geneva, on the lake of Leman, assault it by force, and shall not abandon it nor withdraw his men until he become master and obtain full possession of the said city, putting to the point of the sword, or casting into the lake, every living soul who shall be found therein, without any distinction of age or sex; that all may be taught that the Divine Power in the end hath compensated for the delay of the punishment by the greatness and severity of it."[2790]

The tempest seemed about to burst in the days of Henry II., but the fatal tournament which sent that monarch to a premature grave drew off the storm for a time. It continued, however, to lower in the sky of Europe; the dark cloud would at times approach as if about to break, and again it would roll away. At last it exploded in the St. Bartholomew Massacre, and its awful reverberations were reiterated again and again in the wars of Philip II. in the Low Countries, and in the campaigns and battles which for thirty years continued to devastate Germany.

CHAPTER IX
THE CONFEDERATES OR "BEGGARS"

FINDING that new and more tyrannical orders were every day arriving from Spain, and that the despot was tightening his hold upon their country, the leading nobles of the Netherlands now resolved to combine, in order to prevent, if possible, the utter enslavement of the nation. The "Compromise," as the league of the nobles was called, was formed early in the year 1566. Its first suggestion was made at a conventicle, held on the Prince of Parma's marriage-day (3rd of November, 1565), at which Franciscus Junius, the minister of the Walloon or Huguenot congregation in Antwerp, preached.[2791] This Junius, who was a Frenchman and of noble birth, had studied at Geneva, and though not more than twenty years of age, his great learning and extraordinary talents gave his counsel weight with the Flemish nobles who sometimes consulted him in case of emergency. As he studied Tully, *De Legibus*, in his youth, there came one who said to him, in the words of the epicure, "God cares for none of us," and plied Junius with arguments so subtle that he sucked in the poison of this dreary belief. Libertinism laid the reins on the neck of passion. But a marvellous escape from death, which he experienced at Lyons about a year afterwards, arrested him in his wickedness. He opened the New Testament, and the passage on which his eyes first lighted was this: "In the beginning was the Word, and the Word was with God, and the Word was God," &c. As the stars grow dim and vanish when the sun rises, so the wisdom and eloquence of the pagans paled before the surpassing majesty and splendour of the Gospel by St. John. "My body trembled," said he, "my mind was astonished, and I was so affected all that day that I knew not where nor what I was. Thou wast mindful of me, O my God, according to the multitude of thy mercies, and calledst home thy lost sheep into the fold." From that day he studied the Scriptures; his life became pure; and his zeal waxed strong in proportion as his knowledge enlarged. He possessed not a little of the fearless spirit of the great master at whose feet he had sat. He would preach, at times, with the stake standing in the square below, and the flames in which his brethren were being burned darting their lurid flashes through the windows of the apartment upon the faces of his audience.[2792] On the present occasion the young preacher addressed some twenty of the Flemish nobles, and after sermon a league against the "barbarous and violent Inquisition" was proposed. All Brussels was ringing with the marriage festivities of Parma. There were triumphal arches in the street, and songs in the banquet-hall; deep goblets were drained to the happiness of Parma, and the prosperity of the great monarchy of Spain. At the same moment, in the neighbouring town of Antwerp, those movements were being initiated which were to loosen the foundations of Philip's empire, and ultimately cast down the tyrant from the pinnacle on which he so proudly, and as he deemed so securely, stood.

The aims of the leaguers were strictly constitutional; they made war only against the Inquisition, "that most pernicious tribunal, which is not only contrary to all human and divine laws, but exceeds in cruelty the most barbarous institutions of the most savage tyrants in the heathen world." "For these reasons," say they, "we whose names are here subscribed have resolved to provide for the security of our families, goods, and persons; and for this purpose we hereby enter into a secret league with one another, promising with a solemn oath to oppose with all our power the introduction of the above-mentioned Inquisition into these Provinces, whether it shall be attempted secretly or openly, or by whatever name it shall be called. . . . We likewise promise and swear mutually to defend one another, in all places, and on all occasions, against every attack that shall be made, or prosecution that shall be raised, against any individual among us on account of his concern in this Confederacy."[2793] The first three who took the pen to sign this document were Count Brederode, Charles de Mansfeld, and Louis of Nassau. Copies were circulated over the country, and the subscribers rapidly multiplied. In the course of two months, 2,000 persons had appended their names to it. Tidings of the league were wafted to the ears of the governor, and it was added—a slighted exaggeration, it may be—that it was already 15,000 strong.[2794] Roman Catholics as well as Protestants were permitted to sign, and the array now gathering round this uplifted standard was, as may be supposed, somewhat miscellaneous.

The Duchess of Parma was startled by the sudden rise of this organisation, whose numbers increased every day. Behind her stood Philip, whose truculent orders left her no retreat; before her was the Confederacy, a less formidable but nearer danger. In her perplexity the governor summoned the Knights of the Fleece and the Stadtholders of the Provinces, to ask their advice touching the steps to be taken in this grave emergency. Two courses, she said, appeared to be open to her—the one was to modify the edicts, the other was to suppress the Confederacy by arms; the latter course, she said, was the one to which she leaned, especially knowing how inexorable was the will of the king, but her difficulty lay in finding one to whom she could safely entrust the command of the troops. Orange was disqualified, having pronounced so strongly against the edicts and in favour of liberty of conscience; and Egmont had positively declined the task, saying that "he would never fight for the penal laws and the Inquisition."[2795] What was to be done?

While the Council was deliberating, the Confederates arrived in a body at Brussels. On the 3rd of April, 1566, a cavalcade of 200 nobles and knights, headed by the tall, military form of Broderode, rode into Brussels. The nobleman who was foremost in the procession traced his lineage backwards 500 years, in unbroken succession, to the old sovereigns of Holland. Amid the chances and turnings of the contest now opening, who could tell whether the sovereignty of the old country might not return to the old line? Such was the vision that may have crossed the mind of Brederode. The day following the number of Confederates in Brussels was augmented by the arrival of about 100 other cavaliers. Their passage through the streets was greeted, as that of the first had been, by the acclamations of the populace. "There go," said they, "the deliverers of our country." Next day, the 5th of April, the whole body of Confederates, dressed in their richest robes, walked in procession to the old palace of Brabant, and passing through the stately hall in which Charles V. eleven years before had abdicated his sovereignties, they entered the audience chamber of the Regent of the Netherlands. Margaret beheld not without emotion this knightly assemblage, who had carried to her feet the wrongs of an oppressed nation. Brederode acted as spokesman. The count was voluble. Orange possessed the gift of eloquence, but the latter had not yet enrolled himself among the Confederates. William the Silent never retraced his steps, and therefore he pondered well his path before going forward. He could not throw down the gauntlet to a great monarchy like Spain with the light-hearted, jaunty defiance which many of the signatories of the Confederacy were now hurling against the tyrant, but whose heroism was likely to be all expended before it reached the battlefield, in those Bacchanalian meetings then so common among the Flemish nobles.

Brederode on this occasion was prudently brief. After defending himself and his associates from certain insinuations which had been thrown out against their loyalty, he read the petition which had been drafted in view of being presented to the duchess, in order that she might convey it to Philip. The petition set forth that the country could no longer bear the tyranny of the edicts: that rebellion was rearing its head, nay, was even at the palace-gates; and the monarch was entreated, if he would not imperil his empire, to abolish the Inquisition and convoke the States-General. Pending the king's answer, the duchess was asked to suspend the edicts, and to stop all executions for religious opinion.[2796]

When Brederode had finished, the duchess sat silent for a few minutes. Her emotion was too great to be disguised, the tears rolling down her cheeks.[2797] As soon as she had found words she dismissed the Confederates, telling them that she would consult with her councillors, and give her answer on the morrow. The discussion that followed in the council-hall, after Brederode and his followers had withdrawn, was a stormy one. The Prince of Orange argued strongly in favour of liberty of conscience, and Count Berlaymont, a keen partisan of Rome and Spain, argued as vehemently, if not as eloquently, against the Confederates and the liberty which they craved. This debate is famous as that in which Berlaymont first applied to the Confederates an epithet which he meant should be a brand of disgrace, but which they accepted with pride, and wore as a badge of honour, and by which they are now known in history. "Why, madam," asked Berlaymont of the duchess, observing her emotion, "why should you be afraid of these beggars?" The Confederates caught up the words, and at once plucked the sting out of them. "Beggars, you call us," said they; "henceforth we shall be known as beggars."[2798] The term came soon to be the distinguishing appellation for all those in the Netherlands who declared for the liberties of their country and the rights of conscience. They never met at festival or funeral without saluting each other as "Beggars." Their cry was "Long live the Beggars!" They had medals struck, first of wax and wood, and afterwards of silver and gold, stamped on the one side with the king's effigies, and on the other with a beggar's script or bag, held in two clasped right hands, with the motto, "Faithful to the king, even to beggary." Some adopted grey cloth as livery, and wore the common felt hat, and displayed on their breasts, or suspended round their beavers, a little beggar's wooden bowl, on which was wrought in silver, *Vive le Gueux*. At a great entertainment given by Brederode, after drinking the king's health out of wooden bowls, they pledged themselves at each potation to play their part manfully as "Beggars," and ever to yield a loyal adherence and stout defence to the Confederacy.[2799]

The duchess gave her answer next day. She promised to send an envoy to Spain to lay the petition of the Confederates before Philip. She had no power, she said, to suspend the Inquisition, nevertheless she would issue orders to the inquisitors to proceed with discretion. The discretion of an inquisitor! Much the Beggars marvelled what that might mean. The new project shortly afterwards enlightened them. As elaborated, and published in fifty-three articles, that project amounted to this: that heretics, instead of being burned, were to be beheaded or hanged; but they were to be admitted to this remarkable clemency only if they did not stir up riots and tumults. The people appear to have been but little thankful for this uncommon "moderation," and nicknamed it "murderation." It would appear that few were deemed worthy of the Government's mercy, for not only did blood continue to flow by the axe, but the stake blazed nearly as frequently as before. About this time, four martyrs were burned at Lille. "They all four," says Brandt, "sung as with one mouth the first verse of the twenty-seventh Psalm, and concluded their singing and their life together with the hymn of Simeon, 'Now lettest thy servant depart in peace.'" A tapestry weaver of Oudenard, near Ghent, by name John Tiscan, who had committed the indiscretion of snatching the wafer from the hand of the priest and crumbling it into bits, to show the people that it was bread and not God, had his hand cut off, and afterwards his body cast into the flames. Some there were, however, who were judged to fall within the scope of the Government's indulgence, and were permitted to die by the sword. John Cornelius Winter had been minister in the town of Horn, and had spent some thirty years in the quiet but zealous diffusion of the truth. He was apprehended and thrown first into prison at the Hague, and afterwards into the Bishop of Utrecht's prison, and now this year he was brought forth to be beheaded. He submitted himself cheerfully, and it was observed that, singing the *Te Deum* on the scaffold, the executioner struck, and his head was severed from his body just as he had finished the line, "All the martyrs praise thee."[2801]

CHAPTER X

THE FIELD-PREACHINGS

THE Confederates had been given proof of what was meant by the discretion of the inquisitors, and the Protestants were able to judge how far their condition was likely to be improved under the promised "Moderation of the Placards." It neither blunted the sword nor quenched the violence of the stake. If the latter blazed somewhat less frequently, the former struck all the oftener; and there was still no diminution of the numbers of those who were called to seal their testimony with their blood. Despairing of a Government that was growing daily milder in word, but more cruel in act, the Protestants resolved that from this time forward they would hold their worshipping assemblies in public, and try what effect a display of their numbers would have upon their oppressors. At a meeting held at Whitsuntide, 1566, at which the Lord of Aldegonde—who was destined to play the most distinguished part, next to Orange, in the coming drama—was present, it was resolved that "the churches should be opened, and divine service publicly performed at Antwerp as it was already in Flanders." This resolution was immediately acted upon. In some places the Reformed met together in the number of 7,000, in others to that of 15,000.[2800] From West Flanders, where preaching in public took its rise, it passed into Brabant, and thence into other provinces. The worshippers at the beginning sought the gloom and seclusion of wood and forest. As they grew bolder, they assembled in the plains and open places; and last of all, they met in villages, in towns, and in the suburbs of great cities. They came to these meetings, in the first instance, unarmed; but being threatened, and sometimes attacked, they appeared with sticks and stones, and at last provided themselves with the more formidable weapons of swords, pistols, and muskets.[2802]

It is said that the first field-preaching in the Netherlands took place on the 14th of June, 1566, and was held in the neighbourhood of Ghent. The preacher was Herman Modet, who had formerly been a monk, but was now the Reformed pastor at Oudenard. "This man," says a Popish chronicler, "was the first who ventured to preach in public, and there were 7,000 persons at his first sermon."[2803] The Government "scout," as the head of the executive was named, having got scent of the meeting, mounted his horse and galloped off to disperse it. Arriving on the scene, he boldly rode in amongst the multitude, holding a drawn sword in one hand and a pistol in the other, and made a dash at the minister with intent to apprehend him. Modet, making off quickly, concealed himself in a neighbouring wood. The people, surprised and without arms, appeared for a moment as if they would disperse; but their courage rallying, they plentifully supplied themselves with stones, in lack of other weapons, and saluted the officer with such a shower of missiles on all sides that, throwing away his sword and pistol, he begged for quarter, to which his captors admitted him. He escaped with his life, although badly bruised.

The second great field-preaching took place on the 23rd of July following, the people assembling in a large meadow in the vicinity of Ghent. The "Word" was precious in those days, and the people, thirsting to hear it, prepared to remain two days consecutively on the ground. Their arrangements more resembled an army pitching their camp than a peaceful multitude assembling for worship. Around the worshippers was a wall of barricades in the shape of carts and waggons. Sentinels were planted at all the entrances. A rude pulpit of planks was hastily run up, and placed aloft on a cart. Modet was the preacher, and around him were many thousands of hearers, who listened with their pikes, hatchets, and guns lying by their side, ready to be grasped on a sign from the sentinels who kept watch all around the assembly. In front of the entrances were erected stalls, whereat pedlars offered prohibited books to all who wished to buy. Along the roads running into the country were stationed certain persons, whose office it was to bid the casual passenger turn in and hear the Gospel. After sermon, water was fetched from a neighbouring brook, and the Sacrament of baptism dispensed. When the services were finished, the multitude would repair to other districts, where they encamped after the same fashion, and remained for the same space of time, and so passed through the whole of West Flanders. At these conventicles the Psalms of David, which had been translated into Low Dutch from the version of Clement Marot, and Theodore Beza, were always sung. The odes of the Hebrew king, pealed forth by from five to ten thousand voices, and borne by the breeze over the woods and meadows, might be heard at great distances, arresting the ploughman as he turned the furrow, or the traveller as he pursued his way, and making him stop and wonder whence the minstrelcy proceeded.

Heresy had been flung into the air, and was spreading like an infection far and near over the Low Countries. The contagion already pervaded all Flanders, and now it appeared in Brabant. The first public sermon in this part of the Netherlands was preached on the 24th of June, in a wood belonging to the Lord of Berghen, not far from Antwerp. It being St. John's-tide, and so a holiday, from four to five thousand persons were present. A rumour had been circulated that a descent would be made on the worshippers by the military; and armed men were posted at all the avenues, some on foot, others on horseback: no attack, however, took place, and the assembly concluded its worship in peace.[2804] Tiding having reached the ear of the governor that field-preachings had commenced at Antwerp, she wrote to the magistrates of that city, commanding them to forbid all such assemblies of the people, and if holden, to disperse them by force of arms. The magistrates replied that they had not the power so to do, nor indeed had they; the burgher-guard was weak, some of them not very zealous in the business, and the conventicle-holders were not only numerous, but every third man went armed to the meeting. And as regards the Protestants, so little were they terrified by the threats of the duchess, that they took forcible possession of a large common, named the *Laer*, within a mile of Antwerp, and having fortified all the avenues leading into it, by massing waggons and branches of trees in front, and planting armed scouts all around, they preached in three several places of the field at once.[2805]

The pestilence, which to the alarm and horror of the authorities had broken out, they sought to wall in by placards. Every day, new and severer prohibitions were arriving from the Duchess of Parma against the field-preachings. In the end of June, she sent orders to the magistrates of Antwerp to disperse all these assemblies, and to hang all the preachers.[2806] Had the duchess accompanied these orders with troops to enforce them, their execution might have been possible; but the governor, much to her chagrin, had neither soldiers nor money. Her musketeers and cross-bowmen were themselves, in many instances, among the frequenters of these illegal meetings. To issue placards in these circumstances was altogether idle. The magistrates of Antwerp replied, that while they would take care that no conventicle was held in the city, they must decline all responsibility touching those vast masses of men, amounting at times to from fifteen to twenty thousand, that were in the practice of going outside the walls to sermon.

About this time Tournay became famous for its field-preachings. Indeed, the town may be said to have become Protestant, for not more than a sixth of its population remained with the Roman Church. Adjoining France its preachers were Walloons—that is, Huguenots—and on the question of the Sacrament, the main doctrinal difference between the Lutheran and the Reformed, the citizens of Tournay were decided Calvinists. Nowhere in the Netherlands had the Protestants yet ventured on preaching publicly within the walls of a city, and the inhabitants of Tournay, like those of all the Flemish towns, repaired to the fields to worship, leaving for the time the streets silent. One day in the beginning of July, 1566, some 10,000 citizens passed out at its gates to here Peregrine de la Grange, an eloquent preacher from Provence. La Grange had brought to the Low Countries the warm and impulsive temperament and lively oratory of the South; he galloped with the air of a cavalier to the spot where thousands, gathered round a hastily prepared pulpit, waited his coming; and when he stood up to begin, he would fire a pistol over the heads of his immense audience as a signal to listen. Other two days passed, and another enormous conventicle assembled outside Tournay. A preacher even more popular than Peregrine de la Grange was this day to occupy the pulpit in the fields, and the audience was twice as large as that which had assembled two days before.

Ambrose Wille had sat at the feet of Calvin, and if the stream of his eloquence was not so rapid, it was richer and deeper than that of the Provençal; and what the multitudes which thronged to these field-preachings sought was not so much to have their emotions stirred as to have their understandings informed by the truths of Scripture, and above all, to have their consciences set at rest by hearing the way of pardon clearly explained to them. The risks connected with attendance were far too tremendous to be hazarded for the sake of mere excitement. Not only did the minister preach with a price set upon his head, but every one of these 20,000 now before him, by the mere fact of hearing him, had violated the edicts, and incurred the penalty of death. Their silence bespoke their intense anxiety and interest, and when the sermon had ended, the heartiness of their psalm testified to the depth of their joy. It was at the peril of their lives that the inhabitants of the Netherlands sought, in those days, the bread of their souls in the high places of the fields.

The movement steadily maintained its march northwards. It advanced along the famous seaboard, a mighty silent power, bowing the hearts of young and old, of the noble and the artisan, of the wealthy city merchant and the landward tiller of the soil, and gathering them, in defiance of fiery placards, in tens of thousands round that tree whereon was offered the true Sacrifice for the sins of the world. We have seen the movement advance from Flanders into Brabant, and now we are to follow it from Brabant into Holland. In vain does Philip bid it stop; in vain do the placards of the governor threaten death; it continues its majestic march from province to province, and from city to city, its coming, like that of morning, heralded by songs of joy. It is interesting to mark the first feeble beginnings of Protestant preaching in a country where the Reformation was destined to win so many brilliant triumphs. In an obscure street of Amsterdam, there lived at that time Peter Gabriel, formerly of Bruges, with his wife Elizabeth, who was childless. He had been a monk, but having embraced the Protestant faith, he threw off the frock, and was now accustomed to explain the Heidelberg catechism every Sunday to a small congregation, who came to him by twos and threes at a time for fear of the magistrates, who were animated by a sanguinary zeal against the Reformation, and trembled lest the plague of field-preaching should invade their city. There also dwelt at Kampen at the same time John Arentson, a basket-maker by trade, but gifted with eloquence, and possessed of a knowledge of the Scriptures. Him a few pious burghers of Amsterdam invited to meet them, that they might confer touching the steps to be taken for commencing the public preaching of the Gospel in Holland. They met near St. Anthony's Gate, outside Amsterdam, for Arentson durst not venture into the city. They were a little congregation of seven, including the preacher; and having prayed for Divine guidance in a crisis so important for their country, they deliberated; and having weighed all the difficulties, they resolved, in spite of the danger that threatened their lives, to essay the public preaching of the Word in Holland.

Before breaking up they agreed to meet on the same spot, the same afternoon, to devise the practical steps for carrying out their resolution. As they were re-entering Amsterdam, by separate gates, they heard the great bell of the Stadthouse ring out. Repairing to the market-place they found the magistrates promulgating the last placard which had been transmitted from the court. It threatened death against all preachers and teachers, as also against all their harbourers, and divers lesser penalties against such as should attend their preaching. The six worthy burghers were somewhat stumbled. Nevertheless, in the afternoon, at the appointed hour, they returned to their old rendezvous, and having again earnestly prayed, they decided on the steps for having the Gospel openly preached to the people in all parts of Holland. On the 14th of July the first sermon was preached by Arentson, in a field near Horn, in North Holland, the people flocking thither from all the villages around. In the humble basket-maker we see the pioneer of that numerous band of eloquent preachers and erudite divines, by which Holland was to be distinguished in days to come.[2807]

The movement thus fairly commenced soon gathered way. News of what had taken place at Horn spread like lightning all over Holland, and on the following Sunday, the 21st of July, an enormous gathering took place at Overeen, near Haarlem. Proclamation of the intended field-preaching had been made on the Exchange of Amsterdam on the previous day. The excitement was immense; all the boats and waggons in Amsterdam were hired for the transport of those who were eager to be present. Every village and town poured out its inhabit-

Book Eighteenth   1439

ants, and all the roads and canals converging on Haarlem were crowded. The burgomasters of Amsterdam sent notice to the magistrates of Haarlem of what was impending. The Stadthouse bell was rung at nine o'clock of the evening of Saturday, and the magistrates hastily assembled, to be told that the plague of which they had heard such dreadful reports at a distance, was at last at their gates. Haarlem was already full of strangers; not an inn in it that was not crowded with persons who purposed being present at the field-preaching on the coming day. The magistrates deliberated and thought that they had found a way by which to avert the calamity that hung over them: they would imprison the whole multitude within the walls of their town, and so extinguish the projected conventicle of tomorrow. The magistrates were not aware, when they hit on this clever expedient, that hundreds had already taken up their position at Overeen, and were to sleep on the ground. On Sunday morning, when the travellers awoke and sallied out into the street, they found the city gates locked. Hour passed after hour, still the gates were kept closed. The more adventurous leaped from the walls, swam the moat, and leaving their imprisoned companions behind them, hastened to the place of meeting. A few got out of the town when the watch opened the gates to admit the milk-women, but the great bulk of the conventiclers were still in durance, and among others Peter Gabriel, who was that day to be preacher. It was now eleven o'clock of the forenoon; the excitement on the streets of Haarlem may be imagined; the magistrates, thinking to dispel the tempest, had shut themselves in with it. The murmurs grew into clamours, the clamours into threatenings, every moment the tempest might be expected to burst. There was no alternative but to open the gates, and let the imprisoned multitude escape.

Citizens and strangers now poured out in one vast stream, and took the road to Overeen. Last of all arrived Peter Gabriel the minister. Two stakes were driven perpendicularly into the ground, and a bar was laid across, on which the minister might place his Bible, and rest his arms in speaking. Around the rude pulpit were gathered first the women, then the men, next those who had arms, forming an outer ring of defence, which however was scarcely needed, for there was then no force in Holland that would have dared to attack this multitude. The worship was commenced with the singing of a psalm. First were heard the clear soft notes of the females at the centre; next the men struck in with their deeper voices; last of all the martial forms in the outer circle joined the symphony, and gave completeness and strength to the music. When the psalm had ended, prayer was offered, and the thrilling peals that a moment before had filled the vault overhead were now exchanged for a silence yet more thrilling. The minister, opening the Bible, next read out as his text the 8th, 9th, and 10th verses of the second chapter of the Epistle to the Ephesians: "For by grace are ye saved through faith; and that not of yourselves: it is the gift of God. Not of works lest any man should boast. For we are his workmanship, created in Christ Jesus unto good works, which God hath before ordained that we should walk in them." Here in a few verses, said the minister, was the essence of the whole Bible—the "marrow" of all true theology:—"the gift of God," salvation; its source, "the grace of God;" the way in which it is received, "through faith;" and the fruits ordained to follow, "good works."

It was a hot midsummer day; the audience was not fewer than 5,000; the preacher was weak and infirm in body, but his spirit was strong, and the lightning-power of his words held his audience captive. The sermon, which was commenced soon after noon, did not terminate till past four o'clock. Then again came prayer. The preacher made supplication, says Brandt, "for all degrees of men, especially for the Government, in such a manner that there was hardly a dry eye to be seen."[2608] The worship was closed as it had been commenced, with the melodious thunder of 5,000 voices raised in praise.

So passed the great movement through Holland in the course of a few weeks. Wherever it came it stirred the inhabitants not into wrath, nor into denunciation of the Government, and much less into seditions and insurrections; it awoke within them thoughts which were far too serious and solemn to find vent in tumult and noise. They asked, "What must we do to be saved?" It was the hope of having this the greatest of all questions answered, that drew them out into the woods and wildernesses, and open fields, and gathered them in thousands and tens of thousands around the Book of Life and its expositor. While Brederode and his fellow Confederates were traversing the country, making fiery speeches against the Government, writing lampoons upon the bishops, draining huge bowls of wine, and then hanging them round their necks as political badges—in short, rousing passions which stronger passions and firmer wills were to quell—these others, whom we see searching the Scriptures, and gathering to the field-preachings, were fortifying themselves and leavening their countrymen with those convictions of truth, and that inflexible fidelity to God and to duty, which alone could carry them through the unspeakably awful conflict before them, and form a basis strong enough to sustain the glorious fabric of Dutch liberty which was to emerge from that conflict.

By the middle of August there was no city of note in all Holland where the free preaching of the Gospel had not been established, not indeed within the walls, but outside in the fields. The magistrates of Amsterdam, of all others, offered the most determined resistance. They convoked the town militia, consisting of thirty-six train-bands, and asked them whether they would support them in the suppression of the field-conventicles. The militia replied that they would not although they would defend with their lives the magistrates and city against all insurrections.[2809] The authorities were thus under the necessity of tolerating the public sermon, which was usually preached outside the Haarlem gate. The citizens of Delft, Leyden, Utrecht, and other places now took steps for the free preaching of the Gospel. The first sermon was preached at Delft by Peter Gabriel at Hornburg, near the city. The concourse was great. The next city to follow was the Hague. Twenty waggons filled with the burghers of Delft accompanied the preacher thither; they alighted before the mansion of the president, Cornelius Suis, who had threatened the severest measures should such a heretical novelty be attempted in his city. They made a ring with the waggons, placing the preacher in the centre, while his congregation filled the enclosure. The armed portion of the worshippers remained in the waggons and kept the peace. They sang their psalm, they offered their prayer, the preaching of the sermon followed; the hostile president surveying all the while, from his own window, the proceedings which he had stringently forbidden, but was quite powerless to prevent.

There were only four Protestant ministers at this time in all Holland. Their labours were incessant; they preached all day and journeyed all night, but their utmost efforts could not overtake the vastness of the field. Every day came urgent requests for a preacher from towns and villages which had not yet been visited. The friends of the Gospel turned their eyes to other countries; they cried for help; they represented the greatness of the crisis, and prayed that labourers might be sent to assist in reaping fields that were already white, and that promised so plenteous a harvest. In answer to this appeal some ten pastors were sent, mainly from the north of Germany, and these were distributed among the cities of Holland. Other preachers followed, who came from other lands, or arose from amongst the converts at home, and no long time elapsed till each of the chief towns enjoyed a settled ministration of the Gospel.

CHAPTER XI
THE IMAGE-BREAKINGS

WE have seen the procession of the 300 noblemen who, with Count Brederode at their head, on the 5th of April, 1566, walked two and two on foot to the old palace of Brabant in Brussels, to lay the grievances under which their nation groaned at the feet of Margaret, Regent of the Netherlands. We have also heard the answer which the regent returned. She promised to send their petition by special envoys to Philip, with whom alone the power lay of granting or withholding its request; and meanwhile, though she could not close the Inquisition, she would issue orders to the inquisitors to proceed "with discretion." The noblemen whom Margaret selected to carry the Confederate Petition to Spain were the Marquis de Berghen and the Baron de Montigny. They gladly undertook the mission entrusted to them, little suspecting how fruitless it would prove for their country, and how fatally it would end for themselves. The tyrant, as we shall afterwards see, chose to consider them not as ambassadors, but as conspirators against his Government. Philip took care, however, to keep the dark purpose he harboured in connection therewith in his breast; and meanwhile he professed to be deliberating on the answer which the two deputies, who he purposed should see the Netherlands no more, were to carry back. While Philip was walking in "leaden shoes," the country was hurrying on with "winged feet."

The progress of the movement so far had been peaceful. The psalms sung and the prayers offered at the field-preachings, and above all the Gospel published from the pulpits, tended only to banish thoughts of vengeance, and inspire to amity and good-will. The consideration of the forgiveness of Heaven, freely accorded to the most enormous offences, disposed all who accepted it to forgive in their turn. But numerous other causes were in operation tending to embroil the Protestant movement. The whole soil of the Netherlands was volcanic. Though the voice of the pulpit was peace, the harangues which the Confederates were daily firing off breathed only war. The Protestants were becoming conscious of their strength; the remembrances of the thousands of their brethren who had been barbarously murdered, rankled in their minds—nay, they were not permitted to forget the past, even had they been willing so to do. Did not their pastors preach to them with a price set on their heads, and were not their brethren being dragged to death before their eyes? With so many inflammable materials all about, it needed only a spark to kindle a blaze. A mighty conflagration now burst out.

On the 14th of August, the day before the fête of the Assumption of the Virgin, there suddenly appeared in Flanders a band of men armed with staves, hatchets, hammers, ladders, and ropes; some few of them carried guns and swords.[2810] This party was composed of the lowest of the people, of idlers, and women of disreputable character, "hallooed on," says Grotius, "by nobody knows whom."[2811] They had come forth to make war upon images; they persecuted the campaign with singular energy, and, being unopposed, with complete success. As they marched onwards the crosses, shrines, and saints in stone fell before them. They entered the villages and lifted up their hammers upon all their idols, and smote them in pieces. They next visited the great towns, where they pulled down the crucifixes that stood on the corners of the streets, and broke the statues of the Virgin and saints. The churches and cathedrals they swept clean of all their consecrated symbols. They extinguished the tapers on the altars, and mounting the wall of the edifice with their ladders, pulled down the pictures that adorned it. They overturned the Madonnas, and throwing their ropes around the massive crosses that surmounted altars and chapels, bore them to the ground; the altars too, in some cases, they demolished; they took a special delight in soiling the rich vestments of the priests, in smearing their shoes with the holy oil, and trampling under foot the consecrated bread; and they departed only when there was nothing more to break or to profane. It was in vain that the doors of some churches and convents were hastily barricaded. This iconoclast army was not to be withstood. Some sturdy image-hater would swing his hammer against the closed portal, and with one blow throw it open. The mob would rush in, and nothing would be heard but the clang of axes and the crash of falling pictures and overturned images. A few minutes would suffice to complete the desolation of the place. Like the brook when the rains descend, and a hundred mountain torrents keep pouring their waters into it, till it swells into a river, and at last widens into a devastating flood, so this little band of iconoclasts, swelled by recruits from every village and town through which they passed, grew by minutes into an army, that army into a far-extending host, which pursued its march over the country, bursting open the doors of cathedrals and the gates of cities, chasing burgomasters before it, and striking monk and militia-man alike with terror. It seemed even as if iconoclasts were rising out of the soil. They would start up and begin their ravages at the same instant in provinces and cities widely apart. In three days they had spread themselves over all the Low Countries, and in less than a week they had plundered 400 churches.[2812] To adapt to this destroying host the words of the prophet, descriptive of the ravages of another army—before them was a garden, clothed in the rich blossoms of the Gothic genius and art, behind them was a wilderness strewn over with ruins.

These iconoclasts appeared first in the district of St. Omer, in Flanders, where they sacked the convent of the Nuns of Wolverghen. Emboldened by their success, the cry was raised, "To Ypres, to Ypres!"[2813] "On their way thither," says Strada, "their number increased, like a snowball rolling from a mountain-top into the valley."[2814] They purged the roads as they advanced, they ravaged the churches around Ypres, and entering the town they inflicted unsparing demolition upon all the images in its sanctuaries. "Some set ladders to the walls, with hammers and staves battering the pictures. Others broke asunder the iron-work, seats and pulpit. Others casting ropes about the great statues of Our Saviour Christ, and the saints, pulled them down to the ground."[2815] The day following there gathered "another flock of the like birds of prey," which directed their flight towards Courtray and Douay, ravaging and plundering as they went onward. Not a penny of property did they appropriate, not a hair of the head of monk or nun did they hurt. It was not plunder but destruction which they sought, and their wrath if fierce was discharged not on human beings, but on graven images. They smote and defaced, and broke in pieces, with exterminating fury, the statues and pictures in the churches, without permitting even one to escape, "and that with so much security," says Strada, "and with so little regard of the magistrate or prelates, as you would think they had been sent for by the Common Council, and were in the pay of the city."[2816]

Tidings of what was going on in Flanders were speedily carried into Brabant, and there too the tempest gathered with like suddenness, and expended itself with like fury. Its more terrific burst was in Antwerp, which the wealth and devotion of preceding ages had embellished with so many ecclesiastical fabrics, some of them of superb architectural magnificence, and all of them filled with the beautiful creations of the chisel and the pencil. The crowning glory of Antwerp was its cathedral, which, although begun in 1124, had been finished only a few years before the events we are narrating. There was no church in all Northern Europe, at that day, which could equal the Notre-Dame of the commercial capital of Brabant, whether in the imposing grandeur of its exterior, or in the variety and richness of its internal decorations. The magnificence of its statuary, the beauty of its paintings, its mouldings in bronze and carvings in wood, and its vessels of silver and gold, made it the pride of the citizens, and the delight and wonder of strangers from other lands. Its spire shot up to a height of 500 feet, its nave and aisles stretched out longitudinally the same length. Under its lofty roof, borne up by columns of gigantic stature, hung round with escutcheons and banners, slept mailed warriors in their tombs of marble, while the boom of organ, the chant of priest, and the whispered prayers of numberless worshippers, kept eddying continually round their beds of still and deep and never-ending repose.

When the magistrates and wealthy burghers of Antwerp heard of the storm that was raging at no great distance from their gates, their hearts began to fail them. Should the destructive cloud roll hither, how much will remain a week hence, they asked themselves, of all that the wealth and skill and penitence of centuries have gathered into the Church of our Lady? It needed not that the very cloud that was devastating Flanders should transport itself to the banks of the Scheldt; the whole air was electrical. In every quarter of the firmament the same dark clouds that hung over Flanders were appearing, and wherever stood Virgin, or saint, or crucifix, there the lightnings were seen to fall. The first mutterings of the storm were heard at Antwerp on the fête-day of the Assumption of the Virgin. "Whilst," says Strada, "her image in solemn procession was carried upon men's shoulders, from the great church through the streets, some jeering rascals of the meaner sort of artificers first laughed and hissed at the holy solemnity, then impiously and impudently, with mimic salutations and reproachful words, mocked the effigies of the Mother of God."[2818] The magistrates of Antwerp in their wisdom hit upon a device which they thought would guide the iconoclast past their unrivalled cathedral. It was their little manœuvre that drew the storm upon them.

The great annual fair was being held in their city;[2818] it was usual during that concourse for the image of the Virgin to stand in the open nave of the cathedral, that her votaries might the more conveniently offer her their worship. The magistrates, thinking to take away occasion from those who sought it, bade the statue be removed inside the choir, behind the iron railing of its gates. When the people assembled next day, they found "Our Lady's" usual place deserted. They asked her in scorn "why she had so early flown up to the roost?" "Have you taken fright," said they sarcastically, "that you have retreated within this enclosure?" As "Our Lady" made them no reply, nor any one for her, their insolence waxed greater. "Will you join us," said they, "in crying, 'Long live the Beggars'?" It is plain that those who began the iconoclast riots in Antwerp were more of Confederates than Reformers. A mischievously frolicsome lad, in tattered doublet and old battered hat, ascended the pulpit, and treated the crowd to a clever caricature of the preaching of the friars. All, however, did not approve of this attempt to entertain the multitude. A young sailor rushed up the stairs to expel the caricature preacher. The two struggled together in the pulpit, and at last both came rolling to the ground. The crowd took the part of the lad, and some one drawing his dagger wounded the sailor. Matters were becoming serious when the church officers interfered, and with the help of the margrave of the city, they succeeded with some difficulty in ejecting the mob, and locking the cathedral-doors for the night.[2819]

The governor of the city, William of Orange, was absent, having been summoned a few days before to a council at Brussels; and the two burgomasters and magistrates were at their wits' end. They had forbidden the Gospel to be preached within the walls of Antwerp, having rejected the petition lately presented to that effect by a number of the principal burghers; but the gates which the Gospel must not enter, the iconoclast tempest had burst open without leave of the Senate. Where the psalm could not be sung, the iconoclast saturnalians lifted up their hoarse voices. The night passed in quiet, but when the day returned, signs appeared of a renewal of the tempest. Crowds began to collect in the square before the cathedral; numbers were entering the edifice, and it was soon manifest that they had come not to perform their devotions, but to stroll irreverently through the building, to mock at the idols in nave and aisle, to peer through the iron railings behind which the Virgin still stood ensconced, to taunt and jeer her for fleeing, and to awaken the echoes of the lofty roof with their cries of "long live the Beggars!" Every minute the crowd was increasing and the confusion growing. In front of the choir, sat an ancient crone selling wax tapers and other things used in the worship of the Virgin. Zealous for the honour of Mary, whom Antwerp and all Brabant worshipped, she began to rebuke the crowd for their improper behaviour. The mob were not in a humour to take the admonition meekly. They turned upon their reprover, telling her that her patroness' day was over, and her own with it, and that she had better "shut shop." The huckster thus baited was not slow to return gibe for gibe. The altercation drew the youngsters in the crowd around her, who possibly did not confine their annoyances to words. Catching at such missiles as lay within her reach, the stall-woman threw them at her tormenters. The riot thus begun rapidly extended through all parts of the church. Some began to play at ball, some to throw stones at the altar, some to shout, "Long live the Beggars!" and others to sing psalms. The magistrates hastened to the scene of uproar, and strove to induce the people to quit the cathedral. The more they entreated, the more the mob scowled defiance. They would remain, they said, and assist in singing *Ave Maria* to the Virgin. The magistrates replied that there would be no Vespers that night, and again urged them to go. In the hope that the mob would follow, the magistrates made their own exit, locking the great door of the cathedral behind them, and leaving open only a little wicket for the people to come out by. Instead of the crowd within coming out, the mob outside rushed in at the wicket, and the uproar increased. The margrave and burgomasters re-entered the church once more, and made yet another attempt to quell the riot. They found themselves in presence of a larger and stormier crowd, which they could no more control than they could the waves of an angry sea. Securing what portion they could of the more valuable treasures in the church, they retired, leaving the cathedral in the hands of the rioters.[2820]

All night long the work of wholesale destruction still went on. The noise of wrenching, breaking, and shouting, the blows of hammers and axes, and the crash of images and pictures, were heard all over the city; and the shops and houses were closed. The first object of vengeance of the rioters, now left sole masters of the building and all contained in it, was the colossal image of the Virgin, which only two days before had been borne in jewelled robes, with flaunt of banner, and peal of trumpet, and beat of drum, through the streets. The iron railing within which she had found refuge was torn down, and a few vigorous blows from the iconoclast axes hewed her in pieces and smote her into dust. Execution being done upon the great deity of the place, the rage of the mob was next discharged on the minor gods. Traversing nave and side-aisle, the iconoclast paused a moment before each statue of wood or stone. He lifted his brawny arm, his hammer fell, and the image lay broken. The pictures that hung on the walls were torn down, the crosses were overturned, the carved work was beaten into atoms, and the stained glass of the windows shivered in pieces. All the altars—seventy in number—were demolished;[2821] in short, every ornament was rifled and destroyed. Tapers taken from the altar lighted the darkness, and enabled the iconoclasts to continue their work of destruction all through the night.

The storm did not expend itself in the cathedral only, it extended to the other churches and chapels of Antwerp. These underwent a like speedy and terrible purgation. Before morning, not fewer than thirty churches within the walls had been sacked. When there remained no more images to be pulled down, the rabble laid their hands on other things. They strewed the wafers on the floor; they filled the chalices with wine, and drank to the health of the Beggars; they donned the gorgeous vestments of the priests, and, breaking open the cellars, a vigorous tap of the hammer set the red wine a-flowing. A Carmelite, or bare-footed monk, who had languished twelve year in the prison of his monastery, received his liberty at the hands of these image-breakers. The nunneries were invaded,[2822] and the sisters, impelled by fright, or moved by the desire of freedom, escaped to the houses of their relatives and friends. Violence was offered to no one. Unpitying towards dead idols, these iconoclasts were tender of living men.

When the day broke a body of rioters sallied out at the gates, and set to work on the abbeys and religious houses in the open country. These they ravaged as they had done those of the city. The libraries of some of these establishments they burned. The riotings continued for three days. No attempt to put them down was made by any one. The magistrates did nothing beyond their visit to the cathedral on the first day. The burghal militia were not called out. The citizens kept themselves shut up in their houses, the Protestants because they suspected that the Roman Catholics had conspired to murder them, and the Roman Catholics because they feared the same thing of the Protestants. Though the crowd was immense, the actual perpetrators of these outrages were believed not to number over a hundred. A little firmness on the part of the authorities at the beginning might have restrained them. "All these violences, plunderings, and desolations," said those of the Spanish faction, "were committed by about a hundred unarmed rabble at the most." The famous Dutch historian, Hooft, says: "I do not think it strange, since there are good and bad men to be found in all sects, that the vilest of the [Reformed] party showed their temper by these extravagances, and that others fed their eyes with a sport that grew up to a plague, which they thought the clergy had justly deserved by the rage of their persecutions." "The generality of the Reformed," he adds, "certainly behaved themselves nobly by censuring things which they thought good and proper to be done, because they were brought about by improper methods."[2823] In an Apology which they published after these occurrences had taken place the Reformed said: "The Papists themselves were at the bottom of the image-breaking, to the end they might have a pretext for charging those of the Religion with rebellion: this, they added, plainly appeared by the tumult renewed at Antwerp by four Papists, who were hanged for it next day."[2824]

It is light and not axes that can root out idols. It is but of small avail to cast down the graven image, unless the belief on which the worship of it is founded be displaced from the heart. This was not understood by these zealous iconoclasts. Cast images out of the breast, said Zwingle, and they will soon disappear from the sanctuary. Of this opinion were the Protestant preachers of the Low Countries. So far from lifting axe or hammer upon any of the images around them, they strove to the utmost of their power to prevent the rabble doing so. The preacher Modet, in an Apology which he published soon after these disorders, says "that neither he himself nor any of his consistory had any more knowledge of this design of destroying images when it was first contrived than of the hour of their death." It was objected against him that he was in the church while the mob was breaking and defacing the images. This he owns was true; but he adds that "it was at the desire of the magistrates themselves, and at the peril of his own life, that he went thither to quiet the mob, though he could not be heard, but was pulled down from the pulpit, and thrust out of the church; that, moreover, he had gone first to the convent of the Grey Friars, and next to the nunnery of St. Clara, to entreat the people to depart; that of this matter fifty or sixty nuns could testify. That was all the concern he had in that affair." A written address was also presented to the burgomaster by the ministers and elders of the Dutch and Walloon congregations, in which "they called God to witness that what happened in the taking away and destroying of images was done without either their knowledge or consent; and they declared their detestation of these violent deeds."[2825]

This destroying wind passed on to Breda, Bergen-op-Zoom, and other towns of Brabant. Eight men presented themselves at the gates of Lier, and said they had come to ascertain whether the idols had been taken down. The magistrates admitted two of them into the city, led them from church to church, and removed whatever they ordered, without once asking them by whose authority they had come.[2826] At Tournay the churches were stripped to the very walls; the treasures of gold and silver which the priests had buried in the earth, exhumed; and the repositories broken into, and the chalices, reliquaries, rich vestments, and precious jewels scattered about as things of no value. At Valenciennes the massacre of the idols took place on St. Bartholomew's Day. "Hardly as many senseless stones," says Motley, "were victims as there were to be living Huguenots sacrificed in a single city upon a Bartholomew which was fast approaching. In the Valenciennes massacre not a human being was injured."[2827]

The storm turned northward, and inflicted its ravages on the churches of Holland. Hague, Delft, Leyden, the Brill, and other towns were visited and purged. At Dort, Gouda, Rotterdam, Haarlem, and other places, the magistrates anticipated the coming of the iconoclasts by giving orders beforehand for the removal of the images. Whether the pleasure or the mortification of the rioters was the greater at having the work thus taken off their hands, it would be hard to affirm. At Amsterdam the matter did not pass off so quietly. The magistrates, hearing that the storm was travelling northwards, gave a hint to the priests to remove their valuables in time. The precaution was taken with more haste than good success. The priests and friars, lading themselves with the plate, chalices, patens, pyxes, and mass-vestments, hurried with them along the open street. They were met by the operatives, who were returning from their labour to dinner. The articles were deemed public property, and the clergy in many cases were relieved of their burdens. The disturbances had begun. The same evening, after vespers had been sung, several children were brought for baptism. While the priest was performing the usual exorcisms one of the crowd shouted out, "You priest, forbear to conjure the devil out of him; baptise the child in the name of Jesus, as the apostles were wont to do." The confusion increased; some mothers had their infants hastily baptised in the mother tongue, others hurried home with theirs unbaptised. Later in the evening a porter named Jasper, sauntering near that part of the church where the pyx is kept, happened to light upon a placard hanging on the wall, having reference to the mystery of the pyx. "Look here," said he to the bystanders, at the same time laying hold on the board and reading aloud its inscription, which ran thus: "Jesus Christ is locked up in this box; whoever does not believe it is damned." Thereupon he threw it with violence on the floor; the crash echoed through the church, and gave the signal for the breaking to begin. Certain boys began to throw stones at the altar. A woman threw her slipper at the head of a wooden Mary—an act, by the way, which afterwards cost her her own head. The mob rushed on: images and crucifixes went down before them, and soon a heap of pictures, vases, crosses, and saints in stone, broken, bruised, and blended indistinguishably, covered with their sacred ruins the floors of the churches.[2828]

It does not appear from the narratives of contemporary historians that in a single instance these outrages were stimulated, or approved of, by the Protestant preachers. On the contrary, they did all in their power to prevent them. They wished to see the removal of images from the churches, knowing that this method of worship had been forbidden in the Decalogue; but they hoped to accomplish the change peacefully, by enlightening the public sentiment and awakening the public conscience on the matter. He is the true iconoclast, they held, who teaches that "God is a Spirit, and must be worshipped in spirit." This is the hammer that is to break in pieces the idols of the nations.

Nor can the destruction of these images, with truth, be laid at the door of the Protestant congregations of the Low Countries. There were fanatical persons in their ranks, no doubt, who may have aided the rioters by voice and hand; but the great body of the Reformers—all, in short, who were worthy of the name, and had really been baptised into the spirit of Protestantism—stood aloof from the work of destruction, knowing it to be as useless as it was culpable. These outrages were the work of men who cared as little for Protestantism, in itself, as they did for Roman Catholicism. They belonged to a class found in every Popish country, who, untaught, vindictive, vicious, are ever ready to break out into violence the moment the usual restraints are withdrawn. These restraints had been greatly relaxed in the Low Countries, as in all the countries of Christendom, by the scandals of the priesthood, and yet more by the atrocious cruelty of the Government, which had associated these images in the minds of the people with the 30,000 victims who had been sacrificed during the three or four decades past. And most of all, perhaps, had Protestantism tended to relax the hold which the Church of Rome exercised over the masses. Protestantism had not enlightened the authors of these outrages to the extent of convincing them of its own truth, but it had enlightened them to the extent of satisfying them that Popery was a cheat; and it is of the nature of the human mind to avenge itself upon the impositions by which it has been deluded and duped. But are we therefore to say that the reign of imposture must be eternal? Are we never to unmask delusions and expose falsehoods, for fear that whirlwinds may come in with the light? How many absurdities and enormities must we, in that case, make up our minds to perpetuate! In no one path of reform should we ever be able to advance a step. We should have to sternly interdict progress not only in religion, but in science, in politics, and in every department of social well-being. And then, how signally unjust to blame the remedy, and hold it accountable for the disturbances that accompany it, and acquit the evil that made the remedy necessary! Modern times have presented us with two grand disruptions of the bonds of authority; the first was that produced by Protestantism in the sixteenth century, and the second was that caused by the teachings of the French Encyclopædists in the end of the eighteenth century. In both cases the masses largely broke away from the control of the Roman Church and her priesthood; but every candid mind will admit that they broke away not after the same fashion, or to the same effect. The revolt of the sixteenth century was attended, as we have seen in the Low Countries, by an immense and, we shall grant, most merciless execution of images; the revolt of the eighteenth was followed by the slaughter of a yet greater number of victims; but in this case the victims were not images, but living men. Both they who slew the images in the sixteenth century, and they who slew the human beings in the eighteenth, were reared in the Church of Rome; they had learned her doctrines and had received their first lessons from her priests; and though now become disobedient and rebellious, they had not yet got quit of the instincts she had planted in them, nor were they quite out of her leading-strings.

CHAPTER XII
REACTION—SUBMISSION OF THE SOUTHERN NETHERLANDS

THE first effect of the tumults was favourable to the Reformers. The insurrection had thoroughly alarmed the Duchess of Parma, and the Protestants obtained from her fear concessions which they would in vain have solicited from her sense of justice. At a conference between the leading nobles and the governor at Brussels on the 25th of August, the following treaty was agreed to and signed:—The duchess promised on her part "that the Inquisition should be abolished from this time forward for ever," and that the Protestants should have liberty of worship in all those places where their worship had been previously established. These stipulations were accompanied with a promise that all past offences of image-breaking and Beggar manifestoes should be condoned. The nobles undertook on their part to dissolve the Confederacy, to return to the service of the State, to see that the Reformed did not come armed to their assemblies, and that in their sermons they did not inveigh against the Popish religion.[2829] Thus a gleam broke out through the cloud, and the storm was succeeded by a momentary calm.

On the signing of this treaty the princes went down to their several provinces, and earnestly laboured to restore the public peace. The Prince of Orange and Counts Egmont, Horn, and Hoogstraten were especially zealous in this matter, nor were their efforts without success. In Antwerp, where Orange was governor, and where he was greatly beloved, quiet was speedily re-established, the great cathedral was again opened, and the Romish worship resumed as aforetime. It was agreed that all the consecrated edifices should remain in the possession of the Roman Catholics, but a convention was at the same time made with the Dutch and Walloon congregations, empowering them to erect places of worship within the city-walls for their own use. The latter arrangement,—the privilege, namely, accorded the Reformed of worshipping within the walls—was a concession which it cost the bigotry of Margaret a grudge to make. But Orange, in reply to her remonstrances, told her that, in the first place, this was expedient, seeing assemblies of 20,000 or 25,000 persons were greater menaces to the public peace outside the walls, where they were removed from the eye of the magistrate, than they could possibly be within the city, where not only were their congregations smaller, their numbers seldom exceeding 10,000, but their language and bearing were more modest; and, in the second place, this concession, he reminded the duchess, was necessary. The Reformed were now 200,000 strong, they were determined to enjoy their rights, and he had no soldiers to gainsay their demands, nor could he prevail on a single burgher to bear arms against them.[2830] In a few days the Walloon congregation, availing themselves of their new liberties, laid the first stone of their future church on a spot which had been allotted them; and their example was speedily followed by the Dutch Reformed congregation. Through the efforts of Orange the troubles were quieted all over Holland and Brabant. His success was mainly owing to the great weight of his personal character, for soldiers to enforce submission he had none. The churches were given back to the priests, who, doffing the lay vestments in which many of them had encased themselves in their terror, resumed the public celebration of their rites; and the Protestants were contented with the liberty accorded them of worshipping in fabrics of their own creation, which in a few places were situated within the walls, but in the great majority of cases stood outside, in the suburbs, or the open country.

Meanwhile the news of churches sacked, images destroyed, and holy things profaned was travelling to Spain. Philip, who during his stay in Brussels had been wont to spend his nights in the stews, or to roam masked through the streets, satiating his base appetites upon their foul garbage, when the tidings of the profanation reached him, first shuddered with horror, and next trembled with rage. Plucking at his beard, he exclaimed, "It shall cost them dear, I swear it by the soul of my father."[2381] For every image that had been mutilated hundreds of living men were to die; the affront offered to the Roman Catholic faith, and its saints in stone, must be washed out in the blood of the inhabitants of the Netherlands. So did the tyrant resolve.

Meanwhile keeping secret the terrible purpose in his breast, he began to move toward it with his usual slowness, but with more than his usual doggedness and duplicity. Before the news of the image-breaking had arrived, the king had written to Margaret of Parma, in answer to the petition which the two envoys, the Marquis of Berghen and the Count de Montigny, had brought to Madrid, saying to her—so bland and gracious did he seem—that he would pardon the guilty, on certain conditions, and that seeing there was now a full staff of bishops in the Provinces, able and doubtless willing vigilantly to guard the members of their flock, the Inquisition was no longer necessary, and should henceforth cease. Here was pardon and the abolition of the Inquisition: what more could the Netherlanders ask? But if the letter was meant to read one way in Brussels, it was made to read another way in Madrid. No sooner had Philip indited it than, summoning two attorneys to his closet, he made them draw out a formal protest in the presence of witnesses to the effect that the promise of pardon, being not voluntary but compulsory, was not binding, and that he was not obliged thereby to spare any one whom he chose to consider guilty. As regarded the Inquisition, Philip wrote to the Pope, telling him that he had indeed said to the Netherlanders that he would abolish it, but that need not scandalise his Holiness, inasmuch as he neither could nor would abolish the Inquisition unless the Pope gave his consent. As regarded the meeting of the Assembly of the States for which the Confederates had also petitioned, Philip replied with his characteristic prudence, that he forbade its meeting for the moment; but in a secret letter to Margaret he told her that that moment meant for ever. The two noblemen who brought the petition were not permitted to carry back the answer: that would have been dangerous. They might have initiated their countrymen into the Spanish reading of the letter. They were still, upon various pretences, detained at Madrid.

Along with this very pleasant letter, which the governor was to make known to all Philip's subjects of the Netherlands, that they might know how gracious a master they had, came another communication, which Margaret was not to make known, but on the contrary keep to herself. Philip announced in this letter that he had sent the governor a sum of money for raising soldiers, and that he wished the new battalions to be enlisted exclusively from Papists, for on these the king and the duchess might rely for an absolute compliance with their will. The regent was not remiss in executing this order; she immediately levied a body of cavalry and five regiments of infantry. As her levies increased her fears left her, and the conciliatory spirit which led her to consent to the Accord of the 25th of August, was changed to a mood of mind very different.

But if the Accord was to be kept, the good effects of which had been seen in a pacified country, and if the guilty were to be pardoned and the Inquisition abolished, as the king's letter had promised, where was the need of raising armaments? Surely these soldiers are not merely to string beads. A great treachery is meditated, said Orange and his companions, Egmont and Horn. It is not the abolition of the Inquisition, but a rekindling of its fires on a still larger scale, that awaits us; and instead of a resurrection of Flemish liberty by the assembling of the States-General, it is the entire effacement of whatever traces of old rights still remain in these unhappy countries, and the establishment of naked despotism on the ruins of freedom by an armed force, that is contemplated. Of that these levies left Orange in no doubt. In the Council all three nobles expressed their disapprobation of the measure, as a rekindling of the flames of civil discord and sedition.

Every day new proofs of this were coming to light. The train-bands of the tyrant were gathering round the country, and the circle of its privileges and its liberties was contracting from one hour to another. The regent had no cause to complain of the lukewarmness of Egmont and Horn, whatever suspicions she might entertain of Orange. The prince was now a Lutheran, and he had calmed the iconoclastic tumults all over Brabant, Holland, and Zealand, without staining his hands with a single drop of blood. The Counts Egmont and Horn were Romanists, and their suppression of the image-breakings in Flanders and Tournay had been marked by great severity towards the Reformers. Egmont showed himself an ardent partisan of the Government, and his proceedings spread terror through Flanders and Artois. Thousands of Protestants fled the country; their wives and families were left destitute; the public profession of the Reformed religion was forbidden, despite the Accord; and numbers of its adherents, including ministers, hanged. The chief guilt of these cruelties rests with Egmont's secretary, Bakkerzeel, who had great influence over the count, and who, along with his chief, received his reward in due time from the Government they so zealously and unscrupulously served.

It was much after the same fashion that Tournay was pacified by Count Horn. Five-sixths of the inhabitants of that important place were Calvinists; Horn, therefore, feared to forbid the public preachings. But no church and no spot inside the walls would Horn permit to be defiled by the Protestant worship; nevertheless, three places outside the gates were assigned for sermon. The eloquent Ambrose Wille, whom we have already met, was the preacher, and his congregation generally numbered from fifteen to twenty thousand hearers. Permission was at last given for the erection of churches on the three spots where the field-preachings had been held; and Councillor Taffen made what he judged an eminently reasonable proposal to the magistrates touching the cost of their erection. The Papists, he said, who were not more than a fourth of the citizens, retained all the old churches; the other three-fourths, who were Protestants, were

Book Eighteenth

compelled to build new ones, and in these circumstances he thought it only fair that the community should defray the expense of their erection. The Romanists exclaimed against the proposal. To be compelled to refrain from burning the heretics was much, but to be taxed for the support of heresy was an unheard-of oppression. Money and materials, however, were forthcoming in abundance: the latter were somewhat too plentiful; fragments of broken images and demolished altars were lying about everywhere, and were freely but indiscreetly used by the Protestants in the erection of their new fabrics. The sight of the things which they had worshipped, built into the walls of a heretical temple, stung the Romanists to the quick as the last disgrace of their idols.

The levies of the regent were coming in rapidly, and as her soldiers increased her tone waxed the bolder. The Accord of the 25th of August, which was the charter of the Protestants, gave her but small concern. She had made it in her weakness with the intention of breaking it when she should be strong. She confiscated all the liberties the Reformed enjoyed under that arrangement. The sermons were forbidden, on the ridiculous pretext that, although the liberty of preaching had been conceded, that did not include the other exercises commonly practised at the field assemblies, such as singing, praying, and dispensing the Sacraments. Garrisons were placed by the regent in Tournay, in Valenciennes, and many other towns; the profession of the Reformed religion was suppressed in them; the Roman temples were re-opened, and the Popish rites restored in their former splendour.

The fall of Valenciennes as a Protestant city exerted so disastrous and decisive an influence upon the whole country, that it must detain us for a little while. In the end of the year 1566—the last year of peace which the Netherlands were to see for more than a generation—the regent sent the truculent Noircarmes to demand that Valenciennes should open its gates to a garrison. Strongly fortified, Protestant to all but a fourth or sixth of its population, courageous and united, Valenciennes refused to admit the soldiers of Margaret. Her general thereupon declared it in a state of siege, and invested it with his troops. Its fate engaged the interest of the surrounding villages and districts, and the peasants, armed with pitchforks, picks, and rusty muskets, assembling to the number of 3,000, marched to its relief. They were met by the troops of Noircarmes, discomfited, and almost exterminated. Another company also marching to its assistance met a similar fate. Those who escaped the slaughter took refuge in the church of Watrelots, only to be overtaken by a more dreadful death. The belfry, into which they had retreated, was set on fire, and the whole perished. These disasters, however, did not dispirit the besieged. They made vigorous sallies, and kept the enemy at bay. To cut off all communication between the city and the surrounding country, and so reduce the besieged by famine, orders were given to the soldiers to lay the district waste. The villages were pillaged or burned, the inhabitants slaughtered in cold blood, or stripped naked in the dead of winter, or roasted alive over slow fires to amuse a brutal soldiery. Matrons and virgins were sold in public auction at tuck of drum. While these horrible butcheries were being enacted outside Valenciennes, Noircarmes was drawing his lines closer about the city. In answer to a summons from Margaret, the inhabitants offered to surrender on certain conditions. These were indignantly rejected, and

Noircarmes now commenced to bombard Valenciennes. It was the morning of Palm-Sunday. The bells in the steeples were chiming the air to which the 22nd Psalm, "My God, my God, why has thou forsaken me?" as versified by Marot, was commonly sung. The boom of the cannon, the quaking of the houses, the toppling of the chimneys, mingling with the melancholy chimes of the steeples, and the wailings of the women and children in the streets, formed a scene depressing indeed, and which seems to have weighed down the spirits of the inhabitants into despair. The city sent to Noircarmes offering to surrender on the simple condition that it should not be sacked, and that the lives of the inhabitants should be spared. The general gave his promise only to break it. Noircarmes closed the gates when he had entered. The wealthy citizens he arrested; some hundreds were hanged, and others were sent to the stake.[2833] There was no regular sack, but the soldiers were quartered on the inhabitants, and murdered and robbed as they had a mind. The elders and deacons and principal members of the Protestant congregation were put to death.[2834] The two Protestant preachers, Guido de Bray and Peregrine de la Grange, the eloquent Huguenot, made their escape, but being discovered they were brought back, cast into a filthy dungeon, and loaded with chains.

In their prison they were visited by the Countess of Reux, who asked them how they could eat and drink and sleep with so heavy a chain, and so terrible a fate in prospect. "My good cause," replied De Bray, "gives me a good conscience, and my good conscience gives me a good appetite." "My bread is sweeter, and my sleep sounder," he continued, "than that of my persecutors." "But your heavy irons?" interposed the countess. "It is guilt that makes a chain heavy," replied the prisoner, "innocence makes mine light. I glory in my chains, I account them my badge of honour, their clanking is to my ear as sweet music; it refreshes me like a psalm."[2835]

They were sentenced to be hanged. When their fate was announced to them, says Brandt, "they received it as glad tidings, and prepared as cheerfully to meet it as if they had been going to a wedding-feast." De Bray was careful to leave behind him the secret of his sound sleep in heavy irons and a filthy dungeon, that others in like circumstances might enjoy the same tranquillity. "A good conscience, a good conscience!" "Take care," said he to all those who had come to see him die, "Take care to do nothing against your conscience, otherwise you will have an executioner always at your heels, and a pandemonium burning within you." Peregrine de la Grange addressed the spectators from the ladder, "taking heaven and earth to witness that he died for no cause save that of having preached the pure Word of God." Guido de Bray kneeled on the scaffold to pray; but the executioner instantly raised him, and compelled him to take his place on the ladder. Standing with the rope round his neck he addressed the people, bidding them give all due reverence to the magistrate, and adhere to the Word of God, which he had purely preached. His discourse was stopped by the hangman suddenly throwing him off. At the instant a strange frenzy seized the soldiers that guarded the market-place. Breaking their ranks, they ran about the town in great disorder, "nobody knowing what ailed them," firing off their muskets, and wounding and killing Papists and Protestants indiscriminately.[2836]

We stand on the threshold of a second great era of persecution to the Church of the Netherlands. The horrors of this era, of which the scaffolds of these two learned and eloquent divines mark the commencement, were to be so awful that the sufferings of the past forty years would not be remembered. The severities that attended the fall of the powerful and Protestant Valenciennes discouraged the other cities; they looked to see the terrible Noircarmes and his soldiers arrive at their gates, offering the alternative of accepting a garrison, or enduring siege with its attendant miseries as witnessed in the case of Valenciennes. They made up their minds to submission in the hope of better days to come. If they could have read the future: if they had known that submission would deepen into slavery; that one terrible woe would depart only to make room for another more terrible, and that the despot of Spain, whose heart bigotry had made hard as the nether millstone, would never cease emptying upon them the vials of his wrath, they would have chosen the bolder, which would also have been the better part. Had they accepted conflict, the hardest-fought fields would have been as nothing compared with the humiliations and inflictions that submission entailed upon them. Far better would it have been to have died with arms in their hands than with halters round their necks; far better would it have been to struggle with the foe in the breach or in the field, than to offer their limbs to the inquisitor's rack. But the Flemings knew not the greatness of the crisis: their hearts fainted in the day of trial. The little city of Geneva had withstood single-handed the soldiers of the Duke of Savoy, and the threats of France and Spain: the powerful Provinces of Brabant and Flanders, with their numerous inhabitants, their strong and opulent cities, and their burghal militias, yielded at the first summons. Even Valenciennes surrendered while its walls were yet entire. The other cities seem to have been conquered by the very name of Noircarmes. The Romanists themselves were astonished at the readiness and abjectness of the submission. "The capture of Valenciennes," wrote Noircarmes to Granvelle, "has worked a miracle. The other cities all come forth to meet me, putting the rope round their own neck."[2837] It became a saying, "the governor has found the keys of all the rest of the cities at Valenciennes."[2838] Cambray, Hasselt, Maseik, and Maestricht surrendered themselves, as did also Bois-le-Duc. The Reformed in Cambray had driven away the archbishop; now the archbishop returned, accompanied with a party of soldiers, and the Reformed fled in their turn. In the other towns, where hardly a single image had escaped the iconoclast tempest, the Romish worship was restored, and the Protestants were compelled to conform or leave the place. The Prince of Orange had hardly quitted Antwerp, where he had just succeeded in preventing an outbreak which threatened fearful destruction to property and life, when that commercial metropolis submitted its neck to the yoke which it seemed to have cast off with contempt, and returned to a faith whose very symbols it had so recently trampled down as the mire in the streets. Antwerp was soon thereafter honoured with a visit from the governor. Margaret signalised her coming by ordering the churches of the Protestants to be pulled down, their children to be re-baptised, and as many of the church-plunderers as could be discovered to be hanged. Her commands were zealously carried out by an obsequious magistracy.[2839] It was truly melancholy to witness the sudden change which the Southern Netherlands underwent. Thousands might be seen hurrying from a shore where freedom and the arts had found a home for centuries, where proud cities had arisen, and whither were wafted with every tide the various riches of a world-wide commerce, leaving by their flight the arts to languish and commerce to die. But still more melancholy was it to see the men who remembered casting themselves prostrate before altars they had so recently thrown down, and participating in rites which they had repudiated with abhorrence as magical and idolatrous.

CHAPTER XIII
THE COUNCIL OF BLOOD

WHIRLWINDs from the terrible land of the South"—in literal terms, edicts and soldiers from Spain—were what might now be looked for. The land had been subjugated, but it had yet to be chastised. On every side the priests lifted up the head, the burghers hung theirs in shame. The psalm pealed forth at the field-preaching rose no longer on the breeze, the orison of monk came loud and clear instead; the gibbets were filled, the piles were relighted, and thousands were fleeing from a country which seemed only now to be opening the dark page of its history. The future in reserve for the Low Countries was not so closely locked up in the breast of the tyrant but that the Prince of Orange could read it. He saw into the heart and soul of Philip. He had studied him in his daily life; he had studied him in the statesmen and councillors who served him; and he had studied him in those secret pages in which Philip had put on record, in the depth of his own closet, the projects that he was revolving, and which, opened and read while Philip slept, by the spies which William had placed around him, were communicated to this watchful friend of his country's liberties; and all these several lines of observation had led him to one and the same conclusion, that it was Philip's settled purpose, to be pursued through a thousand windings, chicaneries, falsehoods, and solemn hypocrisies, to drag the leading nobles to the scaffold, to hang, burn, or bury alive every Protestant in the Low Countries, to put to death every one who should hesitate to yield absolute compliance with his will, and above the grave of a murdered nation to plant the twin fabrics of Spanish and Romish despotism. That these were the purposes which the tyrant harboured, and the events which the future would bring forth, unless means were found to prevent them, William was as sure as that the revolution of the hours brings at length the night.

Accordingly he invited Horn, Egmont, Hoogstraaten, and Count Louis to an interview at Dendermonde, in order to concert the measures which it might be advisable to take when the storm, with which the air was already thick, should burst. The sight of Egmont and the other nobles unhappily was not so clear as that of William, and they refused to believe that the danger was so great as the prince represented. Count Egmont, who was not yet disenthralled from the spell of the court, nor fated ever to be till he should arrive at the scaffold, said that "far from taking part in any measure offensive to the king, he looked upon every such measure as equally imprudent and undutiful." This was decisive. These three seigniors must act in concert or not at all. Combined, they might have hoped to make head against Philip; singly, they could accomplish nothing—nay, in all likelihood would be crushed. The Prince of Orange resigned all his offices into the hands of the regent, and retired with his family to his ancestral estate of Nassau in Germany, there to await events. Before leaving, however, he warned Count Egmont of the fate that awaited him should he remain in Flanders. "You are the bridge," said he, "by which the Spanish army will pass into the Netherlands, and no sooner shall they have passed it than they will break it down."[2840] The warning was unheeded. The two friends tenderly embraced, and parted to meet no more on earth.

No sooner was William gone (April, 1567) than a cloud of woes descended upon the Netherlands. The disciples of the Reformation fled as best they could from Amsterdam, and a garrison entered it. At Horn, Clement Martin preached his farewell sermon a month after the departure of William, and next day he and his colleagues were expelled the town. About the same time the Protestants of Enkhuizen heard their last sermon in the open air. Assemblies were held overnight in the houses of certain of the burghers, but these too were discontinued in no long time. A deep silence—"a famine of hearing the Word of the Lord"— fell upon the land. The ministers were chased from many of the cities. The meetings held in out-of-the-way places were surprised by the soldiers; of those present at them some were cut in pieces or shot down on the spot, and others were seized and carried off to the gallows. It was the special delight of the persecutors to apprehend and hang or behead the members of the consistories. "Thus," says Brandt, "the gallows were filled with carcases, and Germany with exiles." The minister of Cambray first had his hand cut off, and was then hanged. At Oudenard and other towns the same fate was inflicted on the pastors. Monks, who had ceased to count beads and become heralds of the glorious Gospel rather than return to the cloister, were content to rot in dungeons or die on scaffolds. Some villages furnished as many as a hundred, and others three hundred victims.[2841] A citizen of Bommel, Hubert Selkart by name, had the courage to take a Bible to the market-place, and disprove the errors of Popery in presence of the people assembled there. A night or two thereafter he was put into a sack and thrown into the river Wael. There were no more Scripture expositions in the market-place of Bommel. All the Protestant churches in course of erection were demolished, and their timbers taken for gallows to hang their builders. Two young gentlewomen of the Province of Over-Issel were sentenced to the fire. One of the sisters was induced to abjure on a promise of mercy. She thought she had saved her life by her abjuration, whereas the mercy of the placards meant only an easier death. When the day of execution arrived, the two sisters, who had not seen each other since they received their sentence, were brought forth together upon the scaffold. For the one who remained steadfast a stake had been prepared; the other saw with horror a coffin, half filled with sand, waiting to receive her corpse as soon as the axe should have severed her head from her body. "This," said the strong sister to the weak one, "this is all you have gained by denying Him before whom you are within an hour to appear.": Conscience-stricken she fell upon her knees, and with strong cries besought pardon for her great sin. Then rising up—a sudden calm succeeding the sudden tempest—she boldly declared herself a Protestant. The executioner, fearing the effect of her words upon the spectators, instantly stopped her by putting a gag into her mouth, and then he bound her to the same stake with her sister. A moment before, it seemed as if the two were to be parted for ever; but now death, which divides others, had united them in the bonds of an eternal fellowship:[2842] they were sisters evermore.

As regarded the Netherlands, one would have thought that their cup of suffering was already full; but not so thought Philip. New and more terrible severities were in course of preparation at Madrid for the unhappy Provinces. The

Book Eighteenth

King of Spain, after repeated deliberations in his council, resolved to send a powerful army under the command of the Duke of Alva, to chastise those turbulent citizens whom he had too long treated with gentleness, and exact a full measure of vengeance for that outbreak in which they had discovered an equal contempt for the true religion and the royal authority. The Duke of Alva, setting sail from Carthagena (May 10th, 1567), landed in the north of Italy, and repairing to Asti, there assembled under his standard about 10,000 picked soldiers from the army in Italy, consisting of 8,700 foot and 1,200 cavalry.[2843] He now set out at the head of this host to avenge the insulted majesty of Rome and Spain, by drowning Netherland heresy in the blood of its professors. It was a holy war: those against whom it was to be waged were more execrable than Jews or Saracens: they were also greatly richer. The wealth of the world was treasured up in the cities of the Netherlands, and their gates once forced, a stream of gold would be poured into the coffers of Spain, now beginning to be partially deplenished by the many costly enterprises of Philip.

A fitter instrument for the dreadful work which Philip had now in hand than the Duke of Alva, it would have been impossible to find in all Europe. A daring and able soldier, Alva was a very great favourite with the Emperor Charles V., under whom he had served in both Europe and Africa, and some of the more brilliant of the victories that were gained by the armies of Charles were owing to his unquestionable ability, but somewhat headlong courage. He had warred against both the Turks and the Lutherans, and of the two it is likely that the latter were the objects of his greatest aversion and deepest hatred. He was now sixty, but his years had neither impaired the vigour of his body nor quenched the fire of his spirit. In person he was thin and tall, with small head, leathern face, twinkling eyes, and silvery beard.[2844] He was cool, patient, cruel, selfish, vindictive, and though not greedy of wine and the pleasures to which it often incites, was inflamed with a most insatiable greed of gold. Haughty and overbearing, he could not tolerate a rival, and the zeal he afterwards showed in dragging Count Egmont to the scaffold is thought to have been inspired, in part at least, by the renown Egmont had acquired over the first generals of France, and which had thrown Alva somewhat into the shade, being compelled to occupy an inglorious position in the north of Italy, while his rival was distinguishing himself on a far more conspicuous theatre. But the master-passion of this man's soul was a ferocious fanaticism. Cruel by nature, he had become yet more cruel by bigotry. This overbearing passion had heated his instincts, and crazed his judgment, till in stealthy bloodthirstiness he had ceased to be the man, and become the tiger.

As was the general, so were the soldiers. The Duke of Alva was, in fact, leading an army of Alvas across the Alps. Their courage had been hardened and their skill perfected in various climes, and in numerous campaigns and battles; they were haughty, stern, and cruel beyond the ordinary measure of Spanish soldiers. Deeming themselves champions of the Cross, the holy war in which they were fighting not only warranted, but even sanctified in their eyes, the indulgence of the most vindictive and sanguinary passions against those men whom they were marching to attack, and whom they held to be worthy of death in the most terrible form in which they could possibly inflict it.

Climbing the steep sides of Mont Cenis, the duke himself leading the van, this invading host gained the summit of the pass. From this point, where nothing is visible save the little circular lake that fills the crater of a now exhausted volcano, and the naked peaks that environ it, the Spaniards descended through the narrow and sublime gorges of the mountains to Savoy. Continuing their march, they passed on through Burgundy and Lorraine,[2845] attended by two armies of observation, the French on this side and the Swiss on that, to see that they kept the straight road. Their march resembled the progress of the boa-constrictor, which, resting its successive coils upon the same spot, moves its glittering but deadly body forwards. Where the van-guard had encamped this night, the main body of the army was to halt the next, and the rear the night following. Thus this Apollyon host went onward.

It was the middle of August when the Spaniards arrived at the frontier of the Low Countries. They found the gates open, and their entrance unopposed. Those who would have suffered the invaders to enter only over their dead bodies were in their graves; the nobles were divided or indifferent; the cities were paralysed by the triumph of the royal arms at Valenciennes; thousands, at the first rising of the tempest, had retreated into the Church of Rome as into a harbour of safety; tameness and terror reigned throughout the country, and thus the powerful Netherlands permitted Philip to put his chain upon its neck without striking a blow. The only principle which could have averted the humiliation of the present hour, and the miseries of the long years to come, had meanwhile been smitten down.

Cantoning his soldiers in the chief cities, the Duke of Alva in the end of August took up his residence in Brussels, Count Egmont riding by his side as he entered the gates of the Belgian capital. He soon showed that he had arrived with a plenitude of power; that, in fact, he was king. Margaret felt her authority overtopped by the higher authority of the duke, and resigned her office as regent. She accompanied her retirement with a piece of advice to her brother, which was to the effect that if the measures that she feared were in contemplation should be carried out, the result would be the ruin of the Netherlands. Although Philip had been as sure of the issue as Margaret was, he would have gone forward all the same. Meanwhile his representative, without a moment's delay, opened his career of tyranny and blood. His first act was to arrest the Counts Egmont and Horn, and in manner as crafty as the deed was cruel. He invited them to his house on pretence of consulting with them respecting a citadel which he meant to erect at Antwerp. When the invitation reached these noblemen, they were seated at a banquet given by the Prior of the Knights of St. John. "Take the fleetest horse in your stable," whispered the prior in the ear of Egmont, "and flee from this place." The infatuated nobleman, instead of making his escape, went straight to the palace of the duke. After the business of the citadel had been discussed, the two counts were conducted into separate rooms. "Count Egmont," said the captain of the duke's guard, "deliver your sword; it is the will of the king." Egmont made a motion as if he would flee. A door was thrown open, and he was shown the next apartment filled with Spanish musketeers. Resistance was vain. The count gave up his sword, saying, "By this sword the cause of the king has been oftener than once successfully defended."[2846] He was conducted up-stairs to a temporary prison; the windows were closed; the walls were hung in black, and lights were burned in it night and day—a sad presage of the yet gloomier fate that awaited him. Count Horn was treated in a precisely similar way. At the end of fourteen days the two noblemen were conducted, under a strong guard, to the Castle of Ghent. At the same time two other important arrests were made—Bakkerzeel, the secretary of Egmont; and Straalen, the wealthy Burgomaster of Antwerp.[2847]

These arrests spread terror over the whole country. They convinced Romanists equally with Protestants that the policy to be pursued was one of indiscriminate oppression and violence. Count Egmont had of late been, to say the least, no lukewarm friend of the Government; his secretary, Bakkerzeel, had signalised his zeal against Protestantism by spilling Protestant blood, yet now both of these men were on the road to the scaffold. The very terror of Alva's name, before he came, had driven from the Low Countries 100,000 of their inhabitants. The dread inspired by the arrests now made compelled 20,000 more to flee. The weavers of Bruges and Ghent carried to England their art of clothmaking, and those of Antwerp that of the silk manufacture. Nor was it the disciples of the Reformation only that sought asylum beyond seas. Thomas Tillius forsook his rich Abbey of St. Bernard, in the neighbourhood of Antwerp, and repaired to the Duchy of Cleves. There he threw off his frock, married, and afterwards became pastor, first at Haarlem, and next at Delft.[2848]

Every day a deeper gulf opened to the Netherlands. The death of the two Flemish envoys, the Marquis of Berghen and the Baron de Montigny, was immediately consequent on the departure of the duke for the Low Countries. The precise means and manner of their destruction can now never be known, but occurring at this moment, it combined with the imprisonment of Egmont and Horn in prognosticating times of more than usual calamity. The next measure of Alva was to erect a new tribunal, to which he gave the name of the "Council of Tumults," but which came to be known, and ever will be known in history, by the more dreadful appellative of the "Council of Blood." Its erection meant the overthrow of every other institution. It proscribed all the ancient charters of the Netherlands, with the rights and liberties in which they vested the citizens. The Council of Tumults assumed absolute and sole jurisdiction in all matters growing out of the late troubles, in opposition to all other law, jurisdiction, and authority whatsoever. Its work was to search after and punish all heretics and traitors. It set about its work by first defining what that treason was which it was to punish. This tribunal declared that "it was treason against the Divine and human Majesties to subscribe and present any petition against the new bishops, the Inquisition, or the placards; as also to suffer or allow the exercise of the new religion, let the occasion or necessity be what it would."[2849] Further, it was treason not to have opposed the field-preachings; it was treason not to have opposed the presenting of the petition of the Confederate nobles; in fine, it was treason to have said or thought that the Tribunal of Tumults was obliged to conform itself to the ancient charters and privileges, or "to have asserted or insinuated that the king had no right to take away all the privileges of these Provinces if he thought fit, or that he was not discharged from all his oaths and promises of pardon, seeing all the inhabitants had been guilty of a crime, either of omission or of commission." In short, the King of Spain, in this fulmination, declared that all the inhabitants of the Low Countries were guilty of treason, and had incurred the penalty of death. Or as one of the judges of this tremendous tribunal, with memorable simplicity and pithiness, put it, "the heretical inhabitants broke into the churches, and the orthodox inhabitants did nothing to hinder it, therefore they ought all of them to be hanged together."[2850]

The Council of Blood consisted of twelve judges; the majority were Spaniards, and the rest fast friends of the Spanish interest. The duke himself was president. Under the duke, and occupying his place in his absence, was Vargas, a Spanish lawyer. Vargas was renowned among his countrymen as a man of insatiable greed and measureless cruelty. He it was who proposed the compendious settlement of the Netherlands question to which we have just referred, namely, that of hanging all the inhabitants on one gallows. "The gangrene of the Netherlands," said the Spaniards, "has need of a sharp knife, and such is Vargas."[2851] This man was well mated with another Spaniard nearly as cruel and altogether as unscrupulous, Del Rio. This council pronounced what sentences it pleased, and it permitted no appeal.

It would be both wearisome and disgusting to follow these men, step by step, in their path of blood. Their council-chamber resembled nothing so much as the lair of a wild beast, with its precincts covered with the remains of its victims. It was simply a den of murder; and one could see in imagination all its approaches and avenues soaked in gore and strewn with the mangled carcases of men, women, and children. The subject is a horrible one, upon which it is not at all pleasant to dwell.

All was now ready; Alva had erected his Council of Blood, he had distributed his soldiers over the country in such formidable bodies as to overawe the inhabitants, he was erecting a citadel at Antwerp, forts in other places, and compelling the citizens to defray the cost of the instruments of their oppression; and now the Low Countries, renowned in former days for the mildness of their government and the happiness of their people, became literally an Aceldama. We shall permit the historian Brandt to summarise the horrors with which the land was now overspread. "There was nothing now," says he, "but imprisoning and racking of all ages, sexes, and conditions of people, and oftentimes too without any previous accusation against them. Infinite numbers (and they not of the Religion neither) that had been but once or twice to hear a sermon among the Reformed, were put to death for it. The gallows, says the Heer Hooft in his history, the wheels, stakes, and trees in the highways were loaden with carcases or limbs of such as had been hanged, beheaded, or roasted, so that the air which God had made for the respiration of the living, was now become the common grave or habitation of the dead. Every day produced fresh objects of pity and mourning, and the noise of the bloody passing-bell was continually heard, which by the martyrdom of this man's cousin, or t'other's friend or brother, rung dismal peals in the hearts of the survivors. Of banishment of persons and confiscations of goods there was no end; it was no matter whether they had real or personal estates, free or entailed, all was seized upon without regarding the claims of creditors or others, to the unspeakable prejudice both of rich and poor, of convents, hospitals, widows and orphans, who were by knavish evasions deprived of their incomes for many years."[2852]

Bales of denunciations were sent in. These were too voluminous to be read by Alva or Vargas, and were remitted to other councils, that still retained a nominal existence, to be read and reported on. They knew the sort of report that was expected from them, and took care not to disappoint the expectations of the men of the Blood Council. With sharp reiterated knell came the words, "Guilty: the gallows." If by a rare chance the accused was said to be innocent, the report was sent back to be amended: the recommendation to death was always carried out within forty-eight hours. This bloody harvest was gathered all over the country, every town, village, and hamlet furnishing its group of victims. Today it is Valenciennes that yields a batch of eighty-four for the stake and the gallows; a few days thereafter, a miscellaneous crowd, amounting to ninety-five, are brought in from different places in Flanders, and handed over by the Blood Council to the scaffold; next day, forty-six of the inhabitants of Malines are condemned to die; no sooner are they disposed of than another crowd of thirty-five, collected from various localities by the sleuth-hounds of the Blood Council, are ready for the fire. Thus the horrible work of atrocity went on, prosecuted with unceasing vigour and a zeal that was truly awful.

Shrovetide (1568) was approaching. The inhabitants of the Netherlands, like those of all Popish countries, were wont to pass this night in rejoicings. Alva resolved that its songs should be turned into howlings. While the citizens should be making merry, he would throw his net over all who were known to have ever been at a field-preaching, and prepare a holocaust of some thousand heads fittingly to celebrate the close of "Holy Week." At midnight his myrmidons were sent forth; they burst open the doors of all suspected persons, and dragging them from their beds, hauled them to prison. The number of arrests, however, did not answer Alva's expectations; some had got timely warning and had made their escape; those who remained, having but little heart to rejoice, were not so much off their guard, nor so easy a prey, as the officers expected to find them. Alva had enclosed only 500 disciples or favourers of the Gospel in his net—too many, alas! for such a fate, but too few for the vast desires of the persecutor. They were, of course, ordered to the scaffold.[2853]

Terror was chasing away the inhabitants in thousands. An edict was issued threatening severe penalties against all carriers and ship-masters who should aid any subject of the Netherlands to escape, but it was quite ineffectual in checking the emigration; the cities were becoming empty, and the land comparatively depopulated. Nevertheless, the persecution went on with unrelenting fury. Even Viglius counselled a little lenity; the Pope, it is said, alarmed at the issue to which matters were tending, was not indisposed to moderation. Such advisers ought to have had weight with the King of Spain, but Philip refused to listen even to them. Vargas, whom he consulted, declared, of course, for a continuance of the persecution, telling his sovereign that in the Netherlands he had found a second Indies, where the gold was to be had without even the trouble of digging for it, so numerous were the confiscations. Thus avarice came to the aid of bigotry. Philip next submitted a "Memorial and Representation" of the state of the Low Countries to the Spanish Inquisition, craving the judgment of the Fathers upon it. After deliberating, the inquisitors pronounced their decision on the 16th of February, 1568. It was to the effect that, "with the exception of a select list of names which had been handed to them, all the inhabitants of the Netherlands were heretics or abettors of heresy, and so had been guilty of the crime of high treason." On the 26th of the same month, Philip confirmed this sentence by a royal proclamation, in which he commanded the decree to be carried into immediate execution, without favour or respect of persons. The King of Spain actually passed sentence of death upon a whole nation. We behold him erecting a common scaffold for its execution, and digging one vast grave for all the men, and women, and children of the Low Countries. "Since the beginning of the world," says Brandt, "men have not seen or heard any parallel to this horrible sentence."[2854]

CHAPTER XIV
WILLIAM UNFURLS HIS STANDARD—EXECUTION OF EGMONT AND HORN

THE Prince of Orange had fled from the Netherlands, as we have already seen, and retired to his patrimonial estates of Nassau. Early in the year 1568 the Duke of Alva cited him to appear before the Council of Blood. It was promised that the greatest lenity would be shown him, should he obey the summons, but William was far too sagacious to walk into this trap. His brother Louis of Nassau, his brother-in-law Count van den Berg, and the Counts Hoogstraaten and Culemberg were summoned at the same time; thrice fourteen days were allowed them for putting in an appearance; should they fail to obey, they were, at the expiration of that period, to incur forfeiture of their estates and perpetual banishment. It is needless to say that these noblemen did not respond to Alva's citation, and, as a matter of course, their estates were confiscated, and sentence of banishment was recorded against them.

Had they succeeded in ensnaring William of Orange, the joy of Philip and Alva would have been unbounded. His sagacity, his strength of character, and his influence with his countrymen, made his capture of more importance to the success of their designs than that of all the rest of the Flemish nobility. Their mortification, when they found that he had escaped them, was therefore extreme. His figure rose menacingly before them in their closets; he disturbed all their calculations; for while this sagacious and dauntless friend of his country's liberties was at large, they could not be sure of retaining their hold on the Netherlands, their prey might any day be wrested from them. But though his person had escaped them, his property was within their reach, and now his numerous estates in France and the Low countries were confiscated, their revenues appropriated for the uses of Philip, and his eldest son, Count van Buren, a lad of thirteen, and at the time a student in the University of Louvain, was seized as a hostage and carried off to Spain.

There was but one man to whom the inhabitants, in the midst of their ever-accumulating misery and despair, could look with the smallest hope of deliverance. That was the man whom we have just seen stripped of his property and declared an outlaw. The eyes of the exiles abroad were also turned to William of Orange. He began to be earnestly importuned by the refugees in England, in Germany, in Cleves and other parts, to unfurl the standard and strike for his country's liberation. William wished to defer the enterprise in the hope of seeing Spain involved in war with some other nation, when it would be more easy to compel her to let go her hold upon the unhappy Netherlands. But the exiles were importunate, for their numbers were being daily swelled by the new horrors that were continually darkening their native country. William therefore resolved to delay no longer, but instantly to gird himself in obedience to the cry from so many countries, and the yet louder cry, though expressed only in groans, that was coming to him from the Netherlands.

His first care was to raise the necessary funds and soldiers. He could not begin the war with a less sum in hand than two hundred thousand florins. The cities of Antwerp, Haarlem, Amsterdam, and others contributed one-half of that sum; the refugee merchants in London and elsewhere subscribed largely. His brother, Count John of Nassau, gave a considerable sum; and the prince himself completed the amount needed by the sale of his plate, furniture, tapestry, and jewels, which were of great value. In this way were the funds provided.

For troops the chief reliance of William was on the Protestant princes of Germany. He represented to them the danger with which their own prosperity and liberties would be menaced, should the Netherlands be occupied by the Spaniards, and their trade destroyed by the foreign occupation of the sea-board and the conversion of its great commercial cities into camps. The German princes were not insensible to these considerations, and not only did they advance him sums of money—they winked at his levying recruits within their territories. He reckoned, too, on receiving help from the Huguenots of France; nor would the Protestant Queen of England, he trusted, be lacking to him at this crisis. He could confidently reckon on the Flemish refugees scattered all over the northern countries of Europe. They had been warriors as well as traders in their own country, and he could rely on their swelling his ranks with brave and patriotic soldiers. With these resources—how diminutive when compared with the treasures and the armies of that Power to which he was throwing down the gage of battle!—William resolved on beginning his great struggle.

By a fiction of loyalty this war against the king was made in the name of the king. William unfurled his standard to drive out the Spaniards from Philip's dominions of the Netherlands, in order that he might serve the interests of the king by saving the land from utter desolation, the inhabitants from dire slavery, the charters and privileges from extinction, and religion from utter overthrow. He gave a commission to his brother, dated Dillenburg, 6th April, 1568, to levy troops for the war to be waged for these objects. Louis of Nassau was one of the best soldiers of the age, and had the cause as much at heart as the prince himself. The count was successful in raising levies in the north of Germany. The motto of his arms was "The freedom of the nation and of conscience," and blazoned on his banners were the words "Victory or death."[2855]

Besides the soldiers recruited in the north of Germany by Count Louis, levies had been raised in France and in the Duchy of Cleves, and it was arranged that the liberating army should enter the Netherlands at four points. One division was to march from the south and enter by Artois; a second was to descend along the Meuse from the east; Count Louis was to attack on the north; and the prince himself, at the head of the main body of liberators, was to strike at the heart of the Netherlands by occupying Brabant. The attacking forces on the south and east were repulsed with great slaughter; but the attack on the north under Count Louis was signally successful.

On the 24th April, 1568, the count entered the Provinces and advanced on Dam, on the shores of the Bay of Dollart, the site of thirty-three villages till drowned in a mighty inundation of the ocean. Troops of volunteers were daily joining his standard. Here Count Aremberg, who had been sent by Alva with a body of Spanish and Sardinian troops to oppose him, joined battle with him. The Count of Nassau's little army was strongly posted. On the right was placed his cavalry, under the command of his brother Count Adolphus. On the left his main army was defended by a hill, on which he had planted a strong band of musketeers. A wood and the walls of a convent guarded his rear; while in front stretched a morass full of pits from which peat had been dug. When the Spaniards came in sight of the enemy drawn up in two little squares on the eminence, they were impatient to begin battle, deeming it impossible that raw levies could withstand them for a moment. Their leader, who knew the nature of the ground, strove to restrain their ardour, but in vain; accusations of treachery and cowardice were hurled at him. "Let us march," said Aremberg, his anger kindled, "not to victory, but to be overcome." The soldiers rushed into the swamp, but though now sensible of their error, they could not retreat, the front ranks being pushed forward by those in the rear, till they were fairly under the enemy's fire. Seeing the Spaniards entangled in the mud, Count Louis attacked them in front, while his brother broke in upon their flank with the cavalry. The musketeers poured in their shot upon them, and one of the squares of foot wheeling round the base of the hill took them in the rear; thus assailed on all sides, and unable to resist, the Spanish host was cut in pieces. Both Adolphus, brother of Louis of Nassau, and Aremberg, the leader of the Spaniards, fell in the battle. The artillery, baggage, and military chest of the Spaniards became the booty of the conquerors.[2856]

This issue of the affair was a great blow to Alva. He knew the effect which the prestige of a first victory was sure to have in favour of William. He therefore hastened his measures that he might march against the enemy and inflict on him summary vengeance for having defeated the veteran soldiers of Spain. The first burst of the tyrant's rage fell, however, not on the patriot army, but on those unhappy persons who were in prison at Brussels. Nineteen Confederate noblemen, who had been condemned for high treason by the Council of Blood, were ordered by Alva for immediate execution. They were all beheaded in the horse-market of Brussels. Eight died as Roman Catholics, and their bodies received Christian burial; the remaining eleven professed the Reformed faith, and their heads stuck on poles, and their bodies fastened to stakes, were left to moulder in the fields.[2857] The next day four gentlemen suffered the same fate. Count Culemberg's house at Brussels was razed to the ground, and in the centre of the desolated site a placard was set up, announcing that the ill-omened spot had been made an execration because the great "Beggar Confederacy" against king and Church had been concocted here. These minor tragedies heralded a greater one.

The last hours of Counts Egmont and Horn were now come. They had lain nine months in the Castle of Ghent, and conscious of entire loyalty to the king, they had not for a moment apprehended a fatal issue to their cause; but both Philip and Alva had from the first determined that they should die. The secretary of Egmont, Bakkerzeel, was subjected to the torture, in the hope of extorting from him condemnatory matter against his master. His tormentors, however, failed to extract anything from him which they could use against Egmont, whereat Alva was so enraged that he ordered the miserable man to be pulled in pieces by wild horses. The condemnation of the unfortunate nobleman was proceeded with all the same. They were brought from Ghent to Brussels under a strong escort. Alva, taking up one of the blank slips with Philip's signature, of which he had brought a chestful from Spain, drafted upon it the sentence of Egmont, condemning him to be beheaded as a traitor. The same formality was gone through against Count Horn. The main accusation against these noblemen was, that they had been privy to the Confederacy, which had been formed to oppose the introduction of the Inquisition and edicts; and that they had met with the Prince of Orange at Dendermonde, to deliberate about opposing the entrance of the king's army into the Netherlands. They knew indeed of the Confederacy, but they had not been members of it; and as regarded the conference at Dendermonde, they had been present at that meeting, but they had, as our readers will remember, disapproved and opposed the proposition of Louis of Nassau to unite their endeavours against the entrance of the Spanish troops into Flanders. But innocence or guilt were really of no account to the Blood Council, when it had fixed on the victim to be sacrificed. The two counts were roused from sleep at midnight, to have the sentence of death intimated to them by the Bishop of Ypres.

At eleven o'clock of the following day (5th of May) they were led to execution. The scaffold had been erected in the centre of the great square of Brussels, standing hard by if not on the identical spot where the stake of the first martyrs of the Reformation in the Netherlands had been set up. It was covered with black cloth; nineteen companies of soldiers kept guard around it; a vast assembly occupied the space beyond, and the windows of the houses were crowded with spectators, among whom was Alva himself, who had come to witness the tragedy of his own ordering. Count Egmont was the first to ascend the scaffold, accompanied by the Bishop of Ypres. He had walked thither, reciting the 51st Psalm: "In the multitude of thy compassions, O God, blot out all mine iniquities," &c. He conducted himself with dignity upon the scaffold. It was vain to think of addressing the spectators; those he wished to reach were too far off to hear him, and his words would have fallen only on the ears of the Spanish soldiers. After a few minutes' conversation with the bishop, who presented him with a silver cross to kiss, and gave him his benediction, the count put off his black mantle and robe of red damask, and taking the Cross of the Golden Fleece from his neck, he knelt down and put his head on the block. Joining his hands as if in the act of supplication, he cried aloud, "O Lord, into thy hands I commit my spirit." Thereupon the executioner emerged from underneath the scaffold, where till that moment he had been concealed, and at one blow severed the head from his body.

Count Horn was next led upon the scaffold. He inquired whether Egmont were already dead. His eye was directed to a black cloth, which had been hastily thrown over the trunk and severed head of that nobleman, and he was told that the remains of Egmont were underneath. "We have not met each other," he observed, "since the day we were apprehended." The crucifix presented to him he did not kiss; but he kneeled on the scaffold to pray. His devotions ended, he rose up, laid his head on the block, and uttering in Latin the same exclamation which Egmont had used, he received the stroke of the sword. The heads of the two counts were stuck up on iron poles on the scaffold, between burning torches, and exhibited till late in the afternoon. This horrible deed very much deepened the detestation and abhorrence in which both Philip and Alva were held by the Netherlanders.[2858]

The dismal tragedy ended, Alva was at liberty to turn his attention to the war. He set out from Brussels with an army of 12,000 foot and 3,000 horse to meet Louis of Nassau. He came up with him (14th of July, 1568) in the neighbourhood of Groningen. On the approach of the duke, Count Louis retreated to the small town of Gemmingen on the Ems, where he encamped. His position was not unlike that in which he had joined battle with Aremberg, being strongly defended by morasses and swamps. The soldiers under him were somewhat inferior in numbers, but far more inferior in discipline, to the troops led by Alva. But Count Louis was more in want of money than men. The pay of his soldiers was greatly in arrear, and when they saw the Spaniards approach, and knew that a battle was imminent, they refused to fight till first their arrears had been paid. Intelligence of this mutinous disposition was duly carried to Alva by spies, and he accordingly chose that moment to attack. Count Louis and the Flemish exiles fought bravely, but deserted by the German mutineers, they were compelled at last to retreat. The Spanish army rushed into the camp; most of the Germans who had refused to fight were put to the sword; Count Louis, with the remains of his routed host, escaped across the river Ems, and soon thereafter, in company with Count Hoogstraaten, he set out for Germany to join his brother, the Prince of Orange.[2859]

CHAPTER XV
FAILURE OF WILLIAM'S FIRST CAMPAIGN

FROM the battlefield of Gemmingen, Alva went on his way by Amsterdam and Utrecht and Bois-le-Duc to Brussels, instituting inquiries in every district through which he passed, touching those of the inhabitants who had been concerned in the late tumults, and leaving his track marked throughout by halters and stakes. At Bois-le-Duc he passed sentence on sixty refugees whom he found in that town, sending some to the gallows and others to the fire. Some noblemen and councillors of Utrecht were at the same time executed, and their estates confiscated. Many in those days perished for no other crime but that of being rich. A gentlewoman of eighty-four years, widow of Adam van Dieman, a former Burgomaster of Utrecht, and who had received under her roof for a single night the minister John Arentson, was sentenced to die. When the day came, the executioner made her sit in a chair till he should strike off her head. Being a Romanist she knew that her great wealth had as much to do with her death as the night's lodging she had given the Reformed pastor, for when brought upon the scaffold she asked if there was no room for pardon. The officer answered, "None." "I know what you mean," replied the brave old lady; "the calf is fat, and must therefore be killed." Then turning to the executioner, and jesting playfully on her great age, which ought to have procured her respect and favour, she said, "I hope your sword is sharp, for you will find my neck somewhat tough." The executioner struck, and her head fell.[2860]

A month after (25th of September) the widow of Egbert van Broekhuissen, a wine merchant at Utrecht, was beheaded. Her sentence set forth that she had been at a conventicle, but it was strongly rumoured that her real offence was one on which the judicial record was silent. One of the commissioners on the Council of Blood was a customer of her husband's, and was said to be deep in his debt. It would seem that the judge took this way of paying it, for when the effects of the widow were confiscated for the king's use, the ledger in which the debt was posted could not be found.[2861] About the same time three persons were hanged at Haarlem. One of them had mutilated an image; another had been a soldier of Brederode's, the Confederate leader; the third had written a poem, styled the *Eecho*, satirising the Pope. This man was the father of eight children, whose mother was dead. His own mother, a woman of eighty years, earnestly interceded that he might be spared for his children's sake. But no compassion could be shown him. His two companions had already been strangled; his own foot was on the ladder, when a sudden tumult arose round the scaffold. But the persecutors were not to be defrauded of their prey. They hurried off their victim to the burgomaster's chamber; there they tied him to a ladder, and having strangled him, they hung up his corpse on the public gallows beside the other two. At Delft, Herman Schinkel, one of the lettered printers of those days, was condemned to die for having printed the "Psalm-book, the Catechism, and the Confession of Faith," or short confession of the Christian doctrine from the Latin of Beza. He made a powerful defence before his judges, but of what avail was it for innocence and justice to plead before such a tribunal? He composed some verses in Latin on his death, which he sent to a friend. He wrote a letter to his infant son and daughters, breathing all the tenderness of a father; and then he yielded up his life.[2862]

In Brabant and Flanders the persecution was still more severe. At Ghent, Giles de Meyer, the Reformed pastor, was condemned to the gallows. But the Spaniards who lay there in garrison, deeming this too good a death for the heretical preacher, changed it to one more befitting his demerits. Putting a gag into his mouth, and throwing him in, bound hand and foot, among a stack of faggots, they set fire to the heap, and burned him. Meyer was one of the four ministers who all sealed their doctrine with their blood in the same diocese. In the towns and villages around Ghent, men and women were being every day hanged—some simply for having taught children to sing psalms; others for having two years before given the use of their barns for sermon. At Bois-le-Duc, on the 28th of August, 1568, 116 men and three women were cited by toll of bell. Every few days a little batch of prisoners were brought forth, and distributed between the gallows and the block, on no principle that one can see, save the caprice or whim of the executioners. Thus the altars of persecution continually smoked; and strangled bodies and headless trunks were perpetually before the eyes of the miserable inhabitants.

Peter van Kulen, a goldsmith by trade, and an elder of the congregation at Breda, was thrown into prison. He had a maid-servant, a fellow-disciple of the same Lord and Master, who ministered to him in his bonds. She brought him his daily meal in the prison; but other Bread, which the guards saw not, she also conveyed to him—namely, that destined for the food of the soul; and many a sweet and refreshing repast did he enjoy in his dungeon. His faith and courage were thereby greatly strengthened. This went on for nine months. At last the guards suspected that they had a greater heretic in the servant than in the master, and threw her also into prison. After two months both of them were condemned, and brought out to be burned. As, with cheerful and constant aspect, they were being led to the scaffold, some of their townsmen forced their way through the guards to take their last farewell of them. Van Kulen had the commiseration shown him of being first strangled, and then committed to the fire; but for his pious maid-servant the more pitiless doom was reserved of being burned alive. This woman continued to encourage her master so long as he was capable of understanding her; when her words could no longer be useful to him, she was heard by the bystanders, with invincible courage, magnifying the name of God in the midst of the flames.[2863]

It was now that a more dreadful instrument than any which the quick invention of the persecutor had yet devised, was brought into play to prevent the martyrs speaking in their last moments. It was seen how memorable were words spoken in circumstances so awful, and how deep they sank into the hearts of the hearers. It has been usual to put a wooden gag or ball into the mouth of the person to be burned, but the ball would roll out at times, and then the martyr would confess his faith and glorify God. To prevent this, the following dreadful contrivance was resorted to: two small bits of metal were screwed down upon the tongue; the tip of the tongue was then seared with a red-hot iron; instant swelling ensued, and the tongue could not be drawn out of its enclosure. The pain of burning made it wriggle to and fro in the mouth, yielding a "hollow sound," says Brandt, "much like that of the brazen bull of the tyrant of Sicily." "Arnold van Elp," continues the historian, "a man of known sincerity, relates that whilst he was a spectator of the martyrdom of some who were thus tongue-tied, he heard a friar among the crowd saying to his companion, 'Hark! how they sing: should they not dance too?'"[2863]

From this horrible though to Alva congenial, work, the viceroy was called away by intelligence that William of Orange was approaching at the head of an army to invade Brabant. To open the gates of the Netherlands to his soldiers, William issued a manifesto, setting forth the causes of the war. "There was," he said, "no resource but arms, unless the ancient charters were to be utterly extinguished, and the country itself brought to ruin by a tyranny exercised, not by the king" (so he still affected to believe), "but by Spanish councillors in the king's name, and to the destruction of the king's interest." To avert this catastrophe was he now in arms. The cause, he affirmed, was that of every man in the Low Countries, and no Netherlander "could remain neutral in this struggle without becoming a traitor to his country." In this manifesto the prince made the first public announcement of that great change which his own religious sentiments had undergone. All that is noble in human character, and heroic in human achievement, must spring from some great truth realised in the soul. William of Orange gave a forecast of his future career—his unselfish devotion, his unwearied toil, his inextinguishable hope of his country—when he avowed in this manifesto his conviction that the doctrines of the Reformed Church were more in accordance with the Word of God than were those of the Roman Church. This elevated the contest to a higher basis. Henceforward it was no longer for ancient Flemish charters alone, it was also for the rights of conscience; it allied itself with the great movement of the human soul for freedom.

The Prince of Orange, advancing from Germany, crossed the Rhine near Cologne, with an army, including horse and foot, not exceeding 20,000. The Spanish host was equal in numbers, but better furnished with military stores and provisions. William approached the banks of the Meuse, which he crossed, much to the dismay of Alva, by a bold expedient, to which Julius Cæsar had had recourse in similar circumstances. He placed his cavalry in the river above the ford, and the force of the current being thus broken, the army was able to effect a passage. But Alva declined battle. He knew how slender were the finances of William, and that could he prolong the campaign till the approach of winter, the prince would be under the necessity of disbanding his army. His tactics were completely successful. Whichever way William turned, Alva followed him; always straitening him, and making it impossible for him to enter any fortified town, or to find provisions for his army in the open country. The autumn wore away in marches and counter-marches, Alva skilfully avoiding battle, and engaging only in slight skirmishes, which, barren of result to William, were profitable to the Spanish general, inasmuch as they helped to consume time. William had expected that Brabant and Flanders would rise at the sight of his standards, and shake off the Spanish yoke. Not a city opened its gates to him, or hoisted on its walls the flag of defiance to the tyrant. At last both money and provisions failed him. Of the 300,000 guilders which the Flemish Protestants at home and abroad had undertaken to furnish towards the deliverance of the country, barely 12,000 were forthcoming. His soldiers became mutinous, and the prince had no alternative but to lead back his army into Germany and there disband it. The Flemings lost far more than William did. The offer of freedom had come to their gates with the banners of William, but they failed to perceive the hour of their opportunity. With the retreating standards of the Deliverer liberty also departed, and Belgium sank down under the yoke of Spain and Rome.

The Duke of Alva was not a little elated at his success, and he set about rearing a monument which should perpetuate its fame to after-ages. He caused the cannon taken in the battle of Gemmingen to be melted, and a colossal bronze statue of himself to be cast and set up in the citadel of Antwerp. It pleased Alva to be represented in complete armour, trampling on two prostrate figures, which were variously interpreted, but from the petitions and axes which they held in their hands, and the symbolic devices of the Beggars hung round their necks, they were probably meant to denote the image-breaking Protestants and the Confederates. On the pedestal was the following inscription in Latin: "To the most faithful minister of the best of kings, Ferdinand Alvarez, Duke of Alva, Governor of the Low Countries for Philip II., King of Spain, who, after having extinguished the tumults, expelled the rebels, restored religion, and executed justice, has established peace in the nation." A truly modest inscription! The duke, moreover, decreed himself a triumphal entry into Brussels, in the cathedral of which a *Te Deum* was sung for his victory. Nor was this all. Pius V. sent a special ambassador from Rome to congratulate the conqueror, and to present him with a consecrated hat and sword, as the special champion of the Roman Catholic religion. The sword was richly set, being chased with gold and precious stones, and was presented to the duke by the hands of the Bishop of Mechlin, in church after the celebration of mass. The afternoon of the same day was devoted to a splendid tournament, the place selected for the spectacle being the same square in which the bloody tragedy of the execution of Counts Egmont and Horn had so recently been enacted.[2865]

It was in the midst of these troubles that the persecuted disciples of the Gospel in the Netherlands met to perfect the organisation of their Church. A synod or assembly was at this time held in Embden, at which Jasper von Heiden, then minister at Franken-deal, presided. At this synod rules were made for the holding of consistories or kirk-sessions, of classes or presbyteries, and synods. The first article of the constitution ordained for the Netherland Church was as follows:— "No Church shall have or exercise dominion over another; no minister, elder, or deacon shall bear rule over another of the same degree; but every one shall beware of his attempting or giving the least cause of suspicion of his aiming at such dominion." "This article," says Brandt, "was levelled chiefly at the prelatic order of Rome, as also at the episcopacy established in some of the countries of the Reformation." The ministers assembled signed the Confession of Faith of the Church of the Netherlands, "as an evidence of their uniformity in doctrine;" as also the Confession of the Churches of France, "to show their union and conformity with them." It was agreed that all the ministers then absent, and all who should thereafter be admitted to the office of the ministry, should be exhorted to subscribe these articles. It was also agreed that the Geneva catechism should be used in the French or Walloon congregations, and the Heidelberg catechism in those of the Dutch; but if it happened that any of the congregations made use of any other catechism agreeable to the Word of God, they were not to be required to change it.[2866] While Alva was scattering and burning the Netherland Church, its members, regardless of the tyrant's fury, were linking themselves together in the bonds of a scriptural organisation. While his motto was "Raze, raze it," the foundations of that spiritual edifice were being laid deeper and its walls raised higher than before.

CHAPTER XVI
THE "BEGGARS OF THE SEA," AND SECOND CAMPAIGN OF ORANGE

WILLIAM, Prince of Orange, having consecrated his life to the great struggle for the rights of conscience, carried the first offer of deliverance to Brabant. Had its great and powerful cities heartily entered into his spirit, and risen at the sound of the advancing steps of their deliverer, the issue would have been far different from what it was. But Brabant saw that the struggle must be tremendous, and, rather than gird itself for so terrible a fight, preferred to lie still ingloriously in its chains. Sad in heart, William retired to a distance, to await what further openings it might please that great Power, to whose service he had consecrated himself, to present to him.

The night of horrors which had descended on the Low Countries continued to deepen. The triumph of Alva, instead of soothing him, made him only the more intolerant and fierce. There came new and severer edicts from Spain; there were gathered yet greater crowds of innocent men for the gallows and the stake, and the outflowing tide from that doomed shore continued to roll on. A hundred thousand houses, it is thought, were now left empty. Their inmates transported their trade and handicrafts to other nations. Wives must not correspond with their exiled husbands; and should they venture to visit them in their foreign asylum, they must not return to their native land. The youth of Flanders were forbidden to go abroad to acquire a foreign tongue, or to learn a trade, or to study in any university save that of Rome.

The carelessness with which the trials of the Blood Council were conducted was shocking. Batches were sent off to the gallows, including some whose cause had not been tried at all. When such were inquired for to take their trial, and it was found that their names had been inserted in the death-list, and that they had been sent to the gallows—a discovery which would have startled and discomposed most judges—the news was very coolly received by the men who constituted this terrible tribunal. Vargas on those occasions would console his fellow-judges by saying that "it was all the better for the souls of such that they were innocent."

One member of the Blood Council, John Hassels by name, was accustomed on the bench to sleep through the examinations of the prisoners, and when awakened to give his vote, he would rub his eyes and exclaim, "To the gallows! to the gallows!"[2867] In Valenciennes, in the space of three days, fifty-seven citizens of good position were beheaded. But Alva wanted more than their blood. He had boasted that he would make a stream of gold, three feet in depth, flow from the Netherlands to Spain, and he proceeded to make good his words. He imposed heavier subsidies upon the inhabitants. He demanded, first, the hundredth penny of every man's estate; secondly, the twentieth penny of all immovable property; and, thirdly, the tenth penny of all movable goods. This last was to be paid every time the goods were sold. Thus, if they changed hands five times it is clear that one-half their value had passed to the Government; and if, as sometimes happened, they changed hands ten times, their entire value was swallowed up by the Government tax. Under such a law no market could be kept open; all buying and selling must cease. The Netherlanders refused to submit to the tax, on the ground that it would bring what remained of their commerce to an utter end, and so defeat itself. After many cajoleries and threats, Alva made a virtue of necessity, and modified the tax.

Such is the melancholy record of the year 1568. Its gloom deepened as the months rolled on. First came the defeat of Count Louis, and the overcasting of the fair morning of a hoped-for deliverance for the miserable Provinces. Next were seen the scaffolds of Egmont and Horn, and of many others among the more patriotic of the Flemish nobility. Then followed the disastrous issue of the attempt of William to emancipate Brabant, and with it the loss of all his funds, and many thousands of lives, and a tightening of the tyrant's grasp upon the country. Wherever one turned one's eye there was a gibbet; wherever one planted one's foot there was blood. The cities were becoming silent; the air was thick with terror and despair. But if 1568 closed in gloom, 1569 rose in a gloom yet deeper.

In the beginning of this year the sword of persecution was still further sharpened. There came a new edict, addressed to the Stadtholders of the Provinces, enjoining that "when the Host or the holy oil for extreme unction was carried to sick people, strict notice should be taken of the behaviour, countenance, and words of every person, and that all those in whom any signs of irreverence were discovered should be punished; that all such dead bodies to which the clergy thought fit to deny Christian burial and the consecrated ground, should be thrown out on the gallows-field; that notice of it should be given to him (Alva), and their estates registered; and that all midwives should report every birth within twenty-four hours after the child had come into the world, to the end that it might be known whether the children were baptised after the Roman manner."[2868] The carrying out of this order necessitated the creation of a new class of agents. Spies were placed at the corners of all the streets, whose duty it was to watch the countenances of passers-by, and pounce on those whose looks were ill-favoured, and hale them to prison. These spies were nick-named the "Sevenpenny Men," because the wages of their odious work was paid them in pieces of that value. Thus the gallows and the stake continued to be fed.

The crowd of martyrs utterly defies enumeration. Many of them were of low estate, as the world accounts it, but they were rich in faith, noble in spirit, and heirs of a greater kingdom than Philip's, though they had to pass through the fire to receive possession of it. The deaths of all were the same, yet the circumstances in which it was endured were so varied, and in many cases so peculiar and tragic, that each differs from the other. Let us gave a very few examples. On the 8th of July, 1569, William Tavart was led to the place of execution in Antwerp, in order to undergo death by burning. While his executioners were binding his hands, and putting the gag into his mouth, being a man of eighty years and infirm, he fainted in their hands. He was thereupon carried back to his prison, and drowned. Another martyr, also very aged, worn out moreover by a long imprisonment, was kneeling on the faggots in prayer before being bound to the stake. The executioner, thinking that he was spending too much time in his devotions, rushed forward to raise him up and put him into the fire. He found that the old man was dead. The martyr had offered up his life in intention, and his gracious Master, compassionating his age and frailties, had given him the crown, yet spared him the agony of the stake. Richard Willemson, of Aspern, being pursued by an officer of the Blood Council, was making his escape on the ice. The ice gave way, and the officer fell in, and would have been drowned but for the humanity of the man whom he was pursuing, who, perceiving what had happened, turned back, and stretching out his hand, at the risk of being himself dragged in, pulled out his enemy. The magnanimous act touched the heart of the officer, and he would have let his deliverer escape; but unhappily the burgomaster happened to come up at the moment, and called out sharply, "Fulfil your oath." Thereupon he seized the poor man who but a moment before had saved his life, and conducted him to prison. He was condemned to the fire, and burned without the walls of Aspern, on the side next to Leerdam. While at the stake, a strong east wind springing up, the flames were blown away from the upper part of his body, leaving the lower extremities exposed to the torment of a slow fire. His cries were heard as far as Leerdam. In this fashion was he rewarded for saving his enemy's life at the peril of his own.

About the same time, four parish priests were degraded and burned at the Hague. The bishop first clothing them with their mass-garments, and then stripping them, as is usual on such occasions, said, in the Latin tongue, "I divest you of the robe of righteousness." "Not so," replied one of the four; "you divest us of the robe of Unrighteousness." "Nor can you," added the other three, "strip us of our salvation as you strip us of these vestments." Whereupon the bishop, with a grave countenance, laid his hand upon his breast, and calling on God, solemnly declared that "he believed from his heart that the Romish religion was the most certain way to salvation." "You did not always think so," replied Arent Dirkson, a man of seventy years, and known to be learned and judicious; "you knew the truth formerly, but you have maliciously rejected it, and you must answer for it at the great Day of Judgment." The words of the old man found a response in the conscience of the apostate. The bishop shook and trembled before his own prisoner. Nevertheless he went on with the condemnation of the four men, delivering them to the temporal arm with the usual prayer that the magistrate would deal tenderly with them. Upon this, the grey-haired pastor again burst out, "*Quam pharisaice!* How pharisaically do they treat us!" They were sent back to prison. The same night they celebrated the Lord's Supper for their mutual consolation, and continued till break of day in singing psalms, in reading the Holy Scriptures, and in prayer. The hour of execution being come, the father of one of the martyrs, mingling in the crowd, waited till his son should pass to the stake, that he might whisper a few words of encouragement. "My dear son," said he, when he saw him approach, "fight manfully for the crown of everlasting life." The guards instantly dragged the old man away to prevent him saying more. His sister now came forward, and spoke to him with equal courage. "Brother," cried she, "be constant; it will not last long; the gate of eternal life is open for you." The scene made a deep impression upon the spectators.

A burgher and bargeman of Amsterdam, Gerrit Cornelison by name, was one day brought out to be burned. In prison he had twice been tortured to force him to betray his associates, but no pain could overcome his constancy. Turning to the people at the stake, he cried, "Good people, eternity is so long, and our suffering here is so short, and yet the combat is very sharp and cruel. Alas! how am I distressed! O my flesh, bear and resist for a little, for this is thy last combat." This, his last battle, he fought courageously, and received the crown.[2869]

While these humble men were dying for their faith, Providence was preparing in high quarters for the deliverance of the country. After the close of his first unsuccessful campaign, William of Orange retired for a short time to France, and was present at the battle of Jarnac, where he witnessed the disaster which there befell the Huguenot arms. It seemed as if a thick cloud was everywhere gathering above the Protestant cause. In a few months he was recalled by his friends to Germany. Disguising himself as a peasant, and accompanied by only five attendants, he crossed the French lines, traversed Flanders in safety, and reached his principality of Nassau. He there learned all that had passed in the Netherlands during his absence. He was told that every day the tyranny of Alva waxed greater, as did also the odium in which both his person and government were held. The unhappy country had but one hope, and if that should misgive it, it must abandon itself to utter despair. That hope was himself. From all sides, from Roman Catholics as well as Protestants, from the exiles abroad and from the sufferers at home, came the most urgent appeals to him to again unfurl the standard of battle. He had consecrated his life to the defence of the Reformed religion, and the maintenance of his country's liberties, and was ready to respond to the appeal of those who had no human help save in his wisdom and courage. But he recollected what had so largely contributed to the failure of his first attempt, and before unsheathing the sword he set about collecting the sinews of war. William had already all but beggared himself in his attempt to break the yoke from the neck of the Netherlands; his plate and jewels and furniture had all been sold to pay his soldiers; his paternal estates were heavily burdened; he would give what remained of his possessions, together with his courage and blood, in promotion of the cause; but others also, at home and abroad, must contribute both their money and their blood, and in no stinted measure, if success was to crown their efforts. William took the first step by forming a comprehensive plan for raising the necessary funds.

The Flemish refugees in London and other parts had united together, and had fitted out a great number of armed vessels. These they sent to cruise on the English and Flemish seas, and make prize of all Spanish ships that came in their way. Their skill and daring were rewarded by numerous rich captures. As the growing fury of Alva swelled the number of refugees in London and other cities, so did the strength of the privateering fleet continue to increase. While Alva was gathering his taxes on land, they were reaping a rich harvest at sea. They scoured the English Channel, they hovered on the coast of the Netherlands, and preyed upon the merchandise of Spain. These cruisers became renowned under the title of the "Sea Beggars." It occurred to the Prince of Orange that these "terrible beggars" might do good service in the cause of their country's emancipation; and it was ultimately arranged that a fifth of the value of all the prizes which they made should be given to officers appointed by William, and the sum devoted to the support of the war of liberation.

Measures were at the same time adopted to improve the *morale* and discipline of a fleet that was becoming the terror of Alva and the Spaniards. No one was to exercise authority in it, save those to whom William himself should grant commissions. Every ship was to carry a Protestant minister on board, whose duty it was to conduct regular religious service; and no one who had ever been convicted of a crime was to be permitted to serve in the fleet. The ships of all friendly Powers were to pass untouched, and Alva and his adherents only were the Sea Beggars to regard as lawful prey.

At the same time the prince adopted another method of improving his finances in prospect of the coming war of independence. Commissions were given to the Protestant preachers, who traversed the Provinces in disguise, and collected money from all who were disaffected to the Spanish Government, or inimical to the Romish religion. None knew so well as they to whom to apply, or were so able by their eloquence to recommend the cause. William, besides, acquired by their means an intimate and accurate knowledge of the dispositions of all classes in the Netherlands. Their mission was specially successful in Holland and Zealand, where the Reformed religion had made greater progress than in the southern Provinces, and where the people, enjoying the natural defences of canals, rivers, and sea-friths, felt less the terror of the Spaniards. On these grounds, too, William resolved to seek in these northern parts a first footing for his enterprise. While these measures were being vigorously prosecuted in Holland, a trustworthy agent, Sonoy, was sent to canvass the Governments and people of Germany, adjuring them in the name of a common faith and a common liberty to put their shoulder to the great enterprise. Not a whisper of what was in preparation was wafted to the ears of Alva, although the prince's designs must have been known to a vast number of persons, so universal was the detestation in which the tyrant was held. Alva himself unconsciously helped to prepare the way for William, and to draw down the first blow of the great conflict.

It was about the end of March, 1572, and the fleet of the Beggars of the Sea was lying off Dover. Spain, smarting from the damage that these daring sea-rovers were constantly inflicting on her merchandise, complained to England that she opened her harbours to Flemish pirates, and permitted the goods stolen by them from Spanish subjects to be sold in her dominions, and so violated the treaties subsisting between the Spanish and English crowns. Elizabeth, though secretly friendly to the Flemish exiles, was yet unwilling to come to an open rupture with Philip, and accordingly she ordered their ships to quit her ports,[2870] and forbade her subjects to supply provisions to their crews. The Sea Beggars instantly weighed anchor, and shot across the German Sea. Half famished they arrived off the mouth of the Meuse, and sailed up its broad channel to Brill. The fleet was under the command of Admiral de la Marck, who held a commission from William of Orange. Coming to anchor opposite Brill, De la Marck sent a herald to summon the town to surrender. "The people," says Strada, "supposed them at first to be merchantmen cast upon their coast by storm, but before they were aware they brought war, not merchandise."[2871] Brill, though a small place, was strongly fortified, but the summons of the Beggars of the Sea inspired such a terror that the magistrates fled, and were followed by many of the inhabitants. De la Marck's soldiers battered open the gates, and having entered they hoisted their flag, and took possession of Brill, in the name of William of Orange. Thus on the 1st of April, 1572, were laid the foundations of the Free Protestant Holland, and thus was opened a conflict whose course of thirty years was to be marked by alternate defeats and triumphs, by the tragedies and crimes of a colossal tyranny, and the heroism and self-devotion of a not less colossal virtue and patriotism, till it should end in the overthrow of the mighty Empire of Spain, and the elevation of the little territory of Holland to a more stable prosperity, and a more enviable greatness and renown, than Philip's kingdom could boast in its palmiest days.

Meanwhile Alva was giving reins to a fury which had risen to madness. He was burning the Prince of Orange in effigy, he was dragging his escutcheon through the streets at the tails of horses, and proclaiming William and his offspring infamous to all posterity. At the same time he was fighting with the inhabitants about "the tenth penny." The consequences of enforcing so ruinous a tax, of which he had been warned, had now been realised: all buying and selling was suspended: the shops were shut, and the citizens found it impossible to purchase even the most common necessaries. Thousands were thrown out of employment, and the towns swarmed with idlers and beggars. Enraged at being thus foiled, Alva resolved to read the shopkeepers of Brussels a lesson which they should not soon forget. He made arrangements that when they awoke the next morning they should see eighteen of the leading members of their fraternity hanged at the doors of their own shops. The hangman had the ropes and ladders prepared overnight. But morning brought with it other things to occupy Alva's attention. A messenger arrived with the news that the great Sea Beggar, De la Marck, had made himself master of the town of Brill, and that the standard of William was floating on its walls. Alva was thunderstruck.[2872] The duke instantly dispatched Count Bossu to retake the town. The Spaniards advanced to the walls of Brill and began to batter them with their cannon. A carpenter leaped into the canal, swam to a sluice and with his axe hewed it open, and let in the sea. The rising waters compelled the besiegers to remove to the south side of the town, which chanced to be that on which De la Marck had planted his largest cannon. While the Spaniards were thundering at this gate, La Marck's men, issuing out at the opposite one, and rowing to the Spanish ships, set fire to them. When the Spaniards saw their ships beginning to blaze, and marked the waves steadily rising round them, they were seized with panic, and made a hasty retreat along the dyke. Many perished in the waves, the rest escaping to the fleet crowded into the vessels that remained unburned, weighed anchor and set sail. The inhabitants who had fled at the first surprise now returned, their names were registered, and all swore allegiance to the Prince of Orange, as Stadtholder for Philip.[2873]

Misfortune continued to dog the steps of the Spaniards. Bossu led his troops toward Dort, but the inhabitants, who had heard of the capture of Brill, closed their gates against him.[2874] He next took his way to Rotterdam. There too his demand for admission to a garrison in the king's name was met with a refusal. The crafty Spaniard had recourse to a stratagem. He asked leave for his companies to pass through one by one; this was given, but no sooner had the first company entered than Bossu, regardless of his promise, made his soldiers keep open the gates for his whole army. The citizens attempted to close the gates, but were hewn down; and the Spaniards, giving loose to their fury, spread themselves over the city, and butchered 400 of the inhabitants. The sanguinary and brutal ravages which Bossu's soldiers inflicted on Rotterdam had nearly as great an effect as the capture of Brill in spreading the spirit of revolt over Holland.

Flushing, an important town from its position at the mouth of the Scheldt, was the next to mount the flag of defiance to the Spaniards. They drove out the garrison of Alva, and razed the foundations of a citadel which the governor was preparing as the chain wherewith to bind them. Next day the Spanish fleet appeared in their harbour; the citizens were deliberating in the market-place when a drunken fellow proposed, for three guilders, to mount the ramparts, and fire one of the great guns upon the ships. The effect of that one unexpected shot was to strike the Spanish with panic. They let slip their cables and stood out to sea.

Two hundred years afterwards we find Flushing commemorating its deliverance from the yoke of Alva. The minutes of the consistory inform us "that the minister, Justus Tgeenk, preached [April 5th, 1772] in commemoration of Flushing's delivery from Spanish tyranny, which was stopped here on the 6th April, 1572, when the citizens, unassisted and unsupported by any foreign Power, drove out the Walloons and opened their gates, and laid the corner-stone of that singular and always remarkable revolution, which placed seven small Provinces in a state of indepencency, in despite of the utmost efforts of Philip II., then the most powerful monarch in Europe." The Sunday after (April 12th), the Lord's Supper was dispensed, and "at the table," say the minutes, was used "a silver chalice," the property of the burgomaster, E. Clyver, "wherein two hundred years ago the Protestants in this town had, for the first time, celebrated the Lord's Supper in a cellar here at the head of the Great Market, on account of the unrelenting persecution."[2875]

In a few months all the more important towns of Holland and Zealand followed the example of Brill and Flushing, and hung out upon their walls the standard of the man in whom they recognised their deliverer.[2876] Haarlem, Leyden, Gouda, Horn, Alkmaar, Enkhuizen, and many others broke their chain. No soldier of the prince, no sea-rover of De la Marck's incited them to revolt: the movement was a thoroughly spontaneous one; it originated with the citizens themselves, the great majority of whom cherished a hatred of the Roman faith, and a detestation of Spanish tyranny. Amsterdam was the only exception that is worth noting in Holland. The flame which had been kindled spread into Friesland, and Utrecht and other towns placed their names on the distinguished list of cities that came forth at this great crisis to the help of conscience and of liberty against the mighty.

A small incident which happened at this moment was fraught with vast consequences. Count Louis of Nassau, approaching from France, made himself master of the frontier town of Mons in the south.[2877] Alva was excessively mortified by this mishap, and he was bent on recovering the place. He was counselled to defer the siege of Mons till he should have extinguished the rising in the north. He was reminded that Holland and Zealand were deeply infected with heresy; that there the Prince of Orange was personally popular; that nature had fortified these Provinces by intersecting them with rivers and arms of the sea, and that if time were given the inhabitants to strengthen their canals and cities, many sieges and battles might not suffice to reduce them to their obedience. This advice was eminently wise, but Alva stopped his ear to it. He went on with the siege of Mons, and while "he was plucking this thorn out of his foot," the conflagration in the north of the Netherlands had time to spread. He succeeded eventually in extracting the thorn—that is, he took Mons—but at the cost of losing Holland.

William himself had not yet arrived in the Netherlands, but he was now on his way thither at the head of a new army wellnigh 20,000 strong, which he had raised in Germany. He caused to be distributed before him copies of a declaration, in which he set forth the grounds of his taking up arms. These were, in brief, "the security of the rights and privileges of the country, and the freedom of conscience." In the instructions which he issued to his deputy in Holland, Diedrich Sonoy, he required him, "first of all, to deliver the towns of that Province from Spanish slavery, and to restore them to their ancient liberties, rights and privileges, and to take care that the Word of God be preached and published there, but yet by no means to suffer that those of the Romish Church should be in any sort prejudiced, or that any impediment should be offered to them in the exercise of their religion."[2878]

Meanwhile, Alva was left literally without a penny; finding it hard to prosecute the siege of Mons on an empty military chest, he announced his willingness to remit the tax of the tenth penny, provided the States-General would give him "the annual twenty tuns of gold"[2879] (about two millions of florins) which they had formerly promised him in lieu of the obnoxious tax; and he summoned the States of Holland to meet at the Hague, on the 15th of July, and consider the matter.

The States of Holland met on the day named, not at the Hague, but at Dort; and in obedience to the summons, not of Alva, but of William. Nor had they assembled to deliberate on the proposal of Alva, and to say whether it was the "tenth penny" or the "twenty tuns of gold" that they were henceforth to lay at his feet. The banner of freedom now floated on their walls, and they had met to devise the means of keeping it waving there. The battle was only beginning: the liberty which had been proclaimed had yet to be fought for. Of this we find their great leader reminding them. In a letter which William addressed at this time to the States of Holland, he told them, in words as plain as they were weighty, that if in a quarrel like this they should show themselves sparing of their gold, they would incur the anger of the great Ruler, they would make themselves the scorn of foreign nations, and they would bind a bloody yoke on themselves and their posterity for ever. William was not present in the assembly at Dort, but he was ably represented by St. Aldegonde. This eloquent plenipotentiary addressed the members in a powerful speech, in which he rehearsed the efforts the Prince of Orange had already made for the deliverance of the land from Spanish cruelty; that he had embarked the whole of his fortune in the struggle; that the failure of the expedition of 1568 was owing to no fault of his, but entirely to his not being adequately supported, not a Fleming having lifted a finger in the cause; that he was again in the field with an army, and that supplies must be found if it was to be kept there, or if it was to accomplish anything for the country. "Arouse ye, then," were the thrilling words in which St. Aldegonde concluded his oration, "awaken your own zeal and that of your sister cities. Seize Opportunity by the locks, who never appeared fairer than she does today."

St. Aldegonde was further instructed by the prince to state the broad and catholic aims that he proposed to himself in the struggle which they were to wage together. If that struggle should be crowned with success, the Papist would have not less cause to rejoice than the Protestant; the two should divide the spoils. "As for religion," said St. Aldegonde, "the desires of the prince are that liberty of conscience should be allowed as well to the Reformed as to the Roman Catholics; that each party should enjoy the public exercise of it in churches or chapels, without any molestation, hindrance, or trouble, and that the clergy should remain free and unmolested in their several functions, provided they showed no tokens of disaffection, and that all things should be continued on this footing till the States-General otherwise directed." In these intentions the States expressed themselves as at one with the prince.

A patriotic response was made to the prince's appeal by the Northern Netherlands. All classes girded themselves for the great struggle. The aristocracy, the guilds, the religious houses, and the ordinary citizens came forward with gifts and loans. Money, plate, jewellery, and all kinds of valuables were poured into the common treasury. A unanimous resolution of the States declared the Prince of Orange Stadtholder of Holland. The taxes were to be levied in his name, and all naval and land officers were to take an oath of obedience to him. What a contrast between the little territory and the greatness of the contest that is about to be waged! We behold the inhabitants of a small platform of earth, walled in by dykes lest the ocean should drown it, heroically offering themselves to fight the world's battle against that great combination of kingdoms, nationalities, and armies that compose the mighty monarchy of Spain!

CHAPTER XVII
WILLIAM'S SECOND CAMPAIGN, AND SUBMISSION OF BRABANT AND FLANDERS

WILLIAM, Prince of Orange, Stadtholder and virtual King of Holland, Zealand, and Friesland, if the prayers and suffrages of an entire people can avail to invest one with that august office, was approaching the Netherlands at the head of his newly-enrolled levies. He crossed the Rhine on the 7th of July, 1572, with an army of 17,000 foot and 7,000 horse. Advancing as far as Roermonde, he halted before that town to demand a supply of provisions for his soldiers. The government of the place was in the hands of zealous Roman Catholics, and the refusal of Roermonde to comply with the request of the Liberator was rendered still more ungracious by the haughtiness and insolence with which it was accompanied. William stormed the city and took it. Unhappily his soldiers here dishonoured the cause for which the prince was in arms, by putting to death certain priests and monks under circumstances of great barbarity. Germany was at that time a magazine of mercenary soldiers, from which both the Prince of Orange and Alva drew supplies, and troops of this class were but little amenable to discipline when their pay fell into arrears, as was now the case. But William felt that such excesses must be checked at all hazards, otherwise his cause would be disgraced and ultimately ruined; and accordingly he issued an order forbidding all such barbarities in future under pain of death.[2880]

For some time his march was a triumphal one. The standards of William shed a gleam through the darkness that shrouded Brabant, and the spirits of its terror-stricken inhabitants for a moment revived. On the first occasion when the Deliverer approached their cities, the Flemings abode within their gates, but now they seemed as if they would rise at his call, and redeem themselves from the yoke of Spain. The important city of Mechlin declared in his favour. Louvain refused to admit a garrison of his soldiers, but sent him a contribution of 16,000 ducats. Tirlemont, Termonde, Oudenarde, Nivelles, and many other towns and villages opened their gates to the prince; the most part spontaneously, in the eager hope of deliverance from a tyranny which threatened to cease its ravages only when nothing more should be left in the Netherlands to destroy.

A successful beginning of the great struggle had been made, but now the prince began to be in straits. The friends of the cause had not yet realised its full grandeur or its immense difficulty, and their scale of giving was totally inadequate. If the tide of bigotry and tyranny now overflowing Christendom was to be stemmed, the friends of liberty, both at home and abroad, must not be sparing either of their blood or their gold. But as yet it was hardly understood that all must be parted with if the pearl of freedom was to be won.

But if the States of Holland, and the refugees in England and other countries, were sending supplies which were disproportionate to the enormous expense to which William had been put in levying, equipping, and maintaining his troops, he had the best hopes of succours from France. The net was then being woven for the Huguenots, and their great chief, Admiral Coligny, was being caressed at the court of the Louvre. "I will fight Philip of Spain on the soil of the Netherlands," said that consummate dissembler, Charles IX. "William of Orange

Book Eighteenth

shall not want for money and soldiers," continued he, with a frankness that seemed the guarantee of a perfect sincerity. Coligny suffered himself to be persuaded of the good faith of the king, and laboured to produce the same conviction in the mind of the Prince of Orange, bidding him expect him soon at the head of 15,000 Huguenots. William, believing that France was at his back, thought that the campaign could have but one issue—namely, the expulsion of the Spaniards, and the liberation of the Netherlands from their unbearable yoke. But his hopes were destined to a cruel overthrow. Instead of an army of Huguenots to help him on to victory, there came tidings that felled him to the earth. Three weeks from the date of Coligny's letter, William received the terrible news of the St. Bartholomew Massacre. The men who were to have emancipated the Low Countries were watering with their blood and strewing with their corpses the plains of their native land! The Prince of Orange opened his eyes on blank desolation; he saw the campaign ending in inevitable failure, and the dark night of Spanish oppression again closing in around a country which he had believed to be as good as emancipated. The shock was terrible, but the lesson was salutary. Those instruments whom Providence selects to fight the holy battles of religion and freedom need a higher training than ordinary warriors. To genius and courage heroes of this class must add faith; but this quality they can acquire only in the school of repeated disappointment. They can never learn this virtue in the midst of numerous and victorious hosts, where success is won by mere numbers, and where victory is of that ordinary and vulgar sort which the worst as well as the best of causes can command.

The fate of his second campaign had been decided at Paris when the St. Bartholomew was struck, but William still continued to prosecute the war. His attempts, however, to stem the swelling tide of Spanish tyranny were without success. First, he failed to relieve his brother, who was shut up in the city of Mons, besieged by Alva; next, he himself narrowly escaped being captured by the Spaniards in a night attack on his camp, in which 600 of his soldiers were slain. He owed his escape to a small spaniel which he kept in his bed-chamber, and which awoke him by scratching his face.[2881] There followed a mutiny of his troops, provoked by the repeated disasters that had befallen them, and the arrears due to them, but which the prince was unable to discharge; they talked, indeed, of delivering him up to Alva. They soon became ashamed at having harboured so base a design, but the incident convinced William that he had no alternative but to disband his army and retire to Holland, and this course he now adopted.

The departure of the Prince of Orange was the signal for Alva to take a terrible revenge on those cities in Brabant which had hoisted the flag of the Deliverer. Mons surrendered, but the terms of the capitulation were most perfidiously violated by the Spaniards. The citizens were sent in hundreds to the gallows; murder and spoliation ran riot in its streets; the axe and the halter rested not for well-nigh a whole year, till the awful silence proclaimed that Mons was now little else than a charnel-house. Its commercial prosperity never recovered this terrible blow. Those of its merchants and artisans who had escaped the gibbet were driven away, and only beggars and idlers were left in their room—a meet population, surely, to wear the yoke of Spain.

In the eyes of Alva, the archiepiscopal city of Mechlin was a greater offender than even Mons, and he resolved to wreak upon it, if possible, a yet more terrible vengeance. Considering the strength of its Romanism, and the rank and influence of its clergy, one would have expected that it would be the last city in Brabant to open its gates to William; it was, as we have seen, the first. The conqueror resolved that it should suffer as pre-eminently as it had sinned. His regiments had recently received no pay, and Alva pointed to the rich city of the priests, and bade them seek their wages in it. The soldiers threw themselves upon the town, like a pack of hungry wolves upon their prey. Some swam the moat, others battered open the gates, while hundreds, by the help of scaling-ladders, climbed the walls, and swarmed down into the city. Along every street and lane poured a torrent of furious men, robbing, murdering, violating, without making the least distinction between friend and foe, Papist and Protestant. No age, nor sex, nor rank, nor profession had exemption from the sword, or the worse brutality of the soldiery. Blood flowed in torrents. Churches, monasteries, private dwellings, and public establishments were broken into and pillaged to the last penny. Altars were pulled down, the chalices and other rich vessels used in the mass were carried off, the very Host itself was profaned and trodden under foot by men who professed to regard it as the body and soul of Christ, and who had come from a distant land to avenge the insults which had been offered to it by others. Their rage far exceeded that of the iconoclasts, who had vented their fury on idols alone. Three days this dreadful work went on,[2882] and then the soldiers of Alva collected their booty, and carrying it on board ship, sent it off to Antwerp, to be converted into money.[2883] The inhabitants of the other cities which had submitted to William were permitted to redeem their lives by the payment of an enormous ransom.

Not so, however, the cities of Zutphen and Naarden. Zutphen was subjected to the same shocking barbarities which had been inflicted on Mechlin. Here the spoil to be gathered was less, for the town was not so rich as Mechlin, but the licence given to the sword was on that account all the greater; and when the soldiers grew weary with slaughtering, they threw their victims into the Issel, and indulged themselves in the horrid pastime of pelting the drowning men and women with missiles as they rose to the surface before finally sinking. We record the fate of Naarden last, because its doom was the most appalling of the three; for it is a series of horrors which we are thus briefly tracing to its climax. Naarden opened its gates to Don Frederic de Toledo, the son of Alva, on a promise of immunity from sack for a slight equivalent. The promise of Toledo was violated with a shocking perfidy. First the male population were put to the sword; then their wives and daughters were brutally outraged, and afterwards nearly all were massacred. The dwellings, the convents, and the hospitals were ransacked for treasure and spoil; and when the fiends had satiated to the utmost their bloodthirstiness, lust, and greed, they drove out the few miserable inhabitants that remained into the open fields, and setting fire to Naarden they burned it to the ground. A blackened spot covered with charred ruins, ashes, and the remains of human carcases marked where the city had stood. It was amid these clouds and tempests that the year 1572 closed. What a contrast to the brilliant promise with which it had opened, when city after city was hanging out the banner of William upon its walls, and men were congratulating themselves that the black night of Spanish usurpation and oppression had come to an end, and the fair morning of independence had dawned! Smitten down by the mailed hand of Alva, the cities of Brabant and Flanders are again seen creeping back into their chains.

Occupied in the siege of Mons and the reduction of the revolted towns in the Southern Netherlands, the Spanish army were compelled meanwhile to leave the Northern Provinces in peace. The leisure thus afforded them the Hollanders wisely turned to account by increasing the number of their ships, repairing the fortifications of their towns, and enrolling soldiers. They saw the terrible legions of Alva coming nearer every day, their path marked in ruins and blood; but they were not without hope that the preparations they had made, joined to the natural defences of their country, here intersected by rivers, there by arms of the sea, would enable them to make a more successful resistance than Brabant and Flanders had done. When the tyrant should ask them to bow again their necks to the yoke, they trusted to be able to say, "No," without undergoing the terrible alternative with which Alva chastised refusal in the case of the Brabant cities—namely, halters for themselves, and horrible outrage for their families. Meanwhile they waited anxiously for the coming of William. He would breathe courage into their hearts, ready to faint at the dreaded prowess of the Spaniards.

At length William arrived in Holland; but he came alone; of the 24,000 troops which he had led into the Netherlands at the opening of his second campaign, only seventy horsemen now remained; nevertheless, his arrival was hailed with joy, for the Hollanders felt that the wisdom, patriotism, and bravery of the prince would be to them instead of an army. William met the Estates at Haarlem, and deliberated with them on the course to be taken. It was the darkest hour of the Netherlands. The outlook all round was not only discouraging, but appalling. The wealthy Flanders and Brabant were again under the heel of the haughty and cruel Spaniard. Of their populous cities, blackened ruins marked the site of some; those that existed were sitting in sullen silence with the chain around their neck; the battle for liberty of conscience had been forced back into Northern Holland; here the last stand must be made; the result must be victory or utter extermination. The foe with whom the Hollanders were to do battle was no ordinary one; he was exasperated to the utmost degree; he neither respected an oath nor spared an enemy; if they should resist, they had in Naarden an awful monument before their eyes of what their own fate would be if their resistance were unsuccessful; and yet the alternative! Submission to the Spanish yoke! Rather ten deaths than endure a slavery so vile. The resolution of the Convention was prompt and decided: they would worship according to their consciences or die.

William now began to prepare for the great struggle. His sagacity taught him that Holland needed other defences besides ships and walls and soldiers, if it was to bear the immense strain to which it was about to be subjected. First of all, he settled the boundaries of his own power, by voluntarily agreeing to do nothing but with the consent of the States. By limiting he strengthened his influence. Next he consolidated the union of the nation by admitting twelve new cities into the Convention, and giving them the same voice in public affairs as the older towns. He next set about re-organising the civil service of the country, which had fallen into great disorder during these unsettled times. Many of the principal inhabitants had fled; numbers of the judges and officers of the revenue had abandoned their posts, to the great detriment of justice and the loss of the finances. William filled up these vacancies with Protestants, deeming them the only thoroughly trustworthy persons in a contest that was to determine which of the two faiths was to be the established religion of Holland.

Before opening the campaign, the Prince of Orange took a step toward the settlement of the religious question. It was resolved that both Papists and Protestants should enjoy the public exercise of their worship, and that no one should be molested on account of his religion, provided he lived quietly, and kept no correspondence with the Spaniards.[2884] In this William obeyed the wishes of the great body of the people of Holland, who had now espoused the Reformed faith, and at the same time he laid a basis for unity of action by purging out, so far as he could, the anti-national element from the public service, and took reasonable precautions against surprise and treachery when Holland should be waging its great battle for existence.

At the moment that the Hollanders were not unnaturally oppressed with grave thoughts touching the issue of the struggle for which they were girding themselves, uncertain whether their county was to become the burial-place of their liberties and their persons, or a theatre of a yet higher civilisation, an incident occurred that helped to enliven their spirits, and confirm them in their resolution to resist. The one city in Holland that remained on the side of Alva was Amsterdam, and thither Toledo, after the butchery at Naarden, marched with his army. In the shallow sea around Amsterdam, locked up in the ice, lay part of the Dutch fleet. The Spanish general sent a body of troops over the frozen waters to attack the ships. Their advance was perceived, and the Dutch soldiers, fastening on their skates, and grasping their muskets, descended the ships' sides to give battle to the Spaniards. Sweeping with the rapidity of a cloud towards the enemy, they poured a deadly volley into his ranks, and then wheeling round, they retreated with the same celerity out of reach of his fire. In this fashion they kept advancing and retreating, each time doing murderous execution upon the Spanish lines, while their own ranks remained unbroken. Confounded by this novel method of battle, the Spaniards were compelled to quit the field, leaving some hundreds of their dead upon the ice. Next day a thaw set in, which lasted just long enough to permit the Dutch fleet to escape, while the returning frost made pursuit impossible. The occurrence was construed by the Dutch as a favourable omen.

Established at Amsterdam, the Spanish sword had cut Holland in two, and from this central point it was resolved to carry that sword over North and South Holland, making its cities, should they resist, so many Naardens, and its inhabitants slaves of Alva or corpses. It was agreed to begin with Haarlem, which was some twelve English miles to the south-west of Amsterdam. Toledo essayed first of all to win over the citizens by mediation, thinking that the fate of Naarden had inspired them with a salutary terror of his arms, and that they only waited to open their gates to him. The tragic end of Naarden had just the opposite effect on the citizens of Haarlem. It showed them that those who submitted and those who resisted met the same fearful destruction. Notwithstanding, two of the magistrates, moved by terror and cowardice, secretly opened negotiations with

Toledo for the surrender of Haarlem; but no sooner did this come to the ears of Ripperda, a Friesland gentleman, to whom William had committed the government of the town, than he assembled the citizens and garrison in the market-place, and warned them against entertaining the idea of submission. What have those gained, he asked, who have trusted the promise of the Spaniards? Have not these men shown that they are as devoid of faith as they are of humanity? Their assurances are only a strategem for snatching the arms from your hands, and then they will load you with chains or butcher you like sheep. From the blood-sprinkled graves of Mechlin, of Zutphen, and of Naarden let the voices of our brethren call on you to resist. Let us remember our oath to the Prince of Orange, whom we have acknowledged the only lawful governor of the Province; let us think of the righteousness of our cause, and resolve, rather than live the slaves of the Spaniards, to die with arms in our hands, fighting for our religion and our laws. This appeal was responded to by the stout-hearted citizens with enthusiastic shouts. As one man they proclaimed their resolution to resist the Spaniard to the death.

CHAPTER XVIII
THE SIEGE OF HAARLEM

BOTH sides began to prepare for the inevitable struggle. The Prince of Orange established himself at Leyden, the town nearest Haarlem on the south, and only some ten English miles distant from it. He hoped from this point to be able to direct the defence, and forward provisions and reinforcements as the brave little town might need them. Alva and his son Toledo, on the other hand, when they learned that Haarlem, instead of opening its gates, had resolved to resist, were filled with rage, and immediately gave orders for the march of their troops on that presumptuous little city which had dared to throw down the gage of battle to the whole power of Spain.

Advancing along the causeway which traverses the narrow isthmus that separates the waters of the Haarlem lake from the Zuyder Zee, the Spanish army, on the 11th of December, 1572, sat down before Haarlem. Regiment continued to arrive after regiment till the beleaguering army was swelled to 30,000,[2885] and the city was now completely invested. This force was composed of Spaniards, Germans, and Walloons. The population of Haarlem did not exceed 30,000; that is, it was only the equal in number to that of the host now encamped outside its walls. Its ramparts were far from strong; its garrison, even when at the highest, was not over 4,000 men,[2886] and it was clear that the defence of the town must lie mainly with the citizens, whom patriotism had converted into heroes. Nor did the war-spirit burn less ardently in the breasts of the wives and daughters of Haarlem than in those of their fathers and husbands. Three hundred women, all of them of unblemished character, and some of high birth, enrolled themselves in defence of the city, and donning armour, mounted the walls, or sallying from the gates, mingled with their husbands and brothers in the fierce conflicts waged with the enemy under the ramparts. This army of amazons was led by Kenau Hasselaer, a widow of forty-seven years of age, and a member of one of the first families of Haarlem.[2887] "Under her command," says Strada, "her females were emboldened to do soldiers' duty at the bulwarks, and to sally out among the firelocks, to the no less encouragement of their own men than admiration of the enemy."

Toledo's preparations for the siege were favoured by a thick mist which hung above the Lake of Haarlem, and concealed his operations. But if the haze favoured the Spanish general, it befriended still more the besieged, inasmuch as it allowed provisions and reinforcements to be brought into the city before it was finally invested. Moving on skates, hundreds of soldiers and peasants sped rapidly past the Spanish lines unobserved in the darkness. One body of troops, however, which had been sent by William from Leyden, in the hope of being able to enter the town before its blockade, were attacked and routed, and the cannon and provisions destined for the besieged were made the booty of the Spaniards. About a thousand were slain, and numbers made prisoners and carried off to the gibbets which already bristled all round the walls, and from this time were never empty, relay after relay of unhappy captives being led to execution upon them.

Don Frederic de Toledo had fixed his headquarters at the Gate of the Cross. This was the strongest part of the fortifications, the gate being defended by a ravelin, but Toledo held the besieged in so great contempt that he deemed it a matter of not the least consequence where he should begin his assault, whether at the weakest or at the strongest point. Haarlem, he believed, following the example of the Flemish cities, would capitulate at almost the first sound of his cannon. He allotted one week for the capture, and another for the massacring and ravishing. This would be ample time to finish at Haarlem; then, passing on in the same fashion from city to city, he would lay waste each in its turn, till nothing but ruins should remain in Holland. With this programme of triumph for himself, and of overthrow for the Dutch, he set vigorously to work. His cannon now began to thunder against the gate and ravelin. In three days a breach was made in the walls, and the soldiers were ordered to cross the ditch and deliver the assault. Greedy of plunder, they rushed eagerly into the breach, but the Spaniards met a resistance which they little anticipated. The alarm-bell in Haarlem was rung, and men, women, and children swarmed to the wall to repel the foe. They opened their cannon upon the assailants, the musketry poured in its fire, but still more deadly was the shower of miscellaneous yet most destructive missiles rained from the ramparts on the hostile masses below. Blocks of stone, boiling pitch, blazing iron hoops, which clung to the necks of those on whom the fell, live coals, and other projectiles equally dreadful, which even Spanish ferocity could not withstand, were hurled against the invaders. After contending some time with a tempest of this sort, the attacking party had to retire, leaving 300 dead, and many officers killed or wounded.

This repulse undeceived Toledo. He saw that behind these feeble walls was a stout spirit, and that to make himself master of Haarlem would not be the easy achievement he had fancied it would prove. He now began to make his preparations on a scale more commensurate with the difficulty of the enterprise; but a whole month passed away before he was ready to renew the assault. Meanwhile, the Prince of Orange exerted himself, not unsuccessfully, to reinforce the city. The continuance of the frost kept the lake congealed, and he was able to introduce into Haarlem, over the ice, some 170 sledges, laden with munitions and provisions, besides 400 veteran soldiers. A still larger body of 2,000 men sent by the prince were attacked and routed, having lost their way in the thick mist which, in these winter days, hung almost perpetually around the city, and covered the camp of the besiegers. Koning, the second in command of this expedition, being made prisoner, the Spaniards cut off his head and threw it over the walls into the city, with an inscription which bore that "this Koning or King was on his road, with two thousand auxiliaries, to raise the siege." The rejoinder of the Haarlemers were in a vein of equal barbarity. They decapitated twelve of their prisoners, and, putting their heads into a cask, they rolled it down into the Spanish trenches, with this label affixed:—"The tax of the tenth penny, with the interest due thereon for delay of payment." The Spaniards retaliated by hanging up a group of Dutch prisoners by the feet in view of their countrymen on the walls; and the besieged cruelly responded by gibbeting a number of Spanish prisoners in sight of the camp. These horrible reciprocities, begun by Alva, were continued all the while that he and his son remained in the Netherlands.

By the end of January, 1573, Toledo was ready to resume the operations of the siege. He dug trenches to protect his men from the fire of the ramparts, a precaution which he had neglected at the beginning, owing to the contempt in which he held the foe. Three thousand sappers had been sent him from the mines of Liége. Thus reinforced he resumed the cannonade. But the vigilance and heroism of the citizens of Haarlem long rendered his efforts abortive. He found it hard by numbers, however great, and skill, however perfect, to batter down walls which a patriotism so lofty defended. The besieged would sally forth at unexpected moments upon the Spanish camp, slay hundreds of the foe, set fire to his tents, seize his cannon and provisions, and return in triumph into the city. When Toledo's artillery had made an opening in the walls, and the Spaniards crowded into the breach, instead of the instant massacre and plunder which their imaginations had pictured, and which they panted to begin, they would find themselves in presence of an inner battery that the citizens had run up, and that awaited the coming of the Spaniards to rain its murderous fire upon them. The sappers and miners would push their underground trenches below the ramparts, but when just about to emerge upon the streets of the city, as they thought, they would find their progress suddenly stopped by a counter-mine, which brought them face to face in the narrow tunnel with the citizens, and they had to wage a hand-to-hand battle with them. These underground combats were of frequent occurrence. At other times the Haarlemers would dig deeper than the Spaniards, and, undermining them, would fill the excavation with gunpowder and set fire to it. The ground would suddenly open, and vomit forth vast masses of earth, stones, mining implements, mixed horribly with the dissevered limbs of human beings.

After some days' cannonading, Toledo succeeded in battering down the wall that extended between the Gate of the Cross and that of St. John, and now he resolved to storm the breach with all his forces. Hoping to take the citizens by surprise, he assembled his troops overnight, and assigning to each his post, and particularly instructing all, he ordered them to advance. Before the sentinels on the walls were aware, several of the storming party had gained the summit of the breach, but here their progress was arrested. The bells of Haarlem rang out the alarm, and the citizens, roused from sleep, hurried *en masse* to the ramparts, where a fierce struggle began with the Spaniards. Stones, clubs, fire-brands, every sort of weapon was employed to repel the foe, and the contest was still going on when the day broke. After morning mass in the Spanish camp, Toledo ordered the whole of his army to advance to the walls. By the sheer force of numbers the ravelin which defended the Gate of the Cross was carried—a conquest that was to cost the enemy dear. The besiegers pressed tumultuously into the fortress, expecting to find a clear path into the city; but a most mortifying check awaited them. The inhabitants, labouring incessantly, had reared a half-moon battery behind the breached portion of the wall,[2888] and instead of the various spoil of the city, for which the Spaniards were so greedily athirst, they beheld the cannon of the new erection frowning defiance upon them. The defenders opened fire upon the mass of their assailants pent up beneath, but a yet greater disaster hung over the enemy. The ravelin had been previously undermined, the citizens foreseeing its ultimate capture, and now when they saw it crowded with the besiegers they knew that the moment was come for firing it. They lighted the match, and in a few moments came the peal of the explosion, and the huge mass, with the hundreds of soldiers and officers whom it enclosed, was seen to soar into the air, and then descend in a mingled shower of stones and mangled and mutilated bodies. The Spaniards stood aghast at the occurrence. The trumpet sounded a retreat; and the patriots issuing forth, before the consternation had subsided, chased the besiegers to their encampments.[2889]

Toledo saw the siege was making no progress. As fast as he battered down the old walls the citizens erected new defences; their constant sallies were taxing the vigilance and thinning the numbers of his troops; more of his men were perishing by cold and sickness than by battle; his supplies were often intercepted, and scarcity was beginning to be felt in his camp; in these circumstances he began to entertain the idea of raising the siege. Not a few of his officers concurred with him, deeming the possession of Haarlem not worth the labour and lives which it was costing. Others, however, were opposed to this course, and Toledo referred the matter to his father, the duke.

The stern Alva, not a little scandalised that his son should for a moment entertain such a thought, wrote commanding him to prosecute the siege, if he would not show himself unworthy of the stock from which he was sprung. He advised him, instead of storming, to blockade the city; but in whatever mode, he must prosecute the siege till Haarlem had fallen. If he was unwilling to go on, Alva said he would come himself, sick though he was; or if his illness should make this impossible, he would bring the duchess from Spain, and place her in command of the army. Stung by this sarcasm, Toledo, regardless of all the difficulties, resumed the operations of the siege.

In the middle of February, the frost went off, and the ice dissolving, the Lake of Haarlem became navigable. In anticipation of this occurrence, the Prince of Orange had constructed a number of vessels, and lading them with provisions, dispatched them from Leyden. Sailing along the lake, with a favourable wind, they entered Haarlem in safety. This was done oftener than once, and the spectre of famine was thus kept at a distance. The besieged were in good spirits; so long as they held the lake they would have bread to eat, and so long as bread did not fail them they would defend their city. Meanwhile they gave the besiegers no rest. The sallies from the town, sometimes from one quarter, sometimes from another, were of almost daily occurrence. On the 25th of March, 1,000 of the soldier-citizens threw themselves upon the outposts of Toledo's army, drove them in, burned 300 tents, and captured cannon, standards, and many wagon-loads of provisions, and returned with them to the city. The exploit was performed in the face of 30,000 men. This attacking party of 1,000 had slain each his man nearly, having left 800 dead in the Spanish camp, while only four of their own number had fallen.[2890] The citizens were ever eager to provoke the Spaniards to battle; and with this view they erected altars upon the walls in sight of the camp, and tricked them out after the Romish fashion; they set up images, and walking in procession dressed in canonicals, they derided the Popish rites, in the hope of stinging the champions of that faith into fighting. They feared the approach of famine more than they did the Spanish sword. Alva was amazed, and evidently not a little mortified, to see such valour in rebels and heretics, and was unable to withhold the expression of his astonishment. "Never was a place defended with such skill and bravery as Haarlem," said he, writing to Philip; "it was a war such as never was seen or heard of in any land on earth."[2891]

But now the tide began to turn against the heroic champions of Protestant liberty. Haarlem was more closely invested than ever, and a more terrible enemy than the Spaniards began to make its appearance, gaunt famine namely. Count Bossu, the lieutenant of Toledo, had mustered a fleet of armed vessels at Amsterdam, and entering the Lake of Haarlem, fought a series of naval battles with the ships of the Prince of Orange for the possession of that inland sea. Being a vital point, it was fiercely contested on both sides, and after much bloodshed, victory declared for the Spaniards. This stopped nearly all supplies to the city by water. On the land side Haarlem was as completely blockaded, for Alva had sent forward additional reinforcements; and although William was most assiduous in dispatching relief for the besieged, the city was so strictly watched by the enemy that neither men nor provisions could now enter it. In the end of May bread failed. The citizens sent to make William aware of their desperate straits. The prince employed a carrier pigeon as the bearer of his answer.[2892] He bade them endure a little longer, and to encourage them to hold out he told them that he was assembling a force, and hoped soon to be able to throw provisions into their city. Meanwhile the scarcity became greater every day, and by the beginning of June the famine had risen to a most dreadful height. Ordinary food was no longer to be had, and the wretched inhabitants were reduced to the necessity of subsisting on the most loathsome and abominable substitutes. They devoured horses, dogs, cats, mice, and similar vermin. When these failed, they boiled the hides of animals and ate them; and when these too were exhausted, they searched the graveyards for nettles and rank grass. Groups of men, women, and children, smitten down by the famine, were seen dead in the streets. But though their numbers diminished, their courage did not abate. They still showed themselves on the walls, "the few performed the duties of many;"[2893] and if a Spanish helmet ventured to appear above the earth-works, a bullet from the ramparts, shot with deadly aim, tumbled its owner into the trenches.

They again made the prince aware of the misery to which they were reduced, adding that unless succours were sent within a very short time they would be compelled to surrender. William turned his eyes to the Protestant Queen of England, and the Lutheran princes of Germany, and implored them to intervene in behalf of the heroic little city. But Elizabeth feared to break with Philip; and the tide of Jesuit reaction in Germany was at that moment too powerful to permit of its Protestants undertaking any enterprise beyond their own borders; and so the sorely beleaguered city was left wholly in the hands of the prince. He did all which it was possible for one in his circumstances to do for its deliverance. He collected an army of 5,000, chiefly burghers of good condition in the cities of Holland, and sent them on to Haarlem, with 400 wagon-loads of provision, having first given notice to the citizens by means of carrier pigeons of their approach. This expedition William wished to conduct in person, but the States, deeming his life of more value to Holland than many cities, would not suffer him to risk it, and the enterprise was committed to the charge of Count Battenburg. The expedition set out on the evening of the 8th of July, but the pigeons that carried the letters of Orange having been shot, the plan of relief became known to the Spaniards, and their whole army was put under arms to await the coming of Battenburg. He thought to have passed their slumbering camp at midnight, but suddenly the whole host surrounded him; his fresh troops were unable to withstand the onset of these veterans; 2,000 were slain, including their leader; the rest were dispersed, and the convoy of provisions fell into the hands of the victors. William could do no more—the last hope of Haarlem was gone.[2894] The patriots now offered to surrender on condition that the town were exempt from pillage, and the garrison permitted to march out. Toledo replied that the surrender must be unconditional. The men of Haarlem understood this to mean that Toledo had devoted them to destruction. They had before them death by starvation or death by the Spaniards. The latter they regarded as by much the more dreadful alternative. The fighting men, in their despair, resolved on cutting their way, sword in hand, through the Spanish camp, in the hope that the enemy would put a curb on his ferocity when he found only women and children, and these emaciated and woe-struck, in the city. But the latter, terror-stricken at the thought of being abandoned, threw themselves down before their husbands and brothers, and clinging to their knees, piteously implored them not to leave them, and so melted them that they could not carry out their purpose. They next resolved to form themselves into a hollow square, and placing their wives and children in the centre, march out and conquer or die. Toledo learned the desperate attempts which the men of Haarlem were revolving; and knowing that there was nothing of which they were not capable, and that should it happen that only ruins were left him, the fruits and honours of his dearly-won victory would escape him, he straightway sent a trumpeter to say that on payment of 200,000 guilders the city would be spared and all in it pardoned, with the exception of fifty-seven persons whom he named.[2895]

The exceptions were important, for those who had rendered the greatest service in the siege were precisely those who were most obnoxious to Toledo. It was with agony of mind that the citizens discussed the proposal, which would not have been accepted had not the German portion of the garrison insisted on surrender. A deputation was sent to Toledo on the 12th of July, to announce the submission of the city on the proposed terms. At the very moment that Toledo gave the solemn promise which led to this surrender, he had in his possession a letter from the Duke of Alva, commanding him to put the garrison to the sword, with the exception of the Germans, and to hang all the leading citizens of Haarlem.[2896]

The first order issued to the Haarlemers after the surrender was to deposit their arms in the town-house; the second was to shut themselves up, the men in the Monastery of Zyl, and the women in the cathedral. Toledo now entered the city. Implacable, indeed, must that revenge have been which the sights of woe that now met his gaze could not extinguish. After an exposure for seven months to the Spanish cannon, the city was little better than a heap of burning ruins. The streets were blocked up with piles of rubbish, mingled with the skeletons of animals from which the flesh had been torn, and the unburied bodies of those who had fallen in the defence, or died by the famine. But of all the memorials of the siege the most affecting were the survivors. Their protruding bones, parchment skin, hollow cheeks, and sunken eyes made them seem corpses that still retained the power of moving about. If they had been guilty of a crime in defying the soldiers of Spain, surely they had sufficiently atoned for their presumption.

On the third day after the surrender the Duke of Alva visited Haarlem, rode round it, and then took his departure, leaving it to his son to carry out the sequel. The treachery and barbarity of Naarden were repeated here. We shall not shock our readers with details. The fifty-seven persons excepted from the amnesty were, of course, executed; but the murders were far from ending with these. The garrison, with the exception of the Germans, were massacred; 900 citizens were hanged as if they had been the vilest malefactors; the sick in the hospitals were carried out into the courtyard and dispatched; the eloquent Ripperda, whose patriotic address, already recorded, had so largely contributed to excite the men of Haarlem to resist, was beheaded in company of several noted citizens. Several hundreds of French, English, and Scotch soldiers were butchered. Five executioners, each with a staff of assistants, were kept in constant employment several days. At last, tired of labours and sick with horrors, they took 300 victims that still remained, tied them back to back in couples, and threw them into the lake.[2897] The number put to death is estimated at about 2,300, in addition to the many thousands that perished in the siege.

So awful was the tragedy of Haarlem! It wore outwardly the guise of victory for the Spaniards and of defeat to the Hollanders; and yet, when closely examined, it is seen to be just the reverse. It had cost Alva 12,000 men; it had emptied his treasury; and, what was worse, it had broken the spell of invincibility, which lent such power to the Spanish arms. Europe had seen a little town defy the power of Philip for seven long months, and surrender at last only from pressure of famine. There was much here to encourage the other cities of Holland to stand for their liberties, and the renewed exhibition of perfidy and cruelty on the part of Toledo deepened their resolution to do so. It was clear that Spain could not accept of many such victories without eventually overthrowing her own power, and at the same time investing the cause of the adversary she was striving to crush with a moral prestige that would in the issue conduct it to triumph.

Such was the view taken by the Prince of Orange on a calm survey of all the circumstances attending the fall of Haarlem. He saw nothing in it that should cause him to think for one moment of abandoning the prosecution of his great design, or that should shake his confidence in the ultimate triumph of his cause; and without abating a jot of courage he wrote to his deputy, Sonoy, in North Holland, to inspirit the States to resist the power of Spain to the death. "Though God," he said, "had suffered Haarlem to fall, ought men therefore to forsake his Word? Was not their cause a righteous one? was not the Divine arm still able to uphold both it and them? Was the destruction of one city the ruin of the Church? The calamities and woes of Haarlem well deserved their commiseration, but the blood of the martyrs was the seed of the Church, and having now had a full disclosure made to them of the character and intentions of their enemy, and that in the war he was waging for the utter extirpation of truth, he shrunk from no perfidy and cruelty, and trampled on all laws, Divine and human, they ought the more courageously to resist him, convinced that the great Ruler would in the end appear for the vindication of the cause of righteousness, and the overthrow of wickedness. If Haarlem had fallen, other and stronger towns still stood, and they had been able to put themselves into a better posture of defence from the long detention of the Spaniards under the walls of Haarlem, which had been subdued at last, not by the power of the enemy, but by the force of famine." The prince wound up his address with a reply to a question the States had put to him touching his foreign alliances, and whether he had secured the friendship of any powerful potentate abroad, on whose aid they could rely in the war. The answer of the prince reveals the depth of his piety, and the strength of his faith. "He had made a strict alliance," he informed the States, "with the Prince of princes for the defence of the good Christians and others of this oppressed country, who never forsook those who trusted in him, and would assuredly, at the last, confound both his and their enemies. He was therefore resolved never to forsake his dear country, but by venturing both life and fortune, to make use of those means which the Lord of Hosts had supplied him with."[2898]

CHAPTER XIX
SIEGE OF ALKMAAR, AND RECALL OF ALVA

THE Duke of Alva soon found that if he had taken Haarlem he had crippled himself. The siege had emptied his military chest; he was greatly in arrears with his troops, and now his soldiers broke out into mutiny, and absolutely refused to march to Alkmaar and commence its siege till the sums owing them were paid. Six weeks passed away before the army was reduced to obedience, and the duke enabled to resume his programme of the war. His own prestige as a disciplinarian had also suffered immensely.

Alkmaar was situated at the extremity of the peninsula, amid the lagunes of North Holland. It was late in the season when the Spanish army, 16,000 strong, sat down before this little town, with its garrison of 800 soldiers, and its 1,300 citizens capable of bearing arms. Had it been invested earlier in the summer it must have fallen, for it was then comparatively defenceless, and its population divided between the prince and the duke; but while Alva was quelling the mutiny of his troops, Alkmaar was strengthening its defences, and William was furnishing it with provisions and garrisoning it with soldiers. The commander of the besieging army was still Toledo.

When Governor Sonoy saw the storm rolling up from the south, and when he thought of his own feeble resources for meeting it, he became somewhat despondent, and wrote to the prince expressing a hope that he had been able to ally himself with some powerful potentate, who would supply him with money and troops to resist the terrible Spaniard. William replied to his deputy, gently chiding him for his want of faith. He had indeed contracted alliance, he said, with a mighty King, who would provide armies to fight his own battles, and he bade Sonoy not grow faint-hearted, as if the arm of that King had grown weak. At the very moment that William was striving to inspirit himself and his followers, by lifting his eyes to a mightier throne than any on earth, Alva was taking the most effectual means to raise up invincible defenders of Holland's Protestantism, and so realise the expectations of the prince, and justify his confidence in that higher Power on whom he mainly leaned. The duke took care to leave the people of Alkmaar in no doubt as to the fate in reserve for them should their city be taken. He had dealt gently with Haarlem; he had hanged only 900 of its citizens; but he would wreak a full measures of vengeance on Alkmaar. "If I take Alkmaar," he wrote to Philip, "I am resolved not to leave a single creature alive; the knife shall be put to every throat. Since the example of Haarlem has proved of no use, perhaps an example of cruelty will bring the other cities to their senses."[2899] Alva thought that he was rendering certain the submission of the men over whose heads he hung that terrible threat: he was only preparing discomfiture for himself by kindling in their breasts the flame of an unconquerable courage.

Toledo planted a battery on the two opposite sides of the town, in the hope of dividing the garrison. After a cannonade of twelve hours he had breached the walls. He now ordered his troops to storm. They advanced in overwhelming numbers, confident of victory, and rending the air with their shouts as if they had already won it. They dashed across the moat, they swarmed up the breach, but only to be grappled with by the courageous burghers, and flung headlong into the ditch below. Thrice were the murderous hordes of Alva repulsed, thrice did they return to the assault. The rage of the assailants was inflamed with each new check, but Spanish fury, even though sustained by Spanish discipline, battled in vain against Dutch intrepidity and patriotism. The round-shot of the cannon ploughed long vacant lines in the beleaguering masses; the musketry poured in its deadly volleys; a terrible rain of boiling oil, pitch, and water, mingled with tarred burning hoops, unslaked lime, and great stones, descended from the fortifications; and such of the besiegers as were able to force their way up through that dreadful tempest to the top of the wall, found that they had scaled the ramparts only to fall by the daggers of their defenders. The whole population of the town bore its part in the defence. Not only the matrons and virgins of Alkmaar, but the very children, were constantly passing between the arsenal and the walls, carrying ammunition and missiles of all sorts to their husbands, brothers, and fathers, careless of the shot that was falling thick around them. The apprehension of those far more terrible calamities that were sure to follow the entrance of the Spaniards, made them forgetful of every other danger. It is told of Ensign Solis, that having mounted the breach he had a moment's leisure to survey the state of matters within the city, before he was seized and flung from the fortifications. Escaping with his life, he was able to tell what that momentary glance had revealed to him within the walls. He had beheld no masses of military, no men in armour; on the streets of the beleaguered town he saw but plain men, the most of whom wore the garb of fishermen. Humiliating it was to the mailed chivalry of Spain to be checked, flung back, and routed by "plain men in the garb of fishermen." The burghers of Alkmaar wore their breastplates under their fisherman's coat—the consciousness, namely, of a righteous cause.

The assault had commenced at three of the afternoon; it was now seven o'clock in the evening, and the darkness was closing in. It was evident that Alkmaar would not be taken that day. A thousand Spaniards lay dead in the trenches,[2900] while of the defenders only thirteen citizens and twenty-four of the garrison had fallen. The trumpet sounded a recall for the night.

Next morning the cannonade was renewed, and after some 700 shot had been discharged against the walls a breach was made. The soldiers were again ordered to storm. The army refused to obey. It was in vain that Toledo threatened this moment and cajoled the next, not a man in his camp would venture to approach those terrible ramparts which were defended, they gravely believed, by invisible powers. The men of Alkmaar, they had been told, worshipped the devil, and the demons of the pit fought upon the walls of their city, for how otherwise could plain burghers have inflicted so terrible a defeat upon the legions of Spain? Day passed after day, to the chagrin of Toledo, but still the Spaniards kept at a safe distance from those dreaded bulwarks on which the invisible champions kept watch and ward. The rains set in, for the season was now late, and the camping-ground became a marsh. A yet more terrible disaster impended over them, provided they remained much longer before Alkmaar, and of this they had certain information. The Dutch had agreed to cut their dykes, and bury the country round Alkmaar, and the Spanish camp with it, at the bottom of the ocean. Already two sluices had been opened, and the waters of the North Sea, driven by a strong north-west wind, had rushed in and partially inundated the land; this was only a beginning: the Hollanders had resolved to sacrifice, not only their crops, but a vast amount of property besides, and by piercing their two great dykes, to bring the sea over Toledo and his soldiers. The Spaniards had found it hard to contend against the burghers of Alkmaar, they would find it still harder to combat the waves of the North Sea. Accordingly Don Frederic de Toledo summoned a council of his officers, and after a short deliberation it was resolved to raise the siege, the council having first voted that it was no disgrace to the Spanish army to retire, seeing it was fleeing not before man, but before the ocean.

The humiliation of Alva did not stop here. To reverses on the land were added disasters at sea. To punish Amsterdam for the aid it had given the Spaniards in the siege of Haarlem, North Holland fitted out a fleet, and blockaded the narrow entrance of the Y which leads into the Zuyder Zee. Shut out from the ocean, the trade of the great commercial city was at an end. Alva felt it incumbent on him to come to the help of a town which stood almost alone in Holland in its adherence to the Spanish cause. He constructed a fleet of still larger vessels, and gave the command of it to the experienced and enterprising Count Bossu. The two fleets came to a trial of strength, and the battle issued in the defeat of the Spaniards. Some of their ships were taken, others made their escape, and there remained only the admiral's galley. It was named the *Inquisition*, and being the largest and most powerfully armed of all in the fleet, it offered a long and desperate resistance before striking its flag. It was not till of the 300 men on board 220 were killed, and all the rest but fifteen wounded, that Bossu surrendered himself prisoner to the Dutch commander.[2901] Well aware that it was of the last consequence for them to maintain their superiority at sea, the Dutch hailed this victory with no common joy, and ordered public thanks to be offered for it in all the churches of Holland.

With the turn in the tide of Spanish successes, the eyes of Philip began to open. Alva, it is true, in all his barbarities had but too faithfully carried out the wishes, if not the express orders, of his master, but that master now half suspected that this policy of the sword and the gallows was destined not to succeed. Nor was Philip alone in that opinion. There were statesmen at Madrid who were strongly counselling the monarch to make trial of more lenient measures with the Netherlanders. Alva felt that Philip was growing cold toward him, and alleging that his health had sustained injury from the moist climate, and the fatigues he had undergone, he asked leave to retire from the government of the Low Countries. The king immediately recalled him, and appointed the Duke de Medina Cœli, governor in his room. Alva's manner of taking leave of Amsterdam, where he had been staying some time, was of a piece with all his previous career. He owed vast sums to the citizens, but had nothing wherewith to pay. The duke, however, had no difficulty in finding his way out of a position which might have been embarrassing to another man. He issued a proclamation, inviting his creditors to present their claims in person on a certain day. On the night previous to the day appointed, the duke attended by his retinue quitted Amsterdam, taking care that neither by tuck of drum nor salvo of cannon should he make the citizens aware that he was bidding them adieu. He travelled to Spain by way of Germany, and boasted to Count Louis van Koningstein, the uncle of the prince, at whose house he lodged a night, that during his government of five and a half years he had caused 18,000 heretics to be put to death by the hands of the executioner, besides a much greater number whom he had slain with the sword in the cities which he besieged, and in the battles he had fought.[2902]

When the Duke de Medina Cœli arrived in the Netherlands, he stood aghast at the terrible wreck his predecessor had left behind him. The treasure was empty, the commerce of the country was destroyed, and though the inhabitants were impoverished, the taxes which were still attempted to be wrung from them were enormous. The cry of the land was going up to heaven, from Roman Catholic as well as Protestant. The cautious governor, seeing more difficulty than glory in the administration assigned to him, "slipped his neck out of the collar," says Brandt, and returned to Spain. He was succeeded by Don Luis de Requesens and Cuniga, who had been governor at Milan. The Netherlands knew little of their new ruler, but they hoped to find him less the demon, and more the man, than the monstrous compound of all iniquity who for five years had revelled in their blood and treasure. They breathed more freely for a little space. The first act of the new governor was to demolish the statue which Alva had erected of himself in the citadel of Antwerp; Requesens wished the Netherlanders to infer from this beginning that the policy of Alva had been disavowed at headquarters, and that from this time forward more lenient measures were be pursued. William was not to be imposed upon by this shallow device. Fearing that the lenity of Requesens might be even more fatal in the end than the ferocity of Alva, he issued an address to the States, in which he reminded them that the new deputy was still a Spaniard—a name of terrific import in Dutch ears—that he was the servant of a despot, and that not one Hollander could Requesens slay or keep alive but as Philip willed; that in the Cabinet of Madrid there were abysses below abysses; that though it might suit the monarch of Spain to wear for a moment the guise of moderation, they might depend upon it that his aims were fixed and unalterable, and that what he sought, and would pursue to the last soldier in his army, and the last hour of his earthly existence, was the destruction of Dutch liberty, and the extermination of the Protestant faith; that if they stopped where they were—in the middle of the conflict—all that they had already suffered and sacrificed, all the blood that had been shed, the tens of thousands of their brethren hanged on gibbets, burned at stakes, or slain in battle, their mothers, wives, and daughters subjected to horrible outrage and murder, all would have been endured in vain. If their desire of peace should reduce them into a compromise with the tyrant, it would assuredly happen that the abhorred yoke of Spain would yet be riveted upon their necks. The conflict, it was true, was one of the most awful that nation had ever been called to wage, but the part of wisdom was to fight it out to the end, assured that, come when it might, the end would be good; the righteous King would crown them with victory. These words, not less wise than heroic, revived the spirits of the Dutch.

At this stage of the struggle (1573) a question of the gravest kind came up for discussion—namely, the public toleration of the Roman worship. In the circumstances of the Netherlanders the delicacy of this question was equal to its difficulty. It was not proposed to proscribe belief in the Romish dogmas, or to punish any one for his faith; it was not proposed even to forbid the celebration in private of Romish rites; all that was proposed was to forbid their public exercise. There were some who argued that their contest was, at bottom, a contest against the Romish faith; the first object was liberty, but they sought liberty that their consciences might be free in the matter of worship; their opponents were those who professed that faith, and who sought to reduce them under its yoke, and it seemed to them a virtual repudiation of the justness of their contest to tolerate what in fact was their real enemy, Romanism. This was to protect with the one hand the foe they were fighting against with the other. It was replied to this that the Romanist detested the tyranny of Alva not less than the Protestant, that he fought side by side on the ramparts with his Protestant fellow-subject, and that both had entered into a confederacy to oppose a tyrant, who was their common enemy, on condition that each should enjoy liberty of conscience.

Nevertheless, not long after this, the States of Holland, at an assembly at Leyden, resolved to prohibit the public exercise of the Romish religion. The Prince of Orange, when the matter was first broached, expressed a repugnance to the public discussion of it, and a strong desire that its decision should be postponed; and when at last the resolution of the States was arrived at, he intimated, if not his formal dissent, his non-concurrence in the judgment to which they had come. He tells us so in his *Apology*, published in 1580; but at the same time, in justification of the States, he adds, "that they who at the first judged it for the interest and advantage of the country, that one religion should be tolerated as well as the other, were afterwards convinced by the bold attempts, cunning devices, and treacheries of the enemies, who had insinuated themselves among the people, that the State was in danger of inevitable destruction unless the exercise of the Roman religion were suspended, since those who professed it (at least the priests) had sworn allegiance to the Pope, and laid greater stress on their oaths to him than to any others which they took to the civil magistrate." The prince, in fact, had come even then to hold what is now the generally approved maxim, that no one ought to suffer the smallest deprivation of his civil rights on account of his religious belief; but at the same time he felt, what all have felt who have anxiously studied to harmonise the rights of conscience with the safety of society, that there are elements in Romanism that make it impossible, without endangering the State, to apply this maxim in all its extent to the Papal religion. The maxim, so just in itself, is applicable to all religions, and to Romanism among the rest, so far as it is a religion; but William found that it is more than a religion, that it is a government besides; and while there may be a score of religions in a country, there can be but one government in it. The first duty of every government is to maintain its own unity and supremacy; and when it prosecutes any secondary end—and the toleration of conscience is to a government but a secondary end—when, we say, it prosecutes any secondary object, to the parting in twain of the State, it contravenes its own primary end, and overthrows itself. The force with which this consideration pressed itself upon the mind of William of Orange, tolerant even to the measure of the present day, is seen from what he says a little farther on in his *Apology*. "It was not just," he adds, "that such people should enjoy a privilege by the means of which they endeavoured to bring the land under the power of the enemy; they sought to betray the lives and fortunes of the subjects by depriving them not of one, two, or three privileges, but of all the rights and liberties which for immemorial ages had been preserved and defended by their predecessors from generation to generation.[2903]

From this time forward the Reformed religion as taught in Geneva and the Palatinate was the one faith publicly professed in Holland, and its worship alone was practised in the national churches. No Papist, however, was required to renounce his faith, and full liberty was given him to celebrate his worship in private. Mass, and all the attendant ceremonies, continued to be performed in private houses for a long while after. To all the Protestant bodies in Holland, and even to the Anabaptists, a full toleration was likewise accorded. Conscience may err, they said, but it ought to be left free. Should it invade the magistrate's sphere, he has the right to repel it by the sword; if it goes astray within its own domain, it is equally foolish and criminal to compel it by force to return to the right road; its accountability is to God alone.

CHAPTER XX

THIRD CAMPAIGN OF WILLIAM, AND DEATH OF COUNT LOUIS OF NASSAU

THE only town in the important island of Walcheren that now held for the King of Spain was Middelburg. It had endured a siege for a year and a half at the hands of the soldiers of the Prince of Orange. Being the key of the whole of Zealand, the Spanish struggled as hard to retain it as the patriots did to gain possession of it. The garrison if Middelburg, reduced to the last extremity of famine, were now feeding on horses, dogs, rats, and other revolting substitutes for food, and the Spanish commander Mondrogon, a brave and resolute man, had sent word to Requesens, that unless the town was succoured in a very few days it must necessarily surrender. Its fall would be a great blow to the interests of Philip, and his Governor of the Low Countries exerted himself to the utmost to throw supplies into it, and enable it to hold out. He collected a fleet of seventy-five sail at Bergen-op-Zoom, another of thirty ships at Antwerp, and storing them with provisions and military equipments, he ordered them to steer for Middelburg and relieve it. But unhappily for Requesens, and the success of his project, the Dutch were masters at sea. Their ships were manned by the bravest and most skilful sailors in the world; nor were they only adventurous seamen, they were firm patriots, and ready to shed the last drop of their blood for their country and their religious liberties. They served not for wages, as did many in the land armies of the prince, which being to a large extent made up of mercenaries, were apt to mutiny when ordered into battle, if it chanced that their pay was in arrears; the soldiers of the fleet were enthusiastic for the cause for which they fought, and accounted that to beat the enemy was sufficient reward for their valour and blood.

The numerous fleet of Requesens, in two squadrons, was sailing down the Scheldt (27th January, 1574), on its way to raise the siege of Middelburg, when it sighted near Romerswael, drawn up in battle array, the ships of the Sea Beggars. The two fleets closed in conflict. After the first broadside, ship grappled with ship, and the Dutch leaping on board the Spanish vessels, a hand-to-hand combat with battle-axes, daggers, and pistols, was commenced on the deck of each galley. The admiral's ship ran foul of a sand-bank, and was then set fire to by the Zealanders; the other commander, Romers, hastened to his relief, but only to have the flames communicated to his own ship. Seeing his galley about to sink, Romers jumped overboard and saved his life by swimming ashore. The other ships of the Spanish fleet fared no better. The Zealanders burnt some, they sunk others, and the rest they seized. The victory was decisive. Twelve hundred Spaniards, including the Admiral De Glimes, perished in the flames of the burning vessels, or fell in the fierce struggles that raged on their decks. Requesens himself, from the dyke of Zacherlo, had witnessed, without being able to avert, the destruction of his fleet, which he had constructed at great expense, and on which he built such great hopes. When the second squadron learned that the ships of the first were at the bottom of the sea, or in the hands of the Dutch, its commander instantly put about and made haste to return to Antwerp. The surrender of Middelburg, which immediately followed, gave the Dutch the command of the whole sea-board of Zealand and Holland.

Success was lacking to the next expedition undertaken by William. The time was come, he thought, to rouse the Southern Netherlands, that had somewhat tamely let go their liberties, to make another attempt to recover them before the yoke of Spain should be irretrievably riveted upon their neck. Accordingly he instructed his brother, Count Louis, to raise a body of troops in Germany, where he was then residing, in order to make a third invasion of the Central Provinces of the Low Countries. There would have been no lack of recruits had Louis possessed the means of paying them; but his finances were at zero; his brother's fortune, as well as his own, was already swallowed up, and before enlisting a single soldier, Louis had first of all to provide funds to defray the expense of the projected expedition. He trusted to receive some help from the German princes, he negotiated loans from his own relations and friends, but his main hopes were rested on France. The court of Charles IX. was then occupied with the matter of the election of the Duke of Anjou to the throne of Poland, and that monarch was desirous of appearing friendly to a cause which, but two years before, he had endeavoured to crush in the St. Bartholomew Massacre; and so Count Louis received from France as many promises as would, could he have coined them into gold, have enabled him to equip and keep in the field ten armies; but of sterling money he had scarce so much as to defray the expense of a single battalion. He succeeded, however, in levying a force of some 4,000 horse and 7,000 foot[2904] in the smaller German States, and with these he set out about the beginning of February, 1575, for Brabant. He crossed the Rhine, and advanced to the Meuse, opposite Maestrict, in the hope that his friends in that town would open its gates when they saw him approach. So great was their horror of the Spaniards that they feared to do so; and, deeming his little army too weak to besiege so strongly fortified a place, he continued his march down the right bank of the river till he came to Roeremonde. Here, too, the Protestants were overawed. Not a single person durst show himself on his side. He continued his course along the river-banks, in the hope of being joined by the troops of his brother, according to the plan of the campaign; the Spanish army, under Avila, following him all the while on a parallel line on the opposite side of the river. On the 13th of April, Louis encamped at the village of Mook, on the confines of Cleves; and here the Spaniards, having suddenly crossed the Meuse and sat down right in his path, offered him battle. He knew that his newly-levied recruits would fight at great disadvantage with the veteran soldiers of Spain, yet the count had no alternative but to accept the combat offered him. The result was disastrous in the extreme. After a long and fierce and bloody contest the patriot army was completely routed. Present on that fatal field, along with Count Louis, were his brother Henry, and Duke Christopher, son of the Elector of the Palatinate; and repeatedly, during that terrible day, they intrepidly rallied their soldiers and turned the tide of battle, but only to be overpowered in the end. When they saw that the day was lost, and that some 6,000 of their followers lay dead around them, they mustered a little band of the survivors, and once more, with fierce and desperate courage, charged the enemy. They were last seen fighting in the *mêlée*. From that conflict they never emerged, nor were their dead bodies ever discovered; but no doubt can be entertained of their fate. Falling in the general butchery, their corpses would be indistinguishable in the ghastly heap of the slain, and would receive a common burial with the rest of the dead.

So fell Count Louis of Nassau. He was a brilliant soldier, an able negotiator, and a firm patriot. In him the Protestant cause lost an enthusiastic and enlightened adherent, his country's liberty a most devoted champion, and his brother, the prince, one who was "his right hand" as regarded the prompt and able execution of his plans. To Orange the loss was irreparable, and was felt all the more at this moment, seeing that St. Aldegonde, upon whose sagacity and patriotism Orange placed such reliance, was a captive in the Spanish camp. This was the third brother whom William had lost in the struggle against Spain. The repeated deaths in the circle of those so dear to him, as well as the many other friends, also dear though not so closely related, who had fallen in the war, could not but afflict him with a deep sense of isolation and loneliness. To abstract his mind from his sorrows, to forget the graves of his kindred, the captivity and death of his friends, the many thousands of his followers now sleeping their last sleep on the battlefield, his own ruined fortune, the vanished splendour of his home, where a once princely affluence had been replaced by something like penury, his escutcheon blotted, and his name jeered at—to rise above all these accumulated losses and dire humiliations, and to prosecute with unflinching resolution his great cause, required indeed a stout heart, and a firm faith. Never did the prince appear greater than now. The gloom of disaster but brought out the splendour of his virtues and the magnanimity of his soul. The burden of the great struggle now lay on him alone. He had to provide funds, raise armies, arrange the plan of campaigns, and watch over their execution. From a sick-bed he was often called to direct battles, and the siege or defence of cities. Of the friends who had commenced the struggle with him many were now no more, and those who survived were counselling submission; the prince alone refused to despair of the deliverance of his country. Through armies foiled, and campaigns lost, through the world's pity or its scorn, he would march on to that triumph which he saw in the distance. When friends fell, he stayed his heart with a sublime confidence on the eternal Arm. Thus stripped of human defences, he displayed a pure devotion to country and to religion.

It was this that placed the Prince of Orange in the first rank of greatness. There have been men who have been borne to greatness upon the steady current of continuous good fortune; they never lost a battle, and they never suffered check or repulse. Their labours have been done, and their achievements accomplished, at the head of victorious armies, and in the presence of admiring senates, and of applauding and grateful nations. These are great; but there is an order of men who are greater still. There have been a select few who have rendered the very highest services to mankind, not with the applause and succour of those they sought to benefit, but in spite of their opposition, amid the contempt and scorn of the world, and amid ever-blackening and ever-bursting disasters, and who lifting their eyes from armies and thrones have fixed them upon a great unseen Power, in whose righteousness and justice they confided, and so have been able to struggle on till they attained their sublime object. These are the peers of the race, they are the first magnates of the world. In this order of great men stands William, Prince of Orange.

On receiving the melancholy intelligence of the death of his brother on the fatal field of Mook, William retreated northward into Holland. He expected that the Spaniards would follow him, and improve their victory while the terror it inspired was still recent; but Avila was prevented pursuing him by a mutiny that broke out in his army. The pay of his soldiers was three years in arrears, and instead of the barren pursuit of William, the Spanish host turned its steps in the direction of the rich city of Antwerp, resolved to be its own paymaster. The soldiers quartered themselves upon the wealthiest of the burghers. They took possession of the most sumptuous mansions, they feasted on the most luxurious dishes, and daily drank the most delicate wines. At the end of three weeks the citizens, wearied of seeing their substance thus devoured by the army, consented to pay 400,000 crowns, which the soldiers were willing to receive as part payment of the debt due to them. The mutineers celebrated their victory over the citizens by a great feast on the Mere, or principal street of Antwerp. They were busy carousing, gambling, and masquerading when the boom of cannon struck upon their ears. William's admiral had advanced up the Scheldt, and was now engaged with the Spanish fleet in the river. The revellers, leaving their cups and grasping their muskets, hurried to the scene of action, but only to be the witnesses of the destruction of their ships. Some were blazing in e flames, others were sinking with their crews, and the patriot admiral, having done his work, was sailing away in triumph. We have recorded the destruction of the other division of Philip's fleet; this second blow completed its ruin, and thus the King of Spain was as far as ever from the supremacy of the sea, without which, as Requesens assured him, he would not be able to make himself master of Holland.

Another act of the great drama now opened. We have already recorded the fall of Haarlem, after unexampled horrors. Though little else than a city of ruins and corpses when it fell to the Spaniards, its possession gave them great advantages. It was an encampment between North and South Holland, and cut the country in two. They were desirous of strengthening their position by adding Leyden to Haarlem, the town next to it on the south, and a place of yet greater importance. Accordingly, it was first blockaded by the Spanish troops in the winter of 1574; but the besiegers were withdrawn in the spring to defend the frontier, attacked by Count Louis. After his defeat, and the extinction of the subsequent mutiny in the Spanish army, the soldiers returned to the siege, and Leyden was invested a second time on the 26th of May, 1574. The siege of Leyden is one of the most famous in history, and had a most important bearing on the establishment of Protestantism in Holland. Its devotion and heroism in the cause of liberty and religion have, like a mighty torch, illumined other lands besides Holland, and fired the soul of more peoples than the Dutch.

Leyden is situated on a low plain covered with rich pastures, smiling gardens, fruitful orchards, and elegant villas. It is washed by an arm of the Rhine, that, on approaching its walls, parts into an infinity of streamlets which, flowing languidly through the city, fill the canals that traverse the streets, making it a miniature of Venice. Its canals are spanned by 150 stone bridges, and lined by rows of limes and poplars, which soften and shade the architecture of its spacious streets, that present to the view public buildings and sumptuous private mansions, churches with tall steeples, and universities and halls with imposing façades. At the time of the siege the city had a numerous population, and was defended by a deep moat and a strong wall flanked with bastions. The city was a prize well worth all the ardour displayed both in its attack and defence. Its standing or falling would determine the fate of Holland.

When the citizens saw themselves a second time shut in by a beleaguering army of 8,000 men, and a bristling chain of sixty-four redoubts, they reflected with pain on their neglect to introduce provisions and reinforcements into their city during the two months the Spaniards had been withdrawn to defend the frontier. They must now atone for their lack of prevision by relying on their own stout arms and bold hearts. There were scarce any troops in the city besides the burghal guard. Orange told them plainly that three months must pass over them before it would be possible by any efforts of their friends outside to raise the siege; and he entreated them to bear in mind the vast consequences that must flow from the struggle on which they were entering, and that, according as they should bear themselves in it with a craven heart or with an heroic spirit, so would they transmit to their descendants the vile estate of slavery or the glorious heritage of liberty.

The defence of the town was entrusted to Jean van der Does, Lord of Nordwyck. Of noble birth and poetic genius, Does was also a brave soldier, and an illustrious patriot. He breathed his own heroic spirit into the citizens. The women as well as men worked day and night upon the walls, to strengthen them against the Spanish guns. They took stock of the provisions in the city, and arranged a plan for their economical distribution. They passed from one to another the terrible words, "Zutphen," "Naarden," names suggestive of horrors not to be mentioned, but which had so burned into the Dutch the detestation of the Spaniards, that they were resolved to die rather than surrender to an enemy whose instincts were those of tigers or fiends.

It was at this moment, when the struggle around Leyden was about to begin, that Philip attempted to filch by a stratagem the victory which he found it so hard to win by the sword. Don Luis de Requesens now published at Brussels, in the king's name, a general pardon to the Netherlanders, on condition that they went to mass and received absolution from a priest.[2905] Almost all the clergy and many of the leading citizens were excepted from this indemnity. "Pardon!" exclaimed the indignant Hollanders when they read the king's letter of grace; "before we can receive pardon we must first have committed offence. We have suffered the wrong, not done it; and now the wrongdoer comes, not to sue for, but to bestow forgiveness! How grateful ought we to be!" As regarded going to mass, Philip could not but know that this was the essence of the whole quarrel, and to ask them to submit on this point was simply to ask them to surrender to him the victory. Their own reiterated vows, the thousands of their brethren martyred, their own consciences—all forbade. They would sooner go to the halter. There was now scarcely a native Hollander who was a Papist; and speaking in their name, the Prince of Orange declared, "As long as there is a living man left in the country, we will contend for our liberty and our religion."[2906] The king's pardon had failed to open the gates of Leyden, and its siege now went forward.

CHAPTER XXI
THE SIEGE OF LEYDEN

FOR two months the citizens manned their walls, and with stern courage kept at bay the beleaguering host, now risen from 10,000 to three times that number. At the end of this period provisions failed them. For some days the besieged subsisted on malt-cake, and when that was consumed they had recourse to the flesh of dogs and horses. Numbers died of starvation, and others sickened and perished through the unnatural food on which the famine had thrown them. Meanwhile a greater calamity even than would have been the loss of Leyden seemed about to overtake them.

Struck down by fever, the result of ceaseless toil and the most exhausting anxiety, William of Orange lay apparently at the point of death. The illness of the prince was carefully concealed, lest the citizens of Leyden should give themselves up altogether to despair. Before lying down, the prince had arranged the only plan by which, as it appeared to him, it was possible to drive out the Spaniards and raise the siege; and in spite of his illness he issued from his sick-bed continual orders respecting the execution of that project. No force at his disposal was sufficient to enable him to break through the Spanish lines, and throw provisions into the starving city, in which the suffering and misery had now risen to an extreme pitch. In this desperate strait he thought of having recourse to a more terrible weapon than cannon or armies. He would summon the ocean against the Spaniards. He would cut the dykes and sink the country beneath the sea. The loss would be tremendous; many a rich meadow, many a fruitful orchard, and many a lovely villa would be drowned beneath the waves; but the loss, though great, would be recoverable: the waves would again restore what they had swallowed up; whereas, should the country be overwhelmed by the power of Spain, never again would it be restored: the loss would be eternal. What the genius and patriotism of William had dared, his eloquence prevailed upon the States to adopt. Putting their spades into the great dyke that shielded the land, they said, "Better a drowned country than a lost country." Besides the outer and taller rampart, within which the Hollanders had sought safety from their enemy the sea, there rose concentric lines of inner and lower dykes, all of which had to be cut through before the waves could flow over the country. The work was executed with equal alacrity and perseverance, but not with the desired result. A passage had been dug for the waters, but that ocean which had appeared but too ready to overwhelm its barriers when the inhabitants sought to keep it out, seemed now unwilling to overflow their country, as if it were in league with the tyrant from whose fury the Dutch besought it to cover them. Strong northeasterly winds, prevailing that year longer than usual, beat back the tides, and lowering the level of the German Sea, prevented the ingress of the waters. The flood lay only a few inches in depth on the face of Holland; and unless it should rise much higher, William's plan for relieving Leyden would, after all, prove abortive. At great labour and expense he had constructed a flotilla of 200 flat-bottomed vessels at Rotterdam and Delft; these he had mounted with guns, and manned with 800 Zealanders, and stored with provisions to be thrown into the famine-stricken city, so soon as the depth of water, now slowly rising over meadow and corn-field, should enable his ships to reach its gates. But the flotilla lay immovable. The expedition was committed to Admiral Boisot; the crews were selected from the fleet of Zealand, picked veterans, with faces hacked and scarred with wounds which they had received in their former battles with the Spaniards; and to add to their ferocious looks they wore the Crescent in their caps, with the motto, "Turks rather than Spaniards." Ships, soldiers, and victuals—all had William provided; but unless the ocean should co-operate all had been provided in vain.

Something like panic seized on the besiegers when they beheld this new and terrible power advancing to assail them. Danger and death in every conceivable form they had been used to meet, but they had never dreamt of having to confront the ocean. Against such an enemy what could their or any human power avail? But when they saw that the rise of the waters stayed, their alarm subsided, and they began to jeer and mock at the stratagem of the prince, which was meant to be grand, but had proved contemptible. He had summoned the ocean to his aid, but the ocean would not come. In the city of Leyden despondency had taken the place of elation. When informed of the expedient of the prince for their deliverance they had rung their bells for very joy; but when they saw the ships, laden with that bread for lack of which some six or eight thousand of their number had already died, after entering the gaps in the outer dyke, arrested in their progress to their gates, hope again forsook them. Daily they climbed the steeples and towers, and scanned with anxious eyes the expanse around, if haply the ocean was coming to their aid. Day after day they had to descend with the same depressing report: the wind was still adverse; the waters refused to rise, and the ships could not float. The starvation and misery of Leyden was greater even than that which Haarlem had endured. For seven weeks there had not been a morsel of bread within the city. The vilest substitutes were greedily devoured; and even these were now almost exhausted. To complete their suffering, pestilence was added to famine. Men and women every hour dropped dead on the streets. Whole families were found to be corpses when the doors of their houses were forced open in the morning, and the survivors had hardly enough strength left to bury them. The dead were carried to their graves by those who tomorrow would need the same office at the hands of others. Amid the awful reiteration of these dismal scenes, one passion still survived—resistance to the Spaniards. Some few there were, utterly broken down under this accumulation of sorrows, who did indeed whisper the word "surrender," deeming that even Spanish soldiers could inflict nothing more terrible than they were already enduring. But these proposals were instantly and indignantly silenced by the great body of the citizens, to whom neither famine, nor pestilence, nor death appeared so dreadful as the entrance of the Spaniards. The citizens anew exchanged vows of fidelity with one another and with the magistrates, and anew ratified their oaths to that Power for whose truth they were in arms. Abandoned outside its walls, as it seemed, by all: pressed within by a host of terrible evils: succour neither in heaven nor in the earth, Leyden nevertheless would hold fast its religion and its liberty, and if it must perish, it would perish free. It was the victory of a sublime faith over despair.

At last heaven heard the cry of the suffering city, and issued its fiat to the ocean. On the 1st of October, the equinoctial gales, so long delayed, gave signs of their immediate approach. On that night a strong wind sprung up from the north-west, and the waters of the rivers were forced back into their channels. After blowing for some hours from that quarter, the gale shifted into the south-west with increased fury. The strength of the winds heaped up the waters of the German Ocean upon the coast of Holland; the deep lifted up itself; its dark flood driven before the tempest's breath with mighty roar, like shout of giant loosed from his fetters and rushing to assail the foe, came surging onwards, and poured its tumultuous billows over the broken dykes. At midnight on the 2nd of October the flotilla of Boisot was afloat, and under weigh for Leyden, on whose wall crowds of gaunt, famished, almost exanimate men waited its coming. At every short distance the course of the ships was disputed by some half-submerged Spanish fort, whose occupants were not so much awed by the terrors of the deep which had risen to overwhelm them as to be unable to offer battle. But it was in vain. Boisot's fierce Zealanders were eager to grapple with the hated Spaniards; the blaze of cannon lighted up the darkness of that awful night, and the booming of artillery, rising above the voice of the tempest, told the citizens of Leyden that the patriot fleet was on its way to their rescue. These naval engagements, on what but a few days before had been cornland or woodland, but was now ocean—a waste of water blackened by the scowl of tempest and the darkness of night—formed a novel as well as awful sight. The Spaniards fought with a desperate bravery, but everywhere without success. The Zealanders leaped from their flat-bottomed vessels and pursued them along the dykes, they fired on them from their boats, or, seizing them with hooks fixed to the ends of long poles, dragged them down from the causeway, and put them to the sword. Those who escaped the daggers and harpoons of the Zealanders, were drowned in the sea, or stuck fast in the mud till overtaken and dispatched. In that flight some 1,500 Spaniards perished.

Boisot's fleet had now advanced within two miles of the walls of Leyden, but here, at about a mile's distance from the gates, rose the strongest of all the Spanish forts, called Lammen, blocking up the way, and threatening to render all that had been gained without avail. The admiral reconnoitred it; it stood high above the water; it was of great strength and full of soldiers; and he hesitated attacking it. The citizens from the walls saw his fleet behind the fort, and understood the difficulty that prevented the admiral's nearer approach. They had been almost delirious with joy at the prospect of immediate relief. Was the cup after all to be dashed from their lips? It was arranged by means of a carrier-pigeon that a combined assault should take place upon the fort of Lammen at dawn, the citizens assailing it on one side, and the flotilla bombarding it on the other. Night again fell, and seldom has a blacker night descended on more tragic scene, or the gloom of nature been more in unison with the anxiety and distress of man. At midnight a terrible crash was heard. What that ominous sound, so awful in the stillness of the night, could be, no one could conjecture. A little after came a strange apparition, equally inexplicable. A line of lights was seen to issue from Lammen and move over the face of the deep. The darkness gave terror and mystery to every occurrence. All waited for the coming of day to explain these appearances. At last the dawn broke; it was now seen that a large portion of the city walls of Leyden had fallen overnight, and hence the noise that had caused such alarm. The Spaniards, had they known, might have entered the city at the last hour and massacred the inhabitants; instead of this, they were seized with panic, believing these terrible sounds to be those of the enemy rushing to attack them, and so, kindling their torches and lanterns, they fled when no man pursued. Instead of the cannonade which was this morning to be opened against the formidable Lammen, the fleet of Boisot sailed under the silent guns of the now evacuated fort, and entered the city gates. On the morning of the 3rd of October, Leyden was relieved.

The citizens felt that their first duty was to offer thanks to that Power to whom exclusively they owed their deliverance. Despite their own heroism and Boisot's valour they would have fallen, had not God, by a mighty wind, brought up the ocean and overwhelmed their foes. A touching procession of haggard but heroic forms, headed by Admiral Boisot and the magistrates, and followed by the Zealanders and sailors, walked to the great church, and there united in solemn prayer. A hymn of thanksgiving was next raised, but of the multitude of voices by which its first notes were pealed forth, few were able to continue singing to the close. Tears choked their voices, and sobs were mingled with the music. Thoughts of the awful scenes through which they had passed, and of the many who had shared the conflict with them, but had not lived to join in the hymn of victory, rushed with overmastering force into their minds, and compelled them to mingle tears with their praises.

A letter was instantly dispatched to the Prince of Orange with the great news. He received it while he was at worship in one of the churches of Delft, and instantly handed it to the minister, to be read from the pulpit after sermon. That moment recompensed him for the toil and losses of years; and his joy was heightened by the fact that a nation rejoiced with him. Soon thereafter, the States assembled, and a day of public thanksgiving was appointed.

This series of wonders was to be fittingly closed by yet another prodigy. The fair land of Holland lay drowned at the bottom of the sea. The whole vast plain from Rotterdam to Leyden was under water. What time, what labour and expense would it require to recover the country, and restore the fertility and beauty which had been so sorely marred! The very next day, the 4th of October, the wind shifted into the north-east, and blowing with great violence, the waters rapidly assuaged, and in a few days the land was bare again. He who had brought up the ocean upon Holland with his mighty hand rolled it back.

CHAPTER XXII
MARCH OF THE SPANISH ARMY THROUGH THE SEA—SACK OF ANTWERP

HE night of this great conflict was far from being at an end, but its darkest hour had now passed. With the check received by the Spanish Power before the walls of Leyden, the first streak of dawn may be said to have broken; but cloud and tempest long obscured the rising of Holland's day.

The country owed a debt of gratitude to that heroic little city which had immolated itself on the altar of the nation's religion and liberty, and before resuming the great contest, Holland must first mark in some signal way its sense of the service which Leyden had rendered it. The distinction awarded Leyden gave happy augury of the brilliant destiny awaiting that land in years to come. It was resolved to found a university within its walls. Immediate effect was given to this resolution. Though the Spaniard was still in the land, and the strain of armies and battles was upon William, a grand procession was organised on the 5th of February, 1575, at which symbolic figures, drawn through the streets in triumphal cars, were employed to represent the Divine form of Christianity, followed by the fair train of the arts and sciences. The seminary thus inaugurated was richly endowed; men of the greatest learning were sought for to fill its chairs, their fame attracted crowds of students from many countries; and its printing presses began to send forth works which have instructed the men of two centuries. Thus had Leyden come up from the "sea's devouring depths" to be one of the lights of the world.[2907]

There came now a brief pause in the conflict. The Emperor Maximilian, the mutual friend of Philip of Spain and William of Orange, deemed the moment opportune for mediating between the parties, and on the 3rd of March, 1575, a congress assembled at Breda with the view of devising a basis for peace. The prince gave his consent that the congress should meet, although he had not the slightest hope of fruit from its labours. On one condition alone could peace be established in Holland, and that condition, he knew, was one which Philip would never grant, and which the States could never cease to demand—namely, the free and open profession of the Reformed religion. When the commissioners met it was seen that William had judged rightly in believing the religious difficulty to be insurmountable. Philip would agree to no peace unless the Roman Catholic religion were installed in sole and absolute dominancy, leaving professors of the Protestant faith to convert their estates and goods into money, and quit the country. In that case, replied the Protestants, duly grateful for the wonderful concessions of the Catholic king, there will hardly remain in Holland, after all the heretics shall have left it, enough men to keep the dykes in repair, and the country had better be given back to the ocean at once. The conference broke up without accomplishing anything, and the States, with William at their head, prepared to resume the contest, in the hope of conquering by their own perseverance and heroism what they despaired ever to obtain from the justice of Philip.

The war was renewed with increased exasperation on both sides. The opening of the campaign was signalised by the capture of a few small Dutch towns, followed by the usual horrors that attended the triumph of the Spanish arms. But

Book Eighteenth

Governor Requesens soon ceased to push his conquests in that direction, and turned his whole attention to Zealand, where Philip was exceedingly desirous of acquiring harbours, in order to the reception of a fleet which he was building in Spain. This led to the most brilliant of all the feats accomplished by the Spaniards in the war.

In the sea that washes the north-east of Zealand are situated three large islands—Tolen, Duyveland, and Schowen. Tolen, which lies nearest the mainland, was already in the hands of the Spaniards; and Requesens, on that account, was all the more desirous to gain possession of the other two. He had constructed a flotilla of flat-bottomed boats, and these would soon have made him master of the coveted islands; but he dared not launch them on these waters, seeing the estuaries of Zealand were swept by those patriot buccaneers whose bravery suffered no rivals on their own element. Requesens, in his great strait, bethought him of another expedient, but of such a nature that it might well seem madness to attempt it. The island of Duyveland was separated from Tolen, the foothold of the Spaniards, by a strait of about five miles in width; and Requesens learned from some traitor Zealanders that there ran a narrow flat of sand from shore to shore, on which at ebb-tide there was not more than a depth of from four to five feet of water. It was possible, therefore, though certainly extremely hazardous, to traverse this submarine ford. The governor, however, determined that his soldiers should attempt it. He assigned to 3,000 picked men the danger and the glory of the enterprise. At midnight, the 27th September, 1575, the host descended into the deep, Requesens himself witnessing its departure from the shore, "and with him a priest, praying for these poor souls to the Prince of the celestial militia, Christ Jesus."[2908] A few guides well acquainted with the ford led the way; Don Osorio d'Ulloa, a commander of distinguished courage, followed; after him came a regiment of Spaniards, then a body of Germans, and lastly a troop of Walloons, followed by 200 sappers and miners. The night was dark, with sheet-lightning, which bursting out at frequent intervals, shed a lurid glare upon the face of the black waters. At times a moon, now in her fourth quarter, looked forth between the clouds upon this novel midnight march. The soldiers walked two and two; the water at times reached to their necks and they had to hold their muskets above their head to prevent their being rendered useless. The path was so narrow that a single step aside was fatal, and many sank to rise no more. Nor were the darkness and the treacherous waves the only dangers that beset them. The Zealand fleet hovered near, and when its crews discerned by the pale light of the moon and the fitful lightning that the Spaniards were crossing the firth in this most extraordinary fashion, they drew their ships as close to the ford as the shallows would permit, and opened their guns upon them. Their fire did little harm, for the darkness made the aim uncertain. Not so, however, the harpoons and long hooks of the Zealanders; their throw caught, and numbers of the Spaniards were dragged down into the sea. Nevertheless, they pursued their dreadful path, now struggling with the waves, now fighting with their assailants, and at last, after a march of six hours, they approached the opposite shore, and with ranks greatly thinned, emerged from the deep.[2909]

Wearied by their fight with the sea and with the enemy, the landing of the Spaniards might have been withstood, but accident or treachery gave them possession of the island. At the moment that they stepped upon the shore, the commander of the Zealanders, Charles van Boisot, fell by a shot—whether from one of his own men, or from the enemy, cannot now be determined. The incident caused a panic among the patriots. The strangeness of the enemy's advance—for it seemed as if the sea had miraculously opened to afford them passage—helped to increase the consternation. The Zealanders fled in all directions, and the invading force soon found themselves in possession of Duyveland.

So far this most extraordinary and daring attempt had been successful, but the enterprise could not be regarded as completed till the island of Schowen, the outermost of the three, had also been occupied. It was divided from Duyveland by a narrow strait of only a league's width. Emboldened by their success, the Spaniards plunged a second time into the sea, and waded through the firth, the defenders of the island fleeing at their approach, as at that of men who had conquered the very elements, and with whom, therefore, it was madness to contend. The Spanish commander immediately set about the reduction of all the forts and cities on the island, and in this he was successful, though the work occupied the whole Spanish army not less than nine months.[2910] Now fully master of these three islands (June, 1576), though their acquisition had cost an immense expenditure of both money and lives, Requesens hoped that he had not only cut the communication between Holland and Zealand, but that he had secured a rendezvous for the fleet which he expected from Spain, and that it only remained that he should here fix the headquarters of his power, and assemble a mighty naval force, in order from this point to extend his conquests on every side, and reconquer Holland and the other Provinces which had revolted from the sceptre of Philip and the faith of Rome. He seemed indeed in a fair way of accomplishing all this; the sea itself had parted to give him a fulcrum on which to rest the lever of this great expedition, but an incident now fell out which upset his calculations and dashed all his fondest hopes. Holland was never again to own the sceptre of Philip.

Vitelli, Marquis of Cetona, who was without controversy the ablest general at that time in the Netherlands, now died. His death was followed in a few days by that of Governor Requesens. These two losses to Philip were quickly succeeded by a third, and in some respects greater, a formidable mutiny of the troops. The men who had performed all the valorous deeds we have recited, had received no pay. Philip had exhausted his treasury in the war he was carrying on with the Turk, and had not a single guelden to send them. The soldiers had been disappointed, moreover, in the booty they expected to reap from the conquered towns of Schowen. These labourers were surely worthy of their hire. What dark deed had they ever refused to do, or what enemy had they ever refused to face, at the bidding of their master? They had scaled walls, and laid fertile provinces waste, for the pleasure of Philip and the glory of Spain, and now they were denied their wages. Seeing no help but in becoming their own paymasters, they flew to arms, deposed their officers, elected a commander-in-chief from among themselves, and taking an oath of mutual fidelity over the Sacrament, they passed over the mainland, and seizing on Alost, in Flanders, made it their headquarters, intending to sally forth in plundering excursions upon the neighbouring towns. Thus all the labour and blood with which their recent conquests had been won were thrown away, and the hopes which the King of Spain had built upon them were frustrated at the very moment when he thought they were about to be realised.

As men contemplate the passage of a dark cloud charged with thunder and destruction through the sky, so did the cities of Brabant and Flanders watch the march of this mutinous host. They knew it held pillage and murder and rape in its bosom, but their worst fears failed to anticipate the awful vengeance it was destined to inflict. The negotiators sent to recall the troops to obedience reminded them that they were tarnishing the fame acquired by years of heroism. What cared these mutineers for glory? They wanted shoes, clothes, food, money. They held their way past the gates of Mechlin, past the gates of Brussels, and of other cities; but swarming over the walls of Alost, while the inhabitants slept, they had now planted themselves in the centre of a rich country, where they promised themselves store of booty. No sooner had they hung out their flag on the walls of Alost than the troops stationed in other parts of the Netherlands caught the infection. By the beginning of September the mutiny was universal; the whole Spanish army in the Netherlands were united in it, and all the forts and citadels being in their hands, they completely dominated the land, plundered the citizens, pillaged the country, and murdered at their pleasure. The State Council, into whose hands the government of the Netherlands had fallen on the sudden death of Requesens, were powerless, the mutineers holding them prisoners in Brussels; and though the Council prevailed on Philip to issue an edict against his revolted army, denouncing them as rebels, and empowering any one to slay this rebellious host, either singly or in whole, the soldiers paid as little respect to the edict of their king as to the exhortations of the council. Thus the instrument of oppression recoiled upon the hands that were wielding it.

War now broke out between the Flemings and the army. The State Council raised bands of militia to awe the proscribed and lawless troops, and bloodthirsty skirmishes were of daily occurrence between them. The carnage was all on one side, for the disciplined veterans routed at little cost the peasants and artisans who had been so suddenly transformed into soldiers, slaughtering them in thousands. The rich cities, on which they now cast greedy eyes, began to feel their vengeance, but the awful calamity which overtook Antwerp had effaced the memory of the woes which at their hands befell some of the other cities.

Antwerp, since the beginning of the troubles of the Netherlands, had had its own share of calamity; its cathedral and religious houses had been sacked by the image-breakers, and its warehouses and mansions had been partially pillaged by mutinous troops; but its vast commerce enabled it speedily to surmount all these losses, and return to its former flourishing condition. Antwerp was once more the richest city in the world. The ships of all nations unloaded in its harbour, and the treasures of all climes were gathered into its warehouses. Its streets were spacious and magnificent; its shops were stored with silver and gold and precious stones, and the palaces of its wealthy merchants were filled with luxurious and costly furniture, and embellished with precious ornaments, beautiful pictures, and fine statues. This nest of riches was not likely to escape the greedy eyes and rapacious hands of the mutineers.

Immediately outside the walls of Antwerp was the citadel, with its garrison.

The troops joined the mutiny, and from that hour Antwerp was doomed. The citizens, having a presentiment of the ruin that hung above their heads, took some very ineffectual measures to secure themselves and their city against it, which only drew it the sooner upon them. The mutineers in the citadel were joined by the rebellious troops from Alost, about 3,000 in number, who were so eager to begin the plundering that they refused even to refresh themselves after their march before throwing themselves upon the ill-fated city. It was Sunday, the 4th of November, and an hour before noon the portals of Alva's citadel were opened, and 6,000 men-at-arms rushed forth. They swept along the esplanade leading to the city. They crashed through the feeble barrier which the burghers had reared to protect them from the apprehended assault. They chased before them the Walloons and the militia, who had come out to withstand them, as the furious tempest drives the cloud before it. In another minute they were over the walls into the city. From every street and lane poured forth the citizens to defend their homes; but though they fought with extraordinary courage it was all in vain. The battle swept along the streets, the Spanish hordes bearing down all before them, and following close on the rear of the vanquished, till they reached the magnificent Exchange, in which 7,000 merchants were wont daily to assemble. Here an obstinate combat ensued. The citizens fought on the street, or, retreating to their houses, fired from their windows on the Spaniards. The carnage was great; heaps of corpses covered the pavement, and the kennels ran with blood; but courage availed little against regular discipline, and the citizens were broken a second time. The battle was renewed with equal obstinacy in the Grand Place. Here stood the Guildhall, accounted the most magnificent in the world. Torches were brought and it was set fire to and burned to the ground. The flames caught the surrounding buildings, and soon a thousand houses, the finest in the city, were ablaze, their conflagration lighting up the pinnacles and the unrivalled spire of the neighbouring cathedral, and throwing its ruddy gleam on the combatants who were struggling in the area below. The battle had now spread over all the city. In every street men were fighting and blood was flowing. Many rushed to the gates and sought to escape, but they found them locked, and were thrown back upon the sword and fire. The battle was going against the citizens, but their rage and hatred of the Spaniards made them continue the fight. Goswyn Verreyck, the margrave of the city, combated the foe with the burgomaster lying dead at his feet, and at last he himself fell, adding his corpse to a heap of slain, composed of citizens, soldiers, and magistrates. While the fire was devouring hundreds of noble mansions and millions of treasure, the sword was busy cutting off the citizens. The Spaniard made no distinction between friend and foe, between Papist and Protestant, between poor and rich. Old men, women, and children; the father at the hearth, the bride at the altar, and the priest in the sanctuary—the blood of all flooded the streets of their city on that terrible day.

Darkness fell on this scene of horrors, and now the barbarities of the day were succeeded by the worse atrocities of the night. The first object of these men was plunder, and one would have thought there was now enough within their reach to content the most boundless avarice. Without digging into the earth or crossing the sea, they could gather the treasures of all regions, which a thousand ships had carried thither, and stored up in that city of which they were now masters. They rifled the shops, they broke into the warehouses, they loaded themselves with the money, the plate, the wardrobes, and the jewels of private citizens; but their greed, like the grave, never said it was enough. They began to search for hidden treasures, and they tortured their supposed possessors to compel them to reveal what often did not exist. These crimes were accompanied by infamies of so foul and revolting a character, that by their side murder itself grows pale. The narrators have recorded many of these cruel and shameful deeds, but we forbear to chronicle them. For three days the work of murdering and plundering went on, and when it had come to an end, how awful the spectacle which that city, that three days before had been the gayest and wealthiest upon earth, presented! Stacks of blackened ruins rising where marble palaces had stood; yawning hovels where princely mansions had been; whole streets laid in ashes; corpses here gathered in heaps, there lying about, hacked, mutilated, half-burned—some naked, others still encased in armour! Eight thousand citizens, according to the most trustworthy accounts, were slain. The value of the property consumed by the fire was estimated at £4,000,000, irrespective of the hundreds of magnificent edifices that were destroyed. An equal amount was lost by the pillage, not reckoning the merchandise and jewellery appropriated in addition by the Spaniards. Altogether the loss to the mercantile capital of Brabant was incalculable; nor was it confined to the moment, for Antwerp never recovered the prosperity it had enjoyed before the bloody and plundering hand of the Spaniard was laid upon it.[2911]

But this awful calamity held in its bosom a great moral. During fifty years the cry had been going up to heaven from tens of thousands of scaffolds, where the axe was shedding blood like water; from prisons, where numberless victims were writhing on the rack; from stakes, where the martyr was consuming amid the flames; from graveyards, where corpses were rotting above-ground; from trees and door-posts and highway gibbets, where human bodies were dangling in the air; from graves which had opened to receive living men and women; from sacked cities; from violated matrons and maidens; from widows and orphans, reared in affluence but now begging their bread; from exiles wandering desolate in foreign lands—from all these had the cry gone up to the just Judge, and now here was the beginning of vengeance. The powerful cities of the Netherlands, Antwerp among the rest, saw all these outrages committed, and all these men and women dragged to prison, to the halter, to the stake, but they "forbore to deliver," they "hid themselves from their own flesh." A callous indifference on the part of nation to the wrongs and sufferings of others is always associated with a blindness to its own dangers, which is at once the consequence and the retribution of its estranging itself from the public cause of humanity and justice. Once and again and a third time had the Southern Netherlands manifested this blindness to the mighty perils that menaced them on the side of Spain, and remained deaf to the call of patriotism and religion. When the standards of William first approached their frontier, they were unable to see the door of escape from the yoke of a foreign tyrant thus opened to them. A tithe of the treasure and blood which were lost in the "Antwerp Fury" would have carried the banner of William in triumph from Valenciennes to the extreme north of Zealand; but the Flemings cared not to think that the hour had come to strike for liberty. A second time the Deliverer approached them, but the ease-loving Netherlanders understood not the offer now made to them of redemption from the Spanish yoke. When Alva and his soldiers—an incarnated ferocity and bigotry—entered the Low Countries, they sat still: not a finger did they lift to oppose the occupation. When the cry of Naarden, and Zutphen, and Haarlem was uttered, Antwerp was deaf. Wrapt in luxury and ease, it had seen its martyrs burned, the disciples of the Gospel driven away, and it returned to that faith which it had been on the point of abandoning, and which, by retaining the soul in vassalage to Rome, perpetuated the serfdom of the Spanish yoke; and yet Antwerp saw no immediate evil effects follow. The ships of all nations continued to sail up its river and discharge their cargoes on its wharves. Its wealth continued to increase, and its palaces to grow in splendour. The tempests that smote so terribly the cities around it rolled harmlessly past its gates. Antwerp believed that it had chosen at once the easier and the better part; that it was vastly preferable to have the Romish faith, with an enriching commerce and a luxurious ease, than Protestantism with battles and loss of goods; till one day, all suddenly, when it deemed calamity far away, a blow, terrible as the bolt of heaven, dealt it by the champions of Romanism, laid it in the dust, together with the commerce, the wealth, and the splendour for the sake of which it had parted with its Protestantism.

CHAPTER XXIII
THE "PACIFICATION OF GHENT," AND TOLERATION

THE great struggle which William, Prince of Orange, was maintaining on this foot-breadth of territory for the religion of Reformed Christendom, and the liberty of the Netherlands, had now reached a well-defined stage. Holland and Zealand were united under him as Stadtholder or virtual monarch. The fiction was still maintained that Philip, as Count of Holland, was the nominal monarch of the Netherlands, but this was nothing more than a fiction, and to Philip it must have appeared a bitter satire; for, according to this fiction, Philip King of the Netherlands was making war on Philip King of Spain. The real monarch of the United Provinces of Holland and Zealand was the Prince of Orange. In his hands was lodged the whole administrative power of the country, as also wellnigh the whole legislative functions. He could make peace and he could make war. He appointed to all offices; he disposed of all affairs; and all the revenues of the kingdom were paid to him for national uses, and especially for the prosecution of the great struggle in which he was engaged for the nation's independence. These revenues, given spontaneously, were larger by far than the sums which Alva by all his taxation and terror had been able to extort from the Provinces. William, in fact, possessed more than the powers of a king. The States had unbounded trust in his wisdom, his patriotism, and his uprightness, and they committed all into his hands. They saw in him a sublime example of devotion to his country, and of abnegation of all ambitions, save the one ambition of maintaining the Protestant religion and the freedom of Holland. They knew that he sought neither title, nor power, nor wealth, and that in him was perpetuated that order of men to which Luther and Calvin belonged—men not merely of prodigious talents, but what is infinitely more rare, of heroic faith and magnanimous souls; and so "King of Holland" appeared to them a weak title—they called him the "Father of their Country."

The great Powers of Europe watched, with an interest bordering on amazement, this gigantic struggle maintained by a handful of men, on a diminutive half-submerged territory, against the greatest monarch of his day. The heroism of the combat challenged their admiration, but its issues awakened their jealousies, and even alarms. It was no mere Dutch quarrel; it was no question touching only the amount of liberty and the kind of religion that were to be established on this sandbank of the North Sea that was at issue; the cause was a worldwide one, and yet none of the Powers interfered either to bring aid to that champion who seemed ever on the point of being overborne, or to expedite the victory on the powerful side on which it seemed so sure to declare itself; all stood aloof and left these two most unequal combatants to fight out the matter between them. There was, in truth, the same play of rivalries around the little Holland which there had been at a former era around Geneva. The rivalry reduced the Protestant Powers to inaction, and prevented their assisting Holland, just as the Popish Powers had been restrained from action in presence of Geneva. In the case of the little city on the shores of the Leman, Providence plainly meant that Protestantism should be seen to triumph in spite of the hatred and opposition of the Popish kingdoms; and so again, in the case of the little country on the shores of the North Sea, Providence meant to teach men that Protestantism could triumph independently of the aid and alliance of the Powers friendly to it. The great ones of the earth stood aloof, but William, as he told his friends, had contracted a firm alliance with a mighty Potentate, with him who is King of kings; and seeing this invisible but omnipotent Ally, he endured in the awful conflict till at last his faith was crowned with a glorious victory.

In England a crowd of statesmen, divines, and private Christians followed the banners of the Prince of Orange, with their hopes and their prayers. But nations then had found no channel for the expression of their sympathies, other than the inadequate one of the policy of their sovereign; and Elizabeth, though secretly friendly to William and the cause of Dutch independence, had to shape her conduct so as to balance conflicting interests. Her throne was surrounded with intrigues, and her person with perils. She had to take account of the pretensions and partisans of the Queen of Scots, of the displeasure of Philip of Spain, and of the daggers of the Jesuits, and these prevented her supporting the cause of Protestantism in Holland with arms or, to any adequate extent, with money. But if she durst not accord it public patronage or protection, neither could she openly declare against it; for in that case France would have made a show of aiding William, and Elizabeth would have seen with envy the power of her neighbour and rival considerably extended, and the influence of England, as a Protestant State, proportionately curtailed and weakened.

France was Roman Catholic and Protestant by turns. At this moment the Protestant fit was upon it: a peace had been made with the Huguenots which promised them everything but secured them nothing, and which was destined to reach the term of its brief currency within the year. The protæan Medici-Valois house that ruled that country was ready to enter any alliance, seeing it felt the obligation to fidelity in none; and the Duke of Anjou, to spite both Philip and Elizabeth, might have been willing to have taken the title of King of the Netherlands, and by championing the cause of Dutch Protestantism for an hour ruined it for ever. This made France to William of Orange, as well as to Elizabeth, an object of both hope and fear; but happily the fear predominating, for the horror of the St. Bartholomew had not yet left the mind of William, he was on his guard touching offers of help from the Court of the Louvre.

But what of Germany, with which the Prince of Orange had so many and so close relationships, and which lay so near the scene of the great conflict, whose issues must so powerfully influence it for good or for ill? Can Germany fail to see that it is its own cause that now stands at bay on the extreme verge of the Fatherland, and that could the voice of Luther speak from the tomb in the Schlosskirk of Wittemberg, it would summon the German princes and knights around the banner of William of Orange, as it formerly summoned them to the standard of Frederick of Saxony? But since Luther was laid in the grave the great heart of Germany had waxed cold. Many of its princes seemed to be Protestant for no other end but to be able to increase their revenues by appropriations from the lands and hoards of the Roman establishment, and it was hardly to be expected that Protestants of this stamp would feel any lively interest in the great struggle in Holland. But the chief cause of the coldness of Germany was the unhappy jealousy that divided the Lutherans from the Reformed. That difference had been widening since the evil day of Marburg. Luther on that occasion had been barely able to receive Zwingle and his associates as brethren, and many of the smaller men who succeeded Luther lacked even that small measure of charity; and in the times of William of Orange to be a Calvinist was, in the eyes of many Lutherans, to be a heretic. When the death of Edward VI. compelled the celebrated John Alasco, with his congregation, to leave England and seek asylum in Denmark, Westphalus, a Lutheran divine, styled the wandering congregation of Alasco "the martyrs of the devil;" whilst another Lutheran, Bugenhagius, declared that "they ought not to be considered as Christians;" and they received intimation from the king that he would "sooner suffer Papists than them in his dominions;" and they were compelled, at a most inclement season, to embark for the north of Germany, where the same persecutions awaited them, the fondness for the dogma of consubstantiation on the part of the Lutheran ministers having almost stifled in their minds the love of Protestantism.[2912] But William of Orange was an earnest Calvinist, and the opinions adopted by the Church of Holland on the subject of the Sacrament were the same with those received by the Churches of Switzerland and of England, and hence the coldness of Germany to the great battle for Protestantism at its borders.

William, therefore, seeing England irresolute, France treacherous, and Germany cold, withdrew his eyes from abroad, in seeking for allies and aids, and fixed them nearer home. Might he not make another attempt to consolidate the cause of Protestant liberty in the Netherlands themselves? The oft-recurring outbreaks of massacre and rapine were deepening the detestation of the Spanish rule in the minds of the Flemings, and now, if he should try, he might find them ripe for joining with their brethren of Holland and Zealand in an effort to throw off the yoke of Philip. The chief difficulty, he foresaw, in the way of such a confederacy was the difference of religion. In Holland and Zealand the Reformed faith was now the established religion, whereas in the other fifteen Provinces the Roman was the national faith. Popery had had a marked revival of late in the Netherlands, the date of this second growth being that of their submission to Alva; and now so attached were the great body of the Flemings to the Church of Rome, that they were resolved "to die rather than renounce their faith." This made the patriotic project which William now contemplated the more difficult, and the negotiation in favour of it a matter of great delicacy, but it did not discourage him from attempting it. The Flemish Papist, not less than the Dutch Calvinist, felt the smart of the Spanish steel, and might be roused to vindicate the honour of a common country, and to expel the massacring hordes of a common tyrant. It was now when Requesens was dead, and the government was for the time in the hands of the State Council, and the fresh atrocities of the Spanish soldiers gave added weight to his energetic words, that he wrote to the people of the Netherlands to the effect that "now was the time when they might deliver themselves for ever from the tyranny of Spain. By the good providence of God, the government had fallen into their own hands. It ought to be their unalterable resolve to hold fast the power which they possessed, and to employ it in delivering their fellow-citizens from that intolerable load of misery under which they had so long groaned. The measure of the calamities of the people, and of the iniquity of the Spaniards, was now full. There was nothing worse to be dreaded than what they had already suffered, and nothing to deter them from resolving either to expel their rapacious tyrants, or to perish in the glorious attempt."[2913] To stimulate them to the effort to which he called them, he pointed to what Holland and Zealand single-handed had done; and if "this handful of cities" had accomplished so much, what might not the combined strength of all the Provinces, with their powerful cities, achieve?

This appeal fell not to the ground. In November, 1576, a congress composed of deputies from all the States assembled at Ghent, which re-echoed the patriotic sentiments of the prince; the deliberations of its members, quickened and expedited by the Antwerp Fury, which happened at the very time the congress was sitting, ended in a treaty termed the "Pacification of Ghent." This "Pacification" was a monument of the diplomatic genius, as well as the patriotism, of William the Silent. In it the prince and the States of Holland and Zealand on the one side, and the fifteen Provinces of the Netherlands on the other, agreed to bury all past differences, and to unite their arms in order to effect the expulsion of the Spanish soldiers from their country. Their soil cleared of foreign troops, they were to call a meeting of the States-General on the plan of that great assembly which had accepted the abdication of Charles V. By the States-General all the affairs of the Confederated Provinces were to be finally regulated, but till it should meet it was agreed that the Inquisition should be for ever abolished; that the edicts of Philip touching heresy and the tumults should be suspended; that the ancient forms of government should be revived; that the Reformed faith should be the religion of the two States of Holland and Zealand, but that no Romanist should be oppressed on account of his opinion; while in the other fifteen Provinces the religion then professed, that is the Roman, was to be the established worship, but no Protestant was to suffer for conscience sake. In short, the basis of the treaty, as concerned religion, was toleration.[2914]

A great many events were crowded upon this point of time. The Pacification of Ghent, which united all the Provinces in resistance to Spain, the Antwerp Fury, and the recovery of that portion of Zealand which the Spaniards by their feats of daring had wrested from William, all arrived contemporaneously to signalise this epoch of the struggle.

This was another milestone on the road of the Prince of Orange. In the Pacification of Ghent he saw his past efforts beginning to bear fruit, and he had a foretaste of durable and glorious triumphs to be reaped hereafter. It was an hour of exquisite gladness in the midst of the sorrow and toil of his great conflict. The Netherlands, participating in the prince's joy, hailed the treaty with a shout of enthusiasm. It was read at market-crosses of all the cities, amid the ringing of bells and the blazing of bonfires.

But the greatest gain in the Pacification of Ghent, and the matter which the Protestant of the present day will be best pleased to contemplate, is the advance it notifies in the march of toleration. Freedom of conscience was the basis on which this Pacification, which foreshadowed the future Dutch Republic, was formed. Calvin, twenty years before, had laid down the maxim that no one is to be disturbed for his religious opinions unless they are expressed in words or acts that are inimical to the State, or prejudicial to the social order. William of Orange, in laying the first foundations of the Batavian Republic, placed them on the principle of toleration, as his master Calvin had defined it. To these two great men—John Calvin and William the Silent—we owe, above most, this great advance on the road of progress and human freedom. The first had defined and inculcated the principle in his writings; the second had embodied and given practical effect to it in the new State which his genius and patriotism had called into existence.

CHAPTER XXIV
ADMINISTRATION OF DON JOHN, AND FIRST SYNOD OF DORT

THE great battles of religion and liberty have, as a rule, been fought not by the great, but by the little countries of the world. History supplies us with many striking examples of this, both in ancient and in modern times. The Pacification of Ghent is one of these. It defined the territory which was to be locked in deadly struggle with Spain, and greatly enlarged it. By the side of the little Holland and Zealand it placed Brabant and Flanders, with their populous towns and their fertile fields. With this vast accession of strength to the liberal side, one would have expected that henceforth the combat would be waged with greater vigour, promptitude, and success. But it was not so, for from this moment the battle began to languish. William of Orange soon found that if he had widened the area, he had diminished the power of the liberal cause. An element of weakness had crept in along with the new territories. How this happened is easy to explain. The struggle on both sides was one for religion. Philip had made void all the charters of ancient freedom, and abolished all the privileges of the cities, that he might bind down upon the neck of the Netherlands the faith and worship of Rome. On the other hand, William of Orange and the States that were of his mind strove to revive these ancient charters, and immemorial privileges, that under their shield they might enjoy freedom of conscience, and be able to profess the Protestant religion. None but Protestants could be hearty combatants in such a battle; religion alone could kindle that heroism which was needed to bear the strain and face the perils of so great and so prolonged a conflict. But the fifteen Provinces of the Southern Netherlands were now more Popish than at the abdication of Charles V. The Protestants whom they contained at that era had since been hanged, or burned, or chased away, and a reaction had set in which had supplied their places with Romanists; and therefore the Pacification, which placed Brabant alongside of Holland in the struggle with Spain, and which gave to the Dutch Protestant as his companion in arms the Popish Fleming, was a Pacification that in fact created two armies, by proposing two objects or ends on the liberal side. To the Popish inhabitants of the Netherlands the yoke of Spain would in no long time be made easy enough; for the edicts, the Inquisition, and the bishops were things that could have no great terrors to men who did not need their coercion to believe, or at least profess, the Romish dogmas. The professors of the Romish creed, not feeling that wherein lay the sting of the Spanish yoke, could not be expected therefore to make other than half-hearted efforts to throw it off. But far different was it with the other and older combatants. They felt that sting in all its force, and therefore could not stop half-way in their great struggle, but must necessarily press on till they had plucked out that which was the root of the whole Spanish tyranny. Thus William found that the Pacification of Ghent had introduced among the Confederates divided counsels, dilatory action, and uncertain aims; and three years after (1579) the Pacification had to be rectified by the "Union of Utrecht," which, without dissolving the Confederacy of Ghent, created an inner alliance of seven States, and thereby vastly quickened the working of the Confederacy, and presented to the world the original framework or first constitution of that Commonwealth which has since become so renowned under the name of the "United Provinces."

Meanwhile, and before the Union of Utrecht had come into being, Don John of Austria, the newly-appointed governor, arrived in the Low Countries. He brought with him an immense prestige as the son of Charles V., and the hero of Lepanto. He had made the Cross to triumph over the Crescent in the bloody action that reddened the waters of the Lepantine Gulf; and he came to the Netherlands with the purpose and in the hope of making the Cross triumphant over heresy, although it should be by dyeing the plains of the Low Countries with a still greater carnage than that with which he had crimsoned the Greek seas. He arrived to find that the seventeen Provinces had just banded themselves together to drive out the Spanish army, and to re-assert their independence; and before they would permit him to enter they demanded of him an oath to execute the Pacification of Ghent. This was a preliminary which he did not relish; but finding that he must either accept the Pacification or else return to Spain, he gave the promise, styled the "perpetual Edict," demanded of him (17th February, 1577), and entered upon his government by dismissing all the foreign troops, which now returned into Italy.[2915] With the departure of the soldiers the brilliant and ambitious young governor seemed to have abandoned all the great hopes which had lighted him to the Netherlands. There were now great rejoicings in the Provinces: all their demands had been conceded.

But Don John trusted to recover by intrigue what he had surrendered from necessity. No sooner was he installed at Brussels than he opened negotiations with the Prince of Orange, in the hope of drawing him from "the false position" in which he had placed himself to Philip, and winning him back to his side. Don John had had no experience of such lofty spirits as William, and could only see the whims of fanaticism, or the aspirings of ambition, in the profound piety and grand aims of William. He even attempted, through a malcontent party that now arose, headed by the Duke of Aerschot, to work the Pacification of Ghent so as to restore the Roman religion in exclusive dominancy in Holland and Zealand, as well as in the other Provinces. But these attempts of Don John were utterly futile. William had no difficulty in penetrating the true character and real design of the viceroy. He knew that, although the Spanish troops had been sent away, Philip had still some 15,000 German mercenaries in the Provinces, and held in his hands all the great keys of the country. William immovably maintained his attitude of opposition despite all the little arts of the viceroy.

Step by step Don John advanced to his design, which was to restore the absolute dominancy at once of Philip and of Rome over all the Provinces. His first act was to condemn to death Peter Panis, a tailor by trade, and a man of most exemplary life, and whose only crime had been that of hearing a sermon from a Reformed minister in the neighbourhood of Mechlin. The Prince of Orange made earnest intercession for the martyr, imploring the governor "not again to open the old theatres of tyranny, which had occasioned the shedding of rivers of blood;"[2916] notwithstanding the poor man was beheaded by the order of Don John. The second act of the viceroy, which was to seize on the Castle of Namur, revealed his real purpose with even more flagrancy. To make himself master of that stronghold he had recourse to a stratagem. Setting out one morning with a band of followers, attired as if for the chase, but with arms concealed under their clothes, the governor and his party took their way by the castle, which they feigned a great desire to see. No sooner were they admitted by the castellan than they drew their swords, and Don John at the same instant winding his horn, the men-at-arms, who lay in ambush in the surrounding woods, rushed in, and the fortress was captured.[2917] As a frontier citadel it was admirably suited to receive the troops which the governor expected soon to return from Italy; and he remarked, when he found himself in possession of the castle, that this was the first day of his regency: it might with more propriety have been called the first day of those calamities that pursued him to the grave.

Intercepted letters from Don John to Philip II. fully unmasked the designs of the governor, and completed the astonishment and alarm of the States. These letters urged the speedy return of the Spanish troops, and dilating on the inveteracy of that disease which had fastened on the Netherlands, the letters said, "the malady admitted of no remedies but fire and sword." This discovery of the viceroy's baseness raised to the highest pitch the admiration of the Flemings for the sagacity of William, who had given them early warning of the duplicity of the governor, and the cruel designs he was plotting. Thereupon the Provinces a third time threw off their obligation to Philip II., declaring that Don John was no longer Stadtholder or legitimate Governor of the Provinces.[2918] Calling the Prince of Orange to Brussels, they installed him as Governor of Brabant, a dignity which had been bestowed hitherto only on the Viceroys of Spain. As the prince passed along in his barge from Antwerp to Brussels, thousands crowded to the banks of the canal to gaze on the great patriot and hero, on whose single shoulder rested the weight of the struggle with the mightiest empire then in existence. The men of Antwerp stood on this side of the canal, the citizens of Brussels lines the opposite bank, to offer their respectful homage to one greater than kings. They knew the toils he had borne, the dangers he had braved, the princely fortune he had sacrificed, and the beloved brothers and friends he had seen sink around him in the contest; and when they saw the head on which all these storms had burst still erect, and prepared to brave tempests not less fierce in the future, rather than permit the tyranny of Spain to add his native country to the long roll of unhappy kingdoms which it had already enslaved and crushed, their admiration and enthusiasm knew no bounds, and they saluted him with the glorious appellation of the Father of his Country, and the guardian of its liberties and laws.[2919]

This was the third time that liberty had offered herself to the Flemings; and as this was to be the last, so it was the fairest opportunity the Provinces ever had of placing their independence on a firm and permanent foundation, in spite of the despot of the Escorial. The Spanish soldiers were withdrawn, the king's finances were exhausted, the Provinces were knit together in a bond for the prosecution of their common cause, and they had at their head a man of consummate ability, of incorruptible patriotism, and they lacked nothing but hearty co-operation and union among themselves to guide the struggle to a glorious issue. With liberty, who could tell the glories and prosperities of that future that awaited Provinces so populous and rich? But, alas! it began to be seen what a solvent

Romanism was, and of how little account were all these great opportunities in the presence of so disuniting and dissolving a force. The Roman Catholic nobles grew jealous of William, whose great abilities and pre-eminent influence threw theirs into the shade. They affected to believe that liberty was in danger from the man who had sacrificed all to vindicate it, and that so zealous a Calvinist must necessarily persecute the Roman religion, despite the efforts of his whole life to secure toleration for all creeds and sects. In short, the Flemish Catholics would rather wear the Spanish yoke, with the Pope as their spiritual father, than enjoy freedom under the banner of William the Silent. Sixteen of the grandees, chief among whom was the Duke of Aerschot, opened secret negotiations with the Archduke Matthias, brother of the reigning emperor, Rudolph, and invited him to be Governor of the Netherlands. Matthias, a weak but ambitious youth, greedily accepted the invitation; and without reflecting that he was going to mate himself with the first politician of the age, and to conduct a struggle against the most powerful monarch in Christendom, he departed from Vienna by night, and arrived in Antwerp, to the astonishment of those of the Flemings who were not in the intrigue.[2920] The archduke owed the permission given him to enter the Provinces to the man he had come to supplant. William of Orange, so far from taking offence and abandoning his post, continued to consecrate his great powers to the liberation of his country. He accepted Matthias, though forced upon him by an intrigue; he prevailed upon the States to accept him, and install him in the rank of Governor of the Netherlands, he himself becoming his lieutenant-general. Matthias remained a puppet by the side of the great patriot, nevertheless his presence did good; it sowed the seeds of enmity between the German and Spanish branches of the House of Austria, and it made the Roman Catholic nobles, whose plot it was, somewhat obnoxious in the eyes of both Don John and Philip. The cause of the Netherlands was thus rather benefited by it. And moreover, it helped William to the solution of a problem which had occupied his thoughts for some time past—namely, the permanent form which he should give to the government of the Provinces. So far as the matter had shaped itself in his mind, he purposed that a head or Governor should be over the Netherlands, and that under this virtual monarch should be the States-General or Parliament, and under it a State Council or Executive; but that neither the Governor nor the State Council should have power to act without the concurrence of the States-General. Such was the programme, essentially one of constitutionalism, that William had sketched in his own mind for his native land. Whom he should make Governor he had not yet determined: most certainly it would be neither himself nor Philip of Spain; and now an intrigue of the Roman Catholic nobles had placed Matthias of Austria in the post, for which William knew not where to find a suitable occupant. But first the country had to be liberated; every other work must be postponed for this.

The Netherlands, their former Confederacy ratified (December 7th, 1577) in the "New Union" of Brussels—the last Confederacy that was ever to be formed by the Provinces—had thrown down the gauntlet to Philip, and both sides prepared for war. The Prince of Orange strengthened himself by an alliance with England. In this treaty, formed through the Marquis of Havrée, the States ambassador, Elizabeth engaged to aid the Netherlanders with a loan of 100,000 pounds sterling, and a force of 5,000 infantry and 1,000 cavalry, their commander to have a seat in the State Council. Nor was Don John idle. He had collected a considerable army from the neighbouring Provinces, and these were joined by veteran troops from Italy and Spain, which Philip had ordered Alexander Farnese, Duke of Parma, to lead back into the Netherlands. The States army amounted to about 10,000; that of Spain to 15,000; the latter, if superior in numbers, were still more superior in discipline. On joining battle at Gemblours the army of the Netherlands encountered a terrible overthrow, a result which the bulk of the nation attributed to the cabals and intrigues of the Roman Catholic nobles.

At this stage the two great antagonistic principles which were embodied in the respective policies of Philip and William, and whose struggles with one another made themselves audible in this clash of arms, came again to the front. The world was anew taught that it was a mortal combat between Rome and the Reformation that was proceeding on the theatre of the Netherlands. The torrents of blood that were being poured out were shed not to revive old charters, but to rend the chains from conscience, and to transmit to generations unborn the heritage of religious freedom. In this light did Pope Gregory XIII. show that he regarded this struggle when he sent, as he did at this time, a bull in favour of all who should fight under the banner of Don John, "against heretics, heretical rebels, and enemies of the Romish faith." The bull was drafted on the model of those which his predecessors had been wont to fulminate when they wished to rouse the faithful to slaughter the Saracens and Turks; it offered a plenary indulgence and remission of sins to all engaged in this new crusade in the Low Countries. The bull further authorised Don John to impose a tax upon the clergy for the support of the war, "as undertaken for the defence of the Romish religion." The banners of the Spanish general were blazoned with the sign of the cross, and the following motto: *In hoc signo vici Turcos: in hoc signo vincam hereticos* ("Under this sign I have vanquished the Turks: under this sign I will vanquish the heretics"). And Don John was reported to have said that "the king had rather be lord only of the ground, of the trees, shrubs, beasts, wolves, waters, and fishes of this country, than suffer one single person who has taken up arms against him, or at least who has been polluted with heresy, to live and remain in it."[2921]

On the other side Protestantism also lifted herself up. Amsterdam, the capital of Protestant Holland, still remained in the hands of the Romanists. This state of matters, which weakened the religious power of the Northern States, was now rectified. Mainly by the mediation of Utrecht, it was agreed on the 8th of February, 1578, that Amsterdam should enroll itself with the States of Holland, and swear allegiance to the Prince of Orange as its Stadtholder, on condition that the Roman faith were the only one publicly professed in the city, with right to all Protestants to practise their own worship, without molestation, outside the walls, and privilege of burying their dead in unconsecrated but convenient ground, provided that neither was psalm sung, nor prayer offered, nor any religious act performed at the grave, and that the corpse was followed to the tomb by not more than twenty-six persons. To this was added a not less important concession—namely, that all who had been driven away on account of difference of religious opinion should have liberty to return to Amsterdam, and be admitted to their former rights and privileges.[2922] This last stipulation, by attracting back crowds of Protestant exiles, led to a revolution in the government of the city. The Reformed faith had now a vast majority of the citizens—scarcely were there any Romanists in Amsterdam save the magistrates and the friars—and a plot was laid, and very cleverly executed, for changing the Senate and putting it in harmony with the popular sentiment. On the 26th May, 1578, the Stadthouse was surrounded by armed citizens, and the magistrates were made prisoners. All the monks were at the same time secured by soldiers and others dispersed throughout the city. The astonished senators, and the not less astonished friars, were led through the streets by their captors, the crowd following them and shouting, "To the gallows! to the gallows with them, whither they have sent so many better men before them!" The prisoners trembled all over, believing that they were being conducted to execution. They were conveyed to the river's edge, the magistrates were put on board one boat, and the friars, along with a few priests who had also been taken into custody, were embarked in another, and both were rowed out to deep water. Their pallid faces, and despairing adieus to their relations, bespoke the apprehensions they entertained that the voyage on which they had set out was destined to be fatal. The vessels that bore them would, they believed, be scuttled, and give them burial in the ocean. No such martyrdom, however, awaited them; and the worst infliction that befell them was the terror into which they had been put of a watery death. They were landed in safety on St. Anthony's Dyke, and left at liberty to go wherever they would, with this one limitation, that if ever again they entered Amsterdam they forfeited their lives. Three days after these melodramatic occurrences a body of new senators was elected and installed in office, and all the churches were closed during a week. They were then opened to the Reformed by the magistrates, who, accompanied by a number of carpenters, had previously visited them and removed all their images. Thus, without the effusion of a drop of blood, was Protestantism established in Amsterdam. The first Reformed pastors in that capital were John Reuchlin and Peter Hardenberg.[2923] The Lutherans and Anabaptists were permitted to meet openly for their worship, and the Papists were allowed the private exercise of theirs.

With this prosperous gale Protestantism made way in the other cities of Holland and of Brabant. This progress, profoundly peaceful in the majority of cases, was attended with tumult in one or two instances. In Haarlem the Protestants rose on a Communion Sunday, and coming upon the priests in the cathedral while in the act of kindling their tapers and unfurling their banners for a grand procession, they dispossessed them of their church. In the tumult a priest was slain, but the soldier who did the deed had to atone for it with his life; the other rioters were summoned by tuck of drum to restore the articles they had stolen, and the Papists were assured, by a public declaration, of the free exercise of their religion.[2924] The presence of the Prince of Orange in Brussels, and the Pacification of Ghent, which shielded the Protestant worship from violence, had infused new courage into the hearts of the Reformed in the Southern Netherlands. From their secret conventicles in some cellar or dark alley, or neighbouring wood, they came forth and practised their worship in the light of day. In Flanders and Brabant the Protestants were increasing daily in numbers and courage. On Sunday, the

16th of May, in the single city of Antwerp, Protestant sermons were preached in not less than sixteen places, and the Sacrament dispensed in fourteen. In Ghent it was not uncommon for Protestant congregations to convene in several places, of four, five, and six hundred persons, and all this in spite of the Union of Brussels (1577), which touched upon the toleration accorded in the Pacification of Ghent.[2925]

The first National Synod of the Dutch Reformed Church met at Dort on the 2nd of June, 1578. This body, in a petition equally distinguished for the strength of its reasonings and the liberality of its sentiments, urged the States-General to make provision for the free exercise of the Reformed religion, as a measure righteous in itself, and the surest basis for the peace of the Provinces. How truly catholic were the Dutch Calvinists, and how much the cause of toleration owes to them, can be seen only from their own words, addressed to the Archduke Matthias and the Council of State. After having proved that the cruelties practised upon them had led only to an increase of their numbers, with the loss nevertheless of the nation's welfare, the desolation of its cities, the banishment of its inhabitants, and the ruin of its trade and prosperity, they go on to say that the refusal of the free exercise of their religion reduced them to this dilemma, "either that they must live without any religion, or that they must force a way to the public exercise of it." They object to the first alternative as leading to an epicurean life, and the contempt of all laws human and divine; they dread the second as tending to a breach in the union of the Provinces, and possibly the dissolution of the present Government. But do they therefore ask exclusive recognition or supremacy? Far from it. "Since the experience of the past years had taught them," they say, "that by reason of their sins they could not all be reduced to one and the same religion, it was necessary to consider how both religions could be maintained without damage or prejudice to each other. As for the objection," they continue, "that two religions are incompatible in the same country, it had been refuted by the experience of all ages. The heathen emperors had found their account more in tolerating the Christians, nay, even in using their service in their wars, than in persecuting them. The Christian emperors had also allowed public churches to those who were of a quite different opinion from them in religious matters, as might be seen in the history of Constantine, of his two sons, of Theodosius, and others. The Emperor Charles V. found no other expedient to extricate himself from the utmost distress than by consenting to the exercise of both religions." After citing many other examples they continue thus: "France is too near for us to be ignorant that the rivers of blood with which that kingdom is overflowed can never be dried up but by a toleration of religion. Such a toleration formerly produced peace there; whereas being interrupted the said kingdom was immediately in a flame, and in danger of being quite consumed. We may likewise learn from the Grand Seignior, who knows how to tyrannise as well as any prince, and yet tolerates both Jews and Christians in his dominions without apprehending either tumults or defections, though there be more Christians in his territories who neer owned the authority of the Pope, than there are in Europe that acknowledge it." And they concluded by craving "that both religions might be equally tolerated till God should be pleased to reconcile all the opposite notions that reigned in the land."[2926]

In accordance with the petition of the Synod of Dort, a scheme of "Religious Peace," drafted by the Prince of Orange and signed by Matthias, was presented to the States-General for adoption. Its general basis was the equal toleration of both religions throughout the Netherlands. In Holland and Zealand, where the Popish worship had been suppressed, it was to be restored in all places where a hundred resident families desired it. In the Popish Provinces an equivalent indulgence was to be granted wherever an equal number of Protestant families resided. Nowhere was the private exercise of either faith to be obstructed; the Protestants were to be eligible to all offices for which they were qualified, and were to abstain from all trade and labour on the great festivals of the Roman Church. This scheme was approved by the States-General, under the name of the "Peace of Religion." William was overjoyed to behold his most ardent hopes of a united Fatherland, and the vigorous prosecution of its great battle against a common tyranny, about to be crowned.

But these bright hopes were only for a moment. The banner of toleration, bravely uplifted by William, had been waved over the Netherlands only to be furled again. The Roman Catholic nobles, with Aerschot and Champagny at their head, refused to accept the "Peace of Religion." In their immense horror of Protestantism they forgot their dread of the Spaniard, and rather than that heresy should defile the Fatherland, they were willing that the yoke of Philip should be bound down upon it. Tumults, violences, and conflict broke out in many of the Provinces. Revenge begat revenge, and animosity on the one side kindled an equal animosity on the other. Something like a civil war raged in the Southern Netherlands, and the sword that ought to have been drawn against the common foe was turned against each other. These strifes and bigotries wrought at length the separation of the Walloon Provinces from the rest, and in the issue occasioned the loss of the greater part of the Netherlands. The hour for achieving liberty had passed, and for three centuries nearly these unwise and unhappy Provinces were not to know independence, but were to be thrown about as mere political make-weights, and to be the property now of this master and now of that.

Meanwhile the two armies lay inactive in the presence of each other. Both sides had recently received an augmentation of strength. The Netherlands army had been increased to something like 30,000, first by an English levy led by John Casimir, and next by a French troop under the command of the Duke of Alençon, for the Netherlands had become the pivot on which the rival policies of England and France at this moment revolved. The sinews of war were lacking on both sides, and hence the pause in hostilities. The scenes were about to shift in a way that no one anticipated. Struck down by fever, Don John lay a corpse in the Castle of Nemur. How different the destiny he had pictured for himself when he entered this fatal land! Young, brilliant, and ambitious, he had come to the Netherlands in the hope of adding to the vast renown he had already won at Lepanto, and of making for himself a great place in Christendom—of mounting, it might be, one of its thrones. But a mysterious finger had touched the scene, and suddenly changed its splendours into blackness, and transformed the imagined theatre of triumph into one of misfortune and defeat. Fortune forsook her favourite the moment his foot touched this charmed soil. Withstood and insulted by the obstinate Netherlanders, outwitted and baffled by the great William of Orange, suspected by his jealous brother Philip II., by whom he was most inadequately supported with men and money, all his hours were embittered by toil, disappointment, and chagrin. The constant dread in which he was kept by the perils and pitfalls that surrounded him, and the continual circumspection which he was compelled to exercise, furrowed his brow, dimmed his eye, sapped his strength, and broke his spirit. At last came fever, and fever was followed by delirium. He imagined himself upon the battlefield: he shouted out his orders: his eye now brightened, now faded, as he fancied victory or defeat to be attending his arms. Again came a lucid interval,[2927] but only to fade away into the changeless darkness of death. He died before he had reached his thirtieth year. Another hammer, to use Beza's metaphor, had been worn out on the anvil of the Church.[2928]

CHAPTER XXV
ABJURATION OF PHILIP, AND RISE OF THE SEVEN UNITED PROVINCES

DON JOHN having on his death-bed nominated Alexander Farnese, Duke of Parma, to succeed him, and the choice having soon afterwards been ratified by Philip II., the duke immediately took upon him the burden of that terrible struggle which had crushed his predecessor. If brilliant abilities could have commanded corresponding success, Parma would have speedily re-established the dominion of Spain throughout the whole of the Netherlands. His figure was finely moulded, and his features were handsome, despite that the lower part of his face was buried in a bushy beard, and that his dark eye had a squint which warned the spectator to be on his guard. His round compact head was one which a gladiator might have envied; his bearing was noble; he was temperate, methodical in business, but never permitted its pressure to prevent his attendance on morning mass; his coolness on the battlefield gave confidence to his soldiers; and while his courage and skill fitted him to cope with his antagonists in war, his wisdom, cunning, and patience won for him not a few victories in the battles of diplomacy. His conduct and valour considerably retrieved at the beginning the affairs of Philip, but the mightier intellect with which he was confronted, and the destinies of the cause against which he did battle, attested in the end their superiority over all the great talents and dexterous arts of Alexander of Parma, seconded by the powerful armies of Spain. After the toil and watchfulness of years, and after victories gained with much blood, to yield not fruit but ashes, he too had to retire from the scene disappointed, baffled, and vanquished.

A revived bigotry had again split up the lately united Fatherland, and these divisions opened an entrance for the arts and the arms of Parma. Gathering up the wreck of the army of Don John, and reinforcing the old battalions by new recruits, Parma set vigorously to work to reduce the Provinces, and restore the supremacy of both Philip and Rome. Sieges and battles signalised the opening of the campaign; in most of these he was successful, but we cannot stay to give them individual narration, for our task is to follow the footsteps of that Power which had awakened the conflict, and which was marching on to victory, although through clouds so dark and tempests so fierce that a few only of the Netherlanders were able to follow it. The first success that rewarded the arms of Parma was the capture of Maestricht. Its massacre of three days renewed the horrors of former sieges. The cry of its agony was heard three miles off; and when the sword of the enemy rested, a miserable remnant (some three or four hundred, say the old chroniclers)[2929] was all that was spared of its thirty-four thousand inhabitants. Crowds of idlers from the Walloon country flocked to the empty city; but though it was easy to repeople it, it was found impossible to revive its industry and prosperity. Nothing besides the grass that now covered its streets would flourish in it but vagabondism. The loss which the cause of Netherland liberty sustained in the fall of Maestricht was trifling, compared with the injury inflicted by another achievement of Parma, and which he gained not by arms, but by diplomacy. Knowing that the Walloons were fanatically attached to the old religion, he opened negotiations, and ultimately prevailed with them to break the bond of common brotherhood and form themselves upon a separate treaty. It was a masterly stroke. It had separated the Roman from the Batavian Netherlands. William had sought to unite the two, and make of them one nationality, placing the key-stone of the arch at Ghent, the capital of the Southern Provinces, and the second city in the Netherlands. But the subtle policy of Parma had cut the Fatherland in twain, and the project of William fell to the ground.

The Prince of Orange anxiously considered how best to parry the blow of Parma, and neutralise its damaging effects. The master-stroke of the Spaniard led William to adopt a policy equally masterly, and fruitful beyond all the measures he had yet employed; this was the "Union of Utrecht." The alliance was formed between the States of Holland, Zealand, Utrecht, Guelderland, Zutphen, Overyssel, and Groningen. It was signed on the 23rd of January, 1579, and six days thereafter it was proclaimed at Utrecht, and hence its name. This "Union" constituted the first foundation-stone in the subsequently world-renowned Commonwealth of the *United Provinces* of the Low Countries. The primary and main object of the Confederated States was the defence of their common liberty; for this end they resolved to remain hereafter and for ever united as one Province—without prejudice, however, to the ancient privileges and the peculiar customs of each several State. As regarded the business of religion, it was resolved that each Province should determine that question for itself—with this proviso, that no one should be molested for his opinion. The toleration previously enacted by the Pacification of Ghent was to rule throughout the bounds of the Confederacy.[2930] When the States contrasted their own insignificance with the might of their great enemy, seven little Provinces banding themselves against the aggregate of nearly twice that number of powerful Kingdoms, they chose as a fitting representation of their doubtful fortunes a ship labouring amid the waves without sail or oars, and they stamped this device upon their first coins, with the words *Incertum quo fata ferant*[2931] ("We know not whither the fates shall bear us"). Certainly no one at that hour was sanguine or bold enough to conjecture the splendid future awaiting these seven adventurous Provinces.

This attitude on their part made the King of Spain feign a desire for conciliation. A Congress was straightway assembled at Cologne to make what was represented as a hopeful, and what was certainly a laudable, attempt to heal the breach. On the Spanish side it was nothing more than a feint, but on that account it wore externally all the greater pomp and stateliness. In these respects nothing was lacking that could make it a success. The first movers in it were the Pope and the emperor. The deputies were men of the first rank in the State and the Church; they were princes, dukes, bishops, and the most renowned doctors in theology and law. Seldom indeed have so many mitres, and princely stars, and ducal coronets graced any assembly as those that shed their brilliance on this; and many persuaded themselves, when they beheld this union of rank and office with skill in law, in art, and diplomacy, that the Congress would give birth to something correspondingly magnificent. It met in the beginning of May, 1579, and it did not separate till the middle of November of the same year. But the six months during which it was in session were all too short to enable it to solve the problem which so many conventions and conferences since the breaking out of the Reformation had attempted to solve, but had failed—namely, how the absolute demands of authority are to be reconciled with the equally inflexible claims of conscience. There were only two ideas promulgated in that assembly; so far the matter was simple, and the prospect of a settlement hopeful; but these two ideas were at opposite poles, and all the stars, coronets, and mitres gathered there could not bridge over the gulf between them. The two ideas were those to which we have already referred—Prerogative and Conscience.

The envoys of the Netherland States presented fourteen articles, of which the most important was the one referring to religion. Their proposal was that "His Majesty should be pleased to tolerate the exercise of the Reformed religion and the Confession of Augsburg in such towns and places where the same were at that time publicly professed. That the States should also on their part, presently after the peace was declared, restore the exercise of the Roman Catholic religion in all the aforesaid towns and places, upon certain equitable conditions which should be inviolably preserved." "The Christian religion," said the envoys in supporting their proposal, "was a great mystery, in promoting of which God did not make use of impious soldiers, nor of the sword or bow, but of his own Spirit and of the ministry of pastors or shepherds sent by him. That the dominion over souls and consciences belonged to God only, and that he only was the righteous Avenger and Punisher of the abuses committed in matters of religion. They insisted particularly upon the free exercise of religion."[2932]

The deputies on the king's side refused to listen to this proposal. They would agree to nothing as a basis of peace, save that the Roman Catholic religion—all others excluded—should be professed in all the Provinces; and as regarded such as might refuse to return to the Roman faith, time would be given them to settle their affairs, and retire from the country.[2933] Half the citizens well-nigh would have had to exile themselves if this condition had been accepted. Where so large a body of emigrants were to find new seats, or how the towns left empty by their departure were to be re-peopled, or by what hands the arts and agriculture of the country were to be carried on, does not seem to have been provided for, or even thought of, by the Congress.

William of Orange had from the first expected nothing from this Conference. He knew Philip never would grant what only the States could accept—the restoration, namely, of their charters, and the free exercise of their Protestant faith; he knew that to convene such an assembly was only to excite hopes that could not possibly be fulfilled, and so to endanger the cause of the Provinces; he knew that mitres and ducal coronets were not arguments, nor could render a whit more legitimate the claims of prerogative; that ingenious and quirky expedients, and long and wordy discussions, would never bring the two parties one hair's-breadth nearer to each other; and as he had foreseen, so did it turn out. When the Congress ended its sitting of six months, the only results it had to show were the thousands of golden guilders needed for its expenses, and the scores of hogsheads of Rhenish wine which had been consumed in moistening its dusty deliberations and debates.

Contemporaneously with this most august and most magnificent, yet most resultless Congress, attempts were made to detach the Prince of Orange from his party and win him over to the king's side. Private overtures were made to him, to the effect that if he would forsake the cause of Netherland independence and retire to a foreign land, he had only to name his "price" and it should be instantly forthcoming, in honour, or in money, or in both. More particularly he was promised the payment of his debts, the restitution of his estates, reimbursement of all the expenses he had incurred in the war, compensation for his losses, the liberation of his son the Count of Buren, and should William retire into Germany, his son would be placed in the Government of Holland and Utrecht, and he himself should be indemnified, with a million of money as a gratuity. These offers were made in Philip's name by Count Schwartzenburg, who pledged his faith for the strict performance of them.

This was a mighty sum, but it could not buy William of Orange. Not all the honours which this monarch of a score of kingdoms could bestow, not all the gold which the master of the mines of Mexico and Peru could offer, could make William sell himself and betray his country. He was not to be turned aside from the lofty, the holy object he had set before him, the glory of redeeming from slavery a people that confided in him, and of kindling the lamp of a pure faith in the land which he so dearly loved. If his presence were an obstacle to peace on the basis of the country's liberation, he was ready to go to the ends of the earth, or to his grave; but he would be no party to a plot which had only for its object to deprive the country of its head, and twine round it the chain of a double slavery.[2934]

The gold of Philip had failed to corrupt the Patriot: the King of Spain next attempted to gain his end by another and a different stratagem. The dagger might rid him of the man whom armies could not conquer, and whom money could not buy. This "evil thought" was first suggested by Cardinal Granvelle, who hated the prince, as the vile hate the upright, and it was eagerly embraced by Philip, of whose policy it was a radical principle that "the end justifies the means." The King of Spain fulminated a ban, dated 15th March, 1580, against the Prince of Orange, in which he offered "thirty thousand crowns, or so, to any one who should deliver him, dead or alive." The preamble of the ban set forth at great length, and with due formality, the "crimes," in other words the services of liberty, which had induced his patient and loving sovereign to set a price upon the head of William, and make him a mark for all the murderers in Christendom. But the indignation of the virtuous king can be adequately understood only by perusing the words of the ban itself. "For these causes," said the document, "we declare him traitor and miscreant, enemy of ourselves and of the country. As such we banish him perpetually from all our realms, forbidding all our subjects . . . to administer to him victuals, drink, fire, or other necessaries. . . . We expose the said William as an enemy of the human race, giving his property to all who may seize it. And if any one of our subjects, or any stranger, should be found sufficiently generous of heart to rid us of this pest, delivering him to us, dead or alive, or taking his life, we will cause to be furnished to him, immediately after the deed shall have been done, the sum of twenty-five thousand crowns of gold. If he have committed any crime, however heinous, we promise to pardon him; and if he be not already noble we will ennoble him for his valour."

The dark, revengeful, cowardly, and bloodthirsty nature of Philip II. appears in every line of this proclamation. In an evil hour for himself had the King of Spain launched this fulmination. It fixed the eyes of all Europe upon the Prince of Orange, it gave him the audience of the whole world for his justification; and it compelled him to bring forward facts which remain an eternal monument to Philip's inhumanity, infamy, and crime. The Vindication or "Apology" of William, addressed to the Confederated States, and of which copies were sent to all the courts of Europe, is one of the most precious documents of the time, and the exposition it gives of the character and motives of the actors, and more especially of himself and Philip. It is not so much a Defence as an Arraignment, which, breaking in a thunder-peal of moral indignation, must have made the occupant of the throne over which it rolled to shake and tremble on his lofty seat. After detailing his own efforts for the emancipation of the down-trodden Provinces, he turns to review the acts, the policy, and the character of the man who had fulminated against him this ban of assassination and murder. He charges Philip with the destruction, not of one nor of a few of those liberties which he had sworn to maintain, but of all of them; and that not once, but a thousand times; he ridicules the idea that a people remain bound while the monarch has released himself from every promise, and oath, and law; he hurls contempt at the justification set up for Philip's perjuries—namely, that the Pope had loosed him from his obligations—branding it as adding blasphemy to tyranny, and adopting a principle which is subversive of faith among men; he accuses him of having, through Alva, concerted a plan with the French king to extirpate from France and the Netherlands all who favoured the Reformed religion, giving as his informant the French king himself. He pleads guilty of having disobeyed Philip's orders to put certain Protestants to death, and of having exerted himself to the utmost to prevent the barbarities and cruelties of the "edicts." He boldly charges Philip with living in adultery, with having contracted an incestuous marriage, and opening his way to this foul couch by the murder "of his former wife, the mother of his children, the daughter and sister of the kings of France." He crowns this list of crimes, of which he accuses Philip, with a yet more awful deed—the murder of his son, the heir of his vast dominions, Don Carlos.

With withering scorn he speaks of the King of Spain's attempt to frighten him by raising against him "all the malefactors and criminals in the world" "I am in the hand of God," said the Christian patriot, "he will dispose of me as seems best for his glory and my salvation." The prince concludes his Apology by dedicating afresh what remained of his goods and life to the service of the States. If his departure from the country would remove an impediment to a just peace, or if his death could bring an end to their calamities, Philip should have no need to hire assassins and poisoners: exile would be sweet, death would be welcome. He was at the disposal of the States. They had only to speak—to issue their orders, and he would obey; he would depart, or he would remain among them, and continue to toil in their cause, till death should come to release him, or liberty to crown them with her blessings.[2935]

This Apology was read in a meeting of the Confederated Estates at Delft, the 13th of December, 1580, and their mind respecting it was sufficiently declared by the step they were led soon thereafter to adopt. Abjuring their allegiance to Philip, they installed the Prince of Orange in his room. Till this time Philip had remained nominal sovereign of the Netherlands, and all edicts and deeds were passed in his name, but now this formality was dropped. The Prince of Orange had before this been earnestly entreated by the States to assume the sovereignty, but he had persistently declined to allow himself to be clothed with this office, saying that he would give no ground to Philip or to any enemy to say that he had begun the war of independence to obtain a crown, and that the aggrandisement of his family, and not the liberation of his country, was the motive which had prompted him in all his efforts for the Low Countries. Now, however, (5th July, 1581), the dignity so often put aside was accepted conditionally, the prince assuming, at the solemn request of the States of Holland and Zealand, the "entire authority, as sovereign and chief of the land, as long as the war should continue."[2936]

This step was finally concluded on the 26th of July, 1581, by an assembly of the States held at the Hague, consisting of deputies from Brabant, Guelderland, Zutphen, Flanders, Holland, Zealand, Utrecht, Overyssel, and Friesland. The terms of their "Abjuration" show how deeply the breath of modern constitutional liberty had entered the Low Countries in the end of the sixteenth century; its preamble enunciates truths which must have shocked the adherents of the doctrine of Divine right. The "Abjuration" of the States declared "that the people were not created by God for the sake of the prince, and only to submit to his commands, whether pious or impious, right or wrong, and to serve him and his slaves; but that, on the contrary, the prince was made for the good of the people, in order to feed, preserve, and govern them according to justice and equity, as a father his children, and a shepherd his flock: that whoever in opposition to these principles pretended to rule his subjects as if they were his bondsmen, ought to be deemed a tyrant, and for that reason might be rejected or deposed, especially by virtue of the resolution of the States of the nation, in case the subjects, having made use of the most humble supplications and prayers, could find no other means to divert him from his tyrannical purposes, nor to secure their own native rights."[2937]

They next proceeded to apply these principles. They fill column after column with a history of Philip's reign over the Low Countries, in justification of the step they had taken in deposing him. The document is measured and formal, but the horrors of those flaming years shine through its dry technicalities in its cold phraseology. If ever there was a tyrant on the earth, it was Philip II. of Spain; and if ever a people was warranted in renouncing its allegiance, it was the men who now came forward with this terrible tale of violated oaths, of repeated perfidies, of cruel wars, of extortions, banishments, executions, martyrdoms, and massacrings, and who now renounced solemnly and for ever their allegiance to the prince who was loaded with all these crimes.

The act of abjuration was carried into immediate execution. Philip's seal was broken, his arms were torn down, his name was forbidden to be used in any letters-patent, or public deed, and a new oath was administered to all persons in public office and employment.

This is one of the great revolutions of history. It realised in fact, and exhibited for the first time to the world, Representative Constitutional Government. This revolution, though enacted on a small theatre, exemplified principles of universal application, and furnished a precedent to be followed in distant realms and by powerful kingdoms. It is important to remark that this is one of the mightiest of the births of Protestantism. For it was Protestantism that inspired the struggle in the Low Countries, and that maintained the martyr at the stake and the hero in the field till the conflict was crowned with this ever-memorable victory. The mere desire for liberty, the mere reverence for old charters and municipal privileges, would not have carried the Netherlanders through so awful and protracted a combat; it was the new force awakened by religion that enabled them to struggle on, sending relay after relay of martyrs to die and heroes to fight for a free conscience and a scriptural faith, without which life was not worth having. In this, one of the greatest episodes of the great drama of the Reformation, we behold Protestantism, which had been proceeding step by step in its great work of creating a new society—a new world—making another great advance. In Germany it had produced disciples and churches; in Geneva it had moulded a theocratic republic; in France it had essayed to set up a Reformed Church so powerful as to include well-nigh half the nation. Making yet another essay, we see it in the Netherlands dethroning Philip of Spain, and elevating to his place William of Orange. A constitutional State, summoned into being by Protestantism, is now seen amid the despotisms of Christendom, and its appearance was a presage that in the centuries to follow, Protestantism would, in some cases by its direct agency, in others by its reflex influence, revolutionise all the governments and effect a transference of all the crowns of Europe.

CHAPTER XXVI
ASSASSINATION OF WILLIAM THE SILENT

THE Seven United Provinces—the fair flower of Netherland Protestantism—had come to the birth. The clouds and tempests that overhung the cradle of the infant States were destined to roll away, the sun of prosperity and power was to shine forth upon them, and for the space of a full century the number of their inhabitants, the splendour of their cities, the beauty of their country, the vastness of their commerce, the growth of their wealth, the number of their ships, the strength of their armies, and the glory of their letters and arts, were to make them the admiration of Europe, and of the world. Not, however, till that man who had helped above all others to find for Protestantism a seat where it might expand into such a multiform magnificence, had gone to his grave, was this stupendous growth to be beheld by the world. We have now to attend to the condition in which the dissolution of Philip's sovereignty left the Netherlands.

In the one land of the Low Countries, there were at this moment three communities or nations. The Walloons, yielding to the influence of a common faith, had returned under the yoke of Spain. The Central Provinces, also mostly Popish, had ranged themselves under the sovereignty of the Duke of Anjou, brother of Henry III. of France. The Provinces of Holland and Zealand had elected (1581), as we have just seen, the Prince of Orange as their king.[2938] His acceptance of the dignity was at first provisional. His tenure of sovereignty was to last only during the war; but afterwards, at the earnest entreaty of the States, the prince consented that it should be perpetual. His lack of ambition, or his exceeding sense of honour, made him decline the sovereignty of the Central Provinces, although this dignity was also repeatedly pressed upon him; and had he accepted it, it may be that a happier destiny would have been in store for the Netherlands. His persistent refusal made these Provinces cast their eyes abroad in search of a chief, and in an evil hour their choice lighted upon a son of Catherine of Medici. The Duke of Anjou, the elect of the Provinces, inherited all the vices of the family from which he was sprung. He was treacherous in principle, cruel in disposition, profuse in his habits, and deeply superstitious in his faith; but his true character had not then been revealed; and the Prince of Orange, influenced by the hope of enlisting on the side of the Netherlands the powerful aid of France, supported his candidature. France had at that moment, with its habitual vacillation, withdrawn its hand from Philip II. and given it to the Huguenots, and this seemed to justify the prince in indulging the hope that this great State would not be unwilling to extend a little help to the feeble Protestants of Flanders. It was rumoured, moreover, that Anjou was aspiring to the hand of Elizabeth, and that the English queen favoured his suit; and to have the husband of the Queen of England as King of the Netherlands, was to have a tolerable bulwark against the excesses of the Spanish Power. But all these prudent calculations of bringing aid to Protestantism were destined to come to nothing. The duke made his entry (February, 1582) into the Netherlands amid the most joyous demonstrations of the Provinces;[2939] and to gratify him, the public exercise of the Popish religion, which for some time had been prohibited in Antwerp, was restored in one of the churches. But a cloud soon overcast the fair morning of Anjou's sovereignty in the Netherlands. He quickly showed that he had neither the principle nor the ability necessary for so difficult a task as he had undertaken. Bitter feuds sprang up between him and his subjects, and after a short administration, which neither reflected honour on himself nor conferred benefit on the Provinces, he took his departure, followed by the reproaches and accusations of the Flemings. The cause of Protestantism was destined to owe nothing to a son of Catherine de Medici. Matthias, who had dwindled in William's overshadowing presence into a non-entity, and had done neither good nor evil, had gone home some time before. Through neither of these men had the intrigues of the Romanists borne fruit, except to the prejudice of the cause they were intended to further.

The Duke of Anjou being gone, the States of Brabant and Flanders came to the Prince of Orange (August, 1583) with an offer of their crown; but no argument could induce him to accept the sceptre they were so anxious to thrust into his hand. He took the opportunity, however, which his declinature offered, of tendering them some wholesome advice. They must, he said, bestir themselves, and contribute more generously, if they wished to speed in the great conflict in which they had embarked. As for himself, he had nothing now to give but his services, and his blood, should that be required. All else he had already parted with for the cause: his fortune he had given; his brothers he had given. He had seen with pleasure, as the fruit of his long struggles for the Fatherland and freedom of conscience, the fair Provinces of Holland and Zealand redeemed from the Spanish yoke. And to think that now these Provinces were neither oppressed by Philip, nor darkened by Rome, was a higher reward than would be ten crowns, though they could place them upon his head. He would never put it in the power of Philip of Spain to say that William of Orange had sought other recompense than that of rescuing his native land from slavery.[2940]

William, about this time, was deeply wounded by the defection of some friends in whom he had reposed confidence as sincere Protestants and good patriots, and he was not less mortified by the secession of Flanders, with its powerful capital, Ghent, from the cause of Netherland independence to the side of Parma. Thus one by one the Provinces of the Netherlands, whose hearts had grown faint in the struggle, and whose "strength was weakened in the way," crept back under the shadow of Spain, little dreaming what a noble heritage they had forfeited, and what centuries of insignificance, stagnation, and serfdom spiritual and bodily awaited them, as the result of the step they had now taken. The rich Southern Provinces, so stocked with cities, so finely clothed, so full of men, and so replenished with commercial wealth, fell to the share of Rome: the sand-banks of Holland and Zealand were given to Protestantism, that it might convert the desert into a garden, and rear on this narrow and obscure theatre an empire which, mighty in arms and resplendent in arts, should fill the world with its light.

The ban which Philip had fulminated against the prince began now to bear fruit. Wonderful it would have been if there had not been found among the malefactors and murderers of the world some one bold enough to risk the peril attendant on grasping the golden prize which the King of Spain held out to them.

A year only had elapsed since the publication of the ban, and now an attempt was made to destroy the man on whose head it had set a price. Gaspar Anastro, a Spanish banker in Antwerp, finding himself on the verge of bankruptcy, bethought him of earning Philip's reward, and doing the world a service by ridding it of so great a heretic, and helping himself at the same time, by retrieving his ruined fortunes. But lacking the courage to do the bloody deed with his own hand, he hired his servant to execute it. This man, having received from a priest absolution of his sins, and the assurance that the doors of paradise stood open to him, repaired to the mansion of the prince, and waited an opportunity to commit the horrible act. As Orange was crossing the hall, from the dinner-table, the miscreant approached him on pretence of handing him a petition, and putting his pistol, loaded with a single bullet, close to his head, discharged it at the prince. The ball, entering a little below the right ear, passed out through the left jaw, carrying with it two teeth. The wound bled profusely, and for some weeks the prince's life was despaired of, and vast crowds of grief-stricken citizens repaired to the churches to beseech, with supplications and tears, the Great Disposer to interpose his power, and save from death the Father of his Country. The prayer of the nation was heard. William recovered to resume his burden, and conduct another stage on the road to freedom the two Provinces which he had rescued from the paws of the Spanish bear. But if the husband survived, the wife fell by the murderous blow of Philip. Charlotte de Bourbon, so devoted to the prince, and so tenderly beloved by him, worn out with watching and anxiety, fell ill of a fever, and died. William sorely missed from his side that gentle but heroic spirit, whose words had so often revived him in his hours of darkness and sorrow.

The two years that now followed witnessed the progressive disorganisation of the Southern Netherlands, under the combined influence of the mismanagement of the Duke of Anjou, the intrigues of the Jesuits, and the diplomacy and arms of the Duke of Parma. Despite all warnings, and their own past bitter experience, the Provinces of Brabant and Flanders again opened their ear to the "cunning charmers" of Spain and the "sweet singers" of Rome, and began to think that the yoke of Philip was not so heavy and galling as they had accounted it, and that the pastures of "the Church" were richer and more pleasant than those of Protestantism. Many said "Beware!" and quoted the maxim of the old Book: "They who wander out of the way of understanding shall remain in the congregation of the dead." But the Flemings turned away from these counsellors. Divisions, distractions, and perpetual broils made them fain to have peace, and, to use the forcible metaphor of the Burgomaster of Antwerp, "they confessed to a wolf, and they had a wolf's absolution."

It was in the Northern provinces only, happily under the sceptre of William, who had rescued them from the general shipwreck of the Netherlands, that order prevailed, and that anything like steady progress could be traced. But now the time was come when these States must lose the wisdom and courage to which they owed the freedom they already enjoyed, and the yet greater degree of prosperity and power in store for them. Twenty years had William the Silent "judged" the Low Countries: now the tomb was to close over him. He had given the labours of his life for the cause of the Fatherland: he was now to give his blood for it. Not fewer than five attempts had been made to assassinate him. They had failed; but the sixth was to succeed. Like all that had preceded it, this attempt was directly instigated by Philip's proscription. In the summer of 1584, William was residing at Delft, having married Louisa de Coligny, the daughter of the admiral, and the widow of Teligny, who perished, as we have seen, in the St. Bartholomew. A young Burgundian, who hid great duplicity and some talent under a mean and insignificant exterior, had that spring been introduced to the prince, and had been employed by him in some business, though of small moment. This stranger professed to be a zealous Calvinist, the son of a French Protestant of the name of Guion, who had died for his faith. His real name was Balthazar Gérard, and being a fanatical Papist, he had long wished to "serve God and the king" by taking off the arch-heretic. He made known his design to the celebrated Franciscan, Father Géry of Tournay, by whom he was "much comforted and strengthened in his determination." He revealed his project also to Philip's Governor of the Low Countries. The Duke of Parma, who had at that time four ruffians lurking in Delft on the same business, did not dissuade Gérard from his design, but he seems to have mistrusted his fitness for it; although afterwards, being assured on this point, he gave him some encouragement and a little money. The risk was great, but so too were the inducements—a fortune, a place in the peerage of Spain, and a crown in paradise.

It was Tuesday, the 10th of July, 1584. The prince was at dinner with his wife, his sister (the Princess of Schwartzenberg), and the gentlemen of his suite. In the shadow of a deep arch in the wall of the vestibule, stood a mean-looking personage with a cloak cast round him. This was Balthazar Gérard. His figure had caught the eye of Louisa de Coligny as, leaning on her husband's arm, she passed through the hall to the dining-room, and his pale, agitated, and darkly sinister countenance smote her with a presentiment of evil. "He has come for a passport," said the prince, calming her alarm, and passed into the dining-hall. At table, the prince, thinking nothing of the muffled spectre in the ante-chamber, was cheerful as usual. The Burgomaster of Leeuwarden was present at the family dinner, and William, eager to inform himself of the religious and political condition of Friesland, talked much, and with great animation, with his guest. At two o'clock William rose from table, and crossed the vestibule on his way to his private apartments above. His foot was already on the second step of the stairs, which he was ascending leisurely, when the assassin, rushing from his hiding-place, fired a pistol loaded with three balls, one of which passed through the prince's body, and struck the wall opposite. On receiving the shot, William exclaimed: "O my God, have mercy on my soul! O my God, have mercy on this poor people!"[2941] He was carried into the dining-room, laid upon a couch, and in a few minutes he breathed his last. He had lived fifty-one years and sixteen days. On the 3rd of August he was laid in his tomb at Delft, mourned, not by Holland and Zealand only, but by all the Netherlands—the Walloons excepted—as a father is mourned.[2942]

So closed the great career of William the Silent. It needs not that we paint his character: it has portrayed itself in the actions of his life which we have narrated. Historians have done ample justice to his talents, so various, so harmonious, and each so colossal, that the combination presents a character of surpassing intellectual and moral grandeur such as has rarely been equalled, and yet more rarely excelled. But as the ancient tree of Netherland liberty never could have borne the goodly fruit that clothed its boughs in the sixteenth and seventeenth centuries unless the shoot of Protestantism had been grafted upon it, and new sap infused into the old decaying charters, so the talents of William of Orange, varied, beautiful, and brilliant though they were, unless linked with something diviner, could not have evolved that noble character and done those great deeds which have made the name of William the Silent one of the brightest on the page of history. Humanity, however richly endowed with genius, is a weak thing in itself; it needs to be grafted with a higher Power in order to reach the full measure of greatness. In the case of William of Orange it was so grafted. It was his power of realising One unseen, whose will he obeyed, and on whose arm he leaned, that constituted the secret of his strength. He was the soldier, the statesman, the patriot; but before all he was the Christian. The springs of his greatness lay in his faith. Hence his lofty aims, which, rising high above fame, above power, above all the ordinary objects of ambition, aspired to the only and supreme good. Hence, too, that inflexible principle which enabled him, without turning to the right or to the left, to go straight on through all the intricacies of his path, making no compromise with falsehood, never listening to the solicitations of self-interest, and alive only to the voice of duty. Hence, too, that unfaltering perseverance and undying hope that upheld him in the darkest hour, and amid the most terrible calamities, and made him confident of ultimate victory where another would have abandoned the conflict as hopeless. William of Orange persevered and triumphed where a Cæsar or a Napoleon would have despaired and been defeated. The man and the country are alike: both are an epic. Supremely tragic outwardly is the history of both. It is defeat succeeding defeat; it is disaster heaped upon disaster, and calamity piled upon calamity, till at last there stands personified before us an Iliad of woes. But by some marvellous touch, by some transforming fiat, the whole scene is suddenly changed: the blackness kindles into glorious light, the roar of the tempest subsides into sweetest music, and defeat grows into victory. The man we had expected to see prostrate beneath the ban of Philip, rises up greater than kings, crowned with the wreath of a deathless sovereignty; and the little State which Spain had thought to consign to an eternal slavery, rends the chain from her neck; and from her seat amid the seas, she makes her light to circulate along the shores of the islands and continents of the deep, and her power to be felt, and her name reverenced, by the mightiest kingdoms on the earth.

CHAPTER XXVII
ORDER AND GOVERNMENT OF THE NETHERLAND CHURCH

THE development of the religious principle is somewhat overshadowed by the struggle in arms which Protestantism had to maintain in the Low Countries. But the well-defined landing-place at which we have arrived, permits us to pause and take a closer view of the inner and spiritual conflict. Amid the armies that are seen marching to and fro over the soil of the Netherlands; amid the battles that shake it from side to side; amid the blaze of cities kindled by the Spaniard's torch, and fields drowned in blood by the Spanish sword, we can recognize the silent yet not inefficacious presence of a great power. It is here that we find the infant springs of a movement that to the outward eye seems so very martial and complex. It is in the closets where the Bible is being read; it is in the little assemblies gathered in cellar or thicket or cave, where prayer is being offered up and the Scriptures are being searched; it is in the prison where the confessor languishes, and at the stake where the martyr is expiring, that we find the beginnings of that impulse which brought a nation into the field with arms in its hands, and raised up William of Orange to withstand the power of Spain. It was not the old charters that kindled the fire in the Netherlands. These were slowly and silently returning to dust, and the Provinces were sinking with them into slavery, and both would have continued uninterruptedly their quiescent repose had not an old Book, which claims a higher than human authorship, awakened conscience, and made it more indispensable to the men of the Netherlands to have freedom of worship than to enjoy goods or estate, or even life itself. It was this inexorability that brought on the conflict.

But was it not a misfortune to transfer such a controversy to the arena of the battle-field? Doubtless it was; but for that calamity the disciples of the Gospel in the Netherlands are not to blame. They waited long and endured much before they betook them to arms. Nearly half a century passed away after the burning of the first martyrs of Protestantism in Brussels till the first sword was unsheathed in the war of independence. During that period, speaking generally—for the exact number never can be ascertained—from 50,000 to 100,000 men and women had been put to death for religion. And when at last war came, it came not from the Protestants, but from the Spaniards. We have seen the powerful army of soldiers which Alva led across the Alps, and we have seen the terrible work to which they gave themselves when they entered the country. The Blood Council was set up, the preaching of the Gospel was forbidden, the ministers were hanged, whole cities were laid in ashes, and, the gibbets being full, the trees of the field were converted into gallows, and their boughs were seen laden with the corpses of men and women whose only crime was that they were, or were suspected of being, converts to Protestantism. As if this were not enough, sentence of death was passed upon all the inhabitants of the Netherlands. Not even yet had a sword been drawn in opposition to a tyranny that had converted the Provinces, recently so flourishing, into a slaughter-house, and that threatened speedily to make them as silent as a graveyard. Nor did Philip mean that his stranglings, burnings, and massacrings should stop at the Netherlands. The orders to his devastating hordes were to follow the steps of Protestantism to every land where it had gone; to march to the shores of the Leman; to the banks of the Thames; to France, should the Guises fail in the St. Bartholomew they were at that moment plotting: everywhere "extermination, utter extermination" was to be inflicted. Protestantism was to be torn up by the roots, although it should be necessary to tear up along with it all human rights and liberties. It is not the Netherlands, with William at their head, for whom we need to offer vindication or apology, for coming forward at the eleventh hour to save Christendom and the world from a catastrophe so imminent and so tremendous; the parties that need to be defended are those more powerful States and princes who stood aloof, or rendered but inadequate aid at this supreme crisis, and left the world's battle to be fought by one of the smallest of its kingdoms. It is no doubt true, as we are often reminded, that the great Defender of the Church is her heavenly King; but it is equally true that he saves her not by miracle, but by blessing the counsels and the arms, as well as the teaching and the blood of her disciples. There is a time to die for the truth, and there is a time to fight for it; and the part of Christian wisdom is to discern the "times," and the duty which they call for.

Leaving the armed struggles that are seen on the surface, let us look at the under-current, which, from one hour to another, is waxing in breadth and power. Protestantism in the Netherlands does not form one great river, as it did in some other countries. For half a century, at least, it is a congeries of fountains that burst out here and there, and send forth a multitude of streamlets, that are seen flowing through the country and refreshing it with living water. The course of Netherland Protestantism is the exact reverse of that of the great river of the land, the Rhine, which long keeping its floods united, divides at last into an infinity of streams, and falls into the ocean. Netherland Protestantism, long parted into a multitude of courses, gathers at length its waters into one channel, and forms henceforth one great river. This makes it somewhat difficult to obtain a clear view of the Netherland Protestant Church. That Church is first seen in her martyrs, and it may be truly said that her martyrs are her glory, for they are excelled in numbers, and in holy heroism, by those of no Church in Christendom. The Netherland Church is next seen in her individual congregations, scattered through the cities of Flanders, Brabant, and Holland; and these congregations come into view, and anon disappear, according as the cloud of persecution now rises and now falls; and last of all, that Church is seen in her Synods. Her days of battle and martyrdom come at length to an end; and under the peaceful sceptre of the princes of the House of Orange, her courts regularly convene, her seminaries flourish, her congregations fill the land, and the writings of her theologians are diffused throughout Christendom. The schools of Germany have ceased by this time to be the crowded resort of scholars they once were; the glory of the French Huguenots has waxed dim; and the day is going away in Geneva, where in the middle and end of the sixteenth century it had shone so brightly; but the light of Holland is seen burning purely, forming the link between Geneva and the glory destined to illuminate England in the seventeenth century.

The order and government established in the Church of Holland may be clearly ascertained from the "Forty Ecclesiastical Laws," which in the year 1577 were drawn up and published in the name of the Prince of Orange as Stadtholder, and of the States of Holland, Zealand, and their allies. The preamble of the Act indicates the great principle of ecclesiastical jurisprudence entertained by the framers, and which they sought to embody in the Dutch Church. "Having," say then, "nothing more at heart than that the doctrine of the holy Gospel may be propagated in its utmost purity in the towns and other places of our jurisdiction, we have thought fit, after mature deliberation, to make the following rules, which we will and require to be inviolably preserved; and we have judged it necessary that the said rules should chiefly relate to the administration of Church government, of which there are to be found in Holy Scripture four principle kinds: 1. That of Pastors, who are likewise styled Bishops, Presbyters, Ministers in the Word of God, and whose office chiefly consists in teaching the said Word, and in the administration of the Sacraments. 2. That of Doctors, to whose office is now substituted that of the Professors of Divinity. 3. That of Elders, whose main business is to watch over men's morals, and to bring transgressors again into the right way by friendly admonitions; and 4. That of Deacons, who have the care of the sick."

According to this programme of Church government, or body of ecclesiastical canons, now enacted by the States, the appointment of ministers was lodged in the hands of the magistrates, who were to act, however, upon "the information and with the advice of the ministers." Towns whose magistrates had not yet embraced the Reformed religion, were to be supplied with pastors from a distance. No one was to assume at his own hands an office so sacred as the ministry: he must receive admission from the constituted authorities of the Church. The minister "elect" of a city had first to undergo examination before the elders, to whom he must give proofs that his learning was competent, that his pulpit gifts were such as might enable him to edify the people, and, above all, that his life was pure, lest he should dishonour the pulpit, and bring reproach upon "the holy office of the ministry." If found qualified in these three particulars, "he shall be presented," say the canons, "to the magistrate for his approbation, in order to his preaching to the people," that they, too, may be satisfied as to his fitness to instruct them. There still awaits him another ordeal before he can enter the pulpit as pastor of a flock. He has been nominated by the magistrate with the advice of the ministers; he has been examined by the elders; he has been accepted by the people; and thus has given guarantees as to his learning, his life, and his power of communicating instruction; but before being ordained to the office of the ministry, "his name shall be published from the pulpit," say the canons, "three Sundays successively, to the end that if any man has aught to object against him, or can show any cause why he should not be admitted, he may have time to do it." We shall suppose that no objections have been offered—at least none such as to form a bar to his admission—the oath of allegiance is then administered to him. In that oath he swears obedience to the lawful authorities "in all things not contrary to the will of God." To this civil oath was appended a solemn vow of spiritual fidelity, in these words: "Moreover, I swear that I will preach and teach the Word of God after the purest manner, and with the greatest diligence, to the end it may bring forth much fruit in this congregation, as becomes a true and faithful shepherd. . . . Neither will I forsake this ministry on account of any advantage or disadvantage." It was to the ecclesiastical authorities that this promise was commonly given in other Presbyterian Churches, but in Holland it was tendered to the nation through the magistrate, the autonomy of the Church not being as yet complete. The act of ordination was to be preceded by a sermon on the sacred function, and followed by prayers for a blessing on the pastor and his flock. So simple was the ritual, in studied contrast to the shearings, the anointings, and the investitures of the Roman Church, which made the entrance into sacred orders an affair of so much mystic pomp. "This," the canons add, "we think sufficient, seeing that the ancient ceremonies are degenerated into abominable institutions," and they might have added, had failed to guard the purity of the priesthood.[2943]

In these canons we see at least an earnest desire evinced on the part of the civil authorities of Holland to secure learned and pious men for its pulpits, and to provide guarantees, so far as human foresight and arrangement could do so, against the indolent and unfaithful discharge of the office on the part of those entrusted with it. And in this they showed a wise care. The heart of a Protestant State is its Church, and the heart of a Church is its pulpit, and the centuries which have elapsed since the era of the Reformation furnish us with more than one example, that so long as the pulpit retains its purity, the church will preserve her vigour; and while the Church preserves her vigour, the commonwealth will continue to flourish; and that, on the other hand, when languor invades the pulpit, corruption sets-in in the Church, and from the Church the leprosy quickly extends to the State; its pillars totter, and its bulwarks fall.

Following an example first originated at Geneva, the ministers of a city and of the parishes around met every fortnight to confer together on religious matters, as also on their studies, and, in short, on whatever concerned the welfare of the Church and the efficiency of her pastors. Every minister, in his turn, preached before his brethren; and if his sermon was thought to contain anything contrary to sound doctrine, the rest admonished him of his error. In order still more to guard the purity and keep awake the vigilance of the ministry, a commission, consisting of two elders and two ministers of the chief town, was to make a yearly circuit through the dependent Provinces, and report the state of matters to the magistrate on their return, "to the end," say the canons, "that if they find anything amiss it may be seasonably redressed." Not fewer than three sermons a week were to be preached "in all public places," and on the afternoon of Sunday the Heidelberg Catechism was to be expounded in all the churches. Baptism was to be administered by a minister only; it was not to be denied to any infant; it was "pious and praiseworthy" for the parent himself to bring the child to be baptised, and the celebration was to take place in the church in presence of the congregation, unless the child were sick, when the ordinance might be dispensed at home "in presence of some godly persons." The Lord's Supper was to be celebrated four times yearly, care being taken that all who approached the table were well instructed in the faith. The canons, moreover, prescribe the duty of ministers touching the visitation of the sick, the care of prisoners, and attendance at funerals. A body of theological professors was provided for the University of Leyden; and the magistrates planted a school in every town under their jurisdiction, selecting as teachers only those who professed the Reformed faith, "whose business it shall be to instil into them principles of true religion as well as learning."

The elders were chosen, not by the congregation, but by the magistrates of the city. They were to be selected from their own body, "good men, and not inexperienced in the matters of religion;" they were to sit with the pastors, constituting a court of morals, and to report to the Government such decisions and transactions as it might concern the Government to know. To the deacons was assigned the care of the poor. The State arrangements in Holland for this class of the community made the office of deacon well-nigh superfluous; nevertheless, it was instituted as being an integral part of the Church machinery; and so the canons bid the magistrates take care "that fit and godly stewards be appointed, who understand how to assist the poor according to their necessities, by which means the trade of begging may be prevented, and the poor contained within the bounds of their duty; this will be easily brought about as soon as an end shall be put to our miseries by peace and public tranquillity."[2944]

This first framework of the Netherland Reformed Church left the magistrate the highest functionary in it. The final decision of all matters lay with him. In matters of administration and of discipline, in questions of morals and doctrine, he was the court of last appeal. This presents us with a notable difference between the Protestant Church of the Netherlands and the Churches of Geneva and France. Calvin aimed, as we have seen, at a complete separation of the civil and the spiritual domain; he sought to exclude entirely the power of the magistrate in things purely spiritual, and he effected this in the important point of admission to the Communion-table; but in Geneva, the Church being the State, the two necessarily touched each other at a great many points, and the Reformer failed to make good the perfect autonomy which he aimed at conferring on the Church. In France, however, as we have also seen, he realized his ideal fully. He established in that country an ascending gradation of Church courts, or spiritual tribunals, according to which the final legislation and administration of all spiritual affairs lay within the Church herself. We behold the French Protestant Church taking her place by the side of the French Government, and exhibiting a scheme of spiritual administration and rule as distinct and complete as that of the civil government of the country. But in the Netherlands we fail to see a marked distinction between the spiritual and the civil power: the ecclesiastical courts merge into the magistrate's tribunal, and the head of the State is to the Church in room of National Synod and Assembly. One reason of the difference is to be found in the fact that whereas in France the magistrate was hostile, in the Low Countries he was friendly, and was oftener found in the van than in the rear of the Reform. Moreover, the magistrates of Holland could plead a very venerable and a very unbroken precedent for their interference in the affairs of the Church: it had been, they affirmed, the practice of princes from the days of Justinian downwards.[2945]

This was one source of the troubles which afterwards afflicted the States, and which we must not pass wholly without notice. Peter Cornelison and Gaspar Koolhaes, ministers in Leyden, were (1579) the first to begin the war which raged so long and so fiercely in Holland on the question of the authority of the Civil Government in Ecclesiastical matters. Peter Cornelison maintained that elders and deacons ought to be nominated by the Consistory and proposed to the congregation without the intervention of the magistrate. Gaspar Koolhaes, on the contrary, maintained that elders and deacons, on being nominated by the Consistory, should be approved by the magistrates, and afterwards presented to the congregation. The dispute came before the magistrates, and decision was given in favour of the latter method, that elders and deacons elect should receive the approval of the magistrate before being presented to the people. The States of Holland, with the view of preserving the public peace and putting an end to these quarrels, appointed certain divines to deduce from Scripture, and embody in a concise treatise, the *Relations of the Civil and Ecclesiastical Powers*—in other words, to give an answer to the question, what the magistrate may do and what he may not do in the Church. It is almost unnecessary to say that their dissertation on this difficult and delicate question did not meet the views of all parties, and that the tempest was not allayed. The worthy divines took somewhat decided views on the magistrate's functions. His duty, they said, was "to hinder those who corrupt the Word of God from disturbing the external peace of the Church, to fine and imprison them, and inflict corporal punishments upon them." As an illustration Peter Cornelison, the champion of the Consistorial rights, was dismissed from his charge in Leyden, an apology accompanying the act, in which the magistrates set forth that they "did not design to tyrannise over the Church, but to rid her of violent and seditious men," adding "that the Church ought to be governed by Christ alone, and not by ministers and Consistories." This looked like raising a false issue, seeing both parties admitted that the government of the Church is in Christ alone, and only disputed as to whether that government ought to be administered through magistrates, or through ministers and Consistories.[2946]

The National Synod which met at Dort in 1578, and which issued the famous declaration in favour of toleration, noticed in a previous chapter, agreed that a National Synod should be convened once every three years. In pursuance of that enactment, the Churches of Antwerp and Delft, to whom the power had been given of convoking the assembly, issued circular letters calling the Synod, which accordingly assembled in 1581 at Middelburg in Zealand. The constitution of the Netherland Reformed Church—so far framed by the "Ecclesiastical Laws"—this Synod completed on the French model. The Consistories, or Kirk-sessions, it placed under classes or Presbyteries; and the Presbyteries it placed under particular Synods. The other regulations tended in the direction of curtailing the power of the magistrate in Church matters. The Synod entirely shut him out in the choice of elders and deacons, and it permitted him to interfere in the election of ministers only so far as to approve the choice of the people. The Synod likewise decreed that all ministers, elders, deacons, and professors of divinity should subscribe the Confession of Faith of the Netherland Church. In the case of Koolhaes, who had maintained against Cornelison the right of the magistrates to intervene in the election of elders and deacons, the Synod found his doctrine erroneous, and ordained him to make a public acknowledgment. Nevertheless, he refused to submit to this judgment, and though excommunicated by the Synod of Haarlem next year, he was sustained in the spiritual functions and temporal emoluments of his office by the magistrates of Leyden. The matter was abundantly prolific of strifes and divisions, which had all but ruined the Church at

Leyden, until it ended in the recalcitrant resigning his ministry and adopting the trade of a distiller.[2947]

CHAPTER XXVIII
DISORGANISATION OF THE PROVINCES

IN proportion as the Reformed Church of the Netherlands rises in power and consolidates her order, the Provinces around her fall into disorganisation and weakness. It is a process of selection and rejection that is seen going on in the Low Countries. All that is valuable in the Netherlands is drawn out of the heap, and gathered round the great principles of Protestantism, and set apart for liberty and glory; all that is worthless is thrown away, and left to be burned in the fire of despotism. Of the Seventeen Provinces seven are taken to be fashioned into a "vessel of honour," ten are left to become a "vessel of dishonour." The first become the "head of gold," the second are the "legs and feet of clay."

Notwithstanding the efforts of the Synod of Middelburg, the peace at large was not restored; there was still war between the pastors and some of the municipalities. The next move in the battle came from the magistrates of Leyden. Their pride had been hurt by what the Synod of Middelburg had done, and they presented a complaint against it to the States of Holland. In a Synod vested with the power of enacting canons, the magistrates of Leyden saw, or professed to see, another Papacy rising up. The fear was not unwarranted, seeing that for a thousand years the Church had tyrannised over the State. "If a new National Synod is to meet every three years," say the magistrates in their memorial to the States, "the number of ecclesiastical decrees will be so great that we shall have much ado to find the beginning and the end of that link." It was a second canon law which they dreaded. "If we receive the decrees of Synods we shall become their vassals," they reasoned. "We demand," said they in conclusion, "that the civil authority may still reside in the magistrates, whole and undivided; we desire that the clergy may have no occasion to usurp a new jurisdiction, to raise themselves above the Government, and rule over the subjects."

The ministers and elders of the Churches of Holland met the demand for an undivided civil authority on the part of the magistrates by a demand for an undivided spiritual authority on the part of the Church. They asked that "the government of the Church, which is of a spiritual nature, should still reside, whole and undivided, in the pastors and overseers of the Churches, and that politicians, and particularly those who plainly showed that they were not of the Reformed religion, should have no occasion to exercise an unreasonable power over the Church, which they could no more endure than the yoke of Popery." And they add, "that having escaped from the Popish tyranny, it behoved them to see that the people did not fall into unlimited licentiousness, or libertinage, tending to nothing but disorder and confusion. The blunted rod should not be thrown away lest peradventure a sharper should grow up in its room."[2948] It is true that both the Popish and the Protestant Churches claim a spiritual jurisdiction, but there is this essential difference between the two powers claimed—the former is lawless, the latter is regulated by law. The Popish jurisdiction cannot be resisted by conscience, because claiming to be infallible, it is above conscience. The Protestant jurisdiction, on the contrary, leaves conscience free to resist it, should it exceed its just powers, because it teaches that God alone is Lord of the conscience.

But to come to the root of the unhappy strife that now tore up the Netherlands, and laid the better half of the Provinces once more at the feet of Rome—there were two nations and two faiths struggling in that one country. The Jesuits had now had time to bring their system into full operation, and they succeeded so far in thwarting the measures which were concerted by the Prince of Orange with the view of uniting the Provinces, on the basis of a toleration of the two faiths, in a common struggle for the one liberty. Led by the disciples of Loyola, the Romanists in the Netherlands would neither be content with equality for themselves, nor would they grant toleration to the Protestants wherever they had the power of refusing it; hence the failure of the Pacification of Ghent, and the Peace of Religion. The Fathers kept the populations in continual agitation and alarm, they stirred up seditions and tumults, they coerced the magistrates, and they provoked the Protestants in many places into acts of imprudence and violence. On the framing of the Pacification of Ghent, the Roman Catholic States issued an order requiring all magistrates and priests to swear to observe it. The secular priests of Antwerp took the oath, but the Jesuits refused it, "because they had sworn to be faithful to the Pope, who favoured Don John of Austria."[2949] Of the Franciscan monks in the city twenty swore the oath, and nineteen refused to do so, and were thereupon conducted peaceably out of the town along with the Jesuits. The Franciscans of Utrecht fled, as did those of other towns, to avoid the oath. In some places the Peace of Religion was not accepted, and in others where it had been formally accepted, it was not only not kept, it was flagrantly violated by the Romanists. The basis of that treaty was the toleration of both worships all over the Netherlands. It gave to the Protestants in the Roman Catholic Provinces—in all places where they numbered a hundred—the right to a chapel in which to celebrate their worship; and where their numbers did not enable them to claim this privilege, they were nevertheless to be permitted the unmolested exercise of their worship in private. But in many places the rights accorded by the treaty were denied them: they could have no chapel, and even the private exercise of their worship exposed them to molestations of various kinds. The Protestants, incensed by this anti-national spirit and bad faith, and emboldened moreover by their own growing numbers, seized by force in many cities the rights which they could not obtain by peaceable means. Disorders and seditions were the consequence. Ghent, the city which had given its name to the Pacification, led the van in those disgraceful tumults; and it was remarked that nowhere was the Pacification worse kept than in the city where it had been framed. The Reformed in Ghent, excited by the harangues delivered to them from the pulpit by Peter Tathenus, an ex-monk, and now a Protestant high-flier, who condemned the toleration granted to the Romanists as impious, and styled the prince who had framed the treaty an atheist, rose upon the Popish clergy and chased them away, voting them at the same time a yearly pension. They pillaged the abbeys, pulled down the convents, broke the images, melted the bells and cast them into cannon, and having fortified the town, and made themselves masters of it, they took several villages in the neighbourhood and enacted there the same excesses.[2950] These deplorable disorders were not confined to Ghent; they extended to Antwerp, to Utrecht, to Mechlin, and to other towns—the Protestants taking the initiative in some places, and the Romanists in others; but all these violences grew out of the rejection of the Peace of Religion, or out of the flagrant violation of its articles.[2951] The commanding influence of the Prince of Orange succeeded in pacifying the citizens in Ghent and other towns, but the tumults stilled for a moment broke out afresh, and raged with greater violence. The country was torn as by a civil war.

This state of matters led to the adoption of other measures, which still more complicated and embarrassed the movement. It was becoming evident to William that his basis of operations must be narrowed if he would make it stable; that the Pacification of Ghent, and the Peace of Religion, in themselves wise and just, embraced peoples that were diverse, and elements that were irreconcilable, and in consequence were failing of their ends. A few Romanists were staunch patriots, but the great body were showing themselves incapable of sympathising with, or heartily co-operating in, the great struggle for the liberation of their native land. Their consciences, in the guidance of the Jesuits, stifled their patriotism. They were awkwardly placed between two alternatives: if Philip should conquer in the war they would lose their country, if victory should declare for the Prince of Orange they would lose their faith. From this dilemma they could be delivered only by becoming Protestants, and Protestants they were determined not to become; they sought escape by the other door—namely, that of persuading or compelling the Protestants to become Romanists. Their desire to solve the difficulty by this issue introduced still another element of disorganisation and danger. There came a sudden outburst of propagandist zeal on the part of the priests, and of miraculous virtue on the part of statues and relics. Images began to exude blood, and from the bones of the dead a healing power went forth to cure the diseases of the living. These prodigies greatly edified the piety of the Roman Catholics, but they inflamed their passions against their Protestant fellow subjects, and they rendered them decidedly hostile to the cause of their country's emancipation. The prince had always stood up for the full toleration of their worship, but he now began to perceive that what the Flemish Romanists called worship was what other men called political agitation; and though still holding by the truth of his great maxim, and as ready to tolerate all religions as ever, he did not hold himself bound to tolerate charlatanry, especially when practised for the overthrow of Netherland liberty. He had proclaimed toleration for the Roman worship, but he had not bound himself to tolerate everything which the Romanist might substitute for worship, or which it might please him to call worship. The prince came at length to the conclusion that he had no alternative but to withdraw by edict the toleration which he had proclaimed by edict; nor in doing so did he feel that he was trenching on the rights of conscience, for he recognised on the part of no man, or body of men, a right to plead conscience for feats of jugglery and tricks of legerdemain. Accordingly, on the 26th of December, 1581, an edict was published by the prince and the States of Holland, forbidding the public and private exercise of the Roman religion, but leaving opinion free, by forbidding inquisition into any man's conscience.[2952] This was the first "placard" of the sort published in Holland since the States had taken up arms for their liberties; and the best proof of its necessity is the fact that some cities in Brabant, where the bulk of the inhabitants were Romanists—Antwerp and Brussels in particular—were compelled to have recourse to the same measure, or submit to the humiliation of seeing their Government bearded, and their public peace hopelessly embroiled. Antwerp chose six "discreet ecclesiastics" to baptise, marry, and visit the sick of their own communion, granting them besides the use of two little chapels; but even these functions they were not permitted to undertake till first they had sworn fidelity to the Government. The rest of the priests were required to leave the town within twenty-four hours under a penalty of 200 crowns.[2953] In Brussels the suppression of the Popish worship, which was occasioned by a tumult raised by a seditious curate, brought with it an exposure of the arts which had rendered the edict of suppression necessary. "The magistrates," says the edict, "were convinced that the three bloody Hosts, which were shown to the people by the name of the Sacrament of Miracles, were only a stained cloth; that the clergy had exposed to the people some bones of animals as relics of saints, and deceived the simple many other ways to satisfy their avarice; that they had made them worship some pieces of alder-tree as if they had been a part of our Saviour's cross; that in some statues several holes had been discovered, into which the priests poured oil to make them sweat; lastly, that in other statues some springs had been found by which they moved several parts of their bodies."[2954]

These edicts, unlike the terrible placards of Philip, erected no gibbets, and dug no graves for living men and women; they were in all cases temporary, "till public tranquillity should be restored;" they did not proscribe opinion, nor did they deny to the Romanist the Sacraments of his Church; they suppressed the public assembly only, and they suppressed it because a hundred proofs had demonstrated that it was held not for worship but sedition, and that its fruits were not piety but tumults and disturbances of the public peace. Most unwilling was the Prince of Orange to go even this length; it placed him, he saw, in apparent, not real, opposition to his formerly declared views. Nor did he take this step till the eleventh hour, and after being perfectly persuaded that without some such measure he could not preserve order and save liberty.

CHAPTER XXIX
THE SYNOD OF DORT

WILLIAM, Prince of Orange, had just fallen, and the murderous blow that deprived of life the great founder of the Dutch Republic was as much the act of Philip of Spain as if his own hand had fired the bullet that passed through the prince's body, and laid him a corpse in the hall of his own dwelling-house. Grief, consternation, despair overspread the Provinces. The very children cried in the streets. Father William had fallen, and the Netherlands had fallen with him; so did men believe, and for a time it verily seemed as if the calamity had all the frightful magnitude in which it presented itself to the nation in the first moments of its surprise and terror. The genius, wisdom, courage, and patriotism of which the assassin's shot had deprived the Low Countries could not possibly be replaced. William could have no successor of the same lofty stature as himself. While he lived all felt that they had a bulwark between them and Spanish tyranny; but now that he was dead, the shadow of Rome and Spain seemed again to approach them, and all trembled, from the wealthy merchant on the exchanges of Antwerp and Brussels, to the rude fisherman on the solitary coast of Zealand. The gloom was universal and tragical. The diplomacy of Parma and the ducats of Spain were instantly set to work to corrupt and seduce the Provinces. The faint-hearted, the lukewarm, and the secretly hostile were easily drawn away, and induced to abandon the great struggle for Netherland liberty and the Protestant faith. Ghent, the key-stone of that arch of which one side was Roman Catholic and the other Protestant, reconciled itself to Philip. Bruges, Brussels, Antwerp, Mechlin, and other towns of Brabant and Flanders, won by the diplomacy or vanquished by the arms of Parma, returned under the yoke. It seemed as if the free State which the labours and sacrifices of William the Silent had called into existence was about to disappear from the scene, and accompany its founder to the tomb.

But the work of William was not so to vanish; its root was deeper. When the first moments of panic were over, the spirit of the fallen hero asserted itself in Holland. The Estates of that Province passed a resolution, the very day of his murder, "to maintain the good cause, by God's help, to the uttermost, without sparing gold or blood," and they communicated their resolve to all commanders by land and sea. A State Council, or provisional executive board, was established for the Seven Provinces of the Union. At the head of it was placed Prince Maurice, William's second son, a lad of seventeen, who already manifested no ordinary decision and energy of character, and who in obedience to the summons of the States now quitted the University of Leyden, where he had been pursuing his studies, to be invested with many of his father's commands and honours. The blandishments of the Duke of Parma the States strenuously repelled, decreeing that no overture of reconciliation should be received from "the tyrant;" and the city of Dort enacted that whoever should bring any letter from the enemy to any private person "should forthwith be hanged."

It was Protestantism that had fired Holland and her six sister Provinces with this great resolve; and it was Protestantism that was to build up their State in the face of the powerful enemies that surrounded it, and in spite of the reverses and disasters to which it still continued to be liable. But the Hollanders were slow to understand this, and to see wherein their great strength lay. They feared to trust their future to so intangible and invisible a protector. They looked abroad in the hope of finding some foreign prince who might be willing to accept their crown, and to employ his power in their defence. They hesitated some time between Henry III. of France and Elizabeth of England, and at last their choice fell on the former. Henry was nearer them, he could the more easily send them assistance; besides, they hoped that on his death his crown would devolve on the King of Navarre, the future Henry IV., in whose hands they believed their religion and liberty would be safe. Willingly would Henry III. have enhanced the splendour of his crown by adding thereto the Seven United Provinces, but he feared the wrath of the League, the intrigues of Philip, and the ban of the Pope.

The infant States next repaired to Elizabeth with an offer of their sovereignty. This offer the Protestant queen felt she could neither accept nor decline. To accept was to quarrel with Philip; and the state of Ireland at that moment, and the numbers and power of the Roman Catholics in England, made a war with Spain dangerous to the stability of her own throne; and yet should she decline, what other resource had the Provinces but to throw themselves into the arms of Philip? and, reconciled to the Netherlands, Spain would be stronger than ever, and a stage nearer in its road to England. The prudent queen was in a strait between the two. But though she could not be the sovereign, might she not be the ally of the Hollanders? This she resolved to become. She concluded a treaty with them, "that the queen should furnish the States with 5,000 foot and 1,000 horse, to be commanded by a Protestant general of her appointment, and to be paid by her during the continuance of the war; the towns of Brill and Flushing being meanwhile put into her possession as security for the reimbursement to her of the war expenses." It was further stipulated "that should it be found expedient to employ a fleet in the common cause, the States should furnish the same number of ships as the queen, to be commanded by an English admiral."

The force agreed upon was immediately despatched to Holland under the command of Robert Dudley, Earl of Leicester. Leicester possessed but few qualities fitting him for the weighty business now put into his hands. He was vain, frivolous, greedy, and ambitious, but he was an immense favourite with the queen. His showy accomplishments blinded at the first the Hollanders, who entertained him at a series of magnificent banquets (December, 1585), loaded him with honours and posts, and treated him more as one who had already achieved their deliverance, than one who was only beginning that difficult and doubtful task. The Provinces soon began to see that their independence was not to come from the hand of Leicester. He proved no match for the genius and address of the Duke of Parma, who was daily winning victories for Spain, while Leicester could accomplish nothing. His prudence failing him, he looked askance on the grave statesmen and honest patriots of Holland and Zealand, while he lavished his smiles on the artful and the designing who submitted to his caprice and flattered his vanity. His ignorance imposed restrictions on their commerce which greatly fettered it, and would ultimately have ruined it, and he gave still deeper offence by expressing contempt for those ancient charters to which the Dutch were unalterably attached. Misfortune attended all that he undertook in the field. He began to intrigue to make himself master of the country. His designs came to light, the contempt of the Provinces deepened into disgust, and just a year after his first arrival in Holland, Leicester returned to England, and at the desire of Elizabeth resigned his government.

The distractions which the incapacity and treachery of the earl had occasioned among the Dutch themselves, offered a most inviting opportunity to Parma to invade the Provinces, and doubtless he would have availed himself of it but for a dreadful famine that swept over the Southern Netherlands. The famine was followed by pestilence. The number of the deaths, added to the many banishments which had previously taken place, nearly emptied some of the great towns of Brabant and Flanders. In the country the peasants, owing to the ravages of war, had neither horses to plough their fields nor seed wherewith to sow them, and the harvest was a complete failure. In the terrible desolation of the country the beasts of prey so multiplied, that within two miles of the once populous and wealthy city of Ghent, not fewer than a hundred persons were devoured by wolves.

Meanwhile Holland and Zealand presented a picture which was in striking contrast to the desolation and ruin that overspread the Southern and richer Provinces. Although torn by factions, the result of the intrigues of Leicester, and burdened with the expense of a war which they were compelled to wage with Parma, their inhabitants continued daily to multiply, and their wealth, comforts, and power to grow. Crowds of Protestant refugees flocked into the Northern Provinces, which now became the seat of that industry and manufacturing skill which for ages had enriched and embellished the Netherlands. Having the command of the sea, the Dutch transported their products to foreign markets, and so laid the foundation of that world-wide commerce which was a source of greater riches to Holland than were the gold and silver mines of Mexico and Peru to Spain.[2955]

We have seen the throes and agonies amid which the Dutch Republic came to the birth, and before depicting the prosperity and power in which the State culminated, it is necessary to glance at the condition of the Dutch Church. From and after 1603, dissensions and divisions broke out in it, which tended to weaken somewhat the mighty influences springing out of a free conscience and a pure faith, which were lifting the United Provinces to prosperity and renown. Up till the year we have named, the Church of the Netherlands was strictly Calvinistic, but now a party in it began to diverge from what had been the one common theology of the Reformation. It is an error to suppose that Calvin held and propagated a doctrine peculiar to himself or different from that of his fellow-Reformers. His theology contained nothing new, being essentially that of the great Fathers of the early Christian Church of the West, and agreeing very closely with that of his illustrious fellow labourers, Luther and Zwingle. Our readers will remember the battles which Luther waged with the champions of Rome in defence of the Pauline teaching under the head of the corruption of man's whole nature, the moral inability of his will, and the absolute sovereignty of God. It was on the same great lines that Calvin's views developed themselves. On the doctrine of Divine sovereignty, for instance, we find both Luther and Zwingle expressing themselves in terms fully stronger than Calvin ever employed. Calvin looked at both sides of the tremendous subject. He maintained the free agency of man not less strenuously than he did God's eternal fore-ordination. He felt that both were great facts, but he doubted whether it lay within the power of created intelligence to reconcile the two, and he confessed that he was not able to do so. Many, however, have made this attempt. There have been men who have denied the doctrine of God's eternal fore-ordination, thinking thereby to establish that of man's free agency; and there have been men who have denied the doctrine of man's free agency, meaning thereby to strengthen that of the eternal fore-ordination of all things by God; but these reconcilements are not solutions to the tremendous question—they are only monuments of man's inability to grapple with it, and of the folly of expending strength and wasting time in such a discussion. Heedless of the warnings of past ages, there arose at this time in the Reformed Church of Holland a class of divines who renewed these discussions, and attempted to solve the awful problem by attacking the common theology of Luther, and Zwingle, and Calvin[2956] on the doctrines of grace and of the eternal decrees.

The controversy had its beginning thus: the famous Francis Junius, Professor of Divinity at Leyden, died of the plague in 1602; and James Arminius, who had studied theology at Geneva under Beza, and was pastor at Amsterdam, was appointed to succeed him.[2957] Arminius was opposed by many ministers of the Dutch Church, on the ground that, although he was accounted learned, eloquent, and pious, he was suspected of holding views inconsistent with the Belgic Confession and the Heidelberg Catechism, which since 1570 had possessed authority in the Church. Promulgating his views cautiously and covertly from his chair, a controversy ensued between him and his learned colleague, Gomarus. Arminius rested God's predestination of men to eternal life on his foresight of their piety and virtue; Gomarus, on the other hand, taught that these were not the causes, but the fruits of God's election of them to life eternal. Arminius accused Gomarus of instilling the belief of a fatal necessity, and Gomarus reproached Arminius with making man the author of his own salvation. The controversy between the two lasted till the death of Arminius, which took place in 1609. He died in the full hope of everlasting life. He is said to have chosen for his motto, Bona conscientia Paradisus.[2958]

After his death, his disciple Simon Episcopius became the head of the party, and, as usually happens in such cases, gave fuller development to the views of his master than Arminius himself had done. From the university, the controversy passed to the pulpit, and the Church was divided. In 1610 the followers of Arminius presented a Remonstrance to the States of Holland, complaining of being falsely accused of seeking to alter the faith, but at the same time craving revision of the standard books of the Dutch Church—the Belgic Confession and the Heidelberg Catechism—and demanding toleration for their views, of which they gave a summary or exhibition in five points, as follow—I. That the decree of election is grounded on foreseen good works. II. That Christ died for all men, and procured remission of sins for all. III. That man cannot acquire saving faith of himself, or by the strength of his free-will, but needs for that purpose the grace of God. IV. That, seeing man cannot believe at first, nor continue to believe, without the aid of this co-operating grace, his good works are to be ascribed to the grace of God in Jesus Christ. V. That the faithful have a sufficient strength, through the Divine grace, to resist all temptation, and finally to overcome it. As to the question whether those who have once believed to the saving of the soul can again fall away from faith, and lose the grace of God, the authors of the Remonstrance were not prepared to give any answer. It was a point, they said, that needed further examination; but the logical train of the previous propositions clearly pointed to the goal at which their views touching the "perseverance of the saints" must necessarily arrive; and accordingly, at a subsequent stage of the controversy, they declared, "That those who have a true faith may, nevertheless, fall by their own fault, and lose faith wholly and for ever."[2959]

It is the first receding wave within the Protestant Church which we are now contemplating, and it is both instructive and curious to mark that the ebb from the Reformation began at what had been the starting-point of the Reform movement. We have remarked, at an early stage of our history, that the question touching the Will of man is the deepest in theology. Has the Fall left to man the power of willing and doing what is spiritually good? or has it deprived him of that power, and inflicted upon his will a moral inability? If we answer the first question affirmatively, and maintain that man still retains the power of willing and doing what is spiritually good, we advance a proposition from which, it might be argued, a whole system of Roman theology can be worked out. And if we answer the second question affirmatively, we lay a foundation from which it might be contended on the other hand, a whole system of Protestant theology can be educed. Pursuing the one line of reasoning, if man still has the power of willing and doing actions spiritually good, he needs only cooperating grace in the matter of his salvation; he needs only to be assisted in the more difficult parts of that work which he himself has begun, and which, mainly in the exercise of his own powers, he himself carries on to the end. Hence the doctrine of good works, with all the dogmas, rites, penances, and merits that Rome has built upon it. But, following the other line of reasoning, if man, by his fall, lost the power of doing what is spiritually good, then he must be entirely dependent upon Divine grace for his recovery—he must owe all to God, from whom must come the beginning, the continuance, and the end of his salvation; and hence the doctrines of a sovereign election, an effectual calling, a free justification, and a perseverance of life eternal. The point, to an ordinary eye, seems an obscure one—it looks a purely speculative point, and one from which no practical issues of moment can flow; nevertheless, it lies at the foundation of all theology, and as such it was the first great battle-ground at the period of the Reformation. It was the question so keenly contested, as we have already narrated, between Dr. Eck on the one side, and Carlstadt and Luther on the other, at Leipsic.[2960] This question is, in fact, the dividing line between the two theologies.

Of the five points stated above, the third, fourth, and fifth may be viewed as one; they teach the same doctrine—namely, that man fallen still possesses such an amount of spiritual strength as that he may do no inconsiderable part of the work of his salvation, and needs only cooperating grace; and had the authors of the Remonstrance been at Leipsic, they must have ranged themselves on the side of Eck, and done battle for the Roman theology. It was this which gave the affair its grave aspect in the eyes of the majority of the pastors of the Church of Holland. They saw in the doctrine of the "Five Points" the ground surrendered which had been won at the beginning of the Reformation; and they saw seed anew deposited from which had sprung the great tree of Romanism. This was not concealed on either side. The Remonstrants—so called from the Remonstrance given in by them to the States—put forward their views avowedly as intermediate between the Protestant and Roman systems, in the hope that they might conciliate not a few members of the latter Church, and lead to peace. The orthodox party could not see that these benefits would flow from the course their opponents were pursuing; on the contrary, they believed that they could not stop where they were—that their views touching the fall and the power of free-will must and would find their logical development in a greater divergence from the theology of the Protestant Churches, and that by removing the great boundary-line between the two theologies, they were opening the way for a return to the Church of Rome; and hence the exclamation of Gomarus one day, after listening to a statement of his views by Arminius, in the University of Leyden. Rising up and leaving the hall, he uttered these words: "Henceforward we shall no longer be able to oppose Popery."[2961]

Peace was the final goal which the Remonstrants sought to reach; but the first-fruits of their labours were schisms and dissensions. The magistrates, sensible of the injury they were doing the State, strove to put an end to these ecclesiastical wars, and with this view they summoned certain pastors of both sides before them, and made them discuss the points at issue in their presence; but these conferences had no effect in restoring harmony. A disputation of this sort took place at the Hague in 1611, but like all that had gone before it, it failed to reconcile the two parties and establish concord. The orthodox pastors now began to demand the assembling of a National Synod, as a more legitimate and competent tribunal for the examination and decision of such matters, and a more likely way of putting an end to the dissensions that prevailed; but the Remonstrant clergy opposed this proposal. They had influence enough with the civil authorities to prevent the calling of a Synod for several years; but the war waxing louder and fiercer every day, the States-General at last convoked a National Synod to meet in November, 1618, at Dort.

Than the Synod of Dort there is perhaps no more remarkable Assembly in the annals of the Protestant Church. It is alike famous whether we regard the numbers, or the learning, or the eloquence of its members. It met at a great crisis, and it was called to review, re-examine, and authenticate over again, in the second generation since the rise of the Reformation, that body of truth and system of doctrine which that great movement had published to the world. The States-General had agreed that a Synod should consist of twenty-six divines of the United Provinces, twenty-eight foreign divines, five theological professors, and sixteen laymen. The sum of 100,000 florins was set apart to defray its estimated expenses. Its sessions lasted six months.

Learned delegates were present in this Assembly for almost all the Reformed Churches of Europe. The Churches of England, Scotland, Switzerland, Geneva, Bremen, Hesse, and the Palatinate were represented in it. The French Church had no delegate in the Synod. That Church had deputed Peter du Moulin and Andrew Rivet, two of the most distinguished theologians of the age, to represent it, but the king forbade their attendance. From England came Dr. George Carleton, Bishop of Llandaff; Joseph Hall, Dean of Worcester; John Davenant, Professor of Theology and Master of Queen's College, Cambridge; and Samuel Ward, Archdeacon of Taunton, who had been appointed to proceed to Holland and take part in the proceedings at Dort, not indeed by the Church of England, but by the King and the Archbishop of Canterbury. Walter Balcanqual represented Scotland in the Synod.[2962]

The Synod was opened on the 16th of November, 1618, with a sermon by Balthazar Lydius, minister of Dort. Thereafter, the members repaired to the hall appointed for their meeting. Lydius offered a prayer in Latin. The commissioners of the States sat on the right of the president, and the English divines on his left. An empty seat was kept for the French deputies. The rest of the delegates took their places according to the rank of the country from which they came. John Bogerman, minister of Leeuwarden, was chosen president; Daniel Heinsius was appointed secretary. Heinsius was an accomplished Latin scholar, and it had been agreed that that language should be used in all the transactions of the Assembly, for the sake of the foreign delegates. There came thirty-six ministers and twenty elders, instead of the twenty-six pastors and sixteen laymen which the States-General had appointed, besides deputies from other Provinces, thus swelling the roll of the Synod to upwards of a hundred.

The Synod summoned thirteen of the leading Remonstrants, including Episcopius, to appear within a fortnight. Meanwhile the Assembly occupied itself with arrangements for a new translation of the Bible into Dutch, and the framing of rules about other matters, as the catechising of the young and the training of students for the ministry. On the 5th of December, the thirteen Remonstrants who had been summoned came to Dort, and next day presented themselves before the Assembly. They were saluted by the moderator as "Reverend, famous, and excellent brethren in Jesus Christ," and accommodated with seats at a long table in the middle of the hall. Episcopius, their spokesman, saluting the Assembly, craved more time, that himself and his brethren might prepare themselves for a conference with the Synod on the disputed points. They were told that they had been summoned not to confer with the Synod, but to submit their opinions for the Synod's decision, and were bidden attend next day. On that day Episcopius made a speech of an hour and a half's length, in which he discovered all the art and power of an orator. Thereafter an oath was administered to the members of Synod, in which they swore, in all the discussions and determinations of the Synod, to "use no human writing, but only the Word of God, which is an infallible rule of faith," and "only aim at the glory of God, the peace of the Church, and especially the preservation of the purity of doctrine."

The Remonstrants did battle on a great many preliminary points: the jurisdiction of the court, the manner in which they were to lay their opinions before it, and the extent to which they were to be permitted to go in vindicating and defending their five points. In these debates much time was wasted, and the patience and good temper of the Assembly were severely tried. When it was found that the Remonstrants persisted in declining the authority of the Synod, and would meet it only to discuss and confer with it, but not to be judged by it, the States-General was informed of the deadlock into which the affair had come. The civil authority issued an order requiring the Remonstrants to submit to the Synod. To this order of the State the Remonstrants gave no more obedience than they had done to the authority of the Church. They were willing to argue and defend their opinions, but not to submit them for judgment. After two months spent in fruitless attempts to bring the Remonstrants to obedience, the Assembly resolved to extract their views from their writings and speeches, and give judgment upon them. The examination into their opinions, and the deliberations upon them, engaged the Assembly till the end of April, by which time they had completed a body of canons, which were read in the Cathedral of Dort with great solemnity, were a summing-up of the doctrine of the Reformation as it had been held by the first Reformers, and accepted in the Protestant Churches without division or dissent, the article of the Eucharist excepted, until Arminius arose. The decision of the Synod condemned the opinions of the Remonstrants as innovations, and sentenced them to deprivation of all ecclesiastical and academical functions.[2963] The States-General followed up the spiritual part of the sentence by banishing them from their country. It is clear that the Government of the United Provinces had yet a good deal to learn on the head of toleration; but it is fair to say that while they punished the disciples of Arminius with exile, they would permit no inquisition to be made into their consciences, and no injury to be done to their persons or property. A few years thereafter (1626) the decree of banishment was recalled. The Remonstrants returned to their country, and were permitted freely to exercise their worship. They established a theological seminary at Amsterdam, which was adorned by some men of great talents and erudition, and became a renowned fountain of Arminian theology.

The Synod of Dort was the first great attempt to arrest the begun decline in the theology of the Reformation, and to restore it to its pristine purity and splendour. It did this, but not with a perfect success. The theology of Protestantism, as seen in the canons of Dort, and as seen in the writings of the first Reformers, does not appear quite the same theology: it is the same in dogma, but it lacks, as seen in the canons of Dort, the warm hues, the freshness, the freedom and breadth, and the stirring spiritual vitalities it possessed as it flowed from the pens, or was thundered from the pulpits, of the Reformers. The second generation of Protestant divines was much inferior, both in intellectual endowments and in spiritual gifts, to the first. In the early days it was the sun of genius that irradiated the heavens of the Church: now it was the moon of culture that was seen in her waning skies. And in proportion to the more restricted faculties of the men, so the theology was narrow, stinted, and cold. It was formal and critical. Turning away somewhat from the grander, objective, soul-inspiring truths of Christianity, it dealt much with the abstruser questions, it searched into deep and hidden things; it was quicker to discern the apparent antagonisms than the real harmonies between truth and truth; it was prone to look only at one question, or at one side of a question, forgetful of its balancings and modifications, and so was in danger of distorting or even caricaturing truth. The empirical treatment which the doctrine of predestination received—perhaps we ought to say on both sides—is an example of this. Instead of the awe and reverence with which a question involving the character and government of God, and the eternal destinies of men, ought ever to inspire those who undertake to deal with a subject so awful, and the solution of which so far transcends the human faculties, it was approached in a proud, self-sufficient, and flippant spirit, that was at once unchristian and unphilosophical. Election and reprobation were singled out, separated from the great and surpassingly solemn subject of which they are only parts, looked at entirely dissociated from their relations to other necessary truths, subjected to an iron logic, and compelled to yield consequences which were impious and revolting. The very interest taken in these questions marked an age more erudite than religious, and an intellect which had become too subtle to be altogether sound; and the prominence given them, both in the discussions of the schools and the ministrations of the pulpit, reacted on the nations, and was productive of animosities and dissensions.

Nevertheless, these evils were sensibly abated after the meeting of the Synod of Dort. The fountains of truth were again purified, and peace restored to the churches and the schools. The nation again reunited, resumed its onward march in the path of progress. For half a century the university and the pulpit continued to be mighty powers in Holland—the professors and pastors took their place in the first rank of theologians. Abroad the canons of the Synod of Dort met with a very general acquiescence on the part of the Protestant Churches, and continued to regulate the teaching and mould the theology of Christendom. At home the people, imbued with the spirit of the Bible, and impregnate with that love of liberty, and that respect for law, which Protestantism ever engenders, made their homes bright with virtue and their cities resplendent with art, while their land they taught by their industry and frugality to bloom in beauty and overflow with riches.

CHAPTER XXX
GRANDEUR OF THE UNITED PROVINCES

WE have narrated the ill success that attended the government of the Earl of Leicester in the Low Countries. These repeated disappointments rebuked the Provinces for looking abroad for defence, and despising the mightier source of strength which existed within themselves; and in due time they came to see that it was not by the arm of any foreign prince that they were to be holden up and made strong, but by the nurturing virtue of that great principle which, rooted in their land by the blood of their martyrs, had at last found for their nation a champion in William of Orange. This principle had laid the foundation of their free Commonwealth, and it alone could give it stability and conduct it to greatness.

Accordingly, after Leicester's departure, at a meeting at the Hague, the 6th of February , 1587, the States, after asserting their own supreme authority, unanimously chose Prince Maurice as their governor, though still with a reservation to Queen Elizabeth. It was not respect alone for the memory of his great father, which induced the States to repose so great a trust, at so momentous a period of their existence, in one who was then only twenty-one years of age. From his earliest youth the prince had given proof of his superior prudence and capacity, and in the execution of his high command he made good the hopes entertained of him when he entered upon it. If he possessed in lower degree than his illustrious sire the faculty of governing men, he was nevertheless superior to him in the military art, and this was the science most needed at this moment by the States. Maurice became the greatest captain of his age: not only was he famous in the discipline of his armies, but his genius, rising above the maxims then in vogue, enabled him to invent or to perfect a system of fortification much more complete, and which soon became common.[2964] The marvellous political ability of William, now lost to the States, was supplied in some sort by a school of statesmen that arose after his death in Holland, and whose patriotic honesty, allied with an uncommon amount of native sagacity and shrewdness, made them a match for the Machiavellian diplomatists with which the age abounded.

Philip II. was at that time getting ready the Armada for the subjugation of England. The Duke of Parma was required to furnish his contingent of the mighty fleet, and while engaged in this labour he was unable to undertake any operation in the Netherlands. Holland had rest, and the military genius of Prince Maurice found as yet no opportunity of displaying itself. But no sooner had Philip's "invincible" Armada vanished in the North Sea, pursued by the English admiral and the tempests of heaven, than Parma made haste to renew the war. He made no acquisition of moment, however—the gains of the campaign remained with Prince Maurice; and the power of Spain in the Low Countries began as visibly to sink as that of Holland to rise.

From this time forward blow after blow came upon that colossal fabric which for so long a period had not only darkened the Netherlands, but had overshadowed all Christendom. The root of the Spanish Power was dried up, and its branch began to wither. Philip, aiming to be the master of the world, plunged into a multitude of schemes which drained his resources, and at length broke in pieces that mighty empire of which he was the monarch. As his years grew his projects multiplied, till at last he found himself warring with the Turks, the Morescoes, the Portuguese, the French, the English, and the Netherlanders. The latter little country he would most certainly have subdued, had his ambition permitted him to concentrate his power in the attempt to crush it. Happily for the Low Countries, Philip was never able to do this. And now another dream misled him—the hope of seizing the crown of France for himself or his daughter,[2965] Clara Eugenia, during the troublous times that followed the accession of Henry of Navarre. In this hope he ordered Parma to withdraw the Spanish troops from the Netherlands, and help the League to conquer Henry IV. Parma remonstrated against the madness of the scheme, and the danger of taking away the army out of the country; but Philip, blinded by his ambition, refused to listen to the prudent councils of his general. The folly of the King of Spain gave a breathing-space to the young Republic, and enabled its governor, Prince Maurice, to display that resource, prudence, and promptitude which gained him the confidence and esteem of his subjects, and which, shining forth yet more brilliantly in future campaigns, won for him the admiration of Europe.

When Parma returned from France (1590) he found Holland greatly stronger than he had left it: its frontier was now fortified; several towns beyond the boundary of the United Provinces had been seized by their army; and Parma, with a treasury drained by his campaign, and soldiers mutinous because ill-paid, had to undertake the work of recovering what had been lost. The campaign now opened was a disastrous one both for himself and for Spain. After many battles and sieges he found that the Spanish Power had been compelled to retreat before the arms of the infant Republic, and that his own prestige as a soldier had been eclipsed by the renown of his opponent, acquired by the prudence with which his enterprises had been concerted, the celerity with which they had been executed, and the success with which they had been crowned. The Duke of Parma was a second time ordered into France to assist the League, and pave Philip's way for mounting the throne of that country; and foolish though he deemed the order, he had nevertheless to obey it. He returned broken in health, only to find that in his absence the Spanish Power had sustained new losses, that the United Provinces had acquired additional strength, and that Prince Maurice had surrounded his name with a brighter glory than ever. In short, the affairs of Spain in the Low Countries he perceived were becoming hopeless. Worn out with cares, eaten up with vexation and chagrin, and compelled the while to strain every nerve in the execution of projects which his judgment condemned as chimerical and ruinous, his sickness increased, and on the 3rd of December, 1592, he expired in the forty-seventh year of his age, and the fourteenth of his government of the Netherlands. "With the Duke of Parma," says Sir William Temple, "died all the discipline, and with that all the fortunes, of the Spanish arms in Flanders."[2966]

There now opened to the United Provinces a career of prosperity that was as uniform and uninterrupted as their previous period of distress and calamity had been continuous and unbroken. The success that attended the arms of Prince Maurice, the vigour with which he extended the dominions of the Republic, the prudence and wisdom with which he administered affairs at home, the truce with Spain, the League with Henry IV. of France, and the various circumstances and methods by which the prince, and the upright and wise counsellors that surrounded him, advanced the credit and power of the United Provinces, belong to the civil history of the country, and hardly come within the scope of our special design. But the mighty growth of the United Provinces, which was the direct product of Protestantism, is one of the finest proofs which history furnishes of the spirit and power of the Reformation, and affords a lesson that the ages to come will not fail to study, and an example that they will take care to imitate.

On the face of all the earth there is not another such instance of a nation for whom nature had done literally nothing, and who had all to create from their soil upwards, attaining such a pitch of greatness. The Dutch received at the beginning but a sand-bank for a country. Their patience and laborious skill covered it with verdure, and adorned it with cities. Their trade was as truly their own creation as their soil. The narrow limits of their land did not furnish them with the materials of their manufactures; these they had to import from abroad, and having worked them up into beautiful fabrics, they carried them back to the countries whence they had obtained the raw materials. Thus their land became the magazine of the world. Notwithstanding that their country was washed, and not unfrequently inundated, by the ocean, nature had not given them harbours; these, too, they had to create. Their scanty territory led them to make the sea their country; and their wars with Spain compelled them to make it still more their home. They had an infinity of ships and sailors. They sent their merchant fleet over every sea—to the fertile islands of the West, to the rich continents of the East. They erected forts on promontories and creeks, and their settlements were dispersed throughout the world. They formed commercial treaties and political alliances with the most powerful nations. The various wealth that was wafted to their shores was even greater than that which had flowed in on Spain after the discovery of the mines of Mexico and Peru. Their land, which yielded little besides milk and butter, overflowed with the necessaries and luxuries of all the earth. The wheat, and wine, and oil of Southern Europe; the gold and silver of Mexico; the spices and diamonds of the East; the furs of Northern Europe; silk, cotton, precious woods, and marbles—everything, in short, which the earth produces, and which can contribute to clothe the person, adorn the dwelling, supply the table, and enhance the comfort of man, was gathered into Holland. And while every wind and tide were bringing to their shores the raw materials, the persecutions which raged in other countries were daily sending crowds of skilful and industrious men to work them up. And with every increase of their population came a new expansion of their trade, and by consequence a new access to the wealth that flowed from it.

With the rapid growth of material riches, their respect for learning, their taste for intellectual pursuits, and their love of independence still continued with them. They were plain and frugal in habit, although refined and generous in disposition. The sciences were cultivated, and their universities flourished. To be learned or eloquent inferred as great eminence in that country as to be rich or high-born did in others. All this had come out of their great struggle for the Protestant faith.

And, as if to make the lesson still plainer and more striking, by the side of this little State, so illustrious for its virtue, so rich in all good things, and so powerful among the nations of the world, were seen those unhappy Provinces which had retreated within the pale of Rome, and submitted to the yoke of Philip. They were fallen into a condition of poverty and slavery which was as complete as it was deplorable, and which, but a few years before, any one who had seen how populous, industrious, and opulent they were, would have deemed impossible. Commerce, trade, nay, even daily bread, had fled from that so recently prosperous land. Bankers, merchants, farmers, artisans—all were sunk in one great ruin. Antwerp, the emporium of the commerce of Europe, with its river closed, and its harbour and wharves forsaken, was reduced to beggary. The looms and forges of Ghent, Bruges, and Namur were idle. The streets, trodden erewhile by armies of workmen, were covered with grass; fair mansions were occupied by paupers; the fields were falling out of cultivation; the farm-houses were sinking into ruins; and, in the absence of men, the beasts of the field were strangely multiplying. To these evils were added the scourge of a mutinous soldiery, and the incessant rapacious demands of Philip for money, not knowing, or not caring to know, into what a plight of misery and penury his tyranny had already sunk them. Spain itself, towards the close of the nineteenth century, is still as great a wreck; but it required three hundred years for despotism and Popery to ripen their fruits in the Iberian Peninsula, whereas in the Southern Netherlands their work was consummated in a very few years.

We turn once more to their northern sister. The era of the flourishing of the United Provinces was from 1579, when the Union of Utrecht was formed, till 1672—that is, ninety-three years. In the year 1666 we find Holland and her sister States at the acme of their prosperity. They are populous in men; they have a revenue of 40,000,000 florins; they possess a land army of 60,000 men, a fleet of above 100 men-of-war, a countless mercantile navy, a world-wide commerce, and, not content with being one of the great Powers of Europe, they are contesting with England the supremacy of the seas.[2967]

It is hardly possible not to ask what led to the decline and fall of so great a Power? Sir William Temple, who had studied with the breadth of a statesman, and the insight of a philosopher, both the rise and the fall of the United Provinces, lays their decay at the door of the Arminian controversy, which had parted the nation in two. At least, this he makes the primary cause, and the one that led on to the others. The Prince of Orange or Calvinist faction, he tells us, contended for the purity of the faith, and the Arminian faction for the liberties of the nation; and so far this was true, but the historian forgets to say that the contest for the purity of the faith covered the nation's liberties as well, and when the sacred fire which had kindled the conflict for liberty was permitted to go out, the flame of freedom sunk down, the nation's heart waxed cold, and its hands grew feeble in defence of its independence. The decay of Holland became marked from the time the Arminian party gained the ascendancy.[2968] But though the nation decayed, the line of William of Orange, the great founder of its liberty, continued to flourish. The motto of Prince Maurice, *Tandem fit surculus arbor* ("The twig will yet become a tree"), was made good in a higher sense than he had dreamed, for the epics of history are grander than those of fiction, and the Stadtholder of Holland, in due time, mounted the throne of Great Britain.

The History of Protestantism

Book Nineteenth
PROTESTANTISM IN POLAND AND BOHEMIA

CHAPTER I
RISE AND SPREAD OF PROTESTANTISM IN POLAND

WE are now approaching the era of that great "Catholic Restoration" which, cunningly devised and most perseveringly carried on by the Jesuits, who had now perfected the organisation and discipline of their corps, and zealously aided by the arms of the Popish Powers, scourged Germany with a desolating war of thirty years, trampled out many flourishing Protestant Churches in the east of Europe, and nearly succeeded in rehabilitating Rome in her ancient dominancy of all Christendom. But before entering on the history of these events, it is necessary to follow, in a brief recital, the rise and progress of Protestantism in the countries of Poland, Bohemia, Hungary, and parts of Austria, seeing that these were the Churches which fell before the spiritual cohorts of Loyola, and the military hordes of Austria, and seeing also that these were the lands, in conjunction with Germany, which became the seat of that great struggle which seemed as though it were destined to overthrow Protestantism wholly, till all suddenly, Sweden sent forth a champion who rolled back the tide of Popish success, and restored the balance between the two Churches, which has remained much as it was then settled, down to almost the present time.

We begin with Poland. Its Reformation opened with brilliant promise, but it had hardly reached what seemed its noon when its light was overcast, and since that disastrous hour the farther Poland's story is pursued, it becomes but the sadder and more melancholy; nevertheless, the history of Protestantism in Poland is fraught with great lessons, specially applicable to all free countries. Christianity, it is believed, was introduced into Poland by missionaries from Great Moravia in the ninth century. In the tenth we find the sovereign of the country receiving baptism, from which we may infer that the Christian faith was still spreading in Poland.[2969] It is owing to the simplicity and apostolic zeal of Cyrillus[2970] and Methodius, two pastors from Thessalonica, that the nations, the Slavonians among the rest, who inhabited the wide territories lying between the Tyrol and the Danube on the one side, and the Baltic and Vistula on the other, were at so early a period visited with the light of the Gospel.

Their first day was waxing dim, notwithstanding that they were occasionally visited by the Waldenses, when Wicliffe arose in England. This splendour which had burst out in the west, travelled, as we have already narrated, as far as Bohemia, and from Bohemia it passed on to Poland, where it came in time to arrest the return of the pagan night. The voice of Huss was now resounding throughout Bohemia, and its echoes were heard in Cracow. Poland was then intimately connected with Bohemia; the language of the two countries was almost the same; numbers of Polish youth resorted to the University of Prague, and one of the first martyrs of Huss's Reformation was a Pole. Stanislav Pazek, a shoemaker by trade, suffered death, along with two Bohemians, for opposing the indulgences which were preached in Prague in 1411. The citizens interred their bodies with great respect, and Huss preached a sermon at their funeral.[2971] In 1431, a conference took place in Cracow, between certain Hussite missionaries and the doctors of the university, in presence of the king and senate. The doctors did battle for the ancient faith against the "novelties" imported from the land of Huss, which they described as doctrines for which the missionaries could plead no better authority than the Bible. The disputation lasted several days, and Bishop Dlugosh, the historian of the conference, complains that although, "in the opinion of all present, the heretics were vanquished, they never acknowledged their defeat."[2972]

It is interesting to find these three countries—Poland, Bohemia, and England—at that early period turning their faces toward the day, and hand-in-hand attempting to find a path out of the darkness. How much less happy, one cannot help reflecting, the fate of the first two countries than that of the last, yet all three were then directing their steps into the same road. Many of the first families in Poland embraced openly the Bohemian doctrines; and it is an interesting fact that one of the professors in the university, Andreas Galka, expounded the works of Wicliffe at Cracow, and wrote a poem in honour of the English Reformer. It is the earliest production of the Polish muse in existence, a poem in praise of the Virgin excepted. The author, addressing "Poles, Germans, and all nations," says, "Wicliffe speaks the truth! Heathendom and Christendom have never had a greater man than he, and never will." Voice after voice is heard in Poland, attesting a growing opposition to Rome, till at last in 1515, two years before Luther had spoken, we find the seminal principle of Protestantism proclaimed by Bernard of Lublin, in a work which he published at Cracow, and in which he says that "we must believe the Scriptures alone, and reject human ordinances."[2973] Thus was the way prepared.

Two years after came Luther. The lightnings of his Theses, which flashed through the skies of all countries, lighted up also those of Polish Prussia. Of that flourishing province Dantzic was the capital, and the chief emporium of Poland with Western Europe. In that city a monk, called James Knade, threw off his habit (1518), took a wife, and began to preach publicly against Rome. Knade had to retire to Thorn, where he continued to diffuse his doctrines under the protection of a powerful nobleman; but the seed he had sown in Dantzic did not perish; there soon arose a little band of preachers, composed of Polish youths who had sat at Luther's feet in Wittemberg, and of priests who had found access to the Reformer's writings, who now proclaimed the truth, and made so numerous converts that in 1524 five churches in Dantzic were given up to their use.

Success made the Reformers rash. The town council, to whom the king, Sigismund, had hinted his dislike of these innovations, lagged behind in the movement, and the citizens resolved to replace that body with men more zealous. They surrounded the council, to the number of 400, and with arms in their hands, and cannon pointed on the council-hall, they demanded the resignation of the members. No sooner had the council dissolved itself than the citizens elected another from among themselves. The new council proceeded to complete the Reformation at a stroke. They suppressed the Roman Catholic worship, they closed the monastic establishments, they ordered that the convents and other ecclesiastical edifices should be converted into schools and hospitals, and declared the goods of the "Church" to be public property, but left them untouched.[2974] This violence only threw back the movement; the majority of the inhabitants were still of the old faith, and had a right to exercise its worship till, enlightened in a better way, they should be pleased voluntarily to abandon it.

The deposed councillors, seating themselves in carriages hung in black, and encircling their heads with crape, set out to appear before the king. They implored him to interpose his authority to save his city of Dantzic, which was on the point of being drowned in heresy, and re-establish the old order of things. The king, in the main upright and tolerant, at first temporised. The members of council, by whom the late changes had been made, were summoned before the king's tribunal to justify their doings; but not obeying the summons, they were outlawed. In April, 1526, the king in person visited Dantzic; the citizens, as a precaution against change, received the monarch in arms; but the royal troops, and the armed retainers of the Popish lords who accompanied the king, so greatly outnumbered the Reformers that they were overawed, and submitted to the court. A royal decree restored the Roman Catholic worship; fifteen of the leading Reformers were beheaded, and the rest banished; the citizens were ordered to return within the Roman pale or quit Dantzic; the priests and monks who had abandoned the Roman Church were exiled, and the churches appropriated to Protestant worship were given back to mass. This was a sharp castigation for leaving the peaceful path. Nevertheless, the movement in Dantzic was only arrested, not destroyed. Some years later, there came an epidemic to the city, and amid the sick and dying there stood up a pious Dominican, called Klein, to preach the Gospel. The citizens, awakened a second time to eternal things, listened to him. Dr. Eck, the famous opponent of Luther, importuned King Sigismund to stop the preacher, and held up to him, as an example worthy of imitation, Henry VIII. of England, who had just published a book against the Reformer. "Let King Henry write against Martin," replied Sigismund, "but with regard to myself, I shall be king equally of the sheep and of the goats."[2975] Under the following reign Protestantism triumphed in Dantzic.

About the same time the Protestant doctrines began to take root in other towns of Polish Prussia. In Thorn, situated on the Vistula, these doctrines appeared in 1520. There came that year to Thorn, Zacharias Fereira, a legate of the Pope. He took a truly Roman way of warning the inhabitants against the heresy which had invaded their town. Kindling a great fire before the Church of St. John, he solemnly committed the effigies and writings of Luther to the flames. The faggots had hardly begun to blaze when a shower of stones from the townsmen saluted the legate and his train, and they were forced to flee, before they had time to consummate their *auto-da-fé*. At Braunsberg, the seat of the Bishop of Ermeland, the Lutheran worship was publicly introduced in 1520, without the bishop's taking any steps to prevent it. When reproached by his chapter for his supineness, he told his canons that the Reformer founded all he said on Scripture, and any one among them who deemed himself competent to refute him was at liberty to do so. At Elbing and many other towns the light was spreading.

A secret society, composed of the first scholars of the day, lay and cleric, was formed at Cracow, the university seat, not so much to propagate the Protestant doctrines as to investigate the grounds of their truth. The queen of Sigismund I., Bona Sforza, was an active member of this society. She had for her confessor a learned Italian, Father Lismanini. The Father received most of the Protestant publications that appeared in the various countries of Europe, and laid them on the table of the society, with the view of their being read and canvassed by the members. The society at a future period acquired a greater but not a better renown. One day a priest named Pastoris, a native of Belgium, rose in it and avowed his disbelief of the Trinity, as a doctrine inconsistent with the unity of the Godhead. The members, who saw that this was to overthrow revealed religion, were mute with astonishment; and some, believing that what they had taken for the path of reform was the path of destruction, drew back, and took final refuge in Romanism. Others declared themselves disciples of the priest, and thus were laid in Poland the foundations of Socinianism.[2976]

The rapid diffusion of the light is best attested by the vigorous efforts of the Romish clergy to suppress it. Numerous books appeared at this time in Poland against Luther and his doctrines. The Synod of Lenczyca, in 1527, recommended the re-establishment of the "Holy Inquisition." Other Synods drafted schemes of ecclesiastical reform, which, in Poland as in all the other countries where such projects were broached, were never realised, save on paper. Others recommended the appointment of popular preachers to instruct the ignorant, and guide their feet past the snares which were being laid for them in the writings of the heretics. On the principle that it would be less troublesome to prevent the planting of these snares, than after they were set to guide the unwary past them, they prohibited the introduction of such works into the country. The Synod of Lenczyca, in 1532, went a step farther, and in its zeal to preserve the "sincere faith" in Poland, recommended the banishment of "all heretics beyond the bounds of Sarmatia."[2977] The Synod of Piotrkow, in 1542, published a decree prohibiting all students from resorting to universities conducted by heretical professors, and threatening with exclusion from all offices and dignities all who, after the passing of the edict, should repair to such universities, or who, being already at such, did not instantly return. This edict had no force of law, for besides not being recognised by the Diet, the ecclesiastical jurisdiction was carefully limited by the constitutional liberties of Poland, and the nobles still continued to send their sons to interdicted universities, and in particular to Wittemberg. Meanwhile the national legislation of Poland began to flow in just the opposite channel. In 1539 a royal ordinance established the liberty of the press; and in 1543 the Diet of Cracow granted the freedom of studying at foreign universities to all Polish subjects.

At this period an event fell out which gave an additional impulse to the diffusion of Protestantism in Poland. In 1548, a severe persecution, which will come under our notice at a subsequent stage of our history, arose against the Bohemian brethren, the descendants of that valiant host who had combated for the faith under Ziska. In the year above-named Ferdinand of Bohemia published an edict shutting up their churches, imprisoning their ministers, and enjoining the brethren, under severe penalties, to leave the country within forty-two days.

A thousand exiles, marshalling themselves in three bands, left their native villages, and began their march westward to Prussia, where Albert of Brandenburg, a zealous Reformer, had promised them asylum. The pilgrims, who were under the conduct of Sionius, the chief of their community— "the leader of the people of God," as a Polish historian styles him—had to pass through Silesia and Poland on their way to Prussia. Arriving in Posen in June, 1548, they were welcomed by Andreas Gorka, first magistrate of Grand Poland, a man of vast possessions, and Protestant opinions, and were offered a settlement in his States. Here, meanwhile, their journey terminated. The pious wanderers erected churches and celebrated their worship. Their hymns chanted in the Bohemian language, and their sermons preached in the same tongue, drew many of the Polish inhabitants, whose speech was Slavonic, to listen, and ultimately to embrace their opinions. A missionary army, it looked to them as if Providence had guided their steps to this spot for the conversion of all the provinces of Grand Poland. The Bishop of Posen saw the danger that menaced his diocese, and rested not till he had obtained an order from Sigismund Augustus, who had just succeeded his father (1548), enjoining the Bohemian emigrants to quit the territory. The order might possibly have been recalled, but the brethren, not wishing to be the cause of trouble to the grandee who had so nobly entertained them, resumed their journey. But the seed they had sown in Posen remained behind them. In the following year (1549) many of them returned to Poland, and resumed their propagation of the Reformed doctrines. They prosecuted their work without molestation, and with great success. Many of the principal families embraced their opinions; and the ultimate result of their labours was the formation of about eighty congregations in the provinces of Grand Poland, besides many in other parts of the kingdom.

A quarrel broke out between the students and the university authorities at Cracow, which although originating in a street-brawl, had important bearings on the Protestant movement. The breach was found impossible to heal, and the students resolved to leave Cracow in a body. "The schools became silent," says a contemporary writer, "the halls of the university were deserted, and the churches were mute."[2978] Nothing but farewells, lamentations, and groans resounded through Cracow. The pilgrims assembled in a suburban church, to hear a farewell mass, and then set forth, singing a sacred hymn, some taking the road to the College of Goldberg, in Silesia, and others going on to the newly-erected University of Konigsberg, in Prussia. The first-named school was under the direction of Frankendorf, one of the most eminent of Melancthon's pupils; Konigsberg, a creation of Albert, Duke of Prussia, was already fulfilling its founder's intention, which was the diffusion of scriptural knowledge. In both seminaries the predominating influences were Protestant. The consequence was that almost all these students returned to their homes imbued with the Reformed doctrine, and powerfully contributed to spread it in Poland.

So stood the movement when Sigismund Augustus ascended the throne in 1548. Protestant truth was widely spread throughout the kingdom. In the towns of Polish Prussia, where many Germans resided, the Reformation was received in its Lutheran expression; in the rest of Poland it was embraced in its Calvinistic form. Many powerful nobles had abandoned Romanism; numbers of priests taught the Protestant faith; but, as yet, there existed no organisation—no Church. This came at a later period.

The priesthood had as yet erected no stake. They thought to stem the torrent by violent denunciations, thundered from the pulpit, or sent abroad over the kingdom through the press. They raised their voices to the loftiest pitch, but the torrent continued to flow broader and deeper every day. They now began to make trial of coercive measures. Nicholaus Olesnicki, Lord of Pinczov, ejecting the images from a church on his estates, established Protestant worship in it according to the forms of Geneva. This was the first open attack on the ancient order of things, and Olesnicki was summoned before the ecclesiastical tribunal of Cracow. He obeyed the summons, but the crowd of friends and retainers who accompanied him was such that the court was terrified, and dared not open its sittings. The clergy had taken a first step, but had lost ground thereby.

The next move was to convoke a Synod (1552) at Piotrkow. At that Convocation, the afterwards celebrated Cardinal Hosius produced a summary of the Roman faith, which he proposed all priests and all of senatorial and equestrian degree should be made to subscribe. Besides the fundamental doctrines of Romanism, this creed of Hosius made the subscriber express his belief in purgatory, in the worship of saints and images, in the efficacy of holy water, of fasts, and similar rites.[2979] The suggestion of Hosius was adopted; all priests were ordered to subscribe this test, and the king was petitioned to exact subscription to it from all the officers of his Government, and all the nobles of his realm. The Synod further resolved to set on foot a vigorous war against heresy, to support which a tax was to be levied on the clergy. It was sought to purchase the assistance of the king by offering him the confiscated property of all condemned heretics.[2980] It seemed as if Poland was about to be lighted up with martyr-piles.

A beginning was made with Nicholaus, Rector of Kurow. This good man began in 1550 to preach the doctrine of salvation by grace, and to give the Communion in both kinds to his parishioners. For these offences he was cited before the ecclesiastical tribunal, where he courageously defended himself. He was afterwards thrown into a dungeon, and deprived of life, but whether by starvation, by poison, or by methods more violent still, cannot now be known. One victim had been offered to the insulted majesty of Rome in Poland. Contemporary chroniclers speak of others who were immolated to the intolerant genius of the Papacy, but their execution took place, not in open day, but in the secrecy of the cell, or in the darkness of the prison.

The next move of the priests landed them in open conflict with the popular sentiment and the chartered rights of the nation. No country in Europe enjoyed at that hour a greater degree of liberty than did Poland. The towns, many of which were flourishing, elected their own magistrates, and thus each city, as regarded its internal affairs, was a little republic. The nobles, who formed a tenth of the population, were a peculiar and privileged class. Some of them were owners of vast domains, inhabited castles, and lived in great magnificence. Others of them tilled their own lands; but all of them, grandee and husbandman alike, were equal before the law, and neither their persons nor property could be disposed of, save by the Diet. The king himself was subject to the law. We find the eloquent but versatile Orichovius, who now thundered against the Pope, and now threw himself prostrate before him, saying in one of his philippics, "Your Romans bow their knees before the crowd of your menials; they bear on their necks the degrading yoke of the Roman scribes; but such is not the case with us, where the law rules even the throne." The free constitution of the country was a shield to its Protestantism, as the clergy had now occasion to experience. Stanislav Stadnicki, a nobleman of large estates and great influence, having embraced the Reformed opinions, established the Protestant worship according to the forms of Geneva, on his domains. He was summoned to answer for his conduct before the tribunal of the bishop. Stadnicki replied that he was quite ready to justify both his opinions and his acts. The court, however, had no wish to hear what he had to say in behalf of his faith, and condemned him, by default, to civil death and loss of property. Had the clergy wished to raise a flame all over the kingdom, they could have done nothing more fitted to gain their end. Stadnicki assembled his fellow-nobles and told them what the priests had done. The Polish grandees had ever been jealous of the throne, but here was an ecclesiastical body, acting under an irresponsible foreign chief, assuming a power which the king had never ventured to exercise, disposing of the lives and properties of the nobles without reference to any will or any tribunal save their own. The idea was not to be endured. There rung a loud outcry against ecclesiastical tyranny all throughout Poland; and the indignation was brought to a height by numerous apprehensions, at that same time, at the instance of the bishops, of influential persons— among others, priests of blameless life, who had offended against the law of clerical celibacy, and whom the Roman clergy sought to put to death, but could not, simply from the circumstance that they could find no magistrate willing to execute their sentences.

At this juncture it happened that the National Diet (1552) assembled. Unmistakable signs were apparent at its opening of the strong anti-Papal feeling that animated many of its members. As usual, its sessions were inaugurated by the solemn performance of high mass. The king in his robes was present, and with him were the ministers of his council, the officers of his household, and the generals of his army, bearing the symbols of their office, and wearing the stars and insignia of their rank; and there, too, were the senators of the Upper Chamber, and the members of the Lower House. All that could be done by chants and incense, by splendid vestments and priestly rites, to make the service impressive, and revive the decaying veneration of the worshippers for the Roman Church, was done. The great words which effect the prodigy of transubstantiation had been spoken; the trumpet blared, and the clang of grounded arms rung through the building. The Host was being elevated, and the king and his court fell on their knees; but many of the deputies, instead of prostrating themselves, stood erect and turned away their faces. Raphael Leszczynski, a nobleman of high character and great possessions, expressed his dissent from Rome's great mystery in manner even more marked: he wore his hat all through the performance. The priests saw, but dared not reprove, this contempt of their rites.[2981]

The auguries with which the Diet had opened did not fail of finding ample fulfillment in its subsequent proceedings. The assembly chose as its president Leszczynski—the nobleman who had remained uncovered [sic] during mass, and who had previously resigned his senatorial dignity in order to become a member of the Lower House.[2982] The Diet immediately took into consideration the jurisdiction wielded by the bishops. The question put in debate was this—Is such a jurisdiction, carrying civil effects, compatible with the rights of the crown and the freedom of the nation? The Diet decided that it was consistent with neither the prerogatives of the sovereign nor the liberties of the people, and resolved to abolish it, so far as it had force in law. King Sigismund Augustus thought it very possible that if he were himself to mediate in the matter he would, at least, succeed in softening the fall of the bishops, if only he could persuade them to make certain concessions. But he was mistaken: the ecclesiastical dignitaries were perverse, and resolutely refused to yield one iota of their powers. Thereupon the Diet issued its decree, which the king ratified, that the clergy should retain the power of judging of heresy, but have no power of inflicting civil or criminal punishment on the condemned. Their spiritual sentences were henceforward to carry no temporal effects whatever. The Diet of 1552 may be regarded as the epoch of the downfall of Roman Catholic dominancy in Poland, and of the establishment in that country of the liberty of all religious confessions.[2983]

The anger of the bishops was inflamed to the utmost. They entered their solemn protest against the enactment of the Diet. The mitre was shorn of half its splendour, and the crozier of more than half its power, by being disjoined from the sword. They left the Senate-hall in a body, and threatened to resign their senatorial dignities. The Diet heard their threats unmoved, and as it made not the slightest effort either to prevent their departure or to recall them after they were gone, but, on the contrary, went on with its business as if nothing unusual had occurred, the bishops returned and took their seats of their own accord.

CHAPTER II

JOHN ALASCO, AND REFORMATION OF EAST FRIESLAND

WE see the movement marching on, but we can see no one leader going before it. The place filled by Luther in Germany, by Calvin in Geneva, and by men not dissimilarly endowed in other countries, is vacant in the Reformation of Poland. Here it is a Waldensian missionary or refugee who is quietly sowing the good seed which he has drawn from the garner of some manuscript copy of the New Testament, and there it is a little band of Bohemian brethren, who have preserved the traditions of John Huss, and are trying to plant them in this new soil. Here it is a university doctor who is expounding the writings of Wicliffe to his pupils, and there it is a Polish youth who has just returned from Wittemberg, and is anxious to communicate to his countrymen the knowledge which he has there learned, and which has been so sweet and refreshing to himself. Nevertheless, although amid all these labourers we can discover no one who first gathers all the forces of the new life into himself, and again sends them forth over the land, we yet behold the darkness vanishing on every side. Poland's Reformation is not a sunrise, but a daybreak: the first dim streaks are succeeded by others less doubtful; these are followed by brighter shades still; till at last something like the clearness of day illuminates its sky. The truth has visited some nobleman, as the light will strike on some tall mountain at the morning hour, and straightway his retainers and tenantry begin to worship as their chief worships; or some cathedral abbot or city priest has embraced the Gospel, and their flocks follow in the steps of their shepherd, and find in the doctrine of a free salvation a peace of soul which they never experienced amid the burdensome rites and meritorious services of the Church of Rome. There are no combats; no stakes; no mighty hindrances to be vanquished; Poland seems destined to enter without struggle or bloodshed into possession of that precious inheritance which other nations are content to buy with a great price.

But although there is no one who, in intellectual and spiritual stature, towers so far above the other workers in Poland as to be styled its Reformer there are three names connected with the history of Protestantism in that country so outstanding as not to be passed without mention. The first is that of King Sigismund Augustus. Tolerant, accomplished, and pure in life, this monarch had read the *Institutes*, and was a correspondent of Calvin, who sought to inflame him with the ardour of making his name and reign glorious by labouring to effect the Reformation of his dominions. Sigismund Augustus was favourably disposed toward the doctrines of Protestantism, and he had nothing of that abhorrence of heresy which made the kings of France drive the Gospel from their realm with fire and sword; but he vacillated, and could never make up his mind between Rome and the Reformation. The Polish king would fain have seen an adjustment of the differences that divided his subjects into two great parties, and the dissensions quieted that agitated his kingdom, but he feared to take the only effectual steps that could lead to that end. He was surrounded constantly with Protestants, who cherished the hope that he would yet abandon Rome, and declare himself openly in favour of Protestantism, but he always drew back when the moment came for deciding. We have seen him, in conjunction with the Diet of 1552, pluck the sword of persecution from the hands of the bishops; and he was willing to go still further, and make trial of any means that promised to amend the administration and reform the doctrines of the Roman Church. He was exceedingly favourable to a project much talked of in his reign—namely, that of convoking a National Synod for reforming the Church on the basis of Holy Scripture. The necessity of such an assembly had been mooted in the Diet of 1552; it was revived in the Diet of 1555, and more earnestly pressed on the king, and thus contemporaneously with the abdication of the imperial sovereignty by Charles V., and the yet unfinished sittings of the great Council of Trent, the probability was that Christendom would behold a truly Œcumenical Council assemble in Poland, and put the topstone upon the Reformation of its Church and kingdom. The projected Polish assembly, over which it was proposed that King Sigismund Augustus should preside, was to be composed of delegates from all the religious bodies in the kingdom—Lutherans, Calvinists, and Bohemians—who were to meet and deliberate on a perfect equality with the Roman clergy. Nor was the constituency of this Synod to be confined to Poland; other Churches and lands were to be represented in it. All the living Reformers of note were to be invited to it; and, among others, it was to include the great names of Calvin and Beza, of Melancthon and Vergerius. But this Synod was never to meet. The clergy of Rome, knowing that tottering fabrics can stand only in a calm air, and that their Church was in a too shattered condition to survive the shock of free discussion conducted by such powerful antagonists, threw every obstacle in the way of the Synod's meeting. Nor was the king very zealous in the affair. It is doubtful whether Sigismund Augustus was ever brought to test the two creeds by the great question which of the twain was able to sustain the weight of his soul's salvation; and so, with convictions feeble and ill-defined, his purpose touching the reform of the Church never ripened into act.

The second name is that of no vacillating man—we have met it before—it is that of John Alasco. John Alasco, born in the last year save one of the fifteenth century,[2984] was sprung of one of the most illustrious families in Poland. Destined for the Church, he received the best education which the schools of his native land could bestow, and he afterwards visited Germany, France, Italy, and Belgium in order to enlarge and perfect his studies. At the University of Louvain, renowned for the purity of its orthodoxy, and whither he resorted, probably at the recommendation of his uncle, who was Primate of Poland, he contracted a close friendship with Albert Hardenberg.[2985] After a short stay at Louvain, finding the air murky with scholasticism, he turned his steps in the direction of Switzerland, and arriving at Zurich, he made the acquaintance of Zwingle. "Search the Scriptures," said the Reformer of Zurich to the young Polish nobleman. Alasco turned to that great light, and from that moment he began to be delivered from the darkness which had till then encompassed him. Quitting Zurich and crossing the Jura, he entered Basle, and presented himself before Erasmus. This great master of the schools was not slow to discover the refined grace, the beautiful genius, and the many and great acquirements of the stranger who had sought his acquaintance. Erasmus was charmed with the young Pole, and Alasco on his part was equally enamoured of Erasmus. Of all then living,

Erasmus, if not the man of highest genius, was the man of highest culture, and doubtless the young scholar caught the touch of a yet greater suavity from this prince of letters, as Erasmus, in the enthusiasm of his friendship, confesses that he had grown young again in the society of Alasco. The Pole lived about a year (1525) under the roof,[2986] but not at the cost of the great scholar; for his disposition being as generous as his means were ample, he took upon himself the expenses of housekeeping; and in other ways he ministered, with equal liberality and delicacy, to the wants of his illustrious host. He purchased his library for 300 golden crowns, leaving to Erasmus the use of it during his lifetime.[2987] He formed a friendship with other eminent men then living in Basle; in particular, with Œcolampadius and Pellicanus, the latter of whom initiated him into the study of the Hebrew Scriptures.

His uncle, the primate, hearing that his nephew had fallen into "bad company," recalled him by urgent letters to Poland. It cost Alasco a pang to tear himself from his friends in Basle. He carried back to his native land a heart estranged from Rome, but he did not dissever himself from her communion, nor as yet did he feel the necessity of doing so; he had tested her doctrines by the intellect only, not by the conscience. He was received at court, where his youth, the refinement of his manners, and the brilliance of his talents made him a favourite. The pomps and gaieties amid which he now lived weakened, but did not wholly efface, the impressions made upon him at Zurich and Basle. Destined for the highest offices in the Church of Poland, his uncle demanded that he should purge himself by oath from the suspicions of heresy which had hung about him ever since his return from Switzerland. Alasco complied. The document signed by him is dated in 1526, and in it Alasco promises not to embrace doctrines foreign to those of the Apostolic Roman Church, and to submit in all lawful and honest things to the authority of the bishops and of the Papal See. "This I swear, so help me, God, and his holy Gospel."[2988]

This fall was meant to be the first step toward the primacy. Ecclesiastical dignities began now to be showered upon him, but the duties which these imposed, by bringing him into close contact with clerical men, disclosed to him more and more every day the corruptions of the Papacy, and the need of a radical reform of the Church. He resumed his readings in the Bible, and renewed his correspondence with the Reformers. His spiritual life revived, and he began now to try Rome by the only infallible touchstone— "Can I, by the performance of the works she prescribes, obtain peace of conscience, and make myself holy in the sight of God?" Alasco was constrained to confess that he never should. He must therefore, at whatever cost, separate himself from her. At this moment two mitres—that of Wesprim in Hungary, and that of Cujavia in Poland—were placed at his acceptance.[2989] The latter mitre opened his way to the primacy in Poland. On the one side were two kings proffering him golden dignities, on the other was the Gospel, with its losses and afflictions. Which shall he choose? "God, in his goodness," said he, writing to Pellicanus, "has brought me to myself." He went straight to the king, and frankly and boldly avowing his convictions, declined the Bishopric of Cujavia.

Poland was no place for Alasco after such an avowal. He left his native land in 1536, uncertain in what country he should spend what might yet remain to him of life, which was now wholly devoted to the cause of the Reformation. Sigismund, who knew his worth, would most willingly have retained Alasco the Romanist, but perhaps he was not sorry to see Alasco the Protestant leave his dominions. The Protestant princes, to whom his illustrious birth and great parts had made him known, vied with each other to secure his services. The Countess Regent of East Friesland, where the Reformation had been commenced in 1528, urged him to come and complete the work by assuming the superintendence of the churches of that province. After long deliberation he went, but the task was a difficult one. The country had become the battleground of the sectaries. All things were in confusion; the churches were full of images, and the worship abounded in mummeries; the people were rude in manners, and many of the nobles dissolute in life; one less resolute might have been dismayed, and retired.

Alasco made a commencement. His quiet, yet persevering, and powerful touch was telling. Straightway a tempest arose around him. The wrangling sectaries on the one side, and the monks on the other, united in assailing the man in whom both recognised a common foe. Accusations were carried to the court at Brussels against him, and soon there came an imperial order to expel "the firebrand" from Friesland. "Dost thou not hear the growl of the thunder?"[2990] said Alasco, writing to his friends; he expected that the bolt would follow. Anna, the sovereign princess of the kingdom, terrified at the threat of the emperor, began to cool in her zeal toward the superintendent and his work; but in proportion as the clouds grew black and danger menaced, the courage and resolution of the Reformer waxed strong. He addressed a letter to the princess (1543), in which he deemed it "better to be unpolite than to be unfaithful," warning her that should she "take her hand from the plough" she would have to "give account to the eternal Judge." "I am only a foreigner," he added, "burdened with a family,[2991] and having no home. I wish, therefore, to be friends with all, but . . . as far as to the altar. This barrier I cannot pass, even if I had to reduce my family to beggary."[2992]

This noble appeal brought the princess once more to the side of Alasco, not again to withdraw her support from one whom she had found so devoted and so courageous. Prudent, yet resolute, Alasco went on steadily in his work. Gradually the remnants of Romanism were weeded out; gradually the images disappeared from the temples; the order and discipline of the Church were reformed on the Genevan model; the Sacrament of the Lord's Supper was established according to the doctrine of Calvin;[2993] and, as regarded the monks, they were permitted to occupy their convents in peace, but were forbidden the public performance of their worship. Not liking this restraint, the Fathers quietly withdrew from the kingdom. In six years John Alasco had completed the Reformation of the Church of East Friesland. It was a great service. He had prepared an asylum for the Protestants of the Netherlands during the evil days that were about to come upon them, and he had helped to pave the way for the appearance of William of Orange.

The Church order established by Alasco in Friesland was that of Geneva. This awoke against him the hostility of the Lutherans, and the adherents of that creed continuing to multiply in Friesland, the troubles of Alasco multiplied along with them. He resigned the general direction of ecclesiastical affairs, which he had exercised as superintendent, and limited his sphere of action to the ministry of the single congregation of Emden, the capital of the country.

But the time was come when John Alasco was to be removed to another sphere. A pressing letter now reached him from Archbishop Cranmer, inviting him to take part, along with other distinguished Continental Reformers, in completing the Reformation of the Church of England.[2994] The Polish Reformer accepted the invitation, and traversing Brabant and Flanders in disguise, he arrived in London in September, 1548. A six months' residence with Cranmer at Lambeth satisfied him that the archbishop's views and his own, touching the Reformation of the Church, entirely coincided; and an intimate friendship sprang up between the two, which bore good fruits for the cause of Protestantism in England, where Alasco's noble character and great learning soon won him high esteem. After a short visit to Friesland, in 1549, he returned to England, and was nominated by Edward VI., in 1550, Superintendent of the German, French, and Italian congregations erected in London, numbering between 3,000 and 4,000 persons, and which Cranmer hoped would yet prove a seed of Reformation in the various countries from which persecution had driven them,[2995] and would also excite the Church of England to pursue the path of Protestantism. And so, doubtless, it would have been, had not the death of Edward VI. and the accession of Mary suddenly changed the whole aspect of affairs in England. The Friesian Reformer and his congregation had now to quit our shore. They embarked at Gravesend on the 15th of September, 1553, in the presence of thousands of English Protestants, who crowded the banks of the Thames, and on bended knees supplicated the blessing and protection of Heaven on the wanderers.

Setting sail, the little fleet was scattered by a storm, and the vessel which bore John Alasco entered the Danish harbour of Elsinore. Christian III. of Denmark, a mild and pious prince, received Alasco and his fellow-exiles at first with great kindness; but soon their asylum was invaded by Lutheran intolerance. The theologians of the court, Westphal and Pomeranus (Bugenhagen), poisoned the king's mind against the exiles, and they were compelled to re-embark at an inclement season, and traverse the tempestuous seas in quest of some more hospitable shore. This shameful breach of hospitality was afterwards repeated at Lubeck, Hamburg, and Rostock; it kindled the indignation of the Churches of Switzerland, and it drew from Calvin an eloquent letter to Alasco, in which he gave vent not only to his deep sympathy with him and his companions in suffering, but also to his astonishment "that the barbarity of a Christian people should exceed even the sea in savageness."[2997]

Driven hither and thither, not by the hatred of Rome, but by the intolerance of brethren, Gustavus Vasa, the reforming monarch of Sweden, gave a cordial welcome to the pastor and his flock, should they choose to settle in his dominions. Alasco, however, thought better to repair to Friesland, the scene of his former labours; but even here the Lutheran spirit, which had been growing in his absence, made his stay unpleasant. He next sought asylum in Frankfort-on-the-Maine, where he established a Church for the Protestant refugees from Belgium.[2998] During his stay at Frankfort he essayed to heal the breach between the Lutheran and the Calvinistic branches of the Reformation. The mischiefs of that division he had amply experienced in his own person; but its noxious influence was felt far beyond the little community of which he was the centre. It was the great scandal of Protestantism; it disfigured it with dissensions and hatreds, and divided and weakened it in the presence of a powerful foe. But his efforts to heal this deplorable and scandalous schism, although seconded by the Senate of Frankfort and several German princes, were in vain.[2999]

He never lost sight of his native land; in all his wanderings he cherished the hope of returning to it at a future day, and aiding in the Reformation of its Church; and now (1555) he dedicated to Sigismund Augustus of Poland a new edition of an account he had formerly published of the foreign Churches in London of which he had acted as superintendent. He took occasion at the same time to explain in full his own sentiments on the subject of Church Reformation. With great calmness and dignity, but with great strength of argument, he maintained that the Scriptures were the one sole basis of Reformation; that neither from tradition, however venerable, nor from custom, however long established, were the doctrine of the Church's creed or the order of her government to be deduced; that neither Councils nor Fathers could infallibly determine anything; that apostolic practice, as recorded in the inspired canon—that is to say, the Word of God—alone possessed authority in this matter, and was a sure guide. He also took the liberty of urging on the king the necessity of a Reformation of the Church of Poland, "of which a prosperous beginning had already been made by the greatest and best part of the nation;" but the matter, he added, was one to be prosecuted "with judgment and care, seeing every one who reasoned against Rome was not orthodox;" and touching the Eucharist—that vexed question, and in Poland, as elsewhere, so fertile in divisions—Alasco stated "that doubtless believers received the flesh and blood of Christ in the Communion, but by the lip of the soul, for there was neither bodily nor personal presence in the Eucharist."[3000]

It is probable that it was this publication that led to his recall to Poland, in 1556, by the king and nobles.[3001] The Roman bishops heralded his coming with a shout of terror and wrath. "The 'butcher'[3002] of the Church has entered Poland!" they cried. "Driven out of every land, he returns to that one that gave him birth, to afflict it with troubles and commotions. He is collecting troops to wage war against the king, root out the Churches, and spread riot and bloodshed over the kingdom." This clamour had all the effect on the royal mind which it deserved to have—that is, none at all.[3003]

Alasco, soon after his return, was appointed superintendent of all the Reformed Churches of Little Poland.[3004] His long-cherished object seemed now within his reach. That was not the tiara of the primacy—for, if so, he needed not have become the exile; his ambition was to make the Church of Poland one of the brightest lights in the galaxy of the Reformation. He had arrived at his great task with fully-ripened powers. Of illustrious birth, and of yet more illustrious learning and piety, he was nevertheless, from remembrance of his fall, humble as a child. Presiding over the Churches of more than half the kingdom, Protestantism, under his fostering care, waxed stronger every day. He held Synods. He actively assisted in the translation of the first Protestant Bible in Poland, that he might give his countrymen direct access to the fountain of truth. He laboured unweariedly in the cause of union. He had especially at heart the healing of the great breach between the Lutheran and the Reformed—the sore through which so much of the vital force of Protestantism was ebbing away. The final goal which he kept in eye, and at which he hoped one day to arrive, was the erection of a national Church, Reformed in doctrine on the basis of the Word of God, and constituted in government as similarly to the Churches over which he had presided in London as the circumstances of Poland would allow. Besides the opposition of the Roman hierarchy, which was to be looked for, the Refomer found two main hindrances obstructing his path. The first was the growth of anti-Trinitarian doctrine, first broached, as we have seen, in the secret society of Cracow, and which continued to spread widely among the Churches superintended by Alasco, in spite of the polemical war he constantly maintained against them. The second was the vacillation of King Sigismund Augustus. Alasco urged the convocation of a National Synod, in order to the more speedy and universal Reformation of the Polish Church. But the king hesitated. Meanwhile Rome, seeing in the measures on foot, and more especially in the projected Synod, the impending overthrow of her power in Poland, dispatched Lippomani, one of the ablest of the Vatican diplomatists, with a promise, sealed with the Fisherman's ring, of a General Council, which should reform the Church and restore her unity. What need, then, for a National Council? The Pope would do, and with more order and quiet, what the Poles wished to have done. How many score of times had this promise been made, and when had it proved aught save a delusion and a snare? It served, however, as an excuse to the king, who refused to convoke the Synod which Alasco so much desired to see assemble. It was a great crisis. The Reformation had essayed to crown her work in Poland, but she was hindered, and the fabric remained unfinished: a melancholy monument of the egregious error of letting slip those golden opportunities that are given to nations, which "they that are wise" embrace, but they that are void of wisdom neglect, and bewail their folly with floods of tears and torrents of blood in the centuries that come after. In January, 1560, John Alasco died, and was buried with great pomp in the Church of Pintzov.[3005] After him there arose in Poland no Reformer of like adaptability and power, nor did the nation ever again enjoy so favourable an opportunity of planting its liberties on a stable foundation by completing its Reformation.[3006]

After John Alasco, but not equal to him, arose Prince Radziwill. His rank, his talents, and his zealous labours in the cause of Protestantism give him a conspicuous place in the list of Poland's Reformers. Nicholas Radziwill was sprung of a wealthy family of Lithuania. He was brother to Barbara, the first queen of Sigismund Augustus, whose unlimited confidence he enjoyed. Appointed ambassador to the courts of Charles V. and Ferdinand I., the grace of his manners and the charm of his discourse so attracted the regards of these monarchs, that he received from the Emperor Charles the dignity of a Prince of the Empire. At the same time he so acquitted himself in the many affairs of importance in which he was employed by his own sovereign, that honours and wealth flowed upon him in his native land. He was created Chancellor of Lithuania, and Palatine of Vilna. Hitherto politics alone had engrossed him, but the time was now come when something nobler than the pomp of courts, and the prizes of earthly kingdoms, was to occupy his thoughts and call forth his energies. About 1553 he was brought into intercourse with some Bohemian Protestants at Prague, who instructed him in the doctrines of the Reformation, which he embraced in the Genevan form. From that time his influence and wealth—both of which were vast—were devoted to the cause of his country's Reformation. He summoned to his help Vergerius[3007] from Italy. He supported many learned Protestants. He defrayed the expense of the printing of the first Protestant Bible at Brest, in Lithuania, in 1563. He diffused works written in defence of the Reformed faith. He erected a magnificent church and college at Vilna, the capital of Lithuania, and in many other ways fostered the Reformed Church in that powerful province where he exercised almost royal authority. Numbers of the priests now embraced the Protestant faith. "Almost the whole of the Roman Catholic nobles," says Krasinski, "including the first families of the land, and a great number of those who had belonged to the Eastern Church, became Protestants; so that in the diocese of Samogitia there were only eight Roman Catholic clergymen remaining. The Reformed worship was established not only in the estates of the nobles, but also in many towns."[3008] On the other side, the testimony to Radziwill's zeal as a Reformer is equally emphatic. We find the legate, Lippomani, reproaching him thus:— "Public rumour says that the Palatine of Vilna patronises all heresies, and that all the dangerous innovators are gathering under his protection; that he erects, wherever his influence reaches, sacrilegious altars against the altar of God, and that he establishes pulpits of falsehood against the pulpits of truth." Besides these scandalous deeds, the legate charges Radziwill with other heinous transgressions against the Papacy, as the casting down the images of the saints, the forbidding of prayers to the dead, and the giving of the cup to the laity; by all of which he had greatly offended against the Holy Father, and put his own salvation in peril.

Had the life of Prince Radziwill been prolonged, so great was his influence with the king, it is just possible that the vacillation of Sigismund Augustus might have been overcome, and the throne permanently won for the cause of Poland's Reformation; but that possibility, if it ever existed, was suddenly extinguished. In 1565, while yet in the prime of life, and in the midst of his labours for the emancipation of his native land from the Papal yoke, the prince died. When he felt his last hour approaching he summoned to his bedside his eldest son, Nicholas Christopher, and solemnly charged him to abide constant in the profession of his father's creed, and the service of his father's God; and to employ the illustrious name, the vast possessions, and the great influence which had descended to him for the cause of the Reformation.

So ill did that son fulfil the charge, delivered to him in circumstances so solemn, that he returned into the bosom of the Roman Church, and to repair to the utmost of his power the injury his father had done the Papal See, he expended 5,000 ducats in purchasing copies of his father's Bible, which he burned publicly in the market-place of Vilna. On the leaves, now sinking in ashes, might be read the following words, addressed in the dedication to the Polish monarch, and which we who are able to compare the Poland of the nineteenth century with the Poland of the sixteenth, can hardly help regarding as prophetic. "But if your Majesty (which may God avert) continuing to be deluded by this world, unmindful of its vanity, and fearing still some hypocrisy, will persevere in that error which, according to the prophecy of Daniel, that impudent priest, the idol of the Roman temple, has made abundantly to grow in his infected vineyard, like a true and real Antichrist; if your Majesty will follow to the end that blind chief of a generation of vipers, and lead us the faithful people of God the same way, it is to be feared that the Lord may, for such a rejection of his truth, condemn us all with your Majesty to shame, humiliation, and destruction, and afterwards to an eternal perdition."[3009]

CHAPTER III
ACME OF PROTESTANTISM IN POLAND

IN following the labours of those eminent men whom God inspired with the wish to emancipate their native land from the yoke of Rome, we have gone a little way beyond the point at which we had arrived in the history of Protestantism in Poland. We go back a stage. We have seen the Diet of 1552 inflict a great blow on the Papal power in Poland, by abolishing the civil jurisdiction of the bishops. Four years after this (1556) John Alasco returned, and began his labours in Poland; these he was prosecuting with success, when Lippomani was sent from Rome to undo his work. Lippomani's mission bore fruit. He revived the fainting spirits and rallied the wavering courage of the Romanists. He sowed with subtle art suspicions and dissensions among the Protestants; he stoutly promised in the Pope's name all necessary ecclesiastical reforms; this fortified the king in his vacillation, and furnished those within the Roman Church who had been demanding a reform, with an excuse for relaxing their efforts. They would wait "the good time coming." The Pope's manager with skilful hand lifted the veil, and the Romanists saw in the future a purified, united, and Catholic Church as clearly as the traveller sees the mirage in the desert. Vergerius laboured to convince them that what they saw was no lake, but a shimmering vapour, floating above the burning sands, but the phantasm was so like that the king and the bulk of the nation chose it in preference to the reality which John Alasco would have given them.

Meanwhile the Diet of 1552 had left the bishops crippled; their temporal arm had been broken, and their care now was to restore this most important branch of their jurisdiction. Lippomani assembled a General Synod of the Popish clergy at Lowicz. This Synod passed a resolution declaring that heretics, now springing up on every side, ought to be visited with pains and penalties, and then proceeded to make trial how far the king and nation would permit them to go in restoring their punitive power. They summoned to their bar the Canon of Przemysl, Lutomirski by name, on a suspicion of heresy. The canon appeared, but with him came his friends, all of them provided with Bibles—the best weapons, they thought, for such a battle as that to which they were advancing; but when the bishops saw how they were armed, they closed the doors of their judgment-hall and shut them out. The first move of the prelates had not improved their position.

Their second was attended with a success that was more disastrous than defeat. They accused a poor girl, Dorothy Lazecka, of having obtained a consecrated wafer on pretence of communicating, and of selling it to the Jews. The Jews carried the Host to their synagogue, where, being pierced with needles, it emitted a quantity of blood. The miracle, it was said, had come opportunely to show how unnecessary it was to give the cup to the laity. But further, it was made a criminal charge against both the girl and the Jews. The Jews pleaded that such an accusation was absurd; that they did not believe in transubstantiation, and would never think of doing anything so preposterous as experimenting on a wafer to see whether it contained blood. But in spite of their defence, they, as well as the unfortunate girl, were condemned to be burned. This atrocious sentence could not be carried out without the royal *exequatur*. The king, when applied to, refused his consent, declaring that he could not believe such an absurdity, and dispatched a messenger to Sochaczew, where the parties were confined, with orders for their release. The Synod, however, was determined to complete its work. The Bishop of Chelm, who was Vice-Chancellor of Poland, attached the royal seal without the knowledge of the king, and immediately sent off a messenger to have the sentence instantly executed. The king, upon being informed of the forgery, sent in haste to counteract the nefarious act of his minister; but it was too late. Before the royal messenger arrived the stake had been kindled, and the innocent persons consumed in the flames.[3010]

This deed, combining so many crimes in one, filled all Poland with horror. The legate, Lippomani, disliked before, was now detested tenfold. Assailed in pamphlets and caricatures, he quitted the kingdom, followed by the execration of the nation. Nor was it Lippomani alone who was struck by the recoil of this, in every way, unfortunate success; the Polish hierarchy suffered disgrace and damage along with him, for the atrocity showed the nation what the bishops were prepared to do, should the sword which the Diet of 1552 had plucked from their hands ever again be grasped by them.

An attempt at miracle, made about this time, also helped to discredit the character and weaken the influence of the Roman clergy in Poland. Christopher Radziwill, cousin to the famous Prince Radziwill, grieved at his relative's lapse into what he deemed heresy, made a pilgrimage to Rome, in token of his own devotion to the Papal See, and was rewarded with a box of precious relics from the Pope. One day after his return home with his inestimable treasure, the friars of a neighbouring convent waited on him, and telling him that they had a man possessed by the devil under their care, on whom the ordinary exorcisms had failed to effect a cure, they besought him, in pity for the poor demoniac, to lend them his box of relics, whose virtue doubtless would compel the foul spirit to flee. The bones were given with joy. On a certain day the box, with its contents, was placed on the high altar; the demoniac was brought forward, and in presence of a vast multitude the relics were applied, and with complete success. The evil spirit departed out of the man, with the usual contortions and grimaces. The spectators shouted, "Miracle!" and Radziwill, overjoyed, lifted eyes and hands to heaven, in wonder and gratitude.[3011]

In a few days thereafter his servant, smitten in conscience, came to him and confessed that on their journey from Rome he had carelessly lost the true relics, and had replaced them with common bones. This intelligence was somewhat disconcerting to Radziwill, but greatly more so to the friars, seeing it speedily led to the disclosure of the imposture. The pretended demoniac confessed that he had simply been playing a part, and the monks likewise were constrained to acknowledge their share in the pious fraud. Great scandal arose; the clergy bewailed the day the Pope's box had crossed the Alps; and Christopher Radziwill, receiving from the relics a virtue he had not anticipated, was led to the perusal of the Scriptures, and finally embraced, with his whole family, the Protestant faith. When his great relative, Prince Radziwill, died in 1565, Christopher came forward, and to some extent supplied his loss to the Protestant cause.

The king, still pursuing a middle course, solicited from the Pope, Paul IV., a Reformation which he might have had to better effect from his Protestant clergy, if only he would have permitted them to meet and begin the work. Sigismund Augustus addressed a letter to the Pontiff at the Council of Trent, demanding the five following things:—1st, the performance of mass in the Polish tongue; 2ndly, Communion in both kinds; 3rdly, the marriage of priests; 4thly, the abolition of annats; 5thly, the convocation of a National Council for the reform of abuses, and the reconcilement of the various opinions. The effect of these demands on Paul IV. was to irritate this very haughty Pontiff; he fell into a fume, and expressed in animated terms his amazement at the arrogance of his Majesty of Poland; but gradually cooling down, he declined civilly, as might have been foreseen, demands which, though they did not amount to a very great deal, were more than Rome could safely grant.[3012]

This rebuff taught the Protestants, if not the king, that from the Seven Hills no help would come—that their trust must be in themselves; and they grew bolder every day. In the Diet of Piotrkow, 1559, an attempt was made to deprive the bishops of their seats in the Senate, on the ground that their oath of obedience to the Pope was wholly irreconcilable to and subversive of their allegiance to their sovereign, and their duty to the nation. The oath was read and commented on, and the senator who made the motion concluded his speech in support of it by saying that if the bishops kept their oath of spiritual obedience, they must necessarily violate their vow of temporal allegiance; and if they were faithful subjects of the Pope, they must necessarily be traitors to their king.[3013] The motion was not carried, probably because the vague hope of a more sweeping measure of reform still kept possession of the minds of men.

The next step of the Poles was in the direction of realising that hope. A Diet met in 1563, passed a resolution that a General Synod, in which all the religious bodies in Poland would be represented, should be assembled. The Primate of Poland, Archbishop Uchanski, who was known to be secretly inclined toward the Reformed doctrines, was favourable to the proposed Convocation. Had such a Council been convened, it might, as matters then stood, with the first nobles of the land, many of the great cities, and a large portion of the nation, all on the side of Protestantism, have had the most decisive effects on the Kingdom of Poland and its future destinies. "It would have upset," says Krasinski, "the dominion of Rome in Poland for ever."[3014] Rome saw the danger in all its extent, and sent one of her ablest diplomatists to cope with it. Cardinal Comendoni, who had given efficient aid to Queen Mary of England in 1553, in her attempted restoration of Popery, was straightway dispatched to employ his great abilities in arresting the triumph of Protestantism, and averting ruin from the Papacy in the Kingdom of Poland. The legate put forth all his dexterity and art in his important mission, and not without effect. He directed his main efforts to influence the mind of Sigismund Augustus. He drew with masterly hand a frightful picture of the revolts and seditions that were sure to follow such a Council as it was contemplated holding. The warring winds, once let loose, would never cease to rage till the vessel of the Polish State was driven on the rocks and shipwrecked. For every concession to the heretics and the blind mob, the king would have to part with as many rights of his own. His laws contemned, his throne in the dust, who then would lift him up and give him back his crown? Had he forgotten the Colloquy of Poissy, which the King of France, then a child, had been persuaded to permit to take place? What had that disputation proved but a trumpet of revolt, which had banished peace from France, not since to return? In that unhappy country, whose inhabitants were parted by bitter feuds and contending factions, whose fields were reddened by the sword of civil war, whose throne was being continually shaken by sedition and revolt, the king might see the picture of what Poland would become should he give his consent to the meeting of a Council, where all doctrines would be brought into question, and all things reformed without reference to the canons of the Church, and the authority of the Pope. Commendoni was a skilful limner; he made the king to hear the roar of the tempest which he foretold; Sigismund Augustus felt as if his throne were already rocking beneath him; the peace-loving monarch revoked the permission he had been on the point of giving; he would not permit the Council to convene.[3015]

If a National Council could not meet to essay the Reformation of the Church, might it not be possible, some influential persons now asked, for the three Protestant bodies in Poland to unite in one Church? Such a union would confer new strength on Protestantism, would remove the scandal offered by the dissensions of Protestants among themselves, and would enable them in the day of battle to unite their arms against the foe, and in the hour of peace to conjoin their labours in building up their Zion. The Protestant communions in Poland were—1st, the Bohemian; 2ndly, the Reformed or Calvinistic; and 3rdly, the Lutheran. Between the first and second there was entire agreement in point of doctrine; only inasmuch as the first pastors of the Bohemian Church had received ordination (1467) from a Waldensian superintendent, as we have previously narrated,[3016] the Bohemians had come to lay stress on this, as an order of succession peculiarly sacred. Between the second and third there was the important divergence on the subject of the Eucharist. The Lutheran doctrine of consubstantiation approached more nearly to the Roman doctrine of the mass than to the Reformed doctrine of the Lord's Supper. If change there had been since the days of Luther on the question of consubstantiation, it was in the direction of still greater rigidity and tenacity, accompanied with a growing intolerance toward the other branches of the great Protestant family, of which some melancholy proofs have come before us. How much the heart of John Alasco was set on healing these divisions, and how small a measure of success attended his efforts to do so, we have already seen. The project was again revived. The main opposition to it came from the Lutherans. The Bohemian Church now numbered upwards of 200 congregations in Moravia and Poland,[3017] but the Lutherans accused them of being heretical. Smarting from the reproach, and judging that to clear their orthodoxy would pave the way for union, the Bohemians submitted their Confession to the Protestant princes of Germany, and all the leading Reformers of Europe, including Peter Martyr and Bullinger at Zurich, and Calvin and Beza at Geneva. A unanimous verdict was returned that the Bohemian Confession was "conformable to the doctrines of the Gospel." This judgment silenced for a time the Lutheran attacks on the purity of the Bohemian creed; but this good understanding being once more disturbed, the Bohemian Church in 1568 sent a delegation to Wittemberg, to submit their Confession to the theological faculty of its university. Again their creed was fully approved of, and this judgment carrying great weight with the Lutherans, the attacks on the Bohemians from that time ceased, and the negotiations for union went prosperously forward.

At last the negotiations bore fruit. In 1569, the leading nobles of the three communions, having met together at the Diet of Lublin, resolved to take measures for the consummation of the union. They were the more incited to this by the hope that the king, who had so often expressed his desire to see the Protestant Churches of his realm become one, would thereafter declare himself on the side of Protestantism. It was resolved to hold a Synod or Conference of all three Churches, and the town of Sandomir was chosen as the place of meeting. The Synod met in the beginning of April, 1570, and was attended by the Protestant grandees and nobles of Poland, and by the ministers of the Bohemian, Reformed, and Lutheran Churches. After several days' discussion it was found that the assembly was of one heart and mind on all the fundamental doctrines of the Gospel; and an agreement, entitled "Act of the Religious Union between the Churches of Great and Little Poland, Russia, Lithuania, and Samogitia," was signed on the 14th of April, 1570.[3018]

The subscribers place on the front of their famous document their unanimity in "the doctrines about God, the Holy Trinity, the Incarnation of the Son of God, Justification, and other principal points of the Christian religion." To give effect to this unanimity they "enter into a mutual and sacred obligation to defend unanimously, and according to the injunctions of the Word of God, this their covenant in the true and pure religion of Christ, against the followers of the Roman Church, the sectaries, as well as all the enemies of the truth and Gospel."

On the vexed question of the Sacrament of the Lord's Supper, the United Church agreed to declare that "the elements are not only elements or vain symbols, but are sufficient to believers, and impart by faith what they signify." And in order to express themselves with still greater clearness, they agreed to confess that "the substantial presence of Christ is not only signified but really represented in the Communion to those that receive it, and that the body and blood of our Lord are really distributed and given with the symbols of the thing itself; which according to the nature of Sacraments are by no means bare signs."

"But that no disputes," they add, "should originate from a difference of expressions, it has been resolved to add to the articles inserted into our Confession, the article of the Confession of the Saxon Churches, relating to the Lord's Supper, which was sent in 1551 to the Council of Trent, and which we acknowledge as pious, and do receive. Its expressions are as follows: 'Baptism and the Lord's Supper are signs and testimonies of grace, as it has been said before, which remind us of the promise and of the redemption, and show that the benefits of the Gospel belong to all those that make use of these rites. . . . In the established use of the Communion, Christ is substantially present, and the body and blood of Christ are truly given to those who receive the Communion.'"[3019]

There follows a long and brilliant list of palatines, nobles, superintendents, pastors, elders, and deacons belonging to all the three communions, who, forgetting the party-questions that had divided them, gathered round this one standard, and giving their hands to one another, and lifting them up to heaven, vowed henceforward to be one and to contend only against the common foe. This was one of the triumphs of Protestantism. Its spirit now gloriously prevailed over the pride of church, the rivalry of party, and the narrowness of bigotry, and in this victory gave an augury—alas! never to be fulfilled—of a yet greater triumph in days to come, by which this was to be completed and crowned.

Three years later (1573) a great Protestant Convocation was held at Cracow. It was presided over by John Firley, Grand Marshal of Poland, a leading member of the Calvinistic communion, and the most influential grandee of the kingdom. The regulations enacted by this Synod sufficiently show the goal at which it was anxious to arrive. It aimed at reforming the nation in life as well as in creed. It forbade "all kinds of wickedness and luxury, accursed gluttony and inebriety." It prohibited lewd dances, games of chance, profane oaths, and night assemblages in taverns. It enjoined landowners to treat their peasants with "Christian charity and humanity," to exact of them no oppressive labour or heavy taxes, to permit no markets or fairs to be held upon their estates on Sunday, and to demand no service of their peasants on that day. A Protestant creed was but the means for creating a virtuous and Christian people.

There is no era like this, before or since, in the annals of Poland. Protestantism had reached its acme in that country. Its churches numbered upwards of 2,000. They were at peace and flourishing. Their membership included the first dignitaries of the crown and the first nobles of the land. In some parts Romanism almost entirely disappeared. Schools were planted throughout the country, and education flourished. The Scriptures were translated into the tongue of the people, the reading of them was encouraged as the most efficient weapon against the attacks of Rome. Latin was already common, but now Greek and Hebrew began to be studied, that direct access might be had to the Divine fountains of truth and salvation. The national intellect, invigorated by Protestant truth, began to expatiate in fields that had been neglected hitherto. The printing-press, which rusts unused where Popery dominates, was vigorously wrought, and sent forth works on science, jurisprudence, theology, and general literature. This was the Augustan era of letters in Poland. The toleration which was so freely accorded in that country drew thither crowds of refugees, whom persecution had driven from their homes, and who, carrying with them the arts and manufactures of their own lands, enriched Poland with a material prosperity which, added to the political power and literary glow that already encompassed her, raised her to a high pitch of greatness.

CHAPTER IV
ORGANISATION OF THE PROTESTANT CHURCH OF POLAND

THE short-lived golden age of Poland was now waning into the silver one. But before recording the slow gathering of the shadows—the passing of the day into twilight, and the deepening of the twilight into night—we must cast a momentary glance, first, at the constitution of the Polish Protestant Church as seen at this period of her fullest development; and secondly, at certain political events, which bore with powerful effect upon the Protestant character of the nation, and sealed the fate of Poland as a free country.

In its imperfect unity we trace the absence of a master-hand in the construction of the Protestant Church of Poland. Had one great mind led in the Reformation of that country, one system of ecclesiastical government would doubtless from the first have been given to all Poland. As it was, the organisation of its Church at the beginning, and in a sense all throughout, differed in different provinces. Other causes, besides the want of a great leader, contributed to this diversity in respect of ecclesiastical government. The nobles were allowed to give what order they pleased to the Protestant churches which they erected on their lands, but the same liberty was not extended to the inhabitants of towns, and hence the very considerable diversity in the ecclesiastical arrangements. This diversity was still farther increased by the circumstance that not one, but three Confessions had gained ground in Poland—the Bohemian, the Genevan, and the Lutheran. The necessity of a more perfect organisation soon came to be felt, and repeated attempts were made at successive Synods to unify the Church's government. A great step was taken in this direction at the Synod of Kosmin, in 1555, when a union was concluded between the Bohemian and Genevan Confessions; and a still greater advance was made in 1570, as we have narrated in the preceding chapter, when at the Synod of Sandomir the three Protestant Churches of Poland—the Bohemian, the Genevan, and the Lutheran—agreed to merge all their Confessions in one creed, and combine their several organisations in one government.

But even this was only an approximation, not a full and complete attainment of the object aimed at. All Poland was not yet ruled spiritually from one ecclesiastical centre; for the three great political divisions of the country—Great Poland, Little Poland, and Lithuania—had each its independent ecclesiastical establishment, by which all its religious affairs were regulated. Nevertheless, at intervals, or when some matter of great moment arose, all the pastors of the kingdom came together in Synod, thus presenting a grand Convocation of all the Protestant Churches of Poland.

Despite this tri-partition in the ecclesiastical authority, one form of Church government was now extended all over Poland. That form was a modified episcopacy. If any one man was entitled to be styled the Father of the Polish Protestant Church it was John Alasco, and the organisation which he gave to the Reformed Church of his native land was not unlike that of England, of which he was a great admirer. Poland was on a great scale what the foreign Church over which John Alasco presided in London was on a small. First came the Superintendent, for Alasco preferred that term, though the more learned one of *Senior Primarius* was sometimes used to designate this dignitary. The Superintendent, or *Senior Primarius*, corresponded somewhat in rank and powers to an archbishop. He convoked Synods, presided in them, and executed their sentences; but he had no judicial authority, and was subject to the Synod, which could judge, admonish, and depose him.[3021]

Over the Churches of a district a Sub-Superintendent, or Senior, presided. The Senior corresponded to a bishop. He took the place of the Superintendent in his absence; he convoked the Synods of the district, and possessed a certain limited jurisdiction, though exclusively spiritual. The other ecclesiastical functionaries were the Minister, the Deacon, and the Lecturer. The Polish Protestants eschewed the fashion and order of the Roman hierarchy, and strove to reproduce as far as the circumstances of their times would allow, or as they themselves were able to trace it, the model exhibited by the primitive Church.

Besides the Clerical Senior each district had a Civil Senior, who was elected exclusively by the nobles and landowners. His duties about the Church were mainly of an external nature. All things appertaining to faith and doctrine were left entirely in the hands of the ministers; but the Civil Senior took cognisance of the morals of ministers, and in certain cases could forbid them the exercise of their functions till he had reported the case to the Synod, as the supreme authority of the Church. The support and general welfare of churches and schools were entrusted to the Civil Senior, who, moreover, acted as the advocate for the Church before the authorities of the country.

The supreme authority in the Polish Protestant Church was neither the Superintendent nor the Civil Senior, but the Synod. Four times every year a Local Synod, composed not of ministers only, but of all the members of the congregations, was convened in each district. Although the members sat along with the pastors, all questions of faith and doctrine were left to be determined exclusively by the latter. Once a year a Provincial Synod was held, in which each district was represented by a Clerical Senior, two Con-Seniors, or assistants, and four Civil Seniors; thus giving a slight predominance to the lay element in the Synod. Nevertheless, ministers, although not delegated by the Local Synods, could sit and vote on equal terms with others in the Provincial Synod.

The Grand Synod of the nation, or Convocation of the Polish Church, met at no stated times. It assembled only when the emergence of some great question called for its decision. These great gatherings, of course, could take place only so long as the Union of Sandomir, which bound in one Church all the Protestant Confessions of Poland, existed, and that unhappily was only from 1570 to 1595. After the expiry of these twenty-five years those great national gatherings, which had so impressively attested the strength and grandeur of Protestantism in Poland, were seen no more. Such in outline was the constitution and government of the Protestant Church of Poland. It wanted only two things to make it complete and perfect—namely, one supreme court, or centre of authority, with a jurisdiction covering the whole country; and a permanent body or "Board," having its seat in the capital, through which the Church might take instant action when great difficulties called for united councils, or sudden dangers necessitated united arms. The meetings of the Grand Synods were intermittent and irregular, whereas their enemies never failed to maintain union among themselves, and never ceased their attacks upon the Protestant Church.

We must now turn to the course of political affairs subsequent to the death of king Sigismund Augustus, of which, however, we shall treat only so far as they grow out of Protestantism, and exerted a reflex influence upon it. The amiably enlightened, and tolerant monarch, Sigismund Augustus, so often almost persuaded to be a Protestant, and one day, as his courtiers fully hoped, to become one in reality, went to his grave in 1572, without having come to any decision, and without leaving any issue. The Protestants were naturally desirous of placing a Protestant upon the throne; but the intrigues of Cardinal Comendoni, and the jealousy of the Lutherans against the Reformed, which the Union of Sandomir had not entirely extinguished, rendered all efforts toward this effect in vain. Meanwhile Coligny, whom the Peace of St. Germains had restored to the court of Paris, and for the moment to influence, came forward with the proposal of placing a French prince upon the throne of Poland. The admiral was revolving a gigantic scheme for humbling Romanism, and its great champion, Spain. He meditated bringing together in a political and religious alliance the two great countries of Poland and France, and Protestantism once triumphant in both, an issue which to Coligny seemed to be near, the united arms of the two countries would soon put an end to the dominancy of Rome, and lay in the dust the overgrown power of Austria and Spain. Catherine de Medici, who saw in the project a new aggrandisement to her family, warmly favoured it; and Montluc, Bishop of Valence, was dispatched to Poland, furnished with ample instructions from Coligny to prosecute the election of Henry of Valois, Duke of Anjou. Montluc had hardly crossed the frontier when the St. Bartholomew was struck and among the many victims of that dreadful act was the author of that very scheme which Montluc was on his way to advocate and, if possible, consummate. The bishop, on receiving the terrible news, thought it useless to continue his journey; but Catherine, feeling the necessity of following the line of foreign policy which had been originated by the man she had murdered, sent orders to Montluc to go forward. The ambassador had immense difficulties to overcome in the prosecution of his mission, for the massacre had inspired universal horror, but by dint of stoutly denying the Duke of Anjou's participation in the crime, and promising that the duke would subscribe every guarantee of political and religious liberty which might be required of him, he finally carried his object. Firley, the leader of the Protestants, drafted a list of privileges which Anjou was to grant to the Protestants of Poland, and of concessions which Charles IX. was to make to the Protestants of France; and Montluc was required to sign these, or see the rejection of his candidate. The ambassador promised for the monarch.

Henry of Valois having been chosen, four ambassadors set out from Poland with the diploma of election, which was presented to the duke on the 10th September, 1573, in Notre Dame, Paris. A Romish bishop, and member of the embassy, entered a protest, at the beginning of the ceremonial, against that clause in the oath which secured religious liberty, and which the duke was now to swear. Some confusion followed. The Protestant Zborowski, interrupting the proceedings, addressed Montluc thus:— "Had you not accepted, in the name of the duke, these conditions, we should not have elected him as our monarch." Henry feigned not to understand the subject of the dispute, but Zborowski, advancing towards him, said— "I repeat, sire, if your ambassador had not accepted the condition securing religious liberty to us Protestants, we would not have elected you to be our king, and if you do not confirm these conditions you shall not be our king." Thereupon Henry took the oath. When he had sworn, Bishop Karnkowski, who had protested against the religious liberty promised in the oath, stepped forward, and again protested that the clause should not prejudice the authority of the Church of Rome, and he received from the king a written declaration to the effect that it would not.[3022]

Although the sovereign-elect had confirmed by oath the religious liberties of Poland, the suspicions of the Protestants were not entirely allayed, and they resolved jealously to watch the proceedings at the coronation. Their distrust was not without cause. Cardinal Hosius, who had now begun to exercise vast influence on the affairs of Poland, reasoned that the oath that Henry had taken in Paris was not binding, and he sent his secretary to meet the new monarch on the road to his new dominions, and to assure him that he did not even need absolution from what he had sworn, seeing what was unlawful was not binding, and that so soon as he should be crowned, he might proceed, the oath notwithstanding, to drive from his kingdom all religions contrary to that of Rome.[3023] The bishops began to teach the same doctrine and to instruct Henry, who was approaching Poland by slow stages, that he would mount the throne as an absolute sovereign, and reign wholly unfettered and uncontrolled by either the oath of Paris or the Polish Diet. The kingdom was in dismay and alarm; the Protestants talked of annulling the election, and refusing to accept Henry as their sovereign. Poland was on the brink of civil war.

At the coronation a new treachery was attempted. Tutored by Jesuitical councillors, Henry proposed to assume the crown, but to evade the oath. The ceremonial was proceeding, intently watched by both Protestants and Romanists. The final act was about to be performed; the crown was to be placed on the head of the new sovereign; but the oath guaranteeing the Protestant liberties had not been administered to him. Firley, the Grand Marshal of Poland, and first grandee of the kingdom, stood forth, and stopping the proceedings, declared that unless the Duke of Anjou should repeat the oath which he had sworn at Paris, he would not allow the coronation to take place. Henry was kneeling on the steps of the altar, but startled by the words, he rose up, and looking round him, seemed to hesitate. Firley, seizing the crown, said in a firm voice, "Si non jurabis, non regnabis" (If you will not swear, you shall not reign). The courtiers and spectators were mute with astonishment. The king was awed; he read in the crest-fallen countenances of his advisers that he had but one alternative—the oath, or an ignominious return to France. It was too soon to go back; the took the copy of the oath which was handed to him, swore, and was crowned.

The courageous act of the Protestant grand marshal had dispelled the cloud of civil war that hung above the nation. But it was only for a moment that confidence was restored. The first act of the new sovereign had revealed him to his subjects as both treacherous and cowardly; what trust could they repose in him, and what affection could they feel for him? Henry took into exclusive favour the Popish bishops; and, emboldened by a patronage unknown to them during former reigns, they boldly declared the designs they had long harboured, but which they had hitherto only whispered to their most trusted confidants. The great Protestant nobles were discountenanced and discredited. The king's shameless profligacies consummated the discontent and disgust of the nation. The patriotic Firley was dead—it was believed in many quarters that he had been poisoned—and civil war was again on the point of breaking out when, fortunately for the unhappy country, the flight of the monarch saved it from that great calamity. His brother, Charles IX., had died, and Anjou took his secret and quick departure to succeed him on the throne of France.

CHAPTER V
TURNING OF THE TIDE OF PROTESTANTISM IN POLAND

AFTER a year's interregnum, Stephen Bathory, a Transylvanian prince, who had married Anne Jagellon, one of the sisters of the Emperor Sigismund Augustus, was elected to the crown of Poland. His worth was so great, and his popularity so high, that although a Protestant the Roman clergy dared not oppose his election. The Protestant nobles thought that now their cause was gained; but the Romanists did not despair. Along with the delegates commissioned to announce his election to Bathory, they sent a prelate of eminent talent and learning, Solikowski by name, to conduct their intrigue of bringing the new king over to their side. The Protestant deputies, guessing Solikowski's errand, were careful to give him no opportunity of conversing with the new sovereign in private. But, eluding their vigilance, he obtained an interview by night, and succeeded in persuading Bathory that he should never be able to maintain himself on the throne of Poland unless he made a public confession of the Roman faith. The Protestant deputies, to their dismay, next morning beheld Stephen Bathory, in whom they had placed their hopes of triumph, devoutly kneeling at mass.[3024] The new reign had opened with no auspicious omen!

Nevertheless, although a pervert, Bathory did not become a zealot. He repressed all attempts at persecution, and tried to hold the balance with tolerable impartiality between the two parties. But he sowed seeds destined to yield tempests in the future. The Jesuits, as we shall afterwards see, had already entered Poland, and as the Fathers were able to persuade the king that they were the zealous cultivators and the most efficient teachers of science and letters, Bathory, who was a patron of literature, took them under his patronage, and built colleges and seminaries for their use, endowing them with lands and heritages. Among other institutions he founded the University of Vilna, which became the chief seat of the Fathers in Poland, and whence they spread themselves over the kingdom.[3025]

It was during the reign of King Stephen that the tide began to turn in the fortunes of this great, intelligent, and free nation. The ebb first showed itself in a piece of subtle legislation which was achieved by the Roman Synod of Piotrkow, in 1577. That Synod decreed excommunication against all who held the doctrine of religious toleration.[3026] But toleration of all religions was one of the fundamental laws of the kingdom, and the enactment of the Synod was levelled against this law. True, they could not blot out the law of the State, nor could they compel the tribunals of the nation to enforce their own ecclesiastical edict; nevertheless their sentence, though spiritual in its form, was very decidedly temporal in both its substance and its issues, seeing excommunication carried with it many grievous civil and social inflictions. This legislation was the commencement of a stealthy policy which had for its object the recovery of that temporal jurisdiction of which, as we have seen, the Diet had stripped them.

This first encroachment being permitted to pass unchallenged, the Roman clergy ventured on other and more violent attacks on the laws of the State, and the liberties of the people. The Synods of the diocese of Warmis prohibited mixed marriages; they forbade Romanists to be sponsors at the baptism of Protestant children; they interdicted the use of books and hymns not sanctioned by ecclesiastical authority; and they declared heretics incapable of inheriting landed property. All these enactments wore a spiritual guise, and they could be enforced only by spiritual sanctions; but they were in antagonism to the law of the land, and by implication branded the laws with which they conflicted as immoral; they tended to widen the breach between the two great parties in the nation, and they disturbed the consciences of Romanists, by subjecting them to the alternative of incurring certain disagreeable consequences, or of doing what they were taught was unlawful and sinful.

Stretching their powers and prerogatives still farther, the Roman bishops now claimed payment of their tithes from Protestant landlords, and attempted to take back the churches which had been converted from Romanist to Protestant uses. To make trial of how far the nation was disposed to yield to these demands, or the tribunals prepared to endorse them, they entered pleas at law to have the goods and possessions which they claimed as theirs adjudged to them, and in some instances the courts gave decisions in their favour. But the hierarchy had gone farther than meanwhile was prudent. These arrogant demands roused the alarm of the nobles; and the Diets of 1581 and 1582 administered a tacit rebuke to the hierarchy by annulling the judgments which had been pronounced in their favour. The bishops had learned that they must walk slowly if they would walk safely; but they had met with nothing to convince them that their course was not the right one, or that it would not succeed in the end.

Nevertheless, under the appearance of having suffered a rebuff, the hierarchy had gained not a few substantial advantages. The more extreme of their demands had been disallowed, and many thought that the contest between them and the civil courts was at an end, and that it had ended adversely to the spiritual authority; but the bishops knew better. They had laid the foundation of what would grow with every successive Synod, and each new edict, into a body of law, diverse from and in opposition to the law of the land, and which presenting itself to the Romanist with a higher moral sanction, would ultimately, in his eyes, deprive the civil law of all force, and transfer to itself the homage of his conscience and the obedience of his life. The coercive power wielded by this new code, which was being stealthily put in operation in the heart of the Polish State, was a power that could neither be seen nor heard; and those who were accustomed to execute their behests through the force of armies, or the majesty of tribunals, were apt to contemn it as utterly unable to cope with the power of law; nevertheless, the result as wrought out in Poland showed that this influence, apparently so weak, yet penetrating deeply into the heart and soul, had in it an omnipotence compared with which the power of the sword was but feebleness. And farther there was this danger, perhaps not foreseen or not much taken into account in Poland at the moment, namely, that the Jesuits were busy manipulating the youth, and that whenever public opinion should be ripe for a concordat between the bishops and the government, this spiritual code would start up into an undisguisedly temporal one, having at its service all the powers of the State, and enforcing its commands with the sword.

What was now introduced into Poland was a new and more refined policy than the Church of Rome had yet employed in her battles with Protestantism. Hitherto she had filled her hand with the coarse weapons of material force—the armies of the Empire and the stakes of the Inquisition. But now, appealing less to the bodily senses, and more to the faculties of the soul, she began at Trent, and continued in Poland, the plan of creating a body of legislation, the pseudo-divine sanctions of which, in many instances, received submission where the terrors of punishment would have been withstood. The sons of Loyola came first, moulding opinion; and the bishops came after, framing canons in conformity with that altered opinion—gathering where the others had strewed—and noiselessly achieving victory where the swords of their soldiers would have but sustained defeat. No doubt the liberty enjoyed in Poland necessitated this alteration of the Roman tactics; but it was soon seen that it was a more effectual method than the vulgar weapons of force, and that if a revolted Christendom was to be brought back to the Papal obedience, it must be mainly, though not exclusively, by the means of this spiritual artillery.

It was under the same reign, that of Stephen Bathory, that the political influence of the Kingdom of Poland began to wane. The ebb in its national prestige was almost immediately consequent on the ebb in its Protestantism. The victorious wars which Bathory had carried on with Russia were ended, mainly through the counsels of the Jesuit Possevinus, by a peace which stripped Poland of the advantages she was entitled to expect from her victories. This was the last gleam of military success that shone upon the country. Stephen Bathory died in 1586, having reigned ten years, not without glory, and was succeeded on the throne by Sigismund III. He was the son of John, King of Sweden, and grandson of the renowned Gustavus Vasa. Nurtured by a Romish mother, Sigismund III. had abandoned the faith of his famous ancestor, and during his long reign of well-nigh half a century, he made the grandeur of Rome his first object, and the power of Poland only his second. Under such a prince the fortunes of the nation continued to sink. He was called "the King of the Jesuits," and so far was he from being ashamed of the title, that he gloried in it, and strove to prove himself worthy of it. He surrounded himself with Jesuit councillors; honours and riches he showered almost exclusively upon Romanists, and especially upon those whom interest had converted, but argument left unconvinced. No dignity of the State and no post in the public service was to be obtained, unless the aspirant made friends of the Fathers. Their colleges and schools multiplied, their hoards and territorial domains augmented from year to year. The education of the youth, and especially the sons of the nobles, was almost wholly in their hands, and a generation was being created brimful of that "loyalty" which Rome so highly lauds, and which makes the understandings of her subjects so obdurate and their necks so supple. The Protestants were as yet too powerful in Poland to permit of direct persecution, but the way was being prepared in the continual decrease of their numbers, and the systematic diminution of their influence; and when Sigismund III. went to his grave in 1632, the glory which had illuminated the country during the short reign of Stephen Bathory had departed, and the night was fast closing in around Poland.

CHAPTER VI
THE JESUITS ENTER POLAND—DESTRUCTION OF ITS PROTESTANTISM

*T*HE Jesuits had been introduced into Poland, and the turning of the Protestant tide, and the begun decadence of the nation's political power, which was almost contemporaneous with the retrogression in its Protestantism, was mainly the work of the Fathers. The man who opened the door to the disciples of Loyola in that country is worthy of a longer study than we can bestow upon him. His name was Stanislaus Hosen, better known as Cardinal Hosius. He was born at Cracow in 1504, and thus in birth was nearly contemporaneous with Knox and Calvin. He was sprung of a family of German descent which had been engaged in trade, and become rich. His great natural powers had been perfected by a finished education, first in the schools of his own country, and afterwards in the Italian universities. He was unwearied in his application to business, often dictating to several secretaries at once, and not unfrequently dispatching important matters at meals. He was at home in the controversial literature of the Reformation, and knew how to employ in his own cause the arguments of one Protestant polemic against another. He took care to inform himself of everything about the life and occupation of the leading Reformers, his contemporaries, which it was important for him to know. His works are numerous; they are in various languages, written with equal elegance in all, and with a wonderful adaptation in their style and method to the genius and habit of thought of each of the various peoples he addressed. The one grand object of his life was the overthrow of Protestantism, and the restoration of the Roman Church to that place of power and glory from which the Reformation had cast her down. He brought the concentrated forces of a vast knowledge, a gigantic intellect, and a strong will to the execution of that task. History has not recorded, so far as we are aware, any immorality in his life. He could boast the refined manners, liberal sentiments, and humane disposition which the love and cultivation of letters usually engender. Nevertheless the marvellous and mysterious power of that system of which he was so distinguished a champion asserted its superiority in the case of this richly endowed, highly cultivated, and noble-minded man. Instead of imparting his virtues to his Church, she transferred her vices to him. Hosius always urged on fitting occasions that no faith should be kept with heretics, and although few could better conduct an argument than himself, he disliked that tedious process with heretics, and recommended the more summary one of the lictor's axe. He saw no sin in spilling heretical blood; he received with joy the tidings of the St. Bartholomew Massacre, and writing to congratulate the Cardinal of Lorraine on the slaughter of Coligny, he thanked the Almighty for the great boon bestowed on France, and implored him to show equal mercy to Poland. His great understanding he prostrated at the feet of his Church, but for whose authority, he declared, the Scriptures would have no more weight than the Fables of Æsop. His many acquirements and great learning were not able to emancipate him from the thrall of a gloomy asceticism; he grovelled in the observance of the most austere performances, scourging himself in the belief that to have his body streaming with blood and covered with wounds was more pleasing to the Almighty than to have his soul adorned with virtues and replenished with graces. Such was the man who, to use the words of the historian Krasinski, "deserved the eternal gratitude of Rome and the curses of his own country," by introducing the Jesuits into Poland.[3027]

Returning from the Council of Trent in 1564, Hosius saw with alarm the advance which Protestantism had made in his diocese during his absence. He immediately addressed himself to the general of the society, Lainez, requesting him to send him some members of his order to aid him in doing what he despaired of accomplishing by his own single arm. A few of the Fathers were dispatched from Rome, and being joined by others from Germany, they were located in Braunsberg, a little town in the diocese of Hosius, who richly endowed the infant establishment. For six years they made little progress, nor was it till the death of Sigismund Augustus and the accession of Stephen Bathory that they began to make their influence felt in Poland. How they ingratiated themselves with that monarch by their vast pretensions to learning we have already seen. They became great favourites with the bishops, who finding Protestantism increasing in their dioceses, looked for its repression rather from the intrigues of the Fathers than the labours of their own clergy. But the golden age of the Jesuits in Poland, to be followed by the iron age to the people, did not begin until the bigoted Sigismund III. mounted the throne. The favours of Stephen Bathory, the colleges he had founded, and the lands with which he had endowed them, were not remembered in comparison with the far higher consideration and vaster wealth to which they were admitted under his successor. Sigismund reigned, but the Jesuits governed. They stood by the fountain-head of honours, and they held the keys of all dignities and emoluments. They took care of their friends in the distribution of these good things, nor did they forget when enriching others to enrich also themselves. Conversions were numerous; and the wanderer who had returned from the fatal path of heresy to the safe fold of the Church was taught to express his thanks in some gift or service to the order by whose instructions and prayers he had been rescued. The son of a Protestant father commonly expressed his penitence by building them a college, or bequeathing them an estate, or expelling from his lands the confessors of his father's faith, and replacing them with the adherents of the Roman creed. Thus all things were prospering to their wish. Every day new doors were opening to them. Their missions and schools were springing up in all corners of the land. They entered all houses, from the baron's downward; they sat at all tables, and listened to all conversations. In all assemblies, for whatever purpose convened, whether met to mourn or to make merry, to transact business or to seek amusement, there were the Jesuits. They were present at baptisms, at marriages, at funerals, and at fairs. While their learned men taught the young nobles in the universities, they had their itinerant orators, who visited villages, frequented markets, and erecting their stage in public exhibited scenic representations of Bible histories, or of the combats, martyrdoms, and canonisations of the saints. These wandering apostles were furnished, moreover, with store of relics and wonder-working charms, and by these as well as by pompous processions, they edified and awed the crowds that gathered round them.

They strenuously and systematically laboured to destroy the influence of

Protestant ministers. They strove to make them odious, sometimes by malevolent whisperings, and at other times by open accusation. The most blameless life and the most venerated character afforded no protection against Jesuit calumny. Volanus, whose ninety years bore witness to his abstemious life, they called a drunkard. Sdrowski, who had incurred their anger by a work written against them, and whose learning was not excelled by the most erudite of their order, they accused of theft, and of having once acted the part of a hangman. Adding ridicule to calumny, they strove in every way to hold up Protestant sermons and assemblies to laughter. If a Synod convened, there was sure to appear, in no long time, a letter from the devil, addressed to the members of court, thanking them for their zeal, and instructing them, in familiar and loving phrase, how to do their work and his. Did a minister marry, straightway he was complimented with an epithalamium from the ready pen of some Jesuit scribe. Did a Protestant pastor die, before a few days had passed by, the leading members of his flock were favoured with letters from their deceased minister, duly dated from Pandemonium. These effusions were composed generally in doggerel verse, but they were barbed with a venemous wit and a coarse humour. The multitude read, laughed, and believed. The calumnies, it is true, were refuted by those at whom they were levelled; but that signified little, the falsehood was repeated again and again, till at last, by dint of perseverance and audacity, the Protestants and their worship were brought into general hatred and contempt.[3028]

The defection of the sons of Radziwill, the zealous Reformer of whom we have previously made mention, was a great blow to the Protestantism of Poland. That family became the chief support, after the crown, of the Papal reaction in the Polish dominions. Not only were their influence and wealth freely employed for the spread of the Jesuits, but all the Protestant churches and schools which their father had built on his estates were made over to the Church of Rome. The example of the Radziwills was followed by many of the Lithuanian nobles, who returned within the Roman pale, bringing with them not only the edifices on their lands formerly used in the Protestant service, but their tenants also, and expelling those who refused to conform.

By this time the populace had been sufficiently leavened with the spirit and principles of the Jesuits to be made their tool. Mob violence is commonly the first form that persecution assumes. It was so in Poland. The caves whence these popular tempests issued were the Jesuit colleges. The students inflamed the passions of the multitude, and the public peace was broken by tumult and outrage. Protestant worshipping assemblies began to be assailed and dispersed, Protestant churches to be wrecked, and Protestant libraries to be given to the flames. The churches of Cracow, of Vilna, and other towns were pillaged. Protestant cemeteries were violated, their monuments and tablets destroyed, the dead exhumed, and their remains scattered about. It was not possible at times to carry the Protestant dead to their graves. In June, 1578, the funeral procession of a Protestant lady was attacked in the streets of Cracow by the pupils of All-hallows College. Stones were thrown, the attendants were driven away, the body was torn from the coffin, and after being dragged through the streets it was thrown into the Vistula. Rarely indeed did the authorities interfere; and when it did happen that punishment followed these misdeeds, the infliction fell on the wretched tools, and the guiltier instigators and ringleaders were suffered to escape.[3029]

While the Jesuits were smiting the Protestant ministers and members with the arm of the mob, they were bowing the knee in adulation and flattery before the Protestant nobles and gentry. In the saloons of the great, the same men who sowed from their chairs the principles of sedition and tumult, or vented in doggerel rhyme the odious calumny, were transformed into paragons of mildness and inoffensiveness. Oh, how they loved order, abominated coarseness, and anathematised all uncharitableness and violence! Having gained access into Protestant families of rank by their winning manners, their showy accomplishments, and sometimes by important services, they strove by every means—by argument, by wit, by insinuation—to convert them to the Roman faith; if they failed to pervert the entire family they generally succeeded with one or more of its members. Thus they established a foothold in the household, and had fatally broken the peace and confidence of the family. The anguish of the perverts for their parents, doomed as they believed to perdition, often so affected these parents as to induce them to follow their children into the Roman fold. Rome, as is well known, has made more victories by touching the heart than by convincing the reason.

But the main arm with which the Jesuits operated in Poland was the school. They had among them a few men of good talent and great erudition. At the beginning they were at pains to teach well, and to send forth from their seminaries accomplished Latin scholars, that so they might establish a reputation for efficient teaching, and spread their educational institutions over the kingdom. They were kind to their pupils, they gave their instructions without exacting any fee; and they were thus able to compete at great advantage with the Protestant schools, and not unfrequently did they succeed in extinguishing their rivals, and drafting the scholars into their own seminaries. Not only so: many Protestant parents, attracted by the high repute of the Jesuit schools, and the brilliant Latin scholars whom they sent forth from time to time, sent their sons to be educated in the institutions of the Fathers.

But the national mind did not grow, nor did the national literature flourish. This was the more remarkable from contrast with the brilliance of the era that had preceded the educational efforts of the Jesuits. The half-century during which the Protestant influence was the predominating one was "the Augustan age of Polish literature;" the half-century that followed, dating from the close of the sixteenth century, showed a marked and most melancholy decadence in every department of mental exertion. It was but too obvious that decrepitude had smitten the national intellect. The press sent forth scarcely a single work of merit; capable men were disappearing from professional life; Poland ceased to have statesmen fitted to counsel in the cabinet, or soldiers able to lead in the field. The sciences were neglected and the arts languished; and even the very language was becoming corrupt and feeble; its elegance and fire were sinking in the ashes of formalism and barbarism. Nor is it difficult to account for this. Without freedom there can be no vigour; but the Jesuits dared not leave the mind of their pupils at liberty. That the intellect should make full proof of its powers by rang-ing freely over all subjects, and investigating and discussing unfettered all questions, was what the Jesuits could not allow, well knowing that such freedom would overthrow their own authority. They led about the mind in chains as men do wild beasts, of whom they fear that should they slip their fetters, they would turn and rend them. The art they studied was not how to educate, but how *not* to educate. They intrigued to shut up the Protestant schools, and when they had succeeded, they collected the youth into their own, that they might keep them out of the way of that most dangerous of all things, knowledge. They taught them words, not things. They shut the page of history, they barred the avenues of science and philosophy, and they drilled their pupils exclusively in the subtleties of a scholastic theology. Is it wonderful that the eye kept perpetually poring on such objects should at last lose its power of vision; that the intellect confined to food like this should pine and die; and that the foot-prints of Poland ceased to be visible in the fields of literature, in the world of commerce, and on the arena of politics? The men who had taken in hand to educate the nation, taught it to forget all that other men strive to remember, and to remember all that other men strive to forget; in short, the education given to Poland by the Jesuits was a most ingenious and successful plan of teaching them not how to think right, but how to think wrong; not how to reason out truth, but how to reason out falsehood; not how to cast away prejudice, break the shackles of authority, and rise to the independence and noble freedom of a rational being, but how to cleave to error, hug one's fetters, hoot at the light, and yet to be all the while filled with a proud conceit that this darkness is not darkness, but light; and this folly not folly, but wisdom. Thus metamorphosed this once noble nation came forth from the schools of the Jesuits, the light of their eye quenched, and the strength of their arm dried up, to find that they were no longer able to keep their place in the struggles of the world. They were put aside, they were split up, they were trampled down, and at last they perished as a nation; and yet their remains were not put into the sepulchre, but were left lying on the face of Europe, a melancholy monument of what nations become when they take the Jesuit for their schoolmaster.

This estimate of Jesuit training is not more severe than that which Popish authors themselves have expressed. Their system was admirably described by Broscius, a zealous Roman Catholic clergyman, professor at the University of Cracow, and one of the most learned men of his time, in a work published originally in Polish, in the beginning of the seventeenth century. He says, "The Jesuits teach children the grammar of Alvar,[3030] which it is very difficult to understand, and to learn; and much time is spent at it. This they do for many reasons: first, that by keeping the child a long time in the school they may receive in gifts from the parents of the children, whom they pretend gratuitously to educate, much more than they would have got had there been a regular payment; second, that by keeping the children a long while in the school they may become well acquainted with their minds; third, that they may train the boy for their own plans, and for their own purposes; fourth, that in case the friends of the boy wish to have him from them, they may have a pretence for keeping him, saying, give him time at least to learn grammar, which is the foundation of every other knowledge; fifth, they want to keep the boys at school till the age of manhood, that they may engage for their order those who show most talent or expect large inheritances; but when an individual neither possesses talents nor has any expectations, they will not retain him."[3031]

Sigismund III., in whose reign the Jesuits had become firmly rooted in Poland, died in 1632, and was succeeded by his eldest son Vladislav IV. Vladislav hated the disciples of Loyola as much as his father had loved and courted them, and he strove to the utmost of his power to counteract the evil effects of his father's partiality for the order. He restrained the persecution by mob riots; he was able, in some instances, to visit with punishment the ringleaders in the burning down of Protestant churches and schools; but that spirit of intolerance and bigotry which was now diffused throughout the nation, and in which, with few exceptions, noble and peasant shared alike, he could not lay; and when he went to his grave, those bitter hatreds and evil passions which had been engendered during his father's long occupancy of the throne, and only slightly repressed during his own short reign, broke out afresh in all their violence.

Vladislav was succeeded by his brother John Casimir. Casimir was a member of the Society of Jesus, and had attained the dignity of the Roman purple; but when his brother's death opened his way to the throne, the Pope relieved him from his vows as a Jesuit. The heart of the Jesuit remained within him, though his vow to the order had been dissolved. Nevertheless, it is but justice to say that Casimir was less bigoted, and less the tool of Rome, than his father Sigismund had been. Still it was vain to hope that under such a monarch the prospects of the Protestants would be materially improved, or the tide of Popish reaction stemmed. Scarcely had this disciple of Loyola ascended the throne than those political tempests began, which continued at short intervals to burst over Poland, till at length the nation was destroyed. The first calamity that befell the unhappy country was a terrible revolt of the Cossacks of the Ukraine. The insurgent Cossacks were joined by crowds of peasants belonging to the Greek Church, whose passions had been roused by a recent attempt of the Polish bishops to compel them to enter the Communion of Rome. Poland now began to feel what it was to have her soul chilled and her bonds loosened by the touch of the Jesuit. If the insurrection did not end in the dethronement of the monarch, it was owing not to the valour of his troops, or to the patriotism of his nobles, but to the compassion or remorse of the rebels, who stopped short in their victorious career when the king was in their power, and the nation had been brought to the brink of ruin.

The cloud which had threatened the kingdom with destruction rolled away to the half-civilised regions whence it had so suddenly issued; but hardly was it gone when it was again seen to gather, and to advance against the unhappy kingdom. The perfidy of the Romish bishops had brought this second calamity upon Poland. The Archbishop of Kioff, Metropolitan of the Greek Church of Poland, had acted as mediator between the rebellious Cossacks and the king, and mainly through the archbishop's friendly offices had that peace been effected, which rescued from imminent peril the throne and life of Casimir. One of the conditions of the Pacification was that the archbishop should have a seat in the Senate; but when the day came, and the Eastern prelate entered the hall to take his place among the senators, the Roman Catholic bishops rose in a body and left the

Senate-house, saying that they never would sit with a schismatic. The Archbishop of Kioff had lifted Casimir's throne out of the dust, and now he had his services repaid with insult.

The warlike Cossacks held themselves affronted in the indignity done their spiritual chief; and hence the second invasion of the kingdom. This time the insurgents were defeated, but that only brought greater evils upon the country. The Cossacks threw themselves into the arms of the Czar of Muscovy. He espoused their quarrel, feeling, doubtless, that his honour was also involved in the disgrace put upon a high dignitary of his Church, and he descended on Poland with an immense army. At the same time, Charles Gustavus of Sweden, taking advantage of the discontent which prevailed against the Polish monarch Casimir, entered the kingdom with a chosen body of troops; and such were his own talents as a leader, and such the discipline and valour of his army, that in a short time the principal part of Poland was in his possession. Casimir had, meanwhile, sought refuge in Silesia. The crown was offered to the valorous and magnanimous Charles Gustavus, the nobles only craving that before assuming it he should permit a Diet to assemble and formally vote it to him.

Had Gustavus ascended the throne of Poland, it is probable that the Jesuits would have been driven out, that the Protestant spirit would have been reinvigorated, and that Poland, built up into a powerful kingdom, would have proved a protecting wall to the south and west of Europe against the barbaric masses of the north; but this hope, with all that it implied, was dispelled by the reply of Charles Gustavus. "It did not need," he said, "that the Diet should elect him king, seeing he was already master of the country by his sword." The self-love of the Poles was wounded; the war was renewed; and, after a great struggle, a peace was concluded in 1660, under the joint mediation and guarantee of England, France, and Holland. John Casimir returned to resume his reign over a country bleeding from the swords of two armies. The Cossacks had exercised an indiscriminate vengeance: the Popish cathedral and the Protestant church had alike been given to the flames, and Protestants and Papists had been equal sufferers in the calamities of the war.

The first act of the monarch, after his return, was to place his kingdom under the special protection of the "Blessed Virgin." To make himself and his dominions the more worthy of so august a suzerainty, he registered on the occasion two vows, both well-pleasing, as he judged, to his celestial patroness. Casimir promised in the first to redress the grievances of the lower orders, and in the second to convert the heretics—in other words, to persecute the Protestants. The first vow it was not even attempted to fulfill. All the efforts of the sovereign, therefore, were given to the second. But the shield of England and Holland was at that time extended over the Protestants of Poland, who were still numerous, and had amongst them some influential families; the monarch's efforts were, in consequence, restricted meanwhile to the conversion of the Socinians, who were numerous in his kingdom. They were offered the alternative of return to the Roman Church or exile. They seriously proposed to meet the prelates of the Roman hierarchy in conference, and convince them that there was no fundamental difference between their tenets and the dogmas of the Roman Church.[3032] The conference was declined, and the Socinians, with great hardship and loss, were driven out of the kingdom. But the persecution did not stop there. England, with Charles II. on her throne, grew cold in the cause of the Polish Protestants. In the treaty of the peace of 1660, the rights of all religious Confessions in Poland had been secured; but the guaranteeing Powers soon ceased to enforce the treaty, the Polish Government paid but small respect to it, persecution in the form of mob violence was still continued; and when the reign of John Casimir, which had been fatal to the Protestants throughout, came to an end, it was found that their ranks were broken up, that all the great families who had belonged to their communion were extinct or had passed into the Church of Rome, that their sanctuaries were mostly in ashes, their congregations all dispersed, and their cause hopeless.[3033]

There followed a succession of reigns which only furnished evidence how weak the throne had become, and how powerful the Jesuits and the Roman hierarchy had grown. Religious equality was still the law of Poland, and each new sovereign swore, at his coronation, to maintain the rights of the anti-Romanists, but the transaction was deemed a mere fiction, and the king, however much disposed, had not the power to fulfil his oath. The Jesuits and the bishops were in this matter above the law, and the sovereign's tribunals could not enforce their own edicts. What the law called rights the clergy stigmatised as abuses, and demanded that they should be abolished. In 1732 a law was passed excluding from all public offices those who were not of the communion of the Church of Rome.[3034] The public service was thus deprived of whatever activity and enlightenment of mind yet existed in Poland. The country had no need of this additional stimulus: it was already pursuing fast enough the road to ruin. For a century, one disaster after another had devastated its soil and people. Its limits had been curtailed by the loss of several provinces; its population had been diminished by the emigration of thousands of Protestants; its resources had been drained by its efforts to quell revolt within and ward off invasion from without; its intelligence had been obscured, and well-nigh extinguished, by those who claimed the exclusive right to instruct its youth; for in that land it was a greater misfortune to be educated than to grow up untaught. Overspread by torpor, Poland gave no signs of life save such as indicate paralysis. Placed under foreign tutelage, and sunk in dependence and helplessness, if she was cared for by her powerful protectors, it was as men care for a once noble palace which they have no thought of rebuilding, but from whose fallen masses they hope to extract a column or a topstone that may help to enlarge and embellish their own dwelling.

Justice requires that we should state, before dismissing this part of our subject, with its many solemn lessons, that though the fall of Protestantism in Poland, and the consequent ruin of the Polish State, was mainly the work of the Jesuits, other causes co-operated, though in a less degree. The Protestant body in Poland, from the first, was parted into three Confessions: the Genevan in Lithuania, the Bohemian in Great Poland, and the Lutheran in those towns that were inhabited by a population of German descent. This was a source of weakness, and this weakness was aggravated by the ill-will borne by the Lutheran Protestants to the adherents of the other two Confessions. The evil was cured, it was thought, by the Union of Sandomir; but Lutheran exclusiveness and intolerance, after a few years, again broke up the united Church, and deprived the Protestant cause of the strength which a common centre always gives. The short lives of John Alasco and Prince Radziwill are also to be reckoned among the causes which contributed to the failure of the Reform movement in Poland. Had their labours been prolonged, a deeper seat would have been given to Protestant truth in the general population, and the throne might have been gained to the Reformation. The Christian chivalry and patriotism with which the great nobles placed themselves at the head of the movement are worthy of all praise, but the people must ever be the mainstay of a religious Reformation, and the great landowners in Poland did not, we fear, take this fact sufficiently into account, or bestow the requisite pains in imbuing their tenantry with great Spiritual principles: and hence the comparative ease with which the people were again transferred into the Roman fold. But an influence yet more hostile to the triumph of Protestantism in Poland was the rise and rapid diffusion of Socinian views. These sprang up in the bosom of the Genevan Confession, and inflicted a blight on the powerful Protestant Churches of Lithuania. That blight very soon overspread the whole land; and the green tree of Protestantism began to be touched with the sere of decay. The Socinian was followed, as we have seen, by the Jesuit. A yet deeper desolation gathered on his track. Decay became rottenness, and blight deepened into death; but Protestantism did not perish alone. The throne, the country, the people, all went down with it in a catastrophe so awful that no one could have effected it but the Jesuit.

CHAPTER VII

BOHEMIA — ENTRANCE OF REFORMATION

IN resuming the story of Bohemia we re-enter a tragic field. Our rehearsal of its conflicts and sufferings will in one sense be sorrowful, in another a truly triumphant task. What we are about to witness is not the victorious march of a nation out of bondage, with banners unfurled, and singing the song of a recovered Gospel; on the contrary, it is a crowd of sufferers and martyrs that is to pass before us; and when the long procession begins to draw to an end, we shall have to confess that these are but a few of that great army of confessors who in this land gave their lives for the truth. Where are the rest, and why are not their deaths recorded? They still abide under that darkness with which their martyrdoms were on purpose covered, and which as yet has been only partially dispelled. Their names and sufferings are locked up in the imperial archives of Vienna, in the archiepiscopal archives of Prague, in the libraries of Leitmeritz, Königgrätz, Wittengau, and other places. For a full revelation we must wait the coming of that day when, in the emphatic language of Scripture, "The earth also shall disclose her blood, and shall no more cover her slain."[3035]

In a former book[3036] we brought down the history of the Bohemian Church[3037] a century beyond the stake of Huss. Speaking from the midst of the flames, as we have already seen, the martyr said, "A hundred years and there will arise a swan whose singing you shall not be able to silence."[3038] The century had revolved, and Luther, with a voice that was rolling from east to west of Christendom, loud as the thunder but melodious as the music of heaven, was preaching the doctrine of justification by faith alone. We resume our history of the Bohemian Church at the point where we broke it off. Though fire and sword had been wasting the Bohemian confessors during the greater part of the century, there were about 200 of their congregations in existence when the Reformation broke. Imperfect as was their knowledge of Divine truth, their presence on the soil of Bohemia helped powerfully toward the reception of the doctrines of Luther in that country. Many hailed his appearance as sent to resume the work of their martyred countryman, and recognised in his preaching the "song" for which Huss had bidden them wait. As early as the year 1519, Matthias, a hermit, arriving at Prague, preached to great crowds, which assembled round him in the streets and market-place though he mingled with the doctrines of the Reformation certain opinions of his own. The Calixtines, who were now Romanists in all save the Eucharistic rite, which they received in both kinds, said, "It were better to have our pastors ordained at Wittemberg than at Rome." Many Bohemian youths were setting out to sit at Luther's feet, and those who were debarred the journey, and could not benefit by the living voice of the great doctor, eagerly possessed themselves, most commonly by way of Nuremberg, of his tracts and books; and those accounted themselves happiest of all who could secure a Bible, for then they could drink of the Water of Life at its fountainhead. In January, 1523, we find the Estates of Bohemia and Moravia assembling at Prague, and having summoned several orthodox pastors to assist at their deliberations, they promulgated twenty articles— "the forerunners of the Reformation," as Comenius calls them—of which the following was one: "If any man shall teach the Gospel without the additions of men, he shall neither be reproved nor condemned for a heretic."[3039] Thus from the banks of the Moldau was coming an echo to the voice at Wittemberg.

"False brethren" were the first to raise the cry of heresy against John Huss, and also the most zealous in dragging him to the stake. So was it again. A curate, newly returned from Wittemberg, where he had daily taken his place in the crowd of students of all nations who assembled around the chair of Luther, was the first in Prague to call for the punishment of the disciples of that very doctrine which he professed to have embraced. His name was Gallus Zahera, Calixtine pastor in the Church of Læta Curia, Old Prague. Zahera joined himself to John Passek, Burgomaster of Prague, "a deceitful, cruel, and superstitious man," who headed a powerful faction in the Council, which had for its object to crush the new opinions. The Papal legate had just arrived in Bohemia, and he wrote in bland terms to Zahera, holding out the prospect of a union between Rome and the Calixtines. The Calixtine pastor, forgetting all he had learned at Wittemberg, instantly replied that he had "no dearer wish than to be found constant in the body of the Church by the unity of the faith;" and he went on to speak of Bohemia in a style that must have done credit, in the eyes of the legate, at once to his rhetoric and his orthodoxy. "For truly," says he, "our Bohemia, supporting itself on the most sure foundation of the most sure rock of the Catholic faith, has sustained the fury and broken the force of all those waves of error wherewith the neighbouring countries of Germany have been shaken, and as a beacon placed in the midst of a tempestuous sea, it has held forth a clear light to every voyager, and shown him a safe harbour into which he may retreat from shipwreck;" and he concluded by promising to send forthwith deputies to expedite the business of a union between the Roman and Calixtine Churches.[3040] When asked how he could thus oppose a faith he had lately so zealously professed, Zahera replied that he had placed himself at the feet of Luther that he might be the better able to confute him: "An excuse," observes Comenius, "that might have become the mouth of Judas."

Zahera and Passek were not the men to stop at half-measures. To pave the way for a union with the Roman Church they framed a set of articles, which, having obtained the consent of the king, they required the clergy and citizens to subscribe. Those who refused were to be banished from Prague. Six pastors declined the test, and were driven from the city. The pastors were followed into exile by sixty-five of the leading citizens, including the Chancellor of Prague and the former burgomaster. A pretext being sought for severer measures, the malicious invention was spread abroad that the Lutherans had conspired to massacre all the Calixtines, and three of the citizens were put to the rack to extort from them a confession of a conspiracy which had never existed. They bore the torment[3041] rather than witness to a falsehood. An agreement was next concluded by the influence of Zahera and Passek, that no Lutheran should be taken into a workshop, or admitted to citizenship. If one owed a debt, and was unwilling to pay it, he had only to say the other was a Lutheran, and the banishment of the creditor gave him riddance from his importunities.[3042]

Branding on the forehead, and other marks of ignominy, were now added to exile. One day Louis Victor, a disciple of the Gospel, happened to be among the hearers of a certain Barbarite who was entertaining his audience with ribald stories. At the close of his sermon Louis addressed the monk, saying to him that it were "better to instruct the people out of the Gospel than to detain them with such fables." Straightway the preacher raised such a clamour that the excited crowd laid hold on the too courageous Lutheran, and haled him to prison. Next day the city sergeant conducted him out of Prague. A certain cutler, in whose possession a little book on the Sacrament had been found, was scourged in the market-place. The same punishment was inflicted upon John Kalentz, with the addition of being branded on the forehead, because it was said that though a layman he had administered the Eucharist to himself and his family. John Lapatsky, who had returned from banishment, under the impression that the king had published an amnesty to the exiles, was apprehended, thrown into prison, and murdered.[3043]

The tragic fate of Nicolas Wrzetenarz deserves a more circumstantial detail. Wrzetenarz was a learned man, well stricken in years. He was accused of Picardism, a name by which Protestant sentiments were at times designated. He was summoned to answer before the Senate. When the old man appeared, Zahera, who presided on the tribunal, asked him what he believed concerning the Sacrament of the altar. "I believe," he replied, "what the Evangelists and St. Paul teach me to believe." "Do you believe," asked the other, "that Christ is present in it, having flesh and blood?" "I believe," replied Wrzetanarz, "that when a pious minister of God's Word declares to the faithful congregation the benefits which are received by the death of Christ, the bread and wine are made to them the Supper of the Lord, wherein they are made partakers of the body and blood of Christ, and the benefits received by his death." After a few more questions touching the mass, praying to the saints, and similar matters, he was condemned as a heretic to the fire. His hostess, Clara, a widow of threescore years, whom he had instructed in the truth, and who refused to deny the faith she had received into her heart, was condemned to be burned along with him.

They were led out to die. Being come to the place of execution they were commanded to adore the sign of the cross, which had been elevated in the east. They refused, saying, "The law of God permits us not to worship the likeness of anything either in heaven or in earth; we will worship only the living God, Lord of heaven and earth, who inhabiteth alike the south, the west, the north, the east;" and turning their backs upon the crucifix, and prostrating themselves toward the west, with their eyes and hands lifted up to heaven, they invoked with great ardour the name of Christ. Having taken leave of their children, Nicolas, with great cheerfulness, mounted the pile, and standing on the faggots, repeated the Articles of the Creed, and having finished, looked up to heaven and prayed, saying with a loud voice, "Lord Jesus Christ, Son of the living God, who was born of a pure Virgin, and didst vouchsafe to undergo the shameful death of the cross for me a vile sinner, thee alone do I worship—to thee I commend my soul. Be merciful unto me, and blot out all mine iniquities." He then repeated in Latin the Psalm, "In thee, O Lord, have I put my trust." Meanwhile the executioner having brought forward Clara, and laid her on the pile, now tied down both of them upon the wood, and heaping over them the books that had been found in their house, he lighted the faggots, and soon the martyrs were enveloped in the flames. So died this venerable scholar and aged matron of Prague, on the 19th December, 1526.[3044]

In the following year Martha von Porzicz was burned. She was a woman heroic beyond even the heroism of her sex. Interrogated by the doctors of the university as well as by the councillors, she answered intrepidly, giving a reason of the faith she had embraced, and upbraiding the Hussites themselves for their stupid adulation of the Pope. The presiding judge hinted that it was time she was getting ready her garment for the fire. "My petticoat and cloak are both ready," she replied; "you may order me to be led away when you please.[3045] She was straightway sentenced to the fire. The town-crier walked before her, proclaiming that she was to die for blaspheming the holy Sacrament. Raising her voice to be heard by the crowd she said, "It is not so; I am condemned because I will not confess to please the priests that Christ, with his bones, hairs, sinews, and veins, is contained in the Sacrament."[3046] And raising her voice yet higher, she warned the people not to believe the priests, who had abandoned themselves to hypocrisy and every vice. Being come to the place where she was to die, they importuned her to adore the crucifix. Turning her back upon it, and elevating her eyes to heaven, "It is there," she said, "that our God dwells: thither must we direct our looks." She now made haste to mount the pile, and endured the torment of the flames with invincible courage. She was burned on the 4th of December, 1527.

On the 28th of August of the following year, two German artificers—one a potter, the other a girdler—accused of Lutheranism by the monks, were condemned by the judges of Prague to be burned. As they walked to the stake, they talked so sweetly together, reciting passages from Scripture, that tears flowed from the eyes of many of the spectators. Being come to the pile, they bravely encouraged one another. "Since our Lord Jesus Christ," said the girdler, "hath for us suffered so grievous things, let us arm ourselves to suffer this death, and let us rejoice that we have found so great favour with him as to be accounted worthy to die for his Gospel;" to whom the potter made answer, "I, truly, on my marriage-day was not so glad of heart as I am at this moment." Having ascended the pyre, they prayed with a clear voice, "Lord Jesus, who in thy sufferings didst pray for thine enemies, we also pray, forgive the king, and the men of Prague, and the clergy, for they know not what they do, and their hands are full of blood." And then addressing the people, they said, "Dearly beloved, pray for your king, that God would give him the knowledge of the truth, for he is misled by the bishops and clergy." "Having ended this most penitent exhortation," says the chronicler, "they therewith ended their lives."

After this the fury of the persecution for a little while subsided. The knot of cruel and bloodthirsty men who had urged it on was broken up. One of the band fell into debt, and hanged himself in despair. Zahera was caught in a political intrigue into which his ambitious spirit had drawn him, and, being banished, ended his life miserably in Franconia. The cruel burgomaster, Passek, was about the same time sent into perpetual exile, after he had in vain thrown himself at the king's feet for mercy. Ferdinand, who had now ascended the throne, changed the Council of Prague, and gave the exiles liberty to return. The year 1530 was to them a time of restitution; their churches multiplied; they corresponded with their brethren in Germany and Switzerland, and were thereby strengthened against those days of yet greater trial that awaited them.[3047]

These days came in 1547. Charles V., having overcome the German Protestants in the battle of Muhlberg, sent his brother, Ferdinand I., with an army of Germans and Hungarians to chastise the Bohemians for refusing to assist him in the war just ended. Ferdinand entered Prague like a city taken by siege. The magistrates and chief barons he imprisoned; some he beheaded, others he scourged and sent into exile, while others, impelled by terror, fled from the city. "See," observed some, "what calamities the Lutherans have brought upon us." The Bohemian Protestants were accused of disloyalty, and Ferdinand, opening his ear to these malicious charges, issued an order for the shutting up of all their churches. In the five districts inhabited mainly by the "Brethren," all who refused to enter the Church of Rome, or at least meet her more than half-way by joining the Calixtines, were driven away, and their landlords, on various pretexts, were arrested.

This calamity fell upon them like a thunder-bolt. Not a few, yielding to the violence of the persecution, fell back into Rome; but the great body, unalterably fixed on maintaining the faith for which Huss had died, chose rather to leave the soil of Bohemia for ever than apostatise. In a previous chapter we have recorded the march of these exiles, in three divisions, to their new settlements in Prussia, and the halt they made on their journey at Posen, where they kindled the light of truth in the midst of a population sunk in darkness, and laid the foundations of that prosperity which their Church at a subsequent period enjoyed in Poland.

The untilled fields and empty dwellings of the expatriated Bohemians awakened no doubts in the king's mind as to the expediency of the course he was pursuing. Instead of pausing, there came a third edict from Ferdinand, commanding the arrest and imprisonment of the pastors. All except three saved themselves by a speedy flight. The greater part escaped to Moravia; but many remained near the frontier, lying hid in the woods and caves, and venturing forth at night to visit their former flocks and to dispense the Sacrament in private houses, and so to keep the sacred flame from going out in Bohemia.

The three ministers who failed to make their escape were John Augusta, James Bilke, and George Israel, all men of note. Augusta had learned his theology at the feet of Luther. Courageous and eloquent, he was a terror to the Calixtines, whom he had often vanquished in debate, and "they rejoiced," says Comenius, "when they learned his arrest, as the Philistines did when Samson was delivered bound into their hands." He and his colleague Bilke were thrown into a deep dungeon in the Castle of Prague, and, being accused of conspiring to depose Ferdinand, and place John, Elector of Saxony, on the throne of Bohemia, they were put to the torture, but without eliciting anything which their persecutors could construe into treason. Seventeen sorrowful and solitary years passed over them in prison. Nor was it till the death of Ferdinand, in 1564, opened their prison doors that they were restored to liberty. George Israel, by a marvellous providence, escaped from the dungeon of the castle, and fleeing into Prussia, he afterwards preached with great success the Gospel in Poland, where he established not fewer than twenty churches.[3048]

Many of the nobles shared with the ministers in these sufferings. John Prostiborsky, a man of great learning, beautiful life, and heroic spirit, was put to a cruel death. On the rack he bit out his tongue and cast it at the tormentors, that he might not, as he afterwards declared in writing, be led by the torture falsely to accuse either himself or his brethren. He cited the king and his councillors to answer for their tyranny at the tribunal of God. Ferdinand, desirous if possible to save his life, sent him a physician; but he sank under his tortures and died in prison.[3049]

Finding that, in spite of the banishment of pastors, and the execution of nobles, Protestantism was still extending, Ferdinand called the Jesuits to his aid. The first to arrive was Wenzel Sturm, who had been trained by Ignatius Loyola himself. Sturm was learned, courteous, adroit, and soon made himself popular in Prague, where he laboured, with a success equal to his zeal, to revive the decaying cause of Rome. He was soon joined by a yet more celebrated member of the order, Canisius, and a large and sumptuous edifice having been assigned them as a college, they began to train priests who might be able to take their place in the pulpit as well as at the altar; "for at that time," says Pessina, a Romish writer, "there were so few orthodox priests that, had it not been for the Jesuits, the Catholic religion would have been suppressed in Bohemia."[3050] The Jesuits grew powerful in Prague. They eschewed public disputations; they affected great zeal for the instruction of youth in the sciences; and their fame for learning drew crowds of pupils around them. When they had filled all their existing schools, they erected others; and thus their seminaries rapidly multiplied, "so that the Catholic verity," in the words of the author last quoted, "which in Bohemia was on the point of breathing its last, appeared to revive again, and rise publicly."

Toward the close of his reign, Ferdinand became somewhat less zealous in the cause of Rome. Having succeeded to the imperial crown on the abdication of his brother, Charles V., he had wider interests to care for, and less time, as well as less inclination, to concentrate his attention on Bohemia. It is even said that before his death he expressed his sincere regret for his acts of oppression against his Bohemian subjects; and to do the monarch justice, these severities were the outcome, not of a naturally cruel disposition, but rather of his Spanish education, which had been conducted under the superintendence of the stern Cardinal Ximenes.[3051]

Under his son and successor, Maximilian II., the sword of persecution was sheathed. This prince had for his instructor John Fauser, a man of decided piety, and a lover of the Protestant doctrine, the principles of which he took care to instil into the mind of his royal pupil. For this Fauser had nearly paid the penalty of his life. One day Ferdinand, in a fit of rage, burst into his chamber, and seizing him by the throat, and putting a drawn sword to his breast, upbraided him for seducing his son from the true faith. The king forbore, however, from murdering him, and was content with commanding his son no further to receive his instructions. Maximilian was equally fortunate in his physician, Crato. He also loved the Gospel, and, enjoying the friendship of the monarch, he was able at times to do service to the "Brethren." Under this gentle and upright prince the Bohemian Protestants were accorded full liberty, and their Churches flourished.

The historian Thaunus relates a striking incident that occurred in the third year of his reign. The enemies of the Bohemians, having concocted a new plot, sent the Chancellor of Bohemia, Joachim Neuhaus, to Vienna, to persuade the emperor to renew the old edicts against the Protestants. The artful insinuations of the chancellor prevailed over the easy temper of the monarch, and Maximilian, although with great distress of mind, put his hand to the hostile mandate. "But," says the old chronicler, "God had a watchful eye over his own, and would not permit so good and innocent a prince to have a hand in blood, or be burdened with the cries of the oppressed."[3052] Joachim, overjoyed, set out on his journey homeward, the fatal missives that were to lay waste the Bohemian Church carefully deposited in his chest. He was crossing the bridge of the Danube when the oxen broke loose from his carriage, and the bridge breaking at the same instant, the chancellor and his suite were precipitated into the river. Six knights struck out and swam ashore; the rest of the attendants were drowned. The chancellor was seized hold of by his gold chain as he was floating on the current of the Danube, and was kept partially above water till some fishermen, who were near the scene of the accident, had time to come to the rescue. He was drawn from the water into their boat, but found to be dead. The box containing the letters patent sank in the deep floods of the Danube, and was never seen more— nor, indeed, was it ever sought for. Thaunus says that this catastrophe happened on the fourth of the Ides of December, 1565.

In Maximilian's reign, a measure was passed that helped to consolidate the Protestantism of Bohemia. In 1575, the king assembled a Parliament at Prague, which enacted that all the Churches in the kingdom which received the Sacrament under both kinds—that is, the Utraquists or Calixtines, the Bohemian Brethren, the Lutherans, and the Calvinists or Picardines—were at liberty to draw up a common Confession of their faith, and unite into one Church. In spite of the efforts of the Jesuits, the leading pastors of the four communions consulted together and, animated by a spirit of moderation and wisdom, they compiled a common creed, in the Bohemian language, which, although never rendered into Latin, nor printed till 1619, and therefore not to be found in the "Harmony of Confessions," was ratified by the king, who promised his protection to the subscribers. Had this Confession been universally signed, it would have been a bulwark of strength to the Bohemian Protestants.[3053]

The reign of the Emperor Maximilian came all too soon to an end. He died in 1576, leaving a name dear to the Protestants and venerated by all parties.

Entirely different in disposition and character was his son, the Emperor Rudolph II., by whom he was succeeded. Educated at the court of his cousin Philip II., Rudolph brought back to his native dominions the gloomy superstitions and the tryannical maxims that prevailed in the Escorial. Nevertheless, the Bohemian Churches were left in peace. Their sleepless foes were ever and anon intriguing to procure some new and hostile edict from the king; but Rudolph was too much engrossed in the study of astrology and alchemy to pursue steadily any one line of policy, and so these edicts slept. His brother Matthias was threatening his throne; this made it necessary to conciliate all classes of his subjects;

hence originated the famous Majestäts-Brief, one object of which was to empower the Protestants in Bohemia to open churches and schools wherever they pleased. This "Royal Charter," moreover, made over to them[3054] the University of Prague, and permitted them to appoint a public administrator of their affairs. It was in virtue of this last very important concession that the Protestant Church of Bohemia now attained more nearly than ever, before or since, to a perfect union and a settled government.

CHAPTER VIII
OVERTHROW OF PROTESTANTISM IN BOHEMIA

THE Protestant Church of Bohemia, now in her most flourishing condition, deserves some attention. That Church was composed of the three following bodies: The Calixtines, the United Brethren, and the Protestants — that is, the Lutheran and Calvinist communions. These three formed one Church under the Bohemian Confession—to which reference has been made in the previous chapter. A Consistory, or Table of Government, was constituted, consisting of twelve ministers chosen in the following manner: three were selected from the Calixtines, three from the United Brethren, and three from the Lutheran and Calvinistic communions, to whom were added three professors from the university. These twelve men were to manage the affairs of their Church in all Bohemia. The Consistory thus constituted was entirely independent of the archiepiscopal chair in Prague. It was even provided in the Royal Charter that the Consistory should "direct, constitute, or reform anything among their Churches without hindrance or interference of his Imperial Majesty." In case they were unable to determine any matter among themselves, they were at liberty to advise with his Majesty's councillors of state, and with the judges, or with the Diet, the Protestant members of which were exclusively to have the power of deliberating on and determining the matter so referred, "without hindrance, either from their Majesties the future Kings of Bohemia, or the party *sub una*"—that is, the Romanist members of the Diet.[3055]

From among these twelve ministers, one was to be chosen to fill the office of administrator. He was chief in the Consistory, and the rest sat with him as assessors. The duty of this body was to determine in all matters appertaining to the doctrine and worship of the Church—the dispensation of Sacraments, the ordination of ministers, the inspection of the clergy, the administration of discipline, to which was added the care of widows and orphans. There was, moreover, a body of laymen, termed Defenders, who were charged with the financial and secular affairs of the Church.

Still further to strengthen the Protestant Church of Bohemia, and to secure the peace of the kingdom, a treaty was concluded between the Romanists and Protestants, in which these two parties bound themselves to mutual concord, and agreed to certain rules which were to regulate their relations to one another as regarded the possession of churches, the right of burial in the public cemeteries, and similar matters. This agreement was entered upon the registers of the kingdom; it was sworn to by the Emperor Rudolph and his councillors; it was laid up among the other solemn charters of the nation, and a protest taken that if hereafter any one should attempt to disturb this arrangement, or abridge the liberty conceded in it, he should be held to be a disturber of the peace of the kingdom, and punished accordingly.[3056]

Thus did the whole nation unite in closing the doors of the Temple of Janus, in token that now there was peace throughout the whole realm of Bohemia. Another most significant and fitting act signalised this happy time. The Bethlehem Chapel—the scene of the ministry of John Huss—the spot where that day had dawned which seemed now to have reached its noon—was handed over to the Protestants as a public recognition that they were the true offspring of the great Reformer and martyr. Bohemia may be said to be now Protestant. "Religion flourished throughout the whole kingdom," says Comenius, "so that there was scarcely one among a hundred who did not profess the Reformed doctrine." The land was glad; and the people's joy found vent in such unsophisticated couplets as the following, which might be read upon the doors of the churches:—

"Oped are the temples; joys Bohemia's lion:
What Max protected, Rudolph does maintain."[3057]

But even in the hour of triumph there were some who felt anxiety for the future. They already saw ominous symptoms that the tranquillity would not be lasting. The great security which the Church now enjoyed had brought with it a relaxation of morals, and a decay of piety. "Alas!" said the more thoughtful, "we shall yet feel the mailed hand of some Ferdinand." It was a true presage; the little cloud was even now appearing on the horizon that was rapidly to blacken into the tempest.

The Archduke Matthias renewed his claims upon the crown of Bohemia, and supporting them by arms, he ultimately deposed his brother Rudolph, and seated himself upon his throne. Matthias was old and had no son, and he bethought him of adopting his cousin Ferdinand, Duke of Styria, who had been educated in a bigoted attachment to the Roman faith. Him Matthias persuaded the Bohemians to crown as their king. They knew something of the man whom they were calling to reign over them, but they relied on the feeble security of his promise not to interfere in religious matters while Matthias lived. It soon became apparent that Ferdinand had sworn to the Bohemians with the mouth, and to the Pope with the heart. Their old enemies no longer hung their heads, but began to walk about with front erect, and eyes that presaged victory. The principal measures brought to bear against the Protestants were the work of the college of the Jesuits and the cathedral. The partisans of Ferdinand openly declared that the Royal Charter, having been extorted from the monarch, was null and void; that although Matthias was too weak to tear in pieces that rag of old parchment, the pious Ferdinand would make short work with this bond. By little and little the persecution was initiated. The Protestants were forbidden to print a single line except with the approbation of the chancellor, while their opponents were circulating without let or hindrance, far and near, pamphlets filled with the most slanderous accusations. The pastors were asked to produce the original titles of the churches in their possession; in short, the device painted upon the triumphal arch, which the Jesuits had erected at Olmutz in honour of Ferdinand—namely, the Bohemian lion and the Moravian eagle chained to Austria, and underneath a sleeping hare with open eyes, and the words, "I am used to it"[3058] —expressed the consummate craft with which the Jesuits had worked, and the criminal drowsiness into which the Bohemians had permitted themselves to fall.[3059]

No method was left unattempted against the Protestants. It was sought by secret intrigue to invade their rights, and by open injury to sting them into insurrection. At last, in 1618, they rushed to arms. A few of the principal barons having met to consult on the steps to be taken in this crisis of their affairs, a sudden mandate arrived forbidding their meeting under pain of death. This flagrant violation of the Royal Charter, following on the destruction of several of their churches, irritated the Reformed party beyond endurance. Their anger was still more inflamed by the reflection that these bolts came not from Vienna, but from the Castle of Prague, where they had been forged by the junto whose headquarters were at the Hardschin. Assembling an armed force the Protestants crossed the Moldau, climbed the narrow street, and presented themselves before the Palace of Hardschin, that crowns the height on which New Prague is built. They marched right into the council-chamber, and seizing on Slarata, Martinitz, and Secretary Fabricius, whom they believed to be the chief authors of their troubles, they threw them headlong out of the window. Falling on a heap of soft earth, sprinkled over with torn papers, the councillors sustained no harm. "They have been saved by a miracle," said their friends. "No," replied the Protestants, "They have been spared to be a scourge to Bohemia." This deed was followed by one less violent, but more wise—the expulsion of the Jesuits, who were forbidden under pain of death to return.[3060]

The issue was war; but the death of Matthias, which happened at this moment, delayed for a little while its outbreak. The Bohemian States met to deliberate whether they should continue to own Ferdinand after his flagrant violation of the Majestäts-Brief. They voted him no longer their sovereign. The imperial electors were then sitting at Frankfort-on-the-Maine to choose a new emperor. The Bohemians sent an ambassador thither to say that they had deposed Ferdinand, and to beg the electors not to recognise him as King of Bohemia by admitting him to a seat in the electoral college. Not only did the electors admit Ferdinand as still sovereign of Bohemia, but they conferred upon him the vacant diadem. The Bohemians saw that they were in an evil case. The bigoted Ferdinand, whom they had made more their enemy than ever by repudiating him as their king, was now the head of the "Holy Roman Empire."

The Bohemians had gone too far to retreat. They could not prevent the electors conferring the imperial diadem upon Ferdinand, but they were resolved that he should never wear the crown of Bohemia. They chose Frederick, Elector-Palatine, as their sovereign. He was a Calvinist, son-in-law of James I. of England; and five days after his arrival in Prague, he and his consort were crowned with very great pomp, and took possession of the palace.

Scarcely had the bells ceased to ring, and the cannon to thunder, by which the coronation was celebrated,. when the nation and the new monarch were called to look in the face the awful struggle they had invited. Ferdinand, raising a mighty army, was already on his march to chastise Bohemia. On the road to Prague he took several towns inhabited by Protestants, and put the citizens to the sword. Advancing to the capital he encamped on the White Hill, and there a decisive battle was fought on the 8th of November, 1620.[3061] The Protestant army was completely beaten; the king, whom the unwelcome tidings interrupted at his dinner, fled; and Bohemia, Moravia, and Silesia lay prostrated at the feet of the conqueror. The generals of Ferdinand entered Prague, "the conqueror promising to keep articles," says the chronicler, "but afterwards performing them according to the manner of the Council of Constance."

The ravages committed by the soldiery were most frightful. Bohemia, Moravia, and Silesia were devastated. Villages were set on fire, cities were pillaged, churches, schools, and dwellings pulled down; the inhabitants were slaughtered, matrons and maidens violated; neither the child in its cradle nor the corpse in its grave was spared. Prague was given as a spoil, and the soldiers boasted that they had gathered some millions from the Protestants; nor, large as the sum is, is it an unlikely one, seeing that all the valuables in the country had been collected for security into the capital.

But by far the most melancholy result of this battle was the overthrow, as sudden as it was complete, of the Protestantism of Bohemia. The position of the two parties was after this completely reversed; the Romanists were now the masters; and the decree went forth to blot out utterly Protestant Bohemia. Not by the sword, the halter, and the wheel in the first instance. The Jesuits were recalled, and the work was committed to them, and so skilfully did they conduct it that Bohemia, which had been almost entirely Protestant when Ferdinand II. ascended the throne, was at the close of his reign almost as entirely Popish. No nation, perhaps, ever underwent so great a change in the short term of fifteen years as Bohemia.

Instead of setting up the scaffold at once, the conquerors published an amnesty to all who should lay down their arms. The proclamation was as welcome as it was unexpected, and many were caught who otherwise would have saved their lives by flight. Some came out of their hiding-places in the neighbourhood, and some returned from distant countries. It was the sweet piping of the fowler till the birds were snared. At length came the doleful 20th of February, 1621.

On that evening fifty chiefs of the Bohemian nation were seized and thrown into prison. The capture was made at the supper-hour. The time was chosen as the likeliest for finding every one at home. The city captains entered the house, a wagon waited at the door, and the prisoners were ordered to enter it, and were driven off to the Tower of Prague, or the prisons of the magistrate. The thing was done stealthily and swiftly; the silence of the night was not broken, and Prague knew not the blow that had fallen upon it.

The men now swept off to prison were the persons of deepest piety and highest intelligence in the land. In short, they were the flower of the Bohemian nation.[3062] They had passed their youth in the study of useful arts, or in the practice of arms, or in foreign travel. Their manhood had been devoted to the service of their country. They had been councillors of state, ambassadors, judges, or professors in the university. It was the wisdom, the experience, and the courage which they had brought to the defence of their nation's liberty, and the promotion of its Reformation, especially in the recent times of trouble, which had drawn upon them the displeasure of the emperor. The majority were nobles and barons, and all of them were venerable by age.

On the day after the transaction we have recorded, writs were issued summoning all now absent from the kingdom to appear within six weeks. When the period expired they were again summoned by a herald, but no one appearing, they were proclaimed traitors, and their heads were declared forfeit to the law, and their estates to the king. Their execution was gone through in their absence by the nailing of their names to the gallows. On the day following sentence was passed on the heirs of all who had fallen in the insurrection, and their properties passed over to the royal exchequer.[3063]

In prison the patriots were strenuously urged to beg pardon and sue for life. But, conscious of no crime, they refused to compromise the glory of their cause by doing anything that might be construed into a confession of guilt. Despairing of their submission, their enemies proceeded with their trial in May. Count Schlik, while undergoing his examination, became wearied out with the importunities of his judges and inquisitors, who tried to make him confess what had never existed. He tore open his vest, and laying bare his breast, exclaimed, "Tear this body in pieces, and examine my heart; nothing shall you find but what we have already declared in our Apology. The love of liberty and religion alone constrained us to draw the sword; but seeing God has permitted the emperor's sword to conquer, and has delivered us into your hands, His will be done." Budowa and Otto Losz, two of his co-patriots, expressed themselves to the same effect, adding, "Defeat has made our cause none the worse, and victory has made yours none the better."[3064]

On Saturday, the 19th of June, the judges assembled in the Palace of Hardschin, and the prisoners, brought before them one by one, heard each his sentence. The majority were doomed to die, some were consigned to perpetual imprisonment, and others were sent into exile. Ferdinand, that he might have an opportunity of appearing more clement and gracious than his judges, ordered the sentences to be sent to Vienna, where some of them were mitigated in their details by the royal pen. We take an instance: Joachim Andreas Schlik, whose courageous reply to his examiners we have already quoted, was to have his hand cut off, then to have been beheaded and quartered, and his limbs exposed on a stake at a cross-road; but this sentence was changed by Ferdinand to beheading, and the affixing of his head and hand to the tower of the Bridge of Prague. The sentences of nearly all the rest were similarly dealt with by the merciful monarch.

The condemned were told that they were to die within two days, that is, on the 21st of June. This intimation was made to them that they might have a Jesuit, or a Capuchin, or a clergyman of the Augsburg Confession, to prepare them for death. They were now led back to prison: the noblemen were conducted to the Castle of Prague, and the citizens to the prisons of the prætor. Some "fellows of the baser sort," suborned for the purpose, insulted them as they were being led through the streets, crying out, "Why don't you now sing, 'The Lord reigneth'?" The ninety-ninth Psalm was a favourite ode of the Bohemians, wherewith they had been wont to kindle their devotion in the sanctuary, and their courage on the battlefield.

Scarcely had they re-entered their prisons when a flock[3065] of Jesuits and Capuchin monks, not waiting till they were called, gathered round them, and began to earnestly beseech them to change their religion, holding out the hope that even yet their lives might be spared. Not wishing that hours so precious as the few that now remained to them should be wasted, they gave the intruders plainly to understand that they were but losing their pains, whereupon the good Fathers withdrew, loudly bewailing their obstinacy, and calling heaven and earth to witness that they were guiltless of the blood of men who had put away from them the grace of God.

The Protestant ministers were next introduced. The barons and nobles in the tower were attended by the minister of St. Nicholas, Rosacius by name. The citizens in the prisons of Old Prague were waited on by Werbenius and Jakessius, and those in New Prague by Clement and Hertwiz. The whole time till the hour of execution was spent in religious exercises, in sweet converse, in earnest prayers, and in the singing of psalms. "Lastly," says the chronicler of the persecutions of the Bohemian Church, "they did prepare the holy martyrs by the administration of the Lord's Supper for the future agony."

On the evening of Sunday, as the prisoners shut up in Old Prague were conversing with their pastor Werbenius, the chief gaoler entered and announced the hour of supper. They looked at each other, and all declared that they desired to eat no more on earth. Nevertheless, that their bodies might not be faint when they should be led out to execution, they agreed to sit down at table and partake of something. One laid the cloth, another the plates, a third brought water to wash, a fourth said grace, and a fifth observed that this was their last meal on earth, and that tomorrow they should sit down and sup with Christ in heaven. The remark was overheard by the Prefect of Old Prague. On going out to his friends he observed jeeringly, "What think ye? These men believe that Christ keeps cooks to regale them in heaven!" On these words being told to Jakessius, the minister, he replied that "Jesus too had a troublesome spectator at his last supper, Judas Iscariot."

Meanwhile they were told that the barons and noblemen were passing from the tower to the courthouse, near to the market-place, where the scaffold on which they were to die had already been erected. They hastened to the windows, and began to sing in a loud voice the forty-fourth Psalm to cheer their fellow-martyrs: "Yea, but for thy sake we are killed all the day long; . . . Rise, Lord, cast us not off for ever." A great crowd, struck with consternation at seeing their greatest and most venerated men led to death, followed them with sighs and tears.

This night was spent as the preceding one had been, in prayers and psalms. They exhorted one another to be of good courage, saying that as the glory of going first in the path of martyrdom had been awarded them, it behoved them to leave an example of constance to their posterity, and of courage to the world, by showing it that they did not fear to die. They then joined in singing the eighty-sixth Psalm. When it was ended, John Kutnauer turned the last stanza into a prayer, earnestly beseeching God that he would "show some token which might at once strengthen them and convince their enemies." Then turning to his companions, and speaking to them with great fervour of spirit, he said, "Be of good cheer, for God hath heard us even in this, and tomorrow he will bear witness by some visible sign that we are the martyrs of righteousness." But Pastor Werbenius, when he heard this protestation, bade them be content to have as sufficient token from God, even this, "that that death which was bitter to the world be made sweet to them."

When the day had broken they washed and changed their clothes, putting on clean apparel as if they were going to a wedding, and so fitting their doublets, and even their frills, that they might not need to re-arrange their dress on the scaffold. All the while John Kutnauer was praying fervently that some token might be vouchsafed them as a testimony of their innocence. In a little the sun rose, and the broad stream of the Moldau, as it rolled between the two Pragues, and the roofs and steeples on either side, began to glow in the light. But soon all eyes were turned upwards. A bow of dazzling brilliance was seen spanning the heavens.[3066] There was not a cloud in the sky, no rain had fallen for two days, yet there was this bow of marvellous brightness hung in the clear air. The soldiers and townspeople rushed into the street to gaze at the strange phenomenon. The martyrs, who beheld it from their windows, called to mind the bow, which greeted the eyes of Noah when he came forth from the Ark. It was the ancient token of a faithfulness more steadfast than the pillars of earth;[3067] and their feelings in witnessing it were doubtless akin to those with which the second great father of the human family beheld it for the first time in the young skies of the post-diluvian world.

The bow soon ceased to be seen, and the loud discharge of a cannon told them that the hour of execution had arrived. The martyrs arose, and embracing, they bade each other be of good cheer, as did also the ministers present, who exhorted them not to faint now when about to receive the crown. The scaffold had been erected hard by in the great square or market-place, and several squadrons of cavalry and some companies of foot were now seen taking up their position around it. The imperial judges and senators next came forward and took their seats on a theatre, whence they could command a full view of the scaffold. Under a canopy of state sat Lichtenstein, the Governor of Prague. "Vast numbers of spectators," says Comenius, "crowded the market-place, the streets, and all the houses.

The martyrs were called to go forth and die one after the other. When one had offered his life the city officers returned and summoned the next. As if called to a banquet they rose with alacrity, and with faces on which shone a serene cheerfulness they walked to the bloody stage. All of them submitted with undaunted courage to the stroke of the headsman. Rosacius, who was with them all the while, noted down their words, and he tells us that when one was called to go to the scaffold he would address the rest as follows: "Most beloved friends, farewell. God give you the comfort of his Spirit, patience, and courage, that what before you confessed with the heart, the mouth, and the hand, you may now seal by your glorious death. Behold I go before you, that I may see the glory of my Lord Jesus Christ! You will follow, that we may together behold the face of our Father. This hour ends our sorrow, and begins our everlasting joy." To whom those who remained behind would make answer and say, "May God, to whom you go, prosper your journey, and grant you a happy passage from this vale of misery into the heavenly country. May the Lord Jesus send his angels to meet thee. Go, brother, before us to our Father's house; we follow thee. Presently we shall reassemble in that heavenly glory of which we are confident through him in whom we have believed.[3069]

The beaming faces and meek yet courageous utterances of these men on the scaffold, exhibited to the spectators a more certain token of the goodness of their cause than the bow which had attracted their wondering gaze in the morning. Many of the senators, as well as the soldiers who guarded the execution, were moved to tears; nor could the crowd have withheld the same tribute, had not the incessant beating of drums, and the loud blaring of trumpets, drowned the words spoken on the scaffold.

But these words were noted down by their pastors, who accompanied them to the block, and as the heroism of the scaffold is a spectacle more sublime, and one that will better repay an attentive study, than the heroism of the battlefield, we shall permit these martyr-patriots to pass before us one by one. The clamour that drowned their dying words has long since been hushed; and the voices of the scaffold of Prague, rising clear and loud above the momentary noise, have travelled down the years to us.

CHAPTER IX

AN ARMY OF MARTYRS

JOACHIM ANDREAS SCHLIK, Count of Passau, and chief justice under Frederick, comes first in the glorious host that is to march past us. He was descended of an ancient and illustrious family. A man of magnanimous spirit, and excellent piety, he united an admirable modesty with great business capacity. When he heard his sentence, giving his body to be quartered, and his limbs to be exposed at a cross-road, he said, "The loss of a sepulchre is a small matter." On hearing the gun in the morning fired to announce the executions, "This," said he, "is the signal; let me go first." He walked to the scaffold, dressed in a robe of black silk, holding a prayer-book in his hands, and attended by four German clergymen.[3069] He mounted the scaffold, and then marking the great brightness of the sun, he broke out, "Christ, thou Sun of righteousness, grant that through the darkness of death I may pass into the eternal light." He paced to and fro a little while upon the scaffold, evidently meditating, but with a serene and dignified countenance, so that the judges could scarce refrain from weeping. Having prayed, his page assisted him to undress, and then he kneeled down on a black cloth laid there for the purpose, and which was removed after each execution, that the next to die might not see the blood of the victim who had preceded him. While engaged in silent prayer, the executioner struck, and the head of Bohemia's greatest son rolled on the scaffold. His right hand was then struck off and, together with his head, was fixed on a spear, and set up on the tower of the Bridge of Prague. His body, untouched by the executioner, was wrapped in a cloth, and carried from the scaffold by four men in black masks.

Scarcely inferior in weight of character, and superior in the variety of his mental accomplishments to Count Schlik, was the second who was called to die—Wenceslaus, Baron of Budowa. He was a man of incomparable talents and great learning, which he had further improved by travelling through all the kingdoms of Western and Southern Europe. He had filled the highest offices of the State under several monarchs. Protestant writers speak of him as "the glory of his country, and the bright shining star of the Church, and as rather the father than the lord of his dependents." The Romanist historian, Pelzel, equally extols his uprightness of character and his renown in learning. When urged in prison to beg the clemency of Ferdinand, he replied, "I will rather die than see the ruin of my country." When one told him that it was rumoured of him that he had died of grief, he exclaimed, "Died of grief! I never experienced such happiness as now. See here," he said, pointing to his Bible, "this is my paradise; never did it regale me with such store of delicious fruits as now. Here I daily stray, eating the manna of heaven, and drinking the water of life." On the third day before receiving his sentence he dreamed that he was walking in a pleasant meadow, and musing on the issue that might be awaiting his affairs, when lo! one came to him, and gave him a book, which when he had opened, he found the leaves were of silk, white as snow, with nothing written upon them save the fifth verse of the thirty-seventh Psalm: "Commit thy way unto the Lord; trust also in him; and he shall bring it to pass." While he was pondering over these words there came yet another, carrying a white robe, which he cast over him. When he awoke in the morning he told his dream to his servant. Some days after, when he mounted the scaffold, "Now," said he, "I attire myself in the white robe of my Saviour's righteousness."

Early on the morning of his execution there came two Jesuits to him, who, complimenting him on his great learning, said that they desired to do him a work of mercy by gaining his soul. "Would," he said, "you were as sure of your salvation as I am of mine, through the blood of the Lamb." "Good, my lord," said they, "but do not presume too much; for doth not the Scripture say, 'No man knoweth whether he deserves grace or wrath'?" "Where find you that written?" he asked; "here is the Bible, show me the words." "If I be not deceived," said one of them, "in the Epistle of Paul to Timothy." "You would teach me the way of salvation," said the baron somewhat angrily, "thou who knowest thy Bible so ill. But that the believer may be sure of his salvation is proved by the words of St. Paul, 'I know whom I have believed,' and also, 'there is laid up for me a crown of righteousness.'" "But," rejoined the Jesuit, "Paul says this of himself, not of others." "Thou art mistaken," said Budowa, "for it continues, 'not for me only, but for all them who love his appearing.' Depart, and leave me in peace."

He ascended the scaffold with undaunted look, and stroking his long white beard—for he was a man of seventy—he said, "Behold! my gray hairs, what honour awaits you; this day you shall be crowned with martyrdom." After this he directed his speech to God, praying for the Church, for his country, for his enemies, and having commended his soul to Christ he yielded his head to the executioner's sword. That head was exposed by the side of that of his fellow patriot and martyr, Schlik, on the tower of the Bridge of Prague.

The third who was called to ascend the scaffold was Christopher Harant, descended from the ancient and noble family of the Harants of Polzicz and Bezdruzicz. He had travelled in Europe, Asia, and Africa, visiting Jerusalem and Egypt, and publishing in his native tongue his travels in these various lands. He cultivated the sciences, wrote Greek and Latin verses, and had filled high office under several emperors. Neither his many accomplishments nor his great services could redeem his life from the block. When called to die, he said, "I have travelled in many countries, and among many barbarous nations, I have undergone dangers manifold by land and sea, and now I suffer, though innocent, in my own country, and by the hands of those for whose good both my ancestors and myself have spent our fortunes and our lives. Father, forgive them." When he went forth, he prayed, "In thee, O Lord, have I put my trust; let me not be confounded." When he stepped upon the scaffold he lifted up his eyes, and said, "Into thy hands, O Lord, I commend my spirit." Taking off his doublet, he stepped upon the fatal cloth, and kneeling down, again prayed. The executioner from some cause delaying to strike, he again broke out into supplication, "Jesus, thou Son of David, have mercy upon me, and receive my spirit." The sword now fell, and his prayer and life ended together.[3070]

The fourth to offer up his life was Gaspar, Baron Kaplirz of Sulowitz, a knight of eighty-six years age. He had faithfully served four emperors. Before going to the scaffold he called for Rosacius, and said, "How often have I entreated that God would be pleased to take me out of this life, but instead of granting my wish, he has reserved me as a sacrifice for himself. Let God's will be done." "Yesterday," said he, continuing his speech, "I was told that if I would petition Prince Lichtenstein for pardon my life would be spared. I never offended the prince: I will desire pardon of Him against whom I have committed many sins. I have lived long enough. When I cannot distinguish the taste of meats, or relish the sweetness of drinks; when I cannot walk unless I lean on a staff, or be assisted by others, what profit would such a life be to me? God forbid that I should be pulled from this holy company of martyrs."

On the day of execution, when the minister who was to attend him to the scaffold came to him, he said, "I laid this miserable body on a bed, but what sleep could so old a man have? Yet I did sleep, and saw two angels coming to me, who wiped my face with fine linen, and bade me make ready to go along with them. But I trust in my God that I have these angels present with me, not by a dream, but in truth, who minister to me while I live, and shall carry my soul from the scaffold to the bosom of Abraham. For although I am a sinner, yet am I purged by the blood of my Redeemer, who was made a propitiation for our sins."

Having put on his usual attire, he made a robe of the finest linen be thrown over him, covering his entire person. "Behold, I put on my wedding garment," he said. Being called, he arose, put on a velvet cloak, bade adieu to all, and went forth at a slow pace by reason of his great age. Fearing lest in mounting the scaffold he should fall, and his enemies flout him, he craved permission of the minister to lean upon him when ascending the steps. Being come to the fatal spot, he had much ado to kneel down, and his head hung so low that the executioner feared to do his office. "My lord," said Pastor Rosacius, "as you have commended your soul to Christ, do you now lift up yourself toward heaven." He raised himself up, saying, "Lord Jesus, into thy hands I commend my spirit." The executioner now gave his stroke, his grey head sank, and his body lay prostrate on the scaffold."[3071]

The fifth to fall beneath the executioner's sword was Procopius Dworschezky, of Olbramowitz. On receiving his sentence, he said, "If the emperor promises himself anything when my head is off, let it be so." On passing before the judges he said, "Tell the emperor, as I now stand at his tribunal, the day comes when he shall stand before the judgment-seat of God." He was proceeding in his address, when the drums beat and drownded his words. When he had undressed for the executioner, he took out his purse containing a Hungarian ducat, and gave it to the minister who attended him, saying, "Behold my last riches! these are unprofitable to me, I resign them to you." A gold medal of Frederick's coronation, that hung round his neck, he gave to a bystander, saying, "When my dear King Frederick shall sit again upon his throne, give it to him, and tell him that I wore it on my breast till the day of my death." He kneeled down, and the sword falling as he was praying, his spirit ascended with his last words to God.[3072]

Otto Losz, Lord of Komarow, came next. A man of great parts, he had travelled much, and discharged many important offices. When he received his sentence he said, "I have seen barbarous nations, but what cruelty is this! Well, let them send one part of me to Rome, another to Spain, another to Turkey, and throw the fourth into the sea, yet will my Redeemer bring my body together, and cause me to see him with these eyes, praise him with this mouth, and love him with this heart." When Rosacius entered to tell him that he was called to the scaffold, "he rose hastily out of his seat," says Comenius, "like one in an ecstacy, saying, 'O, how I rejoice to see you, that I may tell you what has happened to me! As I sat here grieving that I had not one of my own communion [the United Brethren] to dispense the Eucharist to me, I fell asleep, and behold my Saviour appeared unto me, and said, 'I purify thee with my blood,' and then infused a drop of his blood into my heart; at the feeling of this I awaked, and leaped for joy: now I understand what that is, *Believe, and thou hast eaten.* I fear death no longer."

As he went on his way to the scaffold, Rosacius said to him, "That Jesus who appeared to you in your sleep, will now appear to you in his glory." "Yes," replied the martyr, "he will meet me with his angels, and conduct me into the banqueting chamber of an everlasting marriage." Being come to the scaffold, he fell on his face, and prayed in silence. Then rising up, he yielded himself to the executioner.

He was followed on the scaffold by Dionysius Czernin, of Chudenitz. This sufferer was a Romanist, but his counsels not pleasing the Jesuits, he fell under the suspicion of heresy; and it is probable that the Fathers were not sorry to see him condemned, for his death served as a pretext for affirming that these executions were for political, not religious causes. When the other prisoners were declaring their faith, Czernin protested that this was his faith also, and that in this faith did he die. When the others received the Lord's Supper, he stood by dissolved in tears, praying most fervently. He was offered the Eucharistic cup; but smiting on his breast, and sighing deeply, he said, "I rest in that grace which hath come unto me." He was led to the scaffold by a canon and a Jesuit, but gave small heed to their exhortations. Declining the "kiss of peace," and turning his back upon the crucifix, he fell on his face, and prayed softly. Then raising himself, and looking up into the heavens, he said, "They can kill the body, they cannot kill the soul; that, O Lord Jesus, I commend to thee," and died.

There followed other noblemen, whose behaviour on the scaffold was equally courageous, and whose dying words were equally impressive, but to record them all would unnecessarily prolong our narration. We take a few examples from among the citizens whose blood was mingled with that of the nobles in defence of the religion and liberty of their native land. Valentine Kochan, a learned man, a Governor of the University, and Secretary of Prague, protested, when Ferdinand II. was thrust upon them, that no king should be elected without the consent of Moravia and Silesia. This caused him to be marked out for vengeance. In his last hours he bewailed the divisions that had prevailed among the Protestants of Bohemia, and which had opened a door for their calamities. "O!" said he, "if all the States had employed more thought and diligence in maintaining union; if there had not been so much hatred on both sides; if one had not sought preference before another, and had not given way to mutual suspicions; moreover, if the clergy and the laity had assisted each other with counsel and action, in love, unity, and peace, we should never have been thus far misled."[3073] On the scaffold he sang the last verse of the sixteenth Psalm: "Thou wilt show me the path of life; in thy presence is fulness of joy, at thy right hand are pleasures for evermore;" and then yielded his head to the executioner.

Tobias Steffek was a man of equal modesty and piety. He had been chosen to fill important trusts by his fellow-citizens. "Many a cup of blessing, " said he, "have I received from the hand of the Lord, and shall I not accept this cup of affliction? I am going by a narrow path to the heavenly kingdom." His time in prison was mostly passed in sighs and tears. When called to go to the scaffold, he looked up with eyes suffused with weeping, yet with the hope shining through his tears that the same stroke that should sever his head from his body would wipe them away for ever. In this hope he died.

John Jessenius, professor of medicine, and Chancellor of the University of Prague, was the next whose blood was spilt. He was famed for his medical skill all over Europe. He was the intimate friend of the illustrious Tycho Brahe, and Physician in Ordinary to two emperors—Rudolph and Matthias. He it was, it is said, who introduced the study of anatomy into Prague. Being a man of eloquent address, he was employed on an important embassy to Hungary, and this made him a marked object of the vengeance of Ferdinand II.

His sentence was a cruel one. He was first to have his tongue cut out, then he was to be beheaded, and afterwards quartered. His head was to be affixed to the Bridge-tower, and his limbs were to be exposed on stakes in the four quarters of Prague. On hearing this sentence, he said, "You use us too cruelly; but know that there will not be wanting some who will take down the heads you thus ignominiously expose, and lay them in the grave."[3074]

The Jesuits evinced a most lively desire to bring this learned man over to their side. Jessenius listened as they enlarged on the efficacy of good works. "Alas!" replied he, "my time is so short that I fear I shall not be able to lay up such a stock of merits as will suffice for my salvation." The Fathers, thinking the victory as good as won, exclaimed, "My dear Jessenius, though you should die this very moment, we promise you that you shall go straight to heaven." "Is it so?" replied the confessor; "then where is your Purgatory for those who are not able to fill up the number of their good deeds here?" Finding themselves but befooled, they departed from him.

On mounting the scaffold, the executioner approached him, and demanded his tongue. He at once gave it—that tongue which had pleaded the cause of his country before princes and States. It was drawn out with a pair of tongs. He then dropped on his knees, his hands tied behind his back, and began to pray, "not speaking, but spluttering," says Comenius. His head was struck off, and affixed to the Bridge-tower, and his body was taken below the gallows, and dealt with according to the sentence. One of the lights, not of Bohemia only, but of Europe, had been put out.

Christopher Khobr was the next whose life was demanded. He was a man of heroic mind. Speaking to his fellow-sufferers, he said, "How glorious is the memory of Huss and Jerome! And why? because they laid down their lives for the truth." He cited the words of Ignatius—"I am the corn of God, and shall be ground with the teeth of beasts." "We also," he added, "are the corn of God, sown in the field of the Church. Be of good cheer, God is able to raise up a thousand witnesses from every drop of our blood." He went with firm step, and face elate, to the place where he was to die. Standing on the scaffold, he said, "Must I die here? No! I shall live, and declare the works of the Lord in the land of the living." Kneeling down, he gave his head to the executioner and his spirit to God.

He was followed by John Schulz, Burgomaster of Kuttenberg. On being led out to die, he sent a message to his friends, saying, "The bitterness of this parting will make our reunion sweet indeed." On mounting the scaffold, he quoted the words of the Psalm, "Why art thou cast down, O my soul?" When he had gone a few paces forward, he continued, "Trust in God, for I shall yet praise him." Advancing to the spot where he was to die, he threw himself on his face, and spread forth his hands in prayer. Then, rising up, he received that stroke which gave him at once temporal death and eternal life.

In this procession of kingly and glorious spirits who travel by the crimson road of the scaffold to the everlasting gates, there are others whom we must permit to pass on in silence. One other martyr only shall we notice; he is the youngest of them all, and we have seen him before. He is John Kutnauer, senator of Old Prague, the same whom we saw praying that there might be given some "token" to the martyrs, and who, when the bow appeared a little after sunrise spanning the heavens above Prague, accepted it as the answer to his prayer.[3075] No one of all that heroic company was more courageous than Kutnauer. When the Jesuits came round him, he said, "Depart, gentlemen; why should you persist in labour so unprofitable to yourselves, and so troublesome to us?" One of the Fathers observed, "These men are as hard as rocks." "We are so, indeed," said the senator, "for we are joined to that rock which is Christ."

When summoned to the scaffold, his friends threw themselves upon him, overwhelming him with their embraces and tears. He alone did not weep. "Refrain," he said, "let us be men; a little while, and we shall meet in the heavenly glory." And then, says the chronicler, "with the face of a lion, as if going to battle, he set forward, singing in his own tongue the German hymn: 'Behold the hour draws near,' &c."

Kutnauer was sentenced to die by the rope, not by the sword. On the scaffold he gave his purse to the executioner, and then placed himself beneath the beam from which he was to be suspended. He cried, or rather, says the chronicler, "*roared,*" if haply he might be heard above the noise of the drums and trumpets, placed around the scaffold on purpose to drown the last words of the sufferers. "I have plotted no treason," he said; "I have committed no murder; I have done no deed worthy of death. I die because I have been faithful to the Gospel and my country. O God, pardon my enemies, for they know not what they do. Lord Jesus, receive my spirit." He was then thrown off the ladder, and gave up the ghost.[3076]

We close this grand procession of kings, this march of palm-bearers. As they pass on to the axe and the halter there is no pallor on their countenances. Their step is firm, and their eye is bright. They are the men of the greatest talents and the most resplendent virtues in their nation. They belong to the most illustrious families of their country. They had filled the greatest offices and they wore the highest honours of the State; yet we see them led out to die the death of felons. The day that saw these men expire on the scaffold may be said to have witnessed the obsequies of Bohemia.

CHAPTER X
SUPPRESSION OF PROTESTANTISM IN BOHEMIA

THE sufferings of that cruel time were not confined to the nobles of Bohemia. The pastors were their companions in the horrors of the persecution. After the first few months, during which the conqueror lured back by fair promises all who had fled into exile, or had hidden themselves in secret places, the policy of Ferdinand II. and his advisers was to crush out at once the chief men whether of the nobility or of the ministry, and afterwards deal with the common people as they might find it expedient, either by the rude violence of the hangman or the subtle craft of the Jesuit. This astute policy was pursued with the most unflinching resolution, and the issue was the almost entire trampling out of the Protestantism of Bohemia and Moravia. In closing this sad story we must briefly narrate the tortures and death which were inflicted on the Bohemian pastors, and the manifold woes that befell the unhappy country.

Even before the victory of the Weissenberg, the ministers in the various parts of Bohemia suffered dreadfully from the licence of the troops. No sooner had the Austrian army crossed the frontier, than the soldiers began to plunder and kill as they had a mind. Pastors found preaching to their flocks were murdered in the pulpit; the sick were shot in their beds; some were hanged on trees, others were tied to posts, and their extremities scorched with fire, while others were tortured in various cruel ways to compel them to disclose facts which they did not know, and give up treasure which they did not possess. To the barbarous murder of the father or the husband was sometimes added the brutal outrage of the family.

But when the victory of the Weissenberg gave Bohemia and its capital into the power of Ferdinand, the persecution was taken out of the hands of the soldiers, and committed to those who knew how to conduct it, if not more humanely, yet more systematically. It was the settled purpose of the emperor to bring the whole of Bohemia back to Rome. He was terrified at the spirit of liberty and patriotism which he saw rising in the nation; he ascribed that spirit entirely to the new religion of which John Huss had been the great apostle, since, all down from the martyr's day, he could trace the popular convulsions to which it had given rise; and he despaired of restoring quiet and order to Bohemia till it should again be of one religion, and that religion the Bohemian. Thus political blended with religious motives in the terrible persecution which Ferdinand now commenced.

It was nearly a year till the plan of persecution was arranged; and when at last the plan was settled, it was resolved to baptise it by the name of "Reformation." To restore the altars and images which the preachers of the new faith had cast out, and again plant the old faith in the *deformed* churches, was, they affirmed, to effect a real Reformation. They had a perfect right to the word. They appointed a Commission of Reformers, having at its head the Archbishop of Prague and several of the Bohemian grandees, and united with them was a numerous body of Jesuits, who bore the chief burden of this new Reformation. After the executions, which we have described, were over, it was resolved to proceed by kindness and persuasion. If the Reformation could not be completed without the axe and the halter, these would not be wanting; meanwhile, mild measures, it was thought, would best succeed. The monks who dispersed themselves among the people assured them of the emperor's favour should they embrace the emperor's religion. The times were hard, and such as had fallen into straits were assisted with money or with seed-corn. The Protestant poor were, on the other hand, refused alms, and at times could not even buy bread with money. Husbands were separated from their wives, and children from their parents. Disfranchisement, expulsion from corporations and offices, the denial of burial, and similar oppressions were inflicted on those who evinced a disposition to remain steadfast in their Protestant profession. If any one declared that he would exile himself rather than apostatise, he was laughed at for his folly. "To what land will you go," he was asked, "where you shall find the liberty you desire?" Everywhere you shall find heresy proscribed. One's native soil is sweet, and you will be glad to return to yours, only, it may be, to find the door of the emperor's clemency closed." Numerous conversions were effected before the adoption of a single harsh measure; but wherever the Scriptural knowledge of Huss's Reformation had taken root, there the monks found the work much more difficult.

The first great tentative measure was the expulsion of the Anabaptists from Moravia. The most unbefriended, they were selected as the first victims. The Anabaptists were gathered into some forty-five communities or colleges, where they had all things in common, and were much respected by their neighbours for their quiet and orderly lives. They lands were skilfully cultivated, and their taxes duly paid, but these qualities could procure them no favour in the eyes of their sovereign. The order for their banishment arrived in the beginning of autumn, 1622, and was all the more severe that it inferred the loss of the labours of the year. Leaving their fields unreaped and their grapes to rot upon the bough, they arose, and quitted house and land and vineyards. The children and aged they placed in carts, and setting forward in long and sorrowful troops, they held on their way across the Moravian plains to Hungary and Transylvania, where they found new habitations. They were happy in being the first to be compelled to go away; greater severities awaited those whom they left behind.

Stop the fountains, and the streams will dry up of themselves. Acting on this maxim, it was resolved to banish the pastors, to shut up the churches, and to burn the books of the Protestants.

In pursuance of this programme of persecution, the ministers of Prague had six articles laid before them, to which their submission was demanded, as the condition of their remaining in the country. The first called on them to collect among themselves a sum of several thousand pounds, and give it as a loan to the emperor for the payment of the troops employed in suppressing the rebellion. The remaining five articles amounted to an abandonment of the Protestant faith. The ministers replied unanimously that "they would do nothing against their conscience." The decree of banishment was not long deferred. To pave the way for it, an edict was issued, which threw the whole blame of the war upon the ministers. They were stigmatised as "turbulent, rash, and seditious men," who had "made a new king," and who even now "were plotting pernicious confederacies," and preparing new insurrections against the emperor. They must therefore, said the edict, be driven from a kingdom which could know neither quiet nor safety as long as they were in it. Accordingly on the 13th of December, 1621,[3077] the decree of banishment was given forth, ordering all the ministers in Prague within three days, and all others throughout Bohemia and the United Provinces within eight days, to remove themselves beyond the bounds of the kingdom, "and that for ever." If any of the proscribed should presume to remain in the country, or should return to it, they were to suffer death, and the same fate was adjudged to all who should dare to harbour them, or who should in the least favour or help them.[3078]

But, says Comenius, "the scene of their departure cannot be described," it was so overwhelmingly sorrowful. The pastors were followed by their loving flocks, bathed in tears, and so stricken with anguish of spirit, that they gave vent to their grief in sighs and groans. Bitter, thrice bitter, were their farewells, for they knew they should see each other no more on earth. The churches of the banished ministers were given to the Jesuits.

The same sorrowful scenes were repeated in all the other towns of Bohemia where there were Protestant ministers to be driven away; and what town was it that had not its Protestant pastor? Commissaries of Reformation went from town to town with a troop of horse, enforcing the edict. Many of the Romanists sympathised with the exiled pastors, and condemned the cruelty of the Government; the populations generally were friendly to the ministers, and their departure took place amid public tokens of mourning on the part of those among whom they had lived. The crowds on the streets were often so great that the wagons that bore away their little ones could with difficulty move forward, while sad and tearful faces looked down upon the departing troop from the windows. On the 27th of July, 1623, the ministers of Kuttenberg were commanded to leave the city before break of day, and remove beyond the bounds of the kingdom within eight days. Twenty-one ministers passed out at the gates at early morning, followed by some hundreds of citizens. After they had gone a little way the assembly halted, and drawing aside from the highway, one of the ministers, John Matthiades, preached a farewell sermon to the multitude, from the words, "They shall cast you out of the synagogues." Earnestly did the preacher exhort them to constancy. The whole assembly was drowned in tears. When the sermon had ended, "the heavens rang again," says the chronicler, "with their songs and their lamentations, and with mutual embraces and kisses they commended each other to the grace of God."[3079] The flocks returned to the city, and their exiled shepherds went on their way.

The first edict of proscription fell mainly upon the Calvinistic clergy and the ministers of the United Brethren. The Lutheran pastors were left unmolested as yet. Ferdinand II. hesitated to give offence to the Elector of Saxony by driving his co-religionists out of his dominions. But the Jesuits took the alarm when they saw the Calvinists, who had been deprived of their own pastors, flocking to the churches of the Lutheran clergy. They complained to the monarch that the work was only half done, that the pestilence could not be arrested till every Protestant minister had been banished from the land, and the urgencies of the Fathers at length prevailed over the fears of the king. Ferdinand issued an order that the Lutheran ministers should follow their brethren of the Calvinistic and Moravian Communion into exile. The Elector of Saxony remonstrated against this violence, and was politely told that it was very far indeed from being the fact that the Lutheran clergy had been banished—they had only received a "gracious dismissal."[3080]

The razing of the churches in many places was consequent on the expulsion of the pastors. Better that they should be ruinous heaps than that they should remain to be occupied by the men who were now brought to fill them. The lowest of the priests were drafted from other places to enjoy the vacant livings, and fleece, not feed, the desolate flocks. There could not be found so many curates as there were now empty churches in Bohemia; and two, six, nay, ten or a dozen parishes were committed to the care of one man. Under these hirelings the people learned the value of that Gospel which they had, perhaps too easily, permitted to be taken from them, in the persons of their banished pastors. Some churches remained without a priest for years; "but the people," says Comenius, "found it a less affliction to lack wholesome instruction than to resort to poisoned pastures, and become the prey of wolves."[3081]

A number of monks were imported from Poland, that country being near, and the language similar, but their dissolute lives were the scandal of that Christianity which they were brought to teach. On the testimony of all historians, Popish as well as Protestant, they were riotous livers, insatiably greedy, and so shamelessly profligate that abominable crimes, unknown in Bohemia till then, and not fit to be named, says the chronicler, began to pollute the land. Even the Popish historian Pelzel says, "they led vicious lives." Many of them had to return to Poland faster than they had come, to escape the popular vengeance which their misdeeds had awakened against them. Bohemia was doubly scourged: it had lost its pious ministers, and it had received in their room men who were fitter to occupy the culprit's cell than the teacher's chair.

The cleansing of the churches which had been occupied by the Protestant ministers, before being again taken possession of by the Roman clergy, presents us with many things not only foolish, but droll. The pulpit was first whipped, next sprinkled with holy water, then a priest was made to enter it, and speaking for the pulpit to say, "I have sinned." The altars at which the Sacrament of the Lord's Supper had been dispensed were dealt with much in the same way. When the Jesuits took possession of the church in Prague which had been occupied by the United Brethren, they first strewed gunpowder over its floor, and then set fire to it, to disinfect the building by flame and smoke from the poison of heresy. The "cup," the well-known Bohemian symbol, erected over church portals and city gates, was pulled down, and a statue of the Virgin put up in its stead. If a church was not to be used, because it was not needed, it was either razed or shut up. If only shut up it was left unconsecrated, and in that dreadful condition the Romanists were afraid to enter it. The churchyards shared the fate of the churches. The monumental tablets of the Protestant dead were broken in pieces, the inscriptions were effaced, and the bones of the dead in many instances were dug up and burned.[3082]

After the pastors, the iron hand of persecution fell upon the schoolmasters. All teachers who refused to conform to the Church of Rome, and teach the new catechism of the Jesuit Canisius, were banished. The destruction of the Protestant University of Prague followed. The non-Catholic professors were exiled, and the building was delivered over to the Jesuits. The third great measure adopted for the overthrow of Protestantism was the destruction of religious books. A commission travelled from town to town, which, assembling the people by the tolling of the bells, explained to them the cause of their visit, and "exhorted them," says George Holyk, "in kind, sweet and gentle words, to bring all their books." If gentle words failed to draw out the peccant volumes, threats and a strict inquisition in every house followed. The books thus collected were examined by the Jesuits who accompanied the commissioners, and while immoral works escaped, all in which was detected the slightest taint of heresy were condemned. They were carried away in baskets and carts, piled up in the market-place, or under the gallows, or outside the city gates, and there burned. Many thousands of Bohemian Bibles, and countless volumes of general literature, were thus destroyed. Since that time a Bohemian book and a scarce book have been synonymous. The past of Bohemia was blotted out; the great writers and the illustrious warriors who had flourished in it were forgotten; the noble memories of early times were buried in the ashes of these fires; and the Jesuits found it easy to make their pupils believe that, previous to their arrival, the country had been immersed in darkness, and that with them came the first streaks of light in its sky.[3083]

The Jesuits who were so helpful in this "Reformation" were Spaniards. They had brought with them the new order of the Brethren of Mercy, who proved their most efficient coadjutors. Of these Brethren of Mercy, Jacobeus gives the following graphic but not agreeable picture:—"They were saints abroad, but furies at home; their dress was that of paupers, but their tables were those of gluttons; they had the maxims of the ascetic, but the morals of the rake." Other allies, perhaps even more efficient in promoting conversions to the Roman Church, came to the aid of the Jesuits. These were the well-known Lichtenstein dragoons. These men had never faced an enemy, or learned on the battlefield to be at once brave and merciful. They were a set of vicious and cowardly ruffians, who delighted in terrifying, torturing, and murdering the pious peasants. They drove them like cattle to church with the sabre. When billeted on Protestant families, they conducted themselves like incarnate demons; the members of the household had either to declare themselves Romanists, or flee to the woods, to be out of the reach of their violence and the hearing of their oaths. As the Jesuits were boasting at Rome in presence of the Pope of having converted Bohemia, the famous Capuchin, Valerianus Magnus, who was present, said, "Holy Father, give me soldiers as they were given to the Jesuits, and I will convert the whole world to the Catholic faith."[3084]

We have already narrated the executions of the most illustrious of the Bohemian nobles. Those whose lives were spared were overwhelmed by burdensome taxes, and reiterated demands for sums of money, on various pretexts. After they had been tolerably fleeced, it was resolved to banish them from the kingdom. On Ignatius Loyola's day, the 31st of July, in the year 1627, an edict appeared, in which the emperor declared that, having "a fatherly care for the salvation of his kingdom," he would permit none but Catholics to live in it, and he commanded all who refused to return to the Church of Rome, to sell their estates within six months, and depart from Bohemia. Some there were who parted with "the treasure of a good conscience" that they might remain in their native land; but the greater part, more steadfastly-minded, sold their estates for a nominal price in almost every instance, and went forth into exile.[3085] The decree of banishment was extended to widows. Their sons and daughters, being minors, were taken forcible possession of by the Jesuits, and were shut up in colleges and convents, and their goods managed by tutors appointed by the priests. About a hundred noble families, forsaking their ancestral domains, were dispersed throughout the neighbouring countries, and among these was the grey-headed baron, Charles Zierotin, a man highly respected throughout all Bohemia for his piety and courage.

The places of the banished grandees were filled by persons of low degree, to whom the emperor could give a patent of nobility, but to whom he could give neither elevation of soul, nor dignity of character, nor grace of manners. The free cities were placed under a reign of terrorism. New governors and imperial judges were appointed to rule them; but from what class of the population were these officials drawn? The first were selected by the new nobility; the second, says Comenius—and his statement was not denied by his contemporaries—were taken from "banished Italians or Germans, or apostate Bohemians, gluttons who had squandered their fortunes, notorious murderers, bastards, cheats, fiddlers, stage-players, mutineers, even men who were unable to read, without property, without home, without conscience."[3086] Such were the judges to whom the goods, the liberties, and the lives of the citizens were committed. The less infamous of the new officials, the governors namely, were soon removed, and the "gluttons, murderers, fiddlers, and stage-players" were left to tyrannise at pleasure. No complaint was listened to; extortionate demands were enforced by the military; marriage was forbidden except to Roman Catholics; funeral rites were prohibited at Protestant burials; to harbour any of the banished ministers was to incur fine and imprisonment; to work on a Popish holiday was punishable with imprisonment and a fine of ten florins; to laugh at a priest, or at his sermon, inferred banishment and confiscation of goods; to eat flesh on prohibited days, without an indulgence from the Pope, was to incur a fine of ten florins; to be absent from Church on Sunday, or on festival-mass days, to send one's son to a non-Catholic school, or to educate one's family at home, was forbidden under heavy penalties; non-Catholics were not permitted to make a will; if nevertheless they did so, it was null and void; none were to be admitted into the arts or trades unless they first embraced the Popish faith. If any should speak unbecomingly of the "Blessed Virgin the Mother of God," or of the "illustrious House of Austria," "he shall lose his head, without the least favour or pardon." The poor in the hospitals were to be converted to the Roman Catholic faith before the feast of All Saints, otherwise they were to be turned out, and not again admitted till they had entered the Church of Rome. So was it enacted in July, 1624, by Charles, Prince of Lichtenstein, as "the constant and unalterable will of His Sacred Majesty Ferdinand II." [3087]

In the same year (1624) all the citizens of Prague who had not renounced their Protestant faith, and entered the Roman communion, were informed by public edict that they had forfeited their estates by rebellion. Nevertheless, their gracious monarch was willing to admit them to pardon. Each citizen was required to declare on oath the amount of goods which he possessed, and his pardon-money was fixed accordingly. The "ransom" varied from 100 up to 6,000 guilders. The next "thunderbolt" that fell on the non-Catholics was the deprivation of their rights of citizenship. No one, if not in communion with the Church of Rome, could carry on a trade or business in Prague. Hundreds were sunk at once by this decree into poverty. It was next resolved to banish the more considerable of those citizens who still remained "unconverted." First four leading men had sentence of exile recorded against them; then seventy others were expatriated. Soon thereafter several hundreds were sent into banishment; and the crafty persecutors now paused to mark the effect of these severities upon the common people. Terrified, ground down into poverty, suffering from imprisonment and other inflictions, and deprived of their leaders, they found the people, as they had hoped, very pliant. A small number, who voluntarily exiled themselves, excepted, the citizens conformed. Thus the populous and once more Protestant Prague bowed its neck to the Papal yoke.[3088] In a similar way, and with a like success, did the "Commissioners of the Reformation" carry out their instructions in all the chief cities of Bohemia.

After the same fashion were the villages and rural parts "unprotestantised." The Emperor Matthias, in 1610, had guaranteed the peasantry of Bohemia in the free exercise of the Protestant religion. This privilege was now abolished. Beginning was made in the villages, where the flocks were deprived of their shepherds. Their Bibles and other religious books were next taken from them and destroyed, that the flame might go out when the fuel was withdrawn. The ministers and Bibles out of the way, the monks appeared on the scene. They entered with soft words and smiling faces. They confidently promised lighter burdens and happier times if the people would only forsake their heresy. They even showed them the beginning of this golden age, by bestowing upon the more necessitous a few small benefactions. When the conversions did not answer the fond expectations of the Fathers, they changed their first bland utterances into rough words, and even threats. The peasantry was commanded to go to mass. A list of the parishioners was given to the clerk, that the absentees from church might be marked, and visited with fine. If one was detected at a secret Protestant conventicle, he was punished with flagellation and imprisonment. Marriage and baptism were next forbidden to Protestants. The peasants were summoned to the towns to be examined and, it might be, punished. If they failed to obey the citation they were surprised overnight by the soldiers, taken from their beds, and driven into the towns like herds of cattle, where they were thrust into prisons, towers, cellars, and stables; many perishing through the hunger, thirst, cold, and stench which they there endured. Other tortures, still more horrible and disgusting, were invented, and put in practice upon these miserable creatures. Many renounced their faith. Some, unwilling to abjure, and yet unable to bear their prolonged tortures, earnestly begged their persecutors to kill them outright. "No," would their tormentors reply, "the emperor does not thirst for your blood, but for your salvation." This sufficiently accounts for the paucity of martyrs unto blood in Bohemia, notwithstanding the lengthened and cruel persecution to which it was subject. There were not wanting many who would have braved death for their faith; but the Jesuits studiously avoided setting up the stake, and preferred rather to wear out the disciples of the Gospel by tedious and cruel tortures. Those only whose condemnation they could colour with some political pretext, as was the case with the noblemen whose martyrdoms we have recorded, did they bring to the scaffold. Thus they were able to suppress the Protestantism of Bohemia, and yet they could say, with some little plausibility, that no one had died for his religion.

But in trampling out its Protestantism the persecutor trampled out the Bohemian nation. First of all, the flower of the nobles perished on the scaffold. Of the great families that remained 185 sold their castles and lands and left the kingdom. Hundreds of the aristocratic families followed the nobles into exile. Of the common people not fewer than 36,000 families emigrated. There was hardly a kingdom in Europe where the exiles of Bohemia were not to be met with. Scholars, merchants, traders, fled from a land which was given over as a prey to the disciples of Loyola, and the dragoons of Ferdinand. Of the 4,000,000 who inhabited Bohemia in 1620, a miserable remnant, amounting not even to a fifth, were all that remained in 1648.[3089] Its fanatical sovereign is reported to have said that he would rather reign over a desert than over a kingdom peopled by heretics. Bohemia was now a desert.

This is not our opinion only, it is that of Popish historians also. "Until that time," says Pelzel, "the Bohemians appeared on the field of battle as a separate nation, and they not unfrequently earned glory. They were now thrust among other nations, and their name has never since resounded on the field of battle. . . . Till that time, the Bohemians, taken as a nation, had been brave, dauntless, passionate for glory, and enterprising; but now they lost all courage, all national pride, all spirit of enterprise. They fled into forests like sheep before the Swedes, or suffered themselves to be trampled under foot. . . . The Bohemian language, which was used in all public transactions, and of which the nobles were proud, fell into contempt. . . . As high as the Bohemians had risen in science, literature, and arts, in the reigns of Maximilian and Rudolph, so low did they now sink in all these respects. I do not know of any scholar who, after the expulsion of the Protestants, distinguished himself in any learning. . . . With that period the history of the Bohemians ends, and that of other nations in Bohemia begins."[3090]

NOTES TO VOLUME III.

Book Fifteen

2235 Ranke, *Hist. of the Popes*, bk. ii., sec. 4, p. 138; Lond., 1874.
2236 *Ibid.*, pp. 138,139.
2237 Ranke, bk. ii., sec. 4, pp. 138,139.
2238 *Ibid.*, p. 140.
2239 Ranke, bk. ii., sec. 4, p. 143, footnote.
2240 Duller, The Jesuits, pp. 10, 11. Ranke, bk. ii., sec. 4, pp. 143,144.
2241 *Homo Orat.* a J. Nouet, S.J.
2242 Duller, p. 12.
2243 "Raised to the government of the Church Militant"
2244 Bouhours, *Life of Ignatius*, bk. i., p. 248.
2245 See Mariani, *Life of Loyola*; Rome, 1842—English translation by Card. Wiseman's authority; Lond., 1847. Bouhours, *Life of Ignatius*, bk. iii., p. 282.
2246 *Report on the Constitutions of the Jesuits*, delivered by M. Louis René de Caraduc de lo Chalotais, Procureur-General of the King, to the Parliament of Bregagne; 1761. In obedience to the Court. Translated from the French edition of 1762. Lond., 1868. Pages 16, 17.
2247 "Solus præpositus Generalis autoritatem habet regulas condendi." (Can. 3rd., Congreg. i., p. 698, tom. i.)
2248 Chalotais, *Report on the Constitutions of the Jesuits*, pp. 19–23.
2249 Duller, p. 54.
2250 Such was their number in 1761, when Chalotais gave in his *Report* to the Parliament of Bretagne.
2251 Chalotais' *Report*. Duller, p. 54.
2252 *Constit. Societatis Jesu*, pars. i., cap. 4, sec. 1,2.
2253 Examen iii. and iv., sec. 1, and 2—Parroisien, *Principles of the Jesuits*, pp. 16–19; Lond., 1860.
2254 *Constit. Societatis Jesu*, pars. iii., cap. 2., sec. 1, and pars. v., cap. 4, sec. 5—Parroisien, p. 22.
2255 *Ibid.*, pars. iv.,cap. 3, sec. 2.
2256 *Ibid.*, pars. viii., cap. 1, sec. 2.
2257 Examen vi., sec. 1.
2258 *Constit. Societatis Jesu*, pars. i., cap. 2, sec. 2.
2259 *Ibid.*, pars. viii., cap. 3, A.
2260 "Locum Dei tenenti." (*Constit. Societatis Jesu*, pars. v., cap. 4, sec. 2.)
2261 *Constit. Societatis Jesu*, pars. vii., cap. 1, sec. 1.
2262 Chalotais, *Report Const. Jesuits*. p. 62.
2263 *Constit. Societatis Jesu*, pars. vi., cap. 1, sec. 1.
2264 *Constit. Societatis Jesu*, pars. vi., cap. 1, sec. 1.
2265 *The Jesuits*. By Alexander Duff, D.D., LL.D. Pages 19,20. Edin., 1869.
2266 Father Antoine Escobar, of Mendoza. He is said by his friends to have been a good man, and a laborious student. He compiled a work in six volumes, entitled *Exposition of Uncontroverted Opinions in Moral Theology*. It afforded a rich field for the satire of Pascal. Its characteristic absurdity is that its questions uniformly exhibit two faces—an affirmative and a negative—so that *escobarderie* became a synonym in France for *duplicity*.
2267 Ferdinand de Castro-Palao was a Jesuit of Spain, and author of a work on *Virtues and Vices*, published in 1631.

2268 Escobar, tr. 1, ex. 2, n. 21; and tr. 5, ex. 4, n. 8. Sirmond, *Def. Virt.*, tr. 2, sec. 1.
2269 It is of no avail to object that these are the sentiments of individual Jesuits, and that it is not fair to impute them to the society,. It was a particular rule in the Company of Jesus, "that nothing should be published by any of its members without the approbation of their superiors." An express order was made obliging them to this in France by Henry III., 1583, confirmed by Henry IV., 1603, and by Louis XIII., 1612. So that the whole fraternity became responsible for all the doctrines taught in the books of its individual members, unless they were expressly condemned.
2270 Probabilism will be denied, but it has not been renounced. In a late publication a member of the society has actually attempted to vindicate it. See *De l'Existence et de l'Institute des Jésuites.* Par le R. P. de Ravignan, de la Compagnie de Jésus. Paris, 1845. Page 83.
2271 Pascal. *Provincial Letters*, p. 70; Edin., 1847.
2272 *The Provincial Letters.* Letter vii., p. 96; Edin., 1847.
2273 *In Praxi*, livr. xxi., num. 62.
2274 *De Just.*, livr. ii., c. 9, d. 12, n. 79.
2275 *De Spe*, vol. ii., d. 15, sec. 4.
2276 *De Sub, Pecc.*, diff. 9.
2277 Sanchez, *Mor. Theol.*, livr. ii., c. 39, n. 7.
2278 "A quocumque privato potest interfici."—Suarez (k., 6, ch. 4)—Chalotais, *Report Constit. Jesuits*, p. 84.
2279 "There are," adds M. de la Chalotais, in a footnote, "nearly 20,000 Jesuits in the world [1761], all imbued with Ultramontane doctrines, and the doctrine of murder." That is more than a century ago. Their numbers have prodigiously increased since.
2280 Mariana, *De Rege et Regis Institutione*, lib. i., cap. 6, p. 61, and lib. i., cap. 7, p. 64; ed. 1640.
2281 Sanch. *Op. Mor.*, pars. 2, lib. iii., cap. 6.
2282 *Mor. Quæst. de Christianis Oficiis et Casibus Conscientiæ*, tom. ii., tr. 25, cap. 11, n. 321–328; Lugduni, 1633.
2283 It is easy to see how these precepts may be put in practice in swearing the oath of allegiance, or promising to obey the law, or engaging not to attack the institutions of the State, or to obey the rules and further the ends of any society, lay or clerical, into which the Jesuit may enter. The swearer has only to repeat the prescribed words, and insert silently such other words, at the fitting places, as shall make void the oath, clause by clause—nay, bind the swearer to the very opposite of that which the administrator of the oath intends to pledge him to.
2284 Stephen Bauny, *Som. des Pèches*; Rouen, 1653.
2285 *Crisis Theol.*, tom. i., disp. 6, sect. 2, § 1, n. 59.
2286 *Praxis Fori Pœnit.*, tom. ii., lib. xxi, cap. 5, n. 57.
2287 *In Præcep. Decal.*, tom. i., lib. iv., cap. 2, n. 7,8.
2288 *Cursus Theol.*, tom. v., disp. 36, sec. 5, n. 118.
2289 *Cens.*, pp 319,320—*Collation faite à la requêtede l'Université de Paris*, 1643; Paris, 1720.
2290 *Aphorismi Confessariorum—verbo furtum*, n. 3–8; Coloniæ, 1590.
2291 *Instructio Sacerdotum—De Septem Peccat. Mort.*, cap. 49, n. 5; Romæ, 1601.

2292 *Praxis Fori Pœnitentialis*, lib. xxv., cap. 44, n. 555; Lugduni, 1620.
2293 Pascal, Letter vi., pp. 90,91; Edin., 1847,
2294 See Ephesians vi. 14–17.
2295 *Secreta Monita*, cap. 1, sec. 1.
2296 *Ibid.*, cap. 1, sec. 5.
2297 *Ibid.,* cap. 1, sec. 6.
2298 *Ibid.* (tr. from a *French* copy, Lond., 1679), cap.1, sec. 11.
2299 *Secreta Monita*, cap. 2, sec. 2.
2300 *Secreta Monita*, cap. 2, sec. 5.
2301 *Ibid.*, cap. 2, sec. 9,10.
2302 *Ibid.*, cap. 3, sec. 1.
2303 "Præter cantum." (*Secreta Monita*, cap. 3, sec. 3.)
2304 *Secreta Monita*, cap. 4, sec. 1–6.
2305 *Ibid.*, cap. 4, sec. 5.
2306 *Ibid.*, cap. 6, sec. 6.
2307 *Ibid.*, cap. 6, sec. 8.
2308 *Secreta Monita*, cap. vi., sec. 10.
2309 *Secreta Monita*, cap. 7, sec. 23.
2310 *Secreta Monita*, cap. 7, sec. 24.
2311 *Secreta Monita*, cap. 9, sec. 1.
2312 *Ibid.*, sec. 4.
2313 *Ibid.*, sec. 5.
2314 "Contractus et possessiones"—leases and possessions. (Lat. et Ital. ed., Roma. Con approv.)
2315 *Secreta Monita*, cap. 9, secs. 7–10.
2316 "Ostendendo etiam Deo sacrificium gratissimum fore si parentibus insciis et invitis aufugerit." (Lat. ed., cap. 9, secp. 8. L'Estrange's tr., sec. 14.)
2317 *A Master-Key to Popery*, p. 70.
2318 *Secreta Monita*, cap. 8, sec. 18, 19.
2319 *Ibid.*, capl 16 (L'Estrange's tr.); printed as the Preface in the Latin edition.
2320 *Secreta Monita*; Lond., 1850. Pref. by H.M.W., p. ix.
2321 Among the various editions of the *Secreta Monita* we mention the following:—Bishop Compton's translation; Lond., 1669. Sir Roger L'Estrange's translation; Lond., 1679; it was made from a French copy, printed at Cologne, 1678. Another edition, containing the Latin text with an English translation, dedicated to Sir Robert Walpole.Premier of England: Lond., 1723. This edition says, in the Preface, that Mr. John Schipper, bookseller at Amsterdam, bough a copy of the *Secreta Monita*, among other books, at Antwerp, and reprinted it. The Jesuits bought up the whole edition, a few copies excepted. From one of these it was afterwards reprinted. Of late years there have been several English reprints. One of the copies which we have used in this compend of the book was printed at Rome, in the printing-press of the Propaganda, and contains the Latin text page for page with a translation in Italian.
2322 *The Cabinet of the Jesuit's Secrets Opened*; Lond., 1679.
2323 Ranke, *Hist. of the Popes*, bk. ii., sec. 7.
2324 Duller, *Hist. of the Jesuits*, p. 83; Lond., 1845.
2325 Ranke, bk. v., sec. 3.
2326 Ranke, bk. v., sec. 3.

2327 Ranke, bk. v., sec. 3.
2328 *Ibid.*
2329 Krasinski, *Rise, Progress, and Decline of the Reformation in Poland*, vol. ii., p. 196; Lond., 1840.
2330 Krasinski, vol. ii., pp. 197,198.
2331 Sacchinus, lib. vi. p. 172.
2332 Steinmetz, *Hist. of the Jesuits*, vol. ii., pp. 46–48. Sacchinus, lib. iii., p. 129.
2333 Steinmetz, lib. ii., p. 59.
2334 Duller, *Hist. of the Jesuits*, pp. 135–138.
2335 *A Glimipse of the Great Secret Society*, p. lxxix; ed. lond., 1872.
2336 *A Glimpse of the Great Secret Society*, pp. lxxviii.—lxxxi. Chalotais, *Report to Parl. of Bretagne.*
2337 Duller, *Hist. of the Jesuits*, p. 151.
2338 "Sotto-scriviamo la nostra morte."
2339 All the world believed that Clement had been made to drink the *Aqua Tofana*, a spring in Perugia more famous than healthful. Some one has said that if Popes are not *liable to err*, they are nevertheless *liable to sudden death.*
2340 So he himself declared on his death-bed to Bernardino Ochino in 1542. (McCrie, *Prog. and Sup. Ref. in Italy*, p. 220.)
2341 Bromato, *Vita di Paolo*, tom. iv., lib. vii., sec. 3. Ranke, bk. ii., sec. 6.
2342 Ranke, bk. ii., sec. 6.
2343 See McCrie, *Prog. and Supp. Ref. in Italy*, chapt. 3.
2344 Calvin, *Comment. on 1st Corinthians*—Dedication.
2345 *Istoria Conc. Trent*, lib. xiv., cap. 9.
2346 Ranke, bk. ii., sec. 6, p. 157; Lond., 1847.
2347 McCrie's *Italy*, p. 223; Ed., 1833.
2348 *Ibid.*, pp. 318–320.
2349 The Author was conducted over the Inquisition at Nuremberg in September, 1871, and wrote the description given of it in the text immediately thereafter on the spot. Others must have seen it, but he knows of no one who has described it.
2350 The Author has described with greater minuteness the horizontal and upright racks in his account of the dungeons underneatht he town-house of Nuremberg. (See *ante*, bk. ix., chap. 5, p. 501.)

Book Sixteen

2351 Compare Antoine Monastier, *History of the Vaudois Church*, p. 121 (Lond., 1848), with Alexis Muston, *Israel of the Alps*, p. 8 (Lond., 1852).
2352 Monastier, *Hist. Vaudois Church*, p. 123.
2353 Monstier, p. 123.
2354 *Ibid.*
2355 *Ibid.*
2356 *Histoire Générale des Eglises Evangéliques des Vallées de Pidmont, ou Vaudoises.* Par Jean Leger. Pat ii., pp. 6,7. Leyden. 1669. Monastier, pp. 123,124.
2357 The bull is given in full in Leger, who also says that he had made a faithful copy of it, and lodged it with other documents in the University Library of Cambridge. (*Hist. Gén. des Eglises Vaud.*, part ii., pp. 7–15.)

2358 Muston, *Israel of the Alps*, p. 10.
2359 Leger, Livr. ii., p. 7.
2360 *Ibid*. livr. ii., p. 26.
2361 Monastier, p. 128.
2362 Muston, p. 20.
2363 *Ibid.*, part ii., p. 234.
2364 Monastier, p. 129.
2365 Monastier, p. 130.
2366 Monastier, pp. 133, 134.
2367 Monastier, p. 134.
2368 The Author was shown this pool when he visited the chasm. No one of the Valleys of the Waldenses is more illustrated by the sad, yet glorious, scenes of this martyrdom than this Valley of Angrogna. Every rock in it has its story. As you pass through it you are shown the spot where young children were dashed against the stones—the spot where men and women, stripped naked, were rolled up as balls, and precipitated down the mountain, and where caught by the stump of tree, or projecting angle of rock, they hung transfixed, enduring for days the agony of a living death. You are shown the entrance of caves, into which some hundreds of the Vaudois having fled, their enemies, lighting a fire at the mouth of their hiding-place, ruthlessly killed them all. Time would fail to tell even a tithe of what has been done and suffered in this famous pass.
2369 Muston, p. 11.
2370 Leger, livr. ii., p. 26.
2371 Leger, livr. ii., p. 26.
2372 Leger and Gilles say that it was Philip VII. who put and end to this war. Monastier says they "are mistaken, for this prince was then in France, and did not begin to reign till 1496." This peace was granted in 1489.
2373 Monastier, *Hist. of the Vaudois*, p. 138.
2374 *Ibid*.
2375 Gilles, p. 30. Monastier, p. 141.
2376 Ruchat, tom. iii., pp. 176, 557.
2377 *Hist. of the Vaud*., p. 146.
2378 It is entitled, says Leger, "*A Brief Confession of Faith made by the Pastors and Heads of Families of the Valleys of Piedmont.*" "It is preserved," he adds, "with other documents, in the Library of the University of Cambridge." (*Hist. des Vaud*., livr. i., p. 95.)
2379 George Morel states, in his *Memoirs*, that at this time there were more than 800,000 persons of the religion of the Vaudois. (Leger, *Hist. des Vaudois*, livr. ii., p. 27.P He includes, of course, in this estimate the Vaudois in the Valleys, on the plain of Piedmont, in Naples and Calabria, in the south of France, and in the countries of Germany.
2380 Gilles, p. 40. Monastier, p. 146.
2381 Leger, livr. ii., p. 27.
2382 Monastier, p. 153.
2383 Leger, livr. ii., p. 29.
2384 Leger, livr. ii., p. 29. Monastier, p. 168.
2385 Leger, livr. ii., p. 28.
2386 Muston, *Israel of the Alps*, cahp. 8.
2387 Leger, livr. ii., p. 29.
2388 Monastier, chap. 19, p. 172. Muston, chap. 10, p. 52.
2389 Leger, livr. ii., p. 29.

2390 "First, we do protest before the Almighty and All-just God, before whose tribunal we must all one day appear, that we intend to live and die in the holy faith, piety, and religion of our Lord Jesus Christ, and that we do abhor all heresies that have been, and are, condemned by the Word of God. We do embrace the most holy doctrine of the prophets and apostles, as likewise of the Nicene and Athanasian Creeds; we do subscribe to the four Councils, and to all the ancient Fathers, in all such things as are not repugnant to the analogy of faith." (Leger, livr. ii., pp. 30,31.)

2391 See in Leger (livr, ii., pp. 30,31) the petition of the Vaudois presented "Au Sérènissime et très-Puissant Prince, Philibert Emanuel, Duc de Savoye, Prince de Piémont, nôtre très-Clement Seigneur" (To the Serene and most Mighty Prince, Philibert Emmanuel, Duke of Savoy, Prince of Piedmont, our most Gracious Lord).

2392 See in Leger, (livr. ii., p. 32), "A la très-Vertueuse et très-Excellente Dame, Madame Marguerite de France, Duchesse de Savoye et de Berry"—"the petition of her poor and humble subjects, the inhabitants of the Valleys of Lucerna and Angrogna, and Perosa and San Martino, and all those of the plain who call purely upon the name of the Lord Jesus."

2393 Muston, p. 68.
2394 Muston, p. 72.
2395 Muston, p. 69. Monstier, p. 178.
2396 Muston, p. 70. Monastier, pp. 176,177.
2397 Muston, p. 71. Monastier, pp. 177,178.
2398 Muston, p. 72. Monastier, p. 182.
2399 Letter of Scipio Lentullus, Pastor of San Giovanni. (Leger, *Hist. des Eglises Vaud.*, livr. ii., p. 35.)
2400 So says the Pastor of Giovanni, Scipio Lentullus, in the letter already referred to. (Leger, livr. ii., p. 35.)
2401 Letter of Scipio Lentullus. (Leger, livr. ii., p. 35.) Muston, pp. 73, 74.
2402 Leger, livr. ii., p. 35. Monastier, pp. 184,185.
2403 Leger, livr. ii., p. 35.
2404 Muston, p. 77. Monastier, pp. 186,187.
2405 Muston, p. 78.
2406 Monastier, p. 188. Muston, p. 78.
2407 Muston, pp. 78,79.
2408 Monastier, p. 190. Muston, p. 80.
2409 Monastier, p. 191.
2410 Leger, part ii., p. 36. Gilles, chap. 25.
2411 *Ibid.*, part ii., p. 37.
2412 Muston, p. 83.
2413 *Ibid.* Monastier, p. 194.
2414 Leger, part ii., p. 37. Muston, p. 85.
2415 The Articles of Capitulation are given in full in Leger, part ii., pp. 38–40.
2416 Leger, part ii., p. 41.
2417 Muston, p. 37.
2418 Leger, part ii., p. 333.
2419 McCrie, *Italy*, pp. 7,8.
2420 Muston, *Israel of the Alps*, p. 38.
2421 Perrin, *Histoire des Vaudois*, p. 197. Monastier, pp. 203, 204.

2422 Muston, p. 38. Monastier and McCrie say that the application for a pastor was made to Geneva, and that Paschale set out for Calabria, accompanied by another minister and two schoolmates. It is probable that the application was made to Geneva through the intermediation of the home Church.
2423 McCrie, p. 324.
2424 Monastier, p. 205.
2425 McCrie, p. 325.
2426 *Ibid.*, pp. 325–327.
2427 *Ibid.*, pp. 326,327.
2428 Leger, part ii., p. 333. McCrie, p. 303. Muston, p. 41.
2429 Monastier, p. 206.
2430 McCrie, p. 304.
2431 Pantaleon, *Rerum in Eccles. Gest. Hist.*, f.337,338. De Porta, tom. ii., pp. 309,312—ex McCrie, pp. 305,306.
2432 Crespin, *Hist. des Martyrs*, vo. 506–516. Leger, part i, p. 2o4, and part ii., p. 335.
2433 *Sextus Propertius* (Cranstoun's translation), p. 119.
2434 Muston, chap. 16. Monastier, chap. 21.
2435 See the letter in full in Leger, part i., pp. 41–46.
2436 Muston, p. 98.
2437 Monastier, p. 222.
2438 Muston, p. 111.
2439 Monastier, p. 241.
2440 Muston, pp. 112,113. Antoine Leger ws uncle of Leger the historian. He had been tutor for many yhears in the family of the Ambassador of holland at Constantinople.
2441 Monastier, chap. 18. Muston, pp. 242, 243.
2442 Muston, p. 126.
2443 Muston, p. 129.
2444 Leger, part ii., chap. 6, pp. 72,73.
2445 Muston, p. 130.
2446 Leger, part ii., chap. 8, p. 94.
2447 Monastier, p. 265.
2448 Leger, part ii., pp. 95,96.
2449 *Ibid.* part iv., p. 108.
2450 Monastier, p. 267.
2451 Muston, p. 135.
2452 Leger, part ii., pp. 108,.109.
2453 Leger, part ii., p. 110.
2454 So says Leger, who was an eye-witness of these horrors.
2455 Monastier, p. 270.
2456 Leger, part ii., p. 113.
2457 Leger, part ii., p. 111.
2458 Leger, part ii., p. 112.
2459 The book is that from which we have so largely quoted, entitled *Histoire Générale des Eglises Evangéliques des Vallées de Piémont ou Voudoises.* Par Jen Leger, Pasteur dt Modérateur des Eglises des Vallées, et depuis la violence de la Persécution, appelé à l'Eglise Wallonne de Leyde. A Leyde, 1669.
2460 Leger, part ii., p. 113.

2461 The sum collected in England was, in round numbers, £38,000. Of this, £16,000 was invested on the security of the State, to pension pastors, schoolmasters, and students in the Valleys. This latter sum was appropriated by Charles II., on the pretext that he was not bound to implement the engagements of a usurper.

2462 The *History of the Evangelical Churches of the Valleys of Piedmont:* containng a most exact Geographical Description of the place, and a faithful Account of the Doctrine, Life, and Persecutions of the ancient Inhabitants, together with a most naked and punctual Relation of the late bloody Massacre, 1655. By Samuel Morland, Esq., His Highness' Commissioner Extraordinary for the Affairs of the said Valleys. London, 1658.

2463 Leger, part ii., chap. 11, p. 186.

2464 Leger, part ii., pp. 186,187.

2465 *Ibid.*, part ii, p. 187. Muston, pp. 146, 147..

2466 Leger, part ii., p. 188. Muston, pp. 148, 149.

2467 *Ibid.* part ii., p. 189. Monastier, p. 277.

2468 Leger, part ii., p. 182.

2469 Leger, part ii., p.. 275.

2470 Monastier, p. 311.

2471 Monastier, p. 317. Muston, p. 199.

2472 Muston, p. 200.

2473 Muston, p. 202.

2474 Monastier, p. 320.

2475 Monastier, p. 336.

2476 So named by the author of the *Rentrée*, from the village at its foot, but which without doubt, says Monastier (p. 349), "is either the Col Joli (7,240 feet high) or the Col de la Fénêtre, or Portetta, as it was named to Mr. Brockedon, who has visited these countries, and followed the same road as the Vaudois."

2477 Monastier, p. 352.

2478 Monastier, p. 356.

2479 Monastier, pp. 364,365.

2480 The author was conducted over the ground, and had all the memorials of the siege pointed out to him by two most trustworthy and intelligent guides—M. Turin, then Pastor of Macel, whose ancestors had figured in the "Glorious Return;" and the late M. Tron, Syndic of the Commune. The ancestors of M. Tron had returned with Henri Arnaud, and recovered their lands in the Valley of San Martino, and here had the family of M. Tron lived ever since, and the precise spots where the more memorable events of the war had taken place had been handed down from father to son.

2481 Monastier, pp. 369,370'

2482 Cannon-balls are occasionally picked up in the neighbourhood of the Balsiglia. In 1857 the Author was shown one in the Presbytère of Pomaretto, which had been dug up a little before.

2483 Monastier, p. 371.

2484 Monastier, p. 389. The Pope, Innocent XII., declared (19th August, 1694) the edict of the duke re-establishing the Vaudois null and void, and enjoined his inquisitors to pay no attention to it in their pursuit of the heretics.

2485 Muston, pp. 220,221. Monastier, pp. 388,389.
2486 *Waldensian Researches*, by William Stephen Gilly, M.A., Prebendary of Durham; p. 158; Lond., 1831.
2487 So deep was the previous ignorance respecting this people, that Sharon Turner, speaking of the Waldenses in his *History of England*, placed them on the shores of the Lake Leman, confounding the Valleys of the Vaudois with the Canton de Vaud.
2488 The Author may be permitted to bear his personal testimony to the labours of General Beckwith for the Waldenses, and through them for the evangelisation of Italy. On occasion of his first visit to the Valleys in 1851, he passed a week mostly in the society of the general, and had the detail from his own lips of the methods he was pursuing for the elevation of the Church of the Vaudois. All through the Valleys he was revered as a father. His commen appellation among them was "The Benefactor of the Vaudois."
2489 *General Beckwith: his Life and Labours*, &c. By J.P.Meille, Pastor of the Waldensian Church at Turin. Pate 26. Lond., 1873.
2490 "Totius Italiæ lumen."

Book Seventeen

2491 Millot, *Elements of History*, vol. iv., p. 317; Lond., 1779.
2492 Félice, *History of the Protestants of France*, vol. i., p. 61; Lond., 1853.
2493 Félice, vol. i., p. 45.
2494 *Ibid.*, vol. i., p. 44.
2495 Millot, vol. iv., pp. 317,318.
2496 Abbe Anquetil, *Histoire de France*, Tom. iii., pp. 246-249; Paris, 1835.
2497 Sleidan, bk. xix., p. 429. Beza, *Hist. Eccles. des Eglises Réformées du Royaume de France*, livr. i., p. 30; Lille, 1841. Laval, *Hist. of the Reformation in France*, vol. i., bk. i., p. 55; Lond., 1737.
2498 Davila, *Historia delle Guerre Civili di Francia*, livr. i., p. 9; Lyons, 1641. Maimbourg, *Hist. du Calvinisme*, livr. ii., p. 118; Paris, 1682.
2499 Davila, p. 14.
2500 Laval. vol. i., pp. 70,71.
2501 Thaunus, *Hist.*, lib. iii. Laval, vol. i., p. 71.
2502 Davila, lib. i., pp. 13,14.
2503 Laval, vol. i., p. 73.
2504 Laval, vol. i., p. 73.
2505 Beza, tom. i., livr. ii., p. 50.
2506 Beza, tom. i., livr. ii., p. 51. Laval, vol. i., p. 76.
2507 Laval, vol. i., p. 78.
2508 Beza, tom. i., pp. 51,52.
2509 *Ibid.*, tom. i., p. 52.
2510 Maimbourg, *Hist. Calv.*, livr. ii., p. 94; Paris, 1682.
2511 *Ibid.*, livr. ii., pp. 94,95. Laval, vol. i., p. 80.
2512 Laval, vol. i., p. 81.
2513 Laval, vol. i., p. 82. Beza, tom. i., p. 59.
2514 Beza, tom. i., p. 59.
2515 Maimbourg, livr. ii., p. 95.
2516 Beza, tom. i., pp. 62–64.
2517 Laval, vol. i., pp. 83,84.
2518 Beza, tom. i., p. 72. Laval, vol. i., pp. 85,86.

2519 Davila, *Hist. delle Guerre Civili de Francia*, lib. i., p. 13.
2520 Laval, vol. i., p. 107.
2521 Mezeray, *Abr. Chr.*, tom. iv., p. 720. Laval, vol. i., p. 107.
2522 Laval, vol. i., pp. 109,110.
2523 Beza, tom. i., pp. 122,123.
2524 Davila, lib. i., pp. 17,18. Laval, vol. i., p. 142.
2525 Beza, tom. i., p. 124.
2526 Flor. de Ræmond, *Hist. de la Naissance, &c., de l'Hérésie de ce Siècle*, lib. vii., p. 931.
2527 Flor. de Ræmond, lib. vii., p. 864.
2528 Beza, tom. i., p. 124.
2529 Laval, vol. i., p. 146. Beza, tom. i., p. 125.
2530 Beza, tom. i., p. 135.
2531 Beza, tom. i., p. 108.
2532 Laval, vol. i., p. 149.
2533 Laval, vol. i., pp. 150–152—*ex* Vincent, *Recherches sur les Commencemens de la Réf. à la Rochelle*.
2534 Beza, tom. i., p. 109.
2535 Félice, vol. i., p. 70.
2536 Beza, tom. i., pp. 109-118. Laval, vol. i., pp 118-132.
2537 Beza, tom. i., pp. 118-121. Laval, vol. i., pp 132-139.
2538 *Synodicon in Gallia Reformata*, Introduction, v., vi.; Lond., 1692.
2539 Davila, *Hist. del. Guer. Civ,. Franc.*, p. 20.
2540 Davila, p. 19.
2541 Davila, pp. 7, 8.
2542 Maimbourg, livr. ii., p. 123. Laval, vol. i., p. 170.
2543 *Ibid.*, livr. ii., p. 124. Laval, vol. i., p. 171.
2544 Félice, vol. i., p. 83.
2545 Brantôme, tom. iv., p. 204.
2546 Beza, livr. iii., p. 133.
2547 Maimbourg, livr. ii., p. 121.
2548 Beza, livr. iii., p. 156. Laval, vol. i., pp. 176-181.
2549 Laval, vol. i., pp. 194,195.
2550 Laval, vol. i., pp. 193,194.
2551 Félice, vol. i., p. 91.
2552 Beza, livr. i., p. 145.
2553 *Ibid.*, livr. i., p. 146. Laval, vol. i., p. 198.
2554 Beza, livr. i., p. 147.
2555 Laval, vol. i., p. 200. Félice, vol. i., p. 91.
2556 Félice, vol. i., p. 91.
2557 Davila, livr. i., p. 33. With Davila on this point agree Pasquier, De Thou, and D'Aubigné.
2558 Bungener, *Calvin's Life*, &c., p. 304; *Calvin's Letters*, iv. 107.
2559 Davila, livr. i., p. 35.
2560 *Ibid.*, livr i., p. 36. Laval, vol. i., p. 222.
2561 Laval, vol. i., p. 223.
2562 Laval, vol. i., p. 226.
2563 Guizot, vol. iii., pp. 302,303.
2564 Laval, vol. i., p. 234. DAvila, lib. i., p. 40.
2565 Beza, livr. iii., pp. 162-166. Laval, vol. i., p. 236.
2566 Rev. xvi.

2567 Beza, livr. iii., pp. 183,184.
2568 Davila, livr. ii., pp. 47,48.
2569 Beza, livr. iii., pp. 220-222.
2570 Laval, vol. i., pp. 318,319.
2571 Beza, livr. iii., p. 249.
2572 Laval. vol. i., p. 336.
2573 The origin of this word has been much discussed and variously determined. In both France and Geneva the Protestants were called *Huguenots*. Laval tells us that each city in France had a word to denominate a bugbear, or hobgoblin. At Tours they had their King Hugo, who used, they said, every night to ride through the uninhabited places within and without the walls, and carry off those he met. And as the Protestants of Tours used to resort to these places at night to hold their meetings, they were here first of all in FRance called Huguenots. Beza, De Thou, and Pasquier agree in this etymology of the word. Others, and with more probability, derive it from the German word Eidgenossen, which the French corrupt to Eignots, and which signifies sworn confederates. It strengthens this supposition that the term was first of all applied to the sworn confederates of liberty in Geneva. Of this opinion are Maimbourg and Voltaire.
2574 See Laval, for report of the speeches in the States-General (vol. i., pp. 384–424).
2575 Laval, vol. i., p. 482.
2576 *Ibid.*, vol. i., pp. 484, 485.
2577 Fynes Moryson, *Itinerary*, part i., p. 181: Lond., 1617.
2578 See very lengthened accounts of the debates and whole proceedings of this Conference in Beza's *Histoire des Eglises Réformées au Royaume de France*, tom. i., pp. 308-390; Lille, 1841; and Laval's *History of the Reformation in France*, vol. i., pp. 482-587; Lond., 1737.
2579 The important part played by colporteurs in the evangelisation of France is attested by an edict of Francis II., 1559, in whichhe attributes the troubles of his kingdom to "certain preachers from Geneva," and also to "the malicious dispersion of condemned books brought from thence, which had infected those of the populace who, through want of knowledge and judgment, were unable to discern doctrines." (*Mémoires de Condé*, tom. i., p. 9; Londres, 1743.)
2580 *Œuvres Complètes de Barnard Palissy*, par Paul-Antoine, *Récepte Véritable*, p. 108; Paris, 1844.
2581 Laval, vol. i., p. 604.
2582 Davila, lib. ii., p. 78.
2583 Laval, vol. i., p. 623. Félice, vol. i., pp. 139,140. Bayle, *Dict.*, art. Hôpital, note 45.
2584 Davila, lib. ii., p. 80. Félice, vol. ii., p. 146.
2585 Laval, vol. i., p. 625.
2586 Davila, lib. iii., p. 86.
2587 Crespin, *Hist. des Martyrs*, livr. viii., p. 615; à Genève, 1619.
2588 Thaunus, *Hist.*, lib. xxix., p. 78.
2589 Félice, vol. i., p. 151.
2590 Thaunus, *Hist.*, lib. xxix., p. 78.
2591 Crespin, livr. viii., p. 616.
2592 Félice, vol. i., p. 153.

2593 Laval, vol. i., p. 34.
2594 Laval, vol. ii., pp. 57,58.
2595 Félice, vol. i., pp. 174–176.
2596 Laval, vol. ii., p. 42.
2597 *Mémoires de Condé*, tom. i., p. 89.
2598 Félice, vol. i., p. 163.
2599 *Ibid.*
2600 The terrible array of these edicts and outrages may be seen in *Mémoires de Condé*, tom. i., pp. 70-100.
2601 Agrippa d'Aubigné, *Univ. Hist.*, tom. i., lib. iii., cap. 2.
2602 Laval, vol. ii., p. 49.
2603 *Memoirs of Castelnau*; Le Labereaur's Additions—*apud* Laval, vol. ii., pp. 59–64.
2604 Gaberel, *Histoire de l'Eglise de Généve*, tom. i., pp. 352–354.
2605 Laval. vo.. i., p. 64.
2606 Davila, lib. iii., p. 93. *Mém. de Condé*, vol. iii., pp. 222,319.
2607 Laval, vol. ii., pp. 71, 72.
2608 Laval, vol. ii., pp. 77, 86.
2609 It is a curious fact that the Franco-German war of 1870 divided France almost exactly as the first Huguenot war had done. The Loire became the boundary of the German conquests to the south, and the region of France beyond that river remained almost untouched by the German armies: the provinces that rallied round the Triumvirate in 1562, to fight the battle of Romanism, were exactly those that bore the brunt of the German arms in the campaign of 1870.
2610 Félice, vol. i., p. 161.
2611 *Ibid.*, p. 162. Laval, vol. ii., pp. 114,115.
2612 Félice, vol. i., p. 172.
2613 Davila, lib. iii., p. 105.
2614 Laval. vol. ii., p. 171.
2615 *Mém. de Condé*, tom. i., p. 97.
2616 Laval. vol. ii., p. 194. Félice, vol. i., p. 165.
2617 Laval, vol. ii., p. 182.
2618 Brantôme, vol. iii., p. 112. Laval, vol. ii., p. 221. Browning, *Hist. of the Huguenots*, vol. i., p. 151; Lond., 1829.
2619 Laval, vol. ii., p. 225.
2620 *Ibid.*, vol. ii., p. 224. Guizot, vol. iii., p. 335.
2621 Laval, vol. ii., p. 234.
2622 Félice, vol. i., p. 166.
2623 Laval, vol. ii., pp. 237,238.
2624 *Mém. de Condé*, tom. i., p. 125.
2625 Guizot, vol. iii., p. 339.
2626 Thaun., *Hist.*, lib. xxxiv., p. 234. Laval, vol. ii., p. 235.
2627 Laval, vol. ii., p. 255.
2628 Félice, vol. i., p. 169.
2629 Davila, lib. iii., p. 147.
2630 This château has a special and dreadful interest, and as the Author had an opportunity on his way to Spain, in 1869, to examine it, he may here be permitted to sketch the appearance of its exterior. It is situated on a low mound immediately adjoining the city ramparts, hard by the little harbour on which it looks down. The basement storey is loopholed for cannon and musketry, and the upper part is simply a two-storey house

in the style of the French château of the period, with two rows of small windows, with their white jalousies, and a roof of rusty brown tiles. The front is ornamented with two terminating round towers: the whole edifice being what doubtless Holyrood Palace, Edinburgh, was in the days of Queen Mary Stuart—that is, a quadrangular building with a castellated front. The place is now a barrack, but the French sentinel at the gate kindly gives permission for the visitor to inspect the interior. It is a small paved court, having a well in the centre, shaded by two tall trees, while portions of the wall are clothed with a vine and a few flowering shrubs. Such is the aspect of this old house, neglected now, and abandoned to the occupancy of soldiers, but which in its time has received many a crowned head, and whose chief claim to glory or infamy must lie in this—that it is linked for ever with one of the greatest crimes of an age of great crimes.

2631 De Thou, livr. 37 (vol. v., p. 35)
2632 Davila, lib. iii., p. 145.
2633 *Ibid.*, lib. iii., p. 146.
2634 *Mém. de Tavannes*, p. 282.
2635 Maimbourg, *Hist. du Calvinisme*, livr. v., p. 354.
2636 Davila, lib. iv., p. 168.
2637 *Ibid.*, iv., pp. 173–175. Mezeray, tom. v., p. 104.
2638 *Vie de Coligny*, p. 346. Davila, lib. iv., p. 193. Guizot, tom. iii., p. 353.
2639 Davila, lib. iv., p. 196.
2640 *Ibid.*, lib. iv., p. 211.
2641 Davila, lib. v., pp. 243,244.
2642 Félice, vol. i., p. 193.
2643 Davila, lib. v., p. 253.
2644 "Cominciarono ad adoporarsi le machine destinate nell' animo del Rè, e della Reina condurre nella rete i principali Ugonotti." (Davila, lib. v., p. 254.).
2645 Maimbourg, *Hist. du Calvinisme*, lib. vi., p. 453.
2646 Félice, vol. i., pp. 195,196.
2647 Gaberel, vol. ii., p. 341.
2648 *De Vita et Rebus Gestis, Pii V., Pont. Max.* Auctore Io Antonio Gabutio, Novariensi Presbytero Congregationis Clericorum Regularium S. Pauli. Lib. i., p. 5; Romæ, 1605.
2649 *Ibid.*, lib. i., p. 7.
2650 *Ibid.*, lib. i., p. 8.
2651 Gabutius, *Vita Pii V.*, lib. i., cap. 5.
2652 *Ibid.*, lib vi., cap. 13–17.
2653 *Epp. PiiV. a Goubau*. The letters of Pius V. were published at Antwerp in 1640, by Fancis Goubau, Secretary to the Spanish Embassy at Rome.
2654 *Epp. Pii V. a Goubau.* This letter is dated 28th March, 1569.
2655 "Ad internecionem usque."
2656 "Deletis omnibus."
2657 Edit. Goubau, livr. iii., p. 137.
2658 These letters are dated 13th April, 1569.
2659 Adriani (continuator of Guicciardini) drew his information from the *Journal* of Cosmo de Medici, who died in 1574. (Guizot, vol. iii., p. 376.)
2660 *Mémoires de* Tavannes, p. 282.
2661 Guizot, vol. iii., p. 376. Nouë, *Discours Polit. et Milit.*, p. 65.

2662 Guizot, vol. iii., pp. 376,377.
2663 Davila, lib. v., p. 254.
2664 *Mémoires de Sully*, tom. i., livr. i., p. 28; Londres, 1752.
2665 Davila, lib. v., p. 262.
2666 Davila, lib. v., p. 266. Davila says that she died on the fourth day. Sully says, "le cinquième jour de sa maladie," and that the reputed poisoner was a Florentine named René, perfumer to the Queen-mother. (*Mémoires*, tom. i., livr. i., p. 53.)
2667 Sully, tom. i., livr. i., p. 36.
2668 Guizot, vol. iii., p. 380.
2669 Gabutius, *Vita Pii V.*, lib. iv., cap. 10, p. 150; Romæ, 1605.
2670 *Lettr. d'Ossat à Roma*, 1599. Besides the letters of Cardinal d'Ossat, ambassador of Henry IV. at Rome, which place the facts given in the text beyond all reasonable doubt, there is also the work of Camillo Capilupi, published at Rome in October, 1572, entitled, *Lo Stratagema di Carolo IX., Re di Francia, contra gli Ugonotti rebelli di Dio et suoi: descritto dal Signor Camillo Capilupi.* See Mendham, *Life of Pius V.*, pp. 184–187; Lond., 1832.
2671 Guizot, vol. iii., p. 383.
2672 Sully, tom. i., l.ivr. i., pp. 37,38.
2673 The Abbé Anquetil was the first, or among the first, to propound this theory of the massacre in the interests of the Church of Rome. He lays the blame entirely on Catherine, who was alarmed at the confidence her son placed in the admiral. The same theory has since been elaborately set forth by others, especially by the historian Lingard. The main evidence on which it rests is the statement of the Duke of Anjou to his physician Miron, on his journey to Poland, which first appeared in the *Mémoires d'Etat de Villeroy*. That statement is exceedingly apocryphal. There is no proof that it ever was made by Anjou. The same is to be said of the reported conversation of Charles IX. with his mother on their return from visiting Cologny. It is so improbable that we cannot believe it. Opposed to these we have the clear and decided testimony of all contemporary historians, Popish and Protestant, confirmed by a hundred facts. The interior mechanism of the plot is shrouded in mystery, but the result establishes premeditation. The several parts of this plan all coincide: each piece falls into its place, each actor does his part, and the one end aimed at is effected, so that we no more can doubt pre-arrangement than, to use Paley's illustration, we can doubt design when we see a watch. If farther it is asked, Who is the arranger in this case? the argument of *Cui bono?* leaves only one answer possible.
2674 Sully, tom. i., livr. i., p. 43.
2675 Guizot, vol. iii., p. 378.
2676 Margaret is thought to have had a preference for the young Duke of Guise.
2677 Platina, *Vit. Som. Pont.*, p. 300; Venetia, 1600. Both Platina and Gabutius have given us lives of Pius V.; they are little else than a record of battles and bloodshed.
2678 Sully, tom. i., livr. i., p. 54.
2679 Brantôme, vol. viii., p. 184.
2680 Davila, lib. v., p. 269.
2681 Maimbourg says that the former occupants were turned out to make room for the new-comers. (*Hist. du Calvinisme*, livr. vi., p. 469.)

2682 Davila, livr. v., p. 270. Mezeray.
2683 Ag. d'Aubigné, *Mém.*, p. 30.
2684 Maimbourg, livr. vi., p. 472.
2685 Maimbourg, livr. vi., p. 471.
2686 Davila, lib. v., p. 271.
2687 Perefixe, *Hist. de Henri le Grand*—Brantôme, vol. i., p. 261.
2688 De Thou, livr. lii.
2689 Villeroy, vol. ii., p. 88.
2690 Sully, *Mémoires*, tom. i., livr. i., p. 62.
2691 Davila, Maimbourg, De Thou, and others, all agree in these facts.— "After having been subjected, in the course of three centuries, at one time to oblivion, and at others to diverse transferences, these sad relics of a great man, a great Christian, and a great patriot have been resting for the last two-and-twenty years in teh very Castle of Châtillon-sur-Loing, his ancestors' own domain having once more become the property of a relative of his family, the Duke of Luxembourg." (Guizot, vol. iii., p. 398; Lond., 1874.)
2692 Davila, lib. v., pp. 272,273.
2693 Voltaire states in one of the notes to the *Henriade*, that he heard the Marquis de Tessé say that he had known an old man of ninety, who in his youth had acted as page to Charles IX., and loaded the carbine with which he shot his Protestant subjects.
2694 Maimbourg, livr. vi., p. 478. Brantôme, livr. ix., p. 427.—The arquebus is preserved in the museum of the Louvre. Two hundred and twenty years after the St. Bartholomew, Mirabeau brought it out and pointed it at the throne of Louis SVI.—*"visiting the iniquities of the fathers upon the children."*
2695 Sully, tom. i., livr. i.
2696 Maimbourg, livr. vi., p. 485.
2697 Guizot, vol. iii., p. 405.
2698 Sully, livr. i., p. 74. De Thou, livr. lii., lv.
2699 Fénelon's *Despatches—apud* Carte.
2700 Gaberel, tom. ii., pp. 321,322.
2701 McCrie, *Life of Knox*, vol. ii., p. 217.
2702 De Thou informs us that the Cardinal of Lorraine, at that time in Rome, gave the messenger a thousand gold crowns.
2703 *Consiliorum ad rem datorum*. The Author's authority for this statement is a book in the Bodleian Library which contains an official account of the "order of Solemn Procession made by the Sovereign Pontiff in the Eternal City of Rome, for the most happy destruction of the Huguenot Party." The book was printed "At Rome by the heirs of Antonio Blado, printers to the Chamber, 1572."
2704 When the Author was in the Library of the Vatican a few years ago, he observed that the inscriptions below Vasari's frescoes had been removed. Other travellers have observed the same thing. On that account, the Author has thought right to give them in the text.
2705 Gaspar Coligny, the Admiral, is carried home wounded. In the Pontificate of Gregory XIII., 1572."
2706 "The slaughter of Coligny and his companions."
2707 "The king approves Coligny's slaughter."
2708 "The slaughter of the Huguenots, 1572."—The group before the exterminating angel consists of six figures; of which two are dead warriors,

the third is dying, the fourth is trying to make his escape, a women in the background is holding up her hands in an attitude of horror, and a figure draped as a priest is looking on. The letters F. P. are probably the initials of the artist, Frederic Bonzagna, called Parmanensis," from his being a native of Parma.
2709 See Laval, vol. iii. pp. 479–481.
2710 Davila, lib. v.
2711 Maimbourg, lib. vi., p. 489.
2712 Davila, lib. v.
2713 "Mourut de chagrin et de langueur en la fleur de son âge." (Maimbourg, lib. vi., p. 490.)
2714 Laval, vol. iv., p. 530.
2715 *Inventaire des Meubles de Catherine de Médicis*. Par Edmond Bonnaffé. Pages 3, 4. Paris, 1874. (From old MS in Bib. Nationale.)
2716 It is scarcely necessary to remind our readers that this battle formed the subject of Lord Macaulay's well-known ballad-song of the Huguenots.
2717 "Le saut périlleux." (*Mém. de Sully*, tom. ii., livr. v., p. 234, footnote.)
2718 *Mém. de Sully*, tom. ii., livr. v., p. 239.
2719 *Mém. de Sully*, tom. iii., livr. x., pp. 204, 358.
2720 P. de L'Estoile, *apud Mém. de Sully*, tom. vii., pp. 406, 407.
2721 L'Estoile, Mathieu, Perefixe, &c.—*apud Mém. de Sully*, tom. vii., pp. 404–412. Malherbe, *apud* Guizot, vol. iii., pp. 623, 624.
2722 *Mém. de Sully*, tom. vii., p. 418.

Book Eighteen

2723 Cæsar, *Comment. de Bello Gallico*, lib. ii., cap. 15–30. "Hoc prælio facto, et prope ad internecionem gente, ac nomine Nerviorum redacto," are the words of the conqueror (lib. ii., cap 28). Niebuhr, *Lectures on Roman History*, vol. iii., pp. 43, 44; Lond. and Edin., 1850.
2724 Müller, *Univ. Hist.*, vol. ii., bk. xiv., sec. 13–18.
2725 Stevens, *Hist. of the Scot. Church, Rotterdam*, pp. 259, 260; Edin., 1833.
2726 *Ibid.*, p. 260.
2727 See "Historical Introduction" to *Rise of the Dutch Republic*, by John Lothrop Motley; Edin. and Lond., 1859.
2728 Müller, *Univ. Hist.*, p. 230.
2729 *Relationi del Cardinal Bentivoglio*, in Pareigi, 1631; lib. i., cap. 7, p. 32.
2730 Misson, *Travels*, vol. i., p. 4.
2731 *Relat. Card. Bentiv.*, lib. i., cap. 7, p. 32: "Che sia non solo in Europa, ma in tutto il mondo."
2732 The Papal nuncio, Bentivoglio, willingly acknowledges their great physical and mental qualities, and praises them alike for their skill in arts and their bravery in war. "Gli huomini, che produce il pæse, sono ordinariamente di grancde statura; di bello, e candido aspetto, e di corpo vigorose, e robusto. Hanno gli animi non men vigorosi de' corpi; e cio s' è veduto in quella si lunga, e si pertinacè resistenza, che da loro s' è fatta all' armi Spagnuole," &c. (*Relat. Card. Bentiv.*, lib. i., cap. 3, pp. 4,5.)
2733 Brandt, *History of the Reformation in the Low Countries*, vol. i., p. 14; Lond., 1720.
2734 Brandt, vol. i., p. 14.
2735 *Ibid.*
2736 Gerdesius, *Hist. Evan. Ren.*, tom. iii., p. 3; Groning., 1749.

2737 Gerdesius, tom. iii., p. 3.
2738 "If Lyra had not piped, Luther had not danced."
2739 Brandt, bk. i., *passim*.
2740 *Ibid.*, vol. i., p. 17.
2741 Brandt, vol. i., p. 19.
2742 Sleidan, bk. xvi., p. 342; Lond., 1689.
2743 Grot., *Annal.*, lib. i., 17; Amsterdanm, 1658. Watson, *Philip II.*, vol. i., p. 113.
2744 Sleidan, bk. xvi., p. 343.
2745 See *ante*, vol. I., bk. ix., chap. 3, p. 490.
2746 Gerdesius, tom. iii., pp. 23–25.
2747 "Totum peccatum tolerans et tollens." (Gerdesius, tom. iii., Appendix, p. 18.)
2748 Gerdesius, tom. iii., pp. 28–30.
2749 See *ante*, vol. I., bk. ix., chap. 6, p. 506.
2750 "Dirutum est epenitusque eversum." (Gerdesius, tom. iii., p. 29.)
2751 See *ante*, vol. I., bk. ix., chap. 3, p. 490.
2752 Brandt, vol. i., p. 45.
2753 Gerdesius, tom. iii., p. 37. Brandt, vol. i., p. 51.
2754 Gerdesius, tom. iii., p. 39.
2755 Brandt, vol. i., p. 56. Gerdesius, tom. iii., p. 56.
2756 Brandt, vol. i., pp. 57, 58.
2757 *Ibid.*
2758 See *ante*, vol. I., bk. ix., chap. 8; and vol. II., bk. xii., chap. 2.
2759 Brandt, vol. i., p. 79; Gerdesius, tom. iii., p. 143.
2760 Brandt, vol. i., p. 42.
2761 Brandt, vol. i., p. 52.
2762 Brandt, vol. i., p. 53.
2763 Badovaro MS., *apud* Motley, *Rise of the Dutch Republic*, pt. i., chap. 1; Edin., 1859.
2764 Watson, *Philip II.*, vol. i., p. 118.
2765 *Relat. Card. Bent.*, lib. ii., cap. 1, p. 45.
2766 Motley, *Rise of the Dutch Republic*, pt. i., ch. 3, p. 110.
2767 Bentivoglio. "Chegli voleva piu tosto restar senza regni che possedergli con heresia."
2768 Brandt, vol. i., pp. 132,133.
2769 Bentivoglio.
2770 Motley, *Rise of the Dutch Republic*, vol. i., p. 170; Edin., 1859.
2771 Brandt, vol. i., pp. 108, 109.
2772 *Ibid.*, vol. i., p. 93.
2773 Brandt, vol. i., p. 94.
2774 *Ibid.*, vol. i., p. 93.
2775 Brandt, vol. i., p. 135.
2776 Brandt, vol. i., pp. 138, 139.
2777 Hooft, ii. 42—*apud* Motley, i. 178. Brandt, i. 127, 128.
2778 Strada, bk. iv., p. 79; Lond., 1667.
2779 Strada, bk. iv., p. 280.
2780 Brandt, vol. i., p. 142.
2781 Brandt, vol. i., 158.
2782 Brandt, vol. i., pp. 158, 159.
2783 Brandt, vol. i., p. 149.

2784 Brandt, vol. i., p. 150.
2785 Strada, p. 183—*apud* Brandt, vol. i., pp. 150,151. Laval, vol. iii., p. 134.
2786 Brandt, vol. i., p. 154. Laval, vol. iii., p. 134.
2787 Brandt, vol. i., p. 153.
2788 Brandt, vol. i., pp. 154, 155. Laval, vol. iii., pp. 36, 137.
2789 Sleidan, *Continuation*, bk. ii., p. 27.
2790 *Discours des Conjurations de ceux de la Maison de Guise, contre le Roy, son Royaume, les Princes de son Sang, et ses Etats*; printed in 1565, and republished at Ratisbon in 1712, among the proofs of *Satyre Menipée*, tom. iii.
2791 So Brandt affirms, on the authority of a MS. Journal on Junius's own handwriting (vol. i., p. 162.)
2792 Brandt, vol. i., p. 163.
2793 Watson, *Philip II.*, vol. i., pp. 255, 256.
2794 Motley, vol. i., p. 224. Laval, vol. iii., p. 138.
2795 Brandt, vol. i., p. 165.
2796 Brandt, vol. i., pp. 165, 166.
2797 Pontus Peyen, ii., MS.—*apud* Motley, vol. i., p. 254.
2798 *Gueux*. It is a French word, "and seems to be derived," says Brandt, "from the Dutch *Guits*, which signifies as much as rogues, vagabonds, or sturdy beggars."
2799 Brandt, vol. i., p. 167. Laval, vol. iii., p. 139.
2800 Laval, vol. iii., p. 140.
2801 Brandt, vol. i., pp. 168, 169.
2802 *Ibid.*, p. 171.
2803 N. Burgund. *Hist. Belg.*, lib. iii., p. 213—*apud* Brandt, vol. i., p. 171.
2804 Brandt, vol. i., p. 172.
2805 *Ibid.*, p. 173.
2806 *Ibid.*, p. 174.
2807 Brandt, vol. i., pp. 178, 179.
2808 *Memoirs* of Laurence Jacobson Real, an eye-witness—*apud* Brandt, vol. i., pp. 179–181.
2809 Brandt, vol. i., p. 183.
2810 Strada, liv. v.
2811 Grotius, *Annales*, lib. i., p. 22—*apud* Brandt, vol. i., p. 191.
2812 Hooft, lib. iii., p. 99. Strada, lib. v., p. 260. Brandt, vol. i., p. 191.
2813 Strada, lib. v.
2814 *Ibid.*
2815 *Ibid.*
2816 Strada, lib. v.
2817 Strada, lib. v.
2818 Hooft, Strada, &c.—*apud* Brandt, vol. i., p. 192.
2819 Brandt, vol. i., p. 192.
2820 Strada, p. 254—*apud* Brandt, vol. i., p. 193.
2821 *Ibid.*, lib. v.
2822 *Ibid.*, pp. 255, 260—*apud* Brandt, vol. i., p. 193.
2823 Brandt, vol. i., p. 194.
2824 *Ibid.*, p. 258.
2825 Brandt, vol. i., p. 196.
2826 *Ibid.*, p. 197.
2827 Motley, i., 282.

2828 Hooft, lib. iii.—*apud* Brandt, vol. i., pp. 199, 200.
2829 Grotius, *Annales*, lib. i., p. 23. Brandt, vol. i., pp. 204, 205.
2830 Hooft, p. 111. Strada, p. 268. Brandt, vol. i., p. 206.
2831 Letter of Morillon to Granville, 29th September, 1566, in Gachard, *Annal. Belg.*, 254—*apud* Motley, vol. i., p. 284.
2832 Brandt, vol. i., p. 249.
2833 Valenciennes MS. (Roman Catholic), quoted by Motley, vol. i., p. 325.
2834 Laval, vol. iii., p. 143.
2835 Brandt, vol. i., pp. 250, 251.
2836 Brandt, vol. i., p. 251. Pontus Peyen MS.—*apud* Motley, vol. i., p. 325.
2837 Gachard, Preface to *William the Silent*—*apud* Motley, vol. i., p. 326.
2838 Brandt, vol. i., p. 251.
2839 Brandt, vol. i., p. 254.
2840 Strada, bk. vi., p. 286.
2841 Meteren, vol. ii., f. 45.
2842 Brandt, vol. i., p. 257.
2843 Strada, bk. vi., p. 29.
2844 Badovaro MS.—*apud* Motley, vol. i., p. 339.
2845 Strada, bk. vi., p. 30. Le Clerq, *Hist. des Provinces Unies des Pays Bas*, tom. i., livr. ii., p. 13; Amsterdam, 1723.
2846 Strada.
2847 Bentivoglio, lib. ii., cap. 3, pp. 50, 51. Hooft, vol. iv., pp. 150, 151. Brandt, vol. i., p. 260.
2848 Brandt, vol. i., p. 260.
2849 Brandt, vol. i., p. 260. Meteren, lib. iii., p. 66.
2850 *Ibid.*, vol. i., p. 261.
2851 Le Clerq, *Hist. des Provinces Unies*, &c., tom i., livr. ii., p. 14.
2852 Brandt, vol. i., p. 261.
2853 Brandt, vol. i., p. 263.
2854 *Ibid.*, p. 266.
2855 Brandt, vol. i., p. 267.
2856 Bentivoglio, lib. ii., cap. 3, p. 52. Strada, lib. vii. Brandt, vol. i., p. 267.
2857 Strada, lib. vii.
2858 Strada, lib. vii. Brandt, vol. i., p. 267.
2859 Strada, lib. vii. Watson, *Philip II.*, vol. i., pp. 329, 330.
2860 Brandt, vol. i., pp. 269, 270.
2861 *Ibid.*
2862 Brandt, vol. i., p. 271.
2863 Brandt, bol. i., p. 275.
2864 *Ibid.*
2865 Strada, lib. vii. Brandt, vol. i., p. 276.
2866 Brandt, vol. i., p. 294.
2867 "Ad patibulum, ad patibulum." (Brandt.)
2868 Brandt, vol. i., p. 280.
2869 Brandt, vol. i., pp. 286, 287.
2870 Strada, lib. vii.
2871 *Ibid.*
2872 Brandt, vol. i., p. 295.
2873 Watson, *Philip II.*, vol. i., pp. 426–431.\
2874 Strada, lib. vii.
2875 Steven, *Hist. Scottish Church, Rotterdam*, p. 304.

2876 Strada, lib. vii.
2877 Bentivoglio, lib. ii., p. 54.
2878 Brandt, vol. i., p. 298.
2879 Brandt, vol. i., p. 298.
2880 Bor, vi. 398, 399. Strada, vii. 75; Lond., 1667.
2881 Strada, vii. 76.
2882 Strada, vii. 77.
2883 Bor, vi. 409–415.
2884 Brandt, vol. i., bk. x., p. 298.
2885 Motley, vol. ii., p. 58.
2886 Strada, vii. 74.
2887 Strada, vii. 74.
2888 Hooft, vii. 293.
2889 *Ibid.*
2890 Thaunus, tom. iii., p. 218.
2891 *Correspondance de Philippe II.*, ii. 1230.
2892 "They revived," says Strada, "the ancient invention of carrier pigeons. For a while before they were blocked up they sent to the prince's fleet, and to the nearest towns of their own party, some of these pigeons. . . . By these winged posts the Prince of Orange encouraged the townsmen to hold out for the last three months; till one of them, tired with flying, lighted upon a tent, and being shot by a soldier, ignorant of the stratagem, the mystery of the letters was discovered." (Bk. vii., p. 74.)
2893 Strada, bk. vii, p. 74.
2894 Bor, vi. 440. Hooft, viii. 312. Motley, vool ii., p. 68. Watson, vol. ii., pp. 82, 83.
2895 Hooft, viii. 313.
2896 *Correspondance de Philippe II.*, ii. 1253.
2897 Brandt, vol. i., p. 303. Bor, vi. 441. Hooft, viii. 315, 316. Motley, vol. ii., p. 70.
2898 Brandt, vol. i., p. 304.
2899 *Correspondance de Philippe II.*, ii. 1264.
2900 Hooft, viii. 324. Bor, vi. 453. Watson, ii. 95, 96.
2901 Thaunus, lib. lv., sec. 7. Meteren, p. 25. Watson, vol. ii., p. 99.
2902 Hooft, lib. viii. 332. Brandt, vol. i., p. 306.
2903 Brandt, vol. i., pp. 307, 308.
2904 Thaunus, lib. lv. Meteren, p. 133.
2905 Brandt, vol. i., p. 310.
2906 *Archives de la Maisond'Orange*, v. 27—*apud* Motley, vol. ii., p. 122.
2907 Brandt, vol. i., pp. 312, 313.
2908 Strada, bk. vii., p. 11.
2909 Bor, lib. viii., pp. 648–650. Strada, bk. viii., pp. 11, 12.
2910 Strada, bk. viii., pp. 13, 14.
2911 Bor, ix. 728–732. Hooft, xi. 460–465. Meteren, vi. 110. Strada, viii. 21, 22. Brandt., i. 325. Motley, ii. 185–195.
2912 Krasinski, *Slavonia*, p. 213.
2913 WAtson, *Philip II.*, vol. ii., p. 180. See also Letter to States of Brabant, in Bor, lib. ix., p. 695.
2914 Bor, lib. ix., pp. 738–741. Brandt, vol. i., pp. 327, 328. Sir William Temple, *United Provinces of the Netherlands*, p. 38; Edin., 1747. Watson, *Philip II.*, vol. ii., pp. 193–195.

2915 Strada, bk. ix., p. 32.
2916 Brandt, vol. i., p. 333.
2917 Bentivoglio, lib. x., pp. 192–195.
2918 Bor, lib. xi., p. 916.
2919 Watson, *Philip II.*, vol. ii., p. 221.
2920 Bor, lib. xi., p. 900. Strada, bk. ix., p. 38.
2921 Brandt, vol. i., p. 333.
2922 Brandt, vol. i., p. 334.
2923 Brandt, vol. i., p. 338.
2924 *Ibid.* p. 339.
2925 *Ibid.* p. 339.
2926 Brandt, vol. i., pp. 339–341.—Motley in his great history, *The Rise of the Dutch Republic*, when speaking of the intolerance and bigotry of the religious bodies of the Netherlands, specially empasises the intolerance of the Calvinists. It is strange, with the above document and similar proofs before him, that the historian should be unable to see that the French Huguenots and the Dutch Calvinists were the only champions of toleration then in Christendom.
2927 Strada, bk. x., p. 16.
2928 Of the transport of the body through France, and its presentation to Philip II. in the Escorial, Strada (bk. x.) gives a minute but horrible account. "To avoid those vast expenses and ceremonious contentions of magistrates and priests at city gates, that usually waylay the progress of princes whether alive or dead, he caused him to be taken in pieces, and the bones of his arms, thighs, legs, breast, and head (the brains being taken out), with other the severed parts, filling three mails, were brought safely into Spain; where the bones being set again, with small wires, they easily rejointed all the body, which being filled with cotton, armed, and richly habited, they presented Don John entire to the king as if he stood only resting himself upon his commander's-staff, looking as if he lived and breathed." On presenting himself thus before Philip, the monarch was graciously pleased to permit Don John to retire to his grave, which he had wished might be beside that of his father, Charles V., in the Escorial.
2929 Bor, lib. xiii., p. 65; Hooft, lib. xv., p. 633.
2930 See Articles of Union in full in Brandt; Sir W. Temple; Watson, *Philip II.*; Motley, *Dutch Republic*, &c.
2931 Temple, *United Provinces*, &c., chap. i., p. 38.
2932 Brandt, vol. i., p. 366.
2933 Bor, lib. xiii., pp. 58, 59. Brandt, vol. i., p. 366.
2934 Reidanus, ann. ii., 29. Gachard, *Correspondance de Guillaume le Tacit*, vol. iv., Preface. Bor, lib. xiii., p. 95.
2935 The Apology is given at nearly full length in Watson, *Philip II.*, vol. iii., Appendix.
2936 Bor, lib. xv., pp. 181–185.
2937 Brandt, vol. i., p. 383.
2938 Bor, lib. xv., pp. 185, 186.
2939 Bor. lib. xvii., pp. 297–301. Hooft, lib. xix., p. 295.
2940 Message of William to the States-General, MS.—*apud* Motley, vol. ii., p. 437.
2941 "Mon Dieu, ayez pitié de mon âme ! mon Dieu, ayez pitié de ce pauvre peuple !"

2942 The original authority from which the historians Bor, Meteren, Hooft, and others have drawn their details of the assassination of William of Orange is the "Official Statement," compiled by order of the States-General, of which there is a copy in the Royal Library at the Hague. The basis of this "Statement" is the Confession of Balthazar Gérard, written by himself. There is a recent edition of this Confession, printed from an old MS. copy, and published by M. Gachard.
2943 Brandt, vol. i., pp. 318, 319.
2944 Brandt, vol. i., pp. 321, 322.
2945 See "Reasons for prescribing these Ecclesiastical Laws"—Brandt, vol. i., p. 322.
2946 Abridgement of Brandt's *History*, vol. i., pp. 200—202.
2947 Brandt, vol. i., pp. 381, 382.
2948 Brandt, vol. i., pp. 384–386.
2949 Abridgement of Brandt's *History*, vol. i., p. 185.
2950 Brandt, vol. i., p. 342.
2951 Abridgement of Brandt's *History*, vol. i., p. 196.
2952 Brandt, vol. i., p. 383.
2953 *Ibid.*, p. 382.
2954 Abridgement of Brandt, vol. i., p. 207.
2955 Meteren, lib. iv., p. 434.
2956 See Calv., *Inst.*, lib. iii., cap. 21, 22, &c.
2957 Brandt (abridg.), vol. I., bk. xviii., p. 267.
2958 Brandt— "A good conscience is Paradise."
2959 Brandt (abridg.), vol. I., bk. xix., pp. 307, 308.
2960 See *ante*, vol. I., bk. v., chap. 15.
2961 Brandt (bridg.) vol. I., bk. xviii., p. 285.
2962 Brandt (abridg.), vol. II, bk. xxiii., p. 394.
2963 Brandt (abridg.), vol. II., bks. xxiii.–xxviii., pp. 397–504.
2964 Müller, *Universal History*, iii. 67. Sir William Temple, *United Provinces*, chap. i., p. 48; Edin., 1747.
2965 Müller, iii. 68.
2966 *The United Provinces*, chap. i., p. 49.
2967 Sir William Temple, chap. 7, p. 174.
2968 Sir William Temple. Compare chap. i., p. 59, with chap. viii., p. 179.

Book Nineteen

2969 Krasinski, *History Reform. in Poland*, vol. i., p. 2; Lond.; 1838.
2970 A remarkable man, the inventor of the Slavonic alphabet.
2971 Krasinski, *Hist. Reform. Poland*, vol.. i., p. 61.
2972 Krasinski, *Slavonia*, p. 174.
2973 Krasinski, *Slavonia*, p. 182; Lond., 1849.
2974 Krasinski, *Hist. Reform. Poland*, vol. i., pp. 115, 116.
2975 Karsinski, *Slavonia*, p. 185.
2976 Krasinski, *Hist. Reform. Poland*, vol. i., pp. 138–140.
2977 *Constitutiones Synodorum—apud* Krasinski.
2978 Zalaszowski, *Jus Publicum Regni Poloniæ*, Krasinski, *Hist. Reform. Poland*, vol. i., p. 157.
2979 *Vide Hosii Opera*, Antverpiæ, 1571; and *Stanislai Hosii Vita autore Rescio*, Romæ, 1587. Subscription to the above creed by the clergy was enjoined because many of the bishops were suspected of heresy— "quod multi inter episcopos erant suspecti."

Notes to Volume III.

2980 Bzovius, ann. 1551.
2981 Krasinski, *Hist. Reform. Poland*, vol. i., pp. 186—188.
2982 This nobleman was the descendant of that Wenceslaus of Leszna who defended John Huss at the Council of Constance. He had adopted for his motto, *Malo periculosam libertatem quam tutum servitium*— "Better the dangers of liberty than the safeguards of slavery."
2983 *Vide* Krasinski, *Hist. Reform. Poland*, vol. i., pp. 188, 189, where the original Polish authorities are cited.
2984 Gerdesius, *Hist. Reform.*, voll iii., p. 146.
2985 *Ibid.* This is the date (1523) of their friendship as given by Gerdesius; it is doubtful, however, whether it began so early.
2986 "Is in iisdem cum Erasmo ædibus vixerat Basilaæ." (Gerdesius, vol. iii., p. 146.)
2987 Krasinski, *Hist. Reform. Poland*, vol. i., p. 247.
2988 Alasco, *Opp.*, vol. ii., p. 548—*apud* D'Aubigné, vii. 546.
2989 Gerdesium, Hist. Reform., vol. iii., p. 147.
2990 Alasco, *Opp.*, vol. ii., p. 558.
2991 In 1540, Alasco had married at Mainz, to put an insurmountable barrier between himself and Rome.
2992 Alasco, *Opp.* vol. ii., p. 560.
2993 Gerdesius, *Hist. Reform.*, vol. iii., p. 148.
2994 Gerdesius, *Hist. Reform.*, vol. iii., p. 150.
2995 Stype, *Cranmer*, pp. 234–240. The young king granted him letters patent, erecting Alasco and the other ministers of the foreign congregations into a body corporate. The affairs of each congregation were managed by a minister, ruling elders and deacons. The oversight of all was committed to Alasco as superintendent. He had greater trouble but no more authority than the others, and was subject equally with them to the discipline of the Church. Although he allowed no superiority of office or authority to superintendents, he considered that they were of Divine appointment, and that Peter held this rank among the apostles. (*Vide* McCrie; *Life of Knox*, vol. i., p. 407, notes.)
2996 Gerdesius, vol. iii., p. 151. Krasinski, *Hist. Reform. Poland*, vol. i., pp. 264–266.
2997 *Vide* Letter of Calvin to John Alasco–Bonnet, vol. ii., p. 432.
2998 Gerdesius, vol. iii., p. 151.
2999 Krasinski, *Slavonia*, pp. 214, 215.
3000 Krasinski, *Slavonia*, p. 217; and *Hist. Reform. Poland*, vol. i., pp. 272, 273.
3001 Gerdesius, vol. iii., p. 151.
3002 "Carnifex."
3003 Krasinski, *Slavonia*, pp. 217, 218.
3004 Poland was divided politically into Great and Little Poland. The first comprehended the western parts, and being the original seat of the Polish power, was called Great Poland, although actually less than the second division, which comprehended the south-eastern provinces, and was styled Little Poland.
3005 Gerdesius, vol. iii., p. 152.
3006 Krasinski says that but scanty materials exist for illustrating the last four years of John Alasco's life. This the count explains by the fact that his descendants returned into the bosom of the Roman Church after his

death, and that all records of his labours for the Reformation of his native land, as well as most of his published works, were destroyed by the Jesuits.

3007 There were two brothers of that name, both zealous Protestants. The one was Bishop of Capo d'Istria, and set about writing a work against "the apostates of Germany," which resulted in his own conversion to Protestantism. He communiated his change of mind to his brother, Bishop of Pola, who at first opposed, and at last embraced his opinions. The Bishop of Pola soon after met his fate, though how is shrouded in mystery. The Bishop of Capo d'Istria was witness to the horrors of the death-bed of Francis Spira, and was so impressed by them that he resigned his bishopric and left Italy. He it was that now came to Poland. (*See* McCrie, *Italy*.)

3008 Krasinski, *Slavonia*, p. 227.
3009 Krasinski, *Hist. Reform. Poland*, vol. i., p. 309,. footnote.
3010 Raynaldus, ad ann. 1556. Starowolski, *Epitomæ Synodov.—apud* Krasinski, *Hist. Reform. Poland*, vol. i., p. 305.
3011 Krasinski, *Hist. Reform. Poland*, vol. i., pp. 310, 311. Bayle, art. "Radziwill."
3012 Pietro Soave Polano, *Hist. Counc. Trent*, lib. v., p. 399; Lond, 1629.
3013 "Episcopi sunt non custodes sed proditores reipublicæ." (Krasinski, *Hist. Reform. Poland*, vol. i., p. 312.)
3014 Krasinski, *Slavonia*, p. 232, footnote.
3015 *Vie de Commendoni, par Gratiani*, Fr. Trans., p. 213 *et seq.—apud* Krasinski, *Slavonia*, pp. 232–234.
3016 See *ante*, bk. iii., chap. 19, -p. 212.
3017 Krasinski, *Hist. Reform. Poland*, vol. i., p. 368.
3018 This union is known in history as the *Consensus Sandomiriensis*.
3019 These articles are a compromise between the Lutheran and Calvinistic theologies, on the vexed question of the Eucharist. The Lutherans soon began loudly to complain that though their phraseology was Lutheran their sense was Calvinistic, and the union, as shown in the text, was short-lived.
3020 Krasinski, *Hist. Reform: Poland*, vol. i., chap. 9.
3021 Krasinski, *Hist. Reform. Poland*, vol. ii., p. 294.
3022 Krasinski, *Hist. Reform. Poland*, vol. ii., pp 15–34.
3023 Hosius wrote in the same terms from Rome to the Archbishop and clergy of Poland: "Que ce que le Roi avait promis à Paris n'était qu'une feinte et dissimulation; et qu'aussitôt qu'il serait couronné, il chasserait hors du royaume tout exercice de réligion autre que la Romaine." (MS. of Dupuis in the Library of Richelieu at Paris—*apud* Krasinski, *Hist. Reform. Poland*, vol. ii., p. 39.)
3024 The fact that Bathory before his election to the throne of Poland was a Protestant,and not, as historians commonly assert, a Romanist, was first published by Krasinski, on the authority of a MS. history now in the Library at St. Petersburg, written by Orselski, a contemporary of the events. (Krasinski, *Hist. Reform. Poland*, vol. ii., p. 48.)
3025 Krasinski, *Hist. Reform. Poland*, vol. ii., p. 53.
3026 *Ibid.*, vol ii., pp. 49, 50.
3027 See his Life by Rescius (Reszka), Rome, 1587. Numerous editions have been published of his works; the best is that of Cologne, 1584, containing his letters to many of the more eminent of his contemporaries.

3028 Lukaszewicz (a Popish author), *History of the Helvetian Churches of Lithuania*, vol. i., pp. 47, 85, and vol. ii., p. 192; Posen, 1842, 1843—*apud* Krasinski, *Slavonia*, pp. 289,. 294.
3029 Albert Wengiersi.
3030 A Spanish Jesuit who compiled a grammar which the Jesuits used in the schools of Poland.
3031 *Dialogue of a Landowner with a Parish Priest.* The work, published about 1620, excited the violent anger of the Jesuits; but being unable to wreak their vengeance on the author, the printer, at their instigation, was publicly flogged, and afterwards banished. (See Krasinski, *Slavonia*, p. 296.)
3032 Krasinski, *Slavonia*, p. 333.
3033 Krasinski, *Hist. Reform. Poland*, vol. ii., chap. 12.
3034 Krasinski, *Slavonia*, p. 356.
3035 Isaiah xxvi. 21.
3036 See *ante*, vol. i., bk. iii.
3037 We have in the same place narrated the origin of the "United Brethren," their election by lot of three men who were afterwards ordained by Stephen, associated with whom, in the laying on of hands, were other Waldensian pastors. Comenius, who relates this transaction, terms Stephen a chief man or bishop among the Waldenses. He afterwards suffered martyrdom for the faith.
3038 See *ante*, vol. i., bk. iii., chap. 7, p. 162.
3039 Comenius, *Historia Persecutionum Ecclesiæ Bohemica*, cap. 28, p. 98; Lugd. Batav., 1647.
3040 *Ibid.*, cap. 28, p. 29.
3041 "Placide expirarunt." (Comenius, cap. 30, p. 109.)
3042 Comenius, cap. 29, p. 102.
3043 *Ibid.*, cap. 29, p. 105.
3044 Comenius, cap. 30, pp. 105, 106.
3045 "Parata mihi sunt et indusium et palliu, quando lubet duci jubete." (Comenius, p. 107.)
3046 "Cum ossibus, capillis, nervis et venis in Sacramento contineri." (Comenius, p. 108.)
3047 Comenius, p. 110. *The Reformation and Anti-Reformation in Bohemia* (from the German), vol. i., pp. 66, 67; Lond., 1845.
3048 Comenius, cap. 36.
3049 Comenius, cap. 37.
3050 *Reform. and Anti-Reform. in Bohem.*, vol. i., p. 75.
3051 Krasinski, *Slavonia*, p. 145.
3052 Comenius, cap. 39, pp. 126, 127.
3053 Comenius, cap. 39. *Reform. and Anti-Reform. in Bohem.*, vol. i., pp. 105, 107.
3054 Krasinski, *Slavonia*, pp. 145, 146.
3055 *Reform. and Anti-Reform. in Bohem.*, vol. i., p. 187.
3056 Comenius, cap. 40. *Reform. and Anti-Reform. in Bohem.*, vol. i., p. 193 *et seq.*
3057 Comenius, cap. 40, pp. 134–136.
3058 "Adsuevi." (Comenius.)
3059 Comenius, cap. 42. Krasinski, *Slavonia*, p. 146.

3060 Balbin assures us that some Jesuits, despite the order to withdraw, remained in Prague disguised as coal-fire men. (*Reform. and Anti-Reform. in Bohem.*, vol. i., p. 336.)
3061 Comenius, cap. 44, p. 154.
3062 "Lumina et columina patriæ." (Comenius, cap. 59.)
3063 Comenius, pp. 209–211. *Reform. and Anti-Reform. in Bohem.*, pp. 287–290.
3064 Comenius, pp. 211, 212.
3065 "Ut muscæ advolabant." (Comenius.)
3066 "Nuntiatur formosissimus cælum cinxisse arcus." (Comenius.)
3067 Comenius, pp. 223, 224.
3068 Comenius, p. 225.
3069 *The Reformation and Anti-Reformation in Bohemia*, vol. i., p. 401.
3070 Comenius, cap. 63.
3071 Comenius, cap. 64. *The Reformation and Anti-Reformation in Bohemia*, vol. i., pp. 416, 417.
3072 Comenius, cap. 65.
3073 *The Reformation and Anti-Reformation in Bohemia*, vol. i., p. 423.
3074 This anticipation was realised in 1631. After the victory of Gustavus Adolphus at Leipsic, Prague was entered, and Count Thorn took down the heads from the Bridge-tower, and conveyed them to the Tein Church, followed by a large assemblage of nobles, pastors, and citizens, whohad returned from exile. They were afterwards buried, but the spot was concealed from the knowledge of the Romanists. (Comenius, cap. 73.)
3075 This bow is mentioned by both Protestant and Popish writers. The people, after gazing some time at it, admiring its beauty, were seized with fear, and many rushed in terror to their houses.
3076 Comenius, cap. 78. *The Reformation and Anti-Reformation in Bohemia*, vol. i., pp. 429, 430.
3077 Comenius, cap. 51, p. 184.
3078 *Ibid*.
3079 "Tandem cantu et fictu resonante cælo, amplexibus et osculis mutuis Divinæ se commendarunt gratiæ." (Comenius, p. 195.)
3080 *The Reformation and Anti-Reformation in Bohemia*, vol. ii., pp. 32, 33.
3081 Comenius, cap. 54, p. 192.
3082 *The Reformation and Anti-Reformation in Bohemia*, vol. ii., pp. 16–19.
3083 Comenius, cap. 105. *The Reformation and Anti-Reformation in Bohemia*, vol. ii., chap. 3.
3084 *The Reformation and Anti-Reformation in Bohemia*, vol. ii., p. 114.
3085 Comenius, cap. 89.
3086 "Lurcones qui sua decoxerant, homicidas infames, spurios, mangones, fidicines, comædos, ciniflones, quosdam etiam alphabeti ignaros homines," &c. (Comenius, cap. 90, p. 313.)
3087 Comenius, cap. 91.
3088 Comenius, cap. 92.
3089 Ludwing Häusser, *Period of the Reformation*, vol. ii., p. 107; Lond., 1873.
3090 Pelzel, *Geschichte von Böhmen*, p. 185 *et seq.* Krasinski, *Slavonia*, p. 158.